The Knights
of the Crown

Dédié à feu mon très cher et très aimé père
Dacre Fiennes Boulton Gentilhomme sans Reproche
Chef de son Nom et de ses Armes
1906–1984

The Knights of the Crown

The Monarchical Orders of Knighthood in Later Medieval Europe 1325–1520

D'ARCY JONATHAN DACRE BOULTON

St. Martin's Press
New York

First published in the United States of America in 1987

Printed in Great Britain

ISBN 0-312-45842-8

Library of Congress Cataloging-in-Publication Data

Boulton, D'Arcy Jonathan Dacre, 1946–
  The knights of the crown
  Bibliography: p.
  Includes index.
  1. Orders of knighthood and chivalry – Europe –
History.   2. Europe – Kings and rulers.   I. Title.
CR4513.B68   1986b   929.7'1'094   86-1820
ISBN 0-312-45842-8

Contents

List of Illustrations

Acknowledgements

A book of this length could not have been written without the assistance of many people, and I am happy to be able to acknowledge here my gratitude to all of those who have helped me during the long years I have worked on putting it together. Most of the research for the book was done in the Bodleian Library in Oxford, the British Library in London, the Van Pelt Library of the University of Pennsylvania, the Widener Library of Harvard University, the Bibliothèque Nationale and Archives Nationales in Paris, and the Biblioteca Nazionale Universitaria and Archivio di Stato in Turin. I should first of all express my thanks to the many librarians and archivists of those institutions who have helped me during my visits. I should also like to thank the Penfield Foundation and the American Philosophical Society for funding the trips to the European libraries just mentioned.

More especial thanks are due to Sir Richard Southern, who while president of my college at Oxford gave me advice and assistance during the formative stages of the study, to Mr C. A. J. Armstrong, who as the supervisor of my doctoral thesis guided me throughout the composition of its earliest redaction, to the late Rev. Gervase Mathew and Mr Michael Maclagan, who as my examiners gave me much useful advice, and to Dr Maurice Keen, without whose help the book in its present form might never have seen the light of day. Finally, I should like to acknowledge the constant support given to me by my parents, Mr and Mrs Dacre Boulton, from whom I learned to enjoy both heraldry and chivalry, by my wife's parents Mr and Mrs Wallace McCann, and her brother David, who helped with the preparation of the typescript, and by my wife Maureen, a scholar in her own right, who has helped me at every stage of the project, and supported me in every possible way. *Errare humanum est*, and for whatever mistakes have escaped my vigilance, I alone am responsible.

D'A. J. D. B.
Harvard University
St George's Day 1985

A Note on Conventions

I have consistently followed the following conventions in the text of this study. I have given all dates in New Style to the extent of considering every year to begin on 1 January, whatever the local usage. I have quoted all extensive passages from primary sources in English, on the theory that few of my readers will be equally adept in seven or eight medieval languages, but have given the original form of all key words and phrases. Unless otherwise specified, the translation is my own. In keeping with recent practice, I have given all forenames (including those of kings) in the form (if not always the spelling) normally employed by their bearers; I have thus preferred *Amé* to both the Latin *Amadeus* and the Modern French *Amédée*, but have preferred the modern spelling *Jean* to the spelling *Jehan*. On the other hand, for the sake of clarity I have modernized the spelling of all territorial surnames. When quoting words and passages in medieval languages, I supplied accents in keeping with the usual editorial conventions rather than modern usage. When introducing princes and important barons I have generally identified them with a full dynastic name based on a system of nomenclature of my own devising. In this system (a modification of one which has long been in use among the royal and baronial houses of Europe) the earliest surname of the earliest known agnatic (or male-line) ancestor, or some other name commonly used of the whole patrilineage, serves as the basic surname for all members of the dynasty, and a further surname (derived in general from the principal dominion held) is added after this basic name for every younger son in every generation who did not succeed an older brother as the head of his branch, according to the principles of heraldic cadency. Thus all the kings of France between 987 and 1328 bear the simple surname 'Capet', while the Kings of mainland Sicily in the Late Middle Ages, who belonged to various cadet branches and sub-branches of the Capetian dynasty, are surnamed 'Capet d'Anjou', 'Capet d'Anjou-Calabria', 'Capet d'Anjou-Durazzo-Gravina', and 'Capet de Valois-Anjou'. When a completely different surname was actually used by the prince in question, I have given this name in inverted commas following the dynastic name; thus, Pierre de Toulouse-Antioch 'de Lusignan' (a King of Cyprus who was a Lusignan only in the female line). With dates, d. = 'died', v. = 'lived'; r. = 'reigned'.

xii

Preface

The period of roughly a century and a half between 1325 and 1470[1] witnessed the creation in most parts of Western Christendom of numerous more or less formally constituted bodies whose principal class of members was restricted to laymen of noble birth and knightly profession. The more eminent of these bodies were commonly designated 'orders of knighthood' by contemporaries,[2] who seem to have seen them as lay versions of the religious orders of knights founded in the previous two centuries, and still very much in evidence at the time. Later historians, including those of the present century, have generally been content to retain this term, modified by such adjectives as 'temporal' or 'secular' to distinguish them from the religious orders. Since they were composed of lay rather than religious knights I shall call them 'lay' orders of knighthood – a term more felicitous than 'temporal' and less ambiguous than 'secular'.

In the seventeeth, eighteenth, and nineteenth centuries, when the ideals of chivalry they were felt to embody were still admired in the dominant class of European society, and royal and princely courts continued to vie with one another in the creation of new 'orders' whose members were called knights, the medieval knightly 'orders', both religious and lay, received a considerable amount of attention from historians. Indeed, the antiquarian historians of this period produced a small library of books on the subject, of which André Favyn's *Le Théâtre d'Honneur et de Chevalerie* (1620), Joseph Micheli Márquez' *Tesoro Militar de Cavallería* (1642), Andrés Mendo's *De ordinibus militaribus* (1648, 1668), Elias Ashmole's *The Institution, Laws, and Ceremonies of the Most Noble Order of the*

---

[1] Despite the assertions of early historians and the claims of various orders themselves to a more ancient origin, I have found no evidence for the existence of any lay order before 1325/6, when the Fraternal Society of St George was founded in Hungary. I have similarly found no evidence that any true lay orders were founded between 1470 and 1578, when Henri III of France founded his Order of the Holy Spirit.

[2] The earliest society of lay knights to use the title 'order' seems to have been the Castilian order of the Band, founded in 1330. The earliest use of the generic term 'order of knighthood' to describe a lay society that I have found is in the prologue to the statutes of the Order of the Ship, composed in 1381, where it appears in the form *une ordre de chevalerie*. To judge from the comments of Olivier de la Marche cited below (n. 10), the generic term was commonly used in the latter part of the fifteenth century to refer to all sorts of groupings of lay knights. I should perhaps mention here that I have preferred to translate the second element of the contemporary terms *ordo militiae*, *ordre de chevalerie*, and so forth with the word 'knighthood' rather than the cognate word 'chivalry' because the latter has come to refer specifically to the ideology or social ethos of the late medieval nobility, and while many of the lay orders were intended at least in part to promote behaviour in keeping with that ideology or ethos, the religious orders of knighthood were positively hostile to many of its elements.

Garter (1672), and Harris Nicolas' *History of the Orders of Knighthood of the British Empire* (1842) are probably the most important.[3] Most of these works were of a general nature, and consisted of short accounts of the organization, insignia, and history of all of the knightly orders of both sorts known or believed by the author to have been founded by Christians. Unfortunately, only a handful of the lay orders known to have been founded before the Reformation (principally those of the Garter, the Golden Fleece, and the Annunciation) received more extensive, and thus more careful, treatment from the antiquarian historians. As a result their accounts of most of the other orders suffered not merely from extreme brevity and lack of documentation, but from numerous inaccuracies, and indeed the admixture of palpable fictions – for such early writers as Favyn were not above inventing information when their sources failed them, and later writers (who seldom did any original research) merely passed on these inventions from one work to the next.[4] In fact, a number of the orders listed in the works of most antiquarian historians appear themselves to have been the products of the fertile imaginations of Favyn and his contemporaries, so even the lists of orders contained in such books must be treated with considerable caution.[5]

The potential for achieving a more accurate knowledge and understanding of the lay orders of the later medieval period was increased in the nineteenth century by the publication of new critical studies of several individual orders, and of transcriptions of the statutes of these and other previously neglected orders. For a variety of reasons, however, interest in such orders waned after the First World War, and little was done with these texts. The new academic historians of the late nineteenth and early twentieth centuries tended to avoid the later medieval period in general, and moreover preferred to concern themselves only with those institutions that they perceived to be of some political, military, or economic importance. While the religious orders of knighthood, with their vast endowments and hundreds of knights, clearly fell into this category, the lay orders – which were believed to have been relatively small and essentially frivolous – did not. Johan Huizinga (whose short chapter on these orders in his highly influential book *The Waning of the Middle Ages* was for many years the most influential general discussion

---

[3] For an extensive but still far from complete list of such works, see Lessurios, *Histoire de l'ordre du Saint Sépulchre, son origine, son but et sa destination . . .* (Maestricht, 1872, after the 2nd edn. by J. J. Hermens), pp. I–IV.

[4] In his *Tesoro Militar de Cavallería* (Madrid, 1642), for example, Joseph Micheli Márquez referred to a society founded by Carlo III of mainland Sicily in 1381 as the Order of the Argonauts of St Nicholas, and said that it was placed under the patronage of St Nicholas, and that its members assembled every year on his feast day in the cathedral church of St Nicholas in Bari vested in a formal habit of white. In fact the society was called the Order of the Ship, had no connection with the Argonauts, St Nicholas, or Bari, and had a habit of several colours, including red and green. At least thirteen of the collars assigned by Ashmole (op. cit., ch. 3) to the thirty-one historical orders he treats on the basis of earlier accounts bear a similar lack of resemblance to the insignia actually used in these orders.

[5] To cite but one example, Favyn (who was the source of most of the misinformation passed down by later historians) described not only the perfectly historical order of the Broom-Pod (*Cosse de Geneste*) but a completely fictitious Order of the Genet (*Gennette*), evidently based on a misinterpretation of the word for 'broom' in some source, and assigned to it a collar, a costume, a constitution, and a history with no basis in fact.

of their nature) described them as little more than atavistic games or exclusive clubs whose 'real importance ... was very slight',[6] and most of the serious historians of his own and the next generation seem to have accepted his opinion without much question. In any case, for more than four decades after the appearance of Huizinga's book in 1919 very little was written on the medieval lay orders. A scattering of articles and chapters examining some of the lesser known (and in some cases completely forgotten) lay orders appeared in most of the countries and tongues of western Europe, and some notice was taken of still others, but as little as ten years ago the great majority of the lay orders founded before the Reformation had received almost no attention from modern scholarship in any language,[7] and no attempt had been made to sift the reliable facts from the mass of errors and fictions that marred almost all of the pre-critical accounts and continue to deceive historians.[8] In the last twenty years a few historians – stimulated in part by the revival of interest in knighthood and chivalry in general – have again attempted to write brief treatments of the lay orders as a phenomenon, but their treatments, though progressively better informed than that of Huizinga and more positive in their assessment of the importance of these orders, have inevitably suffered from the continuing dearth of reliable information about most of the individual orders, including many of the most important.[9]

---

[6] First Dutch edn. 1919; first English edn. 1924; London, 1965, ch. 6 'Orders of Chivalry and Vows' pp. 91–103.

[7] Most of the modern scholars who have written about these orders have been heraldists or numismatists primarily interested in their insignia. The most important general studies of the insignia of the medieval orders are to be found in the comte de Marsy, 'La collection de décorations militaires françaises du musée d'artillerie' *RNHB* sér. 3, 2 (1887), 109–128, 361–375; Alwin Schultz, *Deutsches Leben im XIV. und XV. Jahrhundert* (Vienna, 1892), II, pp. 541–551; Paul Ganz, 'Die Abzeichen der Ritterorden', *AHS* (1905), 28–37, 52–67, 134–140; (1906) 16–25; Camille Enlart, *Manuel d'archéologie française* (Paris, 1916), III, pp. 401–409; and Ottfried Neubecker, 'Ordensritterliche Heraldik', *Der Herold* 1 (1940), 115–127. None of these is either complete or free from error. The insignia of some of the medieval lay orders are also discussed and depicted in the handbooks of 'orders and decorations' that have continued to be published with some regularity in most of the languages of Europe, but for the last century at least most of these works have concentrated on 'orders' still extant at the time of writing.

[8] Huizinga, *Waning*, p. 85, follows most of the early writers in declaring that the 'chain of Pierre de Lusignan's Sword-order was made of gold S's which meant silence'; in fact the order had no collar until the mid-fifteenth century, and the 'S's' were actually phylacteries wrapped around the sword device. Similarly Raymond Cazelles, *Société politique, noblesse et couronne sous Jean le Bon et Charles V* (Paris, 1982), p. 145, repeats without comment the legend invented by Favyn that the French royal order of the Star was first established by Robert 'the Pious' in 1022, and only revived by Jean II (its true founder) in 1351.

[9] Brief treatments of the lay orders founded in France were published by P. S. Lewis in 'Une devise de chevalerie inconnue, créée par un comte de Foix? Le *Dragon*' *Annales du Midi* 76 (1964), pp. 77–84, esp. pp. 77–79; by M. G. A. Vale in 'A fourteenth-century order of chivalry: the "Tiercelet"', *EHR* 323 (1967), 332–341, and in *War and Chivalry* (Athens, Georgia, 1981), ch. 2, pp. 33–62; and by Philippe Contamine in *Guerre, état et société à la fin du Moyen Age. Etudes sur les armées des rois de France 1337–1494* (Paris, 1972), pp. 193–195, and in 'Points de vue sur la chevalerie en France à la fin du Moyen Age', *Francia* 4 (1976),

The present book is intended to fill only part of the *lacuna* I have just described. When I first undertook this study in 1972 I quickly discovered that the lay orders were not only far too numerous to be studied in detail in a single book, but also – in striking contrast to the religious orders – far too disparate to be studied as a single phenomenon. Although the vast majority restricted their principal class of members to lay persons of knightly birth, and used a badge of some sort from which they commonly took their popular name, no other characteristic was shared by as many as half of these bodies, including the formal title 'order' itself. Before the lay orders could be studied in any systematic way, therefore, they had first to be divided into intelligible classes whose members had enough in common to permit meaningful generalizations.

The need for some method of classifying the lay orders was recognized (though for rather different reasons) as long ago as 1502, when Olivier de la Marche, sometime *maître d'hôtel* to Duke Philippe 'the Rash' of Burgundy, suggested in a letter addressed to that duke's grandson Philippe 'the Handsome'[10] that a fundamental distinction should be drawn between those bodies of knights which (like his master's own order of the Golden Fleece) had both corporate statutes and a limited membership, and those bodies of knights which (like the Order of the Camail or Porcupine of the Dukes of Orléans) had neither; and that the title 'order' should be restricted to bodies of the former class. By the beginning of the next century, however, (when most of the surviving medieval orders had been laicized and attached to the crowns of kings) the need for a classification of the lay orders had been forgotten,[11] and in 1919 Huizinga still felt able to discuss them as if they were all essentially the same. So far as I have been able to discover it was not until as recently as 1964 that the question of dividing these orders into distinct classes was raised even tentatively by a professional historian. In that year P. S. Lewis, in an article discussing two previously unknown orders,[12] devoted two pages to a

---

283–284, n. 122. More general treatments were published by Richard Barber in *The Knight and Chivalry* (London, 1st edn. 1970, 2nd edn. Cardinal, 1974) ch. 20 'The Secular Orders', pp. 303–310; by Gunnar Boalt et al. in *The European Orders of Chivalry* (Stockholm, 1971), pp. 41–51; and by Bernard Guenée in *L'Occident aux XIVe et XVe siècles: Les Etats* (Paris, 1971), pp. 234–235. The best treatment of the subject published to date is that in Maurice Keen, *Chivalry* (New Haven, 1984), ch. 10 'The Secular Orders of Chivalry', pp. 179–99, which was based in part on my Oxford thesis.

[10] *Epistre pour tenir et celebrer la noble feste du Thoison d'Or*, preserved as Paris, B.N., ms. fr. 5046, published by H. Beaune and J. Arbaumont in *Mémoires d'Olivier de la Marche*, IV (Paris, 1888), pp. 158–189.

[11] In his *Origine des chevaliers et ordres militaires* (Antwerp, 1609), Aubert le Mire (*alias* Albertus Miraeus) merely divided lay knights into two classes: Knights of the Collar (*du Collier*), who belonged to what La Marche would have called true orders, maintained by princes; and knights of the Golden Spur (*de l'Esperon d'or*), who belonged to no order at all. The former term seems to have been in use by 1437, as it was employed in a letter of that year issued by the Duke of Brittany to describe the order founded by his father in 1381. See below p. 276.

[12] Cited in n. 9 above.

general discussion of the 'orders' known to have been established by French lords between 1350 and 1450, and – inspired directly by La Marche's letter of 1502 – raised and attempted to answer the question of whether the title 'order' should be accorded to all of them. Although a brief examination of two of the 'orders' erroneously rejected by La Marche from his class of true orders[13] led him not merely to see the latter's categories as too rigid, but to doubt that any rigid scheme was possible, Lewis nevertheless recognized that some sort of distinction ought to be made between societies that were more and those that were less formally constituted, and between those that were intended to be permanent and those that were not. A few years later Richard Barber, in a chapter of his general study *The Knight and Chivalry* devoted to what he called the 'secular orders', divided these orders into three loosely-defined classes: (1) princely orders of openly high intent'; (2) orders whose only *raison d'être* was a chivalrous whim on their founder's part'; and (3) 'practical associations'. He also recognized that certain 'orders' were 'not unlike the liveries of English retinues . . . applied on a higher level, badges of personal alliance rather than membership in an order'.[14]

Barber's classification was a great improvement upon anything that had preceded it, but I found on closer investigation that, as it stood, it was neither sufficiently rigorous nor sufficiently comprehensive to be used by an historian who was particularly interested in these orders. After reading the statutes and examining the other contemporary sources of several dozen lay orders founded all over Western Christendom, I decided that the lay orders could usefully be divided on the combined basis of their constitutional form, principal purpose, and intended longevity into at least six distinct and clearly definable classes. In my scheme of classification, as in that of Olivier de la Marche, a primary division is made between those lay 'orders' which, like the religious orders of knighthood, were endowed with some sort of rule, constitution, or statutes, intended to govern the daily lives and corporate activities of their members; and those so-called 'orders' which had no corporate statutes, and as a result no real corporate existence. I have called the former societies 'true orders' and the latter (which were in effect mere sets of noblemen without any formal ties to one another) 'pseudo-orders'. The true orders are then divided on the basis of the principle stated into four classes which I have called 'monarchical', 'confraternal', 'fraternal', and 'votive', and the pseudo-orders into two classes which I have called 'cliental' and 'honorific'. These classes may be defined and described as follows.

(1) *The Monarchical Orders*.[15]   The first class is composed of those orders which were characterized by a monarchical constitution, according to which the presidential office was normally attached to the crown of the principal dominion of

---

[13] Specifically the Order of the Crescent of Anjou and the Order of the Ermine of Brittany. The former was certainly and the latter probably endowed with formal statutes, contrary to La Marche's belief.

[14] Cited above in n. 9.

[15] In my thesis I called these orders 'curial' because of their association with royal and princely courts, but I have since decided that the term 'monarchical' is preferable because it is more suggestive both of their defining characteristic and of their association with lay princes. The term 'princely', often applied to these orders, could equally well be applied to orders of several other classes founded by princes.

its founder (usually a king and always an effectively sovereign prince), and was in every case intended to pass by hereditary succession to its founder's descendants or heirs. The only goal common to all of these societies was the promotion and reward of loyal service to the princely president, and the president normally exercised a considerable degree of control both over the order's activities and over the selection of new members. The members, though often bound to one another by a variety of mutual obligations, were usually bound primarily by cliental oaths of loyalty and service to the president of the order, who in his turn normally undertook various patronal duties towards them. Although inspired in part by the older religious orders of knighthood, and in part by the various legendary societies of knights described in the prose romances which were then at the height of their popularity, the founders of the monarchical orders borrowed the general constitutional format of their orders from the lay devotional confraternity – a highly flexible form of organization in which a great variety of religious and secular obligations and activities could be combined. The monarchical class included most of the better-known lay orders founded before the Reformation, among them those of the Garter and the Golden Fleece.

(2) *The Confraternal Orders.* This class is made up of those orders which took the form of a devotional confraternity but, unlike the monarchical orders, were endowed with a formally democratic constitution under which the chief office was elective rather than hereditary. This was in fact normal in confraternities, and no clear distinction can be drawn between confraternal 'orders' (which did not always use the title 'order') and the more numerous confraternities of knights who did not consider their society to be an 'order'. The confraternal orders can nevertheless be divided into two distinct subclasses: one, which I have called 'princely', made up of orders founded either directly or indirectly by princes (usually subordinate but effectively sovereign princes in France and the Empire) and associated more or less closely with the court or dynasty of their founder; and a second, which I have called 'baronial', made up orders founded by members of the baronial class, and not closely associated with any princely court or dynasty. The orders of the former subclass bore a superficial resemblance to the monarchical orders, but were always formally independent of their princely founder and his heirs, and chose their own members. The orders of the baronial subclass were generally founded to promote chivalrous conduct and festivities in their region, and may usefully be seen as an aristocratic version of the professional guilds which were then at the height of their influence. The earliest known orders of the princely subclass are those of St George, founded by King Károly I of Hungary in 1325 or 1326, and the Order of St Catherine, founded in the Dauphiné of Viennois at some time between 1330 and 1340,[16] but most of the known confraternal orders date from the fifteenth century. Among the more prominent of the later orders that can definitely be classed as confraternal were the Order of St Hubert, created in the Duchy of Bar out of the earlier fraternal order of the Hound in 1422, the Society of Our Lady, or Order of the Swan, founded by Friedrich II, Elector-Marquis of Brandenburg, in 1440, the Order of St Hubert, founded by Duke Gerhard V of Jülich and Berg in 1444, and the Order of the Crescent, founded by Duke René of Anjou in 1448.[17] The best

[16] See below p. 45.
[17] On these orders, see below, pp. 397–398.

known baronial order is the Noble Order of St George of Rougemont, established in the County-Palatine or Franche Comté of Burgundy around 1440.[18]

(3) *The Fraternal Orders.* The third of my classes is made up of orders characterized by a simple democratic constitution lacking most of the characteristic features of the devotional confraternity, under which the members – generally drawn from the upper and middle nobility of a particular principality or region, especially in France – were bound to one another on more or less equal terms by oaths of mutual loyalty and aid, especially in time of war. Since most of their ordinances seem to have been inspired by the contemporary relationship called 'brotherhood-in-arms', I have called these societies 'fraternal orders'. Unlike the monarchical and confraternal orders, which were always intended by their founders to be perpetual, the fraternal orders seem in general to have been created to deal with a particular war or political crisis, and were intended to endure only while that situation lasted. In fact they were distinguished from other temporary alliances only by the use of a distinctive device and the title 'order'. As a result these orders have left little evidence of their existence, and only four are currently known to scholarship: the *Compaignie* of the Black Swan, created by three princes and eleven knights in Savoy in 1350;[19] the *Corps et Ordre du Tiercelet* or 'Young Male Falcon', founded by the Viscount of Thouars and seventeen minor barons in south-western Poitou at some time between 1377 and 1385;[20] the *Ourdre de la Pomme d'Or* or 'Golden Apple', established by fourteen knights and squires in Auvergne in 1394;[21] and the *Alliance et Compagnie du Levrier* or 'Hound', founded by 44 knights and squires in the Barrois in 1416 for a period of five years, and converted in 1422 into a confraternal order under the patronage of St Hubert.[22]

(4) *The Votive Orders.* The orders of my fourth and last class of true orders were characterized by a set of ordinances of the sort normally associated with those individual projects of formal heroism called *emprinses* or 'enterprises' of arms.[23] Their members undertook a collective vow to perform certain specific chivalrous deeds, under specific conditions and within a specific period of time, after the completion of which the society simply dissolved. Like the individual enterprises upon which they were modelled, these orders – which from their origin in a collective vow I have called 'votive' – were in effect chivalrous games in which their members were the players and the statutes the rules of play. Founded by princes and lords who saw themselves as paragons of chivalric virtue in the image of the heroes of the romances, the votive orders were intended primarily to enhance the heroic reputations of their participants. Not surprisingly, these orders have left even less evidence of their existence than the fraternal orders, and although they

---

[18] Statutes in Gollut, *Mémoires de la République Séquanoise et des Princes de la Franche Comté*, ed. A. Javel (Arbois, 1864), cols. 440–442; study in Baron A. Pidoux de la Maduère, 'Le noble ordre de Saint-Georges au comté de Bourgogne', *Rivista del Collegio araldico* (1905), 464–472.

[19] On this order, see below, pp. 250–251.

[20] Statutes and study in M. G. A. Vale, 'A fourteenth-century order of chivalry'.

[21] Statutes in A. Jacotin, *Preuves de la maison de Polignac* (Paris, 1898–1905), II, no. 283; study in A. Bossuat, 'Un ordre de chevalerie auvergnat: l'Ordre de la Pomme d'or', *Bulletin historique et scientifique de l'Auvergne* (1944), 83–98.

[22] See below, p. 326.

[23] On these, see below, p. 14.

may well have been quite numerous around the beginning of the fifteenth century, only three are currently known to scholarship, all on the basis of their statutes alone: the *Emprise de l'Escu vert a la Dame Blanche* or 'Enterprise of the Green Shield with the White Lady', created in 1399 by the famous French soldier Jean le Maingre 'de Boucicaut', Marshal of France, and twelve other knights for a period of five years;[24] the enterprise of the *Fer de Prisonnier* or 'Prisonner's Iron' undertaken along with sixteen other knights by Jean Capet de Bourbon, Duke of Bourbon, for a period of up to two years, beginning on 1 January 1415;[25] and the enterprise of the Dragon, undertaken at about the same time by another French prince – probably Jean de Grailly, Count of Foix – along with 'a certain number of ladies, damsels, knights, and squires', for a period of one year.[26]

(5) *The Cliental Pseudo-Orders.* In the class of pseudo-order I have called 'cliental' belong those whose 'members' were bound by an oath of clientship to the prince who bestowed the 'order' in the form of a badge. The oath required was generally similar to that sworn by indentured retainers in England and inferior *alliés* in France in the same period,[27] and the pseudo-orders of this class were in effect glorified retinues, distinguished from other such groupings only by the misleading title 'order' applied to them by the prince who distributed their badge.[28] A number of the better-known princely 'orders' belong in this class, including the Order of the Camail or Porcupine created by Duke Louis of Orléans in 1394.[29] Various other well-known orders – including the Orders of the Scale of the Kings of Castile and the Thistle of the Kings of Scots – probably belonged to this class, and other orders that began their existence as monarchical orders – including the Order of the Band of the Kings of Castile, the Order of the Sword of the Kings of Cyprus, and the Order of the Ermine of the Dukes of Brittany – may have been converted into cliental pseudo-orders at some point in their history. Indeed, as we shall see, the statutes of several orders that were technically monarchical were of so simple a nature that they were virtually pseudo-orders even when their statutes were still in force.

---

[24] Statutes in *Le livre des faicts du bon messire Jean le Maingre dit Boucicaut*, ed. J. Michaut, B. Poujoulat (Paris, 1881), pp. 255–257.

[25] Statutes in *Choix de pièces inédites relatives au règne de Charles VI*, ed. L. Douët-d'Arcq (Soc. de l'hist. de France, Paris, 1863), no. CLXVI, t. I, pp. 370–374; trans. by C. T. Allmand in *Society at War: The Experience of England and France During the Hundred Years War* (Edinburgh, 1973), pp. 25–27. I know of no study, but Huizinga comments upon it in the context of a passage on vows (op. cit., p. 89).

[26] Statutes and study in P. S. Lewis, 'Une devise de chevalerie', pp. 77–84. In *L'ordonnance et maniere des chevaliers errants* (B.N., ms. fr. 5241, f. 107r), Merlin de Cordebeuf mentions what may have been a fourth order of this type: the *seigneurs de l'ordre de la Rose blanche ou de serment de la Targe*.

[27] On these relationships, see below, pp. 1–2.

[28] The term 'order' had come to be applied to the badges of true orders in French, at least, by 1380 or so, for the badge of the Order of the Ship is frequently referred to as the *ordre et devise* in the statutes of that order, composed in 1381, and the badge of the order of the Golden Apple is similarly called an *ourdre* in its statutes, composed shortly thereafter.

[29] On this order see Charles d'Orlac, 'Les chevaliers du Porc-Epic ou du Camail, 1394–1498' *RNHB* n.s. 3 (1867), 337–50; and 'Lettres du duc d'Orléans qui confèrent l'ordre du Camail à Louis Chabot (1400)' *RNHB* n.s. 2 (1886), 13.

(6) *The Honorific Pseudo-Orders.* In the second class belong those bodies of knights (generally called 'orders' only by later historians) whose members undertook no special obligations at the time of their admission, beyond those implicitly undertaken with the general order of knighthood. In fact, membership in these bodies was often bestowed along with the accolade of knighthood, either during the course of some festive occasion like a coronation, or upon the completion of a pilgrimage to a shrine whose guardians had received the right to confer knighthood upon noble pilgrims. Like many modern 'orders', these pseudo-orders consisted of nothing more than a badge or title borne by those who received them, and served merely to honour their recipients. I have therefore called them 'honorific pseudo-orders'. Most prominent among these bodies were the knights of the Holy Sepulchre,[30] the knights of St Catherine of Mount Sinai,[31] the papal knights of the *Militia Aurata* or of the Golden Spur,[32] and the English knights of the Bath.[33]

In this book I shall be concerned only with the orders of the first of these six classes – those I have called 'monarchical' – and shall look at orders belonging to the other classes only in relationship to them. I chose to concentrate on the monarchical class because the orders comprising it were not only the best-documented of the lay orders, but the most complex, the most prominent, the best endowed, the longest-lived, and (no doubt in consequence of all these advantages) the most influential. Indeed, the lay orders of all the other classes almost certainly borrowed the title 'order' from the early monarchical orders, and the later confraternal orders founded by princes and all of the cliental pseudo-orders seem to have been inspired by them. The monarchical orders may thus be regarded as the orders of knighthood *par excellence* of the later Middle Ages, and as such particularly worthy of a careful examination.

I initially approached the subject of the monarchical orders with a suspicion that Huizinga's low estimate of their political and military importance was ill-founded, and I have accordingly attempted to see them in relationship to the whole set of institutions and practices employed by kings and princes of the later medieval period to secure the loyalty and service of their noble subjects, especially the contract of retinue investigated in the middle decades of this century by A. E. Prince, N. B. Lewis, Bryce Lyon, and others. Since they were made up largely of knights and intended by their founders to promote chivalric virtues, I have also tried to see them in relation to the general history of knighthood as both a military and a social status, on which so much has been written in recent years by

---

[30] On this pseudo-order see M. H. A. D'Assemani, *The Cross on the Sword* (Chicago, 1944).

[31] I have found no general study of this pseudo-order, but it is discussed briefly in such works as Schultz, *Deutsches Leben*, p. 547; Ganz, 'Die Abzeichen', pp. 34–36; Rabino, 'Le Monastère de Sainte-Catherine (Mont-Sinai)' *Bulletin de la Société de Géographie d'Egypte* 19 (Cairo, 1935), pp. 121–126; and D. L. Galbreath and Leon Jéquier, *Manuel du Blason* (Lausanne, 1977), p. 206.

[32] On this so-called order see D. L. Galbreath, 'Deux ordres de chevalerie du moyen-âge' *AHS* (1927) 25–28; and H. C. de Zeininger in *Rivista Araldica* (1935) pp. 52ff, and 'L'Ordre de l'Eperon d'Or' *AHS* (1939) pp. 91–95.

[33] On the history of this 'order' see John Anstis, *Observations Introductory to an Historical Essay upon the Knighthood of the Bath* (London, 1725).

such scholars as Georges Duby, Joachim Bumke, Philippe Contamine, and Jean Flori, and to the general history of chivalry, the ethos or code of the knightly class, which has also received a good deal of attention of late both from historians (including Richard Barber, Maurice Keen, and Malcolm and Juliet Vale) and from students of literature (including Larry Benson, John Leyerle, and Martín de Riquer). Since the monarchical orders were clearly adjuncts of royal and princely courts, I have finally tried to view them as an element of the international court culture that emerged in Western Christendom in the fourteenth century, investigated in recent years by such historians of literature, art, costume, and ceremony as Gervase Mathew, Stella Mary Newton, Françoise Piponnier, and Colette Beaune.

While bearing in mind these broad themes of historical investigation, I have tried in this book both to examine the monarchical orders as a general phenomenon and to present as thorough and reliable an account of the nature and history of each of the individual orders as the state of the documentation and the exigencies of modern publishing permit. Of the twenty knightly orders founded in our period that were either certainly or probably monarchical, only six have been examined at any length by critical historians, and most are known only on the basis of accounts that are not merely brief and outdated, but positively riddled with errors and inventions. As a result, no general account could have been attempted until the history of most of the individual orders had been reconstructed on the basis of the primary sources so far discovered. Since each order was founded in particular circumstances by a particular prince to accomplish particular goals, and was in consequence peculiar in many ways, I felt that scholarship would be better served if I examined each order separately before I attempted to discuss the orders in a strictly thematic way.

I have in general devoted a full chapter to each of the monarchical orders whose statutes I was able to discover, and a section of a collective chapter to each of the others. I have also examined several orders which, though not strictly monarchical, occupied an important place in the history of the orders of the monarchical class. Since I felt that each order could be best understood in its own historical context, and especially in relationship to the earlier orders of the same class (which were often used as models), I have arranged these chapters chronologically, and begun each with a brief account of the character, life, and political situation of the order's founder on the eve of its creation, to the extent that they are currently understood.[34] In each chapter I have provided a short narrative history of the order from the time of its foundation to the time of its dissolution (if it dissolved before the Reformation) or to the outbreak of the Reformation around 1520 (if it survived to that date or beyond), and have then tried to paint as clear a picture as possible of the order during this period. I have attempted in each case to determine (and, as far as possible, to explain) the names and titles the order used; the role of its patron saint; the role of its princely president and the obligations he undertook toward the order as a whole and the ordinary members individually; what distinctions, if any, were made among the ordinary members; what sort of men were admitted to

---

[34] As a result of the aversion felt until recently by most critical historians for the later medieval period, very few of the founders have been the subject of full length studies.

ordinary membership, how they were admitted and received and what obligations they undertook by accepting admission; what the corporate activities of the order were meant to be; what buildings if any were set aside for the order's use; what officers or clergy, if any, were appointed to serve the order; and finally, what insignia and costumes were worn by those who belonged to or served the order, and in what circumstances. In every case I have also attempted to determine the extent to which the obligations and activities envisioned in the statutes were actually carried out. Throughout each examination I have tried to establish which elements were either inspired by or directly borrowed from the usages of earlier orders and other contemporary institutions, both real and fictional, and which had their origin in the imagination of the founder himself. Finally I have tried – on the basis of this analysis – to determine what the founder hoped to accomplish by establishing the order, and whether it could possibly have achieved all or part of his purposes.

In treating the history of most of the monarchical orders I have concentrated on questions of this nature because the primary evidence for the history of most of these orders does not allow one to say much about what the orders and their members actually did, as distinct from what they were meant to do. Indeed, for most of the orders in question, and for all of the orders in the period before 1430, the only important contemporary source that has come down to us in any form is the order's corporate statutes or constitution. Narrative sources for all of the orders throughout the period of nearly two centuries with which we are concerned are both rare and relatively poor. Most of the orders are mentioned in at least one general chronicle, but the chronicle accounts are without exception both unreliable and brief, and rarely describe more than the foundation of the order or its first general meeting. This was to be expected, for (as we shall see) the normal corporate activities envisioned for most orders of this class were not particularly newsworthy, and most chroniclers were interested in recording only what would now be front-page news. Many of the orders in question kept (or were meant to keep) official records of the meetings of their chapter, but only those of the Garter (from 1416) and the Golden Fleece (from 1431) have been preserved, and both are far from complete. Most of the orders were also meant to keep a book in which the deeds of the members were recorded each year, but although there is evidence to suggest that some of these books were actually maintained, none of them is known to have survived.

Most of the other written evidence for the history of the monarchical orders takes the form of statements made in household account books to the effect that specific sums of money were disbursed to pay for festivities associated with the order's annual assembly or for the provision of badges, costumes, or funerals to individual members. This sort of evidence is certainly useful, since it allows us to know when and where (and indeed whether) the prescribed meetings were held, and to identify at least some of the members present on those occasions, but it does not tell us much about what actually went on. For most orders some physical evidence – in the form of seals, coins, badges, portraits, tomb-monuments, and stained-glass windows in some way associated with the order – also survives, and this can be useful not merely for reconstructing the form of the badge or costume of an order, but for compiling a list of members. Such evidence is of little value for any other purpose, however, and is in any case surprisingly rare for the period before about 1430. As a result even the membership of most orders before that year is only very imperfectly known. Nor do we know much about what most of the members felt about their membership in these orders, for very few private documents even mentioning such orders survive from our period, and we are left to judge attitudes very largely from actions. Contemporary commentary on the purpose, nature, and value of the orders is confined almost entirely to the prologues that generally precede their statutes, and these were of course written either by the founder himself or by one of his servants.

Thus we are left to depend very heavily on the statutes, which at least give us an idea of what the order was meant to do. Fortunately the statutes of at least thirteen of the monarchical orders founded before 1520 have been preserved in at least one contemporary redaction. A few of these redactions are known today only from later printed transcriptions, but most of them are preserved in at least one manuscript roughly contemporary with the time of their adoption. All but two of the redactions I have identified have been published at some time in the last three hundred years, but unfortunately only those of the Castilian order of the Band had been properly edited at the time I began my investigation. I therefore attempted to consult the surviving manuscripts of the statutes, and have at least laid the groundwork for critical editions of most of them. In order to facilitate reference to the statutes both by myself and by others, and to make comparative study possible, I have in every case assigned Arabic numerals to the chapters into which the statutes are formally divided, and minuscule letters to the ordinances that did not correspond precisely to chapters. I have identified as ordinances all statements that ordained, either explicitly or by implication, a discrete action, establishment, right, obligation, or exception to some previously stated rule.

Although my study of the monarchical orders is thus based largely on the statutes of each order, I have not of course neglected the other forms of evidence. Indeed, I have made use of every scrap of contemporary material that I could find that seemed to shed some light on any one of them. I found the earlier scholarship on those orders that had been studied before to be quite useful for locating this material, but unlike most earlier writers in this field I have based all of my arguments on a fresh reading of the primary sources, and have frequently disagreed with the interpretations of earlier scholars.

In order that the background common to all of the orders might be understood, I have included in an introductory chapter a brief consideration of the relationships between kings, princes, and lesser nobles in the later Middle Ages; of the nature and condition of both knighthood and chivalry in the same period; and of certain institutions which seem to have had a major influence upon the form and regulations of the monarchical orders: the religious orders of knighthood, the fictional orders of knighthood depicted in the romances then current, and the lay devotional confraternities. After examining each of the orders individually, I have attempted in a single concluding chapter to examine them all in a more general way, to examine their relationship to other contemporary institutions and to the ideas and practices of those who founded them and accepted election to them, to sum up my findings, and to come to a few general conclusions about their place and their importance in their world.

Although I have tried to be as careful and as comprehensive as possible, I do not for a moment imagine that this book will be the final word on the subject of monarchical orders; my own experience would suggest that many documents containing information relevant to the history of one or another of the orders remain to be discovered or published, and that references lurk in many documents already published which I have not yet had occasion to examine. The discovery of such documents will inevitably require the revision of some of the conclusions I have reached, especially those whose evidential basis is rather thin. If I have done what I meant to do, however, this book will serve both as a useful work of reference and as a point of departure for future studies, as well as shedding new light upon the relationships between princes and nobles and the chivalrous culture of the court in the later medieval period.

Chapter 1

Introduction

1 Kings, Courts, and Courtiers in the Later Middle Ages

In most of the realms of Western Christendom, the period of roughly two centuries conventionally designated the Late Middle Ages was in the sphere of high politics an era of transition between a highly decentralized régime in which the king had shared much of his power with a class of barons bound only loosely to him by ties of feudo-vassality, and a highly centralized régime in which the supremacy of royal authority was unchallenged throughout the kingdom. Between the late thirteenth and the early sixteenth century most Western kings and (especially in Germany) certain effectively sovereign princes of lesser rank, aided by an ever-swelling army of lawyers, administrators, and petty functionaries, and commonly supported once again by taxes granted more or less willingly by newly-formed assemblies representative of the three 'orders' or 'estates' of Clergy, Nobility, and Commonality, slowly but inexorably converted their dominions into unified, sovereign, and bureaucratic states.

In order to accomplish this transformation, the would-be sovereign princes were generally obliged to reduce their baronial vassals from the condition of virtual independence which they had long enjoyed, first to the condition of relatively tractable clients, and finally to that of wholly dependent subjects. In most kingdoms individual princes and makeshift leagues of barons were occasionally driven to resist the encroachment of royal or princely power by armed rebellion, and frequently sought to preserve their traditional independence by supporting an alternative candidate to the throne. Such resistence ultimately proved as futile as it was dangerous, however, and by 1520 the barons of every country but Germany had been reduced to a relatively docile dependence on their royal lords through a judicious combination of legal and military intimidation balanced by generous inducements to loyalty and service to the state. Exceptionally unruly or untrustworthy barons (and those who backed the wrong prince in one of the numerous succession wars) were usually deprived of their estates and imprisoned or even executed as a warning to their fellows, while those who served their prince faithfully were rewarded with gifts of land, dignities, offices, and annuities, and invited to enjoy the lavish hospitality of the princely court. Princes also sought to bind their barons to their service in a variety of more formal ways, intended either to supplement or replace the traditional ties of seigniorio-vassality based on a landed fief, whose effectiveness was in a state of more or less advanced decline throughout Western Christendom. In addition to the knightly orders with which we are here specially concerned, the instruments adopted for this purpose included

1

the *fief-rente* or feudal annuity,[1] and non-feudal contracts of retinue[2] and alliance,[3] in which the obligations of the retainer or ally were often spelled out in considerable detail, but the extent to which any of these instruments was employed, and the time when it was first introduced, varied considerably from one region to another.

Gradually deprived of their traditional means of increasing their wealth and power, often suffering from declining agricultural incomes, and obliged by social conventions promoted by their princely lords to maintain an ever more costly standard of living, the barons were easily seduced by princely *largesse*, and eagerly sought salaried service with princes not only as captains in their armies but as officials in their civil administrations. In order to secure advancement in the prince's service, noblemen of all ranks also spent ever-longer periods of time each year waiting upon the prince in his court, and princes used the opportunity this presented to influence their attitudes and behaviour in a variety of ways.

The princely household (the functional core of the somewhat amorphous body of servants, officials, and visitors who formed the court as a whole) had long served the function of impressing the world at large with the wealth, importance, and noble qualities of the prince it served, both by overwhelming visitors with vast quantitites of rare foods and costly entertainments, and by enveloping the prince and his family in an elaborate daily ritual, enhanced by magnificent and luxurious costumes and settings. In the later medieval period, when the courts of many princes began to spend increasing periods of time in castles and palaces built in or near the princely capital, the food, entertainments, costumes and settings were made ever more magnificent, and the ceremonies – influenced by those of the Byzantine and Islamic courts – grew ever more elaborate and refined. By the end of the fourteenth century most sovereign princes were attended at all times by a small troop of liveried servants, including noble counsellor-chamberlains and armed bodyguards, and even the simple daily acts of rising in the morning, hearing mass in the chapel, dining and supping in the hall, and retiring again in the great chamber, were surrounded by rituals of almost ecclesiastical solemnity.[4]

---

[1] See Bryce Lyon, *From Fief to Indenture. The Transition from Feudal to Non-Feudal Contract in Western Europe* (Cambridge, Mass., 1957).

[2] See especially K. B. McFarlane, 'Bastard Feudalism', *Bulletin of the Institute of Historical Research* 20 (1943–45), pp. 161–80; N. B. Lewis, 'The Organization of Indentured Retinues in Fourteenth-Century England', Transactions of the Royal Historical Society, 4th Ser., 27 (1945), pp. 29–39, and 'Indentures of Retinue with John of Gaunt, Duke of Lancaster, Enrolled in Chancery, 1367–1399', *Camden Miscellany* 22 (1964), pp. 77–112; and W. H. Dunham, Jr., *Lord Hastings, Indentured Retainers, 1461–1483. The Lawfulness of Livery and Retaining under the Yorkists and Tudors* (New Haven, 1955).

[3] See P. S. Lewis, 'Decayed and Non-Feudalism in Later Medieval France', *Bulletin of the Institute of Historical Research* 37 (1964), pp. 156–84.

[4] On medieval courts and households in general, see A. G. Dickens, 'Monarchy and Cultural Revival: Courts in the Middle Ages', and Sydney Anglo, 'The Courtier: The Renaissance and changing ideals', in *The Courts of Europe: Politics, Patronage, and Royalty, 1400–1800*, ed. A. G. Dickens (London, 1977), pp. 8–53, and Mark Girouard, *Life in the English Country House: A Social and Architectural History* (London, 1980), pp. 13–80. For particular courts and households, see Otto Cartellieri, *The Court of Burgundy* (London, 1929); A. R. Myers, *The Household of Edward IV. The Black Book and the Ordinance of 1478*

These ceremonies required an enormous support staff, and princely households tended in consequence to grow steadily in size and complexity throughout the fourteenth century. The household of the King of France (which served as a model for many lesser households) already included about 400 servants when Jean II came to the throne in 1350, and by the death of his grandson Charles VI in 1422 it had grown to include nearly 800 servants of various sorts, organized into half a dozen departments, each of which was in its turn subdivided into various specialized services. Each department and service was organized into a hierarchy of several degrees, of which the higher were in some departments restricted to persons of noble or 'gentle' birth, and the household as a whole presented the appearance of a vast pyramid in which the prince at the pinnacle was supported by ever widening layers of gentlemen, yeomen, and grooms or valets. As early as 1261, King Louis IX of France had found it necessary to issue a special ordinance fixing the duties and salaries of his household servants, and from the 1330s – the decade which saw the creation of the first monarchical order – such ordinances became increasingly common.

Whatever their rank or terms of employment, the members of a princely household were all regarded as personal servants of the prince. As such, they were paid a regular allowance or *livree* of food, drink, and clothing, the amount and quality of which varied in accordance with their social and official rank. In France and England, the term *livree* or 'livery' was especially applied to the clothing distributed to the household servants. At first this clothing was probably not distinguished in any systematic way from that normally worn at court by non-servants of the same rank, but from about 1350 onwards it became increasingly common for princes and barons in England, France, and adjoining regions to distribute liveries that were consistently of one or several particular colours, so that the livery constituted a sort of uniform. Amé VI the 'Green Count' of Savoy, for example (the founder of the monarchical order of the Collar) distributed liveries of green to all his household servants from 1352 until his death in 1383, and Edward the 'Black Prince' of Wales (one of the founder knights of the Garter) probably gave liveries of black between about 1360 and his death in 1376. Livery uniforms of this sort were given by many princes and barons not only to their household servants, but to all those who had been retained by them by some form of written contract, and so became symbolic of their service in general.

The same princes who began the practice of distributing livery uniforms seem to have begun the closely related practice of distributing one or more *devises* or 'badges' distinctive of their service to both household servants and contractual retainers. These badges (which took the form of real or imaginary beasts, plants, and objects, both terrestrial and celestial, and were often accompanied by a cryptic verbal *devise* or motto), were probably derived in part from the very similar devices worn by teams of knights at tournaments in the 1330s and 1340s, in part from the

(Manchester, 1959); Gervase Mathew, *The Court of Richard II* (London, 1968); C. A. J. Armstrong, 'The Golden Age of Burgundy: Dukes that outdid kings', in *The Courts of Europe*, pp. 55–75; and Alan Ryder, *The Kingdom of Naples under Alfonso the Magnanimous* (Oxford, 1976), pp. 54–90.

devices used by craft-guilds and other confraternities since the late thirteenth century, and in part from the devices of the orders of knighthood founded in the 1340s and 1350s. In any case the use of livery badges seems to have begun in England around 1360, and to have spread to France by 1369. Like the badges worn by guild members and pilgrims, and the members of many knightly orders founded between 1350 and 1430, the livery badges worn by household servants in the fourteenth and early fifteenth century commonly took the form of a small metal brooch, which was worn pinned or sewn to the breast of the surcoat, hood-cape, or mantle. The metallic badges given to lesser servants could be made of so base a metal as lead (normal for pilgrims' badges), while those given to servants of noble birth were often made of silver or gold and enriched with enamel and precious stones. From about 1390, when heavy metal collars came into vogue in many courts, metallic badges were often worn pendant from such a collar, or incorporated into the collar itself.[5]

Although centred upon the person of the prince himself, the ceremoniousness of the later medieval court tended to engulf all those who were obliged for one reason or another to attend upon the prince for any period of time. Wishing to surround themselves with a society that reflected not only their grandeur but their refinement, and at the same time to compensate their grander courtiers for the reduction of their independence and power, most princes imposed upon their courts a comprehensive code of etiquette in which minute distinctions of rank and precedence were recognized in a variety of formal ways. Definite ranks were assigned to such traditional dominical statuses as count and baron (common to most countries in 1300), and princes began to bestow these and other similar 'dignities' (ultimately including those of prince, duke, marquis, and viscount) upon their children, their close relatives, and other barons they wished for some reason to reward or favour, in order to increase their formal rank.[6] The precise position of

---

[5] Very little of a critical nature has been written on the use of livery colours or badges in the fourteenth and fifteenth centuries. There is a brief but useful discussion of the problem in Michel Pastoureau, *Traité d'héraldique* (Paris, 1979), pp. 215–20. The best local study is Colette Beaune, 'Costume et pouvoir en France à la fin du Moyen Age: Les Devises royales vers 1400', *Revue des Sciences Humaines* 183 (1981), pp. 125–146. The best source for the badges used in this period outside of England is the chapter in J. Woodward's *Treatise on Heraldry, British and Foreign* (London, 1892), Chapter 18. For English badges see especially Arthur Charles Fox-Davies, *Heraldic Badges* (London, 1907), H. S. London, *Royal Beasts* (London, 1958), and Richard Marks and Ann Payne, *British Heraldry from its Origins to c. 1800* (London, 1978), pp. 30–42. For the use of badges in warfare, see Robert Gayre of Gayre and Nigg, *Heraldic Standards and Other Ensigns: Their development and history* (London, 1959), pp. 45–85. A useful discussion of the decorative use of badges and mottoes can be found in Joan Evans, *Pattern. A Study of Ornament in Western Europe, 1180–1900* (Oxford, 1931), I, pp. 90–104. The use of badges seems to have been closely related to the use of elaborate symbolic crests on helms, especially in tournaments, which spread rapidly between about 1325 and 1340. On the use of devices and mottoes in tournaments, see Juliet Vale, *Edward III and Chivalry. Chivalric Society and its Context 1270–1350* (Woodbridge, 1982).

[6] On the subject of the distribution of dominical dignities, see my forthcoming study, *Lordship and Hierarchy in Later Medieval France: The Development and Effects of the Royal Practice of Bestowing Fiefs and Titles of Dignity, 1202–1515*, which is based upon my University of Pennsylvania Ph.D. dissertation, *Dominical Titles of Dignity in France, 1223–1515: A Study of the Formalization and Hierarchization of Status in the Upper Nobility in the Later Middle Ages* (1978).

the courtier within the steadily growing hierarchy of established ranks came to be clearly indicated in most courts by the cut and material of his clothing and personal adornments, and came to determine where (and indeed whether) he could sit, stand, or walk in any particular gathering, and how he should address and be addressed by others in various circumstances. From 1336 onwards it became increasingly common for the rules of etiquette to be set forth, along with those governing the daily ceremonies of the court, in the household ordinance, and as we shall see, some of them were incorporated into the statutes of knightly orders.[7]

One further characteristic of the culture of princely courts in the later Middle Ages that must be noted here is the marked taste displayed by princes and courtiers alike for historical and quasi-historical literature, especially of the genre that we now call the romance. This genre, popular in Classical times, had been revived in the princely courts of northern France around 1150, and by the end of the century had virtually displaced the traditional epic as the normal form of narrative composition. The earliest French romances, now referred to as *romans d'antiquité*, were based loosely on works composed in the Classical period in Greek or Latin, but although works of this sort continued to be both written and read, they were soon eclipsed in popularity by a series or 'cycle' of romances based even more loosely on Celtic legends, and set in the time of the semi-legendary British king Arthur. The immediate source for much of the legend of Arthur himself was the *Historia Regum Britanniae* composed by the Welsh bishop Geoffrey of Monmouth in 1136, and loosely rendered into French by the Norman poet Wace in 1155, but the cycle of romances associated with Arthur and his court was begun by the great French poet Chrétien de Troyes, who composed his seminal works (including *Lancelot*, or *Le Chevalier de la Charette*, and *Perceval*, or *Le Conte del Graal*) between about 1170 and 1190. The Arthurian romances of Chrétien and his continuators and imitators in the later twelfth and early thirteenth century quickly gained an immense popularity, and through translation and adaptation came to be known in almost every part of Western Christendom before the end of the latter century. As we shall observe shortly, the ideas about knighthood and knightliness they developed and promoted quickly assumed a central place in the ideology of the emerging knightly class, and their heroes came to be regarded as historical personages and treated as models by knights of all ranks. Such was the appeal of the 'matter of Britain' that new works about Arthur and the knights of his court continued to be written until the latter part of the fifteenth century, and the romances of the Arthurian cycle remained the most popular form of literature in the knightly class until the very end of our period.[8] It is almost impossible to overestimate the influence of these works on the chivalrous culture of the later medieval court, and it is not at all surprising that they provided the most important models for the knightly orders with which this study is particularly concerned.

[7] See Bernard Guenée, *L'Occident aux XIVe et XVe siècle: Les Etats* (Paris, 1971), pp. 148–50; M. Durliat, *La cour de Jacques II, de Majorque (1324–1349) d'après les "lois palatines"* (Paris, 1962); and A. R. Myers, *The Household of Edward IV*.

[8] See John Fox, *A Literary History of France: The Middle Ages* (London and New York, 1974), pp. 134–179, 197–224, and *Arthurian Literature in the Middle Ages*, ed. R. S. Loomis, (Oxford, 1959).

2 Knighthood and Chivalry

Since most of the monarchical orders were restricted to knights and intended to reward or promote the virtues and qualities which had come to be associated with knighthood, we must review briefly what is currently known about the nature of that status, and of the aristocratic ethos that was associated with it, in the period before 1520.[9]

The Latin title *miles* and its vernacular equivalents in the various languages of Western Christendom (knight, *chevalier, caballero, rîter*, and so forth) had been used since the twelfth century exclusively to designate the members of a clearly defined class of professional warriors who had been fully trained to fight on horseback with lance and sword while wearing what was currently regarded as full armour. Mounted warriors of this general type may have been employed as shock troops in the armies of the Frankish kings of western Europe since the middle of the eighth century, but it was only during the troubled years of the tenth century that they began to displace ordinary freemen from the field of battle, and in France and adjacent regions began to constitute a distinct class of rural society between the noble landowners and the peasant tenants who worked their land. In recognition of this fact they had begun in the same period to employ the term which had come to designate their military function – in most languages a word meaning 'horseman'

[9] On the early history of knighthood and chivalry see especially G. Duby, 'Les origines de la chevalerie' in *Ordinamenti militari in Occidente nell'alto medioevo* (Settimane di studio del Centro italiano di Studi sull'alto medioevo 15.1–2: Spoleto, 1968), pp. 739–61, rept. in his *Hommes et structures du moyen âge*, pp. 325–41, and *The Chivalrous Society*, trans. C. Postan (London, 1977); P. Van Luyn, 'Les milites dans la France du XIe siècle', *Le Moyen Age* 77 (1971), pp. 5–51, 193–238; J. Flori, 'La notion de Chevalerie dans les Chansons de Geste du XIIe siècle: étude historique de vocabulaire', *Le Moyen Age* 81 (1975), pp. 211–44, 407–45 and 'Sémantique et société médiévale: le verbe adouber et son évolution au XIIe siècle', *Annales E.S.C.* 31 (1976), pp. 915–40 and 'Chevalerie et liturgie: remise des armes et vocabulaire "chevaleresque" dans les sources liturgiques du XIe au XVe siècle', *Le Moyen Age* 84 (1978), pp. 247–78, 409–42 and 'Les origines de l'adoubement chevaleresque: étude des remises d'armes et du vocabulaire qui les exprime dans les sources historiques latines jusqu'au début du XIIIe siècle', *Traditio* 35 (1979), pp. 209–72, and 'Pour une historie de chevalerie: l'adoubement dans les romans de Chrétien de Troyes', *Romania* 100 (1979), pp. 21–53; Tony Hunt, 'The Emergence of the Knight in France and England 1000–1200', *Forum for Modern Language Studies* 17 (1981), pp. 93–114; Linda Paterson, 'Knights and the Concept of Knighthood in the Twelfth Century Occitan Epic', ibid., pp. 115–30; and W. H. Jackson, 'The Concept of Knighthood in Gerbort von Fritzlar's Liet von Troye', ibid., pp. 131–45; and Joachim Bumke, *The Concept of Knighthood in the Middle Ages*, trans. W. T. H. and E. Jackson (New York, 1982). On the state of knighthood and chivalry in the later medieval period, see especially P. Contamine, 'Points de vue sur la chevalerie en France à la fin du moyen âge', *Francia* 4 (1976), pp. 255–85; Maurice Keen, 'Huizinga, Kilgour, and the Decline of Chivalry', *Medievalia et humanistica* N.S. 8 (1977), pp. 1–20; Juliet Vale, *Edward III and Chivalry*; and the collection of articles published in *Chivalric Literature. Essays on Relations between Literature and Life in the Later Middle Ages*, ed. Larry D. Benson and John Leyerle (Kalamazoo, 1980). The most important general works on knighthood and chivalry are Richard Barber, *The Knight and Chivalry* (London, 2nd edn. 1974), and Maurice Keen, *Chivalry* (New Haven, 1984).

– in association with their personal name, as a title indicative of their social status.

For about a century the status of knight (which in the same period spread gradually throughout the territory of Western Christendom) was claimed in this way principally by vassals of relatively humble background and little personal wealth, who served the heirs of the governors and landed magnates of Carolingian days as soldiers in return for food, horse, armour, and perhaps a small landed fief, and helped their patronal lords to turn themselves into barons and princes at the expense of their neighbours. By about 1050, however, the military status of knight had acquired sufficient *éclat* in some regions that the magnates themselves – at first barons, then princes, and finally even kings – began to claim the title, and by 1200 most sons of the aristocracy throughout Western Christendom who were not destined for the church were formally admitted to knighthood when they were declared to be of full age, and commonly wrote the title 'knight' after their surname thereafter.

Knightage and baronage nevertheless remained quite separate classes in most parts of Europe until the 1180s, when the simple knights of France, now for the most part firmly implanted on landed fiefs, and fortified by the new knightly ideology promoted in the previous decade by the romances of the Arthurian cycle, began to usurp from their baronial lords such attributes of aristocratic status as the prefix *sire* (or *messire*), a distinctive coat of arms, and a fortified house. The subsequent evolution of the noble class or 'estate' followed different courses in the various kingdoms of Western Christendom, but in most kingdoms by about 1300 noble status (whatever privileges had been attached to it by local custom) had come to be defined in terms of descent from knights of any rank rather than (as formerly) from members of the old class of landed magnates, and all members of the landed military class, from kings and princes to the lords of single villages, had come to share in a common aristocratic culture, closely associated with knighthood.

Both the fusion of the knightly and baronial classes, and the triumph of knighthood as the unifying factor of the aristocratic culture that resulted from this fusion, were due in large measure to the ideology of knightliness which began to coalesce around 1150 in the courts of northern France and spread rapidly into the courts of neighbouring countries. This knightly ideology – which from the French word for knighthood and knightliness we have come to call 'chivalry' – had several distinct strands. These, though interwoven in its fabric, were never perfectly blended. The oldest strand, probably best termed 'vassalic' or 'military', went back to the earliest days of knighthood, and embodied the virtues suitable to an élite warrior in the service of a lord: prowess, courage, and loyalty. These qualities were those extolled in the *chansons de geste* of the early twelfth century (when they were summed up by the word *vassalage* rather than *chevalerie*), and were probably the only ones admired in the class of simple knights before its fusion with the old aristocracy.

The second strand, which may be called either 'aristocratic' or 'courtly', originated in the same princely courts for which Chrétien de Troyes and his imitators produced the earliest chivalric romances in the decades between 1170 and 1200. At once appealing to and developing the ideals already accepted by their princely patrons, the authors of the early romances described the adventures of men

7

of exalted birth and refined manners, whose principal goal was to win perpetual honour for themselves through the performance of notable deeds of valour – often (though not necessarily) in the service of a noble lady. In addition to the traditional military virtues of *prouesse* and *loyauté* (now extended to fellow knights and ladies), the romance writers assigned to the model knights they portrayed the aristocratic virtues of *courtoisie* or courtliness, *largesse* or generosity, and *franchise* or frankness – by which they meant that frank bearing which was considered a sign of aristocratic breeding and virtue.

The third strand that came to be woven into the fabric of chivalry, which may be characterized as 'religious', had its origins in the monastery – a social milieu where the behaviour of knights was generally condemned rather than admired. Various monastic writers of the twelfth century sought to turn the turbulent energies of the knights as a class towards a purpose that was at once more lofty and less destructive (at least to Christian society) than that of slaughtering, raping, and pillaging their neighbours at the behest of their lord. In his *De laude novae militiae*, written around 1130 for the benefit of the newly founded order of the knights Templar, the great Cistercian reformer Bernard of Clairvaux argued that the only true knights were those who, making themselves *milites Christi* or 'soldiers of Christ' in the most literal sense, devoted themselves wholly to the Crusade against the enemies of Christ.[10] John of Salisbury, in a treatise called the *Policraticus* composed shortly after 1150, proposed a rather broader set of goals and ideals for the knightly class, based in part on an identification of the contemporary *miles* or knight with the classical Roman *miles* or legionary soldier. He argued that knights should be carefully selected for soundness of blood, vigour of body, and courage of heart, should take an oath of loyal service to their prince when they were admitted to knighthood, and should then receive a thorough training in both bodily fitness and military science. The 'office' of this 'duly ordained soldiery' was 'to defend the church, to assail infidelity, to venerate the priesthood, to protect the poor from injuries, to pacify the province, to pour out their blood for their brothers (as the formula of their oath instructs them), and if need be to lay down their lives.'[11] These lofty conceptions of knighthood, with their emphasis on discipline, sacrifice, and piety, were only gradually and imperfectly integrated into the worldly ideology of knighthood developed in the romances, but by 1250 their more important elements seem to have been accepted, in theory at least, as inseparable parts of the knightly ideal.

Along with this new ideology grew up a new conception of the place of the knights as a body within the Christian commonwealth. Clerical writers had long divided the members of Christian society into three distinct *ordines* or 'orders', each of which had been created by God himself and assigned certain duties with respect to the others. The precise definition of these orders and their duties had differed somewhat from one writer to another, but most had distinguished an order of fighters (*bellatores* or *pugnatores*), whose members were charged not merely with defending but with governing the members of the other two.[12] By about 1175, the

[10] Migne, *Patrologia Latina*, CLXXXII, pp. 921–40.
[11] *Joannis Saresberiensis episcopi Carnotensis Policratici sive de nugis curialium et vestigiis philosophorum*, ed. Clemens C. I. Webb (Oxford, 1909), II, pp. 8–58.
[12] See Georges Duby, *Les trois ordres ou l'imaginaire du féodalisme* (Paris, 1978).

Norman bishop Etienne de Fougères felt justified in identifying this 'order' (restricted by earlier writers to kings and princes) with the knightly class or *chevalerie* as a whole,[13] and this identification soon came to be generally accepted as the theoretical basis for the political supremacy of the new knightly nobility in Western Christian society.

In keeping with this new conception – which put the 'order' of knights on a par with the 'order' of priests – the status of knight came to be conferred through a more or less elaborate rite of ordination, the *adoubement* or delivery of arms. Not surprisingly, the various local rites that came to be employed for this purpose by the end of the thirteenth century were derived from those that had originally been employed to inaugurate the reigns of kings, and had gradually been adopted for the same purpose (at different rates in different countries) by princes and barons. A relatively simple version of the rite emerged in the twelfth century and continued to be used when knights were made on the field of battle, but the rituals employed in conditions of peace tended to become increasingly elaborate and overlain with symbolism. Perhaps the earliest detailed description of a fully developed initiation rite is that in the anonymous French poem *L'Ordene de chevalerie*, probably composed at some time in the first half of the thirteenth century. According to its author, a man about to be made a knight should first be bathed in the bath of courtesy and bounty, to cleanse himself symbolically of all sin. He was then to retire to a fair bed, symbolic of the paradise which was to be the ultimate goal of his knightly endeavours. When he rose from this, he should be vested first in *draps* (presumably either a coat or a coat and surcoat) of white linen, signifying the state of cleanness in which his body was to be kept; a red *robe* (presumably either a surcoat or a mantle), signifying the blood that he was to spill in the service of God; black *chauces* or stockings of silk, representing death and the earth in which his body would eventually lie; a white belt, signifying virginity; and gold spurs, symbolic of the swiftness with which he was to carry out God's commandments. Next, the knight who was to confer the status was to gird the postulant with a sword (whose two edges represented justice and loyalty, and reminded the knight of his duty to defend the poor), and to strike him a light blow on his neck – the *collee* or 'accolade'. Finally, he was to give him the four commandments which every knight was bound to follow throughout his life: to refuse to be a party to false judgement or treason; to honour all ladies and damsels and defend them to the limit of his ability; to hear mass every day, when possible; and to fast every Friday in memory of the Passion of Christ. Since this treatise was to achieve a very wide currency in the thirteenth and fourteenth centuries, it probably had a major influence on the subsequent development both of the rite of *adoubement* and of the theoretical interpretations placed upon its elements. It certainly had an influence on the statutes of some of the earliest knightly 'orders' of the monarchical type, as we shall see.

The *Ordene de chevalerie* was but the first of a series of treatises on chivalry composed when the new ideas about the role of the knight had begun to crystallize into what would become their classical form. One other such work produced in the thirteenth century should also be mentioned here, since its influence can be clearly

---

[13] *Estienne von Fougières' livre des manières*, ed. Joseph Kremer (Ausgaben und Abhandlungen au dem Gebiete der romanischen Philologie, XXIX, Marburg, 1887).

9

seen in the statutes of several monarchical orders: the *Libre del ordre de cavayleria*, written around 1270 by the Catalan knight Ramon Llull, sometime Seneschal of Mallorca. Like the *Ordene*, this work was widely read throughout the fourteenth and fifteenth centuries, and was translated into Castilian, French, Scots, and English. In fact, it became the classic work on knighthood in almost every country west of Germany, and the view of the knight and his obligations it presented were to remain central to the chivalry of the later Middle Ages. After describing the sort of training a knight ought ideally to receive, Llull declared that a candidate for knighthood ought to be of sufficient age and strength to discharge the duties of knighthood, of noble lineage, and rich enough to support his rank, and should furthermore be without known 'reproach'. When he had been found by examination to possess the desired qualities, he could proceed to receive the accolade of knighthood, preferably at a major feast such as Pentecost, Christmas, or Easter. On the vigil of the feast he was to confess and to spend the night in prayer and contemplation, and in the morning was to hear mass with the other candidates, including a sermon on the articles of faith, the ten commandments, and the seven sacraments. Finally he was to receive the arms and accoutrements of knighthood (including spurs and a sword) from someone already a knight. With knighthood he assumed a number of duties: to defend the faith of Christ, as well as his temporal lord; to protect the weak, including women, widows, and orphans; to keep fit by hunting and taking part in jousts and tournaments; and to mete out justice to malefactors.

The evolution of both knighthood and chivalry slowed down considerably after about 1250, but did not stop altogether. The period between 1280 and 1525 witnessed a number of revolutionary developments in military technology and tactics which gradually deprived the knight of his position of absolute dominance on the field of battle. Catalan crossbowmen from about 1280, Swiss halberdiers from 1315, English longbowmen from 1346, and Swiss pikemen from 1476, all proved the effectiveness of lowborn infantry against noble heavy cavalry, and forced knights both to adopt ever more effective forms of defensive armour – including by 1400 an outer layer composed entirely of iron plates – and to fight increasingly on foot. Developments in military recruitment and organization also altered the traditional relationship between knights and princes, and converted a large proportion of the 'strenuous' or active knights first into mercenaries, serving as members of companies organized by professional captains or *condottieri*, and later (especially after 1450) into salaried members of the prince's standing army.[13a]

In the same period a variety of factors tended to discourage the sons of the lesser members of the old knightly class from assuming the burden of knighthood, at least until they had acquired a sufficient income to sustain it, and the virtual closure of the new noble estate in many kingdoms to persons not of knightly ancestry meant that those who were descended from knights no longer had to receive knighthood to enjoy the privileges of nobility. As a result, a steadily growing number of minor noblemen throughout Western Christendom chose to remain in the status of

---

[13a] On late medieval warfare, see especially Michael Howard, *War in European History* (Oxford, 1976), pp. 11–19; Philippe Contamine, *La guerre au Moyen Age* (Paris, 1980), pp. 232–306; and William H. McNeill, *The Pursuit of Power* (Chicago, 1982), pp. 65–83.

'squire' (*armiger, escuier, escudero*) – the title traditionally given to young men training for knighthood – throughout their lives. The consequent decline in the number of dubbed knights was dramatic: it has been estimated that the number of knights in England fell from about 6000 in 1100 to about 1250 in 1300 and 300 in 1420. Only princes and barons could afford to keep up the tradition of having most of their sons made knights when they came of age, at some time between their thirteenth and their twenty-second birthday, and they continued to do so with great regularity throughout the fourteenth and most of the fifteenth century. In fact, a practice arose in a number of princely courts of conferring knighthood upon the sons of the prince when they were young children, or even infants. Thus, as the absolute number of knights continued to decline, the proportion of the knightage made up of scions of the baronial class tended to increase, and knighthood became even more firmly associated with the highest class of Western Christian society, and even more honourable. Indeed, as the squires who avoided formal knighthood continued to function on the field of battle much as their knighted ancestors had done, and to consider themselves an integral part of the knightly class, formal knighthood gradually came to be looked upon as a sort of dignity which could be conferred on those of less than exalted birth as a mark of honour towards the end of a long and successful military career.[14]

Nevertheless, until about the middle of the fifteenth century knighthood continued to be thought of as a functional military status requiring the best available training and equipment, and even knights who held no higher rank were commonly paid a significantly higher wage than squires. The military superiority of the knight (and by extension of the squire) over all other forms of soldier remained an article of faith among the nobles and rulers of most countries until well into the sixteenth century, and 'men-at-arms' (as knights and squires came to be referred to collectively in military contexts) were only slowly displaced from the centre of the battlefield by the various forms of infantry and artillery introduced in the fourteenth century. Indeed, throughout the period with which this study is concerned the knight remained first and foremost a warrior, and the ethos of chivalry remained that of a warrior aristocracy whose principal occupation was fighting, and for whom honour was to be won primarily by displaying courage and prowess in combat.

Like most such classes, the knightly aristocracy of later medieval Europe was intensely conservative, and tended to look for its standards in the past. Since the romances and romanticized histories from which its notions of the past were largely derived had drawn a veil of chivalry over all past ages, and converted virtually every major figure of history or literature into a knight in the image of Arthur or Lancelot, the natural inclination of the aristocracy to regard the chivalry of all past ages as more glorious than that of its own received strong support from its favourite form of literature. The life of the ambitious knight in the fourteenth and fifteenth centuries was accordingly dominated above all by a desire to be held in the same high regard, both by his contemporaries and by all future generations, as the heroes of history and romance, whom he sought to emulate in every possible way. This

[14] On these developments, see N. Denholm-Young, 'Feudal Society in the Thirteenth Century: The Knights', in *Collected Papers on Medieval Subjects* (Oxford, 1946), and *The Country Gentry in the Fourteenth Century, with Special Reference to the Heraldic Rolls of Arms* (Oxford, 1969); and Contamine, 'Points de vue sur la chevalerie'.

element of chivalry inevitably gave rise not only to a good deal of 'heroic' behaviour but to a veritable cult of heroism. In keeping with the backward-looking tendencies of the age, this cult centred at first upon the military saints who had come to be regarded as the heavenly patrons of knighthood – St Michael the Archangel, captain of the hosts of heaven and the prototype of all earthly chivalry, St George of Lydda, and St Maurice of the Theban Legion. After about 1310 the cult was extended to the *Neuf Preux* – the nine most valiant or 'worthy' heroes of pagan, Jewish, and Christian antiquity familiar to contemporaries from history or romance: Hector, Alexander and Caesar; Joshua, David and Judas Maccabaeus; Arthur, Charlemagne and Godfrey de Bouillon.[15] By the end of the century the cult of heroism had been extended to include the greatest heroes of the age itself: Edward 'the Black Prince' of Wales, Bertran du Guesclin, Jean le Maingre de Boucicault, Don Pero Niño 'the Unconquered Knight', and Jacques de Lalaing, among others. The deeds of these latter-day *preux* were usually recorded for the edification of posterity, often by a herald, in a form of a 'chivalric biography' not very different from a romance.[16] The line between romance and reality was thus blurred in the present no less than in the past.

Not surprisingly, perhaps, the heroic chivalry of the Late Middle Ages found its chief active expression not in real warfare but in the sport and pageantry of which the nobility was so fond. Perhaps the most important single vehicle for the expression of heroic chivalry was the tournament, a form of mock battle in which two teams of mounted knights sought to defeat one another under certain agreed conditions, including a specified time and the use of specified weapons. The tournament, since it was fought under the watchful eyes of a crowd of spectators, was an almost ideal setting for winning the heart of one's lady while earning a reputation for knightly prowess and honour, and the romances themselves made much of tournaments for this very reason. By the end of the twelfth century the tournament (which like so many other elements of chivalry seems to have originated in France) had become the most popular diversion of the knightly class in most areas of Western Christendom, and during the thirteenth century it came to serve as a standard element in the festivities held by princes in celebration of great holidays and events. Taking their lead from the romances, the princes of the late twelfth and early thirteenth centuries decided to turn the popularity of the tournament to their own advantage by converting it into a relatively harmless festival of chivalry over which they themselves could preside, and a useful training ground for various military skills. What had begun as a wild mêlée hardly different

---

[15] See Ann McMillan, 'Men's Weapons, Women's War: the Nine Female Worthies, 1400–1640', *Mediaevalia* 5 (1979), pp. 113–39.
[16] See Johan Huizinga, *The Waning of the Middle Ages*, trans. F. Hopman (London, 1924; reiss. 1965), pp. 68–74; and Gervase Mathew, 'The Ideals of Knighthood in Late Fourteenth-Century England', in *Studies in Medieval History Presented to Frederick Maurice Powicke*, ed. R. W. Hunt, W. A. Pantin, R. W. Southern (Oxford, 1948), pp. 354–362. See also *The Life of the Black Prince by the Herald of Sir John Chandos*, ed. M. K. Pope, E. C. Lodge (Oxford, 1910); *Le livre des faicts du bon messire Jean le Maingre dit Boucicaut*, ed. J. Michaud, B. Poujoulat (Paris, 1881); Gutierrez Diaz de Gamez, *The Unconquered Knight: a chronicle of the deeds of Don Pero Niño*, tr. Joan Evans (selections) (London, 1928); *Le Livre des Faits du bon Chevalier Messire Jacques de Lalaing*, ed. Kervyn de Lettenhove, in *Oeuvres de Chastellain* (8 vols.; Brussels, 1863–66), vol. VIII.

from a real battle was gradually converted in the thirteenth century into a carefully regulated sport, in which blunted or 'rebated' weapons were used to prevent serious injury, and technical rules, rather than capture or death, were employed to determine defeat. Partly in order to allow the most accomplished knights a better opportunity to display their skills and win both renown and prize money, individual combats called 'jousts' were commonly added to the programme of events, in addition to the 'tourney' or tournament proper, in which the participants continued to fight in teams. In the second half of the fourteenth century, indeed, jousting gradually replaced tourneying as the principal element of the tournament, and after about 1380 the whole tournament was normally composed of various forms of jousts. From their earliest beginnings in the twelfth century, the tournaments staged by princes were commonly surrounded by pomp and pageantry, the details of which were often derived from the chivalric romances. From at least 1223 tournaments were held in which knights and ladies impersonated characters and even reenacted scenes from the better-known Arthurian romances, and from at least 1230 to 1380 one of the most popular forms of tournament in England, France, and Spain was a highly formalized type called a 'round table'.[17]

The increasingly elaborate rules that governed the various types of combat included in thirteenth-century tournaments came in the same century to be interpreted by a special class of minstrels called 'heralds', who by 1200 had already taken it upon themselves to recognize and describe the armorial bearings displayed on the shields and surcoats of all knights. A particularly striking indication of the importance of the tournament and of the heroic element of the chivalric ethos it represented can be seen in the steady growth in the later medieval period in the status and function of the heralds, who while continuing to proclaim and preside over tournaments and (from about 1250) compile rolls of armorial bearings, came to be attached on an increasingly permanent basis to the households of princes and kings, and to serve the latter both as experts in all areas of the 'Law of Arms', and as sacrosanct emissaries of the prince on many sorts of business in both war and peace. By 1400 the heralds – organized into a hierarchy of three ranks headed by 'kings of arms' with jurisdiction over whole provinces or kingdoms – constituted a sort of priesthood in the secular religion of chivalry, and presided at almost all of its rituals. So close did the relationship between heraldry and chivalry become, indeed, that between 1415 and 1518 the chief heraldic office of several countries came to be attached directly to the order of knighthood maintained by the prince,

---

[17] On the subject of tournaments, see especially Noël Denholm-Young, 'The Tournament in the Thirteenth century', in Hunt et al., Studies . . . Powicke, pp. 240–268; Sydney Painter, French Chivalry. Chivalric Ideas and Practices in Mediaeval France (Ithaca, 1940; reiss. 1957), pp. 45–51; Barber, The Knight and Chivalry, pp. 159–192; and Keen, Chivalry, pp. 83–101. On the influence of the romances on tournaments, see Huizinga, Waning, pp. 79–82; Roger Sherman Loomis, 'Chivalric and Dramatic Imitations of Arthurian Romance', in Medieval Studies in Memory of A. Kingsley Porter, ed. Wilhelm R. W. Koehler (2 vols., Cambridge, Mass., 1939), vol. I, pp. 79–97 (bibliography, p. 79, n. 1); R. H. Cline, 'The Influence of Romances on Tournaments of the Middle Ages', Speculum 20 (1945), pp. 204–211; and Roger Sherman Loomis, 'Arthurian Influence on Sport and Spectacle', Arthurian Literature in the Middle Ages, ed. R. S. Loomis (Oxford, 1959), pp. 553–559 (Bibliography, p. 553, n. 1).

the principal institutional embodiment of chivalry in the state.[18]

Although the tournament was the normal setting for the expression of heroic chivalry in the later Middle Ages, some quite eminent knights seem to have felt compelled to emulate the behaviour of the heroes of the romances in other settings as well, and undertook to perform what came to be called *emprinses* or 'enterprises of arms'.[19] These enterprises took a variety of distinct forms, of which the earliest and longest-lasting was a journey in search of adventure like those of the knights-errant of the romances. One of the first enterprises of this sort, and certainly the most famous, was the *Artusfahrt* of the Styrian knight Ulrich von Lichtenstein, described in his poem the *Frauendienst*.[20] According to that work, Ulrich set out in 1240 disguised as King Arthur, with the intention of challenging all knights he encountered to a joust. Those who accepted his challenge and broke three spears on him he admitted to his 'Order of the Round Table' – probably the earliest neo-Arthurian 'order'. Such journeys were still popular in the fifteenth century, especially among the knights of Spain and Germany. A second form of enterprise, particularly favoured in France and Spain between about 1390 and 1450, was that known in French as the *pas d'armes* or 'passage of arms'. Rather than wandering about, participants in a passage of arms chose a particular spot to defend (often a bridge), and issued a general challenge not unlike that used to announce a tournament. Finally, in the period between about 1390 and 1420, a few ambitious knights undertook enterprises of a particularly elaborate nature in the company of a dozen or more companions and for periods of one or several years, and thus established those ephemeral companies of knights I have termed 'votive orders'.

The idea that the chief goal of knightly activity was to win personal honour was commonly carried over from the playful world of the tournament and the enterprise of arms to the more serious world of warfare, and chivalrous notions often had a significant effect upon the way real battles were fought. Not only individual knights like Jacques de Lalaing but commanders like Marshal Boucicaut and princes like Edward III of England commonly exposed themselves to unnecessary dangers and sacrificed strategic and tactical advantages in order to maintain their heroic reputations or avoid the possibility of appearing less than honourable. Honour demanded that knights act in keeping with the foolhardy vows they often made in a vainglorious spirit before the beginning of campaigns and battles, and that the 'laws' governing the conduct of battles of various classes be obeyed, however

[18] On the role of the heralds in the Middle Ages, see especially A. R. Wagner, *Heralds and Heraldry in the Middle Ages: An Inquiry into the Growth and Armorial Function of Heralds* (Oxford, 1939; 2nd edn. 1956); P. Adam Even, 'Les fonctions militaires des hérauts d'armes: Leur influence sur le développement de l'héraldique', *AHS* (1957), pp. 2–33; A. R. Wagner, *Heralds of England* (London, 1967); O. Neubecker, *Le Grand livre de l'héraldique* (Brussels, 1977), pp. 10–31; and Keen, 'The Decline of Chivalry', pp. 14–15.

[19] On these *emprinses*, see Huizinga, *Waning*, pp. 81, 89; Painter, *French Chivalry*, pp. 51–54; Martín de Riquer, *Cavalleria fra Realtà et Letteratura nel Quatrocento* (Bari, 1970); and R. Vaughan, *Philip the Good. The Apogee of Burgundy* (New York and London, 1970), pp. 147–149.

[20] See Otto Höfler, 'Ulrich von Lichtensteins Venus fahrt und Artus fahrt', in *Studien zur deutschen Philologie des Mittelalters Friedrich Panzer zum 80. Geburtstag . . . dargebracht*, ed. W. R. Kienast (Heidelberg, 1950), pp. 131–152.

disadvantageous they might be. Needless to say, this chivalrous approach to warfare often had disastrous results. The utter rout of the knights of France at Crécy in 1346, at Poitiers in 1356, at Nicopolis in 1396, and at Agincourt in 1415, was largely due in each case to their refusal to see any essential difference between a battle and a tournament, even when the enemy was playing by very different rules. Nevertheless, the attitude which produced these disasters remained general among the nobles of France for at least half a century after Agincourt, and was not uncommon among the knights who followed Charles VIII into Italy at the end of the century.

Most late medieval knights seem to have adopted a more practical attitude when engaged in the more mundane aspects of warfare, however, and took part in the innumerable raids and seiges which the wiser captains of the age preferred to pitched battles, more for the wages they were paid and the booty and ransoms they could win than for any honour they might receive for performing an unusually valorous deed. Nevertheless, even the mercenary and often brutal side of the knight's military activities was effectively regulated by an elaborate code of professional conduct which probably owed a good deal to the chivalrous notions of courtesy and fellowship among knights. This code, generally known as the 'Law of Arms', was an extensive body of customs governing the behaviour of all members of the knightly class in almost every situation even remotely related to combat. It was especially concerned with practical questions relating to military discipline, the taking of prisoners and ransoms, and the distribution of booty, but it also dealt with the proper way to declare war or begin a battle, and the right way to display a particular coat of arms. Although some of its provisions were included in such positive codes as the *Siete Partidas* of Alfonso X of Castile (which contained a whole chapter on knighthood), it was largely unwritten, and was interpreted on the field of battle by commanders with the advice of the more experienced knights and heralds present. The great usually obeyed the received rules out of fear of public dishonour, and the rest of the knightly class out of an equally strong fear of being excluded from the profits of war – one of their most important sources of income.[21]

Warfare could be extremely profitable for an able knight, but it was a risky business, and many knights in the fourteenth and fifteenth centuries sought to decrease the risks by entering into a form of reciprocal relationship known as 'brotherhood-in-arms'. Each of the parties to this form of arrangement solemnly swore to be as a brother to the other and support him in a variety of ways – usually itemized in a written contract – either for life or for some specified period of time. Thomas, Duke of Clarence, on becoming the brother-in-arms of Charles, Duke of Orléans and Valois in 1412, swore to 'serve him, aid him, counsel him, and protect his honour and well-being in all ways and to the best of his powers', reserving his allegiance to his sovereign lord the King of England. A similar contract between Bertrand du Guesclin, Constable of France under Charles V, and Olivier de Clisson, his successor in that office, contains in addition a more specific agreement to divide equally the profits from ransoms of men and lands, and to inform one another as quickly as possible of any matter from which he might incur damage or blame. Like contracts of retinue and alliance (which they closely resembled),

---

[21] On the Law of Arms, see especially Maurice Keen, *The Laws of Arms in the Middle Ages* (London, 1965); and G. C. Squibb, *The High Court of Chivalry* (Oxford, 1959).

contracts of fraternity were not necessarily exclusive, and cases are known of men who had several brothers-in-arms at the same time. From such double and triple relationships, it was a fairly easy step to the creation of a network of a dozen or more, in which every member owed the same fraternal obligations to all the others – and indeed, several associations of precisely this nature are known to have existed in France and adjacent regions between 1350 and 1420. Although the smaller groupings of this sort usually defined themselves quite simply as an 'alliance',[22] groupings of a dozen or more often took the title 'order' or 'company', and adopted a corporate badge or name. It is to the societies of the latter sort that I have given the name 'fraternal orders'.[23]

3 The Religious Orders of Knighthood

The same century that saw the emergence of the idea that the knights of Western Christendom formed one of the general 'orders' of society witnessed the foundation of the first particular 'orders' of knights. In the narrow sense of a body of people bound by a common rule of life and a common corporate government, the term *ordo* had first been applied to the new federations of reformed Benedictine monasteries that had grown up in France and Germany in the tenth and eleventh centuries (most notably the Cluniacs and Cistercians), and was extended in the later eleventh and twelfth century to various similar communities of hermits and canons (Carthusians, Augustinians, and so forth) which adopted rules of life and forms of government peculiar to themselves in order to serve Christ in particular ways. The idea of creating a specialized 'order' of this sort made up of knights seems to have originated with Bernard of Clairvaux, who in 1128 helped compose a rule based on that of his own order for a small body of knights founded in Jerusalem about a decade earlier by the Burgundian baron Hugues de Payens to protect Christian pilgrims to that city from the Muslims. The new 'order', officially called 'the Poor Knights of Christ and of the Temple of Solomon', was an embodiment of Bernard's concept of the 'new knighthood', and its members, bound by the solemn monastic vows of poverty, chastity, and obedience, and living together under the traditional discipline of Benedictine monasticism, were to dedicate themselves wholly to a life of prayer and warfare against the enemies of Christ. The new order proved to have a great appeal for the more devout crusaders, and many knights who did not feel up to joining showed their support by endowing it with lands and goods, both in Syria and in Europe. By 1190 the Order of the Temple had become not only a major military power, with several hundred knights among its professed

---

[22] For example the *alliance* of four Gascon barons formed in 1360 (examined by H. Morel, 'Une association de seigneurs gascons au XIVe siècle', *Mélanges dédiées à Louis Halphen*, ed. C. E. Perrin [Paris, 1951], pp. 523–34), and the equally nameless *liansa* undertaken by the Viscount of Bruniquel and five other barons in Quercy in 1380 (examined by L. d'Alauzier, 'Une alliance des seigneurs de Quercy en 1380', *Annales du Midi* 64 [1952], pp. 149–51).

[23] See Maurice Keen, 'Brotherhood in Arms', *History* 47 (1962), pp. 1–17.

brethren, but a great international corporation, with a vast network of houses stretching from Jerusalem to Portugal.[24]

Successful institutions are almost always imitated, and during the course of the century after 1128 more than a dozen similar orders were created to serve similar purposes. The next two orders were created in Syria itself through the gradual militarization of existing orders of Augustinian hospitallers established there not long before: the Order of the Hospital of St John of Jerusalem, which began to add knights to its establishment in the 1130s;[25] and the Order of the Hospital of St Lazarus of Jerusalem, which had its origins in a hospital for lepers, and probably acquired its first knights from the two older orders in the 1130s or 1140s.[26] At least three further orders were founded in the Holy Land later in the century, primarily to serve the crusaders who were not either French or Italian: the Spanish order of the Knights of Our Lady of Mountjoy (later established in Aragon as the Order of Trafac), by 1180;[27] the English order of the Knights of St Thomas of Acre, founded about 1191 and militarized in 1227/8;[28] and the German order of the Teutonic Knights of the Hospital of St Mary in Jerusalem, founded in 1191 and militarized in 1198.[29] In the same period, several orders were created to support the war against the Infidel currently in progress in the Iberian peninsula: the Order of Calatrava, created by Navarrese Cistercians in 1158, and rapidly endowed with houses in all of the peninsular realms;[30] the Order of St James or Santiago, created by King Fernando II of Leon and the Archbishop of Compostela out of the *Fratres de Carceres* in 1170;[31] the Order of the Knights of St Benedict (later called 'of Aviz'), founded as the Portuguese branch of the Order of Calatrava in 1166/76;[32] the Order of St Julian of Pereiro (later called 'of Alcántara'), founded in Leon by 1176, and affiliated with Calatrava in 1218, when it received Alcántara from the Master of that order;[33] and the Order of St George of Alfama, founded by King Pere II of

---

[24] On the religious orders of knighthood in general, see Hans Prutz, *Die geistlichen Ritterorden* (Berlin, 1908); and Desmond Seward, *The Monks of War* (London, 1972). The latter has an excellent bibliography and a discussion of the principal secondary works. On the Templars, see Marion Melville, *La vie des Templiers* (Paris, 1951), and E. Simon, *The Piebald Standard* (Cassell, 1959).

[25] See esp. Jonathan Riley-Smith, *The Knights of St John in Jerusalem and Cyprus, 1050–1310* (London, 1967); and Ettore Rossi, 'The Hospitallers at Rhodes, 1306–1421' and 'The Hospitallers at Rhodes, 1421–1523', *A History of the Crusades*, ed. Kenneth M. Setton, vol. III (Madison, 1975), pp. 278–339.

[26] See esp. P. Bertrand de la Grassière, *L'Ordre Militaire et Hospitalier de Saint-Lazare de Jérusalem* (Paris, 1960).

[27] See esp. A. J. Forey, 'The Order of Mountjoy', *Speculum* 46 (1971), 250–66.

[28] See esp. A. J. Forey, 'The Military Order of St Thomas of Acre', *English Historical Review* 92 (1977), pp. 481–503.

[29] See esp. A. B. Boswell, 'The Teutonic Order', CMH VII (1932), pp. 248–69; and F. J. Carsten, *The Origins of Prussia* (Oxford, 1954) pp. 52–72.

[30] See esp. Joseph R. O'Callaghan, *The Spanish Military Order of Calatrava and its Affiliates* (London, 1975).

[31] See Derek W. Lomax, *La orden de Santiago, 1170–1275* (Madrid, 1965).

[32] M. de Olivieria, 'A Milicia de Evora e a Ordem de Calatrava', *Lusitania Sacra* 1 (1956).

[33] See esp. O'Callaghan, *The Spanish Military Order*, pt. IV.

Aragon in 1201.[34] Each of these defended some part of the long frontier between the Christian kingdoms and the Moors. Finally, in the first decades of the thirteenth century, two orders were founded on the northern frontier of Christendom, to take a leading role in the new Crusade against the heathen Balts of Livonia and Prussia – the Order of the Brethren of the Sword, in 1204,[35] and the Order of Dobrzyn, in 1228 – but both of these had been absorbed by 1240 by the Teutonic knights from Jerusalem, who had joined the northern Crusade in 1234.

The religious orders of knighthood founded in the twelfth and thirteenth centuries differed from one another in a variety of minor ways, but they all had a great deal in common. All were organized as monastic orders on the Cistercian model, and with the exception of the Spanish order of Santiago had rules that were based directly or indirectly upon either the Rule of St Benedict, independently adapted by the Templars in the Holy Land and by the knights of Calatrava in Spain (in each case under Cistercian influence), or that of St Augustine, adapted by the Hospitallers of St John and St Lazarus before they were militarized. Over the years, the original rules of most of the orders came to be supplemented by a growing number of statutes and customs, both written and unwritten, and by the end of the thirteenth century their statutes (in the broad sense of the term) typically included some hundreds of ordinances, dealing with almost every aspect of their organization and corporate life.[36] In addition to the dominant class of 'brother-knights', (who by 1325 were drawn exclusively from the nobility, and usually numbered anywhere from a few dozen in the smaller orders to several hundred in the larger), most orders included by 1200 several other classes of members: a class of 'half-knights' of less than noble birth (called 'brother-serjeants' by the Templars and 'brother-serjeants-of-arms' by the Hospitallers of St John), who seem to have performed the functions of squires as personal assistants to the knights; a smaller class of clerks in holy orders (called 'brother-chaplains'), who performed the clerical functions necessary for the order's spiritual well-being; and a rather more numerous class of servants of humble origin (called 'brothers-of-work' by the Templars and 'brother-serjeants-of-office' by the Hospitallers), who performed all of the minor tasks at the order's various establishments, including the hospitals that the latter order always maintained. Many of the members of the last class were probably mere hirelings, but the other classes seem to have been made up entirely of 'professed' brethren, who lived under the strict monastic rule of their order in one or another of the order's numerous houses in Syria or western Europe. Some orders (including the Templars and the Hospitallers of St John) also maintained associated lay confraternities or 'third-orders', whose members, called *confratres*, were admitted to all of the order's spiritual privileges in return for certain donations and vows of protection.

The professed brethren of most orders were distinguished from the first by a

---

[34] See Luis Más y Gil, 'La Orden Militar de San Jorge de Alfama, sus Maestres, y la Confradía de Mossen Sent Jordi', *Hildaguía* 6 (1958), pp. 247–56.

[35] See esp. J. G. Herder, *Der Orden Schwertbrüder* (Cologne, 1965).

[36] See J. Delaville Le Roulx, 'Les statuts de l'ordre de St-Jean de Jérusalem', *Bibliothèque de l'Ecole des Chartres* 48 (1887), pp. 341–356; and E. J. King, *The Rule, Statutes, and Customs of the Hospitallers, 1099–1310* (London, 1934); Henri de Curzon, *La Règle du Temple* (Paris, 1886); M. Perlbach, *Statuten des Deutschen Ordens* (Halle, 1890); Enrique Gallego Blanco, *The Rule of the Spanish Military Order of St. James 1170–1493* (Leiden, 1971).

peculiar habit of distinctly monastic cut. By the end of the thirteenth century the more formal version of the habit normally included a long mantle, white in most orders but black in the Order of St John, usually charged on the left breast with a cross of a more or less distinctive shape and colour. In the fourteenth century these crosses tended to become ever more distinctive in shape and to be worn on the breast of the *cappa* and coat as well as the mantle. The mantle and cross were the principal symbols of membership in the order, and in some orders, at least, postulants were solemnly vested with the mantle of the order when they were received.[37]

In keeping with the usual practice of monastic orders, the supreme government of the military orders was vested in a single chief officer, called *Magister* or 'Master' in most orders, and *Magnus Magister* or 'Grand Master' by the Templars and the Teutonic Knights.[38] The Master was elected for life from the brother-knights of the order by a complex process which varied in detail from one order to another, but increasingly tended to involve only those knights who held some administrative office within the order. The Master was charged with the general administration of the order, which usually included the appointment and supervision of subordinate officials, the reception of candidates for admission as brothers or *confratres*, the maintenance of discipline among the members of various classes, and the oversight of the order's finances. He also led the forces of the order on campaign, and both convoked and presided over the meetings of the order's officers, normally referred to as *Capitula Generalia* or 'Chapters General'. Originally the Master of most orders lived in the same community as the ordinary knights of the Order, but as the orders became richer and their houses more and more dispersed, their Masters tended to live apart and to adopt a style of life similar to that of the great secular princes with whom they spent much of their time.

In the day-to-day business of the order, the Master governed with the assistance of the great officers of the order, who resided with him in the order's headquarters, and were charged with the oversight of the various administrative departments into which the central government was divided. At regular intervals, however – about once a year in the great orders in the Holy Land, at Easter, Pentecost, and Christmas in the Spanish Order of Calatrava – the Master was obliged to convene a meeting of the full Chapter General, which in addition to the order's great officers normally included the administrators of the order's outlying possessions, typically called *commendatores* or 'commendors' (but usually referred to in English as 'commanders'). The normal purpose of such meetings (which bore a close resemblance to the similarly-named assemblies of the other great monastic orders of the period) was to consider the general situation of the order, to judge accusations of dereliction of duty and deviation from the Rule made against any of its members, and to assign punishments to those convicted. The members of most orders were also obliged to submit any disputes that had arisen amongst themselves to the binding arbitration of the Chapter General.

---

[37] See Riley-Smith, *The Knights of St John*, pp. 255–6; Lomax, *La Orden de Santiago*, p. 93; and O'Callaghan, *The Spanish Military Order*, I, pp. 33–8.
[38] The title *Magnus Magister* was occasionally used by the Master of the Hospital of St John in the twelfth century, when the usage had not yet stabilized, but did not come into regular use until 1489. (Riley-Smith, *The Knights of St John*, p. 277).

Although quarrels both within and among the military orders were not uncommon, and often posed a serious threat to public order, their constant readiness for war and their discipline and fanatical courage on the field of battle made them the *corps d'élite* of the crusading armies, and the kings of Jerusalem and the various Iberian realms came to rely heavily on their support in all their wars. As we have seen, as early as 1201 the King of Aragon founded an order specifically to defend and extend the southern boundary of his dominions, and later in the century King Alfonso X of Castile and Leon founded a short-lived order (dedicated to St Mary of Cartagena) for much the same purpose. Indeed, as long as the crusading movement continued to gain territory for Western Christendom, and the monastic ideal retained its lustre in the eyes of the Western Christian nobility, most of the existing orders continued to receive both recruits and endowments, and zealots continued to found new orders in their image. For a variety of reasons, however, the crusading and monastic ideals both began to decline in popularity in the second half of the thirteenth century. The utter failure of all the major crusading campaigns organized after 1228, and the loss between 1244 and 1291 of all the lands conquered by the Christians in Syria, undermined the confidence of the Christian nobility in the feasibility of the eastern Crusade, and after the death of the saintly Louis IX of France at Tunis in 1270 no major campaign for the reconquest of the Holy Land was ever launched from western Europe. The very success of the Iberian Crusade or *Reconquista*, which by 1253 had reduced the Muslim possessions on that peninsula to the small kingdom of Granada, greatly reduced the scope for crusading activity in western Europe. The steady growth of lay learning and the simultaneous decline in the discipline and asceticism of monastic life through much of Western Christendom in the same period began to erode the traditional respect of laymen of all classes for the monk, and made the monastic vocation considerably less attractive.

These developments inevitably undermined both the role and the situation of the military orders. Only one new order of this sort was founded outside of Spain between 1228 and 1468, and in 1221 the first of five mergers between lesser and greater orders took place. After the fall of Acre in 1291 the orders based in Syria were all forced to withdraw to their possessions in Cyprus or western Europe, and came under strong pressure to amalgamate in a single great order. The Order of the Temple, oldest and richest of all the military orders, was actually suppressed by papal decree in 1312 (largely because the King of France coveted its estates within his kingdom), and the Hospitallers and Teutonic Knights survived mainly because they succeeded in finding new bases from which to carry on the war against the Infidel: the Hospitallers on the island of Rhodes, from which they harried Muslim commerce from 1308 to 1530, and the Teutonic Knights in Prussia and Livonia, whence they maintained a war of attrition against the still pagan Lithuanians until the latter (converted to Catholic Christianity in 1386) finally crushed them at Tannenberg in 1410.

In Spain the decline was more gradual, because the Spanish kings, if less dedicated to the Reconquest than their predecessors, still feared a counterattack from the Moors of North Africa until about 1350. It is true that the Mercedarians of Aragon (founded in 1233) were demilitarized in 1317, but in the same year a new order (called the Knights of Christ) was founded to assume the functions of the suppressed Templars in Portugal, and two years later a similar order (called the

Knights of Our Lady of Montesa) was established for the same purpose in Aragon.[39] These and the remaining orders continued to exist and even to prosper in the first half of the fourteenth century, but after the successful defence of the peninsula by Alfonso XI of Castile in the second quarter of the century the orders had few opportunities to fight Muslims, and devoted most of their energies to their traditional pastimes of squabbling within and among themselves and interfering in secular politics. After about 1350 their members, like the members of most other religious orders, became increasingly worldly in outlook and behaviour, and the monastic discipline under which they were supposed to live seems to have rested ever more lightly on their shoulders. In the fifteenth century the Iberian kings finally succeeded in bringing the orders within their territories under their effective control, at first by securing the masterships of the orders for their sons and brothers, and after the conquest of Granada in 1492 by annexing the masterships – first in fact and later in law – to their respective crowns.[40]

The decline of the religious orders in the later Middle Ages was due to the decline of the ideals they represented rather than to any inherent defect in their organization. On all three frontiers of Western Christendom, the orders had demonstrated the military value of a disciplined body of carefully trained knights maintained in constant readiness under the unquestioned authority of a single commander, who could require their service whenever he needed it and for as long as he needed it. In all of these respects, the orders compared very favourably with the motley bodies of often recalcitrant and generally unruly vassals who made up a large part of the forces at the disposal of contemporary princes, and as we have seen, several Iberian kings actually founded orders of this sort to assist them in their wars against the Moors. It was probably only a matter of time, therefore, before a king decided to found a body of knights expressly designed to serve him and his successors in their secular wars as well, but the format of the existing orders had several disadvantages for the later medieval king who wished to create such a body. In the first place, their very nature as monastic institutions required that they be given not only a suitably spiritual goal (i.e., the war against the Infidel), but their own Master, elected from among the professed brethren, and inevitably independent to some degree of royal control. Furthermore, the demand of their rules that their members live a communal life required the provision of a vast endowment of lands and buildings, and would turn away most of the more prosperous and eminent members of the knightly class, among whom the religious life was largely out of favour. The kings who felt the need of an order wholly dedicated to their service had thus to think in terms of a strictly lay society, with a rule that included only the more useful and acceptable features of the older type of order. For such a society, they needed both a different model and – in an age which idealized the past and regarded all 'innovation' with the deepest suspicion – an historical precedent.

---

[39] See esp. Aurea L. Javierre Mur, *Privilegios reales de la Orden de Montesa en la Edad Media* (Madrid, 1945).
[40] The masterships of the Castilian orders were granted in perpetuity to Carlos I (*alias* Karl V) by a papal bull of 1523. On the later history of the Spanish military orders, see L. P. Wright, 'The Military Orders in Sixteenth and Seventeenth Century Spanish Society. The Institutional Embodiment of a Historical Tradition', *Past and Present* 43 (May, 1969), pp. 34–70.

As it happened, several precedents for a society of just the sort the kings in question had need of – composed of lay knights and attached directly to the courts of great rulers – existed in the romances from which their knowledge of history was largely drawn, and it is to these fictional societies of knights that we must next turn our attention.

4 The Fictional Orders of Knighthood

The idea that a king should be surrounded by a body of heroic companions was not an invention of the poets of the twelfth century, for the Germanic kings who had ruled over Western Christendom in the centuries after the collapse of the Roman administration had all had their *comitatus*, and their successors in the high and late Middle Ages continued to maintain a body of household knights to serve both as a bodyguard and as the core of the royal troop in battle. Moreover, the anonymous *jongleurs* who composed the *chansons de geste* in the eleventh and twelfth centuries surrounded their hero Charlemagne with a similar body of twelve 'peers', including the famous Roland and Oliver. The later body was well known in the fourteenth century, and may well have served as a direct model for the smaller monarchical orders founded in that period. Nevertheless, the evidence for the thinking of the founders suggests that they drew most of their inspiration from the fictional societies presented in the Arthurian cycle of romances, of which the first and most famous was of course the Round Table of King Arthur himself.

The body of knights that became the society of the Round Table was introduced into the Arthurian legend by Geoffrey of Monmouth, who wrote about it in his *Historia* in the following terms:

> Arthur then began to increase his personal entourage by inviting very distinguished men from far-distant kingdoms to join it. In this way he developed such a code of courtliness in his household that he inspired peoples living far away to imitate him. The result was that even the man of noblest birth, once he was aroused to rivalry, thought nothing at all of himself unless he wore his arms and dressed in the same way as Arthur's knights.[41]

The 'Round Table' around which this noble retinue came to be grouped in all the romances was introduced into the legend by Geoffrey's translator and popularizer, Wace, who thus described its invention in his *Roman de Brut*:

> For the noble barons that he had,
> Of whom each thought himself to be the better,
> Held himself to be the best,
> Nor did any of them know the worst,
> Arthur made the Round Table,
> Of which the Britons speak many fables.
> There sat the vassals,
> All chivalrously, and all equal.[42]

[41] *History of the Kings of Britain*, trans. L. Thorpe (London, 1966), p. 222.
[42] *Le Roman de Brut*, ed. I. Arnold (Paris, 1938–40), vv. 9747–9754.

The image of the Round Table presented by Wace was steadily elaborated in the romances based upon his work.[43] In the earliest romances – those of Chrétien de Troyes and his continuators and imitators in the late twelfth and early thirteenth centuries – it remained little more than a convenient assembly point for the members of Arthur's entourage, and had no particular size or significance. In the *Merlin* of Robert de Boron, however, written at the beginning of the thirteenth century, its origin and nature were transformed completely, and it acquired a more definite form. According to the *Merlin*, the table was instituted first by Arthur's father, King Uther, at the behest of the wizard Merlin, who declared that it was destined to complete a trinity of holy tables of which the other members were the table of the Last Supper and the table of the Holy Grail. The Round Table itself was to be an exact replica of the Grail table (though on a larger scale) with exactly fifty-one places, of which one, the 'siege perilous' (representing that of Judas at the table of the Last Supper), could only be occupied by a knight of outstanding worthiness. Merlin himself was to choose the first fifty knights who were to make up the company of the Round Table, and although unknown to one another previously, after the first common meal they ate at the Table they would hold each other in undying affection. This, broadly speaking, was the image of the Round Table and its company retained in most of the romances of the slightly later Prose Vulgate Cycle, though in some of these the number of knights was raised to 150 or even 250. As the Vulgate Cycle was probably more widely read than any other in the later Middle Ages, its picture of the Round Table company was probably the one with which most people in that period were familiar.

The Round Table was at first the only knightly society in the Arthurian cycle, but at least two others were later added. One of these was the society of the guardians of the Grail, invented by Robert de Boron, but it did not provide a very useful model for later foundations. The other society, that of the *Franc Palais* – the 'Frank' or 'Noble Palace' – was created by the anonymous author of the vast prose romance *Perceforest*, written in the French dialect of Hainault between 1314 and 1325 – immediately before the foundation of the earliest monarchical orders.[44] In that work, Perceforest himself, a companion of Alexander the Great on his British expedition who is given the southern part of the island to rule, is both an ancestor and a pre-Christian prefiguration of Arthur. Unlike Arthur, however, not he but the 'Sovereign God' establishes a society of knights in his court, miraculously building a round tower, the *Franc Palais*, which houses an immense round ivory table surrounded by 300 seats. God himself names the first sixty-three knights who are to sit in these places, each of which is then marked with the occupant's shield-of-arms hanging on the wall behind it. No one unworthy could be admitted to complete the company, and all those admitted were to be as equals – this being the significance of the *franchise* which makes the Palace 'Frank'.

Given their propensity for emulating the heroes of Arthurian romance, it is not unlikely that some fourteenth-century kings would have attached bodies of knights

---

[43] See A. Micha, 'La Table ronde chez Robert de Boron et dans la Queste du Saint Graal', *Les Romans du Graal aux XIIe et XIIIe siècles* (Colloques internationaux du Centre national de la recherche scientifique, III, Paris, 1956), pp. 119–136.
[44] See the summary and study by Jeanne Lods, *Le Roman de Perceforest* (Geneva, Lille, 1951).

to their courts even if the religious orders of knighthood had not existed, and it is clear that both the society of the Round Table and that of the Frank Palace served as precedents and general models for some of the earliest monarchical orders. Unfortunately for the founders of these orders, however, the writers who had invented and modified the fictional societies had failed to describe their rules and structure in any detail, so their value as organizational models was extemely limited. In order to provide their new societies with workable constitutions that did not require a monastic form of discipline, therefore, the kings and princes who founded the earliest monarchical orders were obliged to turn for a model to yet another form of organization, the lay devotional confraternity – a type of society whose members, while undertaking significant obligations and participating in a variety of corporate activities, continued to live normal lives in their own homes, and to support themselves from their own private income or earnings.

5 The Lay Devotional Confraternities

It is not without interest here that the confraternity of the later Middle Ages seems to have had its origin in the *gilda* of the pagan Germans, which was originally a band of warriors who assembled regularly to take part in a sacrificial banquet. At an early date other groups of men with common interests began to organize themselves into similar 'guilds', which under the influence of the Church acquired an increasingly Christian character. Such societies were created in part to permit laymen to practice the piety and spiritual mutuality characteristic of monastic communities, and inevitably borrowed many of their customs from the Benedictine tradition. By 1200 guilds or confraternities were common throughout Latin Christendom, and their numbers continued to grow steadily throughout the later medieval period, eventually involving most of the population.

Their popularity was due in part to the spiritual benefits they offered their members (in a period when lay piety and eschatological fears were also growing steadily), and in part to the ease with which their basic format could be adapted to different 'secondary' functions, including some quite unrelated to devotion. Societies with many different purposes adopted a confraternal form of constitution, including charities concerned with aiding the poor, the sick, or the dying, third-orders and penitential societies concerned with saving their members' souls through corporate asceticism, and craft-guilds whose members banded together under the protection of the patron saint of their trade for mutual assistance in prayer and profit.[45]

Despite their many differences, the confraternities of late medieval and early modern Europe all shared certain basic characteristics which make it possible to

---

[45] There is a considerable literature on medieval confraternities, but relatively little of a general nature. See especially G. Monti, *Le Confraternite Medievali* (Venice, 1927); G. Le Bras, 'Les confréries chrétiennes: Problèmes et propositions', *Revue historique de droit français et étranger*, 4e sér. 19–20 (1940–41), pp. 310–363; E. Coornaert, 'Les Guildes médiévales', *Revue historique*, 99 (1948), pp. 22–55, 206–43; and Jean Bennet, *La mutualité française. Des origines à la révolution de 1789* (Paris, 1981). See also J. Heers, *L'Occident aux XIVe et XVe siècles: Aspects économiques et sociaux* (Paris, 1970), pp. 336–341.

speak of them as a single phenomenon. Each society had its own statutes or constitution which, though formulated to suit its own particular needs and aims, followed for the most part a remarkably standard plan, and was often based directly upon the constitution of some older society known to its founders. The statutes generally dealt with four broad topics, usually arranged in the following order: the goals for which the society was founded; the recruitment and induction of new members; the rights and duties of those who had been admitted; and the activities and administration of the society.

The statutes which dealt with the subject of recruitment normally specified the qualities – religious, moral, physical, and social – required for membership, as confraternities were usually restricted to people of a certain profession, class, or area. Once it had been determined that a candidate met the society's standards, the members voted on whether he should be admitted. If elected, the candidate was generally required to pay some sort of entry fee to the society's treasurer or chaplain, and then to promise, often under oath, to obey the society's statutes. He was then received into the society in some formal way, and only then acquired all the rights and duties of membership.

A significant number of both the rights and the duties of membership in most confraternities were religious in nature. This was due in part to the fact that the society as a whole was almost always placed under the protection of a particular patron in the court of Heaven, for whose aid or advocacy the members had to pay with suitable corporate devotions. The cult of the patron saint usually consisted primarily of a corporate celebration of his annual feast, often accompanied by solemn processions, a lavish banquet, and other forms of profane rejoicing. To this was sometimes added the celebration of weekly masses in his honour. The members of the confraternity were also commonly obliged to assist at certain other masses, recite certain offices and prayers, and perform various works of charity. The spiritual benefits obtained in return for the performance of these religious duties were often considerable. In addition to a variety of spiritual indulgences, the confraternity generally provided solemn funerals for its dead, and numerous prayers and masses for both its dead and its living members.

Most of these religious activities required both a church or chapel in which to perform them and at least one priest to officiate. The majority of confraternities built or acquired their own chapel – dedicated, of course, to the society's patron – and the larger societies employed a college of several priests to perform the statutory rites. The chapel generally served as the centre of the society's corporate life. It often had schools, almshouses, or hospitals attached to it, according to the nature of the confraternity and the extent of its endowment. Normally there was also a hall for the meetings and banquets. The administration of the endowment, which could consist of a great variety of goods, properties, and rents, required the employment of a treasurer, and the performance of the society's various corporate functions often necessitated the employment of several other corporate officers and servants.

Priests and lay officers alike were employees rather than members of the confraternity, but the chief officer was generally elected by the members from among their own number. The lay confraternities as a whole appear to have had a great fear of arbitrary rule, for the chief officers were changed regularly, and their terms seldom exceeded two years. In theory, at least, any member of the society was normally eligible for election to its highest office. Once elected, the presiding officer generally shared his authority to a greater or lesser extent with the assembly or chapter of the society.

Like the monastic orders upon which they were based, confraternities commonly attempted to control the actions of their members, at least with respect to matters covered by their corporate statutes, by holding an examination of conduct during their annual meeting and imposing various penalties, usually in the nature of fines or penances, for infraction of the rules. For particularly grave faults the usual penalty was exclusion from the society. They also frequently attempted to adjudicate disputes and (when possible) to effect reconciliations between members who had quarrelled. It should finally be noted that, from the first decade of the fourteenth century if not earlier, the members of confraternities on festive occasions wore 'liveries' and 'cognizances' very similar to those later worn by members of lordly households and retainers, and it is not unlikely that the idea of adopting such symbolic forms of costume was borrowed by the lords from these organizations.

The great majority of confraternities were made up of members of the Third Estate rather than the nobility, but knightly confraternities dedicated to the promotion of the Crusade are known to have existed in Spain in the mid-twelfth century,[46] and various similar confraternities composed largely of knights took part in the religious and factional wars of Italy in the following century.[47] Some of these confraternities were founded primarily to provide mutual support in warlike endeavours, much like the societies we have distinguished as 'fraternal orders', and by 1326 societies of this sort had become sufficiently common to provoke the condemnation of the Council which met in that year with the Pope in Avignon. By this time, according to the description in the records of the Council, they commonly dressed, like the members of other sorts of confraternity, 'in the same robes, with particular badges or ensigns' to identify them.[48] All of these societies, like most of the numerous more or less elaborate confraternities of knights founded in the later fourteenth and fifteenth centuries, seem to have been founded by knights of middle or lower rank, but it was almost inevitable that some king, moved by admiration both for the religious and the fictional orders of knighthood to establish a society of knights attached directly to his court, would recognize the advantages of the confraternal format, and adapt it to his own peculiar needs.

In fact, the first society of lay knights known to have been founded by a prince was a confraternity called the Fraternal Society of St George, established in Hungary in 1325 or 1326. Although this society lacked a clearly defined presidency of any sort, and thus did not conform precisely with our definition of a monarchical order, there can be no doubt that it was intended to function in the same way as the later orders in which the presidential office was defined in the statutes, and it must thus be considered here as representing the earliest attempt to create an order of knights firmly attached to a princely crown.

---

[46] See P. Rassow, 'La Confradía de Belchite', *Anuario de historia del derecho español* 3 (1926), pp. 200–26.

[47] See Conte Luigi Cibrario, 'Delle società popolari e degli aspize de' nobili nelle città libere piemontesi e specialmente della società di S. Giorgio di Chieri', in *Studi Storici* (Turin, 1851), pp. 343–67; Monti, *Le Confraternite*, I, pp. 7–9; and N. J. Houseley, 'Politics and Heretics in Italy: Anti-Heretical Crusades, Orders and Confraternities, 1200–1500', *Journal of Ecclesiastical History* 33 (1982), pp. 193–208.

[48] See Keen, *Chivalry*, p. 181.

Chapter 2

The Fraternal Society of Knighthood
of St George
Hungary, 1325/6–c.1395?

1 Historical Background

The idea of creating an 'order' composed entirely of lay knights seems to have
originated in the mind of Károly (or Charles) I, King of Hungary and its dependent
realms and territories from 1309 to 1342.[1] Though ruler of a Magyar-speaking
kingdom that had only accepted Christianity in the year 1000 and still retained
three centuries later a social and political culture very different from those of the
other kingdoms of Latin Christendom, Károly I was born a member of the Angevin
branch of the French royal house of Capet established in 1264 on the throne of the
mainland kingdom of Sicily by Count Charles of Anjou and Provence, the younger
brother of the sainted King Louis IX.[2] No fewer than four orders of knighthood
were to be founded by members of this house, which carried the chivalrous culture
of the French royal court to all of the lands they came to rule in southern and
eastern Europe.

The future King Károly of Hungary – christened Carlo Roberto after his birth in
Naples in 1288 and commonly called 'Caroberto' in Italian – was the
great-grandson of Charles of Anjou, and had been for several years the heir
presumptive to the latter's Sicilian throne. His father, Carlo 'Martello', Prince of
Salerno, had been the eldest of the five sons borne to King Charles or Carlo II of
Sicily by his wife Maria, daughter of King István V of Hungary. When Maria's
brother László IV 'the Cuman' died childless in 1290, Carlo 'Martello' had laid
claim to the vacant throne in the right of his mother, but had died without
realizing his claim only four years later. Caroberto, his only son by his wife
Clemencia von Habsburg, was then only eight years old, and in no position to
defend any of his hereditary rights. While he was still a minor he was in fact
excluded from the succession to the throne of Sicily in favour of his father's younger
brother Roberto, on the grounds that the latter was more closely related to the

---

[1] On his life and reign, see Bálint Hóman, *Gli Angioini di Napoli in Ungheria* (Rome, 1938),
and 'Hungary, 1301–1490', *Cambridge Medieval History*, VIII, pp. 592–9; and Emile
G. Léonard, *Les Angevins de Naples* (Paris, 1954).

[2] On this kingdom and its royal house, see below, pp. 211–213.

still-living king, Carlo II. Neither Caroberto nor his heirs ever fully recognized the legitimacy of his exclusion, but Caroberto himself decided that he had a better chance of obtaining the crown of his father's father if he could first conquer the kingdom he claimed in the right of his father's mother.

Following the death of Caroberto's great-uncle King László 'the Cuman' in 1290, the Kingdom of Hungary had lapsed into almost total anarchy. A 'patriotic' party of magnates had succeeded in having the last member of the native dynasty of Árpád crowned as King Endre III, but his rights had been contested by several foreign princes and his ten-year reign was torn by constant civil strife. Caroberto's claim was better than those of the other contestants on strictly genealogical grounds, and he had succeeded in gaining the support of the Pope, Boniface VIII, who as overlord of the kingdom disputed the right claimed by the Hungarian parliament to elect a king in cases of disputed succession. In August 1300 Caroberto set out from Naples under a papal banner to wrest the throne from the 'usurper', Endre III, and on the latter's death in the following year was crowned at Esztergom as King Károly I. Later that same year, however, he was forced to surrender his throne to another of the claimants, King Václav II of Bohemia, who with the support of most of the Hungarian nobility retained control of much of Hungary until 1306. Caroberto, or Károly (as we must now call him) continued to press his claim, supported by the Pope, the Hungarian hierarchy, and some of the greater barons, but was unable to displace either Václav of Bohemia or his successor Otto of Bavaria until June 1309, when he was again installed on the throne. Even this reenthronement was not generally recognized until he was again crowned with the holy crown of St István in August 1310, and much of the kingdom remained outside his control until his great victory over rebel forces at Rozgony on 15 June 1312.

Although Károly's authority as king rested in theory on his election by the Estates assembled in parliament, it depended in reality on a series of pacts privately concluded with certain of the great magnates or 'oligarchs', who in the last decades of the previous century had succeeded in securing effective control over most of the kingdom. These pacts placed significant limitations upon the free exercise of royal authority, restricting among other things Károly's right to appoint persons of his own choice to the high offices of the kingdom. Károly's power to govern was further limited by the fact that some of the most powerful magnates of the realm – among them the Voivod of Transylvania, the Bans of Slavonia and Bosnia, and the Count Palatine of North-West Hungary – remained indifferent or hostile to him even after his coronation.

The young Sicilian prince, who was only twenty-one at the time of his second enthronement, was thus confronted with a formidable task if he wished to secure the effective control of his hard-won kingdom from the magnate 'oligarchs'. Fortunately both for himself and his kingdom his talents and energies were to prove equal to the task. The principal modern historian of his house, Bálint Hóman, attributed to him '. . . a strong disposition to autocracy, perseverance and tenacity, a sagacious and profound intuition of the practical demands of politics, a deep understanding of men, diplomatic tact, adaptability, seductive manners, a balanced temperament as inclined to diversions and pleasures as to serious and tenacious labour, [and] a warlike and chivalrous spirit.'[3] Like others of his house

---

[3] Quoted in translation in Léonard, Les Angevins, p. 300.

who had secured foreign thrones, he sought to assimilate himself to the culture of his new subjects to the extent that he felt was necessary to be accepted by them, while retaining enough of the French culture of his ancestors to maintain close relations with the other branches of his house. His reign and that of his son Lajos (or Louis) 'the Great' (r. 1342–1382), who continued his policies, are now looked back to as the golden age of medieval Hungary – the period when the kingdom reached the historic heights of its power and influence in Europe.

Once securely seated on the throne, Károly set out to destroy the power of the magnate oligarchs, not only by beating them down on the field of battle, but by refusing to summon except on rare occasions the parliament which they dominated, by excluding them systematically from all important offices in the state, and by securing the service and political support of the lesser nobles throughout the kingdom through a generous redistribution of lands confiscated from defeated rebels. Indeed, he introduced into Hungary a whole new pattern of feudo-vassality, in which most of the members of the middle and lower strata of the old nobility, along with new men whom he added to their ranks as a reward for their loyal service to his cause, were bound directly to himself and his house by the closest possible ties. The leaders of this new class of royal vassals, who led the *banderia* or principal units of the new feudal army Károly introduced in the same period, came to be known as *barones naturales seu solo nomine*, in contradistinction to the older *veri barones regni*. Throughout his reign Károly sought to increase the wealth and power of the new *barones naturales* by every means at his disposal, and after the suppression of the last major revolt of the oligarchs in 1324 he reserved to them all the chief offices of both the central and provincial governments.

Like other princes of his time, Károly strove to increase his influence over his noble vassals by creating a brilliant court, and by promoting among them the ideals of chivalry as they were currently understood in Naples.[4] The members of the old magnate class had already begun to adopt both the ethos and the trappings of chivalry in the previous century, but the lesser nobles, from whose ranks Károly drew most of his support, were as yet almost untouched by the knightly ideal when he came to the throne. Károly used a variety of methods to promote chivalry among his vassals, including not only the *barones naturales* but the lesser officers whom he made 'knights of the royal court' (*aule regie milites*). He seems to have encouraged them to improve their knightly skills by taking part in tournaments and jousts, and conferred upon many of them both heraldic arms and (more commonly) crests, specifically 'because in the royal service, that is in the host, in tournaments, and in other military processions and expeditions it has become the custom to distinguish the persons of the *fideles* of the realm from others by means of an *insignium* of their own, and this they cannot obtain from anyone except the royal majesty.'[5] Indeed,

---

[4] On Károly's interest in chivalry, see Hóman, 'Hungary', and Erik Fügedi, 'Turniere im mittelalterlichen Ungarn', in *Das Ritterliche Turniere im Mittelalter. Beiträge zu einer vergleichenden Formen- und Verhaltensgeschichte des Rittertums*, ed. Josef Fleckenstein (Göttingen, 1986), pp. 390–400, esp. pp. 394–5.

[5] The Latin, quoted in Fügedi, 'Turniere', p.394, n.15, reads: 'quia in regalibus servitiis, videlicet in exercitibus, tornamentis et aliis quibuslibet armalibus processibus et expeditionibus regni personas fidelium proprii insignii titulo a diversis consueuerunt distingere et hoc non ab alio aliquo valent opptineri, nisi a regia maiestate.'

under Károly and his son Lajos – who maintained a formal court of honour called the *curia militaris* for the maintenance of the laws of arms – the Magyar-speaking court of Hungary became famous throughout Europe as a school for chivalry in the traditions of northern France. It is against the background of these and other reforms undertaken by Károly in the 1320s and '30s, which gradually restored order and prosperity to the war-torn lands of the Crown of St István, that the creation of the knightly order called the Fraternal Society of Knighthood of St George the Martyr must be seen.

2 Foundation and General History

The precise date of the foundation of the Society of St George (as we shall call it for convenience) is not known, but it was certainly in existence on St George's Day (23 April) 1326, as the sole surviving copy of its statutes records that a series of amendments were adopted on that date.[6] It is likely, judging from the history of most later orders of the same type, that Károly had proclaimed the creation of the new order at some time during the previous year – that is to say, at some time after 23 April 1325.[7] This timing is also probable in the light of what we know of his situation at that time, for as we have seen he had finally broken the power of the oligarchs in 1324, and had begun to distribute offices to his most trusted followers. As we observed in the last chapter, the fact that the first lay order was created less than a decade after the foundation of successors to the suppressed Order of the Temple by the Kings of Portugal (in 1317) and Aragon (in 1319) suggests that its creator drew some inspiration from the actions of the latter monarchs, but Károly's precise role in the establishment of the Society of St George is far from clear. In fact it is not certain that Károly was even present on the occasion of the formal ratification of the original statutes of the Society, which according to the preamble to the statutes took place during a meeting of the chapter of the primatial cathedral of Esztergom in the presence of the Archbishop-Primate, various other prelates, and representatives of the secular and regular clergy. As we shall see, Károly seems to have done his best to conceal his role not merely in the creation but in the governance of the Society, but the statutes nevertheless make it clear that he was to play a leading part in its activities, and it would be difficult to believe that he was not the moving force behind its foundation. He was certainly present on the day

---

[6] Unlike several other short-lived orders founded in the fourteenth century, the Society of St George was unknown to the early historians of knightly orders, and is still virtually unknown to historians outside of Hungary. Although the statutes of the Society were published by Fejér in 1852, the only study I have found of this order is in a general article on knightly orders in Hungary: László Erdélyi, 'Bajtarsi egyesületek a magyar lovagkorban', in *Emlékkönyv Dr Gróf Klebelsberg Kuno Negyszázados Kulturpolitikai Müködésének Emlékére* (Budapest, 1925), pp. 249–58, esp. pp. 253–5. The Society is discussed even more briefly by both Hóman, *Gli Angioini*, p. 529, and 'Hungary', p. 602; by Léonard, *Les Angevins*, p. 30; and by Fügedi, 'Turniere', pp. 394–395.

[7] Fügedi postulates that it was founded in or shortly after 1318, but does not explain why.

30

the (first) amendments to the statutes were adopted, for the preamble to the amendments declares that they were established in his presence and in keeping with his will.

The statutes referred to, preserved in what appears to be the original manuscript in the Hungarian National Archives,[8] are in fact the only evidence I have found for either the nature or the history of the Society. If the Society ever met again after April 1326 it left no record of those meetings, no version of the statutes containing later amendments has survived to prove that the Society did continue to meet, and contemporary chroniclers did not see fit to take note of any of its activities.[9] Hóman postulated that the Society was preserved until the civil wars that followed the death of Károly's son Lajos in 1382, and fell apart following the death of Lajos' daughter Mária, the last member of the Hungarian line of her house, in 1395.[10] Given what we know about the history of all later orders this seems very likely. In any case the Society may reasonably be presumed to have dissolved at some time before the creation of the second Hungarian order, that of the Dragon, founded by the late queen's husband and successor, Zsigmond von Luxemburg-Brandenburg, in 1408.[11]

In the total absence of any other documentation, my account of the Society of St George will of necessity be based entirely on the statutes promulgated at and before the meeting of April 1326. An examination of these should allow us to form a reasonably good idea of what the founder hoped to accomplish by establishing so novel an organization, and to what extent, if any, he borrowed from any of the sources and models outlined in the Introduction. Unfortunately, we have no way of knowing whether the surviving statutes were in effect throughout the history of the Society, and as chapter 8 of the statutes requires the members to add one new article every year, it is quite possible that after seventy years they were transformed almost beyond recognition. The surviving statutes thus permit us to reconstruct the nature of the order and the rights, obligations, and activities of its members only in the years immediately following its foundation. This is a good deal less than we might wish to know about the earliest lay order, but it is considerably better than nothing.

---

[8] Budapest, Országos Levéltar (National Archives), DL. 40 483. Two transcriptions of this document have been published: the first, by György Fejér in his *Codex diplomaticus Hungariae ecclesiasticus ac civilis* (Buda, 1832), VIII/3, no. L, pp. 163–170; the second, accompanied by a facsimile, by Antal Pór, in *Az Anjou Ház örösei (1301–1439)*, vol. III of *A magyar nemzet története* (The History of the Hungarian Nation), ed. Sándor Szilagyi (10 vols., Budapest, 1895), between pp. 138–139. Because the text is badly worn where the document was folded, the two transcriptions do not always agree, and the latter is on the whole more reliable. I hope to publish a critical edition of this and all of the other statutes that have not been edited.

[9] I have found no reference to the Society in any of the chronicles covering the history of Hungary in this period.

[10] *Gli Angioini*, p. 529.

[11] See below, p. 348.

3 The Statutes of the Society

The statutes of the Society were set forth in Latin – the normal vehicle for written expression in Hungary before the 'revival' of Hungarian in the nineteenth century – in a text of about 1700 words taking the form of letters patent. The original statutes – those adopted before the meeting of April 1326 – consist of a prologue followed by fifty-nine ordinances organized (not always logically) into twenty-three chapters, one of which (the last, including three ordinances) is redundant.

Like the prologues that precede the statutes of most later orders, and indeed like the preambles to many contemporary charters of particular solemnity, the Prologue to the statutes of the Society of St George explains the actions of the founders in terms of generally accepted principles and expresses its explanations in relatively complex and grandiloquent language. In it, the *Universitas* or 'Community' of the Society declare, in the presence of the Archbishop of Esztergom, Primate of Hungary, seven other Hungarian bishops, and various abbots, friars, and other clergymen gathered in the presence of the Chapter of Esztergom, that they, moved by the highest ideals of Christianity, had determined to band together in a fraternal union to defend the king and the Holy Crown of the realm from their faithless enemies, who, moved by Satan, lay in ambush throughout the kingdom.

The statutes proper are loosely organized into seven groups. The first eight chapters are concerned with what may loosely be described as the religious or moral obligations of the members, while chapters 9 through 11 set forth what may be termed the secular obligations of the members both to one another and to the king. Chapters 12, 13, and 14 form a group of miscellaneous statutes unrelated either to one another or to those preceding or following them. Chapters 15 and 16 are concerned with obligations related to the Monday meal, and chapter 17 with a related weekly obligation. Chapters 18 and 19 form another miscellaneous group; on the basis of their subject matter they seem to belong in the second group of chapters, after chapter 10. Chapters 20 and 21 set forth the procedures to be followed in electing a new member to the Society. Chapter 22 finally deals with the judgement of those members who failed to observe the statutes. In the manuscript these statutes are followed immediately by a short prologue announcing the additional statutes adopted on 23 April 1326. The latter (which I have numbered continuously with the original chapters) consist of some nine ordinances organized into six chapters, and deal with the number of members the Society was to include, the Society's regular meetings, the rights and duties of the Judges, and relations between members and the enemies of other members. As we shall see, these statutes (like those of some later orders) leave a great deal unsaid, and much of what they do say is not easily interpreted.

4 The Name, Title, and Patron of the Society

In the first prologue the founders refer to themselves as the *universitas societatis fraternalis militiae titulo Sancti Georgii insigniti* – 'The Community of the Fraternal Society of knighthood named for the notable Saint George' – but in the later one the society is referred to more briefly as *societatem beati Georgii*, and in chapter 24 it is called *societate beati Georgii Martyris* – 'the Society of the Blessed George the Martyr'. Throughout the statutes it is referred to simply as *fraternalis societas*, the 'Fraternal Society'. The full title 'fraternal society of knighthood' appears to be a compromise between the traditional title 'order of knighthood' borne by the various religious orders of knights, and the title 'fraternal society' borne by most confraternities, and accurately suggests the hybrid nature of the new institution. Károly presumably chose to avoid the title 'order' because until then it had been borne only by strictly religious bodies, mostly quite unmilitary, and its attachment to a body of lay knights might have been thought inappropriate or even offensive by many clerics. In taking the name of his Society from its patron saint, however, Károly was following the common custom of both religious orders and lay confraternities. In any case, as the Society (so far as we know) had neither a badge nor a permanent seat, it could hardly have had any other name.

Károly's dedication of his new Society to St George was equally in keeping with established practice, for as we have seen the martyred Roman soldier had long been accepted as one of the particular patrons of knighthood, and the Golden Legend had spread his fame and assured his popularity in most parts of Western Christendom in the later Middle Ages.

5 The Judges and the King

Unlike most later kings who founded orders of knighthood, Károly of Hungary chose not to attach the presidential office of his new Society directly to his crown; indeed, he chose not to provide his Society with a formally constituted presidency, but placed it instead under the joint chairmanship of two *Judices* or 'Judges', one lay and one clerical, chosen by the knights themselves.[12] As initially conceived of, the role of the judges was to have been to preside over the trials of the members of the Society in all cases in which they stood accused, but in April 1326 they were charged with summoning the monthly assemblies of the Society as well.

Despite the lack of a monarchical presidency, however, there can be no doubt that the king was to be the effective governor of the Society, as well as the principal beneficiary of its activities. Not only does the first prologue state that the king was to 'make use of' the Society to protect his person and kingdom, but chapters 20 and 21 give him control over the process of electing members, the second prologue implies that he was to have the right to approve all new statutes, chapter 7 states that he was to take the lead in acts of consolation, and chapters 5 to 7 and 15 to 17 imply that the headquarters of the Society was to be permanently attached to the royal court. Even if he did not personally attend every one of the Society's meetings (and he may well have done) he would have been in a position to keep well-informed about all of the Society's activities, and probably exercised a considerable informal influence over them. Certainly it is most unlikely that the Society ever did anything either without his knowledge or contrary to his will.

[12] Chs. 14a, 22a.

6 *The Membership of the Society*

Information about the nature of the Society's membership must be gleaned from a variety of passing references made in the statutes. The ordinary members of the Society are referred to in random alternation as *milites* or 'knights' and as *fratres* or 'brothers'. The use of the title 'knight' to refer to the brothers combined with the use of the term 'knighthood' in the long designation of the Society suggests that formal knighthood was to be a requirement for entry into the Society, but this is nowhere stated explicitly. Since the statutes make no reference to the obligations characteristic of monasticism, it would appear that the Society was to be made up of lay rather than religious knights, but this is not stated either. Chapter 21b implies that candidates for membership had to be both morally upright and of proven loyalty – presumably to the king, and apparently in his opinion.

The restriction of membership to dubbed knights represented a departure from the practices of the earlier orders of knighthood, which as we have seen included substantial numbers of squires and persons of even lesser rank. The limitation of the size of the membership to no more than fifty, introduced in the first chapter adopted at the meeting of April 1326, represented an even greater departure, for all earlier orders seem to have been anxious to have as many members as possible. In combination the two restrictions suggest that the founder intended his Society to include only members of the highest strata of Hungarian society. The combination of knighthood, loyalty, and good character required for candidates for election further suggests that he hoped to limit it to men who had not merely received the accolade of knighthood, but exemplified in their lives the virtues of chivalry that he was attempting to impress on the members of his new nobility. This, and the limitation of the membership to a specific number, lead one to suspect that in founding the Society Károly was at least partly inspired by the image of Arthur and the Round Table. Why he decided upon the precise figure fifty is unclear, for as we have seen, most authors attributed a much higher limit to the society of the Round Table and its offshoots, and the total number of knights in Hungary in 1326 may have been close to twenty times as great. It may be that he felt that fifty – the earliest number attributed to the knights of the Round Table – was the highest limit consonant with the image of exclusiveness he wished his Society to enjoy.

The wording of chapter 21 implies that anyone who felt that he had the right qualities (poorly defined as they were) could apply for membership in the Society simply by informing the Chancellor of the Society of his desire to join. This would have been in keeping with the normal practice of most religious orders and confraternities, which were always looking for new members and were essentially open to talent. To prevent the admission of anyone unacceptable to the king, however, both the king himself and the Justiciar of the kingdom had to approve every candidacy before it was passed on to the ordinary members for their approval. The statutes also required the vote of the knights themselves to be unanimous – a level of agreement demanded by no later order.[13] It is not clear from the statutes exactly when elections were to be held – whether immediately following the death

---

[13] Ch. 20a,c.

or expulsion of a member, at the next annual meeting, or at the next thrice-yearly assembly.

Chapter 12 of the statutes states that a candidate who had been elected to the Society could take a year to decide whether he wanted to accept the burdens of membership. It is not clear from the wording of the chapter whether during this period he was regarded as a full member of the Society, but it is likely that he had a status similar to that of a postulant in a religious order until he 'confirmed his standing' – presumably by taking the oath of obedience to the statutes required in chapter 11b – on the anniversary of his election. Once a member-elect had taken the oath of obedience he was normally to retain his membership for life, unless he was formally excluded from the Society. The statutes specify exclusion as the penalty for three specific breaches of the rules: refusal to be reconciled with one of the other members,[14] and refusal either to be judged by or to accept a decision of the Society's Judges.[15]

In the absence of a list of members, we can only speculate about the question of who or even what sort of person was actually admitted to the Society of St George. The Society was much too limited in numbers to have included more than a small fraction of the knights or even of the barons of Hungary at the time of its foundation, for there were several hundred of the latter in 1326, and the former may have numbered over a thousand.[16] The first group of members – whose number may have been well below the figure of fifty set at the meeting of April 1326 – was probably composed for the most part of those *barones naturales* whom Károly had come to regard as his most important and trustworthy adherents.

7 The Privileges and Obligations of Membership

Once a member-elect had taken the oath of obedience to the statutes, he seems to have acquired all of the privileges and obligations entailed in membership. Presumably in order to make his new Society as attractive as possible to the powerful barons he probably wished to include in its ranks, Károly, like later founders in similar positions, conferred a number of quite significant privileges upon the members of the Society. First and foremost, they were to have the privilege of being judged only by the two Judges they were to elect themselves; even the king was not to 'presume' to sit in judgement upon them. This privilege (a clear sign of Károly's role in the creation of the Society, for no one else could have granted it) exempted the knights of the Society from the ordinary judicial system of the kingdom, and gave them a court in which all complaints against them – civil as well as criminal, if chapter 14 meant what it says – would be heard quickly and sympathetically. In addition the knights of St George were to enjoy two related privileges, both of considerable practical value: the right to ask their own Judges both to command provincial judges to give them satisfaction against non-members

---

[14] Ch. 16d.
[15] Ch. 22b.
[16] On the nobility of Hungary in this period, see Hóman, *Gli Angionini*, pp. 149ff.

who had injured them in any way,[17] and to absolve them of the penalties normally imposed for oath-breaking, without reference to the ecclesiastical courts.[18]

The knights of the Society also benefited from certain other provisions of the statutes which were not specifically set forth as privileges. They were to receive the active aid of all the other members in all of their affairs and against anyone not of their number,[19] and received the promise of the Society (and therefore of the king) that any injury inflicted upon them by anyone at all (presumably including another member) would be severely punished.[20] Since the Society probably included many of the most powerful barons in the kingdom and many of the most important officers of the royal administration, the guaranteed support even of most of its members most of the time would have been an extremely valuable asset in the game of politics as it was then played.

In return for these privileges, the knights of St George were required to undertake an even greater number of obligations, some of which would have been seen as relatively burdensome by most contemporary noblemen. The obligations incurred fell into four broad categories: obligations to persons outside the Society, obligations to their fellow members, obligations to the Society as a whole, and general obligations, not directed towards anyone.

In the first category fall two important obligations only vaguely defined in the statutes. According to the first prologue, the Society had been established primarily to protect the king from his enemies – especially the oligarchs – so the knights must have been obliged, as members, to act in ways that would have been conducive to this end. Most later founders would spell out in some detail what amounted to the cliental obligations of the companions of their orders to themselves and their heirs, but Károly, as we have seen, seems to have been anxious to play down his role within the Society he helped to create. As a result it is not at all clear what he expected the knights of St George to do for him in the way of 'protection', but considering the size of the Society and the probable nature of its membership it is likely that he wanted them to protect his interests by serving as leaders of a sort of royal faction in both the national parliament (of which most would have been members by right) and the new banderial army; in his own *banderium* (which included 1000 men even in times of peace) he already had a much larger and more effective bodyguard than the Society could possibly have supplied, and the knights of the Society would certainly have been more useful to him on the field of battle leading their own *banderia* than forming some sort of élite troop composed largely of barons.

The only strictly cliental obligation of the knights to the king actually specified in the statutes is the obligation to inform the king of anything they heard that might prove detrimental to him or his realm, (ch. 11a) so the knights of the Society were certainly intended to function as a network of royal spies. In addition they were required (by ch. 7) to 'follow the king in an outstanding way in every recreational activity and knightly game (*in omni solatio et in ludo militari precipue regem debeant sequi*)'. Although its precise requirements are obscure, this obligation

---

[17] Ch. 2.
[18] Ch. 27a.
[19] Ch. 18a,b.
[20] Ch. 18c,d.

is clearly related to Károly's programme of promoting chivalry among the nobility as a whole, in which knightly sports seem to have occupied a prominent place. It may well be that the knights of the Society, like those of the contemporary Castilian Order of the Band, were expected to function as a sort of royal tournament team, and as such to set a standard of military discipline and prowess for the rest of the nobility to emulate.

The knights were also supposed to undertake certain other obligations to persons outside the Society. According to chapter 19 the Society as a whole was obliged to defend the Church, so that the Church would in its turn pray for the Society, and thus secure its increase in 'spiritual and temporal things'. In keeping with the normal customs of confraternities, the Society also undertook certain charitable obligations towards 'the poor' – presumably in the form of paupers who presented themselves before the gates of whatever palace or house the king was staying in on any particular day. Chapter 16a requires the members present at each Monday dinner to give the scraps from their communal table to the poor along with one penny for each pauper, and chapter 15c requires any member who failed to join his fellows at one of these meals to pay a penny into the fund maintained by the Society for distribution to the poor.

The obligations of the knights of St George to one another are set forth much more explicitly in the statutes. They were bound to aid and 'promote' one another 'by counsel and favour' against everyone else (including when necessary another member),[21] to abstain from plotting against one another,[22] and from friendly dealings with the known enemies of their brethren,[23] to give aid in particular to any of their number who had either fallen in battle[24] or been captured,[25] to attempt to reconcile any of their brethren who had quarrelled,[26] to console any of their number who had suffered a loss,[27] and to pay for ten masses for the soul of any of their number who died, on the day of his funeral.[28] These obligations – similar in spirit and in some cases in substance to those imposed by many contemporary confraternities – were clearly calculated to promote feelings of solidarity among the members and to increase the benefits that they received from membership. In detail they resembled the mutual obligations undertaken in the same period by brothers-in-arms and somewhat later by the members of what we have called the 'fraternal' orders of knighthood, and gave substance to the formal designation 'Fraternal Society'. Some, but not all later monarchical orders would impose a comparable set of mutual obligations upon their ordinary members, but none would impose quite so many, and the Society of St George must be regarded as the most fraternal of the orders designed to serve the policies of a prince.

Under the heading of obligations to the Society as a whole may be placed the obligations to take part in each of the Society's three annual assemblies unless

[21] Ch. 10a, 18a,b.
[22] Ch. 10b.
[23] Ch. 29.
[24] Ch. 9.
[25] Ch. 4a,b.
[26] Chs. 10a, 16d.
[27] Ch. 6b.
[28] Ch. 2a,b.

excused for some pressing reason, and if excused from the principal feast to send a substitute;[29] when in court to take part in the Society's monthly meetings,[30] and to dine every Monday at the community table, unless excused;[31] to submit to and accept the results of attempts made by other members of the Society to reconcile them with any member against whom they harboured any ill-feelings;[32] to submit to and accept the judgement of the Society's Judges and to turn against any of their number who refused to do so;[33] and finally to improve the Society by one new statute each year.[34] All but the last are in effect obligations to take part in the Society's corporate activities and to accept as binding the results of those activities that involved arbitration or judgement. The founder clearly felt that certain of these obligations were particularly important, for he prescribed significant penalties for any failure to fulfil them. Failure to sit with the other knights at the community table during the weekly dinner was to result in nothing more than a penny fine,[35] but a refusal either to accept the results of an attempt at reconciliation, or to submit to or accept the results of the judgement of the Society's Judges, was to be punished by expulsion from the Society – the most severe punishment imposed by most orders and confraternities – and in the last case by the subsequent enmity of his former brethren.[36] All of the obligations in this category were relatively burdensome, and would at the very least have taken up a good deal of time. Károly clearly hoped to use the Society not merely to secure the loyalty and service of its members, but to promote the best possible relations among the members themselves and avoid as far as possible the feuds and private wars that were all too likely to break out among the barons of his age. Later founders were to impose comparable obligations, but few would impose as many and none would impose more.

The rest of the obligations – those I have called 'general' – fall into two groups. In the first group may be placed what are perhaps best described as the 'spiritual' obligations of the members: to fast every year on the vigil of St George, and help to pay for a mass in his honour on his feast day;[37] to attend mass, go about with a sad expression, say twenty prayers, and give a penny to the Church every Friday;[38] and to go about with a happy countenance every Sunday.[39] Obligations of this general sort were characteristic of lay confraternities, and would be imposed by the statutes of most later monarchical orders. Indeed, several later orders would impose special Friday observances, intended to commemorate the Passion, though the particular observances specified in the Hungarian Society were to my knowledge peculiar. Like the obligations undertaken by the Society as a whole to the Church and the

---

[29] Chs. 3c,d, 25a,b.
[30] Ch. 26.
[31] Ch. 15a,b.
[32] Ch. 16d.
[33] Ch. 22a,b,c.
[34] Ch. 8.
[35] Ch. 15c.
[36] Chs. 16d, 22b,c.
[37] Ch. 3a,b.
[38] Ch. 5a,b,d,e.
[39] Ch. 6a.

2.1 Shield of the Arms of St George (reconstruction)

poor, the religious obligations the knights were required to undertake were by no means onerous (though some members may have found it difficult to maintain fixed expressions on Fridays and Sundays, and probably to refrain from slandering their fellows on Fridays as well), and fell well within the normal standards of lay piety in the period; the more pious members of the Society undoubtedly went well beyond their modest spiritual demands in their daily exercises. It is also significant that Károly did not see fit to prescribe any penalties for failure to observe any of the strictly religious obligations he imposed.

The knights of St George finally had certain obligations with respect to the habit of the Society. They were required to provide themselves with a mantle of the prescribed type – black, knee-length, hooded, and bearing the words *In veritatate iustus sum huic fraternali societati*[40] – and to wear it before the hour of mass every Friday.[41] The mantle was clearly modelled on that of the knights of the Hospital of St John, with the peculiar inscription (clearly not a chivalrous *devise*) replacing the white cross; why the knights did not at first adopt some form of the arms attributed to their patron (and used by all of the other orders placed under his protection) is not clear, but they may have done so later.[42] The knights were also required to bear the 'customary letters' (*litteras consuetas*), and were to pay in case of failure a fine equal to the weight of the letters 'which the greater shall be able to find on some member of the Society'.[43] The meaning of this requirement is obscure, since the

---

[40] Ch. 1. The Latin reads: '. . . cappam habeant ex nigro panno, habentem longitudinem vsque ad genua, et caputium consutum ad eamdem, et in pectore ipsius cappae scribantur hae litterae: in veritate . . .'

[41] Ch. 17a.

[42] According to Iván Bertényi, 'L'Apparition et la première diffusion des armoiries en Hongrie', *Les origines des Armoiries* (Paris, 1983), pp. 43–8, esp. p. 44, the Hungarian knights of St George wore a badge in the form of a shield [?] bearing the arms Gules, a cross argent (a reversal of the usual arrangement of the tinctures), but he gives no source for this statement, and no indication of date. The seal of the Society, of which an example is still attached to the base of the membrane on which the statutes are written, bore a shield charged with an image of St George slaying the dragon.

[43] Ch. 13b.

'customary letters' it alludes to are mentioned nowhere else under that name. It may be that the knights were required to bear with them at all times a document identifying them as members of the Society, just as the knights of most later orders would be obliged to wear at all times the badge which identified them as members of their order, but it is more likely that the 'letters' in question were those of the inscription they were required to wear in place of a badge, described in the Latin text of the first chapter as *litteras*. As we shall see, most later orders imposed some sort of penalty for failure to wear the order's device.

8 The Society's Corporate Activities

As was usual in confraternities, most of the corporate activities of the knights of St George were to take place at regular assemblies held at specified intervals. But while the majority of confraternities seem to have held only one assembly each year, on the feast day of their patron saint, the knights of the Society of St George were to meet with much greater frequency, at three different types of assembly held at intervals of different length: at first one and after April 1326 three general meetings a year, roughly four months apart – on St George's Day (23 April), on the Nativity of the Virgin (8 September), and on the octave of the 'New Year's gifts' or Epiphany (13 January)[44] – a monthly assembly to be convened by the Judges on a Monday or Tuesday as they saw fit;[45] and a corporate dinner to be held every Monday.[46] Only those knights who were already in court were required to take part in the monthly and weekly gatherings, but all members were required to attend the other meetings, unless they were excused because they were too ill to come or were engaged in the service of the king or the realm.[47] The meeting on St George's Day was to be the principal assembly of the year, and any member who found it necessary to be excused from attending it was obliged to send one of his men, presumably to represent both his views and his interests.[48]

In the original version of the statutes, the knights were required to take part in only one general meeting each year, to be held in the usual fashion on the feast day of their patron saint. Precisely what they were meant to do on that day is not known, since chapter 3 merely requires them in rather vague terms to have a mass said in honour of St George and to come together to praise the saint and 'be comforted'. Presumably they were meant to attend the mass in question, but whether they were meant to be 'comforted' by it or after it, at some sort of secular gathering, is unclear. Perhaps in part because of this lack of precision in the original statutes, the same amendment that required the knights to attend two extra general meetings each year also specified that at each of the three general meetings they were to do fealty to the king, to 'reform their status', and to render justice among themselves. Such activities could only have been carried out during

44 Chs. 3c, 25a.
45 Ch. 26.
46 Ch. 15a.
47 Ch. 25b.
48 Ch. 3d.

the course of a business meeting of the type that was usually called a 'chapter', and the second and third activities prescribed – which presumably entailed the punishment of transgressions of the rule and the settlement of internal disputes – were similar in nature to those carried out during the regular meetings of both monastic and confraternal chapters.

At least two other types of business must also have been dealt with during meetings of the chapter: the adoption of amendments to the statutes, and the election of new members. Chapter 8 (which is without parallel in the statutes of later orders) requires the knights to adopt at least one new ordinance each year so that the Society would be continually improved. It says nothing about the procedures to be followed in adopting such ordinances, but as we have noted already, the prologue to the first set of amendments suggests that any proposed alterations to the Society's statutes had to receive the approval of the king. Elections would have been less frequent than the adoption of new statutes, but if the full complement of fifty knights was in fact maintained even approximately, an average of at least one election every two years or so would almost certainly have been necessary.

Aside from those that were to take place during the meeting of the chapter, no other activities were specified for the two minor assemblies, but it is likely that on those occasions too the knights took part in the principal mass of the day. It is also likely that all three assemblies normally culminated in a splendid banquet and other courtly festivities, including processions and jousts, but the statutes – unlike those of most later orders – have nothing to say about such matters, leaving the details of each assembly to those charged with arranging it. Nor do the statutes specify where any of the three general assemblies was to be held, and it must appear that in the first few years of its existence, at least, the Society – unlike most later orders – had no fixed seat. The Society was probably intended to meet wherever the royal court found itself on the appointed day (since the presence of the king was certainly required for some of its business), but how the knights absent from the court in the period immediately preceding the day in question were expected to know precisely where that would be is not explained.

About the monthly meetings of the Society (required by the second amendment of April 1326) the statutes say only that the members present in court were to meet at the command of the Judges 'to treat of the good state of our king and kingdom, and their utility'. The wording suggests that they were meant to discuss pressing political questions and to provide advice to the king as to what policy it would be wise for him to follow in regard to each. If this interpretation is correct, the Society was meant to function as a sort of privy council to the Kings of Hungary, comparable in some respects at least to the bodies which had recently been detached from the old unspecialized *curia regis* in France and England. Since the Society probably included the most important officers of both the central and provincial administrations of the kingdom, such an exalted function is not as unlikely as it might at first appear, and it would not be without parallel in the later monarchical orders. It was also in keeping with the privileges given to the knights of the Society, which as we have seen placed them in a position similar to that enjoyed by the peers of England and France, the principal 'natural' counsellors of their respective kings. It is not clear whether the king was expected to attend all or even any of the monthly meetings of the Society, and therefore how and in what form the advice decided upon was to be tendered to him, but the fact that Károly approved the amendment requiring these meetings (even if he was not in fact its author) strongly suggests that he intended to listen to, if not necessarily to follow, the advice provided.

While the monthly assemblies of the Society seem to have been devoted entirely to serious business, the weekly dinners prescribed by chapter 15 seem to have been primarily social gatherings, though certain of the religious obligations of the members were to be carried out before and after these meals, and the inclusion of ordinances 16d and e in a chapter otherwise concerned with the weekly meal suggests that the knights present at the 'table of the community' were to use the opportunity presented to attempt to settle any minor quarrels that had developed between or among other members present. The location of the 'table of the community' (*mensa communitatis*) is not specified, but in all probability it was merely one of the several tables normally set up before each meal in the great hall of the palace or castle in which the court happened to be staying, reserved on Mondays for the exclusive use of the Society. Weekly (or even less frequent) gatherings of the sort in question here were rare, at least, in the confraternities of the period, and unknown in later monarchical orders, but the knights of the religious orders normally ate together on a daily basis, and the idea of requiring the knights of the Society to participate both regularly and frequently in a communal meal may have been borrowed from the older knightly orders. Presumably the purpose of the requirement was to foster a sense of community among the knights of the Society comparable (within the unavoidable limitations imposed by lay life) to that characteristic of the knights of the religious orders. It may also have been intended to compensate to some extent for the fact that, unlike the knights of the religious orders, the knights of St George were not to fight as a unit.

The knights of St George were thus required to meet at least sixty-seven times every year, on at least fifty-five different days. In addition they were required to attend the funeral of any of their number who had died (or so chapter 2b implies), and to take part in corporate acts of consolation (apparently to be held on Sundays) when any of their number suffered a loss of some kind. Finally, they were probably required to take part as a unit in tournaments and jousts proclaimed by the king at irregular (but possibly frequent) intervals. No other lay order is known to have met with anything approaching this degree of frequency, and if the meetings were actually held when they were supposed to be, the knights of St George must indeed have developed a sense of corporate identity comparable to that felt by the knights of the religious orders in the same period, and unknown in any of the later monarchical orders.

9 Conclusion

Little can be added to what has been said about the Society of St George during the course of the foregoing analysis of its earliest statutes, but it will be useful to sum up our more significant findings and to draw a few tentative conclusions from them. It can hardly be doubted that the Society was effectively founded by King Károly rather than by the 'community' of its first members (as the prologue implies), and that despite its lack of an hereditary presidency, the characteristic title 'order', and the badge or device that was a characteristic feature of most later orders, it represented the first known attempt to create what we have called a 'monarchical order of knighthood' – a corporate body of knights permanently attached to the crown of its founder and dedicated to his service. Presumably because he lacked a clear historical model for a society of the sort he had in mind, Károly chose to leave his relationship to the regular government of the Society ill-defined, but retained to himself and his heirs an effective control over the process of choosing new members, and probably over the process of adopting new statutes as well. Although his assignment of a mantle to the knights of the Society suggests that he drew some inspiration from the religious orders of knighthood, and especially perhaps from the Order of the Hospital of St John, he rejected the constitutional form of the religious orders (along with their characteristic title and cross) in favour of that of the lay confraternities, which was clearly more suitable for the reasons we have already reviewed. In fact most of the obligations and activities of the knights, though peculiar in detail and adapted to the particular ends for which the Society was founded, were typical of confraternities of the period, and the Society could be described without any distortion as a professional confraternity of knights. It differed from most confraternities – including those later confraternities of knights that I have termed 'confraternal orders' – in its lack of a fixed seat, in its close formal association with the royal court of Hungary, in the nature and extent of the privileges its members enjoyed as such, in the frequency of its meetings, and in the limitation of its membership to fifty. The last is the only feature of the Society's fundamental law that appears to have been inspired directly by the fictional societies of knights, though it is likely enough that Károly – who was surely familiar with the romances of chivalry composed in his ancestral homeland – drew some general inspiration for his foundation from the Round Table.

The Society of St George was clearly intended to serve as a sort of royal faction or party within the knightly class, devoted to the interests of the founder and his dynasty, and its members were expected to play a fairly active role in the affairs of state as both spies and political advisors to the king. Despite the obligations it entailed, however, membership in the Society must have been regarded as highly desirable by most members of the Hungarian nobility, not only because of the specific practical privileges conferred by the statutes on members, but because of the other practical advantages that so intimate a form of clientship to the king undoubtedly gave to its members, and because of the immense prestige that membership in so exclusive and privileged a body must have conveyed. Like later founders, Károly may well have treated membership in the Society as a sort of dignity which could be conferred on barons and prominent ministers and provincial governors at least partly to reward them for services rendered as well as to secure their continued loyalty and service. In fact, among the honours at the disposal of the Hungarian king, membership in the Society could well have taken the place both of the largely honorific dominical dignities – dukeships, countships, and so forth – and the more functional peerships, princeships, and baronships which the kings of other Western Christian kingdoms were then beginning to distribute to their more prominent vassals and servants; dignities of the former sort were not to be introduced into Hungary for over a century after the foundation of the Society, and no other body within the Hungarian baronage was to enjoy privileges comparable to those of peers and princes of the Holy Roman Empire until the foundation of the second Hungarian monarchical order in 1408.

The Society of St George was thus both political and honourable. It was also chivalrous. Indeed, it was almost certainly intended to function as a sort of institutional embodiment of the ideals of chivalry which Károly sought to promote among the lesser nobles of his kingdom throughout his reign. As we have observed, by the time Károly inherited a claim to the throne of Hungary, the tournament and its associated games and rituals had come to function as a festival of chivalry, at which most of the qualities attributed to the ideal knight – prowesss, courtesy, *franchise*, and *largesse* – could be both cultivated and displayed. Károly probably required the members of the Society to follow his lead in all such exercises because he hoped that, within the controlled environment of the tournament, they would serve as models of knightly behaviour which the other knights present would be moved, by envy or admiration, to emulate as closely as possible. It would appear that Károly himself – assisted perhaps by certain members of his inner circle who had followed him from Italy – intended to serve as the chivalric model for the knights of the Society, many of whom would presumably have needed as much help as those they were expected to inspire. The Society of St George was thus in all probability expected to fulfil a civilizing mission on two levels: to encourage the highest standards of conduct among its members, and to serve as a pattern of behaviour for the nobility as a whole. In addition to raising the general level of conduct among his noble subjects, Károly may well have hoped thereby to discourage quarrels and to promote loyalty to his crown and house among the nobles of all classes – for loyalty was among the oldest qualities associated with the perfect knight. Since both the fictional company of the Round Table and such contemporary bodies as the Hospitallers of St John and Teutonic knights were in effect élite 'orders' within the general 'order' of knighthood, and required their members to conform strictly to certain of the requirements of the chivalric ethos, Károly's idea of creating such a society to embody the virtues of secular chivalry was probably inspired to some extent by both of the available models.

The extent to which the Society of St George succeeded in accomplishing any of the several goals its founder had in mind cannot be told from the evidence currently at our disposal, but there is no particular reason to believe that it could not have functioned very much as we have surmised it was meant to function throughout the reigns of the founder and his like-minded and even more successful son, Lajos 'the Great'. Certainly both Károly and Lajos managed to retain effective control of their kingdom after the foundation of the Society, and to prevent the outbreak of any serious hostilities among the members of the new baronial class, and although it is unlikely that the Society of St George was solely responsible for their successes in these areas, it may well have played a significant part in both. Only when Lajos died leaving his Hungarian throne disputed between his adolescent daughter and his cousin and former ward King Carlo of mainland Sicily did the kingdom once more dissolve into a civil war which probably divided and finally destroyed the Society his father had founded, and it is interesting to note that as soon as his erstwhile son-in-law and ultimate successor Zsigmond von Luxemburg was securely reestablished on the throne in 1408 he founded a new 'Society' that was intended to function as a sort of royal party within the baronage, and in fact played a major role in the political life of the kingdom throughout his reign and that of his successor. It may also be significant that one of the first acts of Lajos' ward Carlo 'di Durazzo' after seizing the throne of mainland Sicily in 1381 was to found an order of knighthood which was similarly designed to function as a sort of royal party within the baronage of his kingdom, and was almost certainly inspired at least in part by the Society of St George. Clearly these kings felt that the Society of St George had served its founder's purposes reasonably well.

Although both the Order of the Ship and the Society of the Dragon were probably inspired in part by the first Hungarian order, and may have borrowed some of their statutes directly from the latter, the immediate influence of the Society of St George appears to have been slight. It is at least possible that the first known confraternal order, that of St Catherine, founded at some time during the next decade or so in the Dauphiné of Viennois[49] (which was then ruled by Károly's nephew Humbert II), was directly inspired by the Hungarian order, but neither the first truly monarchical order, founded five or six years after it in Castile, nor any of the other monarchical orders founded before 1381 appears to have borrowed anything from it. It is indeed quite possible that the Society was virtually unknown in most of the kingdoms of western Europe, which had only infrequent contacts with Hungary in this period.

---

[49] Statutes in [Cyr]-Ulysse-[Joseph] Chevalier, *Choix de documents historiques inédits sur le Dauphiné* VII (Montbéliard, Lyon, 1874), pp. 35–39.

Chapter 3

The Order of the Band
Castile-Leon, 1330–1474?

1 Historical Background

The first society of knights to conform precisely to our definition of a monarchical order of knighthood appears to have been the *Orden de la Banda* or 'Order of the Band'.[1] This order – the first lay society to use that title – was founded only about five years after the establishment of the Society of St George, on the opposite frontier of Western Christendom, by King Alfonso XI of Castile and Leon, known to history as 'the Implacable'.[2]

Although he had not had to fight to win his throne, Alfonso's youth had been scarcely less difficult than that of the future King Károly of Hungary, and he had been obliged to deal with a political situation of comparable danger to his royal authority at an even earlier age. Alfonso had been born in August 1311 as the first son of the then king Fernando IV, the eighth ruler of Castile of the Frankish house of Ivrea established in Spain in the twelfth century by Count Raymond of Burgundy. Only one year and twenty days after his birth, on 9 September 1312, his father had died unexpectedly and he had been proclaimed king as Alfonso XI. Since he was clearly too young to assume the reins of government, a regency had been formed to exercise the rights of the monarchy until he came of legal age. Following the death of his mother, Constanca of Portugal, in 1313, the leading role in the regency was jointly secured (after a brief power struggle) by his father's mother Queen María de Molina, her twenty-five-year-old son the Infante Don Pedro, and her brother-in-law the Infante Don Juan de Valencia, the only

---

[1] For reasons which will be made clear below, I prefer to translate the Spanish word *banda* by the cognate English word 'band' rather than by the words 'sash' and 'scarf' used by other historians.

[2] According to Charles-Emmanuel Dufourcq and Jean Gautier-Delaché ('Les royaumes chrétiens d'Espagne au temps de la "reconquista" d'après les recherches récentes [1948–1969]' *Revue historique* 504 [1972], p. 395), neither Alfonso XI nor his father Fernando IV has been the subject of a modern critical study, and my discussion of the former's reign is therefore based on the relatively brief accounts in Rafael Altamira, 'Spain, 1252–1410', CMH VII, p. 574 and Joseph F. O'Callaghan, *A History of Medieval Spain* (Ithaca and London, 1975), pp. 403–4, 407–14, which despite their brevity are the most extensive accounts I have found. Both seem to have been based very largely on the official chronicle of his reign.

surviving brother of her late husband Sancho IV. Both *infantes* were killed in battle against the Moors of Granada in 1319, however, and a new and more serious power struggle broke out. Several junior members of the royal family now claimed a share in the regency, most prominent among them being the famous writer Don Juan Manuel, Lord of Peñafiel and Escalona, whose father had been a younger son of Fernando III. The death of the Queen Dowager in 1321 removed the last person capable of maintaining even a semblance of order, and the self-proclaimed regents led by Don Juan Manuel attempted to divide the kingdom among them. The result was such total anarchy and chaos that the young king felt obliged to secure an early termination of the 'regency', and had himself proclaimed of age by the *Cortes* that met at Valladolid in 1325. Although he was still only fourteen years old, Alfonso immediately set about restoring order to his war-torn kingdom, and soon showed himself to be endowed with extraordinary military and political abilities.

With the exception of the strip of territory along the north coast known as Asturias, the complex of realms whose government Alfonso was thus obliged to assume – commonly known as the Lands of the Crown of Castile – had been carved by a slow process of Reconquest (begun around 750 and temporarily stalled around 1260) from the steadily dwindling dominion of the Muslim Moors, first established in 711. As a result of this, and of their relative isolation from the Christian kingdoms beyond the Pyrenees before the twelfth century, the Castilian realms had developed social and political institutions which, while bearing a strong superficial resemblance to those of the transpyrenean realms, were in many ways distinct and peculiar.[3] The king, whose authority was theoretically absolute, was in practice obliged to respect the bodies of customary law known as the *fueros*; the attempts of Alfonso's predecessors to impose a general code of law on all their subjects had been unsuccessful. In 1325 the central adminstration, still relatively rudimentary, continued to be centred in the peripatetic *Casa del Rey* or royal household, and the officers of the household, headed by the *Mayordomo Mayor* or chief steward, continued to play a leading role in the government of the kingdom. As in most kingdoms by this date, the old *Curia Regis* had by 1325 given rise to a number of specialized bodies, including a small inner council which had not yet achieved an institutional form (but in practice generally included the more important officers of the household), and a more formal parliamentary assembly of the three estates known as the *Cortes*, which met when summoned by the king to advise him on important matters and to consent to extraordinary taxation of the third estate, and in practice served as a check on royal absolutism. Regional government was entrusted to a hierarchy of royal officers headed by the four provincial governors exercising the joint offices of *Merino Mayor* and *Adelantado Mayor* of Castile, of Leon, Galicia, and Asturias, of Murcia, and of the Frontier, all of whom – like the officers of the household and of the various specialized offshoots of the royal council – were appointed and removed by the king at his pleasure. A certain number of earlier jurisdictions had been effectively converted in the twelfth century into quasi-baronial dominions called *honores*, but like the other forms of benefice

---

[3] My account of the political institutions of Castile is based primarily on those in O'Callaghan, op. cit., pp. 428–58; and Luis Vicente Díaz Martín, *Los Oficiales de Pedro I de Castilla* (Valladolid, 1975). The latter contains a useful list of major offices at the end of the reign of Alfonso XI.

conferred for various purposes by the Castilian kings and magnates (generically termed *prestimonios* rather than *feudos*), they had never become strictly hereditary, and like ordinary offices were regularly bestowed during the king's pleasure.[4]

Although some of the more important judicial and financial offices were normally entrusted to legally-educated men of relatively humble background, the Kings of Castile had continued to confer most of the great offices of both the central and the regional government of their dominions on members of the noble estate, and especially on members of its dominant upper stratum. As this practice would suggest, the nobility remained by far the most important class in Castilian society, and no king could hope to govern without the cooperation of a substantial portion of its members. The Castilian nobility[5] of the early fourteenth century was made up in part of the descendants of the principal clients of the magnates of the tenth and eleventh centuries, known as *infanzones*, and in part of the descendants of certain lesser men who had been granted the privileges of hereditary *infanzonía* by one or another of the kings of Leon or Castile in the twelfth and thirteenth centuries as a reward for serving as *caballeros villanos* or 'low-born knights' in the campaigns of the Reconquest.[6] The newer nobles were known as *fijos de algo* or *fijosdalgo* ('sons of fortune') – a term which was extended during the course of the fourteenth century to all members of the noble estate. The privileges that *infanzones* and *fijosdalgo* had alike come to enjoy by the end of the thirteenth century were very extensive – more extensive, indeed, than those enjoyed even by the greater members of most contemporary nobilities beyond the Pyrenees. Not only were their persons and properties exempt from all forms of taxation (a privilege characteristic of noble status in most continental kingdoms), but they enjoyed a much higher *calumnia* or composition for injury than lesser men, their domiciles were regarded as inviolate, they could only be judged by their peers according to the *fueros* peculiar to their estate in a special court (established for the purpose by Alfonso X) in which (after 1317) even the judge had to be noble, and they were not obliged to perform any form of service for the king without pay in either land or money. The principal obligation they owed in return for all these privileges was that of performing any military service they owed to their lord or king on horseback, as knights or squires.[7]

The majority of the several thousand *infanzones* and *fijosdalgo* who lived in

[4] See Hilda Grassotti, *Las Instituciones Feudo-Vasalláticas en León y Castilla* (2 vols., Spoleto, 1969), t. 2, pp. 553–720.

[5] On the nobility of Castile in this period see esp. Luis Suárez-Fernández, *Nobleza y Monarquía. Puntos de vista sobre la Historia castellana del siglo XV* (Valladolid, 1959); María del Carmen Carlé, 'Infanzones e Hildagos' *Cuadernos de Historia de España* 33–34 (1961), 56–100; Salvador de Moxó, 'De la Nobleza Vieja a la Nobleza Nueva. La Transformación Nobiliaria Castellana en la Baja Edad Media' *Cuadernos de Historia. Annexos de la Revista Hispania* 3 (1969), 1–210, and 'La Nobleza Castellano-leonesa en la Edad Media: Problematica que suscita su estudio en el marco de una historia social' *Hispania* 30 (114–16) (1970), 5–68.

[6] On the phenomenon of the *caballeros villanos*, see Carmela Pescador, 'La Caballería Popular en León y Castilla' *Cuadernos de Historia de Hispania* 33–34 (1961), 101–238.

[7] On both privileges and obligations see María del Carmen Carlé, op. cit., pp. 82–93.

Castile in the early fourteenth century[8] possessed only small estates in which they enjoyed a very limited form of lordly jurisdiction over their tenants, and participated in the government only if chosen to represent their estate in the *Cortes*. Only the members of the upper stratum of the nobility, those men known since the twelfth century as *ricos omes* or 'rich and powerful men', could expect to play a leading role in the affairs of the kingdom as a whole. The status of *rico ome*, symbolized by a *pendón* or banner and a *caldera* or cauldron,[9] was normally conferred by the king for life upon any *infanzón* or *fijodalgo* who received one of the great offices of the kingdom, and was occasionally conferred as a reward for outstanding services, but in the great majority of cases it was effectively inherited. Of the twenty-nine distinct lineages of *ricos omes* surviving in the last decade of the thirteenth century, all but a handful (including three junior branches of the royal house) were descended from men who had risen to positions of wealth and power as leaders of Castilian forces in the war of Reconquest during the great campaigns of the late eleventh and early twelfth centuries, and most of the lineages in question had continued to increase in both respects through continuing service, administrative as well as military, to the crown.[10] The *ricos omes* of the early fourteenth century were distinguished from the lesser members of the nobility not merely by their illustrious ancestry, but by *privanza* or intimate familiarity with the king, by their *mesnadas* or armed retinues (composed in part at least of their numerous noble vassals), and by their vast allodial estates and quasi-feudal *honores*, within both of which they commonly enjoyed extensive, even regalian rights of jurisdiction. Most *ricos omes* seem to have entered into a vassalic relationship with the king in return for either landed *prestimonios* or a cash salary called a *soldada*, but this relationship was neither automatic nor hereditary as in the transpyrenean realms, and vassalic tenements seldom formed more than a small fraction of their total holdings in land.

As in most of the kingdoms beyond the Pyrenees, nobles of all ranks continued to be theoretically united by the sacred status and profession of knight (*caballero*), the nature and duties of which were defined at length in the twenty-first chapter of the great law-code known as the *Siete Partidas*, composed by or for Alfonso X around 1270.[11] In practice, as in other countries, a large and ever-increasing number of

[8] I have been unable to find even a rough estimate of the number of minor nobles in the lands of the Crown of Castile at any time during the medieval period, but the various works cited above seem to imply that there were several thousand lineages whose members enjoyed hereditary nobility.

[9] See Ch.-E. Dufourcq, J. Gautier Dalché, *Histoire économique et sociale de l'Espagne chrétienne au Moyen Age* (Paris, 1976), p. 125.

[10] These lineages – which constituted most of what Moxó calls the *nobleza vieja* or 'old nobility' – are identified and discussed in his study *De la Nobleza Vieja a la Nobleza Nueva*. This seems to be the most thorough critical treatment of the upper nobility of medieval Castile published to date, and a scholar who, like myself, is more familiar with the contemporary nobilities of England and France, cannot help but be struck by how little is known about the lives of most of the leading members of Castilian society – the equivalents of the counts and dukes in England and France – even in the fourteenth century. Not only the birth-dates but the death-dates of most of the persons listed in Moxó's tables appear to be unknown.

[11] *Las Siete Partidas*, trans. Samuel Parsons Scott (New York, 1931), Introduction by Charles Sumner Lobingier.

minor noblemen were finding the cost of formal knighthood prohibitive, and were obliged to remain squires (*escuderos*) for life,[12] but kings and *ricos omes* continued to prize the status highly, and the royal prince Juan Manuel preferred the title *caballero* to that of *rico ome*.[13] The French model of secular chivalry (*caballería*) was widely disseminated through translations of chivalric romances, and tournaments in the French style were very popular throughout the later medieval period,[14] but despite the romantic foreign trappings it had acquired, knighthood remained a serious and practical profession in fourteenth-century Castile, and the knight was first and foremost a warrior in the service of God and his lord.

The principal duty of the fourteenth-century *caballero*, whatevever his wealth or status, was in fact to serve when summoned in the royal army (*hueste, fonsado*), which continued to be made up very largely of knights and squires. Until 1382 it also continued to be organized much as it had been in the twelfth century. Assisted by his *Alférez Mayor* or 'Chief Lieutenant', the king rode into battle at the head of a rather disorganized troop composed of his own *mesnaderos* and minor vassals, accompanied by similar troops of *mesnaderos* and vassals led by *ricos omes* serving for *soldadas*, by troops of non-noble *caballeros villanos* supplied by the towns and serving under the command of a *juez* bearing the town *pendón*, and by contingents supplied by some or all of the four military orders with garrisons in the kingdom: Calatrava, Santiago, Alcántara, and St John of Jerusalem. By far the most effective of the various troops theoretically at the king's disposal were those provided by the military orders, whose members were drawn to a great extent from the families of the *ricos omes*.

When not actually at odds with the king, the *ricos omes* thus played a vital role in the military organization of the kingdom in the early fourteenth century, and that role was to change relatively little before the end of the following century. Their role in the political life of the kingdom, which had always been considerable, grew even greater in the same period. The rapid growth of the royal administration and the virtual cessation of the war of Reconquest had threatened the political power of the *ricos omes* in the late thirteenth century, but they had reacted strongly to this threat, and with the backing of their vast allodial wealth and their numerous vassals they had actually succeeded in increasing their stranglehold on the organs of government in the troubled days of the minority of Alfonso XI. During the course of Alfonso's long reign many of them decided to reside permanently in the royal court in order to maintain a constant and direct influence upon the decisions of the royal council. Those who disagreed with or felt slighted

---

[12] Dufourcq and Dalché (*Histoire économique et sociale*, p. 126), estimate that by 1300 a very high proportion, perhaps even a majority of the minor noblemen living in the lands of the Crown of Castile could not afford to fulfil the obligations of knighthood. I have been unable to find any estimate of the absolute number of knights in Castile at any time before 1500, but if the proportion of noble lineages in Castile was comparable to that of France in the same period, then Castile, with a population about half that of France, would have had between 2500 and 5000 knights in 1325.

[13] Jole Scudieri Ruggieri, *Cavalleria e cortesia nella vita e nella culture di Spagna* (Modena, 1980), p. 66.

[14] On chivalry in Spain in the Later Middle Ages (especially the fifteenth century), see the collection of articles by Martín de Riquer in his *Cavalleria fra realta et Letteratura nel Quatrocento* (Bari, 1970).

by any aspect of royal policy did not hesitate to rise in rebellion, and as they were constantly quarrelling with one another as well, only a strong king could maintain order among them. The masters and great officers of the three military orders with headquarters in Castile behaved in a similar fashion, and when not intervening to their own advantage in secular politics, spent most of their time squabbling amongst themselves.

Alfonso XI was thus faced with a formidable task when he proclaimed an end to the regency in the summer of 1325. Fortunately his abilities and determination quickly proved more than equal to the challenge, and after a few years of outright warfare against a large part of the nobility, he was able not merely to convince the leading *ricos omes* and their vassals of the futility of opposing his will (he did not hesitate to execute those who refused to see reason), but to direct their turbulent energies to the useful task of conquering what remained of Moorish territory in Spain. As early as 1327 he launched the first of his many successful campaigns against the Kingdom of Granada, and by 1330 had already won a considerable reputation as an *athleta Christi*.

Once firmly in control of the kingdom, Alfonso was able to undertake a number of important reforms in the administration both of public finances and of justice. He also put through a number of reforms of more particular interest to us here, if only because they indicate his attitude towards his noble subjects. At the *Cortes* of Burgos in 1338 he legislated on the subject of the relationship between the vassals of royal vassals and the king, and greatly increased the effective authority of the latter.[15] Somewhat later, at the *Cortes* of Alcala in 1348, he sealed an *ordenamiento* making the *Siete Partidas* part of the general law of the lands of the Crown of Castile.[16] Alfonso also introduced the practice of bestowing dominical titles of dignity upon members of the upper nobility by granting a specially created County of Trastámara, Lemos, and Sarria first (in 1325) to his favourite, Alvar Nuñez Osorio, and later (following Osorio's death) to his own bastard son, Enrique. He does not seem to have regarded the practice as an appropriate way either to reward or secure the loyalty of his *ricos omes* in general, however, and it was not until after the accession of his son Enrique in 1369 that another such title was bestowed.[17]

It should finally be noted here that Alfonso eventually secured effective control of two of the three religious orders of knighthood based in Castile by imposing on them masters of whose loyalty he felt sure: Nuño Chamiro was thus made Master of Alcántara following the forcible deposition and execution of his predecessor in 1335, and in 1340 Alfonso's bastard son Fadrique was made Master of Santiago in similar circumstances at the tender age of ten.[18] The unreliability of all three orders in the first five years of his effective reign may well have been one of the principal factors in his decision of 1330 to found an order of a new type, whose mastership could be annexed directly to the Castilian crown.

---

[15] Grassotti, op. cit., p. 1063.
[16] *Las Siete Partidas*, p. liii.
[17] See Antonio de Vargas-Zúñiga, Marqués de Siete Iglesias, 'Titulos y Grandezas del Reino', *Hidalguía* 1 (1953) 10–24, etc., for a complete list of the titles of dignity bestowed by the Kings of Castile in the later medieval period, and of their holders.
[18] Seward, *The Monks of War*, p. 164.

2 Foundation and General History

We are rather better informed about the history of the Order of the Band than we are about that of St George, but the documentation, though spread over a period of more than a century, is still decidedly sparse, and permits the construction of little more than a sketch of a general history.[19]

Our knowledge of the circumstances in which the Order was founded and of its subsequent history during the reign of its founder is derived entirely from two contemporary documents: the anonymous *Crónica del Rey Don Alfonso el Onceno*, and the prologue attached to each of the two distinct redactions of the statutes that almost certainly date from that period. According to the *Crónica*[20] – which seems to have been written in about 1344, and condensed about twenty years later in order to form part of the official history of the kingdom called the *Crónicas de los Reyes de Castilla*[21] – the Order was founded in the year of the Spanish Era 1368, which corresponded to the year 1330 after the Incarnation. By the beginning of that year Alfonso, still only twenty-two years old, had triumphed over most of his enemies, and was probably already thinking about celebrating his victories and proclaiming his full majority by having himself knighted and crowned. At some time early in 1330 Alfonso was in Burgos, the principal city of the Kingdom of Castile, possibly preparing for his coronation there later in the year. While he was there, representatives of the ruling body of the Basque dominion of Alava, situated about fifty miles to the north-east of Burgos, came to him and offered him the lordship of that land. Alfonso, always happy to add to his territories, accepted the offer with alacrity, and went to Vitoria, the principal city of Alava, to receive the fealty of his new subjects. While he was in Vitoria, the chronicle declares,

> ... because in times past the men of his Kingdoms of Castile and Leon had always been employed in knighthood, and because they had abandoned it, so that they did not practise it in his time, in order that they might practise it

---

[19] Most of the general works on orders of knighthood published in the seventeenth, eighteenth, and nineteenth centuries include a brief chapter on the Order of the Band, but the Order has been the subject of only two critical studies, each of which is in effect an introduction to a critical edition of a redaction of the Order's statutes. The first of these, Lorenzo Tadeo Villanueva's 'Memoria sobre la Orden de Caballería de la Banda de Castilla' (originally read before the Spanish Real Academia de Historia in 1812, and published in the *Boletín de la Real Academia de Historia* 73 (1918), 436–465), is largely concerned with the insignia of the Order. The second, G. Daumet's 'L'ordre castillan de l'Escharpe (Banda)' *Bulletin hispanique* 25 (1923), was written without apparent knowledge of the first, but duplicates relatively little of what Villanueva first said nearly a century earlier. More recently the Order was discussed in an appendix to Richard Barber's general work *The Knight and Chivalry* (pp. 339–44), and in the context of a chapter on Spanish chivalry by Jole Scudieri Ruggieri, *Cavalleria et cortesia*, pp. 74–91.

[20] Ed. Don Francisco Cerda y Rico, (Madrid, 1787), and Don Cayetano Rosell, *Crónicas de los reyes de Castilla desde Don Alfonso el Sabio, hasta los Católicos Don Fernando y Doña Isabel*, vol. I (Madrid, 1875).

[21] See D. Catalán y Menéndez-Pidal, *Un cronista del siglo XIV: La Gran Crónica de Alfonso XI: hallazgo, estilo, reconstrucción* (Granaria, 1955).

more willingly, he ordered that certain knights and squires of his household should wear a band on their clothing, and he himself did the same. And while still in Vitoria, the king ordered those knights and squires whom he had chosen for this to wear clothes that he had given them, with a band. And he also dressed in clothing of the same sort, with a band. And the first vestments that were made for this were white, and the band blackish. And from that time on he gave those knights each year similar vestments with a band. And the band was as wide as a hand, and was placed over the *pellotes* and other vestments from the left shoulder to the skirt. And they were called the knights of the Band, and they had an ordinance amongst themselves of many good matters which were all works of chivalry. And when they gave a band to a knight, they made him swear and promise that he would keep to himself all the matters of chivalry that were written in that ordinance. And this the king did because men, wishing to have the band, had reason to do deeds of chivalry. And thus it happened afterwards that knights and squires who had done some good deed of arms against the enemies of the king, or attempted to perform such deeds, were given the band by the king, who did them great honour, in such a way that each one of the others wanted to do well in chivalry to gain that honour and the good will of the king, even as they had it.[22]

The chronicle goes on to say that shortly after proclaiming the foundation of the Order, Alfonso, having returned to Burgos, was informed by his wife Queen María that she felt herself to be pregnant with their first child. The young king, elated at the thought that he might soon have a son, decided that he would immediately 'receive the honour of coronation, and in addition the honour of knighthood.'[23] Furthermore, since for some time 'all the *ricos omes* and *infanzones* and *fijos dalgo* and those of the towns had all excused themselves from receiving knighthood,'[24] he decided to command them all to receive the accolade of knighthood during the course of the festivities that would attend his coronation, and ordered many rich garments and gilded swords prepared for them to wear during the ceremony. Before those invited had arrived in Burgos, Alfonso himself set forth on a brief pilgrimage to the tomb of the Apostle St James or Santiago, the patron of Spanish chivalry, in the cathedral of Compostela. There, after spending the night in the church with his arms on the altar, he armed himself, and placing his sword in the hand of the statue of Santiago that stood behind the altar, struck himself on the shoulder with it, so that he could say that he had received the accolade from the saint himself. He then returned to Burgos, taking with him the body of the saint, and while waiting for the last of those he had invited to his coronation to arrive, took part with the noblemen who were there in various knightly sports. In these, according to the chronicler, the knights of the newly-created order of the Band played a prominent part.

[22] *Crónica*, ch. 100; ed. Cerda, pp. 178–179; ed. Rosell, p. 321, col. 2.
[23] *Crónica*, ch. 102; ed. Cerda, p. 185.
[24] Ibid.

> Moreover they maintained two *tablas* for jousting, and the knights of the Band, whom the king had made and ordained a short time before, remained all day, four of them armed in each *tabla*, and would joust with all who sought to joust with them.[25]

When everyone had finally arrived Alfonso, having been annointed by the Archbishop of Santiago, crowned himself and his queen in the Cathedral. The next day he commanded all those whom he had summoned to receive knighthood to come to his palace, and there he gave them all the costumes and swords he had had made for them. On the following day they all assembled in the Cathedral, and Alfonso girded each one with his sword, and gave him the accolade (*pescozada*).[26] The chronicle gives the names of twenty-one *ricos omes* and eighty-nine lesser nobles who were knighted on that day,[27] and among the latter were no fewer than twelve of those listed in the earliest surviving statutes of the Order as knights of the Band.[28]

The testimony of the chronicler about the nature of the Order of the Band and about the date and circumstances of its foundation is confirmed in the statement attached to each of the two early redactions of the statutes by way of a preface. It is unclear precisely when this was composed, but as it is included (in gold letters) in a manuscript of the statutes that was almost certainly prepared during the founder's reign, and probably for the founder himself, it must be regarded as both contemporary and authoritative.[29]

> This book was made by the noble king Don Alfonso, son of the noble king Don Fernando and of the Queen Constanza, and it is of the Order of the Band, in which are said the things which the knights of the Band must have in themselves and the things that they must keep. And he placed in this Order all the best knights and squires, young men of [his] lordship, who he believed complied with it, and even some from outside his lordship, who he believed merited it and complied with it. And the reason why he was moved to make this book of this Order, ahead you shall read it in the prologue of this book more completely. And it was made in the year in which he was crowned and in which were made in Burgos the knighthoods of the *ricos omes* and *infançones* and knights who were there. And that was in the Spanish year one thousand, three hundred, and sixty-eight.

There is thus no reason to doubt that the Order was proclaimed by Alfonso XI in Vitoria shortly before his coronation in Burgos at some time in 1330,[30] or that he named the first members of the Order at that time.

---

[25] Ibid., p. 186.
[26] *Crónica*, ch. 104.
[27] Ibid. See also Grassotti, *Las instituciones*, pp. 290–91.
[28] See below, p. 68.
[29] See below, p. 66.
[30] Villanueva, 'Memoria', pp. 440ff, argued that the foundation of the Order and all of the other events just recounted must have taken place in 1332 rather than 1330, because he had found a set of privileges granted by Alfonso XI to the nobles of Alava sealed in Vitoria on 2

The one remaining passage of the founder's chronicle in which the knights of the Band are mentioned is a description of a tournament held at Valladolid at Easter (4 April) 1333.

> This King Don Alfonso of Castile and Leon, although in this time there was no war, always studied how to engage himself in the office of knighthood, holding tournaments and round tables and jousting, and when he did not do any of these things he hunted in the mountains. And in addition, in order that the knights would not lose the use of their arms, and would still be prepared for war when the need arose, while he was in Valladolid he ordered summoned by his letters the knights of the Band, and other knights and squires, nobles of his kingdom, that they should all be with him in that town on the third day before Easter Day, and that they bring all their horses and arms. And all came on the day that the king had appointed. And on the day after Easter the king ordered a tournment of a very great company of knights to be held, in which all of the knights of the Band were on one side, and an equal number of other knights and squires of the venture on the other side. And in this tournament the king entered, incognito, on the side of the knights of the Band. [31]

This passage (which goes on to describe the combat in some detail) confirms not only Alfonso's devotion to the tournament both as an expression of chivalry and as a useful exercise in preparation for war, but his familiarity with the particular type of highly regulated tournament known as a 'round table' (in Castilian *tabla redonda*), which as we have seen was inspired by the Arthurian literature of the previous century. It also reveals that the Order of the Band could function as a team in a major tournament, and that by April 1333 – about three years after the Order's foundation – its membership was sufficiently large to make up half of a company that could be described as 'very great'. All of these facts will prove to be of some importance for understanding the nature of the Order.

We have no further record of the activities of the Order between its foundation and the death of its founder in 1350. We do know that the Order continued to exist in some form throughout Alfonso's reign, however, because there is evidence for its survival for more than a century after his death. There is furthermore reason to believe that its nature did not change while he was alive. As we shall see, the earliest of the three surviving redactions of the statutes of the Order must have been composed in its present form at some time between January 1339 and October 1340, and the second redaction, which differs from the first only in minor ways, was probably composed by 1345. The third redaction, which seems to be a fairly radical revision of the second, must date (if it is genuine) either from the last years of Alfonso's own reign or – and this is more likely – from the first part of the reign

---

April 1332. It is difficult to believe, however, that both the chronicler and the author of the preface to the statutes could have been mistaken about the date of such important events.

[31] *Crónica*, ch. 144; Cerda, pp. 276–7.

of his son and successor Pedro I. If the statutes presented in all three of these redactions were actually observed, the Order of the Band must have remained a true monarchical order from the time of its foundation at least until the early years of the reign of its second Master. Unfortunately, the loss of the Order's records (if any were ever kept), combined with the poverty of all of the other forms of documentation for this period of the history of Castile as a whole, make it impossible to know whether and to what extent the statutes of the Order were enforced or obeyed even during the twenty-odd years when it is fairly certain that they were theoretically in force.

The evidence for the history of the Order in all reigns subsequent to that of the founder is even more sparse, and the absence of any manuscripts of the statutes dating from this period makes it impossible to determine what statutes (if any) were in effect at any point after about 1353. Such evidence as there is, however, indicates quite strongly that the monarchical statutes of the Order were either gradually or suddenly abandoned, and that the Order was eventually converted into what we have called an honorific pseudo-order: a mere device distributed by the king to honour certain favoured persons of noble birth. Exactly when this transformation was completed is not clear, but there is reason to believe that it began, at least, in the reign of the founder's only legitimate son and successor Pedro 'the Cruel', who reigned from 1350 to 1369. There is no unequivocal reference to the activities of the knights of the Band as such in the documents of Pedro's reign, but the device of the Order is referred to in two passages of the chronicle of his reign written many years later by Pero López de Ayala,[32] who at some time before 1367 was made the bearer of the 'banner of the Band', and was later the chancellor of Castile. These passages – both of which describe events in which the writer was personally involved – seem at first sight to indicate that the Order continued to function as a monarchical order through most of Pedro's reign, despite the difficulties that he had with many of the Order's members, and the fact that he himself (barely sixteen at the time of his accession) did not receive the accolade of knighthood until the eve of the Battle of Nájera in 1367.[33]

Like the early years of his father's reign, much of Pedro's reign was torn by civil wars involving the supporters of rival members of the royal house. In this case the rivalry was between Pedro and his bastard half-brothers – Don Enrique, Count of Trastámara, Don Fadrique, Master of the Order of Santiago, Don Tello, later Count of Viscaya, Don Juan, later Lord of Jérez-Badajoz, and Don Pedro – most of whom were knights of the Band.[34] The first (and only certain) reference to the Order during Pedro's reign is found in the description of an incident that ocurred during the first revolt of the royal bastards, which took place in 1353 and was occasioned by Pedro's merciless execution of two rebellious noblemen, Garci Laso de la Vega, and Alfonso Fernández Coronel – both of whom had been knights of

---

[32] *Crónicas de los Reyes de Castilla Don Pedro, Don Enrique II, Don Juan, Don Enrique III por Don Pedro López de Ayala, Chanciller Mayor de Castilla*, ed. Geronimo Zurita, Eugenio de Llaguno Amirola, t. I (Madrid, 1779).

[33] Ibid., t. I, p. 447.

[34] Enrique, Tello, and Juan are listed among the members in all redactions of the statutes, and Pedro was probably admitted to the Order shortly after his birth in 1346.

the Band. On the occasion in question, an army led by King Pedro was confronting the forces led by his half-brother Count Enrique.

> On that day the King saw a knight walking before the lines of the Count reviewing the battle, wearing red ensigns[35] with a Band of gold, and he asked who that was. And certain of his men who knew him told him that he was Pero Carillo. And the king sent one of his young gentlemen to him [who was called Pedro de Ayala],[36] and ordered him to say to Pero Carillo, that since he was not his vassal, he had no reason to wear the Band. For this Order of the Band, which King Don Alfonso founded, was much honoured and much sought after and much prized in the Kingdom of Castile, and even in other places, and no one wore it except very select men, polished in their habits and in their lineage and in their chivalry, being vassals of the King, or of the Infante his first-born son and heir, and in no other manner. And the King's young gentleman came to Pero Carillo, and told him what the King had said he should tell him. And immediately Pero Carillo took off the ensigns that he wore, which was a coloured cloth with a Band of gold, and he spoke thus to the young gentleman: "Say to my lord the King, that when Abulhacen King of Benemarin invested the town of Tarifa, King Don Alfonso his father ordered me among other noble and good men to go to aid and defend it, and I went with them. And one night we had a battle with the Moors, who sought to enter through a breach [in the wall] of the town of Tarifa which the blows of the engineers had opened. And that night died there the Lord of the Bright Mountains, who was a very powerful Moor, and had many men there. And fifteen days after that my lord the King Don Alfonso, whom God pardon, sent me these ensigns from his body, and sent me an order to wear the Band. And since that time I have held it, but from this time onwards I shall not wear it any more without the licence of the King, since it does not please him." And the King was pleased when he saw that he had taken it off, for they were so near to the other side that they could see well. And this rule was always kept in the Order of the Band in the courts of the Kings of Castile, that a man who was not a vassal of the King or of his son and heir apparent did not wear the Band.[37]

This passage is at least as interesting for what it tells us about the Order under Alfonso XI as for what it tells us about its survival under his son, and allows us to etablish fairly precisely the date on which one of the members whose name is not listed in the earliest surviving redaction of the statutes was admitted to the Order: for the siege of Tarifa by the forces of Abu-l-Hasan began in June and ended in October 1340.[38] It is also interesting because it implies that, although the Order was maintained under Pedro (and possibly under his immediate successors) in something like the form it was given by its founder, and continued to enjoy

---

[35] The principal text of the chronicle has *unas sobresenales bermejas*, but the footnote gives *sobrevistas* in place of the second term.
[36] This is added in the abbreviated version.
[37] *Crónica*, ch. 8, entire.
[38] O'Callaghan, *Medieval Spain*, p. 412.

considerable prestige, it was no longer so maintained at the time the chronicle was composed – presumably in the early years of the fifteenth century. As we shall see, the evidence from that period tends to confirm this impression.

The only other references to the device of the Order in the chronicle of Pedro's reign occur in the description of the great battle of Nájera, fought on 13 April 1367 between Pedro (aided by the great French constable Bertrand du Guesclin) and his brother Enrique (aided by Edward 'the Black Prince' of Wales and Aquitaine). In this battle, the Castilian knights of Enrique's force who fought on foot in the vanguard led by Du Guesclin – said to number about a thousand – were preceded by a flag referred to several times as the *pendón de la Vanda* or 'banner of the Band', which was borne by the author of the chronicle himself. Earlier historians of the Order of the Band who were familiar with this passage assumed, not unnaturally, that the 'banner of the Band' referred to by Ayala was that of the Order, and that the knights led by Count Sancho under that banner were therefore the knights of the Band fighting as a company, just as their statutes required them to do.[39] Some of the knights actually listed as fighting under the banner – most notably Don Sancho himself – were certainly knights of the Band, and it is quite possible that most of the other knights of the Order who were present and fighting on Enrique's side also fought under the banner, but there is no particular reason to think so, since Ayala never once refers in the course of his description either to the 'Order' or to the 'knights of the Band'. In fact there is nothing whatever in Ayala's account to indicate that the 'banner of the Band' was that of the Order as such, and one statement made by Ayala suggests on the contrary that by the time of the battle the Band had become a royal badge which – like the cross of St George in England, worn on their mantles by the knights of the Garter – could also be displayed by persons unconnected with the Order as a symbol of their adherence to the king. In his description of the first encounter between the forces of Pedro and Enrique, he declares that:

> And those on the side of King Don Pedro and the Prince of Wales wore as their sign white shields and surcoats with red crosses for St George; and all those on the side of King Don Enrique wore that day bands on their surcoats.[40]

If the band could be used in this way as a device to identify all of the members of Enrique's forces, the banner of the Band might just as easily have been a flag like that of St George which was commonly borne before English forces, without reference to the English royal order of St George, *alias* the Garter. It is thus impossible to say whether the Order of the Band *as an institution* was in any way involved in the battle of Nájera, or whether it shared in the destruction of Enrique's army.

Enrique himself escaped, and on 23 March 1369, after defeating Pedro (again with the aid of Du Guesclin) in the Battle of Montiel, personally stabbed him to death when Du Guesclin brought him by treachery to his tent. The fate of the Order as such during the civil war and Pedro's brief restoration is unknown, but as

---

[39] See Daumet, 'L'Ordre castillan', p. 14.
[40] *Crónica*, ed. Zurita, p. 448.

many of its more prominent members certainly fought for Enrique at Nájera and were subsequently either captured or driven into exile with Enrique, it may well have been formally suppressed by Pedro at some time between 1366 and 1369. If it was suppressed, it must have been reconstituted by the victorious Enrique after his second assumption of the Castilian crown. Unlike Pedro, Enrique had no reason to resent the Order, and must have wished to be seen by the Castilian nobility as the true heir of his illustrious and much-regretted father, who had founded the Order and given it a prominent place in his court. It is quite possible that Enrique rewarded many of his loyal supporters among the *fijosdalgo* with membership in the Order, but he certainly rewarded his most prominent supporters by creating new titles of dignity for them (including 'duke' and 'marquis' as well as 'count'), and there is reason to think that his introduction of this practice reduced in his eyes the value of the Order as an instrument of conferring honour.

Enrique may well have allowed the restored Order to keep the statutes it had enjoyed under his brother, with little or no modification, but in practice he seems to have paid little attention to them. As Ayala indicated (with one slight inaccuracy) in his account of the incident in 1353, all known versions of the Order's statutes restricted membership to men who were the vassals either of the king or of one of his sons, and further required all those admitted to swear never to leave the king's service. In the chivalric biography entitled *Le chronique du bon duc Loys de Bourbon*, however, Enrique is reported to have bestowed the insignia of the Order on each of the seven bannerets who accompanied Duke Louis of Bourbon on a visit to his court in 1375. In the words of the biographer,

> Then King Enrique of Spain, seeing that the Duke of Bourbon for his part did not wish to remain [after the King of Portugal had declared war on Castile], reluctantly gave him licence, praying that he work, for love of him, to pacify the young King of Navarre, who had his sister as a wife, with regard to the King of France. The duke told him that he would do what he could, and at his departure King Enrique presented to the Duke of Bourbon gold, silver, and plate, but he did not wish to take any of these, merely some dogs called allans, some figured leathers, and velvet tapestries, and six fair Spanish horses. And to each of the bannerets he gave a horse, and his *Order of the Band*. Thus departed Duke Louis of Bourbon from King Enrique of Spain. . .[41]

The *Chronique* elsewhere identifies the seven bannerets as Guichard Dauphin; Griffon de Montagu; Hugues de Chastellus, Lord of Chastelmorand; Jean Capet de Bourbon-Rochefort, Bastard of Bourbon and Lord of Rochefort; Girart de Bourbon; and Lionnet d'Araines de Beauvoisin.[42] The first three of these, at least, had been admitted by Duke Louis to his own order of the Golden Shield at the time of its foundation in 1367,[43] and there is no reason to believe that any of them was or became a vassal of either Enrique or his son. That all seven could so casually be

---

[41] Alphonse Chazaud, ed., *La chronique du bon duc Loys de Bourbon, par Jean d'Oronville* (Paris, 1876), p. 111.
[42] Ibid., p. 107.
[43] See below, p. 273.

admitted to the Order of the Band while they were attending upon the founder of the Order of the Golden Shield and preparing to leave Castile in his service strongly suggests that, by 1375, the Order of the Band no longer made very strong claims upon the loyalty or service of its members, and that membership in the Order had come to be seen as little more than an indication of royal favour. The fact that membership in the Order was not offered to Duke Louis himself further suggests that it was not considered sufficiently honourable even for a subordinate prince, but if true this estimation was destined to change, as we shall see.

No further mention of the Order of the Band has yet been discovered in the documents of the reign of Enrique II, though there is at least one contemporary representation of Enrique and his only son Juan wearing what is almost certainly the surcoat of the Order.[44] His son, who succeeded him peacefully on the throne as Juan I in 1379,[45] placed a device which may have been that of the Order on several of his coins,[46] but the only possible mention of the Order in a written document of his reign currently known is to be found in his will, dated 21 July 1385.[47] In that instrument, witnessed by the chronicler Pero López de Ayala in his capacity as bearer of the banner of the Band, Juan declared that Ayala was to keep his office when his son succeeded to the throne: "Otrosi que Pero López de Ayala aya el pendón de la Banda e que sea su alférez asi como lo es agora nuestro."[48] If this banner was indeed that of the Order, it would appear that as late as 1385 the Order of the Band – contrary to the implications of the bestowals discussed in the last pargraph – was still theoretically expected to function as a military unit of some sort, and to continue to function as such for the foreseeable future. It is quite possible, however, that the office of banner-bearer had become purely honorary by this time, or was only theoretically connected with the 'Order' of the Band, to the extent that it survived as such.

In any case the standing of the 'Order' of the Band even as a mark of royal favour suffered the first of several blows only five years later when Juan I, on St James' Day (25 July) 1390, proclaimed the adoption of two new *devisas*: a collar of sun-rays from which a dove representing the Holy Spirit depended, to be given to knights of his household who fulfilled the conditions that he had set forth in a book, and a rose, to be given to squires of his household.[49] The first of these *devisas* may have been that of a new monarchical order, and the very fact that Juan felt the need for such a 'device' suggests that he felt that the 'Order' of the Band was no longer sufficient even as a mark of favour for the knights of his household. It may be, however, that Juan saw his new devices as badges of adherence inferior in honour to the device of the Band, and intended to treat them rather the way Henry IV and his successors on the throne of England, all sovereigns of the Order of the Garter, treated their collars of SS or suns-and-roses. Whatever his intentions were,

---

[44] See below, p. 88.
[45] On his reign see esp. Luis Suárez Fernández, *Juan I, Rey de Castilla (1379–1390)*, (Madrid, 1955).
[46] Villanueva, 'Memoria', p. 460.
[47] Published in Rosell, *Crónicas*, t. II, pp. 186ff.
[48] Ibid., p. 192.
[49] *Crónica del Rey Don Juan Primero de Castilla e de León*, *Crónicas*, ed. Rosell, t. II, p. 145. On these devices, see below pp. 326–7.

however, they came to naught, for Juan was killed accidently less than three months after creating his two devices, on 9 October, and only the Order of the Band seems to have survived his death.

Juan I was followed on the throne by his twelve-year-old son Enrique III, who after a brief but turbulent regency ending in August 1393 managed, like his great-grandfather Alfonso XI in similar circumstances, to restore order to his troubled realm. He even succeeded in resolving the conflict between his own line of the royal house and the heirs of the displaced Pedro 'the Cruel' by marrying Catherine, daughter of Pedro's elder daughter Costanza by John 'of Gaunt', Duke of Lancaster. Not long after the coup that in 1399 placed Gaunt's son Henry 'of Bolingbroke' on the English throne as Henry IV, (and probably in about 1402), Enrique seems to have accepted membership in the English order of the Garter,[50] so he could not have been wholly unaware of the value of monarchical orders, but there is no evidence to suggest that he conferred membership in the Order of the Band on Henry in return.

The only certain reference to the Order as such during the reign of Enrique III (which ended in 1406) occurs in the *Victorial*, the chivalric biography of the 'Unconquered Knight' Don Pero Niño (v.c. 1378–1454, created Count of Buelna in 1431),[51] written by his *alférez* between about 1431 and 1449.[52] According to the *Victorial*, Don Pero's mother Ines Laso de la Vega – whose family had included one of the original knights of the Band – had been made the wet-nurse of the future Enrique III in 1379, and Don Pero had therefore been brought up in the royal household. There he seems to have become one of the closest friends of the young Infante, and shortly after the latter began his personal rule as king in 1393 he gave his own arms to his childhood companion Pero, then about fifteen. Don Pero spent much of his long and distinguished career as a captain in the service of Enrique and his son Juan II, and (although his biographer fails to mention the fact), was probably admitted to the Order of the Band by the former monarch at some time before 1404. In June of that year he went to Marseilles to deal with two Castilian corsairs in the pay of the Antipope Benedict XIII. According to his biographer,

> While he was at Marseilles there was there a squire of rank who bore the device of the Band; Pero Niño went to him and ripped it from him, because he did not hold it from the King of Castile.[53]

As we shall see, all three of the surviving redactions of the Order's statutes include a requirement that the knights of the Band challenge any knight not of their number whom they found wearing the device of their Order.[54] Don Pero's

---

[50] *Complete Peerage*, II, p. 538.
[51] See Siete Iglesias, 'Titulos', *Hidalguía* 2 (1953), p. 228.
[52] Juan de Mata Carriazo, ed., *El Victorial, Crónica de Don Pero Niño, Conde de Buelna, por su Alférez Gutierre Diez de Games* (Madrid, 1940).
[53] Ibid., p. 109. The Spanish reads: 'Estando alli en Marsella, hera alli vn escudero de paraje que traya la devisa de la Banda; e Pero Niño fue a el e tirogela, por quanto non la tenia del rey de Castilla'.
[54] Red. A, ord. 3a; red. B, ord. 8a.

action was not entirely in keeping with the specifications of the statute as we know it, but this may have been due to some peculiar circumstance not explained in the *Victorial*. In any case his action suggests that he knew of the statute in question, and believed that it was still in effect. Don Pero himself seems to have taken his membership in the Order quite seriously at the time of this incident, but the fact that his biographer, writing several decades after the incident, failed even to mention his admission to the Order, suggests that by 1430 or thereabouts the Band had come to be so insignificant that the right to wear it was scarcely worth mentioning.

The next document to mention the Order of the Band dates from the first half of the long and war-torn reign of Enrique III's son Juan II (r. 1406–54), who succeeded to the throne at the tender age of one-and-a-half. From Christmas of 1406 to 1416 Castile was governed by his uncle, the chivalrous and capable Don Fernando 'of Antequera', Duke of Peñafiel and (from 1312) King of Aragon as Ferran I.[55] The chronicle of the reign of Juan II reports that during the course of the year 1415 the young king – as yet barely ten years old and certainly acting at the behest either of his uncle or of his mother – bestowed the 'device of the band' on a succession of distinguished foreign visitors to his court, most of whom had come to help the Emperor Sigismund in his attempt to persuade the Aragonese anti-pope Benedict XIII to abdicate.[56] The wording of the passage in question leaves the reader in some doubt as to which of the persons listed actually received the device, but as the passage explicitly states that only the 'principal' members of each party wore the device, the prestige of the 'Order' during this period must have remained reasonably high. Nevertheless, it is highly unlikely that any of the men named (the Count of Armagnac, the Viscount of Saona, the Duke of Brieg, and the Marshal of Hungary) became a vassal of the King of Castile in order to receive the Order's device, or undertook any of the obligations imposed by the original statutes of the Order.

Indeed, it is not clear that the device of the Band was still thought of or referred to as the badge of an 'order', for no official document of the fifteenth century uses this term in connection with it, and it soon came to be treated as but one device among many. At some time between his assumption of royal power in 1416 and 1430, Juan II adopted a second stable device, that of the collar of the Scale (*Escama*), which according to the chronicler of his reign he gave as a sign of his high regard to 'very few', and which some contemporaries at least referred to as an 'order'.[57] He nevertheless continued to distribute the Band, and it is more than likely that some members of his court bore the insignia of both 'orders' at the same time. By a privilege of 28 December 1330 he conceded to Doña María Alvarez de Lara, wife of Don Juan Alfon de Novoa, a knight of Santiago, and to their children Doña Isabel Alfon and Juan de Novoa, the right to wear '. . . his device of the Band on their clothing and . . . armour, even as the other persons, noble ladies and

---

[55] On this period see Juan Torres Fuentes, 'The Regency of Don Ferdinand of Antequera', in Roger Highfield, ed., *Spain in the Fifteenth Century, 1369–1516; Essays and Extracts by Historians of Spain* (New York, 1972), pp. 114–170.

[56] *La Crónica de serenisimo Principe Don Juan, Segondo Rey deste nombre en Castilla y en León . . .*, in *Crónicas*, ed. Rosell, t. II, pp. 365–6.

[57] *La Crónica de . . . Don Juan*, pp. 482, 525, 535. See below, pp. 327–9.

damsels to whom I have given and do give the said licence to bear my device do wear it.'[58] Two years earlier, in 1428, he had issued a similar privilege in favour of Doña Catalina Nuñez, wife of Don Alonso Alvarez de Toledo – whose families, like that of Doña María, were among the most eminent in the kingdom – and to their children.[59] It is clear both from the identity of the recipients and from the language of these grants – which contain no mention of an order and no suggestion that the recipients undertook any special obligations when they accepted the 'device' of the Band – that by the end of the first century of its existence the Band had come to be treated as little more than a superior sort of livery badge that could be given to anyone whom the king chose for some reason to distinguish, including women and children.

The last references to the Band that I have found occur in two related documents dating from the reign of Juan II's son and successor Enrique IV (r. 1454–1474), whose dissolute ways won him the derisive surname 'the Impotent'. The first of these is the famous diary of the German knight-errant Jörg von Ehingen,[60] who during the course of a long journey undertaken in the company of the young knight Jörg von Ramsyden spent several months fighting the Moors in Granada. After being wounded in the storming of a small town, Von Ehingen and his companion returned to Castile, and spent two months in the court of King Enrique. There, according to the diary,

> We were much honoured with feasting, dancing, hunting, horse-racing, and such-like pastimes. After two months we took leave of the King in order to return to the King of Portugal, and were most graciously dispatched. The King gave us both his orders [orden geselschafften], namely the Spanish Order, which is a broad collar overlapping like large fish-scales, also the Band of Castile [la banda de Kastilla], a red coat of scarlet cloth with a gold band, two thumbs breadth, over the left shoulder, running in front on the right side down to the bottom of the coat, and then at the back of the coat running up again to the left shoulder. The third Order is that of Granada, a granite apple set on a club, with a stalk and some leaves on it. The King gave us almost 300 ducats, and to each of us a fine jennet [a Spanish horse]. So we took our leave most honourably and serviceably from the Christian King Henry, in the year, as one counts from the birth of the Lord, 1457.[61]

The other document is the instrument by which the devices referred to by Von Ehingen were legally conveyed:

---

[58] '. . . la su divisa de la Banda en sus ropas, y divisa [sic] y guarniciones segun que la traen las otras personas y duenas y doncellas hijos-dalgo a quien Yo he dado y do la dicha licencia pare traer la mi divisa.' Published by Don Luis de Salazar y Castro, Historia de la Casa de Lara, lib. xv, quoted in Villanueva, 'Memoria', p. 444, n. 1, and p. 461.

[59] Ibid., p. 444, n. 1. Villanueva gives no source for this statement.

[60] Published as Der Schwaebischen Ritters Georg von Ehingen Reisen nach der Ritterschaft (Stuttgart, 1842), and trans. into English by Malcolm Letts as The Diary of Jörg von Ehingen (London, 1929).

[61] Modified after Letts, op. cit., pp. 38–39.

Privilege of the King of Castile given to Jörg von Ehingen, Knight, and his descendants, to wear the abovesaid insignia on their clothing.

We the King of Castile and Leon, seeking to honour and ennoble the person and estate of you, Jörg von Ehingen, knight of the house of the magnificent and illustrious Duke Albrecht, brother of the Emperor of Germany; by these presents we give you licence and faculty that you and your wife may wear and shall wear, on your clothes and armour, our device, and the Band, and the collar of the Scale, even as knights and gentlemen and the rest wear them and are accustomed to wear them. Given in the noble city of Jaen, on the sixth day of September, in the year fifty-seven.[62]

In both of these documents, as in those of the reign of Juan II, the Band appears as nothing more than a device indicative of the esteem of the King of Castile; indeed, it appears as but one device among several, all apparently of equal value, distributed for this purpose. It can hardly be surprising, therefore, that the chroniclers of the period after 1415 failed to take any note of the bestowal of the Band, and that even those who received the Band in that period failed to record the honour paid to them for posterity by having themselves represented in the coat of the Band in portraits or on tomb effigies. Many German knights of the middle and later decades of the fifteenth century who, like Jörg von Ehingen and his companion, were honoured by the King of Castile with the right to wear his devices, proudly displayed the collar of the Scale (or what may have been a revival of the collar of the Holy Spirit or Dove founded by Juan I), along with the collars and devices they had received from other kings, on armorial tombstones, in stained-glass windows, and in other places, but either because they did not receive it or because its peculiar form did not lend itself to pictorial heraldic display, none of them included the device of the Band among the other souvenirs of their chivalric pilgrimages.[63]

In fact I have found no evidence whatever to indicate that the Band continued to be distributed even as a device beyond the day on which it was given to Jörg von Ehingen. Of course even this total absence of positive evidence does not prove that Enrique IV simply ceased to distribute the device of the Band shortly after 5 September 1457, and it is not only possible but likely that he continued to bestow it, at least on occasion, until his death in 1474. It is also possible that it continued to be granted for some time after his death, but it is more likely that it was finally abandoned as a device at about this time. Precisely why it should have been abandoned, after more than a century, remains a mystery, but it seems not

---

[62] The original, published in Letts, op. cit., p. 67, reads as follows: Privilegium Regis Castellae, Georgio Ehingheno, equiti & posteris eius, datum, Insignia supradicta gestandi in vestitu. Nos el Rey de Castilla y de León, quiriendo honrar & noblessar la persona & estado de vos Iorge d'Ehingen, cauallero de la casa del magnifico & inclito Duci Alberto, Hermanno del Emperador de Alemanna; por la presente vos damos lycentia & facultad: para que vos & vuestra muger podays traher, & trayades, en vuestras ropas & guarniciones, la nuestra devisa, & la Vanda & el colar del escama: segund que lo trahen, & acostumbran traher, los cavalleros, & varones gentiles, &c. Data en la noble cibdad de Iaen, cinco dias de setiembre, anno de cinquanta & siete.

[63] See below, p. 483.

unreasonable to surmise that the Band was one of the victims of the civil war that erupted immediately following Enrique's death between the partisans of his daughter Juana (commonly regarded as the illegitimate child of his old favourite Don Beltrán de la Cueva) and those of his sister Isabel, married since 1469 to the Infant En Ferran of Aragon. Only in 1479 – the year in which her husband succeeded to the thrones of the lands of the Crown of Aragon as Ferran II – did Isabel finally triumph over her niece and assume the government of Castile, and it would not be surprising in the circumstances if she decided not to revive any of the secondary devices associated with her much-despised brother. In any case, as we have seen, she and her husband (who maintained his own quasi-monarchical order of the Stole and Jar until his death in 1516) were soon to annex the masterships of most of the surviving religious orders of knighthood to the Castilian crown. Their grandson, Carlos I von Habsburg, who eventually succeeded them both, was by that time Sovereign of the much more illustrious order of the Golden Fleece, and so had even less use than they for the discredited Castilian 'Order' of the Band.

Even by the time of the accession of Isabel 'the Catholic', of course, the 'Order' of the Band had long ceased to function as a monarchical order. The evidence we have just reviewed suggests that it probably lost that character during the course of the civil wars between the founder's two sons Pedro and Enrique, possibly in the wake of Enrique's defeat at Nájera in 1367, and was revived by Enrique after his final victory in 1369 only as a pseudo-order of some sort. Some recollection of its former nature may have persisted during the reigns of Enrique's son Juan I and his grandson Enrique III, but by the time the latter's son Juan II assumed the reins of power in 1416 the original nature and prestige of the 'order' had probably been forgotten, for thereafter the band was consistently referred to and treated by the Kings of Castile themselves as a mere 'device'. In all likelihood, therefore, the statutes of the Order we are about to examine were fully operative only in the period of just over two decades between 1330 and about 1353 (when Pedro 'the Cruel' began to slaughter its members and drove his own brothers into open rebellion), were effectively abandoned by 1369, and were completely forgotten by 1416.

3 The Statutes of the Order

As usual, the most important evidence by far for the nature and purpose of the Order of the Band during the period when it was a true monarchical order is to be found in the Order's statutes, of which two contemporary redactions have been preserved.[64] The first of these, which we shall call redaction A, survives in a single

---

[64] There is a third redaction, published in Joseph Micheli Márquez, *Tesoro Militar de Cavallería* (Madrid, 1642), ff. 49v–51v, and in M. de Iñigo y Miera and D. S. Costanzo, *Historia de las Ordenes de Caballería, que han existido y existen en España* (Madrid, 1863), II, pp. 115–132. This redaction (which may be referred to as C) appears to be a thorough reworking of B, but the list of members it contains has no additional names. Since the origin of this redaction is unknown, and it is not preserved in any document remotely contemporary with the Order's existence, it must be regarded as suspect, and I shall not consider it here at any length.

fourteenth-century manuscript, lavishly illuminated on its title page, and almost certainly prepared for official use.[65] The second, which we shall call redaction B, is preserved as an insertion in a fifteenth-century book on chivalry (the *Doctrinal de Caballeros* of Alfonso of Burgos, Bishop of Carthagena, published in Burgos in 1487), in a seventeenth-century manuscript evidently copied for private reasons from a lost original,[66] in another manuscript of similar date and origin,[67] and in at least three other manuscripts whose date and provenance I have been unable to discover.[68] Both redactions are preserved exclusively in Castilian.

The table of contents which precedes the text of the statutes in the manuscript of redaction A indicates that that version originally included twenty-five distinct *capitulos* or chapters, but the fourth and fifth folios of the manuscript are now missing, and with them the last part of chapter 2, all of chapters 3 to 6, and what appears to be the first line of chapter 7. The text of redaction B was divided into only twenty-three chapters, all of which survive in their entirety. Most of the chapters in both redactions (distinguished in the manuscripts by roman numerals set before the first letter of their text) include two or more distinct ordinances, and although these are not distinguished in any way from one another in the text, we will distinguish them here with lower-case letters. If (as seems likely on the basis of the table of contents of A) the missing chapters of redaction A were essentially similar in content to the corresponding chapters of redaction B, then redaction A originally contained exactly one hundred and thirty-six ordinances, and redaction B one hundred and twenty-one. A careful comparison of the two redactions reveals that (when the missing chapters of A are supplied from B) most of the ordinances included in each are also included in the other, with only insignificant variations in wording, while the arrangement and division of the chapters differ significantly. These differences in arrangement are not random: on the basis of their subject matter, the chapters of each redaction can be divided into a number of sequences or sections, each dealing with a single broad topic such as membership or corporate activities, and while the ordering of the various sections in the two redactions is almost completely different, the content and internal organization of the individual sections is largely identical in both.

---

[65] Paris, B.N., ms. esp. 33 (anc. 464). Published by Daumet, 'L'Ordre castillan', pp. 21–32. I checked his edition carefully against the original manuscript, and found it to be quite accurate.

[66] Paris, B.N., ms. esp. 335 (anc. 465). Daumet, 'L'Ordre castillan', p. 18, gives a brief description of this manuscript.

[67] Paris, B.N., ms. esp.150 (anc.466), ff.1–29. Daumet seems to have missed this copy.

[68] Villanueva alludes to three manuscripts, one taken by Don Pedro de Guzmán el Bueno, Duke of Medina Sidonia, from the archives of the city of Toledo, ('Memoria', p. 439), and two others in the library of the King of Spain (ibid., p. 465, n. 1), none of which is more precisely described or identified. The text published as an appendix to his paper (ibid., pp. 552–575) is evidently based on the first of these, and the text of the version printed in the *Doctrinal* is given there in the form of footnoted variants. I have compared Villanueva's text with that preserved in B.N. ms. esp. 335, and found the differences between them to be very minor. Villanueva was evidently unaware of the existence of the manuscripts preserved in Paris, and Daumet of the existence of those preserved in Spain. Daumet recognized that there were two distinct redactions, but did not compare them carefully, and dismissed the differences as insignificant.

Table 3.1

A Concordance of Redactions A and B of
the Statutes of the Order of the Band

Concordance based on Redaction A			Concordance based on Redaction B		
I	Introduction	P= P 1= B.1	I	Introduction	P= P 1= A.1
II	Membership	2= B.7 [3]= B.8? [4]= B.9?	II	General Obligations	2= [A.5a?] 3= [A.5b?] 4= [A.5c?] 5a–d= [A.5d–g?] 5h= [A.6?] 6= A.7, 8, 25
III	General Obligations	[5]= B.2–B.5g? [6]= B.5h? 7= B.6a–c 8= B.6d–g	III	Membership	7= A.2 8= [A.3] 9= [A.4]
IV	Corporate Activities	9= B.14 10= – (rep. B.15)	IV	Internal Conflicts	10= A.13b, 14, 15 11a= –; 11b = A.17 12= A.18 13= A.19
V	Mutual Obligations	11= B.18 12= B.19	V	Corporate Activities	14= A.9 15= – (rep. A.10)
VI	Internal Conflicts	13a–c= B.17; 13d= B.10a 14= B.10b 15= B.10d 16= – (rep. B.11a–c) 17= B.11b 18= B.12 19= B.13	VI	Miscellaneous	16= A.21 17= A.13a 18= A.11 19= A.12 20= A.20
VII	Attendance at Tourneys	20= B.20 21= B.16	VII	Obedience	21a= A.22a; 21b=–
VIII	Obedience	22a= B.21a; 22bc=–	VIII	Rules for Tourneys	22= A.23 23= A.24
IX	Rules for Tourneys	23= B.22 24= B. 23			
X	Members	25= B.6c			

Missing: B.15, B.11a,c, B.21c Missing: A.10, A.16, A.22c

The exact relationship between both the chapters and the sections contained in the two redactions can best be shown in a table of concordances. As Table 3.1 indicates, the two redactions differ principally in that sections V and VII and the first half of chapter 13 in section VI of redaction A are conflated into one completely disorganized section (VI) in redaction B, while chapter 25 (in section X) of redaction A has been included in the last chapter of section II in redaction B. The two redactions also differ in that each contains exactly four ordinances or sequences of ordinances that the other does not. Each of the four ordinances or sequences peculiar to B corresponds in its relative positioning to one of the four peculiar to A, and three of the four deal with essentially the same subject as the ordinances they replace, but all four differ in detail to a greater or lesser extent from the corresponding ordinances in A. Ordinance B.21e, which sets forth the right of the Master to impose penalties on knights who failed to obey any of the Order's statutes, is a reduced version of ordinances A.22e–m, in which specific penalties are prescribed for specific faults, while ordinances B.21f–h, which set forth the punishment for revealing the Order's rules to outsiders, represent an expanded version of A.22n, which requires that the rule be kept secret, but prescribes no punishment for failure to do so. Similarly, the fourteen ordinances of chapter A.10 and the three ordinances of chapter B.15 describe the Order's regular meetings, but the former call for only one annual meeting, while the latter call for three. Finally, while the single ordinance of chapter A.16 deals with the exemption of the knights of the Order from certain taxes, ordinances B.11a–c, which replace it, deal with a wholly different matter, the settlement of disputes involving the king.

The most natural explanation for the kinds of differences that exist between these two versions of the statutes is that one is an earlier and the other a later, amended, form. This is probably true in this case, but the specific differences in the text itself are such that it is difficult to use them to determine which is the earlier version. In fact the only useful evidence for the time of composition for either of the two redactions is to be found in the list of members which each contains (in chapters A.25 and B.6 respectively). Both lists begin with the name of the founder himself, followed by that of his one legitimate son, the Infante Don Pedro (b. 1334, king from 1350), and those of four of his bastard sons by Leonor de Guzmán: Don Enrique (b. 1333, Count of Trastámara before 1350[69]), Don Fernando (b. 1336, d.v.p.), Don Tello (b. 1337/8) and Don Juan (b. 1338/40).[70] Since Don Pedro is entitled 'infante' rather than 'king' in both lists, and Don Enrique is not called Count of Trastámara, it is likely that both lists were compiled several years before the founder's death in 1350. Similarly, the inclusion in both

---

[69] The precise date on which he was given this county by his father seems to be unknown, but he may have received it when he turned fourteen in 1347.

[70] The first three dates are given in Daumet, 'L'Ordre castillan', p. 30 n. 1. According to Daumet the precise dates of the births of Don Tello and Don Juan are unknown, but they are known to have been alive in June 1341. As Don Fernando was born in November 1336, it is unlikely that Don Tello was born before November 1337, and thus unlikely that Don Juan was born before November 1338. The omission from the list of knights in redaction A of the name of Pero Carillo, who had certainly been admitted to the Order by November 1340, suggests that Don Juan was born before the latter date. The younger bastards, who did not receive titles from their father, were not yet fourteen when he died.

lists of the bastard Don Juan, who was not even born until the autumn of 1338 at the earliest, means that neither list could have been compiled before that time, and that both were probably compiled somewhat later. Most of the remaining names in the list in redaction A also occur in the list in redaction B, but the latter does not contain three of the names included in the former, and contains in addition, following the set of names both have in common, some thirty-one other names. This alone strongly suggests that the list in B was compiled at a later date than that in A. Inasmuch as one of the knights whose name is omitted from A but included in B – Don Pero Carillo – is known to have been admitted to the Order at some time during the summer or early autumn of 1340,[71] it seems very likely that the list in A was compiled before the latter date, while that in B must have been compiled after it. The list in redaction A, therefore, (and therefore redaction A as a whole) must have been composed at some time between January 1339 and November 1340, and was probably composed toward the end of that period. From the fact that one of the three men whose name is included in the list in A but omitted from the list in B – Don Lope de Haro – is known to have died shortly before the end of 1343,[72] we may similarly conclude that the list in B (and therefore redaction B as a whole) was probably composed at some time during or after 1343. The fact that neither of the founder's youngest bastards – Don Pedro (b. 1346) and Don Sancho (b. 1349) – is included suggests that it was composed in or before 1346, since the older bastards all seem to have been admitted to the Order within a short time of their births.

Redaction A – the only redaction to be preserved in a manuscript written in the fourteenth century (and almost certainly during the founder's reign) – is thus in all probability the earliest form of the statutes of the Order to survive. It is possible that the ordinances it contains are precisely those assigned to the new Order by Alfonso in 1330, but it is equally possible that several of them were added or modified at some time between 1330 and 1340, and all that can be said with any confidence is that they represent the form of the statutes in effect in the latter year, and are probably quite similar to the original statutes of the Order. Redaction B must be presumed to be a later version produced by a series of amendments adopted (not necessarily simultaneously) at some time after October 1340. It was probably current in 1344 or 1345, and may well have been maintained in force with little further modification until the end of the founder's reign. Why it should have been amended in such a way as to destroy the generally logical and consistent organization of its original is not at all clear.

In summarizing and citing the statutes of the Order of the Band, I shall follow the more logical order of redaction A, and simply supply from redaction B the four chapters missing from A. As we have seen, both early redactions of the statutes begin with a table of contents (in redaction A headed *Estos son los capitulos del libro de la Vanda*), followed by a short preface which serves primarily to identify the contents of the book and to introduce the rather longer prologue (numbered as chapter 1), in which Alfonso set forth the reasons for which he founded the Order. The prologue – like the preface virtually identical in the two redactions – may be translated as follows:

[71] See above, p. 57.
[72] Daumet, 'L'Ordre castillan', p. 30 n. 8.

(1) Here begins the book of the Band which King Alfonso of Castile and Leon made. And it was founded for two reasons: to glorify first knighthood, and second loyalty.[73] The reason why he decided to make it is that the highest and most precious order that God made is knighthood. This is true for many reasons, but especially for two: first, because because God made it to defend his faith, and secondly, moreover, to defend each of His regions, His lands, and His states. And for this you will discover in the ancient chronicles about the great deeds that were done, that clearly God took a hand in the deeds of the battles that were done by the hands of the knights. And thus it is proved that God prizes this order more than any of the others, because it defends His faith and kingdoms and dominions. And for this, he who is of good fortune and regards himself as a knight, according to his estate he should do much to honour knighthood and to advance it. And furthermore, loyalty is one of the greatest virtues that there could be in any person, and especially in a knight, who ought to keep himself loyal in many ways. But the principal ways are two: the first to keep loyalty to his lord, the second to love truly whomever he has to love, especially her in whom he has placed his heart. Man is also bound to love himself and esteem and hold himself as someone. And for this has the Order of the Band been made, so that the knights who seek to be in the Order and who take the band will have in themselves these two virtues more than other knights: to be loyal to their lord, and to love loyally her to whom they have given their heart; and also to maintain knighthood and to hold themselves as knights more than others, in order to do higher deeds of chivalry.[74]

The statutes proper follow this prologue. As table 3.1 indicates, the next three chapters (made up of twenty-nine distinct ordinances) form a section broadly concerned with membership in the Order. The third division of the statutes sets forth the general obligations of the knights of the Order after their admission. This division contains twenty-eight ordinances organized into four chapters (5 to 8), the first two of which have once again to be supplied from redaction B. The fourth section of the statutes, comprising seventeen ordinances organized into the two chapters 9 and 10, describes the Order's corporate activities. Chapters 11 and 12, which together contain only three ordinances, make up a fifth section, concerned with the reciprocal obligations of the knights of the Order. The sixth section, comprising the twenty-four ordinances of chapters 13 through 19, deals with the settlement of various kinds of internal conflict that the founder felt might arise within the Order. The seventh section, composed of the ten ordinances of chapters 20 and 21, defines the obligations of the knights with respect to attendance at tournaments and jousts that were proclaimed by the king or in honour of some solemn event. Chapter 22 (including fourteen ordinances) forms a section by itself, declaring the obligations of the knights to obey and keep secret the Order's rules, and the punishments for failing to do either. The ninth section sets out, in chapters headed 'On the ordering of tourneys' and 'On the ordering of jousts', the rules which the knights of the Order were to follow when engaging in those two forms of

---

[73] The Spanish reads: '. . . la primera alabando cavalleria, la segunda lealtad.'
[74] Daumet, 'L'Ordre castillan', p. 23.

mock combat. Chapter 23 contains ten rules, and chapter 24 nine. Most were clearly designed to reduce the brutality of such combats, and increase what is perhaps best termed 'fair play', but their details are of little interest in the present context. The last chapter in redaction A is a simple list of twenty-eight names, headed: *Estos son los muy nobles et muy corteses cavalleros de la orden de la Vanda* – 'These are the most noble and most courteous knights of the Order of the Band.'

4 The Name and Title of the Order

The surviving sources consistently refer to the society founded by Alfonso in 1330 by the single designation *la Orden de la Banda* (or *Vanda*), 'the Order of the Band'. Unlike Károly of Hungary, Alfonso evidently felt no scruple about giving the title 'order' – hitherto restricted to strictly monastic organizations – to his new lay society, and unlike most later founders felt no need for a secondary title. There is no reason to doubt that Alfonso borrowed the title directly from the three religious orders of knighthood whose masters and great officers spent much of their time in his court, and whose brother knights, when they were not engaged in internal feuds, fought mainly in his service. His attachment of the title 'order' to his new society suggests that he saw the society as being comparable in important ways to the bodies of knights with which that title had traditionally been associated.

Unlike all the existing religious orders and all known confraternities of knights, however, Alfonso's new 'order' took the name that followed its title neither from its heavenly patron nor from its principal fortress, but from the distinctive device its members were to wear on their official habit. Since this device itself seems to have had no particular symbolic significance,[75] it must be presumed that Alfonso chose to name his 'order' for its device simply because he did not plan to give it either a patron or a seat, and the device was the only distinctive attribute remaining. Nevertheless, by naming the first truly monarchical order in this way, Alfonso set the pattern for most later lay orders of all types.

We cannot be sure why Alfonso, alone among the founders of monarchical orders, chose not to give his Order either a patron in the court of heaven or a permanent headquarters with a chapel in which not only the cult of the patron but such other characteristically confraternal activities as prayers for the living and masses for the dead members of the Order could be carried out. The most likely explanation, however, is that he wanted to make the Order as secular as possible in nature, to distinguish it clearly from the religious orders upon which it was partially modelled. It can hardly be coincidental that he also failed to require the knights of the Order to have masses said for their deceased brethren, and imposed only one, relatively easy 'spiritual' obligation upon them: daily attendance at mass. It is also possible that he avoided tying the Order to a particular place, whether religious or secular, because he wanted to be able to convene it wherever his court happened to be, and as neither the court nor the government of Castile had a fixed seat this was liable to be anywhere in the Castilian realms.

[75] See below, pp. 90–91.

5 The Members of the Order: The Master

The 'Order' of the Band is depicted in its statutes as a society of knights and squires under the presidency of a Master (*Maestre*). The latter title was certainly taken over from the religious orders of knighthood, whose chief officers had always been so styled. Alfonso presumably chose the title 'master' because it seemed the most appropriate one for the head of a society of knights, but despite the usage of many later historians (who commonly refer to the heads of all knightly orders as 'masters' or 'grand masters'), no later founder of a lay order was to follow his example for more than two centuries. Alfonso himself may have been less than happy with the title, for in the statutes themselves the head of the Order is usually referred to not as the Master but as the king.

Neither version of the statutes of the Order of the Band declares in so many words that the office of Master of the Order was to be attached permanently to that of King of Castile and Leon, but the statements contained in both versions about the role of the king within the Order leave no room for doubt that this was in fact the case, and this is confirmed by all the other evidence for the history of the Order. The office of Master is not in fact specifically defined or even discussed in the statutes, but its functions and prerogatives are either stated or clearly implied in the ordinances dealing with the numerous situations in which the king was to play some part in the Order's activities. As Master of the Order, the king was evidently to decide, with the advice of at least twelve other knights of the Order, on the worthiness of candidates for admission to the Order, and either to preside over the ceremony through which those deemed worthy were admitted to membership,[76] or to appoint a committee of six member knights to conduct the ceremony in his absence.[77] It would appear that he was to determine the times and places of the Order's meetings,[78] and was probably responsible for summoning the knights. At such meetings he was to examine the horses and equipment of each knight, and if time permitted to review their knightly skills in jousts and tourneys.[79] He was also to hear accusations of misconduct against the members,[80] and when necessary to impose (again with the advice of at least twelve members knights) appropriate penalties.[81] He was similarly to settle disputes arising between members knights and his sons,[82] and to hear and settle complaints against himself.[83] In times of war he was to lead in battle a company formed of those knights who were also his own vassals, or the vassals of one of his absent sons.[84] In times of peace he was to provide appropriate exercise for the knights by staging tournaments to which they were bound to come.[85]

[76] Ch. A.2a.
[77] Ch. A.2m.
[78] Ch. A.10a, B.13a.
[79] Implied in ch. A.10k, stated in ch. B.13c.
[80] Ch. A.19b.
[81] Ch. A.22f.
[82] Ch. A.17.
[83] Ch. B.11.
[84] Ch. A.9.
[85] Ch. A.20a.

The office of Master was thus thoroughly monarchical, though far from despotic. In fact, the king's rights and duties as Master of the Band appear strikingly similar to those attached to the masterships of the older knightly orders in Castile, which must have served as models. Like the Masters of Calatrava, Santiago, and Alcántara, the king as Master of the Band was in theory no less bound by the rules of the Order than the other members, and could hardly do anything without the advice of at least twelve of their number. In practice, however, it is unlikely that either Alfonso or any of the knights of the order he had created ever forgot that he was not only the Master but the king, and his role both in selecting the members and in regulating their behaviour was almost certainly much less fettered than the statutes would suggest. Indeed, like Károly of Hungary and several later founders, Alfonso probably placed such formal restrictions as he did on his powers as Master of the Order simply in order to convey to its members and potential members – most of whom would have been men bred to a tradition of aristocratic independence and knightly equality – the pleasant illusion that their part in the regulation of the Order was at least comparable in importance to his own; it is most improbable that he allowed any of these restrictions to stand in his way, or that many of the knights long remained in any doubt about the relative weight of his opinions and theirs on matters of importance to the Order.

6 The Members of the Order: The Knights and Squires

The ordinary members of the Order of the Band are generally referred to both in the chronicles and the statutes as *caballeros* or 'knights'. Despite this, formal knighthood does not seem to have been required for entry at any time during the period when the statutes were in force, for the preface implies that undubbed squires (*escuderos*) could also be admitted, and chapter 11 requires the members to attend the knighting ceremonies of their fellows. The chronicle of the founder's reign declares that the first habits of the Order were actually given to both knights and squires,[86] and we know furthermore that Alfonso himself was not yet a knight at the time he founded the Order and assumed the role of Master, and that his son and successor Pedro did not receive the accolade of knighthood until many years after his formal admission to the Order, which took place when he was no more than six years old.[87] Since Pedro was not made a knight at the time of his reception, it is unlikely that this honour was extended in the same circumstances to any of his bastard half-brothers, who were similarly admitted when they were infants in the modern as well as the contemporary sense. Moreover, no fewer than twelve of the twenty-two 'knights' of the Band listed in redaction A who are known to have been born by 1330 are listed in the chronicle among those who received the accolade from Alfonso immediately following his coronation in that year, and it is more than likely that some of them at least had been admitted to the Order while still squires at the time of its proclamation earlier in the same year.

Alfonso's own undubbed state might explain why he did not insist on formal

[86] *Crónica*, p. 178.
[87] See above, p. 55.

knighthood as a prerequisite for entry into his Order at the time he proclaimed it, but it does not really explain why he did not do so ten or fourteen years later, especially as he could so easily have conferred the status himself upon any candidate who did not already enjoy it. It may be that he wanted to be free to admit to the Order for political or personal reasons certain individuals – for example his infant sons – who were not yet old enough to fight effectively as knights, and did not wish to debase the value of the accolade itself by conferring it on infants or children. It is also possible that he wanted to be able to admit certain men-at-arms who, though excellent warriors, could not afford to maintain the estate of knighthood. Whatever his reasons, Alfonso was the only founder of a true monarchical order not to require formal knighthood for admission to the order he had created.

Although Alfonso did not make knighthood a condition for admission to the Order, he did require all candidates to be of noble birth (*fidalguía*), and declared that any 'knight' of the Order found not to have that vital quality was to be ejected.[88] This requirement reflects both the fiercely jealous pride taken by the members of the Castilian nobility in the standing of their hereditary estate, and the fact that in Castile the status of knight was still not restricted to members of the nobility, but commonly enjoyed by low-born *caballeros villanos*.[89] *Fidalguía* was thus more important in the eyes of potential members of Alfonso's Order than *caballería*, and had to be required if the Order was to appear truly exclusive. No doubt Alfonso himself felt that true knighthood was incompatible with ignoble birth, and was uninterested in promoting chivalric virtues among the commonality of his realms.

Alfonso finally required that all those admitted to his Order be vassals either of the King of Castile or of one of his sons.[90] Presumably he felt that the oaths of loyalty and service required of the knights as members of the Order would be more likely to be observed if they were supplemented by the traditional oaths required of vassals. He may also have hoped to entice certain *ricos omes* into vassalship – which as we have seen they frequently evaded – by offering them membership in the Order. The wording of ordinance A.2c is ambiguous on this point, but there is no reason to suppose that the status of vassal, like that of knight, could not be acquired by a member-elect immediately before his admission to the Order. Indeed, it would be difficult to believe that Alfonso intended to deny membership to anyone simply because he had not done homage to him (or one of his successors) on some earlier occasion, especially as vassalic clientship in Castile was not in general hereditary, so that each king had in any case to attract a new set of vassals. It is not impossible that most of the knights only became vassals of the king immediately before their formal induction into the Order, but we know too little about the vassals of the crown under Alfonso XI to be sure.[91]

Of course, the knights of the Order were not actually required to be vassals of the king himself, but could instead do homage to one of his sons.[92] This regulation

---

[88] Ch. A.3i.
[89] See Pescador, *Caballería popular*.
[90] Ch. A.2c.
[91] See Grassotti, *Instituciones*, I, p. 290.
[92] Ch. A.2c.

seems to imply that any sons born to Alfonso or any of his successors were themselves to be admitted to the Order by the time they were old enough to have their own vassals, and in fact Alfonso seems to have secured the admission of all but one of his sons – his second bastard, Fadrique, whom he made instead Master of the Order of Santiago[93] – within a short time of their birth. Whether Alfonso included this rule in the earliest form of the statutes in anticipation of having sons or added it only after the birth of his first son Enrique in 1333 or his only legitimate son Pedro in 1334 is uncertain, but as even Enrique was barely old enough to have vassals of his own when Alfonso died in 1350, it was certainly adopted in anticipation of a future situation. Unless the expression 'son of the king' was extended to mean 'son of a king', it is more than likely that the rule was never actually put into effect, for after Alfonso's death his bastard sons were merely the half-brothers of the new king, Pedro 'the Cruel', and Pedro himself – the last king under whom the statutes of the Order seem to have been observed – never had a legitimate son of his own.

It should be noted that, since the obligations of a vassal ceased with the death of his lord, and were not automatically transferred to the lord's successor, the knights of the Band would have had to do homage to each new King of Castile immediately after his accession if they wished to remain members of the Order. It would appear that at least one of the knights appointed to the Order by the founder – Pero Carillo – failed to do homage to his son Pedro 'the Cruel' when he succeeded as king and Master in 1350, for Pedro demanded the return of the Order's habit from him in 1353 specifically because Carillo was not his vassal.[94]

No other qualifications (such as lay status or military profession) were explicitly required for membership in the Order, but according to the preface only the 'best' knights and squires were to be admitted. What precisely Alfonso meant by 'best' is unclear, but it is likely that (as would be the case in many later orders) both birth and moral character were meant to be taken into consideration, and the rules set forth in chapters 3 and 4 suggest that military prowess was to be considered in some cases at least. Indeed, the emphasis placed in the statutes upon preparedness for and participation in jousts and tournaments implies that prowess was the most important quality that Alfonso was looking for in potential members.

Unlike the statutes of the Society of St George and most later monarchical orders, the statutes of the Band placed no limitation on the number of knights who could belong to the Order at the same time. This was in keeping with the customs of all contemporary religious orders of knighthood, and Alfonso may have failed to set a limit upon membership simply because it did not occur to him to do so. On the other hand, he may have avoided imposing a limit of the sort commonly attributed to the various fictional societies of knights either because he wanted to include as many knights as possible in his Order, or because he did not want to create artificial impediments to the admission of individuals who might have been temporarily excluded by such a limit. Many later founders would find the *numerus clausus* they had imposed something of a nuisance.

[93] See above, p. 51. The fact that Fadrique alone was not admitted to the Order strongly suggests that Alfonso regarded membership in his Order as incompatible with membership in a religious order of knighthood.
[94] See above, p. 57.

75

Just how the selection of new members was to be carried out is not explained in the statutes, but the chronicle account of the foundation declares quite plainly that membership was entirely in the gift of the king,[95] and the accounts in the later chronicles all bear this out. It is possible that the king held some sort of formal consultation with the other members of the Order who were with him at the time before naming anyone to the Order, in what the statutes portray as the usual way of doing business in the Order, but the presence of the founder's infant sons and childhood friends among the early members is strongly suggestive that an effectively arbitrary power of appointment was part of the prerogative of the king as Master. Such a power is also suggested by the omission from the generally meticulous statutes of any procedure for electing new members.

Chapters A.3 and 4 do set forth a rather curious method by which would-be members of the Order might, in effect, select themselves, or at least call attention to their desire to be considered for admission. All an aspiring knight had to do, according to these chapters, was to put on a habit similar to that of the Order and ride about looking for knights of the Order to challenge him. He had then to overcome two such challengers, and at least avoid being overcome himself by other members of the Order at the king's court. There is a distinctly romantic ring to the stipulations of these two extraordinary chapters, which have no parallel in the statutes of any other monarchical order. Both the obligation imposed upon the member knights to challenge the stranger to combat, and the business of sending the stranger after the initial combats to the court of the king, the head of their Order, could have been lifted, with only slight modifications, directly from one of the Arthurian romances, in which the knights of the Round Table were constantly challenging (or being challenged by) strange knights, and constantly sending them back to Arthur's court to be admitted (if deemed worthy) to their company. Indeed, the whole notion of demonstrating worthiness for membership in the company by overcoming other knights in single combat is thoroughly Arthurian. Since he devoted two chapters to it, Alfonso must be presumed to have taken this peculiar process of selection quite seriously, but it is unlikely that any knight was ever admitted to the Order as a result of its operation, especially as the rule of secrecy would have prevented most aspiring knights from knowing of its existence.

Once he had been selected, a candidate for membership had to pass through an entry rite of which the most important action was the swearing of the oaths of loyalty and service to the king, fraternity, and obedience to the statutes described in chapter A.2. He then received the insignia of the Order from the Master, and thereby became a member of the Order for life. Only if he abandoned the service of the king or one of his sons was he to be expelled permanently – and in fact one member, Pero Carillo, is known to have been expelled because he had effectively abandoned the king's service to fight for his enemies.[96]

Our knowledge of the membership of the Order during the period in which its statutes were still in effect is derived almost entirely from the lists of members included in the three surviving redactions. A total of sixty-three names are included in these lists. Given the probable dates of their composition, it is likely

---

[95] See above, p. 53.
[96] See above, p. 57.

that they contain the names of most of those admitted to the Order during the reign of its founder, especially during the years after 1340, but it is quite possible that the names of some knights admitted between 1330 and 1340 who died before the latter year have been omitted. The relative length and composition of the three lists gives the impression that the number of members grew rapidly from twenty-seven in about 1340 to nearly sixty in about 1344, and hovered around the latter figure until about 1352, but we cannot be sure that any of the lists is absolutely up to date. Unfortunately, we know relatively little about most of the knights listed, and almost nothing about one third of their number. On the basis of the chronicles of the period Daumet[97] was able to identify and supply some information about all but six of the twenty-seven knights listed in redaction A, and I have succeeded doing the same for one more of these and fourteen of the additional thirty included in redaction B, but in most cases the information that can be provided even about these knights is very sparse.

Those knights who can be identified can be placed into one or more of four distinct categories: members of the royal house, *ricos omes* or members of their families, great officers of the crown, and men who received the accolade of knighthood at the coronation of the founder in 1330. No fewer than ten of the knights of the Band fell into the first category: the founder, his one legitimate son, four of his seven bastard sons by Leonor de Guzmán, and four of his cousins, descended from younger (or elder) sons of his predecessors on the throne: Juan de la Cerda, called 'de Lara', Juan de la Cerda of Gibraleon, Enrique Enriquez, and his son Fernan Enriquez. In fact, only two of the surviving cadet branches of the royal house were not represented among the knights of the Order: those of Valencia and Manuel. Nevertheless, it is not clear that Alfonso sought to include members of his own house as such (outside of his immediate family) in any systematic way, for all four of the cousins admitted to the Order also held particularly important offices either under him or under his son, and they were probably numbered among his most trusted counsellors. Nor is it without significance that Enrique Enriquez was also married to the sister of Alfonso's mistress Leonor de Guzmán.

Eight of the ten members of the royal house included in the Order – all but the founder and his legitimate son Pedro – either were at the time of their admission or later became members of the second of our categories, that of *ricos omes*. Of the fifty-three non-royal knights, a further thirteen were either *ricos omes* or cadets of *ricos omes*, bringing the total number to twenty-one, or exactly one third of the known total. Seen from the other point of view, exactly half of the distinct non-royal lineages of *ricos omes de natura* still surviving in 1344 – ten out of twenty – were represented among the knights of the Order.[98] Clearly most of these men must have been selected for membership at least partly on the basis of their great wealth and power, especially as only two of them (Lope Diaz de Almansa de Froilas and Juan Rodriguez de Cisneros) held high office under the founder, and only a further two (Garci Laso de la Vega and Per Alvarez de Osorio) were given such

[97] Op. cit., pp. 30–32.
[98] Those not represented were the houses of Cameros, Meneses, Giron, Aza or Daza, Limia, Manzanedo, Villalobos, Mendoza, Manrique, and Saldana. See Moxó, *De la nobleza vieja a la nobleza nueva*.

offices by his son Pedro after his accession. Some of them must also have been close friends or political adherents of the founder.

For reasons which are not at all clear, Alfonso did not see fit to bestow high offices upon many of the knights of his Order, or to admit to the Order many men who already held such offices. Aside from the two royal cousins (Fernan Enriquez, *Adelantado Mayor de la Frontera*, and Juan de la Cerda, *Alguacil Mayor* of Seville) and the two *ricos omes* (Lope Diaz de Almansa, his chief bodyguard, and Juan Rodriguez de Cisneros, *Adelantado Mayor* of Leon), only two of the knights are known to have held any high office under the founder: Alfonso Ferrandez Coronel, his *Copero Mayor*, and Fernan Perez Portocarrero, successively *Merino Mayor* and *Adelantado Mayor* of Castile. It is not without significance, however, that the offices these men held included the most important provincial governorships and the posts most intimately associated with the person of the king. Four knights of the Order (including one of these six) were also put in charge of the households of four of the founder's sons, presumably by the founder himself: Juan Alfonso de Benevides, Alfonso Ferrandez Coronel, Garci Laso de la Vega, and the latter's son Gonzalo Ruiz de la Vega, *Mayordomos Mayores* to the Infante Don Pedro, Don Tello, Don Fadrique, and Don Fernando respectively.[99]

As king, the founder's son Pedro was rather more generous in distributing offices to the knights of the Order. He bestowed high offices upon no fewer than seventeen of the known members, only three of whom had held high offices under his father. Twelve of these officers were members neither of the royal house nor of any of the non-royal houses of *ricos omes*. The seventeen knights in question held among them fourteen distinct offices, and these included all of the most important offices in the kingdom. Several key offices – those of *Adelantado Mayor* of the provinces of Castile, Leon, and the Frontier, *Ballestero Mayor del Rey*, *Copero Mayor*, *Guarda Mayor del Cuerpo del Rey*, and *Mayordomo Mayor*, were held by two or three knights of the Order in succession. None of the men in question was appointed to office after about 1360, however, and the great majority were appointed before 1355. All of this suggests that Pedro placed particular confidence in the knights of the Order appointed by his father in the period before the beginning of the civil wars (during most of which real power was in the hands of his former tutor and chancellor, Juan Alfonso de Alburquerque), but preferred to exclude them in favour of his own adherents in the period after his victory at Toro in September 1356. We know, of course, that many of the knights of the Order appointed by his father ultimately joined the ranks of the rebels led by his half-brother Enrique of Trastámara, and that at least one was ejected from the Order and five were killed by Pedro because of this.

We have already observed that twelve of the 110 men who received the accolade of knighthood during the ceremonies immediately following Alfonso's coronation in 1330 either had already been or would later be admitted to the Order of the

---

[99] There does not appear to be a complete list of royal officers under the founder, but Daumet was able to determine which of the knights held the more important offices at least on the basis of the chronicle of his reign. For the reign of the founder's son Pedro I have relied on the useful list of offices and officeholders included in Luis Vicente Diaz Martin, *Los Oficiales de Pedro I de Castilla*. Some of Pedro's officers had also held office under his father, and Diaz often indicates which offices they held.

Band.[100] None of the twelve was a *rico ome*, and only one belonged to a family headed by a member of that élite stratum, but two of them received high offices from Alfonso himself, and three others from his son. Alfonso Ferrandez Coronel, who held office under both Alfonso and Pedro, was certainly a childhood friend of the former, and another, Garci Laso de la Vega, who held two offices under Pedro, was the son of the founder's childhood favourite who was killed just before the foundation of the Order. It is likely that some or all of the others were similarly childhood companions of the founder who retained his friendship in later life. Unfortunately, we do not know when any of them was born, or precisely when most of them were admitted to the Order, so it is impossible to determine whether the Order was in its early years made up largely of Alfonso's contemporaries. Nevertheless, the emphasis in the statutes on knightly prowess makes this more than likely.

About most of the remaining twenty-one knights of the Band – all but four of whom were admitted after 1340 – nothing is known except that they were (presumably) both *fijosdalgo* and vassals of either the king or one of his sons. It is not without significance, however, that eight of the twenty-one bore the same surname as at least one other knight of the Order, and may reasonably be presumed to have belonged to the same lineage. In fact, fully thirty-two of the knights of the Band whose names are recorded – just over half of the total – seem to have belonged to families that supplied the Order with more than one knight in our period. These knights belonged to only ten distinct lineages (including the royal house), and seven of these included no *ricos omes*. Similarly, fifteen of the knights of the Order, including two of the thirteen not otherwise identified (Garci Gutierrez de Grijalba and Diego Ferrandez de Castrillo), had the same surname as at least one other nobleman who received the accolade of knighthood from the founder at his coronation.[101] It does not seem unreasonable to conclude from this that most of the forty knights admitted to the Order who were not either royal princes or *ricos omes* were members of the highest stratum of *fijosdalgo* below the latter, in which several members of a single house could still afford to assume the burdens of knighthood. If not officers themselves (either of high or middle rank) most of these men were probably connected by blood or marriage to such officers, or even to *ricos omes*. Alvar Garcia de Albornoz (successively *Copero Mayor* to Queen Blanca and King Pedro) and Fernan Gomez de Albornoz (knighted by the founder in 1330) were both brothers of the Archbishop of Toledo, and Garci Jufre de Tenorio (who fits in none of our categories but whose presumed relatives Juan and Alfonso Tenorio were also knights of the Order) was the son of the Admiral of Castile, Alfonso Jufre. Even the eleven knights about whom nothing whatever is known may well have belonged to this class, and like the other lesser knights of the Order may even have held minor offices from the Crown.

Precisely why most of these sixty-three men were selected for inclusion in the Order in preference to other members of the higher strata of the Castilian nobility is unclear. In all likelihood a variety of factors, including military prowess and political connections, played a part, but we can only guess which factors were the most important, since in most cases we know nothing whatever about the

---

[100] See above, p. 73.
[101] *Crónica del Rey Don Alfonso*, pp. 189–191.

circumstances in which they were chosen. Membership seems to have been given in some cases at least as a reward for outstanding services to the Crown, for Alfonso is reported to have named Pero Carillo to the Order in recognition of the role he played in the siege of Tarifa,[102] and the chronicle of his reign declares that 'knights and squires who had done some good deed of arms against the enemies of the king, or attempted to perform such deeds, were given the Band by the king.'[103] No doubt other members were chosen for equally individual but completely different reasons.

7 The Privileges and Obligations of Membership

Immediately after his admission, the new member-knight seems to have acquired all the privileges and obligations entailed in membership in the Order; there seems to have been no status comparable to that of novice in the religious orders. If one sets aside the advantages of close association with the king and his court and the rights which arose from the mutual obligations of the members, the knights of the Band seem to have enjoyed only one distinct privilege, and that only in the first decade or so of the Order's history. According to chapter A.16, all the lands held by the knights of the Band (presumably either as *prestimonios* or *feudos*) from either the king or one of his sons were to be exempt from all taxation, even if a tax should be levied (presumably in error) on that land. This sounds like an important privilege, but its significance is in fact unclear, since all lands held by *fijosdalgo* were normally exempt from taxation,[104] and membership in the Order was restricted to *fijosdalgo*. It may be that Alfonso meant to exempt them from extraordinary taxes that would otherwise have fallen on the lands in question. Whatever his intentions, however, he seems (for reasons which are equally obscure) to have rescinded the privilege at some time before 1345, for there is no mention of it in redaction B. The latter redaction contains no compensatory privilege, and it must appear that after about 1345 the knights of the Band enjoyed no peculiar rights save those of wearing the habit of the Order and taking part in its activities.

Even during the brief period when it was in effect the one substantive privilege of the knights of the Band must have been more than offset by the obligations imposed upon them, which were many and varied. These obligations may usefully be organized under three general headings: obligations owed to the Master; obligations owed to their fellow members; and general obligations.

To the king as Master of the Order all of the knights were required to take an oath that they would never leave his service.[105] This implies that they were all expected to serve him in some way, but neither the nature nor the extent of the services required of them is specified in the statutes. Those knights who were also

---

[102] See above, p. 57.
[103] See above, p. 53.
[104] See above, p. 48. It is possible that this rule applied only to lands held allodially.
[105] Ch. A.2b.

the king's vassals were required to fight when summoned under his command,[106] but as vassals they were required to do so in any case, and it is not clear that their military obligations were in any way increased when they accepted membership in the Order. Those knights who were the vassals of the king's sons were required to serve under the king's command whenever – but only when – their own lords were not present in the army.[107] Since these knights would normally have failed to appear at all without a summons from their lord, this was in theory a fairly significant obligation, but as neither the founder nor any of his immediate successors lived to see even one son into adulthood, it is unlikely that it was ever effective. It may be that Alfonso also intended to impose on the knights of his Order very general cliental obligations of the sort commonly imposed by English contracts of retinue on life retainers,[108] and expected them to be at his beck and call for a wide variety of services, social and political as well as military, but if so it is curious that he did not spell out his intentions a little more clearly. The wording of the statutes seems to imply that he would have been quite satisfied to receive the loyal and effective performance of the services the knights already owed him as vassals. It also appears that he expected the knights of the Order to serve him in return for the fiefs they received when they became his vassals, for the statutes make no reference to any other form of payment, and one ordinance specifically requires those knights who had failed to bring appropriate horses and equipment to the Order's annual assembly to pay for new horses and equipment with the income of the land which they had received from the king or one of his sons when they became vassals.[109] It is possible, however, that in practice Alfonso, in order to compensate them for the additional obligations they undertook as members of the Order, gave all newly-admitted members either additional fiefs or some form of cash pension not formally connected to membership in the Order.

The obligations undertaken by the knights to their fellow members were more numerous and rather more significant. They were first of all bound to love their fellows and to refrain from doing them any harm, except in defence of their nearest kinsmen. They were further bound to attempt to settle disputes among their fellow members without taking either side. Finally they were bound (if they were near enough at the time) to attend the knightings, weddings,[110] and obsequies of their fellows, and to mourn a death in the Order by wearing a dark coat for ten days.[111] These obligations were characteristic of confraternities in general, and were almost certainly borrowed from some knightly confraternity with which the founder was familiar. Like the very similar obligations imposed by other founders of monarchical orders, they were probably included in the statutes partly to foster fraternal feelings among the knights, who would thus function more effectively as a company, and partly to reduce feuding among the members of the upper nobility,

---

[106] Ch. A.9a.
[107] Ch. A.9b,c.
[108] See below, p. 98.
[109] Ch. A.10l. The Spanish text reads: . . . *que lo mande el Rey conprar de la tierra que tovere del o de alguno de sus fijos cuyo vasallo fuere* . . .
[110] Ch. 11.
[111] Ch. 12.

which could be wasteful of both lives and property and could interfere with the prosecution of all sorts of royal plans.

The great majority of the obligations imposed by the founder on the knights of the Order were not owed to anyone. The knights were obliged to take part in the Order's corporate activities, to maintain the exclusiveness of the Order by keeping secret its ordinances and by challenging any knight who usurped its habit, and finally to behave in accordance with the rules of conduct set forth in the fifty-seven ordinances of sections III, VII, and IX of redaction A. These rules, which comprise more than a third of the statutes, were clearly designed to set what contemporaries would have regarded as high standards of personal behaviour in both civil and military activities. In civil life the knights were required to be pious (by attending mass daily), honest (by refraining from lying), and courteous (by walking sedately, speaking carefully, eating and drinking properly, speaking no ill of ladies, and protecting ladies from the abuse of their fellows in the king's court). In effect they were called upon to behave as a proper knight of gentle birth behaved in the best romances of the day, rather than like the boors and ruffians who seem to have been more typical of contemporary noble society. In military affairs they were similarly called upon to behave as befitted chosen knights: to provide themselves with the best possible horse and equipment, clearly marked with the Order's device; to keep their arms near them at all times; to present a courageous front when discouraged or wounded; to avoid boasting of their deeds; and to refrain from gambling while in the king's service. Apparently in order that they might keep exercised in the skills of war, they were also obliged to participate in all major tournaments held within ten leagues of wherever they found themselves, as well as in those held especially for this purpose by the king. While taking part in these tournaments they were obliged, finally, to obey an elaborate set of rules whose general effect was to reduce injury and maintain order and fairness.

The set of rules just summarized – which constitute a sort of practical handbook of chivalry – were the most original element of the statutes of the Order of the Band. Although the rules differ in detail from those proposed in such earlier Spanish works on chivalry as the *Siete Partidas* and the *Libre de Cavallería*, they should probably be viewed as a product of the tradition those works helped to establish of spelling out exactly how a proper knight ought to behave. There is no reason to suppose that Alfonso was any less devoted to the 'ancient' ideals of chivalry than Ramon Llull, but his needs and goals were rather different from those of the latter writer, and it cannot be surprising that he chose to emphasize in the statutes of the Order he created those elements of the chivalric 'code' which were of most practical use to himself and his successors as king; widows, orphans, and the church are wholly neglected as objects of knightly solicitude, the crusade against the heathen (whether ultramarine or peninsular) is ignored, and ladies are mentioned only in the context of ordinances concerned with courtly behaviour whose principal effect would have been to enhance the prestige of the king and his court. The chivalric virtues the Order was chiefly intended to promote were loyalty to the king (as both seigniorial lord and Master of the Order) and military prowess and discipline. While none of the chivalric obligations Alfonso imposed can be regarded as onerous, it is not unlikely that many knights would have found many of them both irksome and difficult, if not impossible, to keep.

Alfonso was clearly aware of the difficulties the knights of his Order were likely to have in keeping their oath to obey the statutes, for he provided a variety of penalties for failure to obey specific rules. No fewer than eighteen of the ordinances of redaction A are concerned with such penalties, which range from minor fines to banishment from the kingdom and death. We may obtain some idea of the relative importance of the ordinances in Alfonso's mind from the list of infractions for which he chose to prescribe a specific penalty and from the severity of the penalty prescribed. Failure to attend one of the Order's regular meetings without a good excuse was to be punished only with a fine,[112] but failure to attend an ordinary tournament was to be punished with the disgrace of not wearing the Order's habit for a month and the dangerous exercise of making three jousting runs without a lance,[113] and failure to attend a tournament specially called by the king was to be punished with the even greater disgrace of wearing only half the band for three months and the even more dangerous exercise of making one jousting run stripped of armour.[114] Those who threatened another member with a sword or dagger were to be banished from the court for two months and forbidden to wear more than half the band,[115] while those who actually struck a fellow member were to be deprived of the revenues they received from the king for a whole year, required to wear the half-band of disgrace at all times during that period, and cut off from the conversation of the other knights.[116] In redaction A even more serious penalties were prescribed for aiding anyone other than a father or brother against any other knight of the Order: deprivation of the Order's habit for three years if the other knight was not injured, deprivation and banishment from the kingdom for ten years if the other knight did suffer some injury, and death if the other knight was killed.[117] Departure from the king's service or that of one of his sons, and actions against the king, were to be punished by permanent expulsion from the Order.[118] By the time redaction B had been composed, Alfonso seems to have thought better of the last set of penalties, and replaced the ordinances in question with one declaring that he would assign appropriate penalties (presumably for all infractions for which a specific punishment was not prescribed) in consultation with the other knights of the Order.[119]

8 The Order's Corporate Activities

The knights of the Band were required to take part as a corporate body in three distinct forms of activity: general meetings, tournaments, and military campaigns. Both early redactions mention general meetings of the Order to which all the knights of the Order were bound to come, but the meetings called for by chapter

---

[112] Ch. A.10m,n.
[113] Ch. A.21c,d.
[114] Ch. A.20c,d.
[115] Ch. A.14a–c.
[116] Ch. A.15a–d.
[117] Ch. A.22j–m.
[118] Ch. A.22g–i.
[119] B.21e.

A.10 were to be held annually on the feast of Pentecost, while chapter B.15 required the knights to assemble every two months if possible, but at least on the feasts of Easter, St John (24 June), and Christmas. It appears that the latter, more frequent schedule (requiring between three and six meetings a year) replaced an original annual meeting, which may have been found to be less than adequate for the founder's purposes. All four of the specified dates were major feasts commonly celebrated in royal courts with tournaments and other festivities. At the annual meeting, at least, a solemn mass was to be sung in honour of St James (the patron saint of Castile), the statutes were to be read aloud, the conduct of the knights during the previous year was to be examined and either rewarded or punished, and the assembled knights were to give an offering sufficient for the ransoming of seven captives. They were finally to take part in jousts and tournaments organized by the king. Chapter B.15 describing the more frequent assemblies which seem to have replaced the annual meeting mentions only the last activity, but it is likely that some or all of the others – which unlike the tournaments were characteristic features of the meetings of both religious orders and confraternities – were also carried out at least once a year. The public examination of conduct was of vital importance for maintaining the Order's rule of life, and the solemn mass provided a unique opportunity for corporate devotion which could serve at once to strengthen the bonds of corporate feeling among the knights and to invoke the protection of heaven for the Order – a matter not taken lightly in that intensely religious age. We have no record whatever of any meeting of the Order, so it is impossible to know how often (or for how many years) the Order did in fact meet or what was actually done during such meetings as did take place.

As we have already noted, the knights of the Band were required to take part not only in those tournaments held by the king during the course of their more or less regular meetings, but in all other tournaments to which the king chose to summon them, and all those proclaimed, for whatever purpose, within a day's ride of wherever they happened to be. No other founder was to impose a comparable set of obligations, and the emphasis placed by Alfonso upon participation in tournaments was to remain unique throughout our period. The chronicle of his reign suggests that Alfonso not only regarded the tournament as a useful form of training for war – an activity which occupied a good deal of his time and energy – but, like his contemporaries Philippe VI of France and Edward III of England, enjoyed the tournament as a form of sport in which he personally excelled.[120] We know from the same chronicle that on at least one occasion the knights of the Order, having been summoned in the fashion specified by the statutes, fought in a tournament as a team, and that Alfonso himself took part as a member of that team,[121] and although direct evidence is lacking, there is no reason to doubt that these were fairly frequent occurrences during his reign.

The knights of the Order who were also the vassals of the king or the vassals of his absent sons – and in practice these must always have been the great majority – were also required to fight as a single company or *quadrilla* under the direct command of the king whenever they were summoned to serve in a military campaign. It would appear that the Order was meant to function as a sort of *corps*

---

[120] See above, p. 55.
[121] Ibid.

d'élite in the royal army, roughly comparable to the regiments of noble guards maintained by European monarchs from the later seventeenth century. The knights' experience of fighting as a team in numerous tournaments would have been invaluable preparation for fighting as a company in battle, and as few other companies of knights would have had an equivalent form of training, the *Quadrilla* of the Band would have been one of the most effective in the royal army on that basis alone. Since its members were also (at least in theory) carefully selected for their prowess, were required to supply themselves with the best possible equipment, were kept in fighting trim by their almost constant participation in jousts and tournaments, and were bound to one another by numerous fraternal obligations, the Company of the Band ought to have been by far the best lay unit in the royal army, and comparable to if not better than the units supplied by the religious orders of knighthood. The particular devotion of its members to the king and his family also qualified them to act as a royal bodyguard in battle, and this too may have been part of Alfonso's intention for the Order as a military company.

The statutes say nothing about how the *Quadrilla* of the Band was to be organised, or what precise relationship it was meant to have with the other elements of the royal *mesnada*. In all likelihood it had its own *pendón* or banner and was led by an *alférez* named by the king from the ranks of its members to serve either for a single campaign or during his pleasure. It is unclear whether the various *ricos omes* admitted to the Order were meant to serve as simple members of the Order's *Quadrilla*, as the statutes seem to imply, or were expected to appear at the *hueste* at the head of their own *quadrillas* of household and vassal knights, as they would normally have done and as their vassalic obligations required them to do. Quite possibly they served in the *Quadrilla* when the king required only a small force, and commanded their own troops when he required a larger one. The king's sons, who were members of the Order, were certainly expected to lead their own vassals under their own *pendones* when they were present in the *hueste*.

Even when serving as members of the Order's company, the *ricos omes* would almost certainly have been accompanied by several squires or mounted auxiliaries of less than noble rank, and most of the ordinary knights of the Order would have had two or three such assistants as well.[122] Some and perhaps all of these would have fought in association with (if not as part of) the *Quadrilla*, and the effective size of the latter might thus on occasion have been risen to as high as one hundred and fifty or even two hundred men. Such a force would have been comparable to those fielded by the religious orders, which also included various auxiliaries in addition to professed knights.

There is no unequivocal evidence that the knights of the Band ever served as a military company, but there is no reason to think that Alfonso did not follow through with his stated plans, and the numerous campaigns undertaken by Alfonso between the foundation of the Order in 1330 and his death in 1350 would have given the knights plenty of opportunities to display in battle the prowess and discipline they ought to have acquired on the tournament fields. We do know that a *pendón* or banner called 'the banner of the Band' existed in and after 1367 and was borne at the head of one of the principal divisions of the royal army,[123] and

---

[122] See Contamine, *La Guerre au Moyen Age*, pp. 243–44.
[123] See above, p. 58.

although by 1367 this banner does not seem to have been associated exclusively with the Order of the Band, it is not impossible that it was originally thought of as the banner of the Company of the Band, whose precise significance was gradually forgotten as the Order gradually lost its character as a corporate body and was transformed into a pseudo-order.[124]

9 The Device and Habit of the Order

The device from which the Order took its formal name is designated in all the surviving documents by the single term *banda* or *vanda*. The primary sense of this term in both Middle and Modern Castilian is 'ribbon' or 'strip of cloth', but it is also used to mean 'riband' or 'sash', and as the chronicle of the founder's reign says that the device of the Order was worn on clothing from the shoulder to the hip, most earlier historians (including Villanueva[125] and Daumet[126]) have interpreted *banda* to mean 'sash'. In fact there is no clear evidence that the device of the Order ever took the form of a sash in the usual sense of that word: a detached strip of cloth worn loosely, like a baldric, over whatever clothing the wearer happened to have on. All three of the passages which describe the device of the Order either imply or state unequivocally that the *banda* proper took the form of a stripe or band of contrasting colour applied in some way to some form of coat, and that the coat was as much a part of the habit of the Order as the *banda* itself.

The first passage, in the chronicle of the founder's reign, declares that Alfonso ordered the knights and squires whom he had appointed to the new Order

> . . . to wear clothes with a band (*paños con banda*) which he had given them. And he himself wore clothes of the same sort with a band (*paños de eso mesmo con banda*): and the first clothes that were made for this were white, and the band blackish (*prieto*). And from that time on he gave those knights each year similar sets of clothes with a band for them to wear. And the band was as wide as a hand, and was placed on the *pellotes* (fur-lined coats) and other vestments (*vestiduras*) from the left shoulder to the skirt (*falda*).[127]

Although the wording of this passage is less than pellucid, it certainly implies that the bands distributed by Alfonso were attached to the tunic or coat of each of the several suits of clothing that he gave the knights of the Order every year as a form of livery. The second passage to describe the band, in the chronicle of the reign of the founder's son, similarly implies that the band was inseparable from a coat: Pero Carillo is there said to have worn (presumably over his armour) 'red ensigns with a band of gold' (*sobreseñales bermejas con la Vanda de oro*), and these 'ensigns' – said to have been taken by the founder from his own person in 1340 –

[124] For a different interpretation of the origin of this banner, see below, p. 91.
[125] 'Memoria', pp. 451ff.
[126] 'L'Ordre castillan' , pp. 5–6.
[127] *Crónica*, p. 178.

are later described as 'a coloured cloth (*tapete colorado*) with a band of gold'.[128] The third passage, in the diary of the German knight Jörg von Ehingen,[129] describes the device of the Order in similar terms but even more precisely. 'The Band of Castile' (*la banda de Kastilla*) given to Jörg by Enrique IV in 1457 is therein said to have been 'a red coat of scarlet cloth (*ain roter scharlatrock*) and a gold stipe (*strich*) or band (*band*), two thumbs wide, over the left shoulder, running in front down to the bottom of the coat on the right side, and then at the back of the coat running up again to the left shoulder.'

It is clear from these passages that the device called *la banda* was throughout its history a form of costume or habit rather than a badge, and that it consisted of some sort of coat upon which a strip of cloth or paint in a contrasting colour was applied in almost the same way the heraldic device known in Castilian as a *banda* and in English as a 'bend' would have been applied to a knightly surcoat, but in the opposite direction on the front part of the coat: from the left shoulder to the right lower hem. In the earliest decades of the Order's history the band seems to have been about four inches wide – the normal width of the heraldic bend when worn on a coat – and on the front of the coat would have been described in the language of blason as a 'bend sinister'; by the middle of the fifteenth century (and probably by 1370) its width seems to have diminished to about two inches – half the width of a normal bend – and it would have been called a 'bendlet sinister'. The band of the Order seems to have differed from both of the equivalent heraldic devices, however, in continuing around the body in the fashion of a sash, so that on the back of the coat it would have appeared as a normal bend or bendlet rather than the sinister form; if the device had been a coat of arms the band on the back of the coat would have begun on the right shoulder and run to the left lower hem. It is because of this that I have preferred to refer to it in English by the cognate but non-technical word 'band'.

The chronicle implies that during the founder's reign, at least, the band was applied to several different coats given by the king each year to the knights of the Order; presumably these included a civil surcoat and a military coat of arms. The precise form of these garments during the earliest years of the Order's history is not known, but it is likely that they all bore a close resemblance to the equivalent forms of attire worn at court or on the field of battle by knights who were not members of the Order. It is also likely that their length and cut changed from year to year to keep pace with fashion, since it would not have done for the knights of an élite court society to appear unfashionable. I have found only one representation of knights in what appears to be the habit of the Order, and this tends to confirm both of these judgements.[130] On a retable painted shortly after his triumph over his

---

[128] *Crónica del Rey Don Pedro*, p. 90. See above, p. 57.

[129] See above, p. 63.

[130] Villanueva, 'Memoria', pp. 452–58, presents four seals (dated 1382, 1385, 1392, and 1408) and a portrait (painted for Jörg von Ehingen in 1457) representing Juan I, Enrique III, Juan II, and Enrique IV wearing in each case what appears to be a sash (but in the first two cases could be an appied band) from the right shoulder to the left hip. He believed that this sash was the device of the Order, but it does not conform either in nature or direction to the three descriptions of the device which we have just examined. The sash worn by Enrique IV in the portrait could be the 'stole' of the Aragonese order of the Stole and Jar, founded in

brother in 1369, Enrique of Trastámara and his son are shown crowned and kneeling behind their crested helms, each wearing over his armour a close-fitting, hip-length, sleeveless military surcoat of the type the French called a *jupon*, charged with a stripe or band that in life would have been about two inches wide, running from the left shoulder to the right hem. The surcoat appears to be red and the band gold.[131] This habit is very similar to that described in the diary of Jörg von Ehingen, written nearly ninety years later, but it is cut in a fashion typical of the last decades of the fourteenth century.

The chronicle of the founder's reign states that the habit of the Order was at first white with a dark or blackish band, but the habits given to Pero Carillo in 1340 and Jörg von Ehingen in 1457 and those worn by Enrique of Trastámara and his son in the retable of circa 1370 were red with a gold band. While it is possible that the colours varied from one year to the next through some or all of the Order's history (as would be the case of the habits distributed by the kings of England to the knights of the Garter),[132] it is perhaps more likely that Alfonso decided at some time before 1340 that a fixed arrangement of colours would make the knights more easily recognizable as members of the Order, and chose red and gold as the noblest colours possible.

Every knight of the Band was required by ordinance A.5n [B.5a] to have with him at all times 'some clothes on which there is a band' (*unos paños en que haya vanda*), and to wear these at least once a week, and more often if possible. It would appear that Alfonso was here referring to civilian attire, for by ordinance A.5d [B.3c] he required them further to have at all times 'body and horse ensigns on which there is a band' (*sobreseñales de cuerpo e de cavallo en que aya vanda*), and by these expressions he presumably meant a military surcoat and horse-trapper. Alfonso obviously wanted the knights of the Order to appear in the Order's device as much as possible, but – perhaps because he recognized the need of courtiers to appear in a variety of rich costumes – did not feel that he could require them to wear it all the time. This was the main disadvantage of a device inseparable from a coat; later founders would avoid the problem by assigning to their order a relatively small and detachable badge, which could easily be worn every day with whatever clothes the member chose to wear.

Several of the Order's statutes prescribe as a punishment for misconduct on the part of the knights that they wear for a certain period of time only half the band (*la meytad de la Vanda*).[133] Ordinances 14d and 15d specify that the disgraced knight was not to wear 'any vestment save that of the half-band' (*otra vestidura si non*

1403. This stole, a wide sash of white fabric generally worn over the left but sometimes over the right shoulder, is often confused with the band of the Castilian Order, which may well have inspired it. On this order, see below, pp. 330–7.

[131] This painting, called the retable of the Mother of God of Tobed, is now in the Collection Birk in Barcelona. A detail of the painting showing Enrique and his son was published in monochrome in Martí de Riquer, *L'Arnès del cavaller; Armes i armadures catalanes medievals* (Barcelona, 1968), fig. 116.

[132] See below, p. 162.

[133] Chs. A.14b,d, 15b,d, 20c.

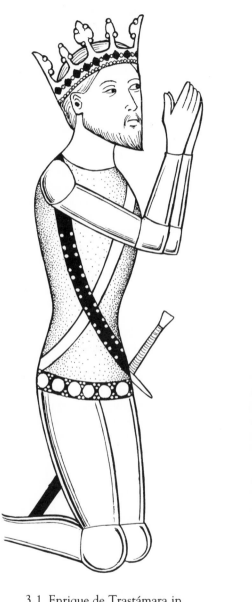

3.1 Enrique de Trastámara in
the surcoat of the Band

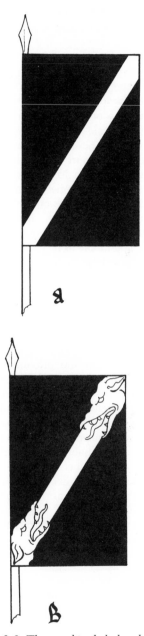

3.2 The *pendón de la banda*
(reconstruction)
a. Simple band   b. *Banda engolada*

aquella de la media vanda) during the period indicated. How the band was to be divided is not specified in the statutes, but in all likelihood it was to be represented as only half as wide as the normal band. The idea of punishing misconduct in this way may have been inspired by a rule common to several of the religious orders of knighthood, that knights in temporary disgrace were forbidden to wear their order's habit for a specified period.[134] In fact both of the early redactions of the Band statutes prescribed precisely that punishment for certain offences rather than the wearing of the half-band.[135]

If Alfonso intended the band of his Order to have some sort of symbolic significance, that significance is now obscure. The band of the Order may have been related in some way to a similar (and equally obscure) device – an heraldic bend swallowed at either end by the head of a dragon – which played an important part in the repertory of royal badges in Castile in the fifteenth century at least. Some older authors maintained that this device, called the *banda engolada*, was borne, in the same colour arrangement as the device of the Order (i.e., gold on red), on the *guiones* or standards of the kings of Castile as early as the reign of Fernando III (d. 1252).[136] If the *banda engolada* was indeed used in this way before the foundation of the Order, it may well have inspired the Order's device, but if (as seems possible) it was not adopted until a later date, the process of inspiration must have been reversed. The earliest direct evidence I have found for the employment of the *banda engolada* as a royal device dates from the reign of the founder's grandson Juan I (r. 1379–90), who placed the device on certain of his coins.[137] There is indirect evidence for its use by about 1375, however, for in the arms presumably assigned by that year to Don Juan, the illegitimate son of the late king Pedro by Juana de Castro, a green *banda engolada* edged in gold was placed along the diagonal partition line separating the lion of Leon from the Castle of Castile.[138] Many other Castilian houses adopted a similar band as part of their arms, including the Laso de la Vega[139] the Grijalba,[140] and the Alvarez de Bohorques,[141] but I have not been able to determine whether they did so before or after the foundation of the Order.[142] It is also possible that the *pendón de la banda* borne before the forces of

[134] See Henri de Curzon, ed., *La Règle du Temple* (Paris, 1886), p. xxxi.

[135] Chs. A.21c, 22j,l, B.21f.

[136] Ignacio Vicente Cascante, *Heraldica general y fuentes de las armas de España* (Barcelona, Madrid, 1956), p. 312, cites Diego Hurtado de Mendoza, *Guerra de Granada hecha por el rey don Felipe II* (Valencia, 1830).

[137] Villanueva, 'Memoria', p. 460. His grandson, Juan II (r. 1406–54), also displayed the device on his coins. See Vicente, *Heraldica general*, figs. 212 and 342.

[138] See Jiri Louda and Michael Maclagan, *Lines of Succession; Heraldry of the Royal Families of Europe* (London, 1981), table 48.

[139] Vicente, *Heraldica general*, fig. 211.

[140] The Marqués del Saltillo, *Catalogo de la exposición de la heraldica en el arte* (Madrid, 1947), No. 66.

[141] Ibid., no. 13.

[142] According to Argote, *Nobleza de Andalucia*, lib. II, cap. 83, 85, 92, 99, Alfonso XI gave the device of the *banda engolada* as an armorial augmentation to the heads of sixteen noble families who had served him with particular distinction in the Battle of Salado in October 1340, but I have been unable to find any contemporary evidence to support this assertion.

Enrique de Trastámara at the Battle of Nájera in 1367 bore a *banda engolada* rather than the simple bend sinister of the Order of the Band, though the earliest royal flag I have found charged with the *banda engolada* dates from the reign of Isabel 'the Catholic' more than a century later.[143] The band of the latter is a bend sinister like that of the Order, but the others just cited are all portrayed issuing from the dexter chief. The relationship of the device of the Order to the royal badge of the *banda engolada* must remain unclear until it can be established with reasonable certainty which came first.

If the band was not intended to allude to the traditional device of the *banda engolada*, it was probably chosen as the device of the Order primarily because it was both clearly visible at a distance and quite distinctive, especially with civil attire. The band proper (as distinct from the coat to which it was attached) was also both cheap and easy to manufacture, and could easily be divided in half to produce a clearly visible, and logical, sign of disgrace. Alfonso probably chose to have the band arranged over the left rather than the right shoulder so that it would not be confused either with an armorial bend or with the guige or belt of the shield, which at the time the Order was founded was normally slung like a baldric around the right shoulder.

In conclusion it can be said that the device and habit assigned by Alfonso to his Order were as original as the Order itself, and owed little or nothing to the devices or costumes of older bodies, knightly or otherwise. Although he clearly drew some inspiration for his Order from the religious orders of knighthood, unlike Károly of Hungary and most later founders he did not see fit to adopt any element of their traditional habit. In fact, the costume he assigned to the knights of the Band seems to have been thoroughly secular in nature, and may be likened more easily to a modern military uniform than a monastic habit. This was in keeping with the nature of the Order as he seems to have conceived it.

10 Conclusions: The Order of the Band

The Order of the Band founded by Alfonso of Castile was a very different sort of order from the Society of St George founded only five years earlier by Károly of Hungary. Unlike the latter, the Order of the Band was (by the standards of the day) a thoroughly secular organization whose members -- most of whom were drawn from the middle ranks of the Castilian nobility, and very few of whom held high political office under the founder -- enjoyed no significant privileges beyond those enjoyed by all *fijosdalgo*, and seem to have had no political responsibilities as members of the Order. Although it was not limited either in theory or practice to men who had been formally admitted to knighthood, the Order's rules were largely concerned with promoting chivalrous activities and behaviour, and the most common form of corporate activity they required of its members was knightly service as part of a tournament team or military company composed exclusively of members.

In fact the Order of the Band as created and maintained with only minor modifications by Alfonso XI was probably conceived of as a secular version of the

143 Ibid., fig. 341.

religious orders of knighthood with which he, as King of Castile, was inevitably quite familiar. Like them it was intended to be an élite body of knights chosen for their prowess, and was endowed with a rule calculated to promote discipline and cooperation among the members (especially on the battlefield), loyalty and obedience to the Master, and high standards of conduct in civil life. Since his Order was to be devoted largely to secular purposes, however, and to be made up entirely of lay knights, Alfonso substituted a confraternal for a religious form of rule, and even omitted from the confraternal format such common religious features as the cult of a patron saint, prayers for living members, and masses for those who had died. Where the religious orders of knighthood sought to promote among their members (when they were not engaged in military activities) the virtues and habits valued by Benedictine or Augustinian monasticism, Alfonso sought to promote among the knights and squires of his Order the virtues and habits most prized by the members of contemporary lay society – especially that exalted segment of lay society that frequented the royal court – all of which had come to be associated with the notion of chivalry or knightliness. Where the religious orders tried to promote discipline, cooperation, and *esprit de corps* on the battlefield through daily participation in a common religious life, Alfonso sought to achieve the same end by requiring the members of his Order to take part in relatively frequent general meetings (three to six a year) and to fight as a team in even more frequent tournaments. Where the religious orders required loyalty and absolute obedience from their knights to their elected masters, Alfonso demanded the same sort of loyalty (if not perhaps the same degree of obedience) from the members of his Order to himself and his heirs as king of Castile and Leon, hereditary Masters of the Order.

In the prologue to the statutes Alfonso actually declared that his principal objects in founding the Order were to promote loyalty and chivalry, and there is no reason to doubt that these were foremost among his conscious goals. By 'loyalty' he clearly meant loyalty to himself as king and Master, despite the lip-service payed in the prologue to the romantic notion of loyalty between lover and lady. Alfonso obviously felt a need for a body of knights upon whose loyalty he could depend in his continuing struggles with the *ricos omes* – a body comparable in size and organization to one of the religious orders of knighthood, whose performance on the battlefield he must have admired, but under his direct control and dedicated solely to his service. Of course loyalty alone would not have been very useful; to serve his purposes the knights of his new model Order had also to be seasoned warriors, and had furthermore to be able to fight effectively as a disciplined unit, like the knights of the religious orders. This was the pragmatic reason behind Alfonso's professed and clearly genuine interest in promoting *caballería*, by which he meant knightly skills in the lists and on the battlefield even more than knightly behaviour in his court. Like most of his contemporaries on the thrones of Europe, Alfonso must have regarded the knight as the most effective type of warrior available to him, and sincerely believed (as the chronicle of his reign reports) that what was wrong with most contemporary noblemen was that they had become careless in their practice of traditional knightly skills. The rules of the Order of the Band were designed to correct that fault among those knights admitted to its ranks, and to make the Order the most efficient military company in the kingdom. With such a body of knights behind him, Alfonso could have confronted almost any local rebellion with confidence that, if he could bring the rebels to open battle, he could easily defeat them.

It is possible that Alfonso also hoped that, by requiring a very high standard of knightly conduct from the members of his Order, he could raise the standard of behaviour of the nobility as a whole. As an élite body of men of proven nobility selected for their prowess and required to demonstrate it regularly in the lists, the knights of the Band could reasonably be expected to attract both admiration and emulation from the younger members of the nobility at least, both on and off the field of combat. It seems likely that Alfonso intended the rules of civil conduct imposed on his knights to be observed by all the noble members of his court, and hoped that those who were not members would ape the manners of those who were, if only to appear à la mode. Some young fijosdalgo would surely have hoped that by behaving like the knights of the Band, they might eventually secure admission to that illustrious company, and enjoy the benefits of a close association with the king.

It is likely that Alfonso also hoped to use the Order to attract into his court and service members of the higher strata of the turbulent Castilian nobility who might otherwise have joined the ranks of his enemies. For this reason he did all that he could to enhance the prestige of the Order, for prestige or 'honour' (as his contemporaries would have called it) was the principal advantage of membership. There can be little doubt that he introduced his sons into the Order when they were still too young even to lift a sword in his service primarily for this purpose – for no one could look down on membership in a body which included most of the king's own sons. Alfonso also identified himself with the Order by regularly wearing its distinctive habit, and this too must have made membership in the Order appear highly desirable in the eyes of young noblemen hungry for honour and distinction. Alfonso seems finally to have granted membership in the Order as a reward for heroic action in the service of the crown, and it is likely that from the beginning it was perceived as a kind of dignity as well as a functional office.

Although the Order of the Band was inspired principally by the religious orders of knighthood (which it resembled more than any later lay order), there is reason to believe that Alfonso was not unmindful, in creating a society of knights attached to his crown, of the precedents for such an action set forth in the quasi-historical romances of the Arthurian cycle. The two chapters describing how an aspiring young knight could win admission to the Order by defeating member knights in single combat were almost certainly inspired by the customs of the Round Table, and it is likely that the emphasis placed in the statutes upon both courtly conduct (especially towards ladies) and prowess in the lists was due at least in part to a desire to promote the sort of behaviour presented in the romances as characteristic of a perfect knight. It is even possible that the idea of making himself the Master of the Order was inspired (and justified) by the action of the heroic King of Britain. In any case, the elements of romantic chivalry that he introduced into the customs of the Order would cetainly have appealed to the young knights and squires he hoped to attract into its ranks, who would have enjoyed being seen as the successors of Arthur's heroic knights.

Indeed, if Alfonso saw himself as acting in the tradition of Arthur when he founded the Order, he must have expected others to see him in the same light, and the Order he had founded as a Castilian successor to the Round Table. Although it had fewer obviously Arthurian elements than several later monarchical orders,[144] its nature and customs were sufficiently like those of the Round Table company that no contemporary prince or nobleman could have failed for long to see the resemblance. To be perceived as a second Arthur served by a company of heroic knights would surely have enhanced Alfonso's prestige and that of his court wherever the chivalrous traditions embodied in the Arthurian legend were still revered – which is to say all of Western Christendom – and this too may have figured among his reasons for establishing the Order.

Nevertheless, it is likely that Alfonso was principally concerned in founding the Order of the Band with the highly practical object of creating a military company on whose loyalty, discipline, and effectiveness he could always rely, and the Order of the Band can best be understood as an élite military unit. If not actually the first – and it might indeed have been – it was certainly one of the earliest formally constituted military companies to be maintained on a permanent footing by a European prince. From about 1350 onwards (but especially in the fifteenth century) princes all over Western Christendom began to create élite military units including a similar number of noble men-at-arms, intending thereby both to assure the security of their person as they travelled about the country and to increase the magnificence of their entourage in the eyes of all who witnessed them on their travels or had occasion to visit their court.[145] It is more than likely that the Order of the Band, many of whose members must have spent much of their time in the royal court, was intended to serve both of these functions, in addition to serving as an élite unit of the field army. Unlike most later units of this type, however, the Order was conservatively restricted to vassals of the king or his sons, and made no formal demands for services beyond those already owed by its members for their fiefs. Furthermore, so far as we can tell its members were expected to serve for their fiefs instead of a cash pension or salary.

Although we have no hard evidence by which to judge the performance of the Order of the Band during the period when its statutes were still in effect, there is no particular reason to doubt that the Order fulfilled all of the functions for which it was created at least reasonably well while the founder himself still lived, and the fact that its habit continued to be distributed as a mark of royal favour (if nothing else) by all of Alfonso's successors on the throne of Castile until the extinction of the male line of his house suggests that it acquired an honourable reputation when it was still a functional military unit. The demise of the Order of the Band both as a military unit and as a true monarchical order probably resulted not from any inherent defect in the Order, but from the civil wars that divided the kingdom, the nobility, and the Order itself for nearly twenty years after the founder's death, destroyed many old families, and gave rise to a new régime which had much less need for an order of the sort Alfonso had created.

In founding an 'order' of lay knights and squires perpetually attached to his own crown, Alfonso set the essential precedent which all the later founders of monarchical orders were to follow, and to this extent at least the Order of the Band almost certainly served as a model for all later monarchical orders. In part because

[144] Most notably perhaps the Companies of the Star and the Knot.
[145] On this, see above, pp. 2–3, and Philippe Contamine, *La Guerre au Moyen Age* (Paris, 1980), pp. 296–306.

of the relative isolation of Castile from the rest of Catholic Christendom in the 1330s and 1340s, however, and in part perhaps because the Order's rule was kept secret from outsiders, very few of Alfonso's more original ordinances (as distinct from those based on the common usages of devotional confraternities) were destined to be incorporated, even in a modified form, into the constitutions of later monarchical orders. Although several later orders were intended to function at least partly as élite military units, their rules contained few if any ordinances specifically calculated to promote military discipline and courtly behaviour, and no later order required its knights either to challenge strangers wearing their order's device or to take part in jousts or tournaments. In fact, no later founder was to go as far as Alfonso of Castile in attempting to make his order a true embodiment of the secular ideals of chivalry as well as a useful instrument of royal policy.

Chapter 4

The Order of St George,
or Society of the Garter
England, 1344/9–present

1 Historical Background

It was not until 1344 – more than a decade after the foundation of the Order of the Band – that a second prince announced his intention to found a similar society of lay knights. The prince was Edward III of England, and the society which finally resulted from his project of 1344 was of course the Order of the Garter, now the oldest and best known of all the princely foundations.[1]

Edward, called 'of Windsor' from his birthplace, was an almost exact contemporary of Alfonso 'the Implacable' of Castile. Born on 13 November 1312, he became the seventh English king of his Angevin house on the deposition of his father Edward II on 13 January 1327, when he was fourteen. The prestige of his kingdom and his house, which had been very high indeed during the long reign of his warlike grandfather Edward I – the conqueror of Wales and hammer of the Scots – was then at its lowest point in centuries. His foolish and unstable father (who had suffered a disastrous defeat in his only full-scale campaign against the Scots in 1314) had alienated the members of the baronage by his avoidance of war and outright scorn for traditional knightly activities and, even more importantly, by his dependence on a succession of hated favourites. His deposition by the 'parliament' convened by his estranged queen Isabella and her lover Roger Mortimer, and his subsequent murder, had been merely the last of a long series of defeats inflicted on him by the leaders of the barons disgusted with his misrule. After being pushed in these unhappy circumstances onto his father's throne, the young Edward III was at first forced to submit to a regency in which real power was retained by his mother and her lover (whom he was obliged to make Earl of March). In order to restore the prestige of the kingdom, Edward was almost immediately put in nominal command of an expedition against the Scots, but like his father's Bannockburn campaign

---

[1] The only thorough critical study of the life and reign of Edward III is James Mackinnon's *The History of Edward III (1327–1377)* (London, 1900; repr. 1974), but this can be supplemented by a number of more recent studies, especially May McKisack's *The Fourteenth Century, 1307–1399* (Oxford, 1959), and Richard Barber's *Edward Prince of Wales and Aquitaine. A Biography of the Black Prince* (London, 1978).

fourteen years earlier this ended in a humiliating defeat, and led to an even more humiliating treaty of peace sealed in his name by the regents in 1328. As if this were not bad enough, Edward was forced in 1329 to accept the election of his cousin Philippe of Valois to the throne of France recently left vacant by the death of the last Capetian of the direct line, and to do homage to him for his duchy of Guyenne, even though his own claim to the French throne – as the proximate male heir of his mother's father King Philippe IV – was arguably better than Philippe's.

When he finally seized effective control of his kingdom and its various dependent dominions in October 1330, the seventeen-year-old Edward was determined to erase the humiliations that he and his kingdom had recently suffered, and to be a truly outstanding ruler according to the standards generally accepted at the time. He quickly distanced himself as much as possible from the policies and practices of his father, and took as his model his heroic grandfather Edward I. Repudiating in rapid succession both his treaty with Scotland and his homage to the 'French king', he spent much of his fifty-year reign leading or organizing highly successful campaigns against the traditional enemies of his kingdom, and in 1337 began the epic struggle now remembered as the Hundred Years War by laying claim to the throne of France. Edward quickly proved himself to be a worthy successor of his grandfather – at once a paragon of knighthood, an able captain, and an astute ruler of men – and by 1344 was one of the most respected rulers in Europe. Since he was blessed in addition with an affable and generous disposition, he also managed to maintain good relations with most of his subjects of all ranks throughout his reign, and died peacefully in his bed in 1377 at the age of sixty-four.

The formal relationship of the King of England to his subjects of the landholding military class had always been rather better than that of any contemporary king to his noble subjects, for the circumstances of the Conquest of 1066 had given the king the upper hand over the baronage, and subsequent kings had steadily built up the already considerable authority of the crown. During the course of the fourteenth century, indeed, the old tenurial baronage – composed of the holders of the 200-odd territorial baronies created by William 'the Conqueror' and his immediate successors[2] – gradually lost what remained of its rights of local jurisdiction, and was wholly superceded as the dominant stratum of English society by a new and more tractable body, composed of those barons and great landholders whom the king chose to summon to sit as 'peers' or 'lords' in the upper chamber of the new national Parliament.[3]

One of the principal reasons for the decline and ultimate disappearance of the tenurial baronage in the fourteenth century was the dissolution of the military system that their baronies had originally been created to support. Although the barons and knights of England continued to hold all their lands as military

[2] On the territorial baronies of England in the period before Edward's accession, see I. J. Sanders, *English Baronies. A Study of their Origin and Descent 1086–1327* (Oxford, 1960).
[3] On the history of the peerage in this period, see especially J. Enoch Powell and Keith Wallis, *The House of Lords in the Middle Ages. A History of the English House of Lords to 1540* (London, 1968).

tenements and to do homage and swear fealty to their landlords until the seventeenth century, the feudal system of military recruitment and organization established in England by the Conqueror proved for a variety of reasons increasingly ineffective. During the reign of Edward I (1273–1307) – who spent much of his time leading or directing campaigns against the Welsh, the Scots, and the French – the old system was gradually abandoned in favour of a new one based upon the payment of wages in cash. Under the new system of recruitment – often called the 'indenture system' but better termed 'retaining by contract' – the king concluded agreements with particular barons in which the baron agreed to provide specified numbers of knights, men-at-arms, and common soldiers of specified types, either for a particular period of time or for a specific military undertaking, and the king for his part agreed to pay daily wages to every member of this company. Barons 'retained' by such contracts (who were rather illogically called 'retainers') commonly raised some of the men promised by retaining lesser captains on similar terms. Most of the contracts entered into on both levels were for a limited period, but some (like that between seigniorial lord and vassal) were for life, and specified that the retainer was to serve his lord either alone or with a specified number of his own retainers, in war and in peace, whenever his lord summoned him. All but a handful of the contracts concluded under Edward I and his son seem to have been purely oral, but under Edward III they were normally written out in the form of an indenture, and many of these have survived. The indentures drawn up between Edward and his principal commanders for particular campaigns were usually quite detailed, the king promising not merely to pay the wages of the commander and his troops, but to pay for other expenses incurred, provide transportation to and from the battlefield, send help in case of need, and allow the commander and his captains to divide such spoils of battle as the ransoms of noble prisoners.[4] The advantages of this form of contract over the feudal contract it replaced were neatly summed up by May McKisack:

> It was almost always short-term; it freed the military tenants from the burden of scutage [a fine or tax paid by military tenants who declined to serve when summoned] and the exchequer from the labour of collecting it; the problems arising from the fragmentation of knight's fees could be ignored; it made even the greatest of the magnates directly dependent upon the king or his appointed representative, while safeguarding all captains against serious loss and offering them the chance of successful profit; and it substituted discipline and a proper subordination of commands for the unruly individualism of the feudal musters.[5]

[4] On the system of retaining by contract in this period, see especially A. E. Prince, 'The Indenture System under Edward III', in *Historical Essays in Honour of James Tait* (Manchester, 1933), pp. 238–97; 'The Payment of Army Wages in Edward III's Reign', *Speculum* 19 (1944), 137–60; N. B. Lewis, 'The Organization of Indentured Retinues in Fourteenth-Century England', *TRHS*, 4th ser., 27 (1945), 29–39; 'The Recruitment and Organization of a Contract Army, May to November 1337', *BIHR* 37 (1964), 1–19; 'Indentures of Retinue with John of Gaunt, Duke of Lancaster, Enrolled in Chancery 1367–1399', *Camden Miscellany*, 4th ser., 1 (1964), 77–97; and H. J. Hewitt, *The Organization of War under Edward III 1338–62* (Manchester, 1966).
[5] *The Fourteenth Century*, p. 236.

In the present context the last two advantages are of particular importance, for they meant that Edward III and his successors on the English throne had no need to create a knightly order or any comparable body to secure the effective military service either of the greatest magnates in their kingdom, or of the most competent and ambitious knights.

The new model army developed by Edward I did resemble the old feudal host in having at its core a large contingent of men drawn from the knightly class or nobility – which though not a legal estate in England, was certainly a recognized social class. Furthermore, rank and wages within the army continued to be closely related to civil rank within the knightly class, and all positions of authority were restricted to knights.[6] At the time of Edward III's accession, the highest-ranking status in the knightly class was that of count or earl, which was then held by nine eminent barons (including four cadets of the royal house and one French prince), and was later conferred by Edward on fifteen other men as a reward for their services. Edward himself introduced the higher status of duke for his eldest son Edward 'of Woodstock' in 1337, and conferred it on his agnatic cousin Henry 'of Grosmont' in 1351, and his younger son John 'of Gaunt' in 1362. He also reintroduced the still higher status of prince for his eldest son in 1343, and it was thereafter the peculiar title of the heir apparent. The status of marquess, ranking between those of duke and earl, was introduced into the kingdom abortively in 1385 and 1397, and successfully in 1444, and the status of viscount, ranking immediately below that of earl, was introduced in 1440. The holders of all five of these essentially honorific statuses were regularly summoned to Parliament as peers, and enjoyed what amounted to state pensions fixed in accordance with their rank. Most members of this class of higher peers (which seldom included more than twenty men at any time in our period) received the accolade of knighthood as soon as they were old enough to function as knights, and those who served in the wars of Edward and his immediate successors were generally given overall command of an army or division. Under Edward dukes on active service were paid a daily wage of one mark (13s 4d), and earls between half a mark and 8s.

Immediately below the higher peers in civil society came the lesser magnates distinguished only by the generic title 'baron', which until about 1400 continued to be applied exclusively to those men who held all or part of a territorial barony. There were several hundred barons in England in the fourteenth century, but fewer than a hundred of these were sufficiently important to be summoned even occasionally as peers, and Edward and his successor Richard II rarely summoned more than sixty of them to any particular Parliament. By the time of Edward's death in 1377 the list of barons who might receive a summons had become virtually fixed, largely through custom, and in the fifteenth century the heirs of the barons on that list came to be thought of as peers with the rank of baron even when they were not sitting in Parliament, and to be distinguished by the title 'lord', prefixed to their surname or that of the ancestor in whose right they received their summons.

As we have seen, the reform of the system of military recruitment and organization deprived the barons as such of their traditional role as leaders of the

---

[6] For this and what follows see McKisack, *The Fourteenth Century*, pp. 184–7, 237–8; and Powell and Wallis, *Lords*.

royal army, but throughout our period many of the more important barons were retained either by the king or by one of the titled magnates to serve as commanders with the new military rank of banneret.[7] Bannerets (so called because they shared with the higher peers the right to display their personal arms on a square banner rather than a triangular pennon) were chosen by the higher commanders from among the whole body of knights on the dual basis of their military skill and their capacity to sustain the considerable expenses associated with the position, and many bannerets were not barons but merely rich knights. A few of these non-baronial bannerets were regularly summoned in the fourteenth century to sit below the barons as peers of the realm, and in military contexts the statuses of baron and banneret were commonly treated as equivalent. Bannerets performed a variety of military tasks, including those of commanding retinues in the field, garrisoning castles, and acting as staff officers. For this they were paid at a rate of 4s a day, or half the pay of an earl.

Almost all bannerets were knights, but only a small minority of the knights in England could aspire to the rank of banneret. Nevertheless, the status of knight itself had come by the time of Edward's accession to be limited to a relatively small number of comparatively wealthy men. It has been estimated that only about 1250 landed gentlemen had actually received the accolade of knighthood in 1300, and that only about half of these were 'strenuous knights' fit to serve in battle. Edward III succeeded in raising the number of strenuous knights to about 1,000 during the first decades of his reign, but thereafter it fell steadily until in 1420 there were only about 300 knights of any sort in the kingdom.[8] Only about a tenth of the knights at the height of Edward's reign were either peers or bannerets, but by 1420 that proportion had risen to nearly a third.

The simple knights who ranked immediately below the bannerets in the Edwardian armies were all called 'knights bachelor', but while some (as the title implies) were young men of little military experience who commanded no one but their own squires and pages, others were old campaigners who were employed as captains of companies, and hoped some day to accumulate enough money to sustain the rank of banneret. Like bannerets, most knights bachelor drew the bulk of their income from their own lands, but a certain number were supported as members of the household of the king or a baron, and with the knights retained on life contracts these household knights formed the core of the royal and baronial retinues in battle. Such knights commonly wore a complete *robe* of their lord's livery. Whatever their experience or position, knights bachelor were paid at a rate of 2s a day under Edward III – half the rate for bannerets, and twice that paid to the squires who made up the bulk of the 'knightly' contingent in the armies of our period.

At the time of Edward's accession the barons and knights of England, though proud and pugnacious to a degree, were far less likely to engage in serious quarrels or rebellions than those of any other kingdom in Europe, and far more likely to act

---

[7] The title first appears in documents of the middle of the thirteenth century.

[8] On the number of knights in England, see N. Denholm-Young, 'Feudal Society in the Thirteenth Century: The Knights', in *Collected Papers on Mediaeval Subjects* (Oxford, 1946); and *The Country Gentry in the Fourteenth Century, with Special Reference to the Heraldic Rolls of Arms* (Oxford, 1969), pp. 15–16.

as loyal and effective servants of the crown. As his father's experience proved, however, they wanted a king who would respect them and their traditional rights and values, would heed their advice in important matters of state, and would lead them in battle against their enemies. Edward proved to be just such a king. Not only did he help the knights of his kingdom win glory and profit by leading them on highly successful campaigns against the Scots and the French, but he treated them as his friends and colleagues, showered them with titles and offices, and entertained them royally in a truly brilliant court. In addition – in part because he felt a genuine personal enthusiasm for the ideals of knighthood and found himself capable of living up to them, and in part because he discovered (like his grandfather and model Edward I) that it was politically advantageous to be seen as a chivalric hero – he took a keen interest in every aspect of the international chivalric culture in which the knights of England had delighted since its inception, and conceits derived from chivalric literature or activities permeated all forms of artistic expression in his court. He also held numerous knightly games and festivals throughout his reign, and staged at least thirty traditional tournaments in the years leading up to the foundation of the Order of the Garter in 1349 alone.

The barons and knights of England responded to all this by giving Edward their unswerving loyalty and devoted service, and Edward's reign was characterized throughout by cooperation rather than confrontation between king and barons. The only serious misunderstanding that arose between Edward and the lords occurred in 1340, when the failure of a home-council to collect enough money forced Edward to cut short a campaign in France, and the king lashed out at those peers he held responsible for his humiliation. It has been suggested that Edward's proclamation of a knightly society in January 1344 was intended in part to smooth the feathers ruffled in this affair, and reduce the possibility of such misunderstandings in the future.[9]

2 The Foundation and History of the Order

Evidence for the history of the Order of the Garter in the fourteenth century is extremely scanty. Because of the loss of its official records in or shortly before 1416, historians have been obliged to piece together its history under its first three 'Sovereigns' on the less than satisfactory basis of a handful of chronicle accounts, occasional references in the financial records of the royal household, and three Latin redactions of the statutes which seem to have been current before 1416. Unfortunately, these sources contain contradictory statements about the time and circumstances of the Order's foundation, and the historians who have attempted over the years to reconstruct some part of the early history of the Order – John

[9] See Juliet Vale, *Edward III and Chivalry. Chivalric Society and its Context 1270–1350* (Woodbridge, 1982). Vale is the first writer to have placed the foundation of the Order against the background not merely of the immediately preceding events of the war in France, but of the chivalrous interests and activities of the founder.

Selden[10] and Sir Elias Ashmole[11] in the seventeenth century, John Anstis[12] in the eighteenth, George Frederick Beltz[13] and Sir Nicholas Harris Nicolas[14] in the ninteenth, and Richard Barber[15] and Juliet Vale[16] in the twentieth – have all had to devote much of their energy to making sense of the inconsistencies, real or apparent, in the primary evidence. The progressive discovery and publication of sources previously unknown, however, and the examination of sources known but previously unexplored, have made it possible for most of these historians to improve upon the accounts of their predecessors, and it is now possible to write a reasonably satisfactory narrative account of the foundation of the Order and of the events which led up to it.

Until shortly after the publication of the works of Beltz and Nicolas – the most recent exhaustive studies of the Order's history – the earliest known chronicle to mention the foundation of the Order of the Garter was that of the Hainaulter Jean Froissart,[17] and his account, full of circumstantial details supposed to have been learned by him during the time (from 1361 to 1366) that he was the secretary to Edward's queen, Philippa of Hainault, was long regarded as the most authoritative. According to Froissart, Edward decided to found the 'order of knights' which the chronicler called the 'Confraternity of St George' towards the end of the year 1343.

> At this time Edward, King of England, resolved to rebuild the great castle of Windsor, formerly built and founded by King Arthur, and where was first set up and established the noble Round Table, from whence so many valiant men and knights had issued forth to perform feats of arms and prowess throughout the world. And the said king created an order of knights, to consist of himself, his children, and the bravest in the land. They were to be forty in number, and were to be called *the knights of the blue Garter*; their feast was to be kept and solemnized annually on St George's Day. And in order to institute this festival, the King of England assembled earls, barons, and knights from his whole realm, and signified to them his purpose and great desire to found the same. In this they joyfully concurred, for it appeared to them to be an honourable undertaking, and calculated to nourish affection among them. Then were elected forty knights known and celebrated as the

---

[10] *Titles of Honor* (London, 1614).

[11] *The Institution, Laws, and Ceremonies of the Most Noble Order of the Garter* (London, 1672; repr. 1971).

[12] *The Register of the Most Noble Order of the Garter . . . called the Black Book* (2 vols., London, 1724).

[13] *Memorials of the Most Noble Order of the Garter* (London, 1841).

[14] *History of the Orders of Knighthood of the British Empire* (4 vols., London, 1842); and 'Observations on the Institution of the Most Noble Order of the Garter', *Archaeologia* 31 (1846), pp. 1–163.

[15] *Edward, Prince of Wales and Aquitaine. A Biography of the Black Prince* (London, 1978), pp. 83–92.

[16] *Edward III and Chivalry. Chivalric Society and its Context 1270–1350* (Woodbridge, 1982), pp. 76–91.

[17] *Chroniques* (1307–1400), ed. Baron Kervyn de Lettenhove, 25 vols. in 26 (Brussels, 1867–77; repr. 1967).

bravest of them all, and they bound themselves to their king, under their seals, by oath and fealty, to keep the feast, and obey the ordinances which should be devised. And the king caused a chapel of St George to be built within the castle of Windsor, established canons therein for the service of God, and provided and endowed them with a good and liberal revenue. And in order that the said feast might be promulgated in all countries, the King of England sent his heralds to publish and proclaim the same in France, Scotland, Burgundy, Hainault, Flanders, Brabant, and the German Empire, granting safe-conduct until fifteen days after the feast. And there was to be held at this feast a joust by forty knights, within the lists, against all comers, and also by forty squires. And this feast was to be celebrated on the following St George's Day, which would be in the year of grace one thousand, three hundred, and forty-four, at Windsor Castle. And the Queen of England, accompanied by three hundred ladies and damsels, all noble and gentle women, and all dressed alike, were to be present.[18]

Unfortunately, Froissart's account conflicts on many points both with other narrative accounts composed closer to the events in question, and with documentary evidence of a more official nature, roughly contemporary with the events. Most of this evidence points to a foundation date for the Order sometime between the autumn of 1347 and St George's Day (23 April) 1350, when a meeting of the Order was certainly held. Scholars were long puzzled by the obvious discrepancies among the primary sources, but since the publication of Nicolas' 'Observations' in 1846 it has been generally agreed that, while Edward III did indeed announce his intention to found some sort of knightly society early in the year 1344, as Froissart and most other chroniclers state, the society in question was meant to have been a revival of the Round Table of King Arthur (merely alluded to by Froissart), was not to have been dedicated to St George, and was not initially intended to have a garter as its device. Since Nicolas wrote his study two chronicles have been published which contain almost contemporary accounts of the tournament of 1344 – the chronicles of Adam of Murimuth[19] and Jean le Bel[20] – and these have not only confirmed Nicolas' conclusions but shown that the Round Table society proclaimed at that tournament bore little resemblance either to the body of forty knights described by Froissart or to the Order eventually founded. Nevertheless, the fact that Froissart and virtually all of the other chroniclers writing after 1350 (when the Order of the Garter had certainly assumed its definitive form) identified that Order absolutely with the Round Table society proclaimed in 1344 suggests that contemporaries, including members of Edward's immediate entourage, generally regarded the historic Order as the ultimate product of Edward's project to revive the Round Table. Since the opinions of well-informed contemporaries can hardly be disregarded completely – and since the Round Table project of 1344 is in any case almost as interesting in the present context as the very different order that was eventually founded – we will begin our examination of the history of the Order of the Garter, like Froissart, toward the end of the year 1343.

[18] Tr. by Beltz, *Memorials*, pp. xxxvi–xxxvii.
[19] First edn. 1846.
[20] First edn. 1863.

Edward had returned in March of that year from a successful four-month campaign in Brittany, and had immediately gone on a pilgrimage on foot to Canterbury and by horse to Gloucester and Walsingham. After dealing rapidly with the pressing business of government at a Parliament convened at Westminster on 28 April (where he invested his twelve-year-old son Edward 'of Woodstock', Duke of Cornwall, with the Principality of Wales), he had embarked upon a series of tournaments and hunting parties, presumably intended at least in part to celebrate his victories in France. The culmination of this series of festive events was the great tournament referred to by Froissart, which was held at Windsor, not on St George's Day, but from 19 to 25 January 1344. This tournament was apparently proclaimed well in advance both in England and in neighbouring regions of the continent, and on 1 January letters of safe conduct were issued placing all foreign knights who came to take part under the special protection of the king until the 9th of the following month.[21]

The tournament itself is described in considerable detail in two versions of the *Continuatio Chronicarum* of Adam of Murimuth, written within three years of the event.[22] According to Murimuth, not only knights but all the ladies from the southern parts of the kingdom were invited by royal letters to take part in this festival of chivalry, along with the wives of the burgesses of London, and those ladies who came included two queens (Edward's mother Isabella and his wife Philippa) and nine countesses. The festivities began with a great banquet on Sunday, and on each of the three subsequent days Edward and nineteen other knights defended the enclosed field against all comers. Edward himself was adjudged the most successful of the defending knights, 'not out of royal favour, but because of the great labour which he had sustained, and the luck which he had . . .'[23] After the tourneying on the third day, Edward announced that no one was to depart until they had heard what he would say on the following day. Early on that day, Thursday the 22nd, Edward and his queen appeared for mass in the chapel of the castle crowned and robed in velvet mantles, and after the service everyone present processed solemnly to a place previously appointed, led by Edward's cousin Henry 'of Grosmont', Earl of Derby, in his capacity as Seneschal of England, and by William de Montague, Earl of Salisbury, in his capacity as Marshal of England. There, according to the version of Murimuth's chronicle preserved in the Cotton manuscript,

> . . . the same lord king and all the others stood together, and the lord king, having held up the Book [a Bible] and touched holy things [relics], swore by his body that within a certain limited period of time, provided the ability remained to him, he would found a Round Table (*mensam rotundam*), of the same manner and standing as that which the Lord Arthur, formerly King of England, had relinquished, to the number of three hundred knights, and to support and maintain it for men whose number was never to be increased. The Earls of Derby, Salisbury, Warwick, Arundel, Pembroke, and Suffolk,

---

[21] Rot. Pat. 17 Edw. III, p. 2, m. 2, cited in Nicolas, 'Observations', p. 104.
[22] Ed. Edward Maunde Thompson (London, 1889). Murimuth's chronicle, begun around 1325, was completed in 1347.
[23] Ibid., p. 155.

and many other barons and knights whom prowess and fame have promoted by praise to be worthy, similarly swore to observe, sustain, and promote this project in all its details.[24]

The other version of Murimuth's chronicle contains a different, but essentially complementary, account of these events.

On Thursday, following after the jousts of the young gentlemen, the Lord King held a great feast at which he inaugurated his Round Table, and received the oaths of certain earls, barons, and knights, who wished to be of the said Round Table in the same place on the following Pentecost and thereafter, and he gave licence to all present with actions of grace to return to their homes. He also ordered afterwards that a most noble house should be made there by a certain date, for the building of which masons, carpenters, and other builders were appointed, and both wood and stone began to be supplied, neither labour nor expense being spared. Afterwards for certain reasons this work was stopped.[25]

The reference to Pentecost in this passage is clarified by a statement in another chronicle written in England not long after the tournament in question, the anonymous continuation of the *Brut* chronicle. According to the continuator,

At that tyme [January 1345], whene the iustes had done, the kyng Edward made a grete souper, in the wheche he begone fyrst hys round table, and ordayned stedfastly the day of the forsayd table to be holde ther at Wyndessore in the Whytson wyke evermore yerely.[26]

The account of these events in the chronicle of the Liegeois canon Jean le Bel, probably composed a dozen or more years later, is considerably less detailed, but it is nonetheless of interest both as an independent record of the events and as Froissart's principal written source.[27] In chapter 64 of his chronicle, Le Bel wrote that Edward, after returning home (in 1343) from campaigns in France,

. . . decided out of nobility of heart that he would have remade and rebuilt the castle of Windsor – which King Arthur had constructed, and where the Round Table was first established, because of the valiant knights who were there at that time – and that he would make and establish a similar Round Table, to increase further the honour of his knights, who had served him so well that he held them to be so bold that one could not find their like in any other realm, and it seemed to him that he could not honour them too much,

---

[24] Ibid., p. 232.

[25] Ibid., p. 156.

[26] BL, Egerton MS. 650, quoted in *Chronicon Galfridi le Baker de Swynebroke*, ed. Edward Maunde Thompson (Oxford, 1889), p. 279.

[27] Many passages of Froissart's chronicle down to the year 1361 were lifted with little or no alteration from that of Le Bel, begun around 1356 and covering the period 1272–1361.

so much did he love them. He had proclaimed throughout his whole realm a general feast and full court, to establish this Round Table, and he commanded ladies and damsels, knights and squires through all lands to come without excuse to take part in this great feast at Windsor on Pentecost in the year of grace 1344.[28]

Slightly later in his chronicle, Le Bel reported that Edward did indeed '. . . order and confirm a noble company of knights (who were to be valiant men), which was made according to the manner of the Round Table',[29] but could give no further details.

Two later chronicles, an anonymous work preserved in the manuscript now kept in the British Library as Cotton Vitellius A.XX, and the *Chronicon Angliae* of Thomas of Walsingham, composed around 1376, contribute to our knowledge of the Round Table project. The former merely confirms Murimuth's statement that the number of knights in the proposed company was to have been 300,[30] but the latter contains additional information of considerable interest here.

In the year of grace 1344, which is the eighteenth year of the reign of King Edward, third from the Conquest, King Edward had many workmen summoned to the castle of Windsor, and began to build a house which was to be called the Round Table. Its area had a distance of 100 feet from the centre to the circumference, and thus a diameter of 200 feet. The expenses by the week were at first £100, but afterwards, on account of the news which the king received from France, they were curtailed to £20, because he decided that that much treasure had to be put together for other affairs.[31]

Surviving financial records indicate that work on a building called the 'House of the Round Table' was in fact begun at Windsor under considerable pressure on 16 February 1344.[32] The accounts give little direct information about the form the building was to take, but H. M. Colvin has concluded from the fact that 40,000 tiles and a similar number of tile-pins were ordered *pro coopertura murorum domus tabule rotunde* that it was probably to have taken the form of a large open space enclosed by two concentric, permanently roofed circular walls, rather along the lines of an Elizabethan theatre.[33] When completed this structure would have occupied almost all of the upper bailey of the castle.[34] Apparently an enormous

---

[28] *Chronique de Jean le Bel*, ed. J. Viard, E. Déprez (Paris, 1904), vol. II, p. 26.
[29] Ibid., pp. 34–5.
[30] 'Anno MCMLIII. Rex Angliae Rotundam Tabulam ccc Militum tenuit apud Wyndesoure . . .' Pub. in Nicholas, 'Observations', p. 151.
[31] *Chronicon Angliae, 1328–88, autore monacho quodam Sancti Albani*, ed. Edward Maunde Thompson (London, 1874), p. 17.
[32] Most of our knowledge about the construction of this structure is derived from the enrolled account of Adam of Kilham, the clerk of the works, the draft of that account, and a counter-roll of particulars drawn up by his comptroller, Brother John de Walrand, preserved in the PRO as Pipe roll 18 Edw. III, *rot. comp. 3*, and E 101/492/25 and 26, respectively. See H. M. Colvin, ed., *The History of the King's Works II* (London, 1963), p. 871.
[33] Ibid., pp. 871–2.
[34] Ibid.

round table was to have been set into the open space in the middle of the building, for another account indicates that Edward ordered fifty-two oaks from the Prior of Merton for the construction of such a table at Windsor, and paid the prior £26 13s. 4d. for the wood.[35]

It must appear from the evidence just reviewed that Edward, at some time after his return from France in 1343, decided to establish a society of knights modelled directly and explicitly upon the Round Table society of King Arthur. Although special tournaments called 'round tables' had been held in England (as in Castile) since at least the year 1235,[36] it is clear that Edward had something much grander and more permanent in mind than the temporary fellowships of knights created for the duration of such tournaments by the oath to obey the rules of play. Not only did Edward announce his intention to refound the Round Table at a particularly splendid tournament to which knights and ladies from an unusually wide area had been invited, but he concealed his intentions from practically everyone until the last dramatic moment, and inaugurated his project in the most solemn possible fashion in the presence (and with the sworn support) of many of the most prominent members of the English knightage. Finally, Edward immediately ordered work begun on a vast and expensive building in the upper bailey of his favourite castle, obviously intended to house the proposed society, and of little use for any other purpose. Designs for this unusual building must have been under discussion with a master builder (no doubt sworn to secrecy) for weeks or even months before the day on which the project was announced. All of this suggests that Edward intended to make the proposed society not merely a permanent but an important adjunct of his court.

Since Edward had obviously been working on the project for several months at the time of his proclamation, he must have had some idea of what sort of society he wanted to establish, even if (as it appears) he had not yet decided the precise details of its statutes. Unfortunately, the sources present only the barest outline of his plans, but what they do tell us suggests that he had drawn most of his inspiration from the societies depicted in the prose romances, including not only that of the Round Table but that of the *Franc Palais* described in the exactly contemporary romance *Perceforest*, whose protagonist was an ancestor and prefiguration of Arthur.[37] According to Murimuth, Edward's Round Table was to have been 'of the same manner and standing' as Arthur's society, and the fact that it was to have had a permanent headquarters within the walls of Edward's principal castle suggests that it was indeed to have been, like the fictional society, a perpetual association of lay knights attached permanently to the royal court of England. Arthur was consistently protrayed in the romances as both the founder and the president for life of the 'original' Round Table society, and it is likely that Edward intended to assume a similar role for himself and his successors on the English throne in the 'restored' society. It would appear that Edward's society was to have been made up of 300 knights (twice the highest number commonly assigned in the romances to

---

[35] Issue Roll of the Exchequer, Mich. 30 Edw. III, cited in Nicolas, 'Observations', p. 107. It is possible that this wood was intended for the building itself, rather than the table.

[36] On these, see above, p. 13.

[37] See above, p. 23.

the Round Table company itself, but precisely the number included in the society of the *Franc Palais*), and was to have met annually on Pentecost (the principal feast of the Arthurian romances in general) at a round table in a round hall (very similar to those described in *Perceforest*)[38] in a castle which was not only (like Camelot) the principal palace of the King of England, but was actually identified by Edward as the place where Arthur had founded and maintained his Round Table. It is not unlikely that Edward meant to imitate his literary models in other ways as well – by assigning each of the knights a specific seat at the table, for example, marked with his arms – but we have no way of knowing how far this imitation was to have gone. Since the authors who described the fictional societies failed to discuss the organization of those bodies in any detail, Edward would have been obliged either to invent a wholly new form of constitution for his society or to look for other models, but we have no way of knowing whether his thinking in this area had made much progress before he decided to substitute St George and the Garter for Arthur and the Round Table. Although the order finally established had most of the religious features characteristic of confraternities, including a patron saint and chapel, there is no evidence to suggest that Edward initially planned to assign any of these features – wholly absent both from the fictional companies of knights and from the Order of the Band – to his Round Table society. It is in fact quite possible that Edward intended the knights of his society to do no more than meet once a year for a great feast and tournament (perhaps of the 'round table' variety), for this is the only form of truly corporate activity attributed to the 'original' society of the Round Table in any of the romances.

There can be no doubt that one of Edward's principal objects in thus 'refounding' the Round Table was to associate himself as strongly as possible in the eyes both of his own subjects and of his allies and enemies in Scotland and on the continent with King Arthur. In this he was following in the footsteps of his grandfather and model Edward I, who in separate ceremonies had caused the supposed bones of Arthur and his queen to be solemnly reburied beneath the high altar of Glastonbury Abbey, and his supposed crown, surrendered by the defeated Welsh, to be placed at the shrine of Edward the Confessor at Westminster.[39] The fact that Arthur was not only the earliest and most celebrated of the three Christian 'Worthies', but was believed to have subdued all of Britain and conquered much of France, gave Edward – who could put forward a convincing claim to be Arthur's 'heir' – the strongest possible political motives for promoting this association, which his grandfather had used in similar ways. His status as Arthur's 'heir' also put him in a unique position not merely to found a society of knights loosely modelled upon the Round Table (as his cousin Alfonso of Castile had done and as various other princes were to do), but to 'refound' the Round Table itself, on the very spot where it had originally been created and maintained. There is every reason to believe that the 300 knights who were to be admitted to the 'revived' society would have been highly gratified to be thus made the successors of Arthur's heroic knights, and that such a society – including nearly a third of the militarily active knights in England, and a majority of the earls and major barons – would have

[38] See above, p. 23.
[39] See Vale, *Edward III*, pp. 16–19.

served at the very least to smooth the relations between Edward and the more important members of the English knightly class, still somewhat ruffled by the crisis of 1340.

While Edward's decision to promote his Arthurian connections was in keeping with the policies of his grandfather and needs no further explanation, there is reason to believe that his decision to do so by refounding the Round Table was directly inspired by the foundation of the Order of the Band by his cousin Alfonso of Castile. Immediately following the conclusion of his campaign in Brittany in March 1343, Edward had sent two of his most trusted friends and lieutenants, Henry 'of Grosmont', Earl of Derby, and William de Montague, Earl of Salisbury (who were later to lead the procession at the climax of the Windsor tournament), to propose to Alfonso of Castile a marriage treaty between Alfonso's son Pedro and one of Edward's daughters.[40] Derby and Salisbury had found Alfonso besieging the city of Algeciras, and spent several months not merely negociating with Alfonso but fighting at his side against the Moors. It is inconceivable that they could have failed to note the existence of the Order of the Band, many of whose members must have taken part in the siege, and it is just as inconceivable that they would have failed to mention the existence of this novel society of knights to Edward – who was very interested in all things chivalric – when they returned to England in the early autumn of 1343[41] to report the successful conclusion of their mission. Less than three months later, Edward announced that he had decided to 'refound' the Round Table, and what evidence there is suggests that this was a fairly recent decision, made in all likelihood within the time since the return of Derby and Salisbury from Spain. In the circumstances it would be difficult to believe that his decision was not directly inspired by what he had just heard from his ambassadors about the Castilian order – whose Arthurian character, though disguised, would not have escaped him.[42] How much Derby and Salisbury were able to tell Edward about the Order of the Band beyond its general nature is of course another question, and it is more than likely that they learned very little about the details of its ordinances, which as we have seen were supposed to be kept secret from all outsiders.[43]

Nicholas and Shaw suggested[44] that Edward's decision to create a society of lay knights may have been inspired to some extent by the creation of an association of lay knights in the County of Lincoln in 1344, but this is in fact unlikely. What we know about this association is derived entirely from the letters patent Edward issued

---

[40] On their mission to Castile, see esp. Kenneth Fowler, *The King's Lieutenant. Henry of Grosmont, First Duke of Lancaster 1310–1361* (New York, 1969), pp. 45–6.

[41] They were back by the beginning of November.

[42] Although I presented an earlier version of this argument in my thesis in 1975, Barber, (*Edward*, pp. 87–9) was the first to propose in print the idea that the project of 1344 and the Order of the Garter itself were inspired by the Order of the Band. He also pointed out (on p. 89) that Edward actually wrote to at least four knights of the Band, among other Castilian noblemen, to ask for their support, but it is not clear that he knew of their membership in the Order at the time he wrote, and there is no reason to believe that they would have informed him of it.

[43] See above, p. 76.

[44] 'Observations', p. 128 and W. A. Shaw, *Knights of England*, vol. I (London, 1906), p. i.

in its favour on 18 January and 10 February 1344 – several months after he had almost certainly decided to 'refound' the Round Table. According to the earlier of these documents,[45] issued on the eve of the Windsor tournament, Edward had initially been asked by a group of Lincolnshire knights to allow a certain number of them, elected for the purpose, to meet at the city of Lincoln every year on the Monday of the week of Pentecost, to hold jousts under the captaincy of Henry of Lancaster, Earl of Derby, for as long as he lived, and after his death under the captaincy of whichever of their own number they elected to the position. Edward, responding specifically to the request of the Earl of Derby himself, granted them the right to hold jousts at the proposed time and place, even in time of war, except when he himself announced that he would hold a round table or jousts or other feats of arms at the specified time, in which case the jousts of the association were to be postponed until some time in the following month. Four days later, of course, he announced his plan (apparently kept secret even from Derby) to found his own society of knights which was to meet every year at Pentecost, and about two weeks later he issued new letters agreeing to allow the Lincolnshire association to meet every year on the Monday following the Nativity of St John the Baptist (24 June) rather than Pentecost.[46] In the latter document Edward grandiloquently declared that he had agreed to the request of the knights '. . . remembering the deeds of the ancients, and considering how much the use and love of arms has exalted the name and glory of knightly men, and how much the the royal throne would be strengthened by the numerousness of men expert in arms, and the danger of dissentions which resulted from their unemployment reduced . . .' It is not unlikely that he had expressed the same sentiments two weeks earlier when he proclaimed the reinstitution of Arthur's Round Table – they would have been even more appropriate on that occasion – but this does not mean that the two associations were essentially similar, or that either of them inspired the other. In fact it would appear that Edward and his cousin the Earl of Derby were each independently inspired by the Order of the Band to found a society of knights of a nature and scale suitable to his rank.

Although the idea of creating a society of knights attached to his throne was not original with Edward, his 'refoundation' of the society of the Round Table itself at the time and in the manner in which he did so must be regarded as a political *tour de force*. It is therefore particularly difficult to explain why he abandoned the project of restoring the Round Table – if not that of founding a monarchical order of knights – less than a year after he proclaimed it in the most solemn and binding way. Despite the fact that the first meeting of the new society was to have been held at Pentecost or Whitsun, 23 May 1344, Edward seems to have been at Marlborough rather than Windsor for that feast,[47] and the surviving accounts of the royal household contain nothing to indicate that any great assembly was held in 1344 after the Windsor tournament itself. A document purporting to record the expenses of the royal household for the period from Michaelmas (29 September) 1344 to the summer of 1345[48] contains a record of payments for red velvet garments

[45] Rot. Pat. 18 Edw. III, p. 2, m. 4; published in Nicolas, 'Observations', pp. 153–4.
[46] Rot. Pat. 18 Edw. III, p. 1, m. 44; published in Nicolas, 'Observations', p. 153.
[47] CPR, 1343–45, p. 261.
[48] PRO, E101/390/5; published in Nicolas, 'Observations', p. 6.

lined with fur supplied to the king 'contra festum tabule rotunde apud Wyndesore', but although Nicolas concluded from the organization of the account that this feast was held (possibly at Pentecost) in 1345,[49] Juliet Vale has convincingly argued on the basis of where the royal court is said in the document to have been on certain named feasts that the record is in fact concerned with expenses of the period from Michaelmas 1343 to the summer of 1344, and concluded that the 'feast of the Round Table' it refers to was the Windsor tournament of January 1344,[50] when red velvet robes were certainly worn.[51] There is thus no evidence that the Round Table Society ever met either in 1344 or in 1345. Even the building operations, which were still regarded as urgent early in the autumn of 1344,[52] were finally abandoned altogether on 27 November of that year.[53] No later records contain any mention of the projected society of the Round Table, and there is no reason to believe that it was ever effectively established.

None of the sources gives any specific reason for the abandonment of the Round Table project as a whole, but Walsingham suggested that the construction of the round hall in Windsor Castle was halted because the king needed to use the money being spent on it for other, more pressing purposes. These purposes were undoubtedly related to the war with France, which took an unexpected turn in March 1344 when the King of France, Philippe VI, bestowed the Duchy of Guyenne – Edward's principal French dominion – along with the adjacent County of Poitiers upon his eldest son, Jean, already Duke of Normandy and Count of Anjou and Maine.[54] Edward was obliged to send the Earls of Derby and Arundel to Guyenne shortly after that, and in the summer of 1345 he himself led an expedition to Flanders and sent large armies under the Earls of Derby and Northampton to shore up the English position in Guyenne and Brittany repectively. The death of Edward's chief political ally in Flanders obliged him to return to England shortly after his arrival there, but he spent the next several months preparing to lead an even larger force to the aid of the armies already in France. The fleet that was to carry this army to France was originally to have assembled at Portsmouth by 16 February 1346, but various factors postponed the sailing to the beginning of July. The king thus had little time or money for such projects as the restoration of the Round Table between March 1344 and the beginning of what was to be remembered as the Crécy Campaign in July 1346. Indeed, despite his love for tournaments, it is not clear that he took part in a single one in the four years between January 1344 and January 1348.[55] It may be, therefore, that Edward at first intended merely to postpone the refoundation of the Round Table until the

[49] Ibid., pp. 109–10.
[50] *Edward III*, p. 67.
[51] See Barber, *Edward*, p. 43.
[52] Ibid., p. 44.
[53] Colvin, *King's Works*, p. 871.
[54] The charters effecting these creations appear to have been lost, but see Paris, A.N., JJ 68, no. 100, and Françoise Lehoux, *Jean de France, duc de Berri* (4 vols., Paris, 1966–8), t. I, p. 11, n. 1.
[55] See the provisional list of tournaments held in England during his reign prepared by Juliet Vale, in *Edward III*, pp. 172–4. Barber, (*Edward*, pp. 45–6) maintained that Edward and eleven of his chamber knights took part in a tournament at Lichfield on 9 April 1346, but Vale seems to have concluded that this tournament was not in fact held until April 1348. (List, p. 174.)

political and economic situation was more propitious. If this is true it is entirely possible that the garter and St George displaced the Round Table and King Arthur in Edward's project only gradually, and in several distinct stages, between 1344 and 1348.

Nicolas demonstrated in 1846 that the earliest references to the garter as a device are to be found in a roll of issues from and purchases into the royal wardrobe, drawn up under the clerkship of John Cook between 29 September 1347 and 31 January 1349.[56] Nicolas believed that this roll dealt only with issues and purchases made during the period in which it was composed, and accordingly dated the first reference to garters in the list of issues to the autumn of 1347,[57] but Juliet Vale has recently demonstrated that the roll in question incorporated a number of records drawn up in earlier years as well, including one explicitly stated to have been begun on 21 December 1345.[58] The record in which the first reference to garters occurs – a long list of materials issued from the great wardrobe to the king's armourer John of Cologne – was almost certainly incorporated in this fashion, but as it has no heading indicating either the time or the circumstances in which the issues were made, it is impossible to fix the date on which the garters were issued on the basis of internal evidence alone.

The first of the entries in Cologne's account to mention the garter device reads as follows:

> For making two streamers of worsted, that is to say one of arms quarterly, and the other of arms quarterly with the image of St Lawrence worked in the head of one white pale, powdered with blue garters (*garteriis bluettis*); ...[59]

Nicolas argued from the presence on this streamer of an image of St Lawrence that Edward probably adopted the garter as a temporary device to be worn at a tournament held on St Lawrence's Day (10 August) 1348,[60] but Vale demonstrated that, as the streamer in question was to have required more than sixteen times the amount allotted in the same account to large standards, it must have been intended for a ship (possibly called the *Lawrence*), and could not therefore have been used at a tournament. She argued further from the fact that the streamer in question was issued at the same time as a very large number of pennons and standards that it could only have been intended for use during a major military campaign in France, and that as the only campaign of that scale in which Edward himself took part in the period of three or four years before 31 January 1349 (when Cook's roll was finished) was the Crécy Campaign that began in July 1346, the garter must have been adopted by Edward as a royal device specifically for that campaign.[61]

The record of issues to John of Cologne contains several other references to items powdered with garters, all intended for the king's personal use: a bed of blue taffeta;

[56] 'Observations', p. 119. Most of the relevant parts of this roll were published by Nicolas, ibid., pp. 5–103.

[57] Ibid., p. 116.

[58] *Edward III*, p. 78.

[59] Quoted in Latin in Vale, *Edward III*, p. 79.

[60] 'Observations', p. 127.

[61] Vale, *Edward III*, pp. 77–81.

a mantle, supertunic, tunic, and hood of blue cloth (bearing a total of 168 garters); a jupon of blue taffeta (bearing 62 garters); and a jupon of blue satin (also bearing 62 garters). The garters on the bed, at least, were to have borne the famous legend *Hony soit qui mal y pense.*[62] Vale has argued convincingly that every one of these items could just as easily have been used during a military campaign as on the occasion of a tournament, and has suggested that both the wording of the verbal *devise* and the fact that – unlike all of Edward's other mottoes – it was expressed in French, made it highly appropriate for a campaign in which Edward was seeking to vindicate his right to the throne of France. She concluded that the signal victory won by Edward's forces at Crécy on 16 August 1346, which not only exonerated all of his actions in his cause, but gave moral justification to every participant, 'prompted Edward to make the device he had adopted for the campaign the basis for an order of chivalry. It was an act of complex motiviation: a pious act of thanksgiving; a fitting reward for those who had served him outstandingly in the battle; but also a means of enshrining in perpetuity the symbol of his vindicated claim.'[63]

The only difficulty I have with this theory is that it does not attempt to deal with the meaning of the garter upon which the motto was inscribed, and ignores completely the possiblility that the garter may have been intended from the moment of its adoption by Edward to serve as the badge of a society of knights. Vale's avoidance of this issue is not surprising, for contemporary sources contain no suggestion of why Edward adopted a garter as a device, and most earlier historians of the Order were concerned primarily with casting doubt upon the story recorded nearly two centuries later by Polydore Vergil, in which Edward is said to have picked up a garter dropped by a lady of his court.[64] The only alternative explanation of the garter proposed until very recently is that it was a sort of knot meant to symbolize the ties of loyalty and affection that bound the companions of the Order, but it is much more likely – as I shall attempt to demonstrate below– that the garter was inspired by the essentially similar device of the Castilian order of the Band, and was chosen because it was an obsolescent item of male attire that would be distsinctive when worn. If this was the case – and I shall present below the arguments in favour of this explanation[65] – then it is all but certain that Edward intended from the first to make the garter the device of his proposed society of knights. It is even possible that he intended to make it the device of the proposed society of the Round Table, for the 'historic' Round Table had no device, and the garter had nothing to do with St George.

Unfortunately, we are very ill-informed about the earliest stages of the history of the Order of the Garter as such. Contemporary chroniclers (perhaps distracted by the Black Death, which ravaged England from the summer of 1348 to the autumn of 1349)[66] failed to notice its proclamation, and as the accounts of the great wardrobe covering the period between January 1349 and 1361 have been lost, we are obliged to rely on the far less detailed accounts of the chamber,[67] and those of

---

[62] Nicolas, 'Observations', pp. 119–120.
[63] Vale, *Edward III*, pp. 81–2.
[64] See below, pp. 154–155.
[65] See below, pp. 157–158.
[66] Philip Ziegler, *The Black Death* (London, 1969), pp. 120ff.
[67] On which see Vale, *Edward III*, p. 82.

the household of Edward's eldest son the Prince of Wales, for information about the Order during most of the crucial period between the return of Edward to England following the capture of Calais in the autumn of 1347 and the first recorded meeting of the Order on 23 April 1350. In fact there is no further reference in any surviving record either to a society of knights associated with the English court or to the garter device in the period between Edward's invasion of France in July 1346 and the winter of 1348, by which time the new order had in all probability been proclaimed.

It is unlikely Edward devoted much time to his project to create a knightly society while he was still in France. There is reason to believe, however, that his decision to create an order in the form of a devotional confraternity may have been inspired by what he learned during his stay in France about a society of knights proclaimed by the eldest son of the French king, Duke Jean of Normandy, within months of his own proclamation of January 1344. This society was initially to have been a 'congregation' of 200 lay knights who were to assemble at least twice a year on the feasts of its patron saints the Blessed Virgin Mary and George the Martyr at a collegiate church dedicated to those saints served by twenty-four priests, twelve canons and twelve vicars, and set aside for the exclusive use of the society.[68] It is not clear just how far the Duke of Normandy had progressed in his project by the time he came to the throne as King Jean II in 1350, but it seems reasonable to assume that Edward heard something about it while he was in Normandy, and it is unlikely to have been purely coincidental that the society he founded within a year of his return was a confraternity of knights under the patronage of St George and the Blessed Virgin Mary, and attached initially to a chapel newly dedicated to these saints, served by twenty-four priests, twelve canons and twelve vicars, and set aside for the exclusive use of the society.

A phrase in the papal letters confirming the Duke of Normandy's projected society suggests one possible reason for Edward's abandonment of his original plan to refound the Round Table. The duke's projected society was permitted to meet only for devotion to the society's church, and 'not for jousts or tournaments or for any other act of arms', and it may well be that Edward received a cool response from the papal curia – traditionally hostile to all martial sports – to his own project, which as we have seen may well have been meant to be a tournament society.

Edward returned to London in triumph on 14 October 1347, and seems to have spent most of the next twelve months celebrating his victories with pleasurable activities. Between January and November 1348 (when he returned briefly to Calais) he staged at least six tournaments, at Reading, at Bury St Edmund's, at Lichfield, at Eltham, and at Canterbury. It is more than likely that he announced his newly-revised plan to establish a small society of knights distinguished by the garter device at one of these tournaments, just as he had proclaimed his intention to refound the Round Table in similar circumstances four years earlier, but there is only one reference to garters in any document certainly referring to the year 1348, and it contains no suggestion that the garter had become the badge of a body of knights. The roll of payments from the wardrobe cited above records that twelve garters bearing the famous motto were provided for the Eltham tournament,[69]

---

[68] On this society, see below, pp. 174–7.
[69] Nicolas, 'Observations', pp. 40–1.

probably held in the early summer just before the onset of the Black Death.[70] Nicolas thought that these were intended for distribution to the twelve knights of a tournament team that gradually evolved into the Order of the Garter,[71] but Juliet Vale has recently shown that they were in fact to be used to decorate a single robe worn by Edward himself.[72] The next reference to garters occurs in a record of gifts made by the Prince of Wales in a rather vaguely defined period prior to 31 January 1349, submitted in 1352 by William de Northwell, then the treasurer of the Prince's household and formerly the keeper of his wardrobe.[73] According to this record, on 18 December 1348 the Prince purchased a 'plate, gilt and enamelled, of the company of the Garter' to present to William de Stafford, Herald of Arms of Alvan, and 'twenty-four garters' to present to 'the knights of the company of the Garter'.[74] This is the earliest known reference to a 'company' of knights taking its name from the garter device, and it has been used to argue that the Order of the Garter was given a definitive form by the middle of December 1348. Juliet Vale, however, has demonstrated that the list of expenditures in this account is very confused, so that the date in question could well be off by a year in either direction.[75]

The best evidence that Edward did in fact decide the final form the Order of the Garter was to take before the end of 1348 is to be found in letters patent issued under his name and seal on 6 August of that year, reoganizing the foundation of what was to be the Order's chapel, along lines that were clearly related to the form of the Order ultimately established.[76] The chapel of Windsor Castle, erected by Henry I and dedicated to St Edward the Confessor, was by these letters rededicated to the Blessed Virgin Mary and St George, in addition to its original patron. The same document increased its foundation from eight to twenty-four secular priests (including a *custos* or warden), and twenty-four *milites pauperes*, or 'poor knights', and various other ministers. The number of the canons and poor knights called for in this charter was identical to the number of knights in the 'company of the Garter' mentioned in the register of the Prince of Wales cited above, just as it was to remain until the reforms of Henry VIII, and there can be little doubt that by the time the charter was composed the final form the Order was to take had been decided upon, if not actually established. By the same charter Edward gave the new College of St George's (as it came to be called) an endowment of £1000 and the advowsons of the churches of Wraysbury, South Tawton, and Uttoxeter, and Juliet Vale has argued from the fact that the last two advowsons belonged to the Earls of Warwick and Derby respectively that those earls at least must have been informed of their inclusion in the Order by August 1348.[77]

Even though Edward probably proclaimed the new form of his knightly society and the names of its first twenty-four companions at some time in the spring or

[70] Vale, *Edward III*, p. 82.
[71] Nicolas, *History*, p. 12.
[72] *Edward III*, p. 82.
[73] *Register of Edward the Black Prince*, 4 vols. (London, 1930–3).
[74] Ibid., IV, pp. 72–3.
[75] *Edward III*, pp. 85–6.
[76] CPR 1348–50, p. 144. Published in Ashmole, *Garter*, p. [758].
[77] *Edward III*, p. 83.

summer of 1348, there is nothing to indicate that the Order of the Garter existed as a formally constituted body before the following year. In terms of the definition we have established for a true order of knighthood, the definitive establishment of the Order must be regarded as having taken place on the day when the original statutes were adopted and sworn to by the first companions. The only direct evidence we have for this is a statement found in the prologue attached to all but one of the surviving redactions of the statutes.[78] According to this prologue the Order was founded in the twenty-third year of Edward's reign – that is to say, in the period between 25 January 1349 and 24 January 1350. Juliet Vale has adduced previously neglected entries in the account of John of Cologne and in the accounts of the royal chamber which suggest that a formal meeting of the Order was indeed convened in this period, in conjunction with a tournament held at Windsor on 23 April 1349.[79] Since one of the knights listed among the original companions of the Order in the prologues to the statutes died by 2 September 1349, and two of the others seem to have died at some time during the course of the same year (probably victims of the Black Death), the Order must have been formally constituted before the end of August 1349, and in all likelihood the tournament held at Windsor on St George's Day of that year – for which twenty-four robes powdered with garters were issued along with matching altar-hangings for the chapel[80] – served as the occasion for the promulgation of the statutes and the induction of the first companions.

The first meeting of the Order to be noticed by a contemporary chronicler was that of 23 April 1350. Geoffrey le Baker, writing within a decade of the event,[81] described it in the following terms:

> In this year [1350] on St George's Day, the king held a great feast at Windsor, in the castle, where he had instituted a chantry (*cantariam*) of twelve priests, and founded an almshouse (*zenodochium*) in which impoverished knights, whose own goods were not sufficient for them, could have in the service of the Lord an adequate sustenance from the perpetual alms of the founders of the College. Others besides the king were co-participants in the foundation of this almshouse, namely the king's eldest son, the Earl of Northampton, the Earl of Warwick, the Earl of Suffolk, the Earl of Salisbury, and other barons, as well as simple knights, namely Roger de Mortimer, now Earl of March, Sir Walter de Mauny, Sir William FitzWaryn, John de Lisle, John de Mohun, John de Beauchamp, Walter de Paveley, Thomas Wale, and Hugh de Wrottesley, whose great ability associated them with the said earls. These men were all vested, together with the king, in surcoats (*togis*) of russet powdered with garters of a dark blue (*indie*) colour, with similar garters on their right [*sic*] calves, and mantles of blue (*blueto*) with little shields of the arms of St George. In this costume, with bare heads they heard with devotion a solemn mass sung by the bishops of Canterbury, Winchester, and Exeter,

---

[78] See below, p. 120.
[79] *Edward III*, pp. 83–4.
[80] Ibid.
[81] His chronicle was finished in 1360.

and sat together at a common table, to the honour of the holy martyr to whom the noble fraternity was especially dedicated, calling their company 'St George de la Gartiere'.[82]

Le Baker's account is not entirely accurate,[83] but it does give us a contemporary impression of the nature of the Order and its activities. It is not without significance that he saw the knights of the Garter primarily as the co-founders of what he called a 'chantry' and an almshouse rather than as the members of a new form of knightly order. Other chroniclers (including Froissart) took note of a few later meetings of particular magnificence, but most of what is known about the Order during the following sixty-five years of its history is derived from references in the accounts of the wardrobe and the records of the remembrancers of the current king and queen to the purchase or issue of items of clothing provided for its annual festivities.[84] These records are themselves far from complete, but they do indicate that the annual meeting of the Order was held in most years, at least,[85] between 1350 and 1415, and provide much useful information not only about the habit of the Order but about the changes in its membership during this period. For the activities of the Order after 1415 we have the rather fuller records contained in the earliest surviving register of the Order. At the time Ashmole wrote his famous history of the Order, what was probably the original of this register – a paper codex entitled *Registrum Ordinis Chartaceum* – was still preserved in the Paper Office in Whitehall, but this has since been lost.[86] Fortunately, its contents were copied around 1534 (apparently with only minor alterations) by the Order's current Registrar, Robert Aldridge, into a new register, and this volume (which has come to known as the 'Black Book' of the Order) is still kept in Windsor Castle.[87] Although full of *lacunae*, particularly during the reigns of Richard III and Henry VII, the Black Book contains minutes of most of the chapters held between 1416 and 1509, (both regular and irregular), and provides us with information that would otherwise be lost about elections, degradations, and amendments to the statutes adopted at particular meetings. When it is supplemented with other, strictly contemporary records, it permits us to know considerably more about the activities of the Order of the Garter in the fifteenth century than we know about those of any other contemporary order except the Golden Fleece.

---

[82] Galfridi le Baker de Swynebroke, *Chronicon*, ed. E. Maunde Thompson (Oxford, 1889), pp. 108–9.

[83] See Barber, *Edward*, p. 84.

[84] These are listed in Beltz, *Memorials*, 'Annals of the Order', pp. 2ff.

[85] All but the following seventeen years are accounted for: 1351–2, 1354–7, 1359, 1365–69, 1380–81, 1383, 1385, 1391.

[86] Ashmole, *Institution*, pp. 198–9.

[87] Windsor Aerary MS. G1, published by J. Anstis, *The Register of the Most Noble Order of the Garter . . . called the Black Book*, 2 vols. (London, 1724). Nicolas made extensive use of this document in his *History* of the Order. See also E. Auerbach, 'The Black Book of the Garter', *Report of the Society of the Friends of St George's*, v, no. 4 (1972–3), pp. 149–53, Pls. 1–9 (Windsor, 1975).

3 The Statutes of the Order

The master copy of the original statutes of the Order of the Garter, probably promulgated as we have seen on 23 April 1349, seems to have been lost along with the rest of the Order's official records early in the fifteenth century, and despite the fact that a copy of the statutes was supposed to have been given to each companion for his own use shortly after his election,[88] and returned by his heirs to the College of St George's shortly after his death,[89] no copy dating from the fourteenth century is known to have survived.

Six distinct redactions of the statutes, however, are (or were) preserved in manuscripts of the fifteenth and early sixteenth centuries, three of them exclusively in Latin, the others primarily in French. The French redactions all include the amendments to the statutes adopted (according to the Black Book) in 1418 and 1421, but these amendments are all lacking in the three Latin redactions, and the latter may reasonably be assumed to represent stages in the development of the statutes prior to the commencement of the lost *Registrum Ordinis Chartaceum* in 1416. The first Latin redaction (which we shall call redaction A) was in fact uniquely preserved in that register, from which it was copied by Ashmole and published in the Appendix to his history of the Order.[90] The second Latin redaction (which we shall call redaction B) was similarly published by Ashmole[91] on the basis of a transcription of an otherwise unidentified manuscript then in the private collection of the famous antiquarian Lord Hatton.[92] It is now preserved in two fifteenth-century manuscripts: a small vellum codex now called *Carte et Statuta Ordinis Garterii*, containing nothing but official documents pertaining to the Order copied in a rapid courthand of the early fifteenth century;[93] and an heraldic miscellany now called *Le Droit d'Armes*, written in a semi-formal courthand of the mid fifteenth century.[94] The third Latin redaction (C) is preserved exclusively in the Black Book of the Order, where it replaces redaction A.

The three Latin redactions differ relatively little from one another in either content or organization, but all three express the same ideas in very different words. The differences in phraseology between A and B, at least, can best be explained as the results of independent translations into Latin from original texts in French —

[88] Ord. A.27a.

[89] Ord. A.27c

[90] *Institution*, pp. [721–5]. (Ashmole failed to number the pages of the lengthy Appendix to his history.)

[91] Ibid., pp. [725–29].

[92] I have as yet been unable to identify this manuscript. It is not in the Bodleian, where most of Hatton's antiquarian collection was deposited after his death, and if it is not identical with B.L., Add. MS. 28,549, it may be among the Hatton manuscripts now in the Northamptonshire Record Society.

[93] B.L., Harley MS. 564, ff. 15r–22r. No earlier historian of the Order seems to have been aware of this manuscript, which is probably the oldest surviving document of a quasi-official nature related to the Order.

[94] B.L., Add. MS. 28,549, ff. 64r–79r. The statutes of the Garter contained in this manuscript (which may be the Hatton manuscript used by Ashmole), were probably copied from Harley 564, possibly at the behest of Garter King of Arms.

which at the time the Order was founded was still the vernacular of the royal court and much of the English knightly class, and was to remain the aulic language of chivalry in England until late in the fifteenth century. All three translations were probably made by canons of St George's serving as Registrar of the Order. Redaction A was probably Latinized by John Corringham, Canon and Registrar from 1414 to 1445,[95] since it is the version included in the register of that period. Redaction C, which is expressed in a much more classical form of Latin than the other two versions, may well represent a translation of A into a more acceptable form of the same language by Robert Aldridge, who as we have seen transcribed Corringham's register into the Black Book around 1534. Certainly C contains exactly the same ordinances as A (albeit arranged in a slightly different order),[96] and must represent a French original dating from the same general period. Redaction B may have been translated (possibly from the master copy) by Corringham's immediate predecessor as Registrar, since it is written in an early fifteenth-century hand and preserved in a quasi-official register (the *Carte et Statuta* referred to above) that includes documents from the reigns of Richard II and Henry IV. The division of chapters is slightly different in redactions A and B,[97] but the content of B differs from that of A only in including an additional chapter (numbered as B.33), and since this does not correspond with any of those amendments recorded in the Black Book as having been adopted in or after 1418, it was probably adopted before that date. On the other hand, as redaction A was probably copied into Corringham's lost *Registrum Ordinis Chartaceum* in or about 1416 (possibly before the meeting of that year), it is likely that chapter B.33 was adopted not long before that, for otherwise it would have been added to the copy of the statutes Corringham used as the basis of his translation (probably one recently returned to the College by a companion who had died) after the loss of the earlier registers. Thus in all likelihood redaction B represents the state of the statutes at or shortly after the beginning of the reign of Henry V (who succeeded his father Henry IV on 21 March 1413). The French original of A and C must have been in effect immediately before chapter B.33 was adopted, and was probably the version current during all or most of the reign of Henry IV at least, and possibly during much of the reign of Richard II as well.

---

[95] Ashmole, *Institution*, p. 198.

[96] The organization of C differs from that of A and B in that the material included in chs. A.6 and 7 is placed at the very end in one chapter, C.34, and the last ordinance of A.13 is separated from the corresponding ch. C.11 and numbered as C.12. The latter division is also found in all other fifteenth-century redactions. The two chapters placed at the end logically belong where they are found in all the other redactions, and there is no reason to suppose that they were added after the promulgation of the original statutes, so the most logical explanation for their position in C is that Aldridge simply left out chs. 6 and 7 when he was retranslating the statutes on the basis of A, and rather than acknowledge his error, put them in a renumbered chapter at the end. This version of the statutes was no longer in effect at the time he transferred it into his register, so the renumbering would have had no practical consequences.

[97] The material contained in B is arranged in exactly the same order as that in A, but the ordinances contained in ch. A.13 are divided in B (as in all later redactions) between two chapters, 13 and 14, so that all subsequent chapters are numbered one (and after ch. 33 two) higher than the corresponding chapters in redaction A. B thus has a total of 36 chapters while A and C have only 34.

Redaction A must therefore be regarded as the earliest surviving version of the statutes of the Order. Like most later versions, it begins with a short prologue:

To the honour of Almighty God, the Glorious Virgin Saint Mary, and Saint George the Martyr, our sovereign lord Edward, the third after the Conquest, King of England, in the twenty-third year of his reign, ordained, established and founded a certain knightly society or order (*societatem sive ordinem militarem*)[98] in his castle of Windsor, in the following fashion. First, himself, Sovereign, his eldest son the Prince of Wales, the Duke of Lancaster, the Earl of Warwick, the Captal of Buch, the Earl of Stafford, the Earl of Salisbury, the Lord of Mortimer, Sir John Lisle, Sir Bartholomew de Burgersh the son, Sir John de Beauchamp, the Lord of Mohun, Sir Hugh de Courtenay, Sir Thomas de Holand, Sir John de Grey, Sir Richard FitzSimon, Sir Miles Stapleton, Sir Thomas Wale, Sir Hugh de Wrottesley, Sir Nele Loring, Sir John Chandos, Sir James d'Audley, Sir Otes de Holand, Sir Henry d'Enne, Sir Sanchet d'Abrichecourt, Sir Walter de Pavely.[99]

The prologue is followed by 34 chapters, most beginning with the word *Item*, and distinguished in most manuscripts with marginal numerals. The chapters include a total of 138 distinct ordinances, which are not distinguished in any way in the text. The first seven chapters (which include seventeen ordinances) deal with the membership of the Order in the broadest sense – including not only the companions but the canons and poor knights of St George's College – and describe their respective qualifications, functions, and costumes. The next seven chapters, 8 through 14 (which include twenty-five ordinances), deal with the various activities which were to take place during the Order's annual St George's Day Assembly at Windsor Castle, while chapters 15 and 16 (containing nine ordinances) set forth the obligations of the knights when they came to Windsor on other occasions. Chapters 17 through 25 (comprising fifty-six ordinances) are concerned with matters arising from the death of one of the companions, specifically the singing of masses for his soul (ten ordinances), the setting up of a memorial plaque in his stall (two ordinances), and the election and installation of his successor (respectively twelve and thirty-two ordinances). Chapters 26 to 30 (containing seventeen ordinances) deal with a variety of matters, for the most part related to the use of the Order's common seal, but including the mutual obligations of the Sovereign and the companions. Finally, chapters 31 to 34 (containing fourteen ordinances) are concerned with miscellaneous questions of especial concern to the canons: the right of a companion to live in the Order's house, the right of non-members of the Order to be included in the daily prayers of the canons, the procedure for nominating the successor of a canon who died while the Sovereign was abroad, and the appointment and duties of the canon-Registrar.[100]

---

[98] The French version substitutes for these words the single word *compaignie*.

[99] Ashmole, *Institution*, p. [721]. Nicolas (*History*, p. 24) believed that the Order was founded by letters patent, and if this was the case, this very short prologue may well be a synopsis in the third person of the prologue to the original letters, now lost.

[100] For a fuller summary of the early statutes in English, see Nicolas, *History*, vol. I, pp. 26–31.

How closely redaction A resembles the original version of the statutes, presumably adopted in 1349, it is impossible to say with any certainty. The fact that its ordinances not only reflect what we know of the practices of the Order in the first half-century of its history, however, but consistently refer to the founding knights listed in the prologue as if they were still alive,[101] suggests that the statutes were never subjected to a thorough revision in this period, and that the amendments which were almost certainly adopted from time to time between 1349 and 1416 were for the most part simply interpolated into the existing chapters without altering their wording, just as they would be in the fifteenth and subsequent centuries. Some of the amendments can be at least tentatively identified on the basis of internal evidence. The prologue with which A and every other surviving redaction except C begins was clearly added (or altered) at some time in or after 1351, since Henry 'of Grosmont' and Ralph Stafford are listed therein by the titles Duke of Lancaster and Earl of Stafford, which they only received from Edward in 1351, but as Roger de Mortimer is not called Earl of March, it is likely that the list was composed in its present form before the spring of 1354, when he was restored to his grandfather's title. It is quite possible that the last four chapters were similarly added at some time after the original statutes were adopted, since they deal with a miscellany of questions of the sort that only arise once an organization is actually functioning. Finally, there are statements in chapters 10 and 12 of redaction B which suggest that those chapters contain added ordinances.[102]

Very few amendments were made to the statutes of the Order during the course of the period between the commencement of the register in 1416 and the accession of Henry VIII in 1506, and those that were added merely clarified or modified in some minor way the established usages of the Order, without in any way affecting its fundamental nature or the obligations of its companions. As we have seen, an ordinance was adopted at a Chapter held around the time of the accession of Henry V, and added to the statutes between chs. 31 and 32 as a separate chapter, numbered (because of the division of ch. 13) 33.[103] The Black Book records that an ordinance was added to ch. 3 in 1418,[104] and that one further ordinance was added to each of eight chapters (A.3, 8, 9, 12, 14, 20, 30, and 32) at the Chapter held in 1421.[105] The earliest surviving version of the statutes preserved in French, which we shall call redaction D, differs from redaction B only in incorporating these additional ordinances. The master of this version (commonly called the statutes of Henry V) is again lost, but Ashmole published its text on the basis of a roll then in

---

[101] E.g., in ch. 3.

[102] Ashmole (*Institution*, p. 191) pointed out that B.10 contains a reference to a 'decree extant', and B.12 a reference to an established custom of the order. Although these statements are peculiar to redaction B, the ordinances with which they are associated are actually common to all three Latin redactions.

[103] This ordinance permitted knights who were not members of the Order to reside at the Order's seat.

[104] See Anstis, *Register*, II, pp. 76–7; Nicolas, *History*, I, pp. 58–9. This ordinance required the companions, when entering and leaving St George's chapel or descending from the altar, to make obeisance to the Sovereign or his stall.

[105] See Anstis, *Register*, II, pp. 77–80; Nicolas, *History*, I, pp. 61–3.

the possession of the Earl of Denbigh,[106] and I have found copies of it in three fifteenth-century manuscripts. The oldest of these is probably the copy once owned by Cotton, which seems to date from the early part of the reign of Henry VI,[107] but a copy has also been preserved in a chivalric miscellany probably presented to Marguerite of Anjou on the occasion of her marriage to that king on 23 April 1445,[108] and another copy is to be found in the same late-fifteenth-century heraldic miscellany that contains a copy of Latin redaction B.[109] The variations among the texts contained in these four manuscripts are quite minor, and all but the third preserve the organization into 36 chapters first found in redaction B. A slightly different version of the statutes (E) with 37 chapters is preserved in two heraldic miscellanies of the later fifteenth century; in one it is expressed in French,[110] in the other in English.[111] Finally, there is a version (F) with 41 chapters, preserved in French in an heraldic miscellany of about 1460 once in the collection of Ashmole himself.[112] None of these seems to incorporate the five resolutions adopted at the Assembly of 1423, immediately following the accession of Henry VI,[113] or the seven additional ordinances adopted in 1488, shortly after the accession of Henry VII.[114] The language of the various redactions of the statutes preserved in French differs much less from one version to another than that of the Latin versions, and as it continues to refer to the founders as if they were still alive, it is very likely that the French of the fifteenth-century manuscripts is essentially the same as that of the original version of the statutes.

Ten years after his accession to the throne, at the Assembly held in May 1519, Henry VIII promulgated a whole series of amendments to the statutes as they then stood, adding several wholly new chapters and adding new ordinances to a dozen existing ones.[115] Like those adopted in the fifteenth century, however, most of these amendments merely clarified or put into writing traditional practices, and the few that were truly novel seem to have been introduced primarily to bring the usages of the Order in line with those of the illustrious Burgundian order of the Golden Fleece.[116] Henry's version of the statutes is still officially in effect, though various amendments adopted during the nearly five centuries since its adoption have changed the structure and activities of the Order in a number of important ways. With these, however, we are not here concerned.

---

[106] I have not yet identified this manuscript.

[107] B.L., Cotton MS. Nero D.II.

[108] B.L., Royal MS. 15 E VI, ff. 439–40 (numbered 486–7).

[109] B.L., Add. MS. 28,549, ff. 81r–95v.

[110] B.L., Add. MS. 34,801, ff. 19r–8r.

[111] B.L., Stowe MS. 668, ff. 82r–88v.

[112] Oxford, Bodl., Ashmole MS. 764, ff. 123r–136v. Ch. 40 of this corresponds to D.36.

[113] Anstis, Register, II, pp. 84–7; Nicolas, History, I, p. 67. Some of these were too specific to be incorporated into the statutes in any case.

[114] Anstis, Register, II, p. 230; Nicolas, History, I, p. 111.

[115] Fourteen of the thirty-eight chapters in the statutes of Henry VIII are wholly new or contain at least one new ordinance. See Ashmole, Institution, p. 193, for a summary of the changes.

[116] Nicolas published an edition of the English version of the statutes of Henry VIII in his History, I, pp. 135–56.

4 *The Name and Title of the Order*

Unlike the Order of the Band, the society of knights which eventually came to be called the Order of the Garter was at first referred to by a bewildering variety of names and corporate titles. We have already seen that the *milites de Societate Garterii* or 'knights of the Society of the Garter' were first mentioned in the register of the Black Prince in an entry probably datable to November 1348. An entry in the register of the great wardrobe, probably written early in 1349, refers to the king's *societate . . . de Garteris*, or 'Society of the Garters'.[117] Two entries in the register of the wardrobe recording expenditures made for the feast of St George held at Windsor in 1353 refer to the 'Order' quite simply.[118] According to Geoffrey le Baker, the 'noble fraternity' founded by Edward was called the *comitivam sancti Georgii de la gartiere*, or 'Company of St George of the Garter'. Froissart refers to it both as the 'Confraternity of St George' and as an 'order of knights' called 'the knights of the blue Garter'. In a letter written in 1377, the companion Enguerrand de Coucy calls it *la tres noble Compaignie et Ordre du Jartier*.[119]

These are all somewhat informal references, to be sure, but the oldest surviving official documents of the Order are scarcely more consistent. The prologue of redaction A of the statutes refers to the establishment of a *societas sive ordo militaris* (a 'knightly society or order'), and chapter 1 of that redaction designates it more specifically *Ordo Sancti Georgii sive Societas Garterii* – 'the Order of St George or Society of the Garter'. *Ordo* or 'order' is the usual term in the body of the statutes of A, but *societas sive ordo* is commonly written throughout. The prologue of redaction B calls it simply a *societas*, but in the text it is usually termed a *comitiva* or 'company', less commonly an *ordo*, and occasionally *Ordo Garterii* or *Ordo Sancti Georgii*. In the French of redaction D the Order is designated both *compagnie* and *ordre*, and the companions are referrred to collectively as the *Chevaliers de St George de la Compagnie du Gartier*.

It would thus appear that throughout the first century or so of the Order's history it was called 'order', 'society', and 'company' in more or less random alternation, and that each of these titles could be used in conjunction with the name either of its badge or of its heavenly patron, or both at the same time, to designate the Order as a corporate body. The titles 'company' and 'society' and the use of the name of the patron saint in the corporate style were all characteristic of confraternities in general, but the style 'Order of the Garter' which ultimately prevailed as the normal and official designation for the society was almost certainly inspired by that of the Castilian Order of the Band – the first and only existing lay society to use the title 'order' and the first society of any type to take its name from its badge. Edward may have felt a little less sure than Alfonso about the propriety of calling his confraternity an 'order', and covered himself by adopting in addition a more traditional form of corporate designation.

---

117 Vale, *Edward III*, p. 83.
118 Beltz, *Memorials*, p. 4.
119 Nicolas, *History*, I, p. 43, n. 1.

5 *The Patron of the Order: St George*

In possessing a patron at all the Order of the Garter differed significantly from its Castilian model, so the question of why Edward chose to place his Order under the protection of St George is of considerable interest. There is no indication that Edward's projected Round Table society was to have had any patron but the shade of Arthur, and the first indication that the revised version of the society was to be placed under the patronage of the soldier-martyr St George is to be found in the letters patent of August 1348 rededicating the chapel of St Edward the Confessor to the Blessed Virgin and St George in addition to the English saint. As we noted above, this additional dedication was identical with that of the chapel that was to have been the devotional centre of the society of knights proclaimed by Edward's rival, Duke Jean of Normandy, in the winter of 1344. It is thus very likely that both the specific dedication and the whole idea of centring the activities of the Order on the cult of a saint in the fashion of confraternities were borrowed by Edward from that as yet uncompleted project, with the outline of which he was probably familiar by the time he returned to England in the autumn of 1347. Certainly when Jean finally established his order in 1352, it was dedicated to the Virgin alone, and the most plausible explanation of this change is that Edward had in the meantime expropriated the patronage of St George.[120] It is also possible, of course, that Edward had heard by 1347 of the Hungarian Society of St George, founded more than twenty years earlier, but about this one can only speculate.

The appeal of the warrior saint George had already been felt by Edward's grandfather Edward I, who had begun both the practice of displaying the banner of St George (a red cross on a white field) with those of the English royal saints, Edmund the Martyr and Edward the Confessor, and the practice of displaying the arms of St George (derived from the banner) on the surcoats of his soldiers.[121] Thus St George – by 1325 commonly regarded as the heavenly protector of knighthood in general – had long been regarded as a patron of English arms in particular when Edward III decided to place his new society under the protection of a saint rather than a legendary king. One of Edward's reasons for preferring George to Arthur may have been the simple fact that, as a member of the court of heaven, George was in a better position to give his enterprises active assistance. St George could also serve as the object of a cult in a way that Arthur could not, and gave Edward an excuse to transfer the centre of his proposed society's activities from a huge round hall as yet unbuilt to a small chapel which needed only to be refurbished.

The cult of St George within the Order of the Garter took a number of forms. The Order was of course alternatively named after the saint, and his arms (and later his image) formed part of its insignia. The Order also met annually on his feast day (which had never been solemnly celebrated in the English court before 1349), attended a solemn mass in his honour in a chapel dedicated principally to him, and

---

[120] See below, p. 189.
[121] See F. L. Cross, E. A. Livingston, eds., *The Oxford Dictionary of the Christian Church* (2nd edn., London, 1974), p. 557.

dined afterwards in a hall likewise named in his honour. As a symbol of the Order, however, St George appears to have been rather less prominent than the garter, for his ensigns were worn only on feast days, while the garter was worn all the time.

6 *The Members of the Order: The Sovereign*

According to its statutes, the Order of the Garter was to consist of a chief officer with the title *Souverain* (in French) or *Superior* (in Latin), a college of twenty-six eminent knights (including the *Souverain*) termed *compagnons* or *consocii*, a college of twenty-six secular priests, and a college of twenty-six poor veteran knights.

Edward seems to have felt even more hesitant about the propriety of adopting the title 'master' for himself and his successors as president than about his assignment of the title 'order' to his society, for he adopted instead a title never previously used by the head of any known body. Edward's choice of the title *Souverain* for this purpose is suggestive, for although it was still a generic term meaning something like 'superior', it had already become a term of political currency roughly equivalent to its modern English derivative 'sovereign', and thus had a distinctly monarchical ring to it. The office itself was certainly monarchical in the sense in which we are employing that word, for chapter 1 of the statutes clearly states that the office of *Souverain* or 'Sovereign' (as it has traditionally been called in English) was to be perpetually annexed the the kingship of England. Although the office is not defined in the statutes, its dignity and authority within the Order are quickly apparent. The Sovereign, aside from appointing the original twenty-six companions, also had the right to appoint all but the first twenty-six clerks and all but the first twenty-six veteran knights. He was further to have the final decision in the election of all future companions, so that no one was to obtain membership in the Order against his will, and many would do so through his will alone. He or his deputy was to initiate the proceedings for the election of new companions, to preside over them, and to to install the companion-elect. His permission was required for a companion to absent himself from an annual assembly, a requiem mass, or an election, and his pardon was required for any default. His permission was required before any companion could leave the kingdom. He kept the Order's common seal while he was in England, and its signet seal was inseparable from his person. No new statute could be enacted in his absence, so that he possessed an effective veto over all internal legislation as well. Finally, his costume was distinguished from that of the other companions, and he sat in a special stall and had the place of honour at the end of processions. In sum, his position within the Order was thoroughly monarchical even in the broader sense of the term.

Although no fewer than five of Edward's successors on the English throne were either deposed or killed by political rivals during the period between his death and the end of the fifteenth century, the office of Sovereign of the Order of the Garter seems to have been held without any interruption throughout the later fourteenth and fifteenth centuries, and most of Edward's successors took care to secure the election of their heir apparent to the Order within a short time of making him Prince of Wales.

With characteristic foresight, Edward realised that it would not always be possible for him or his successors as Sovereign to preside in person at Assemblies held at Windsor in April or at electoral assemblies held within six weeks of the death of a companion, and provided in the statutes for the appointment of a deputy to exercise the Sovereign's functions at both types of meeting. Should the Sovereign find that he would be unable to attend the next St George's Day feast, he was to appoint a deputy by letters charging him with holding both the Chapter and the banquet. Such a deputy was to be empowered to 'correct and reform' transgressors against the existing statutes during the meeting of the Chapter, but not to make any new statutes.[122] The statutes do not specify how the deputy for the holding of elections was to be appointed,[123] but in practice the deputies charged with holding the annual Assemblies probably performed this function as well, as most elections seem to have been held during Assemblies.[124] Nothing is known about the naming of deputies before the accession of Henry V in 1413, but the Black Book records that that king and several of his successors were frequently obliged to appoint deputies to preside over the Order's annual meeting in Windsor Castle. In 1418, 1419, and 1420, for example, Henry V was campaigning in France on St George's Day, and although he seems to have observed the feast with those companions who were with him on each occasion, the regular Assembly was held at Windsor by his brother John, Duke of Bedford, who was governing England during his absence.[125] The Duke of Bedford also presided over the first assemblies of the reign of his nephew Henry VI, who was too young to carry out his functions as Sovereign before 1427, and at the Assembly held on 11 May 1454, the Duke of Buckingham presided, because the king was too ill to attend.[126]

7 The Members of the Order: The Companions

Next in rank below the Sovereign were the Order's twenty-five ordinary *compagnons* or 'companions'. The title 'companion' given to the members of this class was no doubt selected partly because it was the natural and normal designation for members of a corporation with the title 'company', but it had the advantage of emphasizing the fraternal relationship that was ideally to exist among the knights, and it is unlikely that this was lost on Edward. The same title was to be used in most later monarchical orders.

Why Edward chose to create a company of merely or precisely twenty-six companions is unknown. His original project had been for an order of 300 companions, a figure in all likelihood derived from the contemporary romance *Perceforest*, and so large that it would have included nearly a third of the active

---

[122] Ch. 8.
[123] Ord. 18a merely refers to a deputy in this context.
[124] See below, pp. 129–30.
[125] Nicolas, *History*, I, pp. 58–60.
[126] Ibid., p. 82.

knights in England. Between the proclamation of the Round Table society in 1344 and the organization of the Order of the Garter in 1348, Edward evidently decided to found, instead of a vast company, a very small society which excluded all but the most eminent knights. Both the smaller scale and the restriction to distinguished knights could have been inspired (or justified) by the practices of the Order of the Band, but the limitation of membership to a precise number of knights was almost certainly inspired directly by the practices of the various fictional societies. A definite and relatively small number was also called for if each knight was to have a stall permanently marked with his sword and crested helm in the chapel of the lower ward of Windsor Castle, which as we shall see replaced the projected Round Table House in the scaled-down version of the society, and it may well be that the figure chosen was determined in large part by the number of stalls that could conveniently be placed in the existing chapel.

As we observed earlier, there is good reason to believe that the number of knights Edward at first intended to include in his revised order was not twenty-six but twenty-four. Twenty-four secular canons and twenty-four poor knights were called for in the letters refounding St George's Chapel in August 1348, the Prince of Wales presented twenty-four garters to the 'knights of the Society of the Garter' about three months later,[127] and John of Cologne was paid for making twenty-four robes powdered with garters and the motto *Hony soit* for the the feast of the Order held in April 1349.[128] Twenty-four, twice the mystical figure of twelve (the number of Christ's own band of followers and of the legendary peers of France), was a more likely number than twenty-six to have been selected arbitrarily, and the extra two must have been added not long before the meeting in April 1349 – probably because of a desire on Edward's part to include in the foundation two particular individuals who could not otherwise have been included. In any case all surviving versions of the statutes present the same list of twenty-six First Founders. Thereafter the size of the college of companions remained fixed until 2 June 1786, and there is no reason to believe that the number of companions ever exceeded twenty-six before that date.[129]

The principle lying behind Edward's selection of the first twenty-five ordinary companions of the Order has long puzzled historians, for although most of the men chosen were known to have played a part in Edward's French campaigns of the 1340s, a high proportion of those included were relatively obscure or inexperienced knights, while a significant number of men who were much more prominent in the military and political affairs of the kingdom, and also much closer to Edward personally – among them most of the earls who had sworn to support the original Round Table project in 1344 and all of the men he had made earls in 1337 – were at least initially excluded from the Order. The most recent research on the problem suggests that Edward chose the 'First Founders' on two distinct bases, of which the first was participation in the campaigns that had culminated in his great victory at Crécy.[130] All but four of the First Founders are now known to have fought with the

---

[127] See above, p. 115. Despite Juliet Vale's discoveries, 1348 is still the most likely year for this gift.
[128] PRO, E372/207, m. 50; cited by Vale, *Edward III*, p. 83, n. 87.
[129] Nicolas, *History*, II, p. 292.
[130] Barber, *Edward Prince of Wales*, pp. 90–1; Vale, *Edward III*, pp. 87–9.

king at Crécy, and two of the other four – Sanchet d'Abrichecourt and Henry d'Enne – could easily have been there as well.[131] The two remaining First Founders, the Earl of Lancaster and the Captal of Buch, had been engaged in leading the Edwardian forces in a vital subsidiary action in Guyenne at the time of the battle in Ponthieu, and could therefore claim some credit for the English victory.

Edward's division of the First Founders between the two parallel sets of stalls prepared for them in St George's Chapel[132] also seems to have been based at least partly on their relationships to him and his son the Prince of Wales, especially though not exclusively in the Battle of Crécy. All twelve of the companions who were placed in stalls on the side presided over by the Prince had fought in the first division, which he had nominally commanded, four of them had served in his personal retinue, and another of them – Richard FitzSimon – had borne his standard there. The six bachelors among them – Pavely, Enne, Audley, Loring, Mohun, and Wale – eventually joined the Prince's household. The companions first placed on the king's side of the chapel were a less homgeneous group, since two of them at least – Chandos and Wrottesley – had fought under his son at Crécy, but five of the remaining ten – Lisle, Grey, Beauchamp, Otes Holand, and Courtney – are known to have been knights of the king's chamber before the battle (in which Beauchamp had carried the royal standard), and Henry of Lancaster was apparently a member of Edward's inner circle of friends.

Edward himself, the Earls of Lancaster and Warwick, and the future Earl of Stafford, had been the principal commanders of the English forces during the Crécy campaign, and the young Prince of Wales had had the nominal command of the first division of the army during the battle itself, but none of the other First Founders had held a major command during the campaign, and more than a third of them had served in the ranks among the bachelors. Edward must therefore have had at least one further principle in mind when he selected these knights in preference to the hundreds of others who had served him in comparable capacities during the Crécy campaign. Juliet Vale has argued from the fact that equal numbers of experienced and inexperienced knights were placed on both sides of the chapel that Edward's choice and distribution of First Founders may have been influenced by the need to form evenly matched tournament teams.[133] This is certainly possible, but a careful examination of the arragement of the knights in the stalls of the chapel suggests that Edward selected the companions not so much on the basis of age and experience as on the basis of rank, and included a considerable number of relatively minor knights among the First Founders specifically in order to give the knights of middle and lower rank a representation in his new Order appropriate to their numerical (and tactical) importance. The companions were arranged in pairs, in strict order of rank, beginning at the west end of the chapel with four pairs of men who either held or were due to receive a title of dignity, followed by four pairs of men with the rank of baron or banneret (which were commonly treated as equivalent), and concluding at the east end with six pairs of mere knights bachelor. The fact that Edward, in the statutes of the Order, required every companion, when submitting nominations to fill a vacated stall, to give the names of three

---

[131] Their whereabouts at the time of the battle are simply unknown.
[132] See below, p. 146.
[133] *Edward III*, pp. 87–8.

knights bachelor as well as three simple barons or bannerets and three men of at least the rank of earl lends further credence to this theory, for it proves that Edward was thinking in terms of these precise categories when he named the first companions himself.

Why he selected most of the individual First Founders who did not serve as captains must remain a mystery, but as Barber has suggested, certain of the companions were probably included among the First Founders for strictly political reasons: the young Roger Mortimer, to avoid alienating a faction of the English nobility; Jean de Grailly, Captal of Buch, and Sanchet d'Abrichecourt, to honour the loyal nobles of Gascony and Picardy respectively; and Henry d'Enne[134] to honour the knights of the Empire who had in the past been so useful to the English cause.[135] Some of the other knights were probably chosen in recognition of the heroic deeds they performed on the field of battle – for as we shall see, the Order was almost certainly meant to be seen as a society of heroes.

It is clear from the rule just cited governing nomination that Edward wanted to keep the Order open to knights of all ranks.[136] To be eligible for election to the Order, it was necessary only to be 'un gentilhomme de sang, et chevalier sans reproche',[137] – that is to say, a knight of knightly birth who had never transgressed against the unwritten code of chivalry. Each companion was also directed to nominate the nine 'plus suffisans chevaliers sans reproche qu'il connoist'.[138] The word *suffisans* here seems to mean 'worthy', and was probably interpreted in chivalric terms. It would thus appear that the Order of the Garter was conceived of by its founder as an order both of 'knighthood' and of 'chivalry' in the strictest sense of those terms. Whatever else its companions were – and from the beginning some of them were princes and many were lords – they were also knights, and it was as knights that they participated, on terms of almost perfect equality, in the activities of the Order.

It was no doubt to encourage feelings of equality among the 'companions' of his Order that Edward gave the First Founders and their successors the right to participate in the election of all future members of the Order.[139] The statutes specify that within six weeks of learning of the death of a companion, the Sovereign was to summon the surviving companions to elect a successor. At least six companions in addition to the Sovereign or his Deputy were required to make a quorum for such an election, and each companion present was required to submit (as we have just observed) a slate of exactly nine candidates – a number probably chosen to represent the Nine Worthies. The votes were to be collected (and presumably tallied) by the senior cleric present, and then presented to the

---

[134] Usually called d'Eam by earlier writers.

[135] *Edward Prince of Wales*, p. 90.

[136] Ord. 18f. The election of 1445 is the first for which the Registrar (new in that year) bothered to record the details of the voting, but in that year and thereafter each companion present did in fact submit the names of three higher peers, three barons, and three bachelors, in keeping with the statutory requirement, and it is likely that this was done throughout the earlier history of the Order. (Nicolas, *History* I, p. 78.)

[137] Ch. 2.

[138] Ord. 18d.

[139] The whole election procedure is described in ords. 18a–j.

Sovereign or his Deputy. The Sovereign was then to declare elected either the candidate who had received the largest number of votes, or the one who seemed to him to be the most honourable and useful to the Order. The last provision effectively gave the Sovereign the right to ignore the votes of the ordinary companions when there was a candidate whom he particularly wished to see 'elected' to the Order – an underaged son, for example – or one whom he particularly wished to exclude. Nothing is known of the details of voting before 12 May 1445,[140] but for most subsequent elections the lists of candidates put forward by each knight present are recorded in the Black Book, and it is clear that the Sovereign often decided in favour of someone who had received fewer votes than several other candidates.[141]

Our knowledge both of the identity of the knights elected to membership in the Order of the Garter in the period before 1416 and of the approximate time of their election is derived in part from the records of expenditure for robes of the Order referred to above, in part from a list compiled by the first Garter King of Arms *circa* 1430, and in part from a pair of tables apparently compiled in the reign of Edward IV (commonly known as the 'Windsor Tables') in which the succession of knights in each of the stalls of the chapel is set forth in French.[142] Unfortunately, the information contained in these sources is neither complete nor consistent, and although considerable labour has been devoted since the time of Ashmole to the problem of establishing a complete succession of knights in this period, the compiler of the most recent list was forced to admit that he could not be sure that every knight included in his list had in fact been elected to the Order, or that the names of several knights who *were* elected had not been omitted. In almost every case the date on which a companion was elected in this period can only be assigned to the period of months or years between the death (or last notice) of the companion he appears to have succeeded and the first date on which his name appears in a contemporary list of knights receiving the Order's livery. For the period beginning in 1416 we are much better informed, since the Black Book records most of the elections held and periodically provides lists of those currently included in the Order.[143]

The first elections may well have taken place before the first recorded meeting in April 1350, as three of the First Founders – Sanchet d'Abrichecourt, Richard FitzSimon, and Hugh de Courtenay – seem to have died by that time.[144] The first companions actually elected were Sir William FitzWaryn, Robert Ufford, Earl of Suffolk, and William de Bohun, Earl of Northampton. Only six further elections

---

[140] Anstis, *Register*, II, pp. 126–8.

[141] At the election held on 12 May 1445, for example, some candidates received six and some seven votes from the eight companions assembled, but the candidate declared elected by the Sovereign had received only five votes. (Ibid.)

[142] Published in Ashmole, *Institution*, pp. [754–7].

[143] Lists of companions with indications of the approximate order of their election were published by Beltz, *Memorials*, pp. cxlix ff.; Nicholas II, pp. lxi–lxxvi; Shaw, *Knights*, I, pp. 1–72; E. H. Fellowes, *The Knights of the Garter, 1348–1939* (Windsor, 1939); and in *The Complete Peerage*, ed. V. Gibbs, H. R. Doubleday (London, 1910–59), II, pp. 534ff. The last – based on those of Beltz and Shaw – appears to be the most complete and accurate.

[144] Beltz, *Memorials*, pp. 393, 60, 96.

seem to have been held in the decade between 1351 and 1360, but sixteen were necessary between 1361 and 1370, and thereafter the number known to have been required in each decade A.D. of our period fluctuated between eight and twenty, and in most decades fell between twelve and eighteen.[145] The first recorded election is that of Sigismund or Zsigmond, King of Hungary and of the Romans, which took place at a meeting held in May 1416,[146] but not all of the elections which must have occurred after 1416 are recorded in the Black Book, and some are recorded only several years after they seem to have taken place.[147] From 1416 until 1445 all of the elections which *were* recorded took place during the Order's annual Assembly, although Henry V seems to have held a special chapter to elect four new companions at some time during his siege of Rouen (which lasted from August 1418 to 13 January 1419).[148] The Black Book records that an extraordinary meeting was held on 11 July 1445 to fill two vacant stalls, and that similar meetings were held in November 1447, August 1450, February 1474, August 1474, November 1476, February 1480, and September 1482. The rule that elections be held within six weeks thus appears to have been ignored completely in the fifteenth century except in two brief periods (1445–50 and 1474–82). Since it was not uncommon in the fifteenth century for three or four companions to die during the course of the period between annual meetings, the number of living companions often fell well below the figure of twenty-six called for in the statutes for periods of several months, but the elections held at the next regular Assembly normally filled all the vacant stalls, and the number of companions does not appear to have fallen below twenty at any time.

If the First Founders were chosen on the basis of the rôles they had played during the Crécy campaign, their English successors seem to have been chosen primarily on the basis of conspicuous service and unswerving loyalty to Edward and his successors as king and Sovereign, though in many cases the particular reasons can only be guessed at. High rank and close personal friendship with the king no doubt influenced the choice of more than one companion in this period. Juliet Vale has shown that Edward probably excluded two of his most prominent commanders – the Earls of Arundel and Huntington – because of their rôle in the crisis of 1340,[149] and other eminent lords and commanders were undoubtedly excluded by his successors for similar personal reasons. Nevertheless, most of the more prominent military and political leaders of our period were eventually elected to the Order.

Table 4.2 indicates briefly the number of companions currently believed to have been elected to the Order during the reigns of the founder and each of his successors down to the death of Henry VII in 1509. Ideally it would show the numbers of companions who fell into each of the three categories specified for nominations, but as it is impossible to determine in most cases whether a knight

---

[145] Elections per decade: 1349–50, 3; 1351–60, 6; 1361–70, 16; 1371–80, 15; 1381–90, 14; 1391–1400, 20; 1401–10, 19; 1411–20, 14; 1421–30, 13; 1431–40, 8; 1441–50, 15; 1451–60, 15; 1461–70, 17; 1471–80, 18; 1481–90, 20; 1491–1500, 12; 1501–09, 13.

[146] Nicolas, *History*, I, p. 57.

[147] Ibid., pp. 75–7.

[148] Ibid., p. 59.

[149] *Edward III*, pp. 89–91.

who was not summoned as a peer was a banneret or a bachelor, mere bannerets and bachelors have been lumped together as knights. The foreign knights have been separated out into a distinct category. The first figure in each column shows the number of companions who held the status indicated at the time of their election, while the second number, in parentheses, shows the number of the companions elected in that reign who either retained or acquired the status indicated by the time of their death. The First Founders and the three kings who later became Sovereign without having been elected are enumerated in parentheses preceded by a + sign, and the cumulative number of companions admitted to the Order by any means at the end of each reign (including Sovereigns) is indicated in parentheses in the last column.

Table 4.1

Classes of Knights elected to the Order of the Garter, 1349–1509

Sovereign	English Knights	English Barons	English High Peers	English Total	Foreign Total	Totals (Cumulative)
Edward III	14 (9)	7 (9)	10 (14)	31 (+23)	4 (+3)	35 (61)
Richard II	15 (12)	4 (3)	7 (11)	26	4	30 (91)
Henry IV	6 (4)	10 (11)	9 (10)	25	3	28 (119)
Henry V	10 (6)	5 (7)	4 (6)	19	2	21 (140)
Henry VI	11 (5)	8 (10)	12 (16)	31 (+1)	13	44 (185)
Edward IV	5 (0)	9 (4)	12 (18)	26 (+1)	10	36 (222)
Richard III	4 (3)	1 (1)	2 (3)	7	0	7 (229)
Henry VII	14 (12)	4 (4)	13 (14)	31 (+1)	6	37 (267)
Totals	79 (51)	48 (49)	69 (92)	196 (+26)	42 (+3)	238 (267)

As this table demonstrates, the proportion of mere knights bachelor, mere barons, and higher peers elected to the Order between 1349 and 1509 fluctuated significantly. Since many companions were promoted into or within the peerage after their election, the proportion of barons and higher peers within the Order tended to increase. Of the English companions elected under Edward III, three quarters were ultimately admitted to the peerage, and nearly half achieved the rank of earl or higher. Of those elected under his successors down to 1509, the proportion ultimately elevated to the peerage varied between half under Richard II and five sixths under Henry VI, while the proportion who ultimately became viscounts or better varied from one third under Henry V to two thirds under Edward IV. Nearly half of the English knights elected in our period – 92 out of 196 – ultimately became higher peers, while roughly a quarter (49) achieved or retained the rank of baron, and the remaining quarter (51) never rose beyond the rank of knight.

Since the number of English peers of the higher ranks seldom surpassed twenty at any one time throughout this period, the proportion of higher peers who belonged to the Order was always relatively high. Indeed, the great majority of the peers of the two highest ranks were eventually elected to membership in our period: all but seven of the forty-six men who received or inherited the status of duke in this period,[150] and all but one of the nine men who received or inherited the status of marquess.[151] Nevertheless, even the higher peers were never assured of admission to the Order on the basis of their rank alone, and most of the dukes were elected not because of their rank in the peerage, but because they were members of the royal house.[152]

Descent in the male line from the founder fell just short of guaranteeing election to the Order in our period: of Edward's agnatic descendants who lived to manhood, only Richard 'of Conisburgh', younger son of Edward's son Edmund 'of Langley', and Henry and Edmund Beaufort, great-grandsons of Edward's son John 'of Gaunt', died without garters about their knees. Royal sons and brothers who reached maturity were elected with unfailing regularity, though even they had to wait until a vacancy occurred. Unlike men of lesser birth, royal children (and agnatic grandchildren) were generally elected when they were still relatively (and after 1376 very) young. Three of the founder's younger sons – Lionel 'of Antwerp', John 'of Gaunt', and Edmund 'of Langley' – were elected in or about 1360 when they were respectively twenty-two, twenty, and eighteen, and his youngest son, Thomas 'of Woodstock', was elected in 1380, when he was twenty-five. Richard 'of Bordeaux', only son of the Black Prince, was elected to the Order in April 1377 at the tender age of nine, having become through the death of his father in the previous year the heir apparent to the throne; only a few months later the death of his grandfather Edward III placed him on the throne as King Richard II, and he became the Order's second Sovereign. John of Gaunt's son Henry IV (who had been elected to the Order in 1377 when he was ten) secured the election of all four of his sons – Henry, Thomas, John, and Humphrey – immediately after his seizure of the throne in the autumn of 1399, when they were respectively twelve, eleven, ten and nine years old. Henry V's only son Henry VI succeeded to the throne at the age of nine months without having been elected a companion, and Henry VI's only son Edward died at seventeen without being elected to membership. Edward IV, who supplanted Henry VI in 1461, secured the election of his two brothers, George and Richard, in 1461 and 1466 respectively, when they were eleven and fourteen, and on the same day in 1475 had both of his sons – Edward and Richard – inducted into the Order, although they were then only four and two years old. Richard III, who deposed his brother Edward's son Edward V in 1483, failed to secure the election of his only son, Edward, before his death at the age of ten or eleven years in 1484, but Henry VII, who supplanted Richard in 1485, had his elder son Arthur elected in 1491, when he was four, and his younger son and eventual successor

---

[150] The exceptions were the sons of Henry VI and Richard III, Dukes of Cornwall; John and Henry Holand, successive Dukes of Exeter; Henry Beaufort, Duke of Somerset; George Neville, Duke of Bedford; and Henry Beauchamp, Duke of Warwick.

[151] The exception was William de Berkeley, Marquess Berkeley.

[152] All but sixteen dukes in this period were members of the royal house, and the remainder were all closely related to the king by descent or marriage.

Henry elected in 1495, when he was four. It would appear that – unlike Edward himself but like Alfonso of Castile and most later founders – most of Edward's successors regarded membership in the Order as a status characteristic of membership in the immediate family of the king, which had therefore to be secured for all royal sons and brothers as soon as possible after their birth.

Although it was in practice primarily a society of English knights, it is clear that, like the society of the Round Table which inspired it (and unlike the two existing monarchical orders) the Order of the Garter was conceived of from the beginning as being in principle an international order. Not only were three foreign knights included among the First Founders, but the statutes actually specified that the companions could nominate foreign as well as English knights.[153] As we have seen, Edward seems to have employed the Order to reward foreign knights both as individuals and as representatives of particular bodies of nobles who had served him loyally in his war with France, but he almost certainly hoped that in appointing or securing the election of eminent foreigners, he and his successors would increase both the prestige and the fame of their Order throughout the Christian world.

Edward's conception of the Order as an international fraternity of knights famous for their birth or deeds seems to have been maintained under all of Edward's successors as Sovereign, for a number of foreign knights were in fact both nominated and elected to membership in the Order in every reign of our period except that of Richard III (which was very short). In most reigns the number of foreigners admitted was quite small (ranging from two to six), but under Henry VI, who reigned for some years as king of northern France as well as of England, their number rose to nearly a third of the total, and under his successor Edward IV it dropped only to a quarter. A few of the foreigners elected were only knights, but most were of at least baronial rank, and more than two thirds of them were princes. The first foreign prince elected to the Order was the founder's son-in-law and ally Jean IV, Duke of Brittany in France and Earl of Richmond in England, whose election seems to have taken place in 1375. Three more foreign princes of less than royal rank (all vassals of the Emperor) were admitted under Richard II,[154] and under Henry IV the first foreign kings were elected, in the persons of Henry's brother-in-law King Enrique III of Castile and Leon (c.1402),[155] his son-in-law King Erik of Denmark, Norway, and Sweden (1404), and his brother-in-law King João I of Portugal (c.1408). A total of fifteen foreign monarchs were elected to the Order before 1509, including five Emperors or future Emperors (two of them Kings of Hungary and Bohemia), four Kings of Portugal, two Kings of Aragon (one of them King of island Sicily and the other of both Sicilies and in the right of his wife of Castile and Leon), two further Kings of Castile and Leon, two Kings of Denmark, Norway, and Sweden, one King of Poland, and one King of mainland

---

[153] Ord. 18e.
[154] Willem, Duke of Guelders and Jülich (by 1399); Wilhelm, Duke of Bavaria and Count of Ostrevant, later Count of Hainault and Holland (by 1399); and Albrecht, Duke of Bavaria, Count of Hainault and Holland (c.1398).
[155] See above, p. 61.

Sicily or Naples.[156] In fact the Order eventually elected to its ranks all of the Emperors chosen after 1410, all of the Kings of Portugal who succeeded to the throne after 1385, and at least one of the sovereigns of every other Western Christian kingdom except France, Navarre, and Scotland, whose rulers were commonly the enemies of the King of England. Nineteen foreign princes of less than sovereign rank, including men of German, Italian, Portuguese, and French nationality, were also elected to the Order before 1509. Most of the foreign companions seem to have been merely friends or allies rather than close relatives of the English king, and most were probably admitted in part to cement the friendship or alliance between themselves and the Sovereign of the Order, and in part to enhance the prestige of the Order both at home and abroad.

As soon as possible after his election, every companion-elect was to be sent a garter,[157] and every foreign companion-elect was to be sent in addition (at the Sovereign's personal expense) a mantle and a copy of the Order's statutes sealed with the Order's common seal.[158] English subjects elected to the Order were evidently expected to accept the honour without demur, but every foreign companion-elect was to signify to the Order within four months of receiving notification of his election whether he wished to accept, and could agree to comply with the statutes.[159] No foreign companion is known to have refused election at any time during our period, though the request of Duke Philippe 'the Good' of Burgundy that his admission be deferred was interpreted by the companions as a refusal.[160]

Election alone did not confer membership in the Order, however: according to chapters 19 and 20, every companion-elect had to be installed, either in person or by proxy, before he would be considered a full member of the Order, and the election of any English resident who failed to be installed within one year would be declared void.[161] The rite of installment is not described in the statutes, but it would appear that during the course of the ceremony the companion-elect was formally invested with his mantle and probably conducted to his stall in the chapel, where the whole rite must have taken place. Normally the Sovereign himself was to preside at the ceremony, but if detained abroad he could appoint one of the other

---

[156] The following foreign monarchs were elected after 1408: Sigismund, King of Hungary and the Romans and later King of Bohemia and Emperor (1416); Duarte I, King of Portugal (1435); Albrecht, Duke of Austria, later King of Hungary and Bohemia and Emperor (1438); Afonso V, King of Portugal (1447); Alfons V, King of Aragon and the two Sicilies (1450); Kazimierz IV, King of Poland and Grand Prince of Lithuania (1450); Friedrich III, Archduke of Austria and Emperor (1457); Ferrante I, King of mainland Sicily (1460); Ferran II, King of Aragon and Castile (1480); João II, King of Portugal (1482); Maximilian I, Archduke of Austria, titular Duke of Burgundy, King and later Emperor of the Romans (1489); Hans, King of Denmark, Norway, and Sweden (1499); and Carlos I or Karl V, Archduke of Austria, titular Duke of Burgundy, King of Castile and Leon, later King of Aragon and the two Sicilies and Emperor (1508).

[157] Ord. 19a.

[158] Ord. 20a.

[159] Ord. 20b.

[160] Nicolas, *History*, I, p. 66.

[161] Ord. 19e.

companions to act as his deputy.[162] At some point in the proceedings the companion-elect was required to take an oath of obedience to the statutes of the Order.[163] This was evidently required even of foreign kings, but as it did not entail any submission to the Sovereign of the Order except in matters pertaining to the Order itself, it was possible for them to take the oath without compromising their position. It would appear that the sword and crested helm of the companion-elect were hung above his stall at some point in the ceremony,[164] and possibly a banner of his arms as well.[165] Finally, before his installation was complete, the companion-elect was required to pay an entry-fee, scaled in accordance with his rank, but in every case fairly considerable. Throughout our period a new Sovereign was required to pay 40 marks (£26 13s 4d); a foreign king, £20; the Prince of Wales, 20 marks (£13 6s 8d); a duke, £10; and earl or count, 10 marks (£6 13s 4d); a mere baron or banneret), £5; and a knight bachelor, 5 marks (£3 6s 4d).[166] Since knights bachelor were paid at the time at a rate of 2s a day the entry fee represented just over one month's pay for companions of this rank; for earls, paid at 8s a day, it represented the pay of about half a month. New scales were later introduced for marquesses and viscounts, once those ranks had become established in England.[167] The statutes declare that this compulsory 'gift' was demanded so that each companion could be worthy of the name 'Founder'. On a more practical level, the entry-fee served to provide a regular stream of donations for the support of the Order's chapel, and to give each companion a feeling of having invested something in the Order. Such fees were common in confraternities in general, but the Order of the Garter was almost unique among monarchical orders in requiring any fee for admission.

Only foreign princes who declared that they could not attend the ceremony in person were initially exempted from either the requirement of personal intallation or from paying the entry-fee.[168] In such cases the fee was to be contributed by the Sovereign himself.[169] Edward obviously wished to make it as easy as possible for foreign princes to accept membership in his Order, undoubtedly feeling that he and his successors had as much to gain from their membership as the princes themselves. No doubt to encourage them to take their membership seriously, however, Edward required princes who could not come themselves to send a procurator of appropriate rank and without reproach, to be installed in their place

---

[162] Ch. 25.

[163] Ch. 24.

[164] Ord. 19f.

[165] See below, p. 147.

[166] Ch. 22.

[167] See Nicholas, *History*, II, p. 389. During the Chapter held on 27 Nov. 1447, the fees were fixed as follows: To the canons, The king 40 marks, a foreign king £20, the Prince 20 marks, a duke £10, a marquess £8 6s 8d, an earl 10 marks, a viscount £5 16s 8d, a baron £5, a knight bachelor 5 marks. In addition the Office of Arms was to receive a fee on an even higher scale, ranging from £40 for the sovereign to £5 for a baron, £4 for a banneret and 4 marks for a bachelor. Finally, fees were paid at a flat rate to the other officers, to the various classes of clergy of the chapel, and to certain servants of the royal household.

[168] In 1421, an amendment was adopted permitting English subjects actively engaged on the king's service abroad to be installed by proxy in the same manner as a foreign prince. (Nicolas, *History*, I, p. 62.)

[169] Ord. 22j.

within seven months of learning of their election.[170] Lest the procurator feel (or later claim) that he himself had been admitted to the Order, Edward cautiously required him to wear the mantle over his right arm rather than in the normal fashion during the ceremony of intallation, and specifically forbade him to wear it again thereafter, or to take any part in the activities of the Order.[171]

The rule requiring installation for full membersip was consistently observed in the fifteenth century. Between 1349 and 1509, at least six elections were declared void by neglect of installation, the first one recorded being that of Duke Wilhelm of Brunswick, elected on 4 August 1450, and replaced on 23 April 1459. All five of the other companions-elect who failed to be installed were also foreign princes: the Emperor Friedrich III (elected in 1467, replaced in 1470/2); King Kazimierz IV of Poland (elected in 1450, replaced in 1472); King Ferran of Aragon and Castile (elected 1482, replaced in 1483); and King João II of Portugal (elected in 1482, replaced in 1482, and reelected in 1488). With the possible exception of Ferran of Aragon, every one of these princes seems to have accepted election to the Order, and each was listed among the companions. Since none was resident in England, the one-year rule did not apply to them, and in every case but one the companions allowed at least three years to elapse before declaring their election void. Clearly the members of the Order were reluctant to lose the companionship of such distinguished foreigners, and wished to give them every opportunity to conform to the ordinance.

It was perhaps to avoid such losses that the Order (emulating the practice of the Order of the Golden Fleece) began in the last third of the fifteenth century to permit foreign princes to be invested with full ceremony in their own courts. The first prince to be inducted into the Order in this way was Charles 'the Rash' of Burgundy, who on 4 February 1470 was invested with the Order's insignia by a special commission led by the companion Galhard de Durfort and the Order's King of Arms. Only two other princes seem to have been invested by such 'Garter Missions' in our period: Maximilian, King of the Romans, on 12 September 1490; and Alfonso, Duke of Calabria, on 19 May 1493.[172]

Once he had been properly installed and paid the appropriate fee, a new companion was normally to retain his membership in the Order for life; unlike those of most other orders, the statutes of the Garter made no provision before 1519 for the expulsion of erring members. Nevertheless, during the course of our period a number of companions were in fact expelled or 'degraded' from the Order, in consequence of some act judged to be treasonous. Ironically, the first companion known to have been formally expelled was a king's favorite: Robert de Vere, Earl of Oxford, successively created Marquess of Dublin and Duke of Ireland by Richard II, and then convicted by the envious Lords on a trumped-up charge of treason in February 1388 and degraded from all his honours. The second formal degradation from the Order was probably that of Thomas de Beauchamp, Earl of Warwick, who was expelled by Richard II in 1397 in retaliation for his part in the events of 1388. In the fifteenth century at least eight further knights were degraded from the Order, generally as a result of similar political turnabouts: Henry Percy, Earl of

---

[170] Ords. 20c,d.
[171] Ords. 20e–j.
[172] For a complete list of these missions, see *Complete Peerage*, II, pp. 581ff.

Northumberland, in 1406/7; Jasper Tudor, Earl of Pembroke, in 1461; Richard Neville, Earl of Warwick and Salisbury, in 1468; Galhard de Durfort, Lord of Duras, in 1476; Thomas Grey, Marquess of Dorset, in 1483; Thomas Howard, Earl of Surrey, in 1485; and Francis Lovell, Viscount Lovell, in the same year. It is interesting to note that three of the ten companions degraded before 1500 – Beauchamp, Tudor, and Howard – were later restored to membership in the Order, following further turns of the political tide.[173]

The statutes of the Order also failed to provide for the possibility that a companion might wish to withdraw voluntarily, but in fact several companions did resign their membership during the centuries with which we are concerned. The first to do so was the founder's son-in-law, Enguerrand de Coucy, Earl of Bedford in England and Lord of Coucy in France, who withdrew from the Order on 23 August 1377, just two months after the founder's death, because membership in the English Order conflicted with his renewed loyalty to the King of France; at the same time he surrendered his English earldom.[174] The other two companions who resigned from the Order before 1509 – François de Surrienne (1450) and Jean de Grailly 'de Foix', Earl of Kendal in England and Count of Bénauges in France (1462) – seem to have done so for precisely the same reason. It would appear that these knights regarded membership in the English Order of the Garter as incompatible with adherence to the archenemy of the English king, and felt compelled to resign as soon as they changed their political allegiance. Since Galhard de Durfort was later expelled for changing his allegiance, the three knights who resigned may have wished to avoid a similar fate.

8 The Privileges and Obligations of Companionship

Once he had been installed, a companion-elect of the Garter acquired all the privileges and obligations of membership in the college of companions. Compared to those enjoyed by the knights of most other orders of the same type, the privileges of the knights of the Garter were quite modest. The purely honorific privileges spelled out in the statutes were inspired by those of the knights of the Round Table and the Frank Palace: the right to hang their sword, helm, and banner (in life) and a stall-plate bearing their name and armorial achievement (after death) in a particular stall in the Order's chapel. Similar privileges were to be extended (at least in theory) to the knights of most later orders, as we shall see. It is not clear whether the knights of the Garter enjoyed as such any special precedence at court during the reign of the founder or any of his successors in our period, but it is possible, as Henry VIII placed them immediately after the peers of the realm in his table of general precedence. Several knights of the Order condemned to death in our period for treason were spared the nastier stages of the process of execution specifically in consideration of their membership (or former membership) in the Order, but this was certainly not a formal privilege of companionship. The

---

173 A complete list of known degradations is printed in *Complete Peerage*, II, p. 581.
174 The letter by which he resigned from the Order is printed in Nicolas, *History*, I, p. 43 n. 1.

companions were finally given the right to live at the Order's seat at their own expense, but it is not clear that any companion availed himself of this honorific privilege.

The more practical privileges of the Garter knights were derived for the most part from the obligations of the other members of the Order, especially the Sovereign. Though the statutes have nothing to say on the subject, Edward like most later founders took it upon himself and his successors as Sovereign to provide the Order's physical establishment, pay for its upkeep, and provide a lavish feast once a year for all the companions. In addition, Edward, like Alfonso of Castile, undertook to provide the badges and habits (except the mantle) of the companions, and also to pay the entry-fee of any foreign companion installed by proxy. Finally he pledged as Sovereign to give preference to the companions of the Order in any honourable enterprise which he required to be undertaken.[175] The last was the only formal patronal obligation owed by the Sovereign as such to the individual companions, and it was as much to his advantage as to theirs.

The cliental obligations of the ordinary companions to their Sovereign were somewhat more encumbering, but by no means burdensome, and certainly much less extensive than those of any other monarchical order founded in the fourteenth century. The companions were first of all bound to observe the 'precepts and admonitions' of the Sovereign[176] – principally, no doubt, those pronounced during the course of the annual Chapter. In addition they were bound to seek the Sovereign's permission to be late or absent from any of the Order's functions,[177] and before leaving the kingdom on any private business.[178] The last obligation – the only one of any real importance – was in effect the other side of the Sovereign's obligation to prefer the companions for honourable employment, for there is no reason to suppose that Edward included this rule to prevent or even discourage his companions from leaving the kingdom. In practice, the companions were also expected to act as loyal subjects or allies of the Sovereign, but this was not specified in the statutes.

The obligations of the companions to one another in life were equally modest, and essentially negative. By chapter 29 they were bound not to bear arms against one another, except in the war of their sovereign lord (whose rights were thus reserved in the fashion customary in alliances) or their own just quarrel. The only other circumstance in which armed conflict was likely to arise between ordinary companions was one in which two companions were 'retained' as mercenaries by opposite combatants, and in such a situation the companion who had been retained at a later date was bound to excuse himself from further service. Thus the fraternal obligations of the companions in life were effectively reduced to an obligation not to bear arms against one another for pay alone – a rather paltry undertaking compared with those imposed by both earlier monarchical orders and most later ones. No specific penalty was imposed for failure to comply with this regulation, and it is not clear that the situation ever arose.

The obligations owed by the companions to those of their number who had died

---

[175] Ch. 28.
[176] Ord. 15b.
[177] Ords. 10f,h, 18l.
[178] Ord. 28a.

were rather more significant. In keeping with the practice of most devotional confraternities, the knights of the Garter undertook to pay for the singing of a certain number of masses for every deceased companion immediately upon learning of his death.[179] This was both a burden and a benefit of membership, and some similar obligation was to be a feature of almost all of the later monarchical orders. Edward, with a characteristic sense of justice, adjusted the burden in accordance with the probable ability of the donor to pay, contracting to have ten times as many masses sung as he expected from a mere knight bachelor. Nevertheless, the number of masses demanded was very high by the standards of the day, and much higher than that imposed in most later orders. The Sovereign was to have 1000 masses sung for the deceased companion; a foreign king, 800 masses; the Prince of Wales, 700 masses; a duke, 600 masses; a count or earl, 300 masses; a mere baron, 200 masses; and a mere knight bachelor, 100 masses. A companion-elect who died before he could be installed was to receive precisely half the number of masses owed to a full companion in each case.[180] If the number of masses owed had not been paid for within three months a quarter of the number owed was to be doubled; if not within six months, half the number; and if not in a whole year, the whole number was to be doubled.[181] The obligation to pay for these masses was undoubtedly the greatest burden undertaken with membership, but the benefits were correspondingly great, as the first companion to die – probably the knight Hugh Courtenay, who died before 2 September 1349 – would have received from his companions no fewer than 5300 masses to hasten his soul through purgatory, without having paid for a single one himself. For a companion who was a mere knight or baron, at least, there was a strong likelihood that many more masses would be sung for him after his death than would be paid for by him in his lifetime, so that membership in the Order entailed a very profitable spiritual investment. Indeed, when the solemn requiem sung annually by the Order's canons, the daily masses said as a matter of course by the canons and vicars, and the daily prayers of the Order's poor knights were all taken into consideration, the spiritual benefits of companionship must have appeared very considerable.

It is striking that, unlike the knights of most other orders, the knights of the Garter undertook no obligations specifically related to chivalry, no regular spiritual exercises, and no obligation to submit disputes among themselves to the arbitration of the Sovereign and Chapter. In fact, all of the remaining obligations of companionship were related to participation in the Order's activities and the wearing of its badge and habit. The companions were bound to attend annual Assemblies[182] and the religious services held during those Assemblies,[183] and to take part in elections whenever held,[184] unless excused by the Sovereign for some good reason;[185] to hear mass or vespers in the Order's chapel whenever they found

179 Ch. 17.
180 Ord. 19d.
181 Ords. 17h–j.
182 Ord. 9e.
183 Ords. 9f, 14b.
184 Ords. 18k–m.
185 Ords. 10f, 18k,l.

themselves in the neighbourhood,[186] wearing a mantle left with the canons for such visits;[187] to wear the garter whenever they appeared in public[188] and the mantle on the feast of St George and during all ceremonies connected with the Order;[189] to provide their own mantles,[190] helms, swords, and stall-plates; and to accept the punishments imposed for infractions of the Order's ordinances. Specific punishments of the types characteristic of confraternities were set forth in the statutes for absence without leave from any of the Order's corporate activities, for late arrival at any of the activities of the annual Assembly, and for failure either to visit the Order's chapel or to wear the garter on some public occasion. Those late for services were to be required to stand below amongst the choristers throughout the service in question, while those who missed an annual Assembly completely without permission were required during the following Assembly to stand outside their stalls until the offertory of the second service, when they could ask the Sovereign's pardon. Any companion resident in England who missed a second Assembly without permission was in addition to offer on the altar a jewel of the value of 20 marks, the sum to be doubled annually until paid.[191] A companion who absented himself without the Sovereign's permission from an election was liable to a fine of one mark payable to the Dean and College, and was further to sit on the floor during the proceedings of the following Chapter until he was pardoned.[192] A companion who failed to enter the Order's seat when he was in the area was to be required to walk to it from a distance of one league and offer there one penny for St George.[193] Failure to wear the garter was to be punished with a fine of half a mark, presumably for each occasion on which it was not worn.[194] It is likely that most of these penalties were in fact imposed at Chapters held during the course of our period.

It should finally be noted in this context that high civil rank, far from being the asset it usually proved to be in this period, was a serious liability for companions of the Order of the Garter. As we have seen, the early statutes distinguished no fewer than six ranks below the Sovereign: foreign king, Prince of Wales, duke, count or earl, baron or banneret, and knight bachelor. Not only did the entry-fees and the number of masses owed to the dead increase significantly with each increase in rank on this scale, but except in the earliest years of the Order, the civil rank of the companions was accorded no positive recognition whatever. Until the reign of Richard II, the rank of the companions seems to have been indicated by the number of garters strewn on their habits, but this practice was discontinued in the early fifteenth century. Furthermore, with the exception of the Sovereign and the heir apparent, (who was always to sit and process across from the Sovereign), the place of a companion in the Order's chapel and in its solemn processions was

---

[186] Ords. 16a,b,e.
[187] Ord. 15a.
[188] Ord. 12a.
[189] Chs. 3, 11.
[190] This is implied by ord. 15a.
[191] Ords. 10c–i.
[192] Ords. 18l,m.
[193] Ord. 16f.
[194] Ord. 12b.

generally determined solely on the basis of the date of his election.[195] Thus the Order was at once strongly hierarchical in matters of obligation, and strongly egalitarian in matters of honour – a remarkable combination for the time.

9 The Ladies of the Order

Though no provision is made for such a practice in the statutes, it appears that, from the year before the founder's death until the tenth year of the reign of Henry VII, certain ladies were issued with the insignia of the Order, and allowed to participate in the Order's ceremonies with the title of *Domina de Secta et Liberatura Garterii* or *Dame de la Fraternité de St Georges*. Since the practice is recorded only in account-books and on tomb effigies, nothing whatever is known of either how or why ladies were chosen for this honour, but from the silence of the statutes and capitular records it must be assumed that the ladies were never considered to be regular members of the Order. Nevertheless, costumes and garters comparable in every respect to those issued to the male companions were issued to the ladies selected for the honour, and in all likelihood they participated actively in some of the annual festivities of the Order. It appears from tomb effigies (notably that of Margaret Byron, wife of the companion Sir Robert Harcourt, in the church of Stanton Harcourt, Oxfordshire) that the garter itself was worn by these ladies on the left arm, above the elbow, rather than below the left knee.[196] Only one other monarchical order – the Aragonese order of the Stole and Jar – was to have a comparable body of ladies associated with it.

10 The College of St George at Windsor: The Clergy of the Order

What we have called the 'college of companions' alone constituted the Order of the Garter in the narrow sense of the phrase, but from the time of the Order's foundation two other bodies of men were so closely associated with the companions that they must be regarded as forming part of the Order's establishment. Both of these bodies – one made up of secular clerics and the other of lay knights – were at first included within the canonical College attached to the royal chapel of St George in Windsor Castle.[197] As we have seen, this College was reorganized both at the time of its attachment to the projected Order in August 1348,[198] and again when the statutes of the Order were formally adopted in or about April 1349. The

---

[195] According to ch. 21a, each companion was to be seated in the stall of the companion he succeeded, but in practice certain companions were placed in higher seats.

[196] On the subject of the Ladies of the Garter, see Beltz, *Memorials*, pp. 244–6. A complete list of the known ladies is printed in *Complete Peerage*, II, pp. 592–6.

[197] On the Order's clerical establishment, see A. K. B. Roberts, *St George's Chapel Windsor Castle, 1348–1946* (Windsor, 1947); and S. L. Ollard, *The Dean and Canons of St George's Chapel* (Windsor, 1950).

[198] Charter *CPR, 1348–50*, p. 144; pub. Ashmole, *Institution*, p. [758].

new organization of the College was duly confirmed by a papal bull of 30 November 1350,[199] and the College was finally granted a formal constitution of its own on 30 November 1352.[200] According to the latter document, the establishment of the College of St George at Windsor was to be made up of a warden (later called dean), twelve other canons, thirteen vicars, four clerks, six choristers, twenty-six poor knights, and a verger. The College thus constituted was to be supported with the income of eleven churches, and the installation fees, fines, offerings, and mass payments of the companions. Edward later endowed it with lands paying an annual income of £655 15s, and granted it an extraordinary series of privileges, including immunity from most forms of taxation; the profits of certain fines, a weekly market, and two annual fairs; and the right to punish offenders arrested on its lands. It was also granted immunity from all forms of episcopal jurisdiction by the Pope in February 1351, and has since that time been a 'royal peculiar'.[201]

The attachment of a college of clerics to the otherwise lay society of the Garter was one of the more novel features of the Order; there is no evidence to suggest that either the Society of St George or the Order of the Band had its own clergy. The order projected by the Duke of Normandy in 1344, however, was certainly intended to have had attached to it a canonical institute, remarkably similar in size, nature and function to that of the Order of the Garter. As there is nothing to indicate that Edward's original project was to have had any kind of clerical establishment, it is more than possible that Edward borrowed the idea, like the dedication of the Order to St George, directly from his French rival. Several later monarchical orders were intended by their founders to have comparable bodies of clerics placed at their service, but only three later orders – those of the Collar, the Ermine of Brittany, and the Golden Fleece – are known to have acquired one.

The number of priests in the college attached to the Order of the Garter was obviously chosen to match that of the companions (having been raised first to twenty-four by the letters of 1348 and then to twenty-six in the statutes of 1349), and it is clear that the priests were in some sense the representatives of the companions. Indeed, the original members of the clerical college were individually nominated by the 'First Founders', though their successors were to be named by the Sovereign alone.[202] The duties of the twenty-six priests were defined partly in the statutes of their own College and partly in those of the Order. The thirteen vicars, at least, were required to reside in the Castle near the chapel, and to celebrate daily masses for the souls of the faithful departed – particularly, though not exclusively, those of the companions.[203] With the poor veteran knights, the canons and vicars

---

[199] Pub. Ashmole, *Institution*, pp. [758–9].

[200] Roberts, *St George's Chapel*, p. 7.

[201] Letters in Ashmole, *Institution*, p. [759].

[202] Ords. 4f,g.

[203] Any knight who was not a companion of the Order, or any other person who wished to be included in the prayers of the Order's canons and knights, could pay £10 or more annually for the privilege of having his name added to the list of benefactors, and his name would be perpetually commemorated. (Ch. 31). In 1422 Henry V amended this provision by declaring that thenceforth the Dean and canons were not to take any further charge upon themselves without the consent of the Sovereign or his Deputy.

made up the Order's resident establishment, and one of their functions was to receive visiting companions and conduct them to the chapel.[204] At the Order's annual Assembly, the canons and vicars joined to sing for the companions the solemn mass of St George, the two offices, and the requiem mass for the Order's dead, and when a companion died they were to conduct his funeral, and presumably to sing the purgatorial masses paid for by the surviving companions. The principal function of the Order's clergy was thus to provide for the spiritual welfare of the companions.

11 The Poor or Veteran Knights of the Order

Chapter 6 of the statutes declared that there were to be twenty-six impoverished knights associated with the Order, who were to be supported in return for their prayers. Like the priests of the College to which they were at first attached, each of the first set of poor knights was to have been chosen by one of the First Founders, and their successors were to have been chosen by the Sovereign of the day.[205] Edward's attachment to his Order of a second body of knights was even more novel than his attachment to it of the college of priests, as there is no indication that the French project of 1344 was to have included any such body.[206] It was not uncommon for professional confraternities to support almshouses for impoverished members of their profession, however, so in all likelihood Edward merely borrowed the idea from the same general source as he borrowed the constitutional format of his revised Order. Edward probably had three main reasons for the creation of this second lay college: first, a desire to give his Order a genuine charitable function, if only for the spiritual benefits to be gained therefrom; second, a desire to provide an honourable retirement for some of the less fortunate veterans of his foreign wars, both out of genuine regard for them, and to encourage others to serve him; and finally, a desire to provide what might be termed lay-vicars for the companions of the Order, to represent them in the Order's chapel during their enforced absences, and to pray both for them and on their behalf. Through this rather ingenious means Edward might have maintained a full complement of knights at the Order's seat at Windsor while the 'companions' of the Order went their separate ways. It is interesting that Edward – unlike his rival the Duke of Normandy – did not encourage any of the companions to reside at Windsor, requiring anyone who wished to do so to support himself.[207]

According to the constitution of the canonical college,[208] the specific duties of the poor knights were to attend mass at the Order's chapel in choir three times a

---

[204] Ords. 16c,d.

[205] Ch. 6.

[206] On the subject of the poor or 'military' knights (as they have been called since 1833), see E. H. Fellowes, *The Military Knights of Windsor, 1352–1944* (Windsor, 1944).

[207] Ch. 30. Ch. B.33 added that any knight who was not a companion could also live in the Order's house at his own expense with the consent of the Sovereign and companions.

[208] For this and what follows, see Fellowes, *Military Knights*, pp. xiv–xxix.

day and to say one hundred and fifty *Aves* and fifteen *Pater nosters* at each of these services. For this they were to be paid a regular income exactly equal to that of the canons, 40s a year plus a daily allowance of 12d. Evidently Edward and his successors found it impossible to provide an endowment sufficient to maintain such a payment to more than a small fraction of the full complement of twenty-six poor knights called for in the statutes; between 1362 and 1399 payment was never made to more than two knights at a time, and for extended periods was made to only one. During the period from 1399 to 1481, when Edward IV incorporated the College of St George by an act of Parliament, the number of poor knights maintained never exceeded three, and there were occasionally none at all.

The act of 1481 removed the poor knights from dependence on the College of St George to relieve it of the burden of supporting them, but did not provide for any other source of maintenance, and such new 'knights' as were appointed thereafter had to be supported by the Sovereign out of his own pocket. Between 1481 and 1515 a tiny complement of two or three poor knights was in fact maintained in this way, but between 1515 and 1558 – despite the fact that Henry VIII retained the poor knights in his revised statutes of 1519, though reduced in theoretical number to thirteen – no appointments at all were made, and it was not until the reign of Elizabeth I that the college of poor knights, even in this reduced form, was finally established.

The succession of poor knights in the reigns of the first two Sovereigns of the Order can be reconstructed only imperfectly, on the basis of financial records. The names of only seven poor knights are known from this period, the earliest being that of Robert Beverley, which first appears in the records in the year 1368. From the beginning of the fifteenth century the succession of knights can be traced fairly completely, since not only the accounts of the Treasurers of the College but the letters patent by which they were appointed have generally been preserved. Relatively little is known about most of the poor knights of our period. During the first century or so the statutory requirement that they be veteran knights impoverished in the royal service was generally observed: of the first nineteen *milites pauperes* whose names are known, all or most were veterans, though only eleven were dubbed knights. Edward IV, who removed the knights from the College of St. George, also chose to abandon the traditional criteria for their selection, and named as 'poor knights' a number of civilians, including one of his personal physicians, a former groom of his chamber, and one of his provincial kings-of-arms. Henry VII and Henry VIII continued the practice of appointing men who were neither knights nor veterans, and the handful of men they named to the status included a barber, a 'Sewer in the King's Hall', a Baron of the Exchequer, and a musical composer. Some of these men were not even poor, and thus conformed in no respect to the requirements of the statutes.

12 The Physical Establishment of the Order in Windsor Castle

The proper functioning of the Order's permanent establishment of priests and poor knights required extensive and costly physical facilities, and it is perhaps more remarkable that Edward succeeded in providing adequate facilities for the priests than that he failed to do so for the knights. Since the College to which both priests and poor knights belonged was attached to the chapel of the lower bailey of Windsor Castle, these facilities were naturally constructed next to the chapel within the walls of that part of the castle. It appears that Edward hoped to have the necessary construction underway before the end of 1348, the year in which the letters patent of reorganization were issued, but the Black Death intervened, and the work did not finally begin until the time of the first recorded feast of the Order, in April 1350.[209] Between that date and the end of 1357, all the buildings intended for the Order's clergy – including a vestry, chapter-house, treasury, and warden's lodge arranged around one cloister, and lodgings arranged around another – were completed, the old great hall and kitchen in the castle's lower bailey were made over to the College, and the old chapel of St Edward was repaired and refurnished for its new role. The completion of this phase of the work was celebrated by the Order on St George's day 1358. Between 1357 and 1365, the royal lodgings in the upper bailey of the castle were completely remodelled, and a magnificent new hall (of the usual rectangular shape) was built for the use of the king and the companions. Thus by 1365 – twenty-one years after the proclamation of the Round Table project – the Order's seat at Windsor had been converted into a sumptuous royal palace. Thereafter the Order's physical establishment changed little until 1475, when the Order's sixth Sovereign, Edward IV, began to build a new and much larger chapel for the Order, just to the west of the existing one, in the perpendicular style of gothic that was then fashionable. The new chapel was eventually completed under Henry VIII, and the old one was pulled down. The Order's buildings were finally completed when Elizabeth I built quarters for the poor knights, more than two hundred years after the Order's effective foundation.

Of the several buildings built or refurbished for the use of the Order, the Chapel of St George was always the most important. It was there that the numerous prayers and masses required by the statutes were to be said, it was there that the most important of the Order's ceremonies were to be held, and it was there, rather than in the hall as originally planned, that each companion had his personal stall, over which, during his lifetime, his sword and crested helm were placed in token of his occupancy,[210] and upon which, after his death, a plaque was to be set bearing his name and armorial achievement, as a perpetual memorial to him.[211] Little is now known about the original chapel of St George or the stalls of the earliest companions (in use from about 1350 to about 1485), but it is clear that that chapel occupied the same area as the present lady-chapel (built mainly upon its foundations), and that it must have been largely occupied by the stalls of the companions, as the present stalls take up a comparable area within the existing chapel. Presumably the stalls were specially constructed for the knights and priests to occupy simultaneously, and were arranged from the first in two tiers with that of the priests below.

It appears that the practice of setting up a memorial plaque or 'stall-plate' at the death of each companion was only rarely observed before the reign of Henry V.

---

[209] See Colvin, *King's Works*, pp. 872–7, for most of what follows.

[210] Ord. 9g.

[211] Ch. 23 specifies that this was to be done as soon as possible after the companion's death.

The 140 companions elected before 1421 are today represented by only forty-six plates, and all but one of these – that of Sir Ralph Basset, set up around 1390 – seem to have been set up by Henry V himself in or about 1421. Thereafter the plates – generally small rectangular plaques of copper-gilt bearing the name, arms, and crested helm of the companion in coloured enamel – were set in place with considerable regularity, but seem to have been attached to the stall during the companion's lifetime rather than after his death, as the statutes continued to specify until 1519.[212] The practice of setting the companion's helm and sword over his stall, by contrast, was observed quite faithfully from the reign of the founder onwards, for the records of the College contain numerous references to the sale of these items. The same records show that the practice of offering up the helm and sword of a deceased companion for the benefit of the College, not formally required until the reign of Henry V, was almost as old as the Order itself. After the completion of the choir of the new chapel in about 1485, the stall-plates, swords, and helms were all transferred to the magnificent new stalls housed within it, where the stall plates may be seen to this day.[213] From at least the year 1424 a banner of the arms of each companion was hung above his stall, probably at the same time that the sword and helm were put in place, but this was not formally required until 1519.[214]

As we shall see, most later founders of monarchical orders – inspired by the splendid and capacious buildings built or refurbished for the use of the Order of the Garter by Edward and his successors – were to announce an intention to provide comparable accomodations for the knights and chaplains of their order. In the event, however, only the Count of Savoy, the Duke of Brittany, and the Duke of Burgundy would succeed in doing so.

13 The Officers of the Order

In addition to providing his Order with an appropriate set of buildings, the founder also created a number of officers for the Order to serve him in his capacity as Sovereign, and his successors added to these at various times during the course of our period. Although confraternities of the more humble sort commonly had one or two officers in their employ, the offices attached to the Order of the Garter seem to have been modelled partly upon those typical of collegiate churches and partly on those of the royal household. The only office clearly defined by the original statutes of the Order was that of the *register* or Registrar, who was to be chosen from among the canons to act as secretary or recorder of the Order's business. He was required by chapter 34 to undertake by oath to be present at all Chapters of the Order, to register all elections, the names of those elected, the punishments meted out, the reconciliations effected, and all other acts of the Order, with their reasons, from

---

[212] See W. H. St. John Hope, *The Stall Plates of the Knights of the Garter, 1348-1485* (London, 1901), for a thorough discussion of the history and nature of the plates, and representations of many of the plates from our period.

[213] Roberts, *St George's Chapel*, p. 13.

[214] Hope, *Stall Plates*, p. 16.

year to year.[215] We know nothing of either the identity or the work of the Registrars before 1416, but eight canons of Windsor have been at least tentatively identified as Registrars of the Order in the period between 1416 and 1509.[216] Most of these men seem to have carried out their sworn task in a somewhat lackadaisical fashion, since the register for that period is full of *lacunae*, as we have seen.

The statutes also mention a *custos sigilli ordinis* or 'keeper of the Order's seal', to be chosen from among the companions,[217] and a 'Prelate'.[218] The Order seems to have been given a corporate seal at the time of its foundation, for it is mentioned in a document of 1353 as well as in the earliest versions of the statutes.[219] The seal was used to authenticate all copies of the Order's statutes, all letters of license or dispensation, and all other documents pertaining to the Order. Henry V ordained in 1422 that a privy or signet seal was to be used by the Sovereign when he was abroad, to distinguish documents issued in his name from those issued by his deputy in England. The office of Prelate was evidently to be attached to the bishopric of Winchester, and in fact all of the Bishops of Winchester since the foundation of the Order have exercised the office of Prelate. The only functions the Prelate of the Order was called upon to perform were the celebration (with the Order's lesser clergy) of the annual services, and when present, the collection and tabulation of the ballots cast in elections. No doubt his real rôle was to enhance the dignity of the Order and its religious services. Why the office was annexed to the see of Winchester is unknown, but the historic importance of the see and its associations with the Arthurian tradition probably played a part in its selection for the honour.[220]

No other officers are mentioned in the early statutes, but by 1351 the founder seems to have created a fourth office: that of verger or usher of the Order. The incumbant of this office was known from the reign of Edward IV as the 'Gentleman Usher of the Black Rod'. He was given an annual pension of £30 and a daily fee of 12*d*, and from the year 1352 he had a house of his own within Windsor Castle. Black Rod later became the Chief Usher of the kingdom, and no one but a gentleman of name and arms could be appointed to the office.[221]

After 1351 the complement of officers formally attached to the Order remained fixed until 1415, when Henry V added a herald, styled *Jartier, Roy d'armes des Angloys* – 'Garter, King of Arms of the English'.[222] As his title implies, Garter King of Arms was to be not only the herald of the Order of the Garter, but also (in the words of the Patent) '. . . sovereign in the office of arms over all the other servants of arms in the most noble kingdom of England.' Henry died before he had time to endow the new office in an appropriate fashion, but immediately following the Assembly of the Order held in April 1423 letters patent were issued granting to its

---

[215] Ords. 34a–i.

[216] For a list with dates, see Nicolas, *History*, II, p. lxxxiv.

[217] Ords. 26b, 30b.

[218] Ord. 18g.

[219] Nicholas, *History*, II, p. 469.

[220] On the office of Prelate, see Ashmole, *Institution*, pp. 234–7.

[221] Ibid., pp. 256–8, and Roberts, *St George's Chapel*, pp. 13–14. For a partial list of Ushers of the Black Rod, see Nicolas, *History*, II, p. lxxxvii.

[222] See Nicolas, *History*, II, pp. 455–6.

incumbant the right to receive each year at the Order's annual Assembly the sum of five marks from the Prelate, six nobles from every companion of the rank of duke, four nobles from every companion of the rank of baron or banneret, and two from every companion of the rank of knight bachelor.[223] The first Garter King of Arms was Sir William Bruges, formerly Guyenne King of Arms, who held the office from 1415 until his death in 1450. He and his immediate successors, John Smert (1450–78), Sir John Wrythe (1478–1504), and Sir Thomas Wrythe or Wriothesley (1505–34), were distinguished heralds, and all but Smert have left us collections of heraldic materials related to the Order.[224]

The sixth and last officer to be attached to the Order of the Garter was the Chancellor, whose office was created – probably in imitation of the Order of the Golden Fleece – by letters patent of Edward IV dated 10 October 1474.[225] The Chancellor assumed the duties of the informally appointed 'keeper of the seal', and the creation of the office did not therefore increase the number of the Order's officers. The office was from the beginning annexed to the bishopric of Salisbury, the diocese within which Windsor lay, and until the reign of Elizabeth I the Bishops of Salisbury did in fact keep the seal of the Order.

No other order was to be provided with a comparable set of corporate officers until 1431, when the Duke of Burgundy gave his Order of the Golden Fleece four officers clearly modelled on those of the Garter. Thereafter most new orders would be provided with officers of this type.

14 The Corporate Activities of the Order

Although the clergy and poor knights acted together on a daily basis, the companions and officers of the Order of the Garter came together only during the Order's single annual Assembly and in rare irregular meetings held to replace a deceased companion. The Assembly (*congregatio* or *assemblee*) was the only activity in which all members of the Order had a part, and was by far the most important corporate activity in which the companions themselves were involved; there is nothing to suggest that the knights of the Garter were ever intended to fight as a unit in battle like the knights of some contemporary monarchical orders. The Assembly was to be held each year whether or not the Sovereign could himself attend,[226] and was to be convened at Windsor if the companions were in England, but otherwise wherever was most convenient.[227] The statutes, with due consideration of the difficulty of convening a meeting during the Easter holiday season, specify that the Assembly was to begin either on St George's Eve or on the eve of

---

223 Letters published in Ashmole, *Institution*, App. V, pp. [760–1].
224 *Bruges' Garter Book*, (B.L., Stowe MS. 594); *Writhe's Book of Knights* (B.L., Add. MS. 46354); and *Sir Thomas Wriothesley's Garter Book* (Windsor Heraldic MS. 2).
225 Pub. in Ashmole, *Institution*, p. [760].
226 Ch. 6.
227 Ords. 9b,c.

the second Sunday after Easter, whichever was later.[228] In 1422 Henry V decreed that, in order to avoid conflict with certain other major feasts, the Order's celebrations were not to begin thenceforth on 24, 25, 26 or 30 April or on any of the first four days of May.

The activities of the members during the annual Assembly were to consist, according to the statutes, of a business meeting, a banquet, and four religious services. The business meeting or Chapter (the name given to such meetings in most ecclesiatical organizations) was held first, beginning at the hour of terce of the day before the feast-day proper (that is, about mid-morning) and continuing until just before vespers in the evening of the same day. The Sovereign or his Deputy presided at these meetings, assisted by the Registrar, who was to record the proceedings, and the other officers of the Order. The Chapter was to begin with a public reading of the minutes of the previous chapter by the Registrar.[229] Unlike the statutes of some orders, those of the Garter have nothing explicit to say about the matters that were to be discussed at its annual Chapter, but as the Registrar was required to record punishments assigned to the companions,[230] it must be presumed that part of the meeting was regularly devoted to an examination of the conduct of the companions during the course of the preceding year. It would appear that this examination was limited to conduct specifically prescribed by the statutes of the Order, as the Deputy was directed only to 'correct and reform' transgressors against the statutes.[231] The Registrar was also required to record reconciliations effected,[232] so part of the meeting must have been devoted to settling disputes between or among companions of the Order. Both of these activities were normal in confraternities, and were to form an important element of the meetings of most monarchical orders. In all likelihood new ordinances were normally adopted during the course of annual chapters, but the statutes say nothing about this important subject except that such ordinances could not be made in the absense of the Sovereign.[233] We know almost nothing about the manner in which any of these matters was discussed or voted upon either before or after 1416. In practice, as we have seen, most of the elections held to replace deceased companions seem to have been held during the meeting of the annual Chapter, but this was technically irregular. There is no evidence that the companions were ever called upon to discuss matters not of direct concern to the Order as such during the course of the Chapter, so it would appear that they were *not* meant to function (like the companions of several contemporary orders) as counsellors to their Sovereign.

The Chapter was followed by the service of vespers, which everyone present was to attend. The next day (which was that of the Feast of St George, either regular or transferred) began with the solemn high mass of St George, sung in the Order's chapel by the Order's clergy and choir and attended by all the members of the Order. Various ceremonies, including the induction of new companions, took place in the context of this service every year. The original statutes specify that at

---

[228] Ord. 9a,d.
[229] Ord. 34j.
[230] Ord. 34e.
[231] Ord. 8c.
[232] Ord. 34f.
[233] Ord. 8b.

the offertory of the mass, the companions were to approach the altar in pairs, each standing beside the companion from the stall opposite him, and that any whose opposite number was absent was to process alone. The Sovereign was to approach the altar in the place of honour, last.[234] Following the mass the members of the Order gathered at a banquet of Arthurian splendour, presumably held between 1349 and 1365 in the old great hall of the castle, and after 1365 in the new great hall built by the founder for the purpose. The banquet in its turn was followed in most years by elaborate entertainments, which must often have included various forms of hastilude. In the 1350s and '60s the knights of the Order may well have taken part in tournaments as an organized team or pair of opposing teams, as the original composition of the Order suggests, but unlike the knights of the Band they were not formally required to take part in any form of military or paramilitary activity, and the only tournament in which they are known to have participated as a team was held in 1390. After the entertainments were over, the companions once again heard vespers in the chapel, sung by clergy and choir. Finally, on the day following the feast, the companions were required to attend a solemn requiem mass for the Order's departed.[235]

As we observed in passing earlier, the evidence of account books (for the period before 1416) and of the Black Book (for the subsequent period) indicates that meetings of the Order were held at the prescribed time and place in most of the years between 1349 and 1520. Lacunae in the accounts make it impossible to be sure that Assemblies were convened in seventeen years of the fourteenth century, however, and no record has been preserved in the Black Book for fully thirty years of the fifteenth. Our sources tell us almost nothing of what the companions did at these Assemblies, but we do know how many were actually present at most of those for which some records survive, and this is not without interest. At the seventeen such meetings held before 1400, the number fluctuated between a high of twenty-four and a low of thirteen, but only fell below nineteen on four occasions. Considering the fact that many of the knights of the Order were frequently abroad on the service of the king, and that several of them were foreigners, the fact that all but a handful (an average of five) managed to attend most meetings must be regarded as indicative of the high importance they placed upon attendance at the Order's meetings under the founder and his grandson Richard II. In the fifteenth century, however, attendance at Assemblies dropped off sharply. At the four feasts in the reign of Henry V for which records survive, the numbers were five, five, nine, and four, and under his son Henry VI attendance varied from a high of fifteen to a low of three, and only surpassed eleven on four occasions. Under Edward IV the number of companions present ranged from seventeen to two, and only surpassed six three times, when the king himself was present. The figures for the reign of Henry VII are very similar: at nine recorded meetings the number of companions present varied from fifteen to two, and only twice passed six. Attendance by the Sovereign fell just as significantly in the fifteenth century. Henry VI missed many meetings because of his youth or distraction, and in the sixty years between 1460

[234] Ch. 13. The ordinance adopted in 1418 specified that the knights were to bow to the Sovereign's stall when they passed it, and the ordinance added to this chapter in 1422 specified that they were also to bow to the altar.
[235] Ch. 14.

and 1520 the presence of the Sovereign is recorded at only twelve Assemblies, four of them in the reign of Henry VIII.

It should finally be noted in this context that companions who were unable for some good reason to attend the annual Assembly were required by the statutes to wear the costume of the Order from Vespers on St George's Eve to Vespers on St George's Day, just as if they were present.[236] Edward, with characteristic realism, recognized the difficulty many companions would have in attending meetings (especially when they were abroad on his service), but did not want them to forget their membership on the Order's most solemn day. The rule also provided an opportunity for foreign companions, especially princes who seldom if ever attended an Assembly, to wear the Order's habit, and there is evidence that some foreign princes regularly wore their garter and mantle on St George's Day.

15 The Badge and Insignia of the Order

The badge from which the Order took its more common name is referred to in the statutes simply as a 'garter' – in French *gartier*, in Latin *subligarium*, *garterium*, or *garterus* – and neither its form nor its colour is described in any official instrument of the Order itself. On the basis of the records of the great wardrobe and representations dating from the second decade of the Order's history, however, we know that from the time of its adoption by Edward the device called a garter normally took the form of a miniature belt with a metal buckle and pendant, and was invariably made of cloth dyed in the light-blue colour officially known as *bleu* or *bluetus*.[237] We also know that the motto *Hony soyt quy mal y pense* (variously spelled) was commonly if not invariably embroidered upon it, usually in gold thread. The garters supplied before the definitive foundation of the Order in 1349 all seem to have been two-dimensional representations, since they were all applied in a decorative fashion to flags, hangings, and items of apparel. After the foundation of the Order both the Sovereign and the companions wore such two-dimensional garters on formal occasions associated with the Order, em-broidered at first on every item of their formal habit, and later on their mantle alone, but the statutes required the companions to wear a three-dimensional garter buckled about their left knee whenever they appeared in public, and this quasi-functional garter was thus the normal form of the device as the badge of the Order. The first garters of this type may have been those referred to in the register of the Black Prince, which were purchased in December 1348.

At the time Ashmole wrote his history of the Order, three fourteenth-century tomb effigies representing knights of the Order wearing the three-dimensional garter still survived, and in each case the device was represented as a miniature belt

---

[236] Ch. 11.

[237] In the register referred to above recording the payments for the items decorated with garters in the period immediately preceding January 1349, the *garteria* are described as *bluetus* and as having in some cases buckles and pendants of silver gilt. One set of these garters was also inscribed with the motto. (See above, p. 112.)

buckled just below the left knee, without any inscription.[238] The oldest surviving representation of the three-dimensional garter with the motto is probably that on the monumental brass of Simon de Felbrigg, set up in 1416.[239] Only two fourteenth-century representations of the two-dimensional garter are currently known, both dating from the founder's reign. A small portrait of the founder knight Nele Loring (d. 1386) in a manuscript of the *Liber vite* in St Alban's Abbey shows him wearing a surcoat and caped hood powdered with eighteen visible garters. Each of the latter is represented as a blue annulus with a small tongue protruding at the right part of the base, rather like a capital Q; no letters or buckles are visible.[240] The two-dimensional garter is represented in considerably more detail (though without colour) in a lead or pewter badge made for some unknown purpose between about 1350 and 1376, in which it encircles a scene showing the Black Prince, supported by two angels bearing his arms and crested helm, adoring the Trinity. The garter is here represented as a broad belt in the form of an annulus with a buckle at the base and a tongue, pierced with decorative grommets and terminating in a pendant, looped behind the annulus to the left of the buckle and then pulled almost straight down between the annulus and the first part of the tongue in such a way that the pendant hangs down at the centre. The annulus is inscribed with the words *hony soyt ke mal y pense* in gothic minuscule letters, beginning at the left base.[241] Fifteenth-century and later examples differ from this only in such minor details as the position and direction of the buckle, the form of the buckle, pendant, and grommets, and the precise arrangement of the words.[242] The oldest actual garter now in existence is the one worn by Maximilian, King of the Romans and later Emperor, who was elected to the Order in 1489.[243] On this the tongue lacks both grommets and pendant and is entirely covered with gold embroidery, and the words of the motto, embroidered in the same gold thread, are separated by small enamelled roses.

As we have seen, it now appears that the blue garter bearing the motto *hony soyt qui mal y pense* – 'shamed be he who thinks ill of it' – was first adopted by Edward as a device for his personal use shortly before his departure for France in the summer of 1346, rather than after his return to England in the autumn of the following year as Nicolas had supposed. Why Edward should have chosen a garter as the principal device for that campaign, however, remains a mystery, since no writer even

[238] The effigies of William FitzWaryn (d. 1361), in Wantage Church, Berks.; Richard Pembrugge (d. 1386), in Hereford Cathedral; and Simon Burley (d. 1388), in St Paul's Cathedral, London (since destroyed). Ashmole, *Institution*, p. 204.

[239] A representation of the whole brass (of which the original is in the church of Felbrigg in Norfolk) was published by Muriel Clayton in *Catalogue of Rubbings of Brasses and Incised Slabs* (London, 1968), Pl. 17. The next oldest is that on the brass of Thomas, Lord Camoys (d. 1419), a detail of which showing the garter tied about the baron's knee was published by W. H. St John Hope in *Heraldry for Craftsmen and Designers* (London, 1913), fig. 152, p. 261. See fig. 4.1.

[240] For a monochrome reproduction of this, see Stella Mary Newton, *Fashion in the Age of the Black Prince. A study of the years 1340–1365* (Woodbridge, 1980), fig. 13, p. 45.

[241] See fig. 4.2.

[242] For example those on the monumental brass of Thomas, Lord Camoys (see above, n. 239), and that on the brass in Constance of Robert Hallam, Bishop of Salisbury (d. 1416) (Hope, *Heraldry*, fig. 155, p. 265).

[243] A monochrome photograph of this garter was published by Richard Marks and Anne Payne, *British Heraldry from its Origins to c.1800* (London, 1978), no. 246, p. 127.

4.1 The three-dimensional garter,
from the tomb of Thomas,
Lord Camoys, c.1419
(after St. John Hope)

4.2 The two-dimensional garter,
on a leaden badge of 1350/76
(after St. John Hope)

4.3 The two-dimensional garter, as represented
a. on the tomb of Thomas, Lord Camoys, c.1419 (after St. John Hope)
b. on the stall-plate of Francis, Viscount Lovell, c.1483

remotely contemporary with the foundation of the Order saw fit to explain its significance. Two stories purporting to recount the origin of the device were later recorded, but one of these – which maintained that the garter of the Order was inspired by a bit of lace given by Richard I to certain of his knights to wear around their legs during his attacks on Cyprus and Acre – can be dismissed as a late invention without any foundation.[244] The other story, which now appears to have been in circulation by the fourth decade of the fifteenth century, has to be taken somewhat more seriously. According to the more familiar version of this story, Edward had at some time before the foundation of the Order picked up from the ground a garter from the stocking of some lady of his court, and when some of the knights present began to jeer, declared that they would soon hold the same garter in the highest honour. This version of the tale was first published in England by the Italian-born historian Polydore Virgil as late as 1534,[245] but the story was hinted at in a treatise on the Order written by the Italian Mondonus Belvaleti in 1463,[246] and a full-blown version of the story somewhat different from that recorded by Vergil was included in a Catalan romance composed about sixty years before his history: *Tirant lo Blanc*, written about 1460 by the Valencian Joannot Martorell.[247] Martorell had been in London in 1438 and 1439, and probably learned the story then, along with the rest of what he knew about the Order of the Garter.[248] In Martorell's version of the story (which is considerably more circumstantial than Vergil's), the lady in question was a damsel of no great beauty, talent, or standing named Madresilva ('Honeysuckle'), and Edward (after taking her garter from the knight who had picked it off the ground) wore it about his knee for four months before his favourite servant told him that everyone in the kingdom was astonished that he would wear the favour of so undistinguished a girl. Rather than explain his strange behaviour, Edward – piqued by this criticism – replied that all who thought ill of it would be punished (rather than shamed), and that he would found an order of knighthood to honour the garter forever. He then had the garter removed for the time being from his knee.[249] Vergil, who regarded the whole story as nothing more than a 'popular tradition', said the lady in the story was supposed to be either Edward's queen or his mistress, but Camden, at the end of the sixteenth century, identified her as a certain Countess of Salisbury,[250] (presumably the widow of Edward's friend William de Montague, who died immediately after the Windsor

---

[244] This story was first recorded by the compiler of the Black Book of the Order in 1534.

[245] *Polydori Vergilii Urbinatis Anglicae Historiae libri XXV* (Basel, 1534), pp. 373–4; quoted in Latin in Germán Colón, 'Premiers échos de l'Ordre de la Jarretière', *Zeitschrift für Romanische Philologie* 81 (1965), pp. 443–4; quoted in part in English in Barber, *Edward*, p. 85.

[246] *Tractatus ordinis serenissimi domini regis Anglie vulgariter dicti la Gerretiere*, preserved as B.L., Harley MS. 5415, and published in Cologne in 1631. The passage in question reads: 'Et sunt plerique nonnulli autumantes hunc ordinem exordium sumpsisse a sexu muliebri.'

[247] Ed. Martí de Riquer (Barcelona, 1957).

[248] Colón, 'Premiers échos', p. 447.

[249] The story is quoted in Catalan and translated into French in Colón, 'Premiers échos', pp. 444–7.

[250] *Britannia*, p. 207.

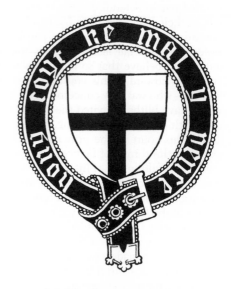

4.4 The garter of the Emperor Maximilian, 1489/15

4.5 The collar of the Garter, from the jousting-cheque for the Field of the Cloth of Gold, 1520

4.6 The device on the breast of the mantle

4.7 Sir Nele Loring in the underhabit of the Order [?], c.1370

4.8 A knight of the Garter depicted in a MS. of c.1450

tournament of 1344), and shortly thereafter Selden specified that the countess in question was rather Joan 'the Fair Maid' of Kent, Edward's cousin, and later the wife both of the founder knight Thomas Holand, and of Edward's son the Black Prince.[251] Joan's name thus entered the tradition, and an attempt was made not long ago to prove that she was indeed the lady whose garter became the badge of the Order.[252]

It is just possible that there is a kernel of truth in this story, for (as Nicolas pointed out in defending it)[253] knights of the fourteenth century did in fact wear bits of their lady's clothing (generally sleeves) as a sign of courtly devotion, and Edward must have had some very particular reason for adopting a garter bearing the words *hony soyt qui mal y pense* as the device of the Order. Nevertheless, it is difficult to believe that so much fuss would have been made over a fallen garter either by Edward or his courtiers, and it is even more difficult to believe that Edward – who was very concerned with his public image both at home and abroad – would have blithely invited the derision of his enemies in France (not to mention the wrath of God) by adopting an item of underclothing publicly dropped by any lady of his court as the principal device, first of an expedition to vindicate his claims to the throne of France, and then of the confraternity of heroic knights he founded in fulfillment of his solemn vow to reestablish the Round Table. Ashmole was probably correct, therefore, when he dismissed the story as a scurrilous invention of someone in the French court, comparable to those told about the origins of the Orders of the Collar and the Golden Fleece.[254] Ashmole[255] and most later historians of the Order[256] have preferred to explain the device as a peculiar form of knot symbolic of the ties that bound the companions to one another, but they have not made any suggestion as to why the knot should have taken the unusual form of a garter buckled like a belt. Barber has recently suggested that the device was meant to represent the belt used in the ceremony by which knighthood was bestowed,[257] but while this explanation is probably correct as far as it goes, it still fails to account for the awkward fact that the device was from the beginning called a garter, even though it was not at first worn about the leg.

In order to understand what might have prompted Edward to adopt a garter as a device one must first of all understand what garters were in the period in question, and how and by whom they were worn. The Anglo-Norman word *gartier* was derived from the Old French word *garret*, 'bend of the knee', and is first attested in Walter Bibbesworth's Glossary (written only about twenty-five years before the foundation of the Order) as the name of an item of clothing worn by fashionable squires to keep up their hose.[258] The garters worn by both men and women for this

---

[251] *Titles of Honor*, p. 793.
[252] Margaret Galway, 'Joan of Kent and the Order of the Garter', *University of Birmingham Historical Journal*, 1 (1947), pp. 18–35. For a corrective see Antonia Gransden, 'The Alleged Rape by Edward III of the Countess of Salisbury', *EHR*, 87 (1972), pp. 333–44.
[253] *History*, I, pp. 17–20.
[254] See the comments of Barber on this, *Edward*, p. 86.
[255] *Institution*, p. 183.
[256] E.g. Beltz, *Memorials*, p. xlvii.
[257] *Edward*, p. 87.
[258] Ibid.

purpose in the first decades of the fourteenth century seem to have taken the form of strips of cloth tied just below the knee, but before about 1330 they were generally invisible, as the hemline of both male tunic and female dress fell well below the knee.[259] During the course of the 1330s and '40s, however, the hemline of the male tunic and supertunic crept steadily upward, exposing ever greater amounts of leg, and for a brief period the garters worn by men were clearly visible. During this period, at least, male garters were commonly decorated with embroidery, and were sometimes tied in such a way that the ends dangled; whether they were occasionally fastened with a buckle like that of a belt rather than a knot is not known, but this was at least unusual. By 1346, garters must have been falling out of use among men of fashion, as the shorter hemline of the tunic and supertunic had begun to require the wearing of full-length hose, and these had to be attached to the tunic rather than supported at the knee. Certainly courtiers are never shown wearing garters (other than that of the Order) after 1350 or so.

Thus, at the time Edward seems to have chosen the garter as a badge, the garter was a traditional item of male apparel which had been worn in a decorative fashion for ten or fifteen years, and was therefore socially unobjectionable, but was also obsolescent or virtually obsolete in court circles, and therefore sufficiently distinctive when worn in the traditional way to serve as a badge of membership in a society of some sort. Reduced to a two-dimensional representation it could also be applied or embroidered like the other devices adopted by Edward and his contemporaries in the 1340s on various forms of clothing, but in this form it was scarcely recognizable as a garter, and it is most unlikely that Edward would have selected a garter as a device (or designated the belt-like device he adopted a garter) if he had intended to display it only in this fashion. In fact, Edward's adoption of a two-dimensional garter of unusual construction as a badge to be displayed on flags, hangings, and royal costumes during the course of his campaign in France in 1346, can only be explained if one postulates that he intended from the beginning to make it the badge of his proposed society of knights, and intended it to be worn in a three-dimensional form about the knee. As a garter, the belt-like device displayed by Edward during the Crécy campaign had no obvious (or easily conceivable) association either with fighting or with his claim to French throne. The three-dimensional garter represented by this device, however, was ideally suited for daily wear as a distinctive badge by the companions of a knightly fraternity, and moreover – as a strip of cloth wrapped about a part of the body – bore a strong resemblance to the device of the only body of lay knights certainly known to Edward at the time, the Order of the Band.

It is indeed more than likely that the garter was inspired by that hitherto peculiar device (which may have been represented by the baldric of green cloth that was adopted by the knights of the Round Table in the poem *Gawain and the Green Knight* composed shortly after the foundation of the Order). Edward could conceivably have chosen an armband, a collar, or a belt rather than a garter, but the first two were not traditional elements of male attire, and the last – which would have been the most appropriate for symbolic reasons – was still a normal part of civil dress and thus would not have been distinctive. Edward seems to have

---

[259] For this and what follows, see C. Willet Cunnington and Phyllis Cunnington, *Handbook of English Medieval Costume* (2nd edn. cor., London, 1973), pp. 55–62.

decided that the most appropriate variant on the band that he could adopt would be a garter in the form of a belt – in effect a miniature belt worn in a highly distinctive fashion below the left knee.

This explains the form the badge of the Order took, but not its colours or its cryptic inscription. For these the explanation first proposed by Ashmole and recently refined by Barber is still the most plausible: that the colours – gold on blue – alluded to the royal arms of France that he had quartered with the arms of England when he asserted his claim to the throne of France, while the inscription alluded to that claim itself, and was intended as a retort to those in France who were spreading propaganda to discredit it.[260]

If this explanation is correct, then the garter must have been intended from the first to serve as the device of a society of knights who had won glory defending Edward's pretensions to the throne of France. Nevertheless, it was probably not proclaimed as such until after the victory at Crécy, and possibly not until after Edward's triumphant return to England. During the campaign itself Edward's intentions for the garter were probably kept secret (though the motto may well have been explained) in case his hopes were not realized. When the garter was finally assigned publicly to the projected society of knights, it had already served for a year or more as the symbol of the campaign, and must have seemed a natural (if still mysterious) symbol for a confraternity composed entirely of the heroes of that campaign and intended to perpetuate the memory of the victories they had won. Whether Edward then offered any further explanation of the meaning of the device we do not know, but if my theory is correct he probably did not, for the garter as such was little more than a clever variant on the band, and had no symbolic meaning of its own. This would certainly account for the lack of any explanation for the device in any contemporary chronicle, and the fact that the historians of the Order in the sixteenth century were so unsure of its significance.

Since a garter (unlike a mantle or a surcoat) could easily be worn with any form of clothing knights of his day were likely to wear, Edward felt free to require that the companions of his Order wear the garter whenever they appeared in public.[261] What little evidence there is, however, suggests that the companions did not wear their garters nearly as frequently as they were required to in the period before the accession of Henry V. Several knights of the Order of this period were represented on their tomb without their garter,[262] and Henry V felt obliged to approve an amendment permitting the companions to wear a simple strip of blue silk in place of their garter when dressed for riding, and forbidding them to enter the annual Chapter of the Order without the garter on their knee.[263] After Henry's death the ordinance requiring that the garter be worn at all times may have been observed rather more faithfully, as most of the companions whose tombs have survived are represented wearing it.

The three-dimensional garter was the only symbol of their status regularly worn

---

[260] Barber, *Edward*, p. 86.

[261] Ord. 12a.

[262] Among them the first three Sovereigns, the Black Prince, and Philip Courtenay, who died in 1409 and is buried beneath a brass in Exeter Cathedral.

[263] Nicolas, *History*, I, p. 63. This suggests that by 1422 the surcoat was short enough for the garter to be visible.

by the companions of the Order until the latter part of the reign of Henry VII. Henry at some time between the first election of the Emperor Maximilian in 1489 and his second election in 1502 added a collar to the insignia of the Order.[264] This collar is described in the revised statues of 1519 as 'a coller of golde . . . waying thyrty ounces of Troy weyght and not above, the whiche coller shall be made by pieces in fashion of Garters, in the myddes of which Garters shal be a double Rose, the one Rose of Red, and the other within White, and the other Rose White, and the other Rose within Red. And at the ende of the said Coller shall be put and fastened the Ymage of Saynt George.'[265] Two almost contemporary representations of this collar give us a rather clearer picture of its form than this official description. One, at the head of a tournament roll prepared for use at the Field of the Cloth of Gold in 1520,[266] depicts the collar as being composed of elements in the form of a two-dimensional blue garter encircling red and white roses like those described in the statutes, alternating with gold love-knots with four loops above and four tasselled ends below. From the pendant of the central garter depends a gold figurine of St George, armed and mounted on a horse, and slaying a dragon with his lance. The second representation, in Sir Thomas Wriothesley's Garter Book, dated to about 1524,[267] differs from the first only in that the roses are alternately red and white, every other rose is replaced by a shield of the arms of St George, and the central rose, below which the 'George' hangs, is dimidiated by a shield of the same arms. In other representations from this period, all the roses are depicted as red,[268] and this has long been the normal practice, despite the specifications of the statutes.[269] One of the earliest representations of the collar is that on the effigy in the church of Holme Pierrepont (Notts.) of Sir Henry Pierrepont, who died in 1499,[270] but this has lost its colour.

The design of this collar was certainly based upon that adopted by Louis XI of France in 1469 for his new order of St Michael the Archangel, which was also composed of badges alternating with gold knots, and supported a golden effigy of the order's patron slaying a monster.[271] The inclusion of such a collar among the insignia of a monarchical order was not original with Louis, however. The fashion of wearing metallic collars of this sort developed in the last quarter of the fourteenth century, and from the last decade of that century almost all new lay orders adopted a collar as one of the principal elements of their insignia. Henry no doubt added a collar to the ensigns of the Garter in order to bring its practices more closely in line with those of the other royal orders of the day.

It is not known what rules, if any, governed the wearing of the collar before

---

[264] Nicolas, *History*, II, pp. 349–50.

[265] Ashmole, *Institution*, p. [751].

[266] See Oswald Barron, 'Heraldry', *E.B.*, XIII, Pl. IV (facing p. 324).

[267] See Marks and Payne, *British Heraldry*, no. 238, p. 124.

[268] For example, the collar worn by Charles Brandon, Duke of Suffolk, in the portrait painted about 1515, reproduced in Neville Williams, *Henry VIII and his Court* (London, 1973), p. 41.

[269] See Paul Hieronymussen, *Orders and Decorations of Europe* (London, 1967), no. 65.

[270] Arthur Gardner, *English Medieval Sculpture* (2nd edn. Cambridge, 1951), fig. 675, p. 399.

[271] See below, p. 441.

1519, when the statutes were revised by Henry VIII, but from that time onward the knights were obliged to wear it on all major feast days. On other days they were to wear instead only the effigy of St George, dependent either from a gold chain or (with military costume) a ribbon of blue silk like that which replaced the garter itself.[272] These rules closely reflect those of the Order of the Golden Fleece, upon which they were certainly modelled.

16 The Formal Costume of the Order

During the various ceremonies that made up the annual Assembly, and on certain other occasions connected with the Order, the members and officers of the Order of the Garter were all required to wear a mantle (*mantellum, manteau*) appropriate to their status and rank. The idea of having a mantle as the principal element of the Order's formal habit was probably borrowed from the Order of the Hospital of St John, whose prior in England regularly sat among the lords in Parliament; it is unlikely that Edward knew of the use of mantles by the knights of St George in Hungary. The mantle assigned to the companions is described in the statutes only as being blue.[273] Since this was a colour generally considered by contemporaries to be more suitable for wear by the clergy and the poor than by members of the higher classes of lay society,[274] and was not one of the colours of the arms of the Order's patron, St George (which were red and white), it was probably chosen, like that of the garter itself, to allude to the arms of France. Several poets, including Guillaume de Machaut,[275] later declared that blue was symbolic of loyalty, but it is more than likely that this was an idea derived from its use by the Order of the Garter rather than the other way around. We know very little about the mantles worn by the companions before the accession of Henry VI in 1422, for no representation of a knight in the formal habit of the Order has come down to us from that period, and since the king as Sovereign was only required to supply his own mantle (and Edward and his heirs seem to have used the same mantle from one year to the next over long periods of time), the records of the great wardrobe contain no references to the mantle of the Order. Geoffrey le Baker, however, described the mantles worn by the companions at the Assembly of 1350 as 'blue with little shields of arms of St George' and this suggests that they were from the first charged on the left breast with a single garter, surrounding a shield of the arms of St George. In all likelihood the mantles were at first made, like that provided to Edward for the Crécy campaign, of blue woolen longcloth and lined, like the hoods worn with them, in ermine or miniver. Not long after the accession of Henry VI, however, the materials were upgraded, and thereafter the mantles of all the companions seem

---

[272] Ch. 38.

[273] Ch. 11: 'mantella sua de blodio'; 'leurs manteaux de bleu dudit ordre'.

[274] For a discussion of the significance of the colour blue and of the use of blue cloth in the English court in this period, see Stella Mary Newton, *Fashion in the Age of the Black Prince*, pp. 43–6. Newton suggests that the blue might have been intended to symbolize humility, but this was not one of the salient characteristics of the Order of the Garter.

[275] See below, p. 242 n. 6.

to have been made of blue silk velvet and lined at first in white damask and later in white satin. The earliest known representations of knights of the Garter in their mantles are those of the First Founders painted in a paper book prepared around 1430 for the first Garter King of Arms, William Bruges, and now know as *Bruges' Garter Book*.[276] In this the mantle is depicted as a floor-length vestment of dark blue lined in white, and charged on the left breast with a single two-dimensional garter that in life would have been about six inches in diameter outlined in gold, encircling a heater-shaped shield of the arms of St George – a red cross on white. The mantles are all worn open at the front, and are held on with a long heavy cord, tasseled at either end and variously coloured, which passes through a pair of eylets just below the throat. The mantles thus depicted closely resembled those of the Order of St John and the other religious orders of knighthood, which were distinguished by the cross of the order embroidered on the left breast, and it is likely that this is the form they had had from the time of the Order's foundation. The mantles depicted on the tomb monuments of companions of the later fifteenth and early sixteenth centuries differ from those in Bruges' book only in such minor details as the size of the garter, the shape of the shield, and the arrangement of the tasseled cords.[277]

From the time of the institution of the Order the companions regularly wore with the mantle a surcoat (*supertunica*) and a hood (*capucium*), both of which were supplied annually by the Sovereign as a form of livery. Neither of the latter items was mentioned in any of the medieval versions of the statutes, but they were always worn, and were finally listed as part of the official habit of the Order in Henry VIII's revised statutes of 1519. From the records of the great wardrobe we know that the surcoat and hood were made at first of woolen longcloth, and later (from some time in the second half of the fifteenth century) of silk velvet. The surcoat and hood were usually of the same colour, but that common colour was changed every year until the later part of the reign of Henry VIII. Through most of our period the usual colours were blue, scarlet, sanguine, and white, though other colours were sometimes used. In some years the surcoat seems to have been embroidered with the arms of the individual companions, in the fashion of a military surcoat, but in general it was of one colour throughout. In the fourteenth century, both surcoat and hood were commonly powdered all over with garters, the number of garters on the whole costume varying from 173 for the Sovereign to 60 for a knight bachelor. From the middle of Henry VI's reign, however, both surcoat and hood were normally devoid of such ornament, and only the mantle still bore a two-dimensional garter. While they were still made of wool, both surcoat and hood were always lined with fur – the Sovereign's with ermine, the companions' with plain miniver. Later, when made of velvet, they were both lined in white cloth – at first sarcenet, later taffeta.

What little we know about the cut of the surcoat and hood in our period is

---

[276] B.L., Stowe MS. 594.

[277] The effigy of Robert Harcourt (d. 1471) in the church of Stanton Harcourt, Oxon., wears a mantle charged with a garter only about three inches wide surrounding an even more diminutive shield, while that of Thomas Bullen (d. 1538) in the church of Hever, Kent, wears a full-sized garter surrounding a scrolled tournament shield. See Gardner, *English Medieval Sculpture*, fig. 673, p. 337; and Clayton, *Catalogue*, Pl. 29.

derived from three miniatures, one of the fourteenth century and two of the fifteenth, representing knights of the Order wearing what seem to be those garments. The first is the portrait already referred to of the founder knight Nele Loring, painted at some time before his death in 1386.[278] Loring is depicted wearing a loosely-cut ankle-length surcoat with wrist-length tubular sleeves and a caped hood pulled over his head. Both are made of some white fabric, probably *blanket*, and both are powdered with garters that in life would have been about four inches wide and would have been set about four inches apart. The cut of this costume is extremely conservative, and bears a much closer resemblance to the monastic habits worn under their mantles by knights of religious orders than to the normal lay costume of the late fourteenth century. How long the hood continued to be worn in the traditional (and natural) fashion is unclear, but by the time Bruges' *Garter Book* was painted around 1430, it had come to be worn in keeping with a fashion dating from around 1380 as a turban-like hat, wrapped around the head with the gorget and liripipe hanging down to either side. The knights in Bruges' book wear knee-length heraldic surcoats under their mantles, but it is not clear whether these were meant to represent the normal civil surcoats of the day, since they are worn over full armour. A miniature in one of the manuscripts containing the statutes of Henry V, probably painted around 1450, depicts a knight of the Garter in a floor-length surcoat powdered with garters, wearing the hood on his head as a hat.[279] Later in the century the hood came to be worn (in keeping with the new fashion of the period) slung over the right shoulder, with the long liripipe tucked into the belt at the front and the head-covering and cape (still arranged in the form of a hat) hanging down loosely at the back. As a head-covering the hood was in the same period replaced by a cap of black velvet, the form of which varied according to fashion. It appears that such a cap was already in use in the fourteenth century, since Loring is depicted wearing one over his hood in his portrait.

Edward III almost certainly based the habit he assigned to the companions of his Order on that of the knights of St John, which suggests that he – like Károly of Hungary and Alfonso of Castile before him – wanted the Order to be seen as a sort of lay version of the familiar religious orders of knighthood. The habit of the Garter was to serve in its turn as the model for the costumes of most, though not all, of the later monarchical orders.

About the formal costumes worn by the canons and poor knights of the Order of the Garter we are less well-informed. According to the statutes the canons were to wear a mantle of purple (*murrey*, *purpurii*) ensigned on the right breast with a roundel of the arms of St George,[280] while the poor knights were to wear a similar mantle of red (*rouge*, *rubeo*) similarly ensigned with a shield of the same arms.[281] Presumably the canons wore the usual priestly habit beneath their mantle, which in cut was very like a clerical cope. What the poor knights wore beneath their mantle is unclear, but in all likelihood they wore a surcoat and hood similar to those of the companions.

The officers of the Order also wore mantles appropriate to their offices while

---

[278] See Newton, *Fashion*, p. 45.
[279] B.L., Add. MS. 28,549, f. 80v.
[280] Ch. 5.
[281] Ch. 7.

participating in the activities of the Order. In the early sixteenth century, at least, these mantles were characterized by wide orphreys embroidered with royal badges, and only the mantles of the Prelate and Chancellor were ensigned on the right shoulder with the badge of the Order. Both the herald and the usher also bore staves of office.[282]

17 Conclusion: The Order of the Garter

Edward III's motives for creating the Order of the Garter seem to have been complex. To begin with, in order to increase his personal prestige both at home and abroad, he wanted to promote an image of himself as a heroic king in the tradition of Arthur by surrounding himself with an international company of heroic knights, and initially attempted to 'restore' the Round Table company itself in a form very similar to that presented in the later romances, in what he proclaimed to be the very castle that had housed the original society. Like its legendary model, the new company was to be an embodiment of the ideal of chivalry he was attempting to realise in his own life and to promote among his courtiers, and Edward may well have hoped that its very brilliance would cause the memory of his father's inglorious reign to fade into oblivion. No doubt he was also concerned from the start with cementing his relations with the knights of his kingdom, whose enthusiasm for chivalry was hardly less than his own, and with celebrating their martial prowess and their achievements in the first camapigns of the war with France. Perhaps to allude to the legendary conquest of France by his 'predecessor' King Arthur, Edward made the belt-like garter he had apparently chosen to distinguish the knights of his new Round Table, the symbol of his campaign to vindicate his own claim to the crown of France, and when this campaign culminated in an overwhelming victory for his forces against vastly superior odds, Edward seems to have decided to make the order itself a perpetual memorial to this victory. Deciding for practical reasons to abandon his original plan to create a society modelled directly on the historic Round Table, he founded instead a much smaller company attached to the already-existing chapel of the same castle, which he rededicated to the patron saint of knighthood. This society still bore a general resemblance to the company of the Round Table, and its small size, though limiting the number of knights who could at any one time be honoured with membership, made the Order even more select, and membership in it all the more desirable in a class of men for whom distinction was one of the chief goals of life.

Edward almost certainly decided to create an order of knights attached to his court because of what he learned about the Order of the Band, but although he gave his society a similar designation and adopted a similar device, he does not seem to have borrowed much else from the statutes of the Castilian order. The society he eventually founded was, like that projected by his rival the Duke of Normandy, a true devotional confraternity, and differed from other such bodies on

---

[282] They are so depicted in a book prepared for the third Garter King of Arms, John Writhe, around 1488. (See Marks and Payne, *British Heraldry*, pp. 122–3 and no. 262, pp. 130–1.)

paper primarily in having an hereditary presidency attached perpetually to his crown. In practice, of course, the role played by Edward and his successors as Sovereign of the Order of the Garter was much more important than that played by the presidents of ordinary confraternities, and bore a closer resemblance to that of the Master of a religious order. Edward's adoption of both the title and the habit characteristic of the religious orders of knighthood suggests that he wished his order to be seen as a lay version of those societies – which still embodied the religious ideals of chivalry – as well as a successor to the more worldly company of the Round Table. Since Edward provided the physical establishment of the Order within the walls of his favourite castle, and he and his successors as king and Sovereign effectively appointed many of the companions, provided the badges and underhabits they wore as a form of livery, and paid for the banquet and festivities that accompanied its annual Assembly, the Order was also in effect a form of contractual retinue annexed to the royal household.[283]

Although the companions of the Garter were thus in some sense retainers or clients of the King of England, and were certainly expected to be scrupulously loyal to him and his interests, Edward did not conceive of his Order as an instrument to compel either loyalty or service from any of the companions. Unlike most contemporary princes, Edward had little need to fear baronial particularism, enjoyed a good personal relationship with most of the leading members of the knightly class, and had inherited from his grandfather and father a set of political and military institutions that were more than adequate for securing the advice and service of his vassals. He thus had no need to impose further cliental obligations on the companions, and used the Order to reward and encourage loyal service rather than to secure it.

The Order of the Garter is probably best seen as a sort of élite club, whose members, selected on the basis of their knightly distinction and their unswerving loyalty to the king, were honoured by their Sovereign with regular ceremonies and lavish entertainments. Membership in the Order was from the first a sign of royal favour, but the Order was by no means either a mere reward for merit or a mere contractual retinue. It was in fact a true corporation and a true fraternity, in which the Sovereign himself was no less a companion than the others. Nor should the religious side of the Order be regarded as mere window-dressing; although it was undoubtedly of secondary importance, the cult of St George was probably taken quite seriously by Edward and his fellow knights, and the prayers and purgatorial masses were almost certainly regarded as being of real value both in this world and the next.

The Order of the Garter was thus a brilliant creation, and within its own carefully limited terms it proved remarkably successful. Unlike many of its imitators, the Order not only survived its founder but has survived twenty-nine subsequent Sovereigns, and retains its lustre and its social preeminence even today. Its initial survival can probably be attributed to a number of factors, most of which were missing from the situations of the abortive orders that immediately succeeded it. In the first place, Edward was an eminently successful prince in the fashion of his

---

[283] It is also possible (if Juliet Vale is correct) that they were initially intended to function as a pair of tournament teams, but it is unlikely that this function continued much beyond 1360.

time, and his personal prestige was inevitably taken on by the society he founded. Secondly, he made sure that his Order was securely endowed financially, and provided with a permanent physical establishment in his castle at Windsor, so that when he died it would carry on with relatively little assistance from his successors. Edward also made the Order very attractive to the contemporary military nobility, and at the same time required very little of the companions that could be regarded as burdensome or restrictive. Next, and perhaps most important, Edward himself survived the foundation of his Order by nearly thirty years, during which time he was able firmly to establish the Order's annual activities as an integral part of the life of his rapidly evolving court. Finally, Edward was peacefully succeeded on his death by his grandson, Richard II, a child who had no reason to wish his grandfather's Order suppressed, and after him by kings whose best claim to the throne was descent in the male line from Edward himself. In these circumstances the Order of the Garter – the preeminent symbol of Edward's reign – was most unlikely to be set aside, and by the end of our period it had become one of the most important symbols of the English monarchy itself.

Unlike the foundation of the Order of the Band, that of the Order of the Garter provoked almost immediate imitation, and within the next decade at least four kings were moved to found orders of the same general type. The situations of these kings were all very different from that of Edward III, however, and neither they nor any of the other princes who founded monarchical orders in the half-century or so after 1349 saw fit to create an order that resembled the Garter except in having a similar badge and corporate designation and a confraternal form of constitution. Only in 1430 was an order created that incorporated most of the features of the Garter constitution – the Burgundian order of the Golden Fleece – but thereafter all of the new foundations whose statutes have survived were modelled either directly on the Garter or on the Golden Fleece, and by the end of our period, all of the surviving orders would have a constitution derived from that created by Edward III in 1349.

Chapter 5

The Company or Society of Our Lady of the Noble House
Commonly Called the Company of the Star
France, 1344/52–1364/80?

1 Historical Background

Some mention has already been made of the project to found a knightly society undertaken in 1344 by Jean Capet de Valois, Duke of Normandy and elder son of King Philippe VI of France. This project, like the one to refound the Round Table which seems to have inspired it, had to be postponed for a number of years, and was only brought to fruition in January 1352 – nearly two years after the first feast of the Order of the Garter, and more than sixteen months after Jean succeeded his father on the French throne as King Jean II. The society then founded – commonly known from its badge as the Company of the Star – was certainly a monarchical order, and if its founder's intentions for it had been fully realized it would probably have become the most important order of its type in Christendom. In the event, however, the first order of knighthood founded by a king of France was abandoned within a few years of its foundation, the victim of events and forces which swept away most of the changes its founder had attempted to effect in the government of his kingdom. The Company of the Star is nevertheless of considerable interest in the present context, not only because its founder was the ruler of France – the richest and most populous kingdom in Europe and the source of most of the literature and practices of chivalry – but because its ordinances were to serve as models for those of at least two later monarchical orders.

The future Jean II, commonly known to contemporaries as 'the Good', was born on 26 April 1319, less than seven years after his second-cousin and life-long rival Edward of England.[1] His father, the future King Philippe VI,[2] was then only

---

[1] Until very recently the most thorough critical study of the life and reign of Jean II was that of A. Coville in the fourth volume of the *Histoire de France depuis les origines jusqu' à la Révolution* edited by Ernest Lavisse, *Les premiers Valois et la Guerre de Cent ans (1328–1422)* (Paris, 1911), Livre II, pp. 89–170, but this has now been superceded by Raymond Cazelles' *Société politique, noblesse et couronne sous Jean le Bon et Charles V* (Geneva, 1982), and unless otherwise indicated the background material included in this chapter is based on that magisterial work.

[2] On his reign, see Raymond Cazelles, *La société politique et la crise de la royauté sous Philippe*

Count of Maine and heir apparent to his own father Charles, Count of Valois, the second son of King Philippe III and younger brother of King Philippe IV. Count Charles died in 1325, so when Philippe IV's youngest son King Charles IV died without male issue in February 1328, his first-cousin Philippe of Valois was the head of the senior cadet line of the royal house, and thus heir male of the late king. As such he was elected by an assembly of prelates and barons that met in April of that year to fill the vacant throne. The circumstances of his accession were quite unprecedented, however, and many people in France were long to harbour doubts about the right of the House of Valois – as his line of the Capetian dynasty was called – to occupy the throne. Most prominent among these were his cousins Edward, Duke of Guyenne and King of England, who was to claim the throne as the son of Charles IV's sister Isabelle, and Charles Capet d'Evreux, Count of Evreux and King of Navarre, who was later to assert his rights as the grandson of Charles IV's eldest brother Louis X.

Philippe VI had himself asserted the right of his elder son Jean to succeed him on the throne in 1332, when he made him titular Duke of Normandy and Count of Anjou and Maine, but he later felt obliged to back away from this position, and Jean was not again referred to as *héritier* until the last year of his father's reign. In the meantime Jean's position had been doubtful at best, and following the defeat of his father's army at Crécy in 1346, he seems to have been constrained to agree to a draught treaty whereby Philippe set aside his rights altogether and made Edward of England his heir. This treaty was never put into effect, but even on his deathbed Philippe VI seems to have expressed doubts about the validity of Jean's right to succeed him, and suggested that he would have to prove it on the field of battle. Although in the event Jean was able to have himself crowned without active opposition from anyone after his father's death in August 1350, his whole fourteen-year reign was to be dominated by the necessity of combatting or conciliating rival claims to his throne. His efforts to do this met with even less success than had those of his father, and Jean was ultimately forced to buy both his crown and his personal freedom from Edward by paying him an enormous cash ransom and ceding him one third of his kingdom in full sovereignty.

Not surprisingly, historians of France have traditionally blamed Jean for the disasters that befell his kingdom during his reign, and have portrayed Jean himself in less than flattering terms.[3] For more than three centuries now he has generally been seen as a dull-witted mediocrity, a 'king of gentlemen' whose undoubted courage and punctillious observance of the code of chivalry did not begin to compensate for his incompetance as a ruler and commander. The careful research of Raymond Cazelles, however, has recently revealed that Jean was not at all the chivalrous fool he has been made out to be, but an intelligent and sensitive man who not only patronized the leading scholars, artists, and musicians of his day, but worked hard to improve the effectiveness of the institutions of the central government of his kingdom, including the royal army, and fought entrenched privileges on every level in the interest of the kingdom as a whole. Furthermore,

---

de Valois (Paris, 1958).
[3] For this and what follows, see Cazelles, *Jean le Bon*, pp. 35–47.

although Jean certainly shared with his noble subjects a high regard for the ideals and conventions of chivalry, his poor health prevented him from developing much skill as a knight himself, and after the disaster of Crécy he seems to have held a low opinion of the character and abilites of most of the other members of the knightly class of his realm. After his accession, indeed, he looked upon the greater members of that class with deep suspicion, systematically excluded them from positions of authority in the royal administrative hierarchy, and did not hesitate to punish them severely when they betrayed him. His character and his relationship with his noble subjects were thus very different from those of the first three founders of monarchical orders, but he was in his own way just as capable a king, and the ultimate failure of his policies was due less to his own shortcomings than to the self-interested disloyalty of a faction of his nobility, and to the knightly indiscipline which led to his defeat and capture by his English enemies in the Battle of Poitiers.

The nobility of France at the time of Jean's accession in 1350 bore a superficial resemblance to that of England in the same period, but was in fact very different, and the differences lay at the heart of Jean's troubles.[4] Unlike the English knightly class, the French *noblesse* or *chevalerie* had become an hereditary caste composed in principle of all those descended in the male line from knights and living in a knightly fashion, and its members both claimed and enjoyed, in addition to the usual forms of deference due to those of high social rank, a number of important practical privileges, including exemption from most forms of taxation, the right to wage private war, and the exclusive right to enjoy the profits of war. Although most of the land possessed by the members of the knightly Estate in France had come by 1350 to be held by some form of feudal tenure either directly or indirectly from the crown, allodial estates were still common in some regions, and many important dominions were still held of some lord other than the king. Even more importantly, the vast majority of the thousands of *seigneuries* or dominions into which the kingdom had come to be divided had evolved, quite independently of any royal control, for the sole benefit of their lords, and even the nobles of middling rank had come to enjoy rights of jurisdiction over their peasant 'subjects' greater than those the English barons had recently lost. The nobles at the summit of the hierarchy, heirs *de facto* if not *de jure* of the provincial governors of the early Carolingian kings, were still virtually sovereign within their large and compact baronies – which in some cases formed blocks of territory as large as kingdoms – and continued to resist the steady encroachment of royal authority.

The hierarchy of wealth and power in the French nobility was in general closely reflected by the hierarchy of dominical titles which had crystallized at the beginning of the previous century, for in France personal titles continued to be associated exclusively with the possession of appropriately titled baronies, and the baronies bearing each of the three recognized titles of dignity were on average significantly larger than those which bore the title below theirs. As in England, the greater lords were referred to collectively as *barons*, but the criteria for baronial status varied considerably from province to province. At the top of the hierarchy of barons stood the five great princes bearing the title *duc* or 'duke', who among

---

4 On the French nobility in this period, see esp. Philippe Contamine, ed., *La Noblesse au Moyen Age XIe–XVe siècles. Essais à la mémoire de Robert Boutruche* (Paris, 1976).

them held the five duchies still in private hands, and five of the fifty-two counties: the Dukes of Guyenne, Burgundy, Brittany, Bourbon, and Orléans.[5] Below them, thirty-seven *contes* or 'counts' held the forty-seven remaining counties still in private hands, and a considerable number of lesser dominions.[6] Four of the dukes and five of the counts were members of cadet branches of the royal house of Capet, and as *seigneurs du sang de France* enjoyed a certain preeminence within the titled class as a whole. Below the counts in rank came the *vescontes* or 'viscounts', several dozen in number,[7] and below them the barons without any title of dignity, who numbered somewhere between 300 and 400 in 1350.[8] Below the barons came several hundred *chastellains* or 'castellans', who like the barons possessed a castle and extensive rights of jurisdiction within their compact castellanies, and below them the thousands of minor lords holding simple *seigneuries* or fractions of *seigneuries*. It has been estimated that the lesser nobility of France in this period included between 40,000 and 50,000 families, and most of these included several adult male members at any particular time.[9] With the exception of a handful of lords who bore unusual titles like *vidame*, *captal*, and *soudan*, all lords below the rank of viscount were described as *sire* or 'lord' of their principal dominions.

The nobility as a whole was still commonly referred to in this period as *la chevalerie* – 'the knightage' – but while virtually every male member of the baronial stratum of the nobility still sought the accolade of knighthood as soon as he was old enough to function effectively as a knight, only a small minority of the nobles of lesser rank could still afford to do so.[10] On the basis of the relative numbers of bannerets and bachelors listed in various documents of the period it has been estimated that there were between 2,000 and 3,700 strenuous knights bachelor in

---

[5] The one remaining duchy in the kingdom, that of Normandy, had reverted to the crown when Jean succeeded his father in August 1350. Gautier VI de Brienne, Count of Brienne in Champagne, was titular Duke of Athens in 1350, but this duchy was not in France.

[6] For some years now I have been working on a study of the distribution of titles in the upper baronage of France in the later Middle Ages, and have prepared the first complete lists of counties and counts in the kingdom. Immediately after his accession, Jean sent letters to three hundred and forty-eight barons, including twenty-seven counts (list published in La Roque, *Du ban et de l'arrière ban* [Paris, 1676], pp. 184ff), but Cazelles (*Jean le Bon*, p. 65) is wrong when he supposes that every count in the kingdom was sent such a letter.

[7] There is nothing resembling a complete list of the viscounts in France in this or any other period. On 23 August 1350 Jean sent letters to sixteen men who bore 'viscount' as their highest title, but there were certainly many others. I have so far identified ninety dominions which bore the title 'viscounty' in France in the period before 1350, and although a number of these had been annexed to the crown, most were still in private hands at the time of Jean's accession.

[8] Jean sent letters to just under 300 simple barons immediately after his accession in 1350, but there were probably several dozen others unknown for one reason or another to the royal chancellery.

[9] Contamine, *La Noblesse au Moyen Age*, p. 31.

[10] On knights and knighthood in France in this period, see esp. Philippe Contamine, 'Points de vue sur la chevalerie en France à la fin du Moyen Age', *Francia* 4 (1976), pp. 255–85.

France at the beginning of Jean's reign.[11] Since the class of barons and non-baronial bannerets seems to have included about 350 strenuous knights in the same period, the total number of such knights could have been as low as 2,350 and as high as 4,000 – about four times the number of strenuous knights in England at the same time.

Until the beginning of the fourteenth century, the kings of France had continued to rely very heavily on the feudo-vassalic obligations of the barons and the knights of their own demesne when they wanted to assemble an army, but although the seigniorio-vassalic relationship continued to serve as the legal basis for holding *seigneuries* of all classes until the Revolution of 1789, by 1350 it had been abandoned completely as the basis for military recruitment and service in France, as in England, except when based on the 'feudal' annuity known as the *fief-rente*.[12] As in England, too, the practice of retaining by special contract, either verbal or written, had come to be widely employed in the first half of the fourteenth century by kings and barons alike to secure the services not merely of soldiers but of councillors, chamberlains, secretaries, and other members of a royal or baronial household. Unlike their English rivals, however, Philippe VI and Jean II made extensive use of two forms of general summons to recruit mounted men-at-arms for military service: the traditional call to all male subjects between fourteen and sixty known as the *ban et arriere ban*, and the more novel *semonce des nobles*, directed to all nobles between fourteen and sixty holding fiefs, regardless of their place in the seigniorio-vassalic hierarchy. Those who answered the latter form of summons – which replaced the former early in Jean's reign – were paid a daily wage similar to that paid to indentured retainers on active service. With these two forms of recruitment at his disposal Jean seems to have had no difficulty securing the service of as many knights and squires as he needed in his war with Edward of England, and for as long as he needed them; all the French army seemed to lack in this period was discipline on the field of battle.

Like his immediate predecessors, Jean also summoned certain barons and representatives of the lesser nobles to advise him on important matters and to give their consent to various important measures, especially new taxes. Unlike his English rival, however, he preferred to confer with them and the representatives of the church and towns in meetings of the Estates of a province (such as Normandy) or region (such as the north-east), and only rarely summoned the Estates General of the *Langue d'ouïl* and *Langue d'oc*, the northern and southern divisions of his kingdom. Thus the upper nobility of France as a whole possessed no regular assembly representative of its interests and views comparable to the House of Lords in England, and the only French barons who enjoyed a status comparable to that of peer or lord of Parliament in England at Jean's accession were the seven great princes (all but one of whom were members of the royal house) who as *Pairs* or

---

[11] Cazelles, *Jean le Bon*, p. 66. Contamine, 'Points de vue sur la chevalerie', p. 259, estimated that there were between 5,000 and 10,000 knights in France around 1300, but this figure included all those who had received the accolade of knighthood, not merely those who were still fit to serve in battle.

[12] On military recruitment and organization in France in this period, see esp. Philippe Contamine, *Guerre, état et société à la fin du moyen âge. Études sur les armées des rois de France 1337–1494* (Paris, 1972), esp. pp. 26–64.

Peers of France enjoyed the hereditary right to sit among the professional judges in the supreme judicial court called the *Parlement*. A certain number of barons and lesser nobles were admitted to the relatively frequent sessions of the king's *Conseil Secret* or Privy Council, in which most of the important decisions touching the government of the kingdom were actually taken, but this was by its very nature a small body, and during Jean's reign it never included more than half a dozen barons at any particular time.

The foundation of the Company of the Star in 1351/2 must of course be seen against the background, not only of the general relationships between king and nobles just outlined, but of the particular situation or series of situations in which its creator found himself in the previous eight years, and of the general political programme he pursued in response to those situations during the same period. In the very year that he first announced his intention to found a society of lay knights, Jean, then about twenty-five, was sent off to the Languedoc as Lieutenant of the King and 'Lord of the Conquest of the Parts of Languedoc'. In March of the following year, 1345, an English army invaded Brittany in support of one of the two rival claimants for the throne of that rich duchy,[13] and Jean was caught up in the disastrous phase of the war with England that culminated in the rout of the French army at Crécy in August 1346. The young Duke of Normandy was apparently humiliated by his father's ignominious flight from the field at the end of this battle, but even more angry at the nobles for their miserable performance. During the autumn and winter following the battle, he and his father were widely reproached for choosing unworthy counsellors and wasting public funds, but from April to October 1347 Jean led a counterattack against the nobles. He publicly reproached them for the inefficacy of their military service, and not only suggested that they ought in consequence to pay taxes like the members of the other two Estates, but actually secured a subsidy from his own Duchy of Normandy that weighed with exceptional heaviness on the nobles of that province. He and his father also surrounded themselves with reform-minded counsellors, who saw the defeat at Crécy as the punishment of God for the sins of the privileged orders,[14] and sought accordingly to promote honesty, justice, and piety, as well as loyalty, among the nobles of the kingdom. Not surprisingly, the nobles reacted strongly to these charges at the meeting of the Estates General that was convened at the end of the year, and rejected the attempt to increase their taxes, but there is no reason to think that Jean (who felt obliged to absent himself from the meeting) changed his opinion of their shortcomings during the next few years. On the contrary, there is good evidence that he continued to hold the nobility as a whole in very low esteem for some time after his accession to the throne, and persisted in his desire to reform their dissolute habits.

Philippe VI died on 22 August 1350, and Jean, fearful that his English rival would try to prevent him from succeeding his father on the throne (as indeed he intended to do), had himself crowned at Reims on the 26th of the following

---

[13] On this conflict, see below, pp. 274–5.

[14] A tract entitled *Traité du gouvernement d'un prince* written in 1347 for Jean accused the nobles of dereliction of duty, living in falsehood, misappropriation of public funds, luxury, and immodesty. See Cazelles, *Jean le Bon*, p. 120.

month.[15] Immediately following his coronation and his *Joyeuse Entree* into his capital, Jean gave an unequivocal demonstration of how he intended to deal with anyone who engaged in treasonable dealings with his enemies, by ordering the arrest, trial, and decapitation of the Constable of France, Raoul II de Brienne, Count of Eu and Guines. The Constable, captured along with many other French knights at the battle of Crécy, had just returned to France, and it appears that one of the conditions of his release had been recognition of Edward's right to succeed the late king on the French throne. None of Jean's predecessors had ever dealt so harshly with a man of the rank of the Constable, who had been one of the most important barons of northern France as well as the commander of the royal army, and his summary execution on 19 November in the presence of leading members of the nobility and the Council sent a shock-wave through the nobility as a whole. Partly in order to assuage their fears and lessen their resentment, Jean convoked the Estates General of the Langue d'oc and the Langue d'ouïl to meet on 8 January and 6 February 1351 respectively, and then summoned a council of notables to take counsel for the reform of the kingdom and the preparation of its defenses against the next English attack.

From mid-February to mid-May, Jean spent most of his time deliberating with his Council, and with their advice instituted a whole series of reforms in the army and central administration. On 30 April he secured the passage of a *reglement pour les gens de guerre* which fixed at twenty-five the minimum number of men-at-arms a *chevetaine* or captain could lead under his banner, established a new scale of wages for knights banneret, knights bachelor, and squires, organized the company of *chevetaines*, fixed their duties, and ordered bi-monthly reviews of the companies they were to maintain, to be held without warning by the marshals' clerks.[16] More gradually but even more importantly, he gave particular members of the various services of the royal government – the *Hôtel*, the *Parlement*, the *Chambre des Comptes* – overall authority within their service (with the new title *premier* prefixed to their old official style), and overcame the traditional conflicts among these services, and between them and the Council, by giving the new 'first' officers a permanent place in the Council alongside the more traditional types of councillor. In order to make this new arrangement work properly, he also abandoned the peripatetic habits of his predecessors, including his father, and spent virtually all of his time in his residences in and around Paris.

After a brief lull the reorganized royal Council returned to a high level of activity in August and September of 1351. It was now joined by three prelates of aristocratic extraction – Guillaume de Melun, Archbishop of Sens, Guillaume Bertran, Bishop of Beauvais, and Jean de Meulan, Bishop of Noyon – who were not only moralists but experienced captains, and thus represented at the same time the views of the higher clergy and of the old nobility. Apparently acting under their influence, Jean in this brief period renewed the truce with England, proclaimed a moratorium on the payment of the debts of the crown for the duration of this truce in order to prepare for the defense of the realm, reissued with modifications the great ordinance for the reformation of the realm first promulgated in 1303 by

---

[15] For this and what follows, see Cazelles, *Jean le Bon*, pp. 127–45.
[16] Edouard Perroy, *The Hundred Years War*, trans. W. B. Wells (New York, 1965), p. 126.

Philippe IV, and finally, on 6 November, issued letters proclaiming the foundation of the knightly company of the Star.

2 The Foundation and Maintenance of the Company, 1344–1364

Before we can examine the foundation of the society of knights proclaimed in November 1351,[17] however, we must first take a closer look at the project of 1344 out of which that society seems to have grown. What little is known about this project is derived entirely from a series of six letters by which Pope Clement VI (pont. 1342–52) – the son of a French nobleman – granted various spiritual privileges to the proposed foundation.[18] All six letters are dated 5 June 1344, and clearly deal with different aspects of the same matter. What appears to be the first letter is by far the most informative. By it the pope, in response to a supplication of unspecified date, granted to the Duke of Normandy the right to establish, with the counsel and assistance of the Duke of Burgundy, a collegiate church, to be endowed by him and built at some suitable location in France, to the honour of the Holy Trinity, the Blessed Virgin, and all saints, under the name of the Virgin and St George. This church was to be served by a chapter of twelve secular canons, of

---

[17] Despite the brevity of its existence, the Company or 'Order' of the Star has never been forgotten by historians, and most of the encyclopaedias and dictionaries concerned with knightly orders contain what purport to be accounts of its history. Almost all of these were based in part upon the account by Favyn in his *Théâtre d'Honneur et de Chevalerie* (Paris, 1620). Favyn maintained that the 'Order' was founded in 1022 by King Robert, who had a special devotion to 'Our Lady of the Star', and that it was merely revived or revitalized by Jean II in 1351. Needless to say, there is not the slightest contemporary evidence for the existence of a Company of the Star in France before 1351, and in several of the letters issued by Jean II referring to the society he states quite unequivocally that he was the founder. Even contemporary critical historians have been misled by Favyn, including Cazelles (*Jean le Bon*, pp. 144–5.) The first critical accounts of the Company were written as long ago as the 1770s by the *érudits* Etienne Lauréault de Foncemagne, (*Recherches historiques sur l'Etablissement et l'Extinction de l'ordre de l'Etoile*, Paris, B.N., ms. nouv. acq. fr. 3294, ff. 63r–96r, unpublished) and M. Dacier, 'Recherches historiques sur l'établissement et l'extinction de l'ordre de l'Etoile', *Mémoires de Littérature tirés des registres de l'Acad. roy. des Inscr. et Belles Lettres* 39 [1777], pp. 662ff.), who refuted Favyn's ideas about the origins of the order. The next critical study of the order to be published was Léopold Pannier's *La Noble Maison de Saint Ouen, la Villa Clipiacum, et l'Ordre de l'Etoile* (Paris, 1878), which is concerned primarily with the history of its buildings, but includes most of the documents relevant to the history of the order. The slightly later article by A. Vattier, 'Fondation de l'Ordre de l'Etoile', *Comité archéologique de Senlis*, 2nd ser., 10 (1885), pp. 37–47, is of value principally because it includes several further documents of great importance for the order's history. The foundation of the order has been noted by several more recent historians, including Cazelles (*Jean le Bon*, pp. 144–5), but the only extensive study published since Pannier's is Yves Renouard's 'L'Ordre de la Jarretière et l'Ordre de l'Etoile. Etude sur la genèse des Ordres laïcs de Chevalerie et sur le développement progressif de leur caractère national', *Le Moyen Age* (1949), pp. 281–300.

[18] These were published in E. Déprez, *Lettres de Clément VI*, in *Bibliothèque des Ecoles françaises d'Athènes et de Rome*, ser. 3, t. 3 (fasc. 1, 1901), cols 31–7, nos 883–8.

whom one was to be treasurer, and twelve priests who were to reside there permanently. They were to say and sing the divine offices according to the rite observed in the Royal Chapel in Paris. Furthermore, the letter declares:

> ... for the greater and more fervent devotion from the faithful there is to be in the same church a communion or congregation of two hundred knights (*communio seu congregatio ducentorum militum*), of which knights those normally absent shall personally come together each year, not for jousts or tournaments or for any other act of arms, but for devotion to the same church, at least on the feasts of the Assumption of the Blessed Virgin Mary and the Blessed George the Martyr in the month of April, together with those of them who, out of pious and loving ordination and right intention, and at the pleasure and will of the aforesaid Duke of Normandy, shall reside there.[19]

The right to appoint the treasurer, canons, and other necessary servants, and the provision of the prebends and chaplaincies, were to belong to the Duke of Normandy himself, and after him to the Kings of France for the time being. The clerics, who were all to be priests, were to say the prescribed offices 'in the presence of the knights of the congregation who resided by the church.'

The other five letters describe the basic project in almost identical terms, adding nothing to the description of the 'congregation' of knights quoted above. By the second letter, Pope Clement granted to the knights of the congregation chosen within ten years of the date of writing, the privilege of receiving absolution *in articulo mortis* from their ordinary confessors. By the next letter he added to this the further privilege of similarly receiving full absolution and the commutation of penance from their confessors even for sins normally reserved to the Holy See.[20] The fourth letter granted to 'any faithful person' the right to found a chapel in the church of the projected congregation, and to present to the Duke or King suitable clerics to serve it.[21] This privilege, while not exclusive to the knights of the congregation, was no doubt intended to pertain particularly to them as the persons most directly interested in the church. The remaining two letters had nothing to do with the knights; one required the canons and priests to reside permanently by the church,[22] and the other conferred on them the right to enjoy the full fruits of their ecclesiastical benefices.[23]

The picture we are able to form of the projected 'congregation' of St Mary and St George on the basis of these letters is one of a large body of knights who were to meet twice a year on the feasts of their two patron saints (15 August and 23 April respectively) at a church especially set aside for them, staffed by a college of twenty-four priests, who were to be appointed by the founder and his successors. Presumably the first group of knights was also to be chosen by the founder. The priests and some of the knights were to reside permanently by the church and to

---

[19] Ibid., no. 883.
[20] Ibid., no. 886.
[21] Ibid., no. 888.
[22] Ibid., no. 887.
[23] Ibid., no. 885.

participate in regular religious services. Both the lay and the clerical personnel were to enjoy a number of significant spiritual privileges, and the ostensible purpose of the semi-annual gatherings was devotion to the church and its heavenly patrons. Nothing is known of any other activities, though it is reasonable to suppose on the basis of later developments that other activities were planned, and that the purpose of the organization was not entirely or even primarily religious. The role of the Duke of Burgundy in the affair is similarly obscure, but it appears to have been purely advisory. The current duke, Eudes IV, was both an agnatic cousin and a maternal uncle of the Duke of Normandy (who was eventually to marry his widowed daughter-in-law), so the role of advisor to the twenty-five-year-old prince would have been natural enough.[24]

We do not know precisely when Jean decided to establish a congregation of knights, but as the Pope would almost certainly have responded fairly promptly to a petition submitted by the eldest son of his former sovereign and principal supporter, it is likely that Jean sent his petition to Avignon at some time during the spring of 1344. It is therefore reasonable to suppose that his decision to create a society of knights was reached at some time during the preceding winter, and that it was taken in direct response to the proclamation made in January of that year by his rival Edward of England at the great tournament held at Windsor.[25] In all likelihood Jean was primarily concerned with offsetting the effects of Edward's projected 'restoration' in the propaganda war between the two rival dynasties, but he may also have hoped to create an alternative Round Table to forstall the defection of individual barons to the English allegiance. Jean's projected congregation resembled the Round Table project in both the number and the quality of its lay members and in having regular general assemblies on high holidays, and it may well have resembled it in other ways as well. It is even possible that the congregation was to have had a round table, for according to the chronicle of Thomas of Walsingham, Jean's father Philippe, '. . . provoked by the action of the King of England, began himself to construct a Table in his own land,'[26] at some time early in 1344, and it is more than likely that Walsingham (writing in England several decades after the event) was confusing Jean with his father. It seems improbable that both Jean and his father would have announced their intention to found different knightly societies at the same time.

It is unclear why Jean should have chosen to found a knightly society himself when he was still Duke of Normandy in title only, and was not even securely established as the heir apparent to his father's throne, but it may be that he felt very strongly about the necessity of founding a counterpart to the society proclaimed by his rival, and found his father unwilling for some reason to undertake such a project. In any case he meant his congregation to be closely associated with his father's successors as King of France, and it is probably safe to presume that he fully intended to claim the throne on his father's death. The fact that Jean and his

[24] Eudes IV Capet de Bourgogne (d. 1349), Duke of Burgundy, Count Palatine of Burgundy, Count of Artois, was through his mother Agnès, a daughter of King St Louis IX, first cousin of Jean's grandfather, Count Charles of Valois. Jean himself was the son of Eudes' sister Jeanne, who had married the future Philippe VI in 1313.

[25] See above, pp. 104–106.

[26] Chronicon, p. 17.

successors as king were to have had the right to nominate the various priests attached to the society's chapel strongly suggests that they were to have played a major role in the society's activities, and that the projected society was to have had a monarchical form of constitution.

Although it was almost certainly inspired by the rival Round Table project, the proposed Congregation of St Mary and St George differed from its English model in several important respects: it was intended from the beginning to be placed under the patronage of saints, to have as the centre of its activities a chapel served by its own clergy, and to have as one of its explicit purposes the encouragement of devotion to those saints at that chapel. In fact, it was almost certainly intended to be a devotional confraternity. We cannot be sure where Jean got the idea of giving his knightly society a confraternal form of constitution, but he could have taken it either from the Hungarian Society of St George (whose founder was a cadet of his own house) or from a confraternity of knights probably founded at some time during the preceding dozen years in the Dauphiné of Viennois: the Order of St Catherine.[27] The latter society, as we have seen,[28] had probably been founded at the encouragement of the current Dauphin, Humbert II de la Tour du Pin (who was the nephew of Károly of Hungary), and was clearly designed to promote his interests. Jean must have known something of the order in 1344, since he had spent part of the previous year conducting negociations with the Dauphin Humbert over the purchase of the Dauphine for his younger brother Philippe, and it would be surprising if the society he proclaimed only a few months after the agreement was ratified was not influenced in some way by the Dauphinois order.[29]

Unfortunately, nothing more is known about Jean's project of 1344, and there is absolutely no evidence to indicate that any part of it was carried out before the death of his father on 22 August 1350. When the demands made upon Jean's time and resources during those years are considered, along with his reaction to the Crécy disaster and the fact that he did not receive full possession of any of the dominions he held in title until just before the onset of the Black Death (which ravaged France throughout 1348 and most of 1349 and carried off nearly a third of the population),[30] it can hardly seem surprising that he was unable to carry out his very ambitious plans until after his accession. Once securely established on the throne, however, he waited only a year before he again announced his intention to establish a society of knights, and although the proclamation of this society seems to have been urged upon him by the reformist prelates of his Council as part of a general programme of political, military, and social reform, it is likely that Jean

[27] Statutes in C. U. J. Chevalier, *Choix de documents historiques inédits sur le Dauphiné*, (Montbéliard, Lyon, 1874), pp. 35–9. On the character and career of the Dauphin Humbert, to whose service the order was dedicated (and who was one of the founder knights of the Star) see Aziz Suryal Atiya, *The Crusade in the Later Middle Ages* (London, 1938), pp. 301–18.

[28] See above, p. 44.

[29] The first treaty of transport was ratified by Philippe VI on 23 April 1343 and by the Dauphin on 30 July. Humbert finally abdicated his titles to Jean's eldest son Charles, the future Charles V, on 16 July 1349, and thereafter the eldest son of the King of France was always invested with the Dauphiné.

[30] See Philip Ziegler, *The Black Death* (London: Pelican, 1970), pp. 63–84.

himself saw the society he proclaimed on 6 November 1351 as the realization of the plans he had first made in 1344. Certainly the society proclaimed in 1351 had most of the known features of the earlier project.[31]

Jean seems to have announced his creation of what he now called a *compaignie de chevaliers* by sending letters close to each of the knights whom he had decided to appoint as a founding member. Unfortunately, no record has been preserved of either the names or even the number of those appointed to the Company at this time, and the only copy of the letter itself that has survived is the one in the register of the *Chambre des Comptes*, addressed to an unnamed *Biau cousin*.[32] The principal objects of this letter were to signal the foundation of the Company and to inform the recipient both that he had been elected to membership and that he was to attend the first meeting of the Company at a specified time and place, bringing with him the badges and costumes prescribed, but the letter included, in addition to a detailed description of the badges and costumes in question, a rapid summary of the principal rights, obligations, and activities that membership in the Company was to involve. The letter was clearly not intended to serve as a formal constitution for the new society, but as no such formal constitution is known to have been adopted, and no other official document containing comparable information about the Company has come down to us, it must be treated here in the same way that the official statutes of other orders have been treated.

As might be expected, the letter was composed (either by Jean himself or by one of the secretaries of his Chancellery on the basis of dictated notes) in continuous prose. The text can be broadly divided into two parts, the first containing a description of the new society, the second informing the recipient of his 'election' to it and of his immediate obligations. Some 33 ordinances can be distinguished in the first part, and although the scribe made no attempt to set them off from one another in any way, it will be useful for the purposes of reference to enumerate these as if they were statutes. Since the majority of the ordinances are arranged in groups of two or three concerned with essentially the same topic, I shall number these groups of ordinances, along with the ordinances which do not fall into such groups, as if they were chapters, and assign lower-case letters to the ordinances within these groups as if they were contained in chapters. The 33 ordinances can be organized in this way into 21 capitular divisions, which to avoid confusion with the equivalent units of formal statutes I shall call 'items'.

The first item is in effect the prologue. In it, Jean set forth the nature, name, and purpose of his foundation in the following terms:

> We, to the honour of God [and] of Our Lady, and to the exaltation of knighthood and the increase of honour, have ordained that a company of

---

[31] It was suggested by Renouard (op. cit., p. 293) that Jean's second wife, Jeanne d'Auvergne-Comté, (the widow of his uncle Eudes' son Philippe), whom he had married in February 1350, reminded Jean of the unfinished business shared by the French and Burgundian courts. This is certainly possible, but it is unlikely that Jean needed much encouragement to complete his project.

[32] This was preserved in Paris, A.N., Mémoires de la Chambre des Comptes, Reg. C, f. 120. It has been published a number of times, most recently in ORF, II, p. 465; Pannier, *La Noble Maison*, pp. 88–90; and Vattier, op. cit., pp. 37–40.

knights be created, who shall be called the knights of Our Lady of the Noble House.

The next five items (2 to 6) contain eight ordinances describing the badges (a brooch and a ring) and the costumes the knights of the Company were to wear, and setting forth the circumstances and manner in which they were to be worn. Items 7 to 9 (containing five ordinances) set forth certain general obligations entailed in membership, while items 10 and 11 (containing four ordinances) specify what the knights were expected to do during the Company's annual Assumption Day assembly. Item 12 contains two ordinances concerned with the banner of the Company and its display, items 13 to 15 three ordinances specifying what was to be done after the death of one of the knights, and items 16 and 17 five ordinances concerned with the display of the arms and crest of each knight above his seat in the Company's hall. Items 18 and 19 seem to be afterthoughts, the former dealing with the selection of knights for the table of honour at the annual banquet, the latter declaring that no member of the Company was to go on a long voyage without the permission of the Prince. Finally, Jean declared in items 20 and 21 that there were to be 500 knights in this Company, of which he, 'as inventor and founder', was to be Prince, and after him all his successors as king.

The last item is followed by what we have called the epilogue, which reads as follows:

> And you have been chosen to be of the number of the said Company. And we plan to hold (if God pleases) the first feast and entry of the said Company at Saint-Ouen on the next eve and day of the Epiphany. Therefore be on the said day at the said place if you can do so well, with your whole habit, ring, and brooch. And at that time this matter will be more fully explained to you and the others. And it is further ordered that each shall bring his arms and his crest painted on a sheet of paper or parchment, so that the painters may put them as soon and as correctly as possible where they should be placed in the Noble House.

Unlike the original project of 1344, that of 1351 was mentioned in at least four fourteenth-century chronicles, two of which – the *Grande Chronique de St Denis*[33] and the *Chronique* of the Liégeois canon Jean le Bel[34] – were almost contemporary with the event. The account in the third, that of Jean Froissart,[35] is almost identical with that in Le Bel's chronicle, and was certainly copied from it.

The St Denis chronicle is not very informative. According to it,

> In this year CCCLI aforesaid, in the month of October, was published the confraternity (*confrarie*) of the Noble House of Saint-Ouen, near Paris, by the said King Jean; and those in it each bore a star (*estoille*) on the front of his

---

[33] *Chronique des règnes de Jean II et de Charles V*, ed. R. Delachenal, Société de l'histoire de France, 4 vols, (Paris, 1910–20).

[34] *Chronique de Jean le Bel*, ed. J. Viard, E. Déprez (Paris, 1904).

[35] *Les chroniques de Jean Froissart*, ed. J. A. Buchon (Paris, 1824), pp. 53–9.

hood (*chaperon*) or on his mantle. And during this feast of the Star the town and castle of Guines were taken, through treason, by the English.[36]

The month given here for the 'publication' of the Company may be inaccurate, but it is possible that a formal proclamation was made in the royal court before the letters were sent out to inform the members officially of their election. The records of the royal *Argenterie* indicate that payment was made for a ring bearing the device of the Company and the name of the king that was delivered on 20 October,[37] so Jean's plans must have been well-advanced, if not absolutely complete, by that date.

Le Bel's chronicle, composed between 1356 and 1361, contains in its eighty-ninth chapter not only an account of the foundation, but a fairly detailed enumeration of the activities and obligations of the knights of the Company as reported to him. His account is so detailed and so generally in conformity with what we know about the Company from other sources that it could only have been based upon a conversation with a member or a clerk closely associated with the Company during its brief existence, and although certain of the statements it contains are at variance in detail with statements contained in official sources, it must be regarded as at least approximately correct. In the absence of any formal statutes, Le Bel's account takes on an added importance in the present context, and the various statements he makes about the Company must therefore be numbered for future reference.

How the King of France Jean ordained a company of knights at the example of the Round Table, and it was called the Company of the Star [1] In the year of grace M CCC LII King Jean of France ordained a fair company, large and noble, after the Round Table which formerly existed in the time of King Arthur. [2] Of the company there were to be 300 knights, of the most worthy (*souffisans*) in the Kingdom of France. [3] And this company was to be called the Company of the Star (*compaignie de le Estoille*). [4] And each knight of the said Company was always to wear a star of gold or of silver gilt or of pearls, in recognition of the Company. [5] And King Jean promised to have made a large and beautiful house near Saint-Denis, [6] at which the companions and brothers (*confreres*) – those who were in the country – were to be on all the solemn feasts of the year, if they had no reasonable excuse. [7] And it was to be called the Noble House of the Star. [8] And there each year, at least, the king was to hold full court with the companions. [9] And there each of the companions was to recount all the adventures, the shameful as well as the glorious, which had come to him in the time since he had been in the noble court. [10] And the king was to establish two or three clerks who were to listen to all these adventures and put them in a book, [11] so that they might be reported there every year before the companions, [12] by which one could know the most valorous (*preux*) and honour those who best deserved it. [13] And no one could enter into this Company if he did not have the consent of

---

[36] *Chronique*, I, pp. 33–4.
[37] Paris, A.N., KK 8, f. 8r. The passages from this register relevant to the Company of the Star were published by Pannier, *La Noble Maison*, Preuves, pp. 63–74.

the king and the greater part of the companions present, [14] and if he was not worthy (*souffisant*), without a failure (*deffaulte*) of reproach. [15] And they were to swear that they would never flee in battle farther than four *arpents* (in their opinion), but would die or surrender; [16] and that each would aid and help the other in all his encounters. [17] And there were several other statutes and ordinances that each had sworn. [18] And the Noble House was almost made. [19] And when anyone became so old that he could no longer go before the country, he was to have his upkeep and his expenses in the said house (*hostel*) with two varlets, for the remainder of his life, if he wished to dwell there, so that the Company might be well maintained (*entretenue*).[38]

Froissart's account, composed around 1373 for Count Robert of Namur and clearly based on that of Le Bel, differs from the latter primarily in employing different words to express the same ideas and in adding explanatory phrases and clauses: it refers to the Company, for example, as *les chevaliers de l'Etoile* rather than *la compaignie de le Estoille*, and specifies that the house of the Company was to be built at the founder's expense. The only addition of any real significance is the qualification inserted into the last statement to the effect that the right of maintenance was to belong only to those enfeebled and in need of being helped, and this may well be a completely unwarranted elaboration of his original, done for the sake of variation alone.

The one remaining chronicle to mention the foundation of the Company is the *Chronique des Quatre Premiers Valois*, composed at some time between 1380 and 1395. Its anonymous author had only this to say on the subject:

Jean, King of France, ordained and made a feast in honour of Our Lady, the which he made at Saint-Ouen near Paris. The which feast was called the Feast of the Star, and was made the day of the Epiphany. At the which feast the highest barons of his kingdom were present, and bore as the device of the king a star. And at this feast, by order of the king, those of the feast were vested in red above and white below. And there were at this feast elected nine worthy knights, of whom Charles de Blois, Duke of Brittany, was named by the country.[39]

The records of the *Argenterie* referred to above indicate that a meeting of the new Company was indeed convened as planned on the eve of the Epiphany (6 January) 1352, and that it was held, as the chroniclers all declared, in the hall and chapel of the royal manor of Saint-Ouen-lès-Saint-Denis just to the north of Paris, newly renamed the *Noble Maison*. The amount of money spent on furnishings for the hall, chamber, and chapel of the manor, suggest that Jean wished to inaugurate his new Company in an atmosphere of unusual splendour, presumably to impress the princes and barons who converged on the manor for the occasion with the importance he attached to it, and to encourage them to take pride in their membership. The same records (which we shall examine in detail below) give us

[38] *Chronique*, II, pp. 204–6.
[39] Luce, *Chronique*, pp. 23–4.

the names of more than a dozen of the original knights of the Company, and indicate the nature and quantity of the materials used to make habits and badges provided by Jean to the knights who were his personal retainers or members of his household.

According to the letter of election, the Company of the Star was to have met again on the feast of the Assumption in August of that year, but the surviving evidence of all types suggests that neither this meeting nor any of the subsequent meetings projected in the letter of election were actually held. Most of this evidence is negative, but both Le Bel and Froissart conclude their chapters on the Company with an account of a disaster that befell it not long after its foundation, and express the opinion that as a result of this disaster the Company was dissolved. According to the former, King Jean, on hearing of the invasion of a large body of English men-at-arms into Brittany in support of the Countess of Montfort in the Breton succession war, sent a large force including many knights of the Company of the Star to combat them. The French knights fell into an English ambush, however, and were all killed or 'discomfited'. Among the dead were no fewer than eighty-nine knights of the Star, who fell

> . . . because they had sworn that they would never flee; for if it had not been for the oath, they could well have withdrawn. Several others died for the love of them, who might have been saved if they had not sworn the oath, and feared thay they would be reproved for it by the Company.[40]

Froissart repeated this account with certain variations, most notably in the time and the number of the slain. According to Le Bel the battle took place in 1353, but Froissart merely said that it was 'fairly soon' after the feast of foundation. In this he was more accurate than his principal source, for the Battle of Mauron, which both appear to have been describing, took place on 14 August 1352, the eve of the feast that was to have witnessed the Company's first regular assembly.

Both Le Bel and Froissart terminated their histories of the Company immediately after the account of the Battle of Mauron, in a fashion which makes it clear that they felt there was nothing further to be said on the subject. In the words of the earlier writer: 'After that time this noble Company was not spoken of, and in my opinion it came to nothing, and the house remained vacant; I shall say no more of it, and speak of other matters.' Froissart is equally definite in his judgement of its collapse. 'Thus,' he wrote, 'was disrupted this noble company of the Star, with the great mischiefs which came afterwards in France, as you have heard recorded earlier in this history.'

The opinions expressed by the two chroniclers are supported fully, if only in a negative fashion, by all of the other sources that survive from the reign of Jean II. The records of the royal *Argenterie* that have been preserved – which cover the critical years 1351–1355[41] – contain no subsequent reference either to the provision of part of the Company's habit or to preparations made for any similar festivities at the 'Noble House', and I have found no mention of a later meeting of the Company

---

[40] *Chronique*, pp. 206–7.
[41] The only surviving register of payments made in Jean's reign is that cited above, A.N., KK 8, which covers this period.

in any other document. Furthermore, there is no record of any knight being elected to the Company of the Star after January 1352, and so far as I have been able to discover, only one knight who died at any time after the foundation of the Company – the Neapolitan Giacomo Bozzuto – saw fit to mention his membership on his tomb or any other form of memorial.[42]

In all probability the meeting scheduled for 15 August 1352 was first postponed because most of the knights of the Company were engaged in active service in Brittany, and then cancelled because all or most of the knights sent to Brittany were killed at Mauron on the very eve of the feast. It is more difficult to understand why Jean did not call a special meeting at some time during the autumn or winter to elect successors to the knights who fell at Mauron, but while Jean might have succeeded in restoring the much-reduced Company of the Star in 1352 or early in 1353, a growing feud between the noble factions supporting his favourite Charles 'd'Espagne' (whom he had made Constable of France in succession to the executed Count of Eu) and his cousin Charles 'the Bad', Count of Evreux and King of Navarre (who hoped to end the war by ceding half the kingdom to Edward of England) would have made it increasingly difficult to do so in the latter year, and after the murder of his favourite in January 1354, Jean had to struggle just to regain control of his own Council from the Navarrist faction. It is less clear why he did not attempt to revive the Company at some time in 1355, when he was again in the ascendency and was attempting to rally support for his policy of defending the kingdom against the inevitable attack from England, but by the spring of 1356 the political situation was once again inauspicious for any such revival, and thereafter a revival would have been all but impossible.

Although Jean's failure to convene a plenary assembly of the Company of the Star when conditions were still relatively favourable might appear to indicate that he simply abandoned the idea of creating an order of knighthood after the disaster of Mauron, there is convincing evidence that in fact he persisted in his intention to maintain the Company, in accordance with his announced plan, right up until his capture at Poitiers, and was only waiting until his political, military, and financial situation made a second general assembly feasible. For several years after the feast of January 1352 he continued to lavish attention upon the manor of Saint-Ouen, now concentrating primarily upon the chapel of the 'Noble House' and upon the college of canons which, in keeping with the initial plan of 1344, he planned to establish there. Pannier has shown that Jean first attempted to provide an endowment for the chapel indirectly, by helping the chaplain he had evidently appointed to the Noble House – Henri de Culent, Lord of Langennerie and Archdeacon of Thérouanne – to endow it from his own lands.[43] Not until October 1352 did Jean finally sign letters creating a 'college of canons, chaplains, and clerks to celebrate

---

[42] The inscription on Bozzuto's tomb in the Cathedral Church of Naples reads: 'Hic iacet egregius miles Jacobus Boczutus qui fuit de societate Stelle illustris domini Johannis Regis Francorum et Collateralis et Consiliarii incliti domini Lodovici ducis Duracii 1358 die . . .' See Matteo Camera, *Elucubrazioni Storico-Diplomatiche su Giovanna Ia Regina di Napoli et Carlo III di Durazzo* (Salerno, 1889), p. 169, n. 3.

[43] Op. cit., pp. 118–19. On pp. 77–82 of the *Preuves*, he publishes the orignial letters by which Jean approved Culent's purchases, preserved in Paris, A.N., JJ 81, nos 367, 362.

... the divine offices ...' at the 'Noble House of Saint-Ouen'.[44] By the same instrument he endowed the college with all of the royal revenues resulting from

> ... all the forfeitures both in property and in goods and all the *épaves* ... which shall befall in our realm and escheat to us, for crimes of *lèse majesté* or for any other cause, whatever their value ...

calling upon his financial officers in Paris and the provinces to send the money without delay to the 'governor or receiver' of the Noble House. In theory the sums involved should have been considerable (especially as the war with England had increased the rate of confiscations for treason), and the extent of the endowment must be regarded as an indication both of Jean's high regard for the Company, and of his determination to maintain it.

The letters of October 1352 are also of interest for quite a different reason, however, for their lengthy preamble contains the best surviving statement of Jean's intentions in founding the Company, expressed in what may well be the king's own words. This preamble is of sufficient interest in the present context to be reproduced here *in extenso*:

> Jean by the Grace of God King of France ... Among the other the preoccupations of our mind, we have many times asked ourself with all the energy of reflection, by what means the knighthood (*milicia*) of our realm has, from ancient times, sent forth into the whole world such a burst of probity, and has been crowned with so lively an aureole of valiance and honour: so well that our ancestors the Kings of France, thanks to the powerful intervention of heaven and to the faithful devotion of this knighthood, which has bestowed upon them the sincere and unanimous concourse of its arms, have always triumphed over all the rebels whom they have wished to reduce; that they have been able, with the aid of divine favour, to restore to the pure paths of the Catholic Faith the numberless victims that the perfidious Enemy of the human race, through ruse and artifice, had made to err against the true faith; and finally that they had established in the realm a peace and security so profound that, after many long centuries, some of the members of this order, unaccustomed to arms and deprived of exercises, or for some other cause unknown to us, have immoderately plunged themselves into the idleness and vanity of the age, to the contempt of honour, alas, and of their good renown, to diminish their gaiety of heart in exchange for the comfort of their persons.
>
> For this reason we, mindful of former times, of the honourable and constant prowess of the aforesaid liegemen, who brought forth so many victorious, virtuous, and fortunate works, have taken it to heart to recall these same liegemen, present and future, to a perfect union, to the end that in this intimate unity they will breathe nothing but honour and glory, renouncing

---

[44] The letter, of which two copies are preserved in the French Archives Nationales (Mém. de la Chambre des comptes, C, f. 121; and Register JJ 81, f. 288r), has been published several times. See Vattier, op. cit., pp. 42–5.

the frivolities of inaction, and will, through respect for the prestige of the nobility and knighthood, restore to our epoch the lustre of their ancient renown and of their illustrious company, and that after they have brought about the reflowering of the honour of knighthood through the protection of divine goodness, a tranquil peace will be reborn for our reign and our subjects, and the praises of their virtue will be published everywhere. Therefore, in expectation of these benefits and of many others, we . . . have founded the Company or Society of the Knights of the Blessed Mary of the Noble House of Saint-Ouen near Saint-Denis in France, and a college of canons, chaplains, and clerks to celebrate there the divine services. And we have firm confidence that with the intercession of the said most glorious Virgin Mary for us and our faithful subjects, the Lord Jesus Christ will mercifully pour out his grace upon the knights of the aforesaid company or association, with the result that the same knights, eager for honour and glory in the exercise of arms, shall bear themselves with such concord and valiance, that the flower of chivalry, which for a time and for the reasons mentioned had faded into the shadows, shall blossom in our realm, and shine resplendent in a perfect harmony to the honour and glory of the kingdom and of our faithful subjects.[45]

The complaints and criticism expressed here are essentially similar to those voiced by Jean and the other critics of the knights of France in 1347 (and indeed by the critics of contemporary knighthood throughout the period) and indicate very clearly that the Company of the Star was intended to form part of the general programme of reform. Pannier has shown that in the four years between the sealing of this instrument and the great disaster of Poitiers in September 1356, several estates were in fact handed over under its provisions to the chapel of the Noble House.[46] It appears, however, that Jean himself did not comply very religiously with his own letters, for in a second instrument sealed in Paris on 17 February 1355 he reiterated his earlier donation, confessing that he had himself given away several estates contrary to his earlier promise, and that the canons he had established were consequently receiving less than their due.[47] Despite this, there is no evidence that the canons received so much as a single forfeiture after February 1355, and the last known donation of land made by Jean to the Noble House – a Manor near Saint-Ouen formerly in the possession of Marie of Castile, Countess of Alençon and Etampes, received in exchange for a lordship in Alençon forfeited for treason in April 1356 – was specifically granted (on 5 June 1356) not to the chapel but 'to embellish and augment' the seat of the Company of the Star.[48]

In addition to the documents recording Jean's benefactions to the seat of his order, there exists one other set of documents which not only indicate his continuing interest in the project, but shed further light on what he hoped to accomplish by founding it. I refer to a set of closely related works on chivalry,

---

[45] Paris, A.N., Reg. JJ 81, no. 570, f. 288r.

[46] Pannier, op. cit., p. 20.

[47] This letter (preserved in Paris, A.N., Mémoires de la Chambre des Comptes, C, f. 158) is also printed in Vattier, op. cit., pp. 45–7, and in several other places.

[48] Paris, A.N., J 169, no. 32; published in Pannier, La Noble Maison, pp. 87–90.

almost certainly written in this period by Geoffroy de Charny, who by his own testimony was one of the founder knights of the Company of the Star: the metrical treatise called the *Livre Charny*, the *Demandes pour la joute, les tournois et la guerre*,[49] and the prose treatise *Livre de Chevalerie*.[50] The author of these works was a veteran knight of obscure origins who had served in several campaigns under the unfortunate Count of Eu from 1337 onward, and had received the accolade at the siege of Aiguillon on 2 August 1346. He was one of the reformers named to the royal Council by Philippe VI after the disaster of Crécy, and as Captain of Saint-Omer had led an ill-fated attempt to recapture Calais from the English on 1 January 1350, and spent more than a year as a prisoner in England. Jean himself paid Charny's ransom on 31 July 1351, made him a *conseiller du roi es parties de Picardie et sur les frontieres de Flandres et d'Artois* on his return to France, and immediately following the Feast of the Star, invited him to take part once again in the deliberations of the Privy Council itself. After serving Jean in various military capacities during the next several years, Charny, as 'le plus preudomme et le plus vaillant de tous les autres'[51] was named the bearer of the Oriflamme on 25 June 1355, and fell defending that sacred banner in the Battle of Poitiers.

A valorous soldier, wise councillor, high-minded gentleman, and loyal servant of the crown, Charny seems to have been the very model of the sort of knighthood that Jean was attempting to promote when he founded the Company of the Star, and it is very probable that Charny composed all three of his works on chivalry at Jean's request. Each of the three sections of the *Demandes* begins with the prologue: 'These are the questions for the joust [or the tournament, or war] which I, Geoffroy de Charny, made for the the high and puissant Prince of the knights of Our Lady of the Noble House, to be judged by you and the knights of our noble company', and it would appear that each of the 133 questions that make up the work – all dealing with such fine points of the laws and customs of arms as whether a prisoner who had sworn faith might escape without reproach, whether a man who did not honour a challenge from another knight might be captured by that knight, and whether knights of a company who did not take part in a battle might share the booty captured by their companions who did – was intended to be the subject of a debate among the knights of the Star, presumably to be held during one of the annual assemblies of the Company. The connection of the other two books with the Company of the Star is less well established, but considering the relationship between Charny and Jean in the last six years of the former's life, and the fact that his works set forth a view of the nature and duties of knighthood which seems to be wholly consistent with that expressed in the prologue to the letters founding the Company's clerical college, there is a strong possiblity that one or both of them were also composed at Jean's explicit request specifically to serve as as handbooks on chivalry for the knights of the Company.

---

[49] Both edited by Michael Anthony Taylor, *A Critical Edition of Geoffroy de Charny's Livre Charny and the Demandes pour la joute, les tournois, et la guerre* (unpublished Ph.D. dissertation, University of North Carolina at Chapel Hill, 1977), pp. 1–76, 77–138.
[50] Published as a sort of appendix by Baron Kervyn de Lettenhove, *Oeuvres de Froissart I*, iii (Brussels, 1873), pp. 463–533. For a discussion of this work, see Maurice Keen, *Chivalry* (New Haven, 1981), pp. 12–15.
[51] Lettenhove, *Oeuvres de Froissart*, V, p. 412.

Jean's act of exchange of 5 June 1356 refers to the manor of Saint-Ouen as the 'principal seat' of his 'knightly congregation', but this seems to be the last contemporary reference to the Company as such. Barely three months after setting his seal to it, Jean was defeated at Poitiers and carried off as a prisoner first to Gascony and then to England. He was to remain a prisoner until freed on parole in October 1360, after which date he was preoccupied until the end of his reign with accumulating the immense sum demanded as his ransom. Despite these setbacks, he does not appear to have given up his idea of reviving the Company of the Star in some form, for in July 1359, while still a captive in England, he had two rings bearing stars made up,[52] and in January 1360 his son Charles, presumably at his request, had the coin bearing the star device (and known in consequence as the *gros denier blanc a l'estoille*) struck again.[53] Early in 1364, however, the defection from Calais of his second son Louis, Duke of Anjou, who had been serving as a hostage for the ransom, obliged him to return to honourable captivity in England, where he died, at the age of only forty-five, on 8 April of that year. There is not a shred of evidence that the society of knights he had founded ever met after his death, and it must be concluded that the Company of the Star, at least as a true order of knighthood, died with him.[54]

Since the seventeenth century it has been generally believed that the Company of the Star survived the death of its founder in some form or other for a century or so, and was only finally dissolved at or shortly before the foundation of the Order of St Michael the Archangel by Louis XI in 1469. In fact there is some evidence to suggest that, like the Order of the Band after the death of Alfonso XI, the star survived as the device of an honorific pseudo-order through most of the reign of the founder's eldest son and successor Charles V (r. 1364–80). In 1739 the Marquis of Courbon presented to the Parlement of Paris a document which he alleged to be letters of that monarch issued on 20 February 1375, in favour of the marquis' ancestor Arnaud de Courbon and four other gentlemen: Robert de Tezac, Pierre le Comte, Antoine de Pontac, and Jean de Lousme. In these letters Charles declared that, 'after being well informed of their good and noble generation, and in consideration of the fact that at their own cost and expense they had besieged and driven the English out of the castle of Mortagne', he was giving 'them and their heirs the power to bear ... the royal Star, in all places they pleased, whether battles, tournaments, feasts, or companies.'[55] Favyn quotes similar letters of Charles V conferring precisely the same rights on his chamberlains Jean II de Rochechouart

---

[52] *Comptes de l'Argenterie des Rois de France*, ed. L. Douët d'Arcq (Paris, 1851), p. 209.

[53] *Ordonnances des Rois de France*, III, p. 397. See below, p. 202.

[54] The *Noble Maison* is last referred to in the Saint-Denis chronicle under the year 1359, the year before Jean's return to France (pp. 162, 184). By April 1367 the land left by the Archdeacon of Thérouanne to the chapel of the Company had been given by Charles V to the Sainte Chapelle in Paris (*ORF*, V, pp. 1–3), and by October 1374 that king had given 'son Hostel de la Noble Maison' itself to his son the Dauphin Charles 'pour son esbatement' (*ORF*, VI, p. 67). This is surely proof that in his reign the Company was completely defunct by the latter date.

[55] Extract published in Aubert de la Chesnaye des Bois [*alias* Desbois], *Dictionnaire de la Noblesse* (2nd. edn, 15 vols, Paris, 1770–86), V, p. 213.

and Jean de Beaumont.[56] In these documents (the phrasing of which sounds genuine) the Star appears as a mere mark of distinction which can be passed on to the heirs of the recipients, and is clearly not the badge of a true order of knighthood. Indeed, the star is not even called an 'order' in the documents just cited.

If Charles V did at first continue to distribute the device of his father's defunct order as a sign of royal favour, as it must appear from these letters, he seems to have given up the practice in the last years of his reign, for there are no references to the star device in any source later than 1375, and while the inventory of jewels made for him in 1363 just before his accession lists among his possessions the 'ring of the star' (*l'anel de l'estelle*) given to him by his father in 1352,[57] neither the account of the *Ecurie* submitted in 1380[58] (the only record of objects distributed by Charles currently surviving), nor the inventory *post mortem* of his jewels made in February 1380,[59] contains a reference to any item associated with the order. The history of the society of knights projected in 1344 and established in 1352 can thus be concluded with confidence on the death of its founder's son in 1380.[60]

3 The Statutes of the Company

Since Le Bel's account of the Company contains what amount to fourteen ordinances not included in the letter of election, it seems reasonable to suppose that the latter document included only those ordinances which Jean felt the knights should know about before the first meeting of the Company, and that he presented a full set of ordinances to the knights who assembled at the Noble House in the following January. Unfortunately, not a single copy of this hypothetical document has survived, so we are obliged to reconstruct the statutes of the Company on the basis of the statements contained in the letter of election and the account in Le Bel's chronicle, quoted above. A careful comparison of the statements these contain reveals only one real discrepancy: the letter states that there were to be 500 knights in the Company, whereas Le Bel maintains that there were to be only 300. Obviously the letter issued by the founder himself is to be believed. Otherwise the statements in Le Bel's account supplement those in the

[56] Favyn, *Théâtre*, p. 576.
[57] Paris, B.N., ms. fr.21447, *Inventaire des meubles de monsieur le duc de Normandie dauphin de Viennois, fait en l'anee 1363* (copy of 17th century), fol. 2r.
[58] Paris, A.N., KK 34.
[59] Paris, B.N., ms. fr.1705.
[60] Foncemagne, *Recherches historiques*, traced to the works of Brantôme and Castelnau the idea, often repeated in later accounts of the order, that the Company of the Star gradually lost its *éclat* through a too generous distribution of stars by Charles VI, and that it was finally abandoned by its members after Charles VII or Louis XI gave its device to the *capitaine du Guet* or Captain of the Watch of Paris. He demonstrated that these ideas were based upon a misinterpretation of the sources by those authors, who supposed that all knighthoods conferred by the king in this period, as in their own, were associated with a royal order, and knew of no other order.

letter, and as none of them seems implausible, they will be treated here as generally if not precisely accurate.

4 The Name, Title, and Patron of the Company

The official designation of the society appears in the prologue to the letter of election as *les Chevaliers de Nostre Dame de la Noble Maison* – 'the Knights of Our Lady of the Noble House'. In the letter founding the society's canonical institute, however, Jean designated it more fully as *consortium seu societatem militem Beate Marie Nobilis Domus apud Sanctum Odoenum prope Sanctum Dyonisium in Francia*, 'the knightly Company or Society of the Blessed Mary of the Noble House at Saint-Ouen near Saint-Denis in France', and in the letters of June 1356 he called it *inclite Stellifere Congregationis nostre militaris apud Sanctum Audoenum in Domo Nobili*, 'our illustrious Starbearing Knightly Congregation in the Noble House at Saint-Ouen'. The confraternal title *compagnie*, used throughout letter of election and also by all of the chroniclers, seems to have been the society's usual title in the vernacular, and it is significant that, unlike its principal rival, the society was never referred to by its founder or any of his contemporaries under the title 'order'. Rather than adopt the characteristic title of the religious orders of knighthood, Jean chose to emulate those bodies by giving his Company a corporate name that combined that of the Company's patron with that of its seat, and in official sources the Company was always referred to by a form of that designation, instead of a name taken from its badge. Nevertheless, it would appear that even in the lifetime of its founder the society was normally referred to as the Company of the Star, for that is the only name given in any of the chronicle accounts.

The Company of the Star was dedicated, like the Order of the Garter, to God and the Blessed Virgin Mary, but not to St George, whose patronage was no doubt dropped from the original plan because of his association with the rival English order; although St George could serve simultaneously as the patron of many different bodies, he could hardly be asked to give aid to two rival bodies of knights. The dedication of an order of knights to the Queen of Heaven alone was entirely appropriate in terms of contemporary ideas of courtly chivalry, and Geoffroy de Charny in his *Livre Charny* rather pointedly declared that every knight ought to ask God and the Blessed Virgin to guide him so that he might act honourably in all his undertakings. Considering the relative standing of the Virgin and St George in the heavenly hierarchy, Jean may well have thought himself the winner in the contest for celestial patronage, even if the choice was forced on him. The position of the Blessed Virgin as patroness of the Company was to have been acknowledged symbolically in a variety of ways by the Company, principally in its name, in the dedication of its chapel, in its annual feast day and weekly fast day, in the blason of its banner, and probably in the iconography of its badge – all the usual ways in which patronage was represented in devotional confraternities.

5 The Membership of the Company

The structure of the Company finally established in 1351/2 retained the two-fold plan of the original project of 1344, with a college of lay knights served by a college of secular priests. Over both colleges the founder set himself and his successors as King of France in the presidential office of *Prince*. At that time the title *prince* still carried the general sense of 'chief' in addition to the more specialized senses of 'ruler' and 'great baron'. In its general sense it was almost synonymous with the term *souverain*, the title adopted by Edward as president of the Order of the Garter, and Jean's 'Prince' – a title never previously employed to designate the chief officer of any organization – may well have been an elegant variation upon Edward's 'Sovereign'.[61] The position Jean and his successors were to have enjoyed as Prince of the Company of the Star seems in to have been very similar in most respects to that of Edward of England as Sovereign of the Garter, but as we shall see the political and military benefits he hoped to gain from his position were considerably greater.

The lay college of the Company of the Star was to have been composed, when complete, of 500 ordinary members, who are referred to in the official sources only as *chevaliers* or 'knights'. Both the idea of such a body and the proposed limit on its membership were probably borrowed from Edward's Round Table project of 1344, which was to have had 300 knights. Jean's project of the same year had called for a membership of only 200 knights, but despite Edward's decision to reduce the size of his projected order by eleven-twelfths to a mere twenty-six, Jean chose for some reason to increase his initial goal by a factor of two and a half. Clearly he did not wish to abandon the advantages of size in favour of those of exclusiveness, and as the number 500 was not significantly greater than the total number of barons and bannerets he had called upon on the day after his accession to be ready to defend the kingdom (346), it was not in theory an impossible goal. As we have seen, the total number of knights of all ranks in France in 1351 was somewhere between 2,500 and 4,000, so the Company would have included between a fifth and and eighth of all the knights in the kingdom if Jean's plan had been fully implemented. Most of the known members were barons or bannerets, and it is possible that Jean set the limit on membership at 500 in order to include, either immediately or eventually, most or all of the barons and bannerets in the kingdom. Even if all the barons and bannerets known to the royal Chancellery in 1351 had been admitted, however, the Company would have had to admit more than 150 knights bachelor to reach the limit of 500, and as knights bachelor made up at least five sixths of the knightage, Jean may well have meant a clear majority of the membership to be drawn from their ranks. Jean seems to have been well aware of the fact that his Company would include knights of several classes, for in the letter of election he declared that each year three princes, three bannerets, and three bachelors of the Company would be placed at the Table of Honour.[62]

Jean almost certainly selected the first lay members of the Company, either alone

---

[61] *Souverain*, from MLat *superanus*, was at first synonymous with *superior*, as the translation of the Garter title indicates.
[62] Item 18.

or in consultation with his Council, but it would appear that, like Edward of England, he intended to give the knights of the Company themselves an active role in the selection of all future members. Jean's letter of 1351 contains no suggestion of how the later members of his Company were to be selected, but Le Bel states quite clearly that no knight was to be admitted to the Company of the Star without the consent not only of the king but of the majority of the companions present,[63] and this suggests that elections were to have been held either during the annual assembly or (as in the Order of the Garter) at special assemblies called for the purpose. Jean's letter has nothing to say of the qualifictions required for membership, but it is likely, given the fact that they are consistently referred to as *chevaliers*, that candidates for membership in the Company of the Star were required to receive the accolade of knighthood before being formally received. In the light of what we know about the Order of the Band, however, it is at least possible that squires were admitted to membership. It may be significant that three of the young princes known to have been admitted as founding members of the Company – the king's younger sons Jean and Philippe and their cousin and companion Louis de Bourbon – received the accolade of knighthood in a ceremony held on the very day of the feast of the Star;[64] this suggests that knighthood was necessary for reception, but not for election to the Company. According to Le Bel, the knights of the Company of the Star were to have been chosen from among the most worthy (*souffisans*) in the kingdom, and (like those of the Garter) were to have been 'sans deffaulte de reproeuche'.[65] If Jean did impose such a restriction he must have done so primarily to make those admitted think more highly of their membership, for (especially given his opinion of most contemporary knights) he cannot possibly have imagined that he would be able to find 500 knights in his kingdom who would qualify for membership if this requirement were followed to the letter.

Unfortunately, our knowledge of the identity and even of the number of the knights actually admitted to the Company during its brief history is very far from perfect. The names or offices of twenty of the original knights are known from the records of the royal *Argenterie*, which indicate that badges and/or habits were provided to them before the Feast of the Star.[66] Nine of these knights were junior members of the royal family who at the time of the proclamation of the Company were being supported as members of the royal household: Jean's four young sons, Charles, Dauphin of Viennois and future Duke of Normandy and King of France (aged fifteen, d. 1380); Louis, future Duke of Anjou and Touraine (aged twelve, d. 1384); Jean, future Duke of Berry and Auvergne (aged eleven, d. 1416); and Philippe, future Duke of Touraine and later of Burgundy (aged nine, d. 1404); Jean's younger brother Philippe, Duke of Orléans and Count of Valois and Beaumont (aged fifteen, d. 1375); and Jean's agnatic cousins Charles Capet d'Artois-Pézenas, later Count of Longueville and of Pézenas (aged about fifteen?, d.p. 1376); Louis Capet de Bourbon, later Duke of Bourbon and *Chambrier* of

---

[63] Statement 13.
[64] See Françoise Lehoux, *Jean de France, duc de Berri*, I (Paris, 1966), pp. 23–4.
[65] Statement 14.
[66] Paris, A.N., KK 8; relevant passages published in Pannier, *La Noble Maison, Preuves*, pp. 63–74.

France (aged fifteen, d. 1410); and the younger brothers of the King of Navarre: Philippe Capet d'Evreux-Longueville, later Count of Longueville (aged about eighteen, d. 1363); and Louis Capet d'Evreux-Beaumont, later Count of Beaumont-le-Roger (aged about fifteen, d. 1372).[67] In addition to these princes, the records mention that badges or habits were provided to eleven men, who were with one exception officers of the household of the king or the dauphin: to the Grand Master of the Household (Jean de Châtillon, Lord of Châtillon-sur-Marne);[68] and to the four *chambellans* who served under him – presumably the *Chambellan* of France Jean de Melun, Viscount of Melun, Constable and Chamberlain of Normandy, and later Count of Tancarville (d. 1382); Jean de Clermont, Marshal of France (d. 1346); Robert de Lorris;[69] and the Lord of Andresel (whose name is not known); to the Lord of Saint Venant, (Robert de Wavrin), the king's former *gouverneur*; to four unnamed *chambellans* of the Dauphin (so far unidentified); and finally to the former Dauphin, Humbert de la Tour du Pin, since January 1351 titular Patriarch of Alexandria (d. 1355). As we have seen, there is convincing evidence that Geoffroy de Charny (d. 1356)[70] and the Neapolitan Giacomo Bozzuto (d. 1358)[71] were admitted to the Company, and there is reason to believe that the Lord of Bevelinghem, Captain of the Castle of Guines, was also included among the first members.[72] According to the *Chronique des quatre premiers Valois*, Charles de Blois (d. 1364), one of the two contenders for the throne of Brittany, was elected as one of the *neuf preux* at the Epiphany feast, so he too must have been named to the Company, even though he had been for some time a captive in England.[73]

Precisely how many others were appointed to the Company in November 1351 we have no way of knowing, but as Le Bel records that more than eighty knights of the Company were killed or wounded in the Battle of Mauron, and none of the known members seems to have been present at that battle, it is quite possible that well over a hundred were named at that time. Who they were is of course another question, but it is more than likely that their number included a high proportion of the titled baronage at least, for it is hardly likely that the emprisoned Duke of Brittany was singled out for inclusion, and the *Chronique des quatre premiers Valois* confidently asserts that 'the highest barons of the kingdom' were present at the feast. Charles of Navarre, who was to marry the founder's daughter within a few

---

[67] Before the death of Philippe VI, Jean's sons, Louis 'de Bourbon' and Louis 'de Navarre' had formed (with Edouard de Mousson-Bar, Count and future Duke of Bar, his brother Robert, and Godefroy de Brabant), the 'company' of the young Duke of Orléans, and all but Jean's two youngest sons and Louis 'de Bourbon' had been knighted together on the day of Jean's coronation. See Françoise Lehoux, *Jean de France, duc de Berri*, I, pp. 19–21.

[68] See Cazelles, *Jean le Bon*, p. 175.

[69] Ibid., p. 46.

[70] See above, p. 186.

[71] See above, p. 183.

[72] He is reported to have left his post to attend the feast of the Star, which he would hardly have done had he not been required to attend. See the *Chronique de Saint-Denis*, VI, p. 56.

[73] See above, p. 181.

weeks of the feast,[74] would certainly have been included, and it would be difficult to believe that Jean failed to appoint his own favourite, Charles 'd'Espagne', Count of Angoulême and Constable of the Kingdom. The Dukes of Bourbon and Burgundy and the Counts of Etampes and Alençon ought also have received appointments among the founder knights of the Company, as *seigneurs du sang royal* closely related by blood and marriage to the king,[75] and one would similarly expect the appointment of such men as the Lord of Craon and the Counts of L'Isle-Jourdain and Armagnac, who were not only important barons, but served in this period as captains or lieutenants general of the king.[76]

The letter of election is silent on the subject of the reception or installation of newly-chosen members of the Company, though it must be assumed that it was upon the occasion of their installation that the oath of membership was to be taken. Presumably the knights who attended the assembly of January 1352 were formally received into the new Company on that occasion, but it is not known whether any other knights were either elected or inducted into the Company during the remainder of its official existence.

6 The Privileges and Obligations of Membership

Our knowledge of the privileges and obligations entailed in membership in the Company of the Star, if less than complete, is considerably better than our knowledge of the identity of the members. Aside from the right to wear the badge and habit of the Company and to participate in its activities, the only known privileges a knight of the Star was to enjoy as such were derived from the obligations of the Prince and the other knights, and consisted of the right to be maintained in his old age along with two servants at the *hostel* of the Company, and to receive, after his death, a solemn funeral in the Company's chapel,[77] and a single mass from each of the surviving companions to speed his soul through purgatory.[78] The first of these privileges is mentioned only in the chronicles of Le Bel and Froissart,[79] but it is in conformity with the suggestion in the papal letters of 1344 that certain members of the originally projected company were to live at the Company's seat. The provision is similar to that included in the Garter statutes for the maintenance of a college of 'poor knights', with the significant difference that in the French order it was set forth as a benefit for the companions themselves to look forward to in their chivalrous dotage, rather than as a charity to be performed by them for persons not of their number. Jean was clearly less interested in charity

---

[74] Cazelles, op. cit., p. 147.
[75] The two young counts, Louis Capet d'Evreux-Etampes and his half-brother Charles Capet de Valois-Alençon, had received the accolade of knighthood at Jean's coronation, and since that time had formed part of the 'company' of the Dauphin Charles. See Lehoux, op. cit., pp. 22–3.
[76] See Cazelles, op. cit., pp. 151–2.
[77] Item 14.
[78] Item 15.
[79] Statement 19.

than in providing privileges calculated to sustain the loyalty of his companions.

The obligations of the Prince of the Company of the Star to the knights were even more diffuse than those of the Sovereign of the Garter. It would appear that he was to provide at his own expense not only the buildings in which the Company's activities were to take place, but the furnishings of both the hall and the chapel, and the food to be consumed at the annual feast. We know that Jean attempted to endow the college of canons entirely out of crown revenues, despite the example set by Edward of providing for their upkeep out of the entry fees and fines of the companions, and the income of several parishes. It is also very likely that the Prince was to pay for the solemn obsequies of the departed knights, and possibly (though this is far from clear) for some sort of memorial involving their badges and rings[80] – though it is just as likely that these were to be sold (like the sword and helm of the Garter knights) for the support of the canons. All of this must be inferred from silence, however, as nothing is said in Jean's letters of the Company's finances.

The obligations of the ordinary members specified in the surviving sources fall as usual into three categories: cliental, fraternal, and general. The obligations in the first of these categories were rather more significant than those imposed in any of the older orders, but still far from onerous. According to the letter of election, the knights of the Company were required to swear (presumably on being admitted to the order) to give to the Prince, to the best of their ability, loyal counsel on any matter he chose to put before them, 'whether of arms or of other things'.[81] It is possible that Jean intended to ask for advice from the knights of the Company only on matters relating to chivalry or of direct concern to the Company as such, but as the Company seems to have included many and perhaps most of the leading members of the nobility of the kingdom, and as there was no other regular assembly in which the king could consult with representatives of the second Estate, it is very likely that Jean meant to ask the knights for 'loyal counsel' on matters of concern to the nobility as a whole, including taxation as well as military organization and service. Thus, the knights of the Star may have been expected to function – like the knights of St George of Hungary – as members of a sort of assembly of the nobility, roughly analogous to the English House of Lords. As far as we know, no more active service was to be demanded of them; despite the mention of military activities in items 12, 17, and 18, there is no indication that the knights of the Company as such were to be required to fight in their Prince's wars or to aid him in any way either against his own enemies or those of the Company as a whole. Why Jean neglected to require military service from the knghts of the Company is unclear, but it may be that he, like his rival Edward III, felt the systems of military recruitment already at his disposal were more than adequate to secure the active service of the knights of the Company whenever and for however long he required it.

Only two further obligations to their Prince were certainly to be assumed by the lay members of the order: to ask his permission before joining any other order,[82]

---

[80] Item 13.

[81] Item 8: 'Jureront que a leur pouoir il donront loyal conseil au prince de ce qu' il leur demandera, soit d'armes ou d'autres choses.'

[82] Item 9.

and before going on any long journey.[83] The first of these was to become a common feature of monarchical orders, as was the rider that, should another order be joined, the present was to come first. It is clear that Jean, like most founders of orders, was anxious to obtain a monopoly of the loyalty of the members of his order, but realistically recognized that the best he could hope for was priority among a number of conflicting loyalties. He was in fact the first founder to have to face the problem of membership in other orders, and could only have had the Garter in mind when framing his requirements. No doubt he was concerned to keep as many of his subjects as possible from being lured into alliance with England, and it is possible, given the wording of item 9, that he hoped to lure French subjects already belonging to Edward's order back into the fold. Chapter 28 of the Garter statutes had required the knights of that order to ask permission of the Sovereign before leaving the country, and it may be that the slightly different requirement in item 19 of the Star letter was a direct borrowing from the earlier foundation. On the other hand, in France it was standard practice in time of war for the king to issue an order forbidding his subjects to leave the kingdom, and this may be the true origin of this rule.[84] It is possible that Jean hoped by imposing this obligation to prevent any illicit intercourse with England, or more generally to keep track of the whereabouts of his knights. There is no suggestion in the sources of a corresponding obligation on the part of Prince to give the knights of his order the most honourable journeys to undertake, such as Edward of England had promised as Sovereign of the Garter.

The fraternal obligations of the Star knights were considerably more extensive than those of the knights of the Garter. Although no oath of fraternity is mentioned in Jean's letter, the chronicle accounts state clearly that the knights of the Star were to swear to aid all their fellow knights 'in all their encounters', in the fashion of brothers-in-arms.[85] The latter was the only fraternal obligation owed by the knights to their fellows in life, but they were also obliged to have a mass said for every deceased member shortly after his death.[86] This was a very minimal version of an obligation common to almost all monarchical orders (and virtually all confraternities), and as it seems to have provided one of the most important practical benefits to be derived from membership in the order, it is surprising the number of masses required was so meagre. It may be that Jean felt the large number of knights to be included in the Company made it unnecessary to require more than one mass of each to provide a large number of masses.

The knights also undertook a number of general obligations. Those that have been recorded seem to have been designed to secure their participation in the corporate activities of the Company and to promote courage and piety. Unless some pressing business made it impossible, they were required to assemble each year at the seat of the Company on the eve of the Assumption and to take part in the various activities of the annual meeting.[87] In order that those knights who could not come would be reminded of their membership on the feast of the Company's

---

[83] Item 19.
[84] See Contamine, *Guerre, état et société*.
[85] Le Bel, statement 16.
[86] Item 15.
[87] Item 10.

patron, Jean, like Edward of England, required them to gather, if possible, in groups of at least five, and hear mass and vespers together at the appointed times, wearing the habit of the Company.[88]

According to Le Bel, the knights were also obliged to swear an oath never to retreat more than four *arpents* (about six acres) from a battle, even if it meant death or capture,[89] and the letter of election gives credence to this assertion by declaring that any knight of the Company who fled shamefully from a battle or ordered encounter was to be suspended from the Company and forbidden to wear its habit, until such time as he was either expelled permanently by the Prince and his council, or held to be cleared by subsequent good deeds. In the meantime his arms and crest in the hall of the Noble House were to be reversed, but not defaced.[90] Such a requirement was certainly in keeping with Jean's expressed desire to promote the highest standards of knightly conduct, and if we can believe Le Bel a considerable number of the knights died trying to live up to it. Jean himself – who remembered with chagrin his father's flight after Crécy – seems to have taken the oath quite seriously, for as we have seen he refused to flee the field at Poitiers when he could easily have done so.

The two remaining obligations imposed on the knights of the Star were 'spiritual' in nature. The first of these, stated in item 7, was that they fast every Saturday of the year, or give the sum of fifteen *deniers* in alms. According to item 5 they were to wear a special version of the order's habit every Saturday as well, no doubt to mark the fast. The fast was the only regular common activity of the knights other than the annual feast, and in addition to providing spiritual benefits it would have served as a frequent reminder to each knight of his membership in the order. It would also have given the knights frequent opportunities to show off the order's splendid costume, and thus to advertise both the order and their membership in it all over western Europe. Two later orders – the Star and the Ship – were to have a very similar practice.

Both the day selected for the Star fast (Saturday, on which a special Office of Our Lady had been said since the twelfth century) and the number of *deniers* or pennies owed in lieu of fasting (fifteen, explicitly for her fifteen joys) were closely associated with the patroness of the order, and the exercise was probably regarded as a form of devotion to her in her patronal capacity. It is possible that in return for this, and the spiritual exercises associated with the annual feast, the knights of the order were to receive some or all of the spiritual privileges conferred by the papal letters of 1344, but nothing is said of this in the later sources.

7 The Clergy and Officer of the Company

The letter of election also fails to mention the Company's ecclesiastical college, which we know from other sources was part of the original project, and was actually established by Jean within a year of the first and only meeting of the lay college. It

---

[88] Item 11.
[89] Statement 15.
[90] Item 17.

would appear that the canonical institute attached by the letters of 1352 to the 'Church of the Noble House' was founded under the authority of the papal letters of 1344, but aside from the fact that it was to be composed of 'canons, chaplains, and clerks' who were to celebrate the divine office in the Company's chapel, nothing is known of either its composition or the activities which Jean intended it to perform. According to the letter of foundation, the function of the Company's clergy was to pray for the chivalrous conduct of the knights of the Company, that it might redound to the greater glory of the kingdom. Presumably they were also to pray, like the canons of the Garter, for the souls of the Company's departed, and to sing both the annual services and the requiem masses for the newly deceased. How many priests, if any, Jean actually appointed to the clerical college of the Company, and whether or not they ever performed any of the functions he intended them to perform, we have no way of knowing.

Unlike the statutes of the Garter, the letter proclaiming the Company of the Star makes no mention of any officers specifically attached to the Company, but we know from the letter founding the college of canons that at least one corporate office was created during the Company's brief history: that of 'Receiver' or 'Governor' of the Noble House. The first and only known Receiver, a bourgeois of Paris named Etienne Lepellier, was appointed by royal letters dated 3 September 1352. His duties, according to the instrument of appointment, were to receive the various forfeited lands and chattels granted to the canonical college from the officers of the royal *Chambre des comptes*, and to convert into cash such property as could be more profitably sold than kept.[91] Lepellier seems to have had little to occupy his time as Receiver of the Noble House, for as we have seen, the Company received very few of the forfeitures promised to it, and received none at all after February 1355.

8 The Physical Establishment of the Company: The Noble House

Like Edward of England, Jean provided his Company with a physical establishment by assigning to it the hall and chapel of one of his own favourite residences, refurbished especially for their new role. The residence in question was the royal *manoir* of Saint-Ouen-lès-Saint-Denis, an estate which had been acquired by Jean's grandfather Count Charles of Valois around the end of the thirteenth century, and had become part of the royal demesne when Jean's father Philippe ascended the throne in 1328. Although it had been neglected by Philippe, the manor of Saint-Ouen was conveniently and symbolically situated mid-way between the two principal seats of the French monarchy, the City of Paris and the Royal Abbey of Saint-Denis, and Jean felt this was important enough to mention in his letter. The manor of Saint-Ouen lacked completely the historic associations with the monarchy enjoyed by Windsor Castle, and with the exception of its hall (which was large enough to require seven fireplaces to heat it)[92] its structures were on a much smaller scale, but its situation and nature as a royal country residence bore a

---

91 Pannier, *La Noble Maison*, p. 120.
92 Ibid., p. 98.

general resemblance to those of the seat of the Order of the Garter, and this may have influenced Jean's choice. The size of its hall and its proximity to Paris were probably its most attractive features, however, for Jean needed a room large enough for 500 knights to eat and deliberate in together, and as we have seen he spent almost all of his time in and around the capital of his kingdom in order to permit the heads of the government services fixed there to participate regularly in the deliberations of his Council. Since Saint-Ouen was not mentioned in the papal letters of 1344, and did not become part of Jean's personal estate until after his accession to the throne in 1350, it was probably chosen for its new role only after the latter event.

The name by which the manor-house of Saint-Ouen is referred to in the sources – la Noble Maison or Nobilis Domus – seems to have been adopted at or shortly before the time of the proclamation of the Company, and was almost certainly meant to recall the very similar name of the great round tower in which the fictional company of the British king Perceforest was said to have gathered: the Franc Palais. The Company's full title, which included the new name of its seat, must also have been intended to evoke the Company of the Frank Palace, and less directly the knights of the Round Table.

According to item 16 of the letter of proclamation, the arms and crest of each knight of the Company were to be painted over what must have been some sort of stall in the sale or hall of the Noble House, presumably arranged around the outer wall in the fashion of a monastic or collegiate chapter house.[93] This practice, though similar to that of the Garter, was probably inspired by that of the fictional company of the Franc Palais, whose knights had special places marked by their arms around a table in the great round hall of their society. In order to accomodate 500 knights in this fashion Jean would have had to install at least 1,000 feet of benches against the walls of the hall, and unless the hall of the Noble House was exceptionaly large, this would have required him to arrange the benches in at least four ranks or tiers all or most of the way around the room.[94] Such an arrangement would have used up a great deal of floor space, and made it difficult to set up tables for a banquet in the same room, but it is difficult to see what else Jean could have done short of building a new and larger hall.

There is no evidence that Jean ever got around to having permanent stalls contructed for the knights of the Company, but it is clear that he did have a great deal of work done to the hall, chapel, and chamber of the newly-named Noble House in the two months between his proclamation of the Company and the Feast of the Star of 6 January 1352. The records of the expenditures made on the preparations for the feast are incomplete, but they show that Jean had the hall hung with curtains of red velvet, and had a dais constructed in it which he first intended

---

[93] The French reads: 'Et est ordené que les armes et timbres de touz les seigneurs et chevaliers de la Noble Maison seront paint en la salle d'icelle, au dessus d'un chacun la ou il sera.'

[94] It would require a hall about 66 feet square to accomodate 1,000 feet of benches arranged against the walls in four tiers. Very few halls were as large as this; those of the castles of Cawdor, Harlech, Caernarvon, and Conway, which were among the largest in Britain at the time, measured 40 x 20 ft., 70 x 18 ft., 98 x 48 ft., and 120 x 40 ft., respectively. See Sidney Toy, The Castles of Great Britain, 4th edn. (London, 1966).

to cover with blue cloth semé of fleurs de lys, and embroidered with three large clouds each surrounding a star, but in the end covered with cloth of gold and silver. The chapel and chamber were provided with similar hangings, and three large stars were made of embroidery to hang on the *coutepointe*, *ciel*, and *cheveciel* of the latter room. Various items of furniture were also made, including several *chaires* for the king and the Dauphin Charles.[95]

The hall of the Noble House may have been large enough to serve as a meeting place for 500 knights, but it would be surprising if the chapel was also sufficiently spacious to accommodate such a number without crowding,[96] and Jean may have laid plans either to extend the existing chapel or to build a new one especially for the Company. In the meantime the Company (which probably included no more than 150 knights on the one occasion it actually assembled) had to make do with the existing building. Curiously enough, this had originally been dedicated to St George, but after the foundation of the Company of the Star it seems to have been rededicated to the patroness of the Company, for in the letters issued by Jean in that period it is referred to as the *ecclesiam Beate Marie Virginis nostre Nobilis Domus*,[97] and as *l'eglise de Nostre Dame de l'Estelle*.[98]

Since Le Bel asserted that the knights of the Star too old to fight any longer were to have the right to be supported at the seat of the Company in some sort of *hostel*, it may be that Jean intended to construct a building or set of buildings for this purpose, comparable to those provided in Windsor Castle for the clergy and (eventually) the poor knights of the Order of the Garter. Not surprisingly, however, there is no evidence that any new building was ever constructed at Saint-Ouen either for the retired companions of the Company or for the various canons and lesser clerics Jean planned to add to the establishment of the chapel.

The 'Noble House' of Saint-Ouen remained the theoretical seat of the Company at least until the time of Jean's capture in 1356, and probably until his death. After the latter event it probably reverted to its original condition as a royal hunting lodge, for it was given by Charles V to his son the Dauphin in 1374.[99] Its estate was eventually engulfed by the northern expansion of Paris, and nothing now remains of its buildings.

9 The Annual Assembly of the Company

As was true in the Order of the Garter, the only corporate activity in which all or most of the knights of the Star were to take part was the annual Assembly of the Company. This was to have been held at the Company's seat between the eve of

---

95 Pannier, *La Noble Maison*, Preuves, pp. 65–9.
96 Even the chapels built within major castles were usually much smaller than the hall. The chapel of Windsor Castle could only accommodate sixty or seventy people at a time.
97 Letter of May 1352, Pannier, op. cit., p. 77.
98 Letters of June 1352, ibid., p. 79.
99 See above, p. 187 n. 54.

the Assumption and the afternoon of the day following the feast, or in other words on 14, 15, and 16 August. The only activities of this Assembly mentioned in the letter of election were religious services of some sort and a banquet. Almost nothing is said about the former, but the fact that those knights who could not attend the Assembly were required to hear vespers and mass together at the appropriate times (item 11) suggests that similar services were to have been included among the activities of the Assembly. The banquet is mentioned only in the context of the item describing the seating arrangements at the Table of Honour. This is not much to go on for reconstructing the nature of the Assembly envisaged by Jean, but as the timing and duration of the Assembly exactly reflected Garter usage, and the religious services and banquet alluded to in Jean's letter corresponded exactly to elements of the Garter Assembly, it seems likely that the occasion was to have had much the same format as that of its English rival: a chapter and vespers on the eve, a solemn mass of the patron followed by a splendid banquet on the feast day proper, and perhaps a requiem mass for the Company's dead on the day after the feast.

The sources refer either directly or indirectly to several activities that were presumably to have taken place during the chapter or business meeting. As we have already noted, Jean apparently intended to ask the advice of the assembled knights on various matters of concern to them as knights and noblemen. It would also appear that he intended to put to them questions relating to fine points of the law of arms, drawn from the set of *Demandes* specially prepared for the purpose by Geoffroy de Charny. The object of the latter exercise was probably to make them think about how knights ought to behave in a variety of real-life situations; no doubt Jean hoped that this would carry over into their behaviour when such situations arose. According to Le Bel, the knights were also to recount at or before each feast their 'adventures' of the past year, shameful as well as meritorious, and these were to be set down in a book so that they might be read out during the chapter, and the various adventures judged by the knights present. Although the idea of writing the deeds of the knights into a book seems to have been original with Jean, the practice of reviewing members' behaviour during the previous year and doling out rewards and punishments was common to many confraternities. At the first Assembly, according to the letter of election, the three *plus souffisanz* or 'most worthy' princes, bannerets, and bachelors present were to be seated at a special *Table d'Onnour* during the dinner that followed the meeting and the banquet on the feast day proper, and every year thereafter their places at the Table were to be taken by the three princes, three bannerets, and three bachelors who had done the most that year in *armes de guerre*.[100] These nine 'worthy' knights were obviously meant to represent the *Neuf Preux* or 'Nine Worthies' of contemporary lore. We know from the *Chronique des quatre premiers Valois* that nine such knights, described therein as *preux*, were actually elected during the course of the Company's first and only meeting. It is significant that Jean wished to reward in this way only knightly deeds performed on the field of battle, and explicitly excluded from consideration all *faits d'armes de paix* – feats, that is to say, performed in tournaments and jousts. This would appear to suggest that Jean, unlike Alfonso of Castile and Edward of England, had little faith in the usefulness of such contests

---

[100] Item 18.

for developing knightly skill and virtue, but this impression is contradicted by the position adopted by Geoffroy de Charny in the works he wrote, in all probability at Jean's request, to serve as textbooks on chivalry for the knights of the Company. In the circumstances, however, it would not be surprising if Jean felt more inclined to reward heroic action against his English enemies than brilliant performances in the lists.

Those knights who were found to have committed disgraceful acts were presumably to be punished in appropriate ways, but the only punishable act mentioned in the sources is flight from the field of battle. This was to be punished, as we have seen, by suspension and the reversal of the offender's armorial achievement in the hall until such time as his good deeds won him restoration to the Company. It is interesting to note in the wording of item 17 of Jean's letter that the punishment of a knight was to be effected by the Prince 'et son Conseil'. What 'council' was meant is not clear, but it is likely that it was to be composed of some or all of the member knights, acting in their advisory capacity. This is the only reference in the sources to participation by anyone other than the Prince in the government of the Company.

Nothing is said in the sources about any other business to be conducted at the annual Assembly, and the whole question of the interpretation and amendment of the statutes themselves is ignored.

10 The Badge of the Company

The badge of the Company of the Star is the first for which we have a precise contemporary description. According to items 3 and 4 of Jean's letter of 1351, the badge of the Company he therein proclaimed was to be 'a white star, in the middle of the star a roundel of azure, in the middle of this roundel of azure a little gold sun'.[101] Unlike the garter of the English order, which as a functional element of male apparel had to be redesigned in two dimensions for display on the various parts of that order's habit, the star adopted by Jean was essentially two-dimensional, and could easily be displayed in any of the various ways that the devices adopted during his reign as livery-badges were commonly displayed. Probably in imitation of Garter usage, Jean nevertheless prescribed two distinct forms for the badge of his Company: a large version in the form of a *fremail* or brooch (very much like those worn by pilgrims and messengers), to be worn on formal occasions pinned to the shoulder of the mantle or caped hood, and at other times in any position in which it could be seen clearly;[102] and a smaller version, set within a red roundel (representing the Company's livery-colour) on a ring, which like the garter

---

[101] The French reads: '[3] Et porteront continuelment un anel entour la verge duquel sera escrit leur nom et surnom; auquel annel aura un esmail plat vermeil; en l'esmail une estoille blanche; au milieu de l'estoille une rondete d'azure; au milieu d'icelle rondeur, un petit soleil d'or. [4] Et au mantel sus l'espaule au devant en leur chaperon un fremail auquel aura un estoille toute telle comme en l'annel est devisé.'

[102] Item 6.

knee-band was to be worn all the time.[103] The ring bearing the badge was also to be inscribed around its edge with the name and surname of its owner, presumably because it was to be sent to the Prince of the Company to inform him of its owner's death.[104] Unlike the garter, neither form of the star-badge had any verbal device associated with it.

Although the letter of election required each of the knights appointed to the Company to provide himself with a brooch and ring, conforming to the description provided therein, before the meeting of January 1352, and the surviving register of the royal *Argenterie* records that both Jean and his son the Dauphin Charles had rings and brooches made for distribution to members of their immediate entourages, not one of these jewels has survived, and we are obliged to reconstruct their appearance on the basis of written descriptions and pictorial representations. The only strictly contemporary representations of the star-badge are to be found on coins; during the period between the proclamation of the Company and his capture at Poitiers, Jean issued three successive coins bearing on one or both sides representations of the device of his new order, and known in consequence as *gros blancs a l'estoille*.[105] As figure 5.1 shows, the 'star' of the Company is depicted on these coins as a mullet of six, seven, or eight rectilinear points, pierced with a circular hole in the centre. Where the star is large enough for this to be represented, a sun in the form of a swirling pinwheel occupies most of the hole, exactly as the letter of election specifies. The only other representation of the badge in either of its forms now known is in a miniature in a manuscript of the Saint-Denis chronicle cited above, prepared for the founder's son at some time between 1364 and 1375, depicting the Assembly of the Company held in January 1352.[106]

In this miniature – which includes depictions of eight brooch-badges – the star is represented as a mullet of eight points of silver rather than white, with a blue roundel bearing a swirling gold sun voided of the field set in its centre. The original miniaturist seems to have represented the badge as a brooch that in reality would have been about eight inches in outer diameter, but at some point the stars in the miniature were overpainted, and the rays of each one were doubled in length. Since this representation not only conforms to the official description but closely resembles the stars depicted on the contemporary coins, it probably presents a reasonably accurate picture of at least some of the star-badges actually worn, but as most of the knights had their badges made at their own expense on the basis of a verbal description, there must have been considerable variation both in the size and in the design of the badges of both types.

The accounts of the *Argenterie* confirm that even the badges ordered by the king and his eldest son the Dauphin Charles varied significantly in weight, material, and decoration, according to the civil rank of the recipient.[107] The brooches (*estoille*)

---

[103] Item 3.

[104] Item 13.

[105] See H. Hoffmann, *Les monnaies royales de France, depuis Hugues Capet jusqu' à Louis XVI* (Paris, 1878), p. 215, Pl. XXI. See figs 5.1, 5.2.

[106] The illumination in question (Paris, B.N., ms. fr.2813, f. 394r) was published in full colour in Kenneth Fowler, *The Age of Plantagenet and Valois* (London, 1967), p. 82. See fig. 5.5.

[107] Paris, A.N., register KK 8; published in Pannier, *La Noble Maison*, Preuves, pp. 71–73.

5.1 The *gros blancs a l'estoille*
(after Hoffmann)

5.2 The star as represented
on the coins

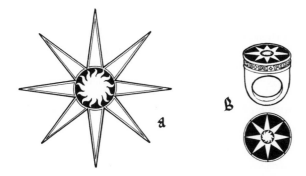

5.3 a. The star badge as represented in the MS. of the *Grands chroniques*
b. The ring of the star (reconstruction)

and rings (*anel*) of the star provided to the king himself, his younger brother, and his four sons, were all of 22 carat gold, and in each case weighed together 4 ounces and 10 *esterlins*; the six brooches provided for the *Grand Maistre d'Ostel* and five *chambellans* of the king were made of a total of 3 marks of silver gilded with 18 *esterlins* of fine gold, and the six rings made for them contained a total of 4 *esterlins* of gold; the ring made for Monseigneur de Saint-Venant was made of 5 *esterlins* of gold, while those made for the four *chambellans* of the Dauphin were each made of 4 *esterlins* of gold, and the brooches made for the latter were made of silver gilt weigning a total of 1 mark 6 ounces, including 12 *esterlins* of fine gold used for gilding. Thus the differences in civil rank among the members were only thinly disguised by the common badges they wore as members of the Company of the Star. Indeed, the Dauphin had made in addition to what must have been his ordinary brooch (which like all of those listed above was *sans perrerie*), two more lavish brooches, one for himself made of 7 ounces and 2 *esterlins* of 22 carat gold, and garnished with six balas rubies and six groups of seven pearls; the other for his uncle the Duke of Orléans, of similar weight but garnished with three balas and seven oriental rubies, and with four groups of three pearls.

The symbolic significance of Jean's star badge is not as obscure as that of Edward's garter, but until now it has been consistently misunderstood. If the device of the Company had been a plain white star it might well have represented the Star of Bethlehem, as both the timing of the Company's first meeting at Epiphany and the verbal device long associated with the star by scholars – *Monstrant regibus astra viam* – seem to suggest. The device was anything but plain, however, the famous motto had no demonstrable connection with the Company,[108] and the regular feast of the Company had no connection with the Nativity or any or its associated commemorations. It is thus exceedingly unlikely that the device was meant to represent the star seen by the three kings, as has been generally supposed.

It is in fact all but certain that the star was intended to represent the patroness of the Company, the Blessed Virgin Mary. Mary was called the 'Star of the Sea' in the very popular hymn *Ave maris stella*, was referred to as *Nostre Dame de l'Estelle* in the letter of 18 May 1352 by which Henry de Culent donated land to the church of the Noble House,[109] and was normally portrayed in this period in paintings of the Siennese school (to which Jean must have been exposed during his visit to the papal court in Avignon in 1347) wearing a star, very much like that represented on the coins and in the chronicle manuscript, on the shoulder of her mantle.[110] If the

---

[108] Pannier, *La Noble Maison*, p. 116, n. 1, convincingly argues that this motto, which appeared on a medal of uncertain date in association with a star quite unlike that of the Company, was associated with the Company by modern historians solely on the basis of the use of the word *astra* (although the device of the Company was invariably called a *stella* in Latin sources). Despite this demonstration, modern authors (including Renouard, 'L'Ordre de la Jarretière', p. 294) have continued to refer to this motto as if it were certainly that of the Company.

[109] Pannier, *La Noble Maison*, Preuves, p. 79.

[110] For example in a painting by Lippo Memmi (v. 1317–1357), now in the Boston Museum of Fine Arts, no. 36.144; and in paintings by Taddeo di Bartolo (not. 1362) and Andrea di Bartolo (not. 1389–1428) now on display in the Sienna Pinacoteca, nos. 131 and 220. Such stars are frequently pierced, and in the last painting the star even has a small sun in its voided centre. See fig. 5.4.

star did represent the Virgin, then the sun set in a circle within the star probably represented Christ, of whom the sun was a recognized symbol. It seems very probable that the star device was also meant to allude to the verse of Revelation (12:1) in which a woman generally identified as Mary is described as crowned with stars and clothed with the sun.

Both the form and the symbolic significance of the badge adopted by Jean for his knightly 'company' were quite different from those of the principal devices worn by the knights of the Band and the Garter, but were very similar to those of the badges commonly used by lay confraternities, from which Jean undoubtedly drew his inspiration.

11 The Habit of the Knights

In what may well have been an attempt to outdo his rival's order in splendour of attire, Jean assigned to the knights of his Company not one but three formal orders of dress, each of them consisting of several defined articles. For the most formal occasions – specifically the ceremony of induction and the annual religious services – the knights of the Star were to wear a habit consisting of black hose, gold shoes, a white *surcote* (probably worn over a white *cote*), and a red mantle lined in *menu vair* – a fur composed of squirrel skins arranged in a pattern in which white belly alternated with grey back.[111] Presumably during the rest of the Assumption Day festivities they were to wear the second order of dress, in which the white *surcote* was replaced by one of red, and the mantle by a *chaperon* of the same colour.[112] It appears that the *chaperon* was not to be worn with the mantle, unlike that of the Garter and those of most later orders. Finally, during the Company's weekly Saturday fast the knights were to wear (if the wording is not confused) a costume in which the colours of the semi-formal habit were reversed.

The elements of the three Star habits were actually the same as those of the Garter's single habit, but their colours were more fixed and more minutely specified, and they could be combined in a greater variety of ways. The significance of the colours – red, white, and black – is uncertain, but the habit is almost identical with that recommended by Geoffroy de Charny in his *Livre de Chevalerie*[113] as appropriate for a squire about to receive the accolade of knighthood, and also to that recommended for the same purpose in the thirteenth-century *Ordene de Chevalerie*, which must have been Charny's source.[114] According to Charny, the white undergarments represented chastity and sinlessness, the red *cote* the blood the knight was to shed in defense of the Church, the red mantle humility, and the black stockings mortality. It is surely not without significance that a very similar costume – including a *cote* and mantle of red samite, lined with vair – was worn by the founder's two younger sons, Jean and Philippe, on the day

---

[111] Item 2b.
[112] Item 2a.
[113] Kervyn de Lettenhove, *Oeuvres de Froissart*, I, iii, pp. 514–15.
[114] Ed. Keith Busby, *Raoul de Houdenc. Le roman des eles; The Anonymous Ordene de Chevalerie* (Amsterdam-Philadelphia, 1983), pp. 105–19, esp. pp. 108–11. See above, p. 9.

5.4 The star represented on the mantle of the Virgin
a. by Taddeo di Bartolo   b. by Andrea di Bartolo

5.5 The formal habit of the Star,
as represented in the MS. of
the *Grands chroniques*

5.6 The banner of the Star
(reconstruction)

before they were admitted to knighthood, while for the knighting ceremony itself (which was held on the very day of the Feast of the Star) they wore *cotes* and mantles of cloth-of-gold, lined with ermine.[115] All of this suggests that the costume of the knights of the Star was meant to represent a condition or state of mind similar to that of a squire about to receive the accolade: one of penitence for past sins and firm commitment to the highest ideals of knighthood.

The accounts of the *Argenterie* referred to above record that a *surcot*, *mantel*, and *chaperon* of red cloth-of-scarlet lined with vair were provided to the Dauphin Charles for the Feast of the Star, along with a *cote* of white and a *surcot*, *mantel*, and *chaperon* of red camocas, similarly lined,[116] and that similar items were provided to the five *chambellans* of the king and the four *chambellans* of the dauphin.[117] In each case the first mantle is described as *fendu a un costé*, or 'open at one side', while the other is described as *a parer*, 'ornamented'.

The only known depiction of the knights of the Star in any of their three habits is the miniature referred to above in the manuscript of the Saint-Denis chronicle, painted during the reign of the founder's son. This miniature, which consists of two panels and occupies most of a page, represents the knights of the Company in what appears to be the most formal of their habits. All ten of the knights in the miniature are depicted wearing hose with black right and red left legs, white ankle-length *surcotes*, gold hip-belts, and scarlet *vair*-lined mantles with attached hoods worn off their heads. The mantles themselves are worn with the opening to the right and are sewn rather than clasped together on the right shoulder. On the left shoulder of the mantle each knight wears a very large eight-pointed star, as described above. King Jean himself is depicted wearing an open crown heightened with fleurons, and all but one of the other knights are crowned with what appear to be narrow circlets of gold studded with jewels. This habit corresponds very closely with that prescribed in the letter and the account book, and it may be a fairly accurate portrayal of the habit actually worn at the meeting of January 1352, based upon the description of an eye-witness. It is significant that the length of the *surcot* depicted in the miniature is very unfashionable both for the time it was painted and for the time of the Feast represented; like that of the Garter, it may well have been intended to suggest the habits worn by the knights of the religious orders.

12 The Banner of the Company

According the item 12 of Jean's letter, the Company of the Star was to have had a corporate banner, or rectangular armorial flag, displaying on a red field sewn with white stars an image of the Blessed Virgin, also in white. Iconographically, the banner was thus made up of representations of the Company's badge and patroness depicted in its livery colours. The possession of a banner, a symbol of corporate identity at that time still primarily military in its uses, was an innovation of Jean's which was probably inspired directly by the practice of the religious orders of

---

[115] Lehoux, *Jean de France*, I, p. 24.
[116] Pannier, *La Noble Maison*, Preuves, p. 65.
[117] Ibid., p. 74.

knights rather than that of the Order of the Band. Jean specified that the banner was to be raised by groups of the Company's knights numbering at least five, 'if it pleased them', 'especially against the enemies of the Faith, or in the war of their rightful lord'. The implications of this statement are not altogether clear, but it would appear that the banner was to be a purely optional addition to the heraldic accoutrements of war of any group of at least five of the Company's knights in any engagement in which a banner might properly be raised. The 'especial' qualification, since it was not mandatory, was little more than a gesture in the direction of the crusading and feudo-vassalic ideals of the age. Certainly there is no suggestion in the passage that the knights were ever to act together in battle as a company, in the fashion of the knights of the Band.

13 Conclusions: The Company of the Star

The society of knights commonly known as the Company of the Star was clearly the final product of the project announced by its founder in 1344, and like that project it was clearly intended to serve as a counterfoil to a similar society proclaimed slightly earlier by Edward of England, its founder's rival for the throne of his kingdom. Certain of the usages of the Company of the Star – its 500 knights, its hall with permanent stalls marked with their arms, its table of honour, its recounting of deeds – were probably inspired by Edward's project of 1344 to restore the Round Table, and the French order bore a much closer resemblance to the fictional companies of the Round Table and the Frank Palace than the order Edward finally founded. Many other usages of the Star were very similar to usages of the Garter, but while a few of these – for example the adoption of a badge in two distinct forms – were almost certainly inspired by those of the latter order, most were probably arrived at by an independent adaptation of the confraternal model which Jean (possibly inspired by the Dauphinois order of St Catherine) had already decided to adopt in 1344.

Although many of the minor differences between the Company of the Star and its English rival can also be explained as the result of independent adaptations of their common models, the more important differences were clearly the result of the different purposes the two founders had in mind when they founded their respective societies. Edward of England had every reason to be happy with the knights of his kingdom in 1346, and was said by Froissart to have created his order primarily 'to increase the honour of his knights, who had served him so well that he held them to be so bold that he could not find their like in any other realm.' Jean of France, on the other hand, had been a bitter critic of the knights of France since their defeat at Crécy in 1346, expressed his continued dissatisfaction with most of them in the letter by which he founded his order's canonical college, and therein declared the purpose of his Company to be the restoration of their military virtue and honour. The Order of the Garter, in other words, was founded to recognize outstanding knightly virtue in a nobility where such virtue was felt to be widespread, while the Company of the Star was founded to promote knightly virtue in a nobility where it was felt to be generally lacking. The annual recounting, recording, and judgement of deeds, the mechanisms of honour (especially for heroic deeds on the field of battle) and disgrace (especially for flight from the field of battle), the discussion of Charny's *Demandes* and the reading of his two manuals of chivalry – all these things were clearly intended to instill in the knights of the Star both a knowledge of and a high regard for the customs and ideals of chivalry, and to promote courageous as well as correct behaviour when engaged in warlike activities. Jean seems to have felt that most of the knights in France were in need of such instruction and encouragement, but as he could hardly include them all in his society, he chose to impose the highest limit that space and money permitted, no doubt justifying the figure on the basis of the similarly high limits imposed in the fictional societies. Since the limit of 500 automatically excluded up to seven-eighths of the knights in the kingdom, he could also maintain that the Company of the Star only admitted to membership the most outstanding knights, and those admitted could enjoy the prestige associated with membership in an exclusive society. No doubt the more overtly romantic elements of the Company's usages were carried over from the original project of 1344 in order to associate the members (both in their own minds and in the minds of their fellow subjects who were not to be included) with the legendary knights of the Round Table and Frank Palace, for this would have served not only to enhance the pride they took in their membership (and thus their willingness to accept the rules associated with it), but to encourage them to follow the examples of those courteous and heroic knights.

The principal purpose of the Company of the Star was thus to promote the highest standards of chivalry among the knights of the kingdom, not in the society of ladies or in the lists, but in the war against the enemies of the king and kingdom. Indeed, when the particular circumstances in which it was conceived are considered, it is clear that it was meant to form part of a general programme of reform designed to improve the government and more particulary the defences of the kingdom, and to be a sort of complement to the wholly practical *reglement pour les gens de guerre* adopted at the end of the previous April. Where the regulation set out new forms of organization and scales of pay for knights of all ranks, the Company of the Star was to provide first a setting in which leading knights in particular could be indoctrinated in what was perceived to be an appropriate set of values, second a closely-related system of rewards and punishments, and finally a place where knights exausted in the service of their king and kingdom could be maintained in honourable retirement.

Among the knightly virtues the Company of the Star was intended to promote among its members was of course loyalty to the king. Jean had at least as much reason to suspect the loyalty of his noble subjects as he had to criticize their discipline and prowess, but for reasons that are not entirely clear, the only oath of loyalty Jean chose to impose upon them was one to give him loyal counsel. Beyond this he merely required them to ask his permission before going on any long journey, and before they joined any other order, and made no specific demands upon them for service except during the annual meeting itself. Jean could hardly have had much faith in the value of the vassalic oaths sworn to him by the more important knights of his Company, but may have felt that the devices he had introduced to promote chivalrous conduct in general made it unnecessary to include a special oath of loyalty. As we have noted, he seems to have felt that the methods of securing the service of his knightly subjects already available to him obviated the need for including among the statutes of the Company any ordinance designed to compel military service.

It appears that Jean did feel a need for some sort of regular forum in which he could discuss with the leading members of the nobility of the kingdom as a whole matters of mutual interest, for it is unlikely that he would have required the knights to swear to give him loyal counsel on whatever matter he put before them if he meant them to discuss nothing more serious than the finances of the Company itself. If my interpretation is correct, Jean and his Council may have hoped that the Company would play an advisory role in some respects comparable to that of the English House of Lords, or that it would serve at the very least to give the leading members of the nobility the feeling that their opinions were of interest to the king, and improve the strained relations between them and their sovereign.

Contrary to the opinion of most earlier historians, therefore, the Company of the Star must be regarded as a wholly serious organization that was very carefully designed by Jean and his principal advisors to fulfil a number of important social, military, and political functions in the context of a general programme of reform. Nor can its failure to achieve any of the goals for which it was founded be blamed on any inherent flaw in its design. Some of the responsibility for its dissolution must be laid on the shoulders of its founder, who failed to pursue his project with sufficient vigour after the discouraging defeat at Mauron on the eve of the Company's first regular meeting, but his situation in the next four years was such that it would have been very difficult to impose the sort of discipline the Company required of its members on the leading members of his divided nobility, and after his capture at Poitiers it would have been impossible. Indeed, the goals Jean set for the Company were probably somewhat unrealistic, but there is no particular reason to doubt that, had Jean been given time to establish the Company more effectively, it would have served to promote both higher standards of conduct among its members and better relations between the king of France and the leading members of the nobility.

Chapter 6

The Company of
the Holy Spirit of Right Desire
Commonly Called the Company of the Knot
Mainland Sicily (Naples), 1352/3–1362?

1 Historical Background

The first and only meeting of the Company of the Star was held in January 1352. Just five months later, on the Day of Pentecost, 27 May 1352, the foundation of a fourth monarchical order was proclaimed in Naples. The ostensible founder of this order, Loysi 'di Taranto' – a first-cousin and almost exact contemporary of Jean II of France – had recently ascended the throne of the mainland kingdom of Sicily as the second husband of Queen Giovanna I, and the occasion for the proclamation was his coronation as king-consort. The order founded in his name was appropriately dedicated to the Holy Spirit and took its formal designation from its patron, but like the Company of the Star (upon which, as we shall see, it was closely modelled) it has usually been referred to by a name taken from its badge: the Company of the Knot.[1]

The kingdom commonly known to contemporaries from its capital as the Kingdom of Naples, but officially called the Kingdom of Sicily beyond the Pharos, represented the mainland portion of a state forged in the eleventh and twelfth centuries by a company of Norman adventurers led by the sons of Tancred de Hauteville. The kingdom was officially created in 1130 by the Pope, and was thereafter legally recognized as a fief of the Apostolic See. The heiress of the last Hauteville king, who died in 1189, carried the throne into the then Imperial house of Hohenstaufen, but after the death of the second Hohenstaufen king in 1250 successive popes were determined to prevent any further member of that anti-papal dynasty from reigning in southern Italy, and for some years hawked the throne of Sicily in the various courts of Western Christendom. In 1265 Pope Clement IV finally found a prince both willing and able to take the throne in the person of

---

[1] The most recent and by far the most thorough study of the reign of Loysi (or Ludovico) 'di Taranto' is to be found in Emile Léonard, *Histoire de Jeanne Ire, reine de Naples* 3 vols. (Paris, 1932–1937), I. A somewhat shorter account is to be found in his book *Les Angevins de Naples* (Paris, 1954), pp. 366–400, which contains the best general survey of the history of the kingdom in the fourteenth century.

Charles Capet d'Anjou, younger brother of King Louis IX of France, Count of Anjou and Maine by apanage and of Provence (in the Kingdom of Burgundy) in the right of his wife. Charles succeeded in defeating the last of the Hohenstaufen and was crowned king as Carlo I in 1265, but the harsh rule of his French officers led to the revolt of the Sicilian Vespers in 1282, which delivered the island of Sicily proper into the hands of the King of Aragon, Pere III, who had married the heiress of the Hohenstaufen kings. For the next century and a half Charles of Anjou and his heirs were to reign from Naples over the boot of Italy and Pere and his heirs were to rule from Palermo over the island of Sicily, but despite an agreement reached between the two kingdoms in 1301 the kings of both lines continued to call themselves King of Sicily and to claim the whole kingdom of the Hautevilles. Kings of both lines attempted to make good their claim to the 'lost' portion of their kingdom, and in 1442 the heirs of Pere of Aragon would finally succeed in reconquering the mainland. The kings of the mainland kingdom also claimed the throne of the kingdom of Jerusalem after 1277, when Charles of Anjou purchased the rights of one of the heiresses of that defunct crusader kingdom, and partly in consequence of this took an active interest in the affairs of the eastern Mediterranean and the Balkans, as well as in Sicily and northern Italy.

Founded by knights from northern France, the Kingdom of Sicily was soon organized into a hierarchy of feudal dominions very similar to that of France, governed by a similar hierarchy of lords. In 1352 a handful of large baronies bearing the titles *principato* or 'principality' and *ducato* or 'duchy' were held by cadets of the royal house, and several dozen baronies bearing the title *contea* or 'county' were held by lay barons of various origins. Many thousands of lesser fiefs were held by members of the middle and lesser nobility, of whom the richer still sought the accolade of knighthood and served their lords in the traditional way. Many of the greater fiefs had changed hands during and after the conquest of the kingdom by Charles of Anjou, and the upper nobility of the kingdom in the fourteenth century was composed of families of French and Provençal origin recently implanted as well as families of Norman and Lombard origin long established there. By 1300, however, the newer arrivals had intermarried with the older families and were well on the way to complete assimilation into the traditional culture of the kingdom. In the knightly class that culture was inevitably very similar to that of the French nobility, and the literature of chivalry originating in France seems to have been both well known and highly regarded.

The Kingdom of Sicily differed from France in one important respect, however: the barons were from the first thoroughly subjected to the central power of the king and his administration, whose institutions owed more to Constantinople than to Paris. The King of mainland Sicily was virtually an absolute monarch, who made laws with the advice of his privy Council alone, and summoned a parliament – under the Angevins composed exclusively of barons – only when he wished to levy some extraordinary tax. Down to the death of the third Angevin sovereign, Roberto 'the Wise', in 1343, royal authority was generally respected by the barons, and rebellions were rare. As a result, the kingdom was long the most powerful state in Italy.

In the years immediately following the death of King Roberto, however, the stable government which the kingdom had so long enjoyed dissolved before the vicious rivalry that erupted among the surviving members of the royal family, descended from the four sons of Roberto's father Carlo II. If we are to understand fully the circumstances in which the Company of the Knot was created in 1352, we must look briefly at the history of the four branches of the royal house, and the origins of the quarrels that divided them. We have already examined the career of Roberto's elder brother, Carlo 'Martello', who on the death of his mother's brother in 1290 laid claim to the vacant throne of Hungary. When he died in his father's lifetime in 1295, his only son Carlo Roberto was excluded from the succession to the throne of Naples, and had to fight for many years to win the throne of Hungary. It was he who, as King Károly I, founded the first effectively monarchical order of knighthood in 1325 or 1326. Neither he nor his eldest son, Lajos 'the Great', who succeeded him on the Hungarian throne in 1342, ever gave up their claim to the throne of mainland Sicily, and Lajos tried on several occasions to make good his claim by diplomacy and by force.

On the death of Carlo II in 1309 his throne had passed in fact to his third (but oldest surviving) son, Roberto, later called 'the Wise'. Roberto's only child, Carlo, Duke of Calabria, died in 1328, leaving by his wife Marie (sister of Philippe VI of France) only two daughters: Giovanna (v. 1326–82) and Maria (v. 1327?–66). Disregarding the very rule which had placed him on the throne, Roberto had declared his elder granddaughter Giovanna to be the heir apparent to the throne, and to buy off the claims of the senior line of his house married her in 1333 to her cousin Endre, younger son of his nephew King Károly of Hungary. The claims of the two elder branches were thus temporarily reconciled.

The third branch of the royal family, the House of Taranto, was descended from Carlo II's fourth son, Filippo, Prince of Taranto and Count of Acerra in mainland Sicily, and Prince of Achaia and Despot of Romania in the Balkans, who had married Catherine, titular Empress of Constantinople, the half-sister of King Philippe VI of France. The 'Empress' Catherine gave Prince Filippo three sons who survived to adulthood: Roberto, who succeeded him in his principal lands and titles in 1331 and died without issue in 1364; Loysi (v. 1320–62), who became king as the second consort of Queen Giovanna in 1348; and Filippo, Count of Acerra, who in 1364 succeeded his eldest brother in all his titles and pretensions and died without surviving issue in 1373.

The junior branch of the Angevin dynasty, the House of Durazzo, was made up of the descendants of Carlo II's youngest son Giovanni, Count of Gravina and Lord of Monte Sant'Angelo in mainland Sicily, and from 1333 first Duke of Durazzo in Albania. By his second wife, Agnès de Périgord, Giovanni had three sons: Carlo, who succeeded him in 1335 and died in 1348 leaving four daughters by his wife Maria, younger granddaughter of King Roberto; Loysi, who died in 1362 leaving one son, the future King Carlo III (founder of the Order of the Ship); and Roberto, who died at Poitiers in 1356, leaving no issue.

When Roberto 'the Wise' died in 1343, his elder granddaughter was allowed to succeed him as Queen Giovanna I, but a council of regency was established, and the court immediately split into factions. A group of courtiers in the pay of King Lajos of Hungary argued for the rights of his brother Endre (or Andrea), the new queen's husband, to receive the title 'king', and when that was granted in 1344, pushed his claim as representative of the senior line of the dynasty to share power equally with his wife. Giovanna herself resisted this strongly, and sought support first from the Durazzo faction, led by the dowager Duchess Agnès, and after her murder in 1345, from their rivals of the Taranto faction. The Pope finally agreed to a double coronation on 20 and 21 September 1345, but King Andrea was murdered on the 18th (probably at the instigation of Loysi 'di Taranto' and with the complicity of Queen Giovanna), and the political situation thereupon dissolved into total chaos. Duke Carlo of Durazzo, who had married Giovanna's sister Maria in 1343, posed as the avenger of the dead king, and allied himself with Lajos of Hungary. Lajos himself wrote to the Pope demanding that the throne be attributed to the Hungarian line of the Angevin dynasty, and when this was refused pending the trial of the queen, declared war and invaded the peninsula with an army. In the meantime the two eldest Tarantos, Roberto and Loysi, had been fighting one another to secure the hand of the newly-widowed queen, but the arrival of Lajos' forces in May 1347 reunited the Neapolitan Angevins, and Loysi was permitted to marry Queen Giovanna. By this time the royal family was held in general contempt by most of the queen's sujects, however, and Lajos had no difficulty crossing the kingdom. Giovanna and Loysi fled to Provence, but Lajos captured all of the remaining Neapolitan princes at Aversa early in 1348, and after causing his erstwhile ally Duke Carlo of Durazzo to be executed, carried the others off to Hungary.

After these discouraging events the fortunes of the exiled Giovanna and her husband Loysi began to improve. The Pope, whose support for his cause Lajos had alienated by his refusal of mediation, gave them absolution for their sins, consent to their long-consummated marriage, and support for the reconquest of their kingdom. Since Lajos had also alienated public opinion in the kingdom of mainland Sicily by his execution of Carlo of Durazzo, when his forces withdrew to fight the Venetians the kingdom rose against his regime and rallied to the banner of its exiled queen. Thus, when Giovanna and Loysi arrived back in Naples in August 1348, they were both warmly received. Loysi, however, immediately had himself proclaimed king and co-regent, and embarked upon a campaign to secure complete control of the government. Early in 1350 Lajos of Hungary again invaded and occupied Naples, but the Pope arranged an armistice, and Lajos again withdrew. The Pope also freed Giovanna, who had been virtually imprisoned by her husband, but Loysi foiled her last attempt to oust him from power, and after concluding a treaty with Lajos for the release of the princes imprisoned in Hungary, received on 23 March 1352 a formal recognition from the Pope both of his royal title and of his right to rule as co-regent. Two months later, on 27 May, he had himself crowned as king, and proclaimed the establishment of the Company of the Knot. For the next ten years, until his death in 1362, real power in the kingdom remained in his hands, and Queen Giovanna – though provided with her own seal and given a generous civil list – was obliged to sit on the sidelines.

The foregoing account of the rise of Loysi 'di Taranto' might easily lead one to believe that the ostensible founder of the Company of the Star was, if somewhat lacking in scruples, at least an active and capable prince. In reality he was quite the opposite. Contemporary writers were unanimous in their low estimation of his abilities as well as of his character. According to Petrarch (who was intimately familiar with the members of the Neapolitan court), he was violent and mendacious, prodigal and avaricious, debauched and cruel, and knew neither how to make his subjects love him nor even that he had need of their love.[2] Immediately

---

[2] Léonard, *Les Angevins*, p. 372.

after his death the chronicler Matteo Villani described him in similarly unflattering terms: 'He was a lord of little weight and even less authority, without any knowledge . . . He took little trouble about feats of arms . . . He was unfaithful to his promises and boasted of this as if it were a virtue. The most hardened sinners among his barons were his counsellors . . . He was changeable, timid, and fearful when fortune was against him . . . He was eager to make money, administered justice softly, and made himself little feared by his barons.'[3] In fact, Loysi's rise to power was almost certainly engineered at every stage by his former tutor and principal counsellor, Nicola Acciaiuoli, a Florentine of bourgeois origins who rose in his service to become a great baron and the virtual prime minister of the kingdom.

Nicola Acciaiuoli had been born in 1310, and was thus an almost exact contemporary of both Alfonso of Castile and Edward of England, and about a decade older than Jean of France and Loysi 'di Taranto'. His family owned one of the most important banking houses in Italy, and as moneylender on a grand scale to King Roberto and his brothers, Nicola's father Acciaiuolo had come to be accepted as an important member of the court of Naples, where he was made a chamberlain to the king in 1333. Nicola himself entered the household of the Empress Catherine, dowager Princess of Taranto and Achaia, by February 1335, and was given the care of her second son, Loysi. Already much more a nobleman than a banker, he was knighted by the king in the same year, and then used his position as creditor to the Principality of Achaia to acquire, by donation or purchase, a whole series of estates in southern Greece. When he returned to Naples in 1341 Nicola was the most influential baron in the Morea, and he and his family were to remain active in that area until the end of the century.[4] After 1341 he took an ever more active part in the political life of his adopted country as the *éminence grise* behind the unworthy Loysi 'di Taranto'. He quickly proved to be one of the most able politicians of his day, and after placing his pupil securely on the throne of Naples was made both Grand Seneschal and Master of the Royal Household. He was also given numerous feudal estates, including the counties of Melfi and Malta and the key barony of Corinth.

According to Emile Léonard (who recently raised his memory from the obscurity into which it had quite unjustly fallen since his death), Nicola Acciaiuoli was in every respect a far more admirable man than his master, joining to the realism, prudence, parsimony, irony, and subtlety that he inherited from his Florentine ancestors, a love of adventure worthy of a knight errant, and a taste for grandeur and an ambition to do great things in the world worthy of a high-born prince. His sense of his own greatness and his princelike magnanimity led him not only to construct magnificent palaces but to pose as an *amateur* and patron of Latin poetry, and to look down upon his countryman Boccaccio (who regarded his success with growing envy) as a vulgar storyteller. It also led him, once he was effectively in control of the affairs of his adopted country, to seek to restore the greatness which it had enjoyed before the death of King Roberto, and he immediately set out to make his sovereign the conqueror both of the island kingdom of Sicily and of the Piedmont, and the nominal leader of the Guelfs of northern Italy. In order to

---

[3] Chronicle, l. x, cap. c.; quoted (in French) in Léonard, loc. cit., n. 2.
[4] See Nicolas Chatham, *Medieval Greece* (New Haven, 1981), pp. 166–8.

impose his ideal of greatness upon the court of his sovereign (whose weaknesses he must have known better than anyone), he decided to create an institution which would both embody and promote that ideal: the society of knights which he grandiloquently called the 'Company of the Holy Spirit of Right Desire'.

2 The Foundation and Maintenance of the Company: 1352–1362?

Unfortunately, we know rather less about the society of knights proclaimed in Naples in May 1352 than we do about the society founded in France a few months earlier.[5] Not only the records kept by the society itself, but all of the registers both of the chancellery and of the household of King Loysi have long since perished in one conflagration or another,[6] so we are obliged to rely for information about the society upon a single manuscript of its statutes, a single copy of the letter by which its first members were informed of their election, brief accounts in two contemporary chronicles, and an allusion to it in a letter of Boccaccio.

Although the Hungarian Society of St George must have been quite familiar to the members of the court of Naples at least from the time of the marriage of its founder's son Endre to the future Queen Giovanna in 1333, there is nothing to indicate, and no reason to believe, that either Loysi or Acciaiuoli had made plans to found an order of any kind much before the time of Loysi's coronation. Indeed, both the contents of the statutes assigned to the order proclaimed in May 1352, and the very words in which they are expressed, are so clearly based upon the letter by which Jean of France announced the foundation of the Company of the Star in November of the previous year that they could not have been composed before the latter date. Both the prologue to the statutes and the Chronicon Siculum[7] declare that the Company was founded on the day of the coronation in 1352, but in all probability this 'foundation' consisted of nothing more substantial than a proclamation. Acciaiuoli is unlikely to have heard about the French order before the end of January 1352, and may not have decided to have his royal master found a similar order until after the treaty recognizing Loysi's right to the royal title was sealed by the Pope, barely a month before the coronation. Thus it is not at all surprising that the chronicler Villani failed to notice the foundation of the Company of the Knot before the feast of Pentecost (12 May) 1353, when the

---

[5] The history of this order was recorded with reasonable accuracy by Pandolfo Collenuccio in his Compendio dell'istoria del Regno di Napoli (Venice, 1539, 1613), and on the basis of that book the order was known to Micheli Márquez, Ashmole, and other antiquarian encyclopedists of knightly orders. The first critical historian to discuss the order was Matteo Camera, who devoted three pages to it in his Elucubrazioni Storico-Diplomatiche su Giovanna Ia Regina di Napoli e Carlo III di Durazzo (Salerno, 1889), p. 171. The only other critical historian who has examined the order is Emile Léonard, who devoted a thirteen-page section to it in his monumental study of the reign of Giovanna I, cited above (I, pp. 12–25), and included variants of this account in several other works, including Les Angevins de Naples, pp. 366–71, and Boccace et Naples (Paris, 1944), pp. 112–16.

[6] Léonard, Histoire, I, Etude des sources.

[7] Ed. Josephus de Blasii (Naples, 1887). Cited in Léonard, Histoire, II, p. 12.

companions met in what appears to have been the Company's first formal assembly.

Villani's account of this assembly is our most important narrative source for the history of the Company. Under the general heading of the year 1353 he wrote:

> King Loysi of Jerusalem and Sicily in this year on the Day of Pentecost held a solemn feast with his barons for the annual renewal of his coronation. And at this feast he ordained a thing new and unused by the crown, choosing sixty of the barons and knights, who swore faith and company together with the said king, under a certain order of their life, and of their activities and vestments. When they had taken the oath, they put on a *cotehardie* and an *assisa* of the same colour throughout, and wore on their breasts a knot of Solomon, those with a more vain spirit wearing a more magnificent *cotehardie* and a knot of gold and silver and precious stones of great cost and grand appearance. And it was called the Company of the Knot. The Prince of Taranto, brother of the king, was not here, but arrived. The king had had made for him a royal *cotehardie*, with a knot of huge pearls of great value, but the Prince did not wish to put it on, and saying that he bore the knot of fraternal love in his heart, gave it to one of his knights. This did not please the king.[8]

Apart from the statutes themselves, the only other evidence we have for the foundation of the Company is a single copy of the letter which Loysi, like Jean of France before him, had sent to those he had nominated as members to inform them of the creation of the Company and of their election to it. Loysi's letter, addressed to the Count of Apice (Loysi di Sabran), was still preserved in the nineteenth century in a collection of acts and letters compiled by one of the secretaries of Queen Giovanna, Nicola d'Alife, and although this collection has since been lost, the letter itself was published by Matteo Camera in 1860. While Jean's letter of election had begun with the briefest of explanations and had gone on to summarize the new order's statutes, Loysi's letter omitted any specific reference to the ordinances of his order (which seem to have been delivered in a separate document at the same time), and contained instead a greatly expanded explanation of the significance of the new order, couched in grandiloquent quasi-theological language. The letter, translated from the Latin of the original, reads as follows:

> O Magnificent Man and beloved subject: In the name of that Holy Spirit who, sent from above to the disciples of Christ, strengthened them in faith, we have made a certain order, distinguished by the name of the Holy Spirit Himself, comprehended under certain Catholic and knightly statutes. Into this order, through us as its institutor and inventor, there have been and shall successively be admitted only those persons whose trustworthy strength in faith and faithful willingness without discrepancy in any activity is known to us. Among these and of their number the choice of our judgement has selected you as a man possessed of the aforesaid qualities, to strengthen the

[8] *Chronica di Matteo Villani*, ed. Ignazio Moutier (Florence, 1877), I, pp. 109–110.

constancy of your faith, in which by the infusion of the same Paraclete you have come to shine in our eyes through the instinct of natural lordship, and you have been made by us a faithful companion, who from Saul, as we believe, shall next be confirmed to be Paul. Behold, therefore, the Knot (*Nodum*) – under whose name the order itself is assumed – which we send to you by the Magnificent Man Nicola Acciaiuoli, to show you the happy signs in our place. He, ordered in our place and name, is to receive from you the oath provided, until with God's guidance we shall, within a short space of time, come ourself to see you, and you shall renew it in our hands. Therefore, taking up in the name of the same Holy Spirit the Knot itself – which even as it figuratively ties together its parts, connects its professors morally in unity – to the sevenfold increase of your strength in faith, and to your strengthening, proceeding from virtue to virtue in work incumbent upon you hereafter, may you embrace the knot (*nexum*) of love, and may you pursue that worthy sign of praise through imitation of the example of your companions, just as through our assignment of these same statutes to you, you shall see how to persevere, so that by the grace of the sevenfold help of the Holy Spirit Himself you may prosper and grow in strength; and may He establish more laudably in you the proof of virtue, and bear away every vestige of past darkness, who in renewing the face of the earth makes new things.[9]

This singular discourse, which extols the personal virtue of the recipient and expounds both the spiritual goals of the new order and the mystical significance of its badge, can be compared to the prologue of the letters by which King Jean founded the clerical college attached to his order, but its tone is even more moralistic. It may well have been composed by its bearer, Acciaiuoli himself, who fancied himself as a Latin stylist.

Nothing more is known about the foundation of the Company, and very little more about its subsequent history. Beyond its first meeting, we have no record of its corporate activities, and although as we shall see there is evidence that at least some of the provisions of its statutes were in fact carried out during the reign of its founder, the sources are completely silent on the subject of the Company of the Knot in the period after his death on 24 May 1362. It must therefore appear that, like the Company of the Star upon which it was based, the Company of the Knot perished with its creator.

It is not difficult to construct a plausible explanation for its dissolution. Its putative founder and president, King Loysi, had little money of his own, and is unlikely to have provided it with an adequate endowment. In addition the Company had existed for a bare ten years at the time of Loysi's death – which occurred two weeks before the tenth Pentecost following its foundation – and though relatively untainted by defeats, was equally unsupported by glorious victories. Acciaiuoli's three concerted attempts to reconquer the island of Sicily were all ultimately unsuccessful, and he was forced to devote much of his energy to putting down revolts by the surviving Durazzos and to defending his own position at court against the schemes of a new faction composed of his master's cronies: Giannotto Estandart, Francesco del Balzo, Count of Andria, and Loysi di Sabran,

---

[9] *Receuil de Nicola d'Alife*, f. 195v; pub. in Camera, *Elucubrazioni*, p. 171.

Count of Ariano. In this he was ultimately successful, but at the very moment when it appeared that Acciaiuoli had triumphed Loysi himself died, probably of the bubonic plague, leaving no heir of his body to maintain the Company for his sake. His consort, Queen Giovanna (who immediately resumed the reins of government which Loysi had snatched from her a decade earlier), had no reason to honour her late husband's memory by maintaining his order, and the other members of the royal house, who seem to have been hostile to the Company from the start, may well have sought its suppression in an active fashion. In these circumstances it could hardly have survived even if its Prince had been one of the best and most well-loved of kings, and the death of Nicola Acciaiuoli himself in 1364 probably removed its last active supporter.

3 The Statutes of the Company

Most of what we now know about the Company of the Knot is derived from its statutes. There must once have been numerous copies of this document, for both the letter of election just quoted and the prologue to the statutes themselves suggest that a copy of the statutes was delivered along with the letter to each of the original knights, but only a single contemporary manuscript of the statutes is known to survive.[10] The elaborate historiation of this manuscript, and the fact that it begins with a full-page miniature depicting King Loysi and Queen Giovanna kneeling before the Trinity, suggest that it was prepared for the ostensible founder himself, and statements attached to chapters 3 and 24 to the effect that the former was 'erased' and replaced by chapters 24 and 25 during the first meeting of the Company held on Pentecost 1353 show that it was drawn up at some time before that date.[11]

---

[10] Paris, B.N., ms. fr.4274. The text of this manuscript has been published several times, most recently by comte Horace [de Salviac] de Viel-Castel as a transcription of a chromo-lithographic facsimile in *Statuts de l'Ordre du Saint-Esprit au Droit Desir ou du Noeud* (Paris, 1853), but they have never been properly edited, and I am currently preparing a critical edition. According to M. Le Febvre, *Mémoire pour servir à l'histoire de France du quatorzième siècle, contenant les statuts de l'ordre du Saint-Esprit au Droit Desir ou du Noeud . . .* (Paris, 1764), a copy of which is now bound with the manuscript, this copy of the statutes was given by the Venetian Republic to the future King Henri III of France in 1574, and later served as the inspiration for the Order of the Holy Spirit that prince founded in 1579, but this story is probably apocryphal, as Henri III had his own reasons for dedicating an order to the Holy Spirit, and the order he founded bore no resemblance whatever to the Neapolitan order here in question. Moreover, the manuscript was still in private hands in 1764.

[11] The illumination which accompanied chapter 3 has been painted out and replaced with the following inscription: 'Cestui chapitre, pour grengnor honnor conquerre, fu rassés y amendés en la maniere qui s'ensuit, a la feste fait l'an de grace m.cccliij.' Chapter 24 begins with the clause: 'Item, il est declaré par ce derrenier chappitres ajousté en la premiere feste passee de la Pentecouste l'an de grace M.cccliij que . . .' In fact it is unlikely that the amendments were meant to replace more than the first of the four ordinances of ch. 3, since the last three deal with the knot retied, and this is not touched upon in the new chapters.

The statutes set forth in this manuscript are divided into a short prologue and twenty-five chapters beginning with the word 'Item'. Every chapter is accompanied by at least one miniature illustrating its subject matter, and these miniatures – unique in the documents of our period – not only give us a clear picture of the costume and ceremonies of the Company, but help us to interpret many of the statements about other subjects. The prologue and the original twenty-three chapters contained some sixty-nine ordinances, but the first ordinance of chapter 3 was cancelled at the first meeting of the Company and replaced by the three ordinances of chapters 24 and 25, bringing the total to seventy-one. Curiously enough, in a court whose vernacular was certainly an Italian dialect,[12] the statutes were written in the Parisian dialect of French. It appears that Acciaiuoli regarded French as the aulic language of chivalry, for as we shall see, the book of deeds maintained by the order was also composed in that language.

The title and prologue may be translated as follows:

These are the chapters made and created by the most excellent prince My Lord the King Loysi, by the grace of God King of Jerusalem and Sicily, to the honour of the Holy Spirit creator and founder of the most noble Company of the Holy Spirit of Right Desire, begun the day of Pentecost, in the year of grace mccclij.
[a] We Loysi, by the grace of God King of Jerusalem and Sicily, to the honour of the Holy Spirit, on whose day by his grace we were crowned of our kingdoms, to the exaltation of knighthood and the increase of honour, have ordered made a company of knights, [b] who shall be called the knights of the Holy Spirit of Right Desire. [c] And the said knights shall be in the number of 300, [d] of whom we, as creator and founder of this company, shall be Prince, as also must be all of our successors, Kings of Jerusalem and Sicily. [e] And to all those whom we have chosen and shall choose to be of the said Company, we make known that we are planning to hold the first feast, if God pleases, in the Castle of the Egg, enchanted of the marvellous peril, on the day of Pentecost next coming. And for this all the aforesaid companions who can do so well are to be on the said day at the said place in such a manner as shall be hereafter devised. And then this matter will be more fully spoken of to all the companions.

The statutes proper, which follow the prologue, are arranged in almost random order, with only a few logical groupings. The first chapter sets forth, in two ordinances, the obligation of the companions to give counsel and aid to the Prince and to obey the statutes. Chapters 2 to 4 contain nine ordinances setting forth the form the badge of the Company was to take and the rules for displaying and augmenting it, one of which was later replaced. Chapter 5 contains two ordinances setting forth the spiritual obligations of the companions, while chapters 6 through 8 contain eleven ordinances concerned with the activities of the knights at the annual assembly of the Company. Chapter 9 sets forth in two ordinances the obligation of the companions to take part in a crusade, chapter 10 sets forth in three ordinances the form of the Company's banner and the rules for its use, chapter 11 sets forth in four ordinances the penalties for shameful conduct, and

---

[12] Léonard, *Histoire*, II, p. 13.

chapter 12 sets forth in three ordinances what the companions were to do when they wished to undertake a long journey. Chapters 14 and 15 revert to the subject of the annual assembly, and discuss in eight ordinances the table of honour and the 'parliament' to be held each year. Chapter 16 contains four ordinances dealing with membership in other orders, and chapter 17 a single ordinance requiring newly-elected members to receive the accolade of knighthood. Chapters 18 to 23, with which the statutes originally concluded, are all concerned with matters related to the death of a companion, and set forth in twelve ordinances the obligations of the companions and the Prince with respect to funerals, tombs, and memorials. Finally, chapters 24 and 25, which were added in May 1353, set forth three new rules for the augmentation of the badge, replacing those deleted from chapter 3.

A careful comparison of the document just outlined with the letter by which Jean of France informed the first companions of his order of their election leaves no room for doubt that the statutes assigned by Acciaiuoli to his master's Company of the Knot were not merely inspired by, but based directly upon the those of the Star, as they were set forth in Jean's letter of November 1351. To begin with, large sections of the prologue were clearly lifted almost word for word from the prologue and epilogue of Jean's letter. In addition, every one of the twenty-one items in the letter proclaiming the French order is clearly represented among the statutes of the Knot, and some of the corresponding ordinances in the latter document are expressed in almost identical words. We are thus obliged to conclude that Acciaiuoli had access to a copy of Jean's letter at some time before the first meeting of the Company of the Knot, and probably before the day on which it was proclaimed. This presents no difficulties, for we know that at least one Neapolitan knight, Giacomo Bozzuto, (whose son Coluccio is known to have been a knight of the Knot) was included among the original companions of the Star, and he could easily have given his copy of the letter of election to the Grand Seneschal on returning to Naples after attending the feast of the Star in January 1351. Indeed, this would explain how several ordinances attributed to the Company of the Star in Le Bel's chronicle but not included in the letter of election also found their way into the statutes of the Knot, for Bozzuto would certainly have mentioned to Acciaiuoli some of the obligations and activities first mentioned at the feast itself.

The men of the fourteenth century had a very different attitude toward originality and plagiarism from that current today, of course, and it was normal practice for new confraternities to base their statutes more or less closely upon those of an older confraternity of the same general type. Nevertheless, Acciaiuoli did not slavishly copy the statutes of the Star as they were known to him, but altered the ordinances they contained in many more or less important ways, and added a considerable number of ordinances that were quite original. Fully thirty-eight of the seventy-two ordinances of the Knot have no equivalents among the forty-two known ordinances of the Star (including the nine reported only by Le Bel), and although some of these might have been based on Star ordinances not mentioned in either souce but reported verbally to Acciaiuoli, some by their very nature must have been peculiar to the Neapolitan order. In examining the nature of the Company of the Knot, therefore, I shall attempt to point out the various ways in which it both resembled and differed from the Company of the Star.

4 The Name, Title, and Patron of the Company

The prologue of the statutes of the Knot faithfully reflects the opening statement of the Star letter. Each king had, to the honour of God and his patron and 'en essaucement de chevalerie et accroissement d'onnour' ordered the creation of a 'compaignie de chevaliers', who were to be called by a name composed of that of the company's patron followed by a modifying phrase. The patron of the Star was 'Our Lady of the Noble House', that of the Knot 'the Holy Spirit of Right Desire'. In both cases the specific title added seems to have been invented for the order. Acciaiuoli gave his foundation the formal title 'company' that he found in Jean's letter, but it is significant that both in the letter of election and in the text of the statutes the Company of the Knot is referred to as an 'order' (ordo, ordre),[13] as this suggests that the word 'order' was beginning to be accepted as a generic term for lay as well as religious societies of knights.

The Holy Spirit was a rather less obvious patron for an order of lay knights than the Blessed Virgin, but the fact that Loysi was crowned on Pentecost suggests that either he or Acciaiuoli felt a special devotion to the Paraclete, possibly due to the influence of the 'spiritual' Franciscans at the Sicilian court during the reign of Queen Giovanna's father Roberto 'the Wise'.[14] The title au Droit Desir bestowed on the generally untitled third Person of the Holy Trinity seems to have referred to the quasi-spiritual goal which Acciaiuoli – in the best Arthurian fashion – set for his master's knights. It appears that where Edward of England had taken the Round Table and Jean of France the Frank Palace as literary models, Acciaiuoli took as his model the Grail-Seekers of the Vulgate Cycle of romances, for the theme of the Quest runs throughout the statutes of the Knot. Chapter 21 makes it clear that the object of the Knot quest was to be 'Right Desire', and chapters 3, 24, and 25 explain how it was to be achieved. Despite its name, the goal set forth in those chapters is not obviously related to the Holy Spirit, whose role as patron was largely formal. Nevertheless, in most of the illuminations illustrating the manuscript of the statutes, a representation of the Holy Spirit, in the form of a dove emitting rays of divine grace, is placed immediately above the head of the Prince, as if to suggest that the latter was to be perpetually under his inspration and guidance, and every year the companions were to pray for the outpouring of his grace upon the Company.

5 The Insignia of the Company

Because of the unprecedented way in which the principal badge was to be altered to indicate the partial and complete fulfilment of the goal of Right Desire, the insignia of the order must be considered here rather than in the usual place towards the end

[13] [16a] 'Item, se aucun chevalier de la dicte Compaignie eust devant entre pris aucune ordre, soit tenus de faire so pouoir de le entrelessier. [b] Et se il ne puet bonnement, ceste ordre doit tous jours aler devant toutes les autres.'
[14] Léonard, Histoire, II, pp. 21–22.

of the chapter. According to chapter 2 of the statutes, the basic badge of the order was a knot, which the companions were to wear at all times, with civilian dress wherever they chose, and with armour in a place where it could be clearly seen. Until a companion had performed certain specified feats of arms and piety he was to wear this knot tied and accompanied by the words *Se Dieux plaist* ('If God pleases'), in 'easily readable letters', either above or below it. According to ordinance 3a, however, the knot was to be worn 'all untied' by a companion who, in an honourable battle or encounter in which a banner was raised (except against the church of Rome), was *encontré*, or touched with the tip of a lance, dagger, or sword, or touched one of his enemies with his own lance, dagger, or sword. The knights of the Company themselves evidently thought that this was too slight an accomplishment to honour, however, for the two chapters adopted as amendments at the first assembly stipulated that the knot could not be untied until a companion, in a battle in which a force of at least fifty enemies was confronted by a company no greater than the enemy force, was either the first to attack the enemy, captured their banner or beat it to the ground, or captured their captain; or else, in a battle in which a force of at least 300 enemy *barbues* was confronted by a company no greater than the enemy force, he was one of the first to attack the front line of the enemy force. The companions also insisted that the knight who wished to untie his knot had to prove to the Prince and his Council that he had performed one of these feats, by 'true signs'.[15] Finally, ordinances 3b and c declare that a knight who had untied his knot could retie it after he had visited the Holy Sepulchre, and had there placed a knot in a clearly visible place, accompanied by his name, as a sort of votive offering. The knot 'retied, as before' was to have below it 'a burning ray of the Holy Spirit', and was to be accompanied by the new motto: *Il a pleeu a Dieu*, 'It has pleased God'.

The knot-badge of the Company is represented many times in the manuscript of the statutes, both in the marginal decoration and in the panels representing the knights of the Company. It usually appears as a single strand of heavy cord about twenty inches long loosely tied in the figure-8 pattern which was termed a 'love-knot', and set like an 8 in an upright or slightly inclining position. In a few cases, however, it is represented as set like an 8 lying on its side, as indicated in figure 6.1. Ordinance 2b, requiring that a knot of plain white silk 'without gold, pearls, or silver' be worn on Fridays 'in remembrance of Our Lord Jesus Christ, and of his Holy Sepulchre', implies that it was otherwise to be heavily bejewelled, probably according to the owner's taste and wealth, and this is confirmed by Villani's description of the knots worn on the occasion of the Company's only recorded banquet. Presumably it was often made of gold or silver wire rather than cord, since this would facilitate the attachment of embellishments. The knots depicted in the manuscript are all of plain gold, and are worn as brooches, pinned or otherwise attached to the cape of the *chaperon* (with civil costume) or the breast of the surcoat (over armour), directly over the heart. None of the illustrations shows an accompanying motto, but this is probably due only to the difficulty of representing letters on so small a scale. Since the statutes do not specify how they were to be displayed, it is likely that both mottoes were represented in a considerable variety of ways, sometimes with and sometimes without a scroll. As

[15] Chs. 24, 25.

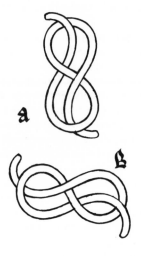

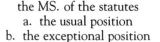

6.1 The knot as represented in
the MS. of the statutes
a. the usual position
b. the exceptional position

6.2 The basic badge of the Knot
(reconstruction)

6.3 a. The knot untied (reconstruction)   b. The knot retied (reconstruction)

the panel illustrating chapter 3 has been overpainted, there is no representation of the irradiated knot retied, but in all likelihood the rays were to have been similar to those associated with the dove of the Holy Spirit throughout the manuscript. (Figs. 6.2, 6.3.)

Like Jean of France, Acciaiuoli also required each companion of the order to possess a smaller version of the Company's badge, encircled by his name. Rather than placing this minor badge on a ring, however, Acciaiuoli had it set into the pommel of the companion's sword, with his crest on the reverse. The appearance of this minor knot is not clearly described, but it was presumably represented, like the star on the ring, in coloured enamel, and was probably set within a roundel around which the name was engraved. Unlike the ring of the Star, this sword was not to be carried by the knight at all times, since the knights of the Knot were obliged to wear their primary badge continually. The sword *was* to be used to fulfill the other functions of the ring, however, namely to inform the Prince of the companion's death, and thereafter to form part of his memorial. The latter function, unclear in the case of the ring, is explicitly described in Knot chapter 18. (Fig. 6.4.)

Despite Villani's statement, the knot of Acciaiuoli's Company seems to have had no connexion with Solomon. According to the letter of election, it was intended to symbolize the fraternal ties which were to bind the companions together in a 'moral unity'. Acciaiuoli, however, almost certainly had another idea in mind when he selected the knot as the badge of his master's order, for as we have just seen he introduced regulations for the untying and retying of the knot as a sign of the progressive accomplishment of deeds associated with the Company's ostensible goal, 'Right Desire', and these suggest that the knot was chosen at least partly because it could be manipulated in this novel way (somewhat reminiscent of the halving of the band as a sign of disgrace), and could thus be tied in with the equally novel idea of a quest for a chivalrous goal. Acciaiuoli rather ingeniously associated the knot with both the Holy Spirit and the goal of Right Desire by attaching to it a motto referring to both, in which the verb (*plaist*) is a play on one of the common words for knot (*plait*). The untied and retied forms of the knot served not merely as a badge identifying the wearer as a member of the Company, but as a sort of medal of honour, proclaiming that the wearer had accomplished some notable feat of arms or piety. This practice was so ingenious that is is surprising that it was imitated by only one later founder, Carlo 'di Durazzo', the supplanter of Loysi's wife. There is evidence that at least one of the companions accomplished the goal of Right Desire, for the tomb of Coluccio Bozzuto in the Cathedral of Naples bears the inscription: 'Hic iacet strenuus miles Colutius Buczutus ... qui fuit de societate Nodi illustris Ludovici Regis Sicilie quem nodum in campali belli victoriose dissolvit, et dictum nodum relegavit in Hierusalem ...'[16]

Although the knot was a fairly common symbol of fraternal union, it is possible that its selection as the device of the order was inspired in part by the device of the Order of the Garter, which must have been known in the court of Naples by 1352. Like the garter – and unlike the star-badge of its French model – the knot was a device not previously associated with the patron of the order, and moreover took the form of a strip of cloth accompanied by a cryptic motto.

In addition to the two knot-badges in their various forms, Acciaiuoli adopted a

---

[16] Camera, *Elucubrazioni*, p. 169.

third device for his master's order. This device took the form of a dove emitting rays – a traditional symbol of the Holy Spirit, who was only rarely represented in human form. In the illuminations illustrating the statutes, the device is represented as a silver dove with wings extended and head downwards, from which a series of golden rays in the form of thin rectilinear wedges extend both outwards and downwards. The device of the dove-and-rays was connected to the regular knot device only through the association of a similar set of rays with the retied knot. Acciaiuoli's adoption of the device was probably inspired by the use in the French order of an image of that order's patron on its banner, but Acciaiuoli's employment of the patronal image went well beyond Jean's, for the dove actually replaced the knot as a symbol of his Company not only on the Company's banner but on the breast of the most formal costume of the companions. (Figs. 6.5–7.) It thus constituted a distinct and independent badge. No other fourteenth-century order was to have such a multiplicity of corporate symbols.

6 *The Membership of the Company*

Like its model, the Company of the Knot was to have been composed of a relatively large number of ordinary members presided over by an officer with the title 'Prince' – written *Prince* or *Princeps* in the statutes, but presumably rendered as *Principe* in the vernacular of the court. The office of 'Prince' is only slightly better defined in the statutes of the Knot than in the corresponding instrument of the French order, but it was unquestionably monarchical in both the narrow and the broad senses of that term. Like the presidential office in all the earlier orders, the princeship of the Knot was to belong to the founder and his heirs as lord of his principal dominion. Unlike the presidents of the earlier orders, however, the Prince of the Company of the Knot was apparently to have had an unrestricted right to appoint the ordinary members, and was certainly to have had the right to command their service at any time and in any situation.

In the body of the statutes the ordinary members of the Company of the Knot are consistently referred to simply as *chevaliers* – the only term used in the official sources for the ordinary members of the Company of the Star – but in the amendments the more fraternal title *compaignon* appears, presumably because it was preferred by the 'companions' themselves. Jean of France may have required that candidates for membership in his order be outstanding knights (as Le Bel maintained), but Acciaiuoli required only that a prospective companion of the Knot receive the accolade of knighthood by the time he was introduced to the other companions at the meeting of the Company following his appointment, which implies that even formal knighthood was not necessary for election to the Company.[17] Chapter 6 of the statutes contains an ordinance specifically concerned with the rights of 'strange knights and bachelors from outside our kingdom', which implies that Acciaiuoli, like Edward of England, intended the Company to include a certain number of distinguished foreigners.

Jean's letter had not touched on the subject of the election of future members.

[17] Ch. 17.

This may explain why Acciaiuoli failed to include in the statutes of his master's order any suggestion as to how future companions were to be selected, but it is not unlikely that he would in any case have preferred to keep the power of appointment in the hands of his master and his successors on the throne, as this was in keeping with the absolutist traditions of the kingdom. The chapter requiring squires admitted to the order to receive the accolade before the next Assembly implies that appointments to the Company could be made (as was theoretically the case in the Order of the Garter) at any time, not just during the annual Assembly. Presumably once the official limit had been achieved such appointments would have been made only after the death of a companion. Acciaiuoli, again influenced by the lacunae in Jean's letter, did not see fit to include in his statutes any mention of a rite of induction into the Company, but according to the letter sent to the Count of Apice the first companions were formally invested with the badge of the Company by Acciaiuoli himself when he informed them of their appointment, and were required to swear both before him and later before King Loysi himself some sort of membership oath. The statutes refer to two such oaths, including one to obey the statutes,[18] and it seems likely that both of these oaths were sworn by all new companions at their induction into the Company. The illustration accompanying the first chapter, indeed, depicts a knight kneeling before the Prince seated on his throne, with his hands placed upon an open book (presumably a Bible) held in the Prince's hands.

According to chapter 16, if any knight elected to the Company had already joined another order, he was to do his best to leave it, but if he could not do so honourably, he was always to place his membership in the present Company first, and was to join no further order without the express permission of the Prince of the Knot. These ordinances Acciaiuoli lifted directly from the Star statutes,[19] but he improved upon his model by adding that no knight who had retied his knot was even to ask for permission to join another order. The implication of Acciaiuoli's refinement seems to be that it would be unworthy of anyone who had actually achieved the goal of Right Desire to think of belonging to a less worthy company, but his real aim was no doubt to assure the exclusiveness of the bond which held the companions to his master.

While the bond was intended to be exclusive, the Company itself was quite the opposite. In the prologue Acciaiuoli projected a membership of 300 knights. This was smaller by 200 than the goal set by Jean of France, but as the mainland kingdom of Sicily probably had well under half the population of France in 1352, and presumably less than half the number of knights, it was in practical terms more ambitious. Whether Acciaiuoli realised this we have no way of knowing, but he must at least have been aware of the fact that the achievement of his goal would have required the admission of a considerable number of simple knights in addition to a large proportion of the baronial class of the kingdom.[20]

---

[18] Ch. 1a,b.

[19] Item 9a,b,c.

[20] I have found no estimate of the number of knights in the kingdom in or about 1350, but if the ratio of knights to the general population was comparable to that in both England and France in the same period, the number of knights would have been between 1,000 and 2,000, so the Company would have included between one third and one sixth of the knights in the kingdom.

How many knights were ever actually appointed to the Company is unknown, but the figure sixty mentioned by Villani seems likely enough for the first promotion, and it would be surprising if no others were admitted during the next several years. Nothing resembling a complete list of members has been preserved, however, and the current state of the documentation makes it all but impossible to reconstruct one. The antiquarian historians of the seventeenth century claimed to have identified some nineteen knights who had belonged to the Company, largely on the basis of funerary monuments, but their works actually list the names only of the following twelve:[21] Bernabò Visconti, Lord of Milan; Loysi di Sabran, Count of Apice; Guglielmo del Balzo (alias Guillaume des Baux), Count of Noja; Loysi Sanseverino (whose family included several counts); Giacomo Carracciolo; Coluccio (or Giovanello) Bozzuto; Roberto di Burgenza (a royal chamberlain in 1349);[22] *Francesco Loffredo; *Roberto Seripando; *Guerello di Tocco; *Nardo Bozzuto; *Cristoforo di Costanzo; and *Matteo Boccapianola. Of these, Coluccio Bozzuto was buried in the cathedral church of St Januarius in a tomb that bore an inscription indicating that in life he had been de Societate Nodi,[23] Roberto di Burgenza was buried in the church of St Clare in Naples in a tomb with a similar inscription,[24] and the last six men named (marked with asterisks) were laid to rest in tombs in the tribune of the church of St Peter the Martyr in Naples, at least two of which (those of Costanzo and Loffredo) still bore signs of membership in the Company.[25] Although none of these men seems to have played a leading role in the politics of the period,[26] they all belonged to families long prominent in the nobility of the kingdom, and there is no particular reason to doubt that any of them was admitted to the Company of the Knot. The letter of election sent to the Count of Apice, an important baron, proves his membership. It is unclear on what basis the names of Guglielmo del Balzo and Bernabò Visconti were included in the list, but the former was a member of the most important baronial family in the County of Provence as well as the lord of a Neapolitan county, and the latter – Lord of Milan from 1354 to 1385 – was the most important ruler in northern Italy. Loysi and Acciaiuoli may well have bestowed membership on foreign rulers like Visconti in order to increase the prestige of the order or to cement alliances, but there is not enough evidence to say much more about the practice.

It would be surprising if Loysi did not also confer membership in his order upon the members of his immediate circle of friends – especially Gianotto Estandart,

---

[21] Eleven of the twelve names are given in Cesare d'Engenio Carracciolo, Napoli Sacra (Naples, 1623). Somewhat shorter lists were published by S. Giovanni Batista Carrafa, Historia del Regno di Napoli (Naples, 1572), Pt. 1a, f. 130v; by Angelo di Costanzo, Storia del Regno di Napoli (Naples, 1581), Lib. 6, p. 175; and by Giovanni Antonio Summonte, Historia della Città e Regno di Napoli (Naples, 1640–75), Pt. 2a, lib. 3, p. 439.

[22] Camera, Elucubrazioni, p. 111 nn. 4, 5.

[23] Ibid., p. 169.

[24] Ibid., p. 170. This church, built in 1310–28 for Sancia, wife of Roberto 'the Wise', was completely burnt out on 4 August 1943 by incendiary bombs, and most of the large monuments were wrecked. Nevertheless, many gothic tombs remain, including those of Roberto himself, his daughter, and his younger granddaughter.

[25] Carrafa, loc. cit.

[26] Only Burgenza is even mentioned by name in Léonard's three-volume history of Giovanna's reign, and he was only a royal chamberlain.

Francesco del Balzo, and Loysi di Sabran of Ariano – but for this we have no evidence at all. On the other hand, there is no reason to believe that any member of the royal house accepted membership in the Company of the Knot. As we have seen, Loysi offered a badge and habit to his older brother Roberto, Prince of Taranto and titular Emperor of Constantinople, but he publicly declined the honour. His younger brother Filippo (who succeeded Roberto in 1354), may have been induced to accept membership, but it is unlikely that either of the two surviving sons of Giovanni of Durazzo – Loysi Count of Gravina and Roberto Prince of Morea – would have been invited to join, as they were almost constantly in rebellion against Loysi. The founder himself had no sons by his wife Queen Giovanna, and his brothers both died without surviving issue, so the question of admitting infant princes did not even arise.

7 The Obligations and Privileges of Membership

The various obligations imposed upon the members of the Company of the Knot are scattered throughout the statutes. They may usefully be discussed under three headings: obligations to the living, obligations to the dead, and general obligations.

Among the obligations to the living the usual distinction must also be made between those owed by the Prince as such and those owed by the ordinary members. The absence of any reference to admission fees or annual dues implies that the Prince was to take upon himself the full burden of paying for the order's buildings and for its annual festivities. The statutes themselves specify only two obligations owed by the Prince to the ordinary companions while they were alive: to pay for the journey to and from the annual Assembly of the order of any foreign knight bachelor who could not otherwise have come;[27] and to maintain any companion impoverished in the pursuit of the Company's goal who informed the Prince of his impoverishment at an annual Assembly and was able to demonstrate the truth of his claim, provided that he live part of the time at the Company's seat.[28] The former undertaking – unique among the orders under consideration here – was obviously intended to encourage participation in the activities of the Company by knights who might not otherwise have done so; the latter (clearly inspired by the obligation undertaken by the founder of the Company of the Star to support companions worn out in his service)[29] was presumably meant to encourage the companions to pursue adventures without regard for their cost.

The statutes set forth three obligations owed by the ordinary companions to their Prince before his death. Two were derived from the statutes of the French order, but the third was a significant innovation. In the very first chapter of the statutes Acciaiuoli, improving upon the eighth item of the Star letter, required all those who were admitted to the Company to swear that they would give, 'with abandon' and 'to all their power and knowledge' both loyal counsel and aid in everything

[27] Ch. 6b.
[28] Ch. 13a,b,c.
[29] Le Bel, statement 14.

the Prince asked of them, 'whether in arms or in other matters'.[30] This oath constituted, in effect, a life contract of retinue, and would in theory have required the companions of the Company to be at the beck and call of the Prince. No earlier order had made a comparable demand for service upon its members, and it is therefore surprising that Acciaiuoli both thought and dared to do so. It may be that he did not expect the more important knights admitted to the order to take this oath much more seriously than the oaths they swore as vassals, but hoped to bind the lesser knights of the Company – who would surely have been the great majority – into a form of service to the crown very similar to that undertaken by life retainers in both England and France.

A less important obligation to the Prince, based directly upon Star item 19, required the companions to obtain the permission of the Prince before going on any long voyage. Acciaiuoli added a further requirement that the companions send a written description of their intended voyage to the chapel of the Company if permission was given. The descriptions submitted were to be presented to the Prince and his Council on the day of the feast, specifically so that the Prince could ask for news of the absent companions from those who were present. It is possible that Acciaiuoli did not understand the original purpose of the obligation imposed by the Star statutes (which was to control the movements of the companions), but it is more likely that he decided to present it in a more acceptable light, and at the same time relate it to the theme of the quest which he introduced into the statutes.

Unlike the knights of the Star, those of the Knot seem to have owed no particular obligations to their fellow knights while the latter still lived. Acciaiuoli may have failed to include any fraternal obligations for no better reason than that they were not mentioned in the letter that was his principal source for the statutes of the Star, but it is nevertheless significant that he did not decide independently to include a single concession to the idea of fraternity-in-arms among the ordinary members of his order, and made no provision even for the avoidance or settlement of disputes among them. Acciaiuoli clearly perceived the knights of the Company primarily as clients of his master rather than as members of a corporate body, and was not interested in their relationships with one another.

The obligations of the Prince and companions of the Company of the Knot to a companion who had died were considerably more extensive than they were to the living companions of the order. As in the Company of the Star, the death of a companion of the Knot was to be signalled by sending his best primary badge (the knot) to the order's chapel and his personalized secondary badge (the sword) to the Prince.[31] The latter was to have a funeral said for him in the Company's chapel,[32] after which the companions were each to have a certain number of masses said for the good of his soul in purgatory.[33] Acciaiuoli here improved upon his model by specifying a time period within which the funeral was to be held (eight days after

---

[30] [1a] 'Primierement, euls sont tenus de jurer que, a tout leur pouoir et savoir, donront abandoneement loyal conceil et aide au Prince de tout ce qu'il leur requerra, soit d'armes, soit d'autres choses, [b] et d'observer les enfrescripts chapitres.'
[31] Ch. 18a,b.
[32] Ch. 19a.
[33] Ch. 23.

the Prince received the sword), by requiring companions within one day's ride to be present, by requiring the Prince and the companions present to accompany the sword to the altar (where it was to be offered up) and to pray there for his soul,[34] and by increasing the number of masses owed by the survivors from one to seven – the number of the gifts of the Holy Spirit. In addition to these improvements, Acciaiuoli had Loysi declare that he and his successors would not only hang up the sword (and, according to the illuminations, the knot) of each deceased companion in the chapel of the Company, as a perpetual memorial,[35] but would also provide a tomb for him in the chapel, inscribed with his name and the place and date of his death. This was to be erected within three months of his death if the Prince was in the kingdom at the time,[36] and within one year if he was abroad.[37] Other orders had provided similar memorials to their departed members, but no other order either had promised or would promise to provide a tomb. Even a relatively simple tomb would have been expensive, and it is unclear where Acciaiuoli expected to find the money to provide tombs for the hundreds of knights the Company was to have included. It may be that he hoped most members would continue to provide for their own tombs, so that the Prince would only have to make good his promise to a few outstanding or impoverished knights.

Acciaiuoli also imposed upon the companions of his master's order several obligations which may be described as 'spiritual'. Most of these are contained in chapter 5, based upon item 7 of the Star letter. In both orders the knights were obliged to fast one day each week of the year, and Acciaiuoli merely changed the day from Saturday to Thursday.[38] As in the Company of the Star the fast could be avoided by a charitable donation, the sum demanded being calculated in numbers related to the Company's patron. The knights of the Knot were obliged to feed three paupers, whose number represented the Trinity. Acciaiuoli elaborated upon his model, however, by setting forth (in chapter 2) a special pious observance for Friday as well, in remembrance of the Passion: the wearing of a black hood and a plain white knot. This had no particular connection to the Holy Spirit, but was of course intimately associated with the Holy Sepulchre, the goal both of the pilgrimage of 'Right Desire', and of the crusade which the companions were obliged to undertake.

The crusading obligations of the knights of the Knot were among Acciaiuoli's more notable innovations. Every companion was obliged (if he could do so *bonnement*) to take part in person in any crusade proclaimed, either by the Holy See or by any Christian prince, to reconquer the Holy Land. Furthermore, if the Prince of the Company, 'to whom the said heritage should reasonably belong', himself either led or personally joined this crusade, the companions were obliged to remain with the crusade for as long as he did, unless they were prevented from doing so by 'an express and apparent necessity'.[39] Acciaiuoli had two very good reasons for introducing these rules. In the first place, the crusade to reconquer the Holy

[34] Ch. 19a–e.
[35] Ch. 20a.
[36] Ch. 20b.
[37] Ch. 22.
[38] Ch. 5a.
[39] Ch. 9a,b.

Sepulchre was in effect the highest form of the spiritual quest he had set for the companions of the order, the pilgrimage of Right Desire, and it would have done the knights of the Company no harm to be seen as sworn crusaders. Although no major crusade had been launched against the Muslims of Syria or North Africa since 1270, the crusading ideal had been kept alive in the intervening period by various propagandists, and many ambitious knights of the fourteenth century travelled to Spain or Prussia (in what amounted to a special sort of enterprise of arms as well as a special sort of pilgrimage) specifically to combat the enemies of Christendom – if only for a few weeks. Two minor crusades whose ultimate object had been to recapture Jerusalem had actually been organized in the 1340s, and such a crusade may have formed a part of Acciaiuoli's ambition to restore the greatness of the kingdom and dynasty he served, for the Kingdom of Jerusalem (as the statutes themselves indicate) was one the the several 'lost realms' he hoped to reconquer. As it turned out the obligation remained purely theoretical, for neither Loysi nor any of his contemporaries led a crusade while the Company of the Knot was effectively in existence.

8 Officers and Clergy

Probably because these matters were not touched upon in the Star letter, the statutes of the Knot make no reference either to a corporate seal or to any corporate officers. The 'clergy of the chapel' (clers de la dicte chappelle)[40] are referred to only in the chapter dealing with the maintenance of the book of deeds, without any suggestion of status or number. It is likely that Acciaiuoli intended to establish a college of priests similar to those of the Star and the Garter, but there is no evidence to indicate whether in fact he did so, or what form he intended it to take.

9 The Physical Establishment of the Company: The Castle of the Egg

Acciaiuoli seems to have selected the seat of his Company in direct imitation of his French model, and thus in indirect imitation of the Company of the Garter. Jean of France had declared that his knights were to assemble at the royal manor of Saint-Ouen 'seated between Paris and Saint Denis', and Acciaiuoli accordingly made the royal Castle of the Egg, 'seated in the sea between Naples and Notre Dame', the centre of his new Company's activities. Like the seats of the two earlier orders, the Castel dell'Ovo – a massive fortress which had been built on a small, egg-shaped island in the Bay of Naples in 1154 – was a royal residence situated at a convenient distance from the urban capital of the kingdom. Unlike the other seats, it had certain magical associations, connected with the popular legends which had made of the Classical Roman poet Vergil a Merlinesque enchanter. Vergil was believed to have caused the castle to appear suddenly on an egg hurled into the sea. In the prologue to the statutes the castle is described as that of 'the Egg, enchanted of the marvellous peril'; in chapter 6 it is said to be situated 'near the hidden grotto of the enchantments of Vergil'; and in chapter 20 it is said that the tombs of the companions were to be placed 'behind the place of the marvellous peril'. As

[40] Ch. 8.

nothing further is said about all this, one must assume that these allusions were merely intended to associate the order's seat with the atmosphere of marvels characteristic of the courts of Arthurian romance.

The statutes imply that Acciaiuoli, like the earlier founders, intended to set aside a hall and a chapel within the castle for the use of the Company, and also some sort of 'hostel' in which the impoverished knights maintained by the Prince could live at least part of the time.[41] Nothing in particular is said in the statutes about the hall, which was presumably to be used both for the chapter or 'parliament' and for the banquet on the feast day. The chapel is specifically mentioned in several chapters, however, and some of its structures are described in detail. The chapel was to be established, according to chapter 7, to the honour of the Holy Spirit of Right Desire, and in it each of the companions was to have a fixed seat (*siege*) or stall, at the top of which his name, surname, arms, and crest were to be painted. The placement of these stalls in the chapel (which was in keeping with the 'spiritual' pretensions of the order) may have been inspired by the custom of the Garter, but the large number of knights to be accomodated would have necessitated an arrangement of stalls similar to that required (if never actually established) in the hall of the Noble House. It would also have required the construction of a very large new chapel, since the existing chapel of the Castel dell'Ovo, like most of the churches in Naples, was much too small to hold 300 stalls of the sort called for. One can only wonder if Acciaiuoli was aware of this problem when he decided to place the stalls in the chapel rather than the hall. The chapel was to have been the site both of the services held during the annual Assembly and of the special memorial service held for each companion after his death. After the latter service, according to chapter 20, the sword of the deceased companion was to have been 'placed in an apparent and permanent place' in the chapel as a form of memorial. The illustration to this chapter shows four swords hanging points down before the altar, each accompanied by a knot hung to the right of the pommel. In practice most of the hundreds of swords that would have accumulated in the chapel if this ordinance had been followed could only have been displayed in this way in the aisles of the chapel behind the stalls.

Chapter 20 also specifies that the tombs that were to be provided for the companions were to be set in the Castel dell'Ovo, but 'behind the place of the enchantment of the marvellous peril' rather than in the chapel (which was already rather overcrowded). Each tomb was to have written over it in letters carved in marble: 'This is the tomb of the remembrance of such a knight who died in such a place at such a time'. The illustration to the chapter depicts three very splendid tombs, each taking the form of an oblong chest with richly carved side-panels, set on four short columns and bearing a *gisant* figure of a knight in full armour wearing a surcoat strewn with knots. The tombs appear to be set end to end against the wall, under a continuous canopy with three arches, and each has an inscription in Latin painted on the wall behind it. According to chapter 21 any knight who had retied his knot was to have carved above his tomb (presumably in addition to this inscription) the words: 'He achieved his part of the Right Desire', irradiated like the knot and the dove. The tomb depicted in the illustration to this chapter is even more elaborate than the other three, and has above it in addition to the specified

---

[41] Ch. 13c.

inscription in French (without any rays) the dove-and-rays and three love-knots set on their sides. As we have already observed, it is difficult to believe that Acciaiuoli planned to pay for or house in the castle hundreds of tombs of this sort, which would have been monstrously expensive and taken up a tremendous amount of space.

I have found no evidence that Loysi actually constructed any new buildings for the Company during his brief reign, so it must be assumed that the Company made use of the existing facilities of the Castel dell'Ovo. If any stalls were ever set up in the chapel, they have not survived. It is just possible, on the other hand, that some or all of the tombs referred to above were paid for by Loysi as Prince of the Company, even though they were not set in the Castel dell'Ovo.

10 The General Assembly of the Company

As had been true in both the Order of the Garter and the Company of the Star, the only corporate activity in which the knights of the Knot were obliged to participate on a regular basis was the annual general Assembly (*Assemblé*). Like the two earlier orders, the Company of the Knot was to meet at its offical seat once every year, on Pentecost, the feast of its patron and the anniversary of the founder's coronation. Although Jean of France had required those knights of his order who could not attend the Assembly to meet in small groups to celebrate the feast, Loysi declared instead that he would pay for the journey to Naples of any foreign knight bachelor, who alone, the chapter implies, might have a legitimate excuse for absence. Thus Acciaiuoli showed himself even more eager than Jean to have all his knights assembled together, and did his best to discourage excuses.

The activities of the knights of the Knot during their annual Assembly, like those of the knights of both the Star and the Garter, were to include a religious service, a banquet, and a business meeting, apparently in that order. It would appear that all three were to be held on the day of Pentecost itself, since this is the day on which the knights were required to convene, and the statutes imply that the knights were to leave immediately following the business meeting, which itself was to follow the banquet. All three activities are described in unprecedented detail.

At the religious service (described only as a mass but presumably a solemn mass of the Holy Spirit) the knights were to hear the office sitting in their stalls, wearing their most formal costume, and holding their swords. When the celebrant had returned to his place after elevating the host, the Prince and all the companions were to kneel and say together the prayer *Veni creator spiritus, mentes tuorum visita, imple superna gracia que tu creasti pectora*, in order that the Holy Spirit might fill and illuminate the whole Company with his grace.[42]

The banquet that was apparently to follow this service was to be an occasion of the greatest pomp, altogether reminiscent of the banquets legendarily held by King Arthur for the knights of the Round Table. Like Arthur, Loysi was to wear his crown and hold a full court, in which those who had done well each year were to be

[42] Ch. 7.

honoured, and those who had done anything shameful were to be punished. The ceremonial means adopted for imposing honour and shame were as usual partly borrowed and partly new. During the banquet, those knights who had untied their knots were to sit at a special table of honour called the *Table Desiree*, arranged in order of their achievement to date. Those who had retied their knot after visiting the Holy Sepulchre were to wear a wreath of laurels 'for more triumphal honour, exactly as the ancient Romans, who conquered the whole world, established to do and did to all the good knights who above all the others deserved and merited to receive the greatest honour'.[43] The table itself clearly represented the Arthurian Round Table, but the idea of having such a table was just as clearly taken from Jean's letter – in which the analogous item of furniture was designated less romantically the *Table d'Onneur*. The new name was of course an allusion to the Company's name and goal. The use of a laurel wreath to set off the knights who had achieved the most – a distinction among the distinguished characteristic of the order – may be seen as a sign of Acciaiuoli's interest in Classical Roman history and letters.

Perhaps more remarkable than these symbolic rewards for virtue was the symbolic punishment for deviation from the Chivalric ideal imposed by the Grand Seneschal. Jean of France had provided for the temporary suspension of any knight who disgraced himself by flying from the field,[44] but Acciaiuoli – adapting a custom of the knights of St John to his purposes[45] – required a knight who had shamefully departed from a battle or *chose ordenee* ('which thing,' he decared, 'the Holy Spirit is unwilling to suffer') to appear at the Assembly each year dressed all in black, and wearing on his breast in place of the dove-and-ray device normally worn during the feast the words *J'ay esperance ou Saint Esperit de ma grant honte amender*, in white letters, clearly visible. During the banquet such a knight was to dine alone in the middle of the hall at a special table of disgrace (which in the illustration to the chapter is represented as small and black). He was to continue to dress and dine this way every year until his good deeds relieved him of his shame, or the Prince and his Council decided to forgive him.[46] Unlike Jean, Acciaiuoli made no provision for the expulsion of companions, perhaps feeling that formal humiliation was a more effective form of punishment.

As in the Company of the Star, the deeds of the knights were to be judged on the basis of the knights' own accounts, submitted before the meeting. Unlike the knights of the Star, however, those of the Knot were to present their accounts in writing to the clerks of the chapel when they arrived at the Assembly each year, and the clerks were to read them out to the Prince and his Council rather than to the assembled knights. Only those deeds judged by them to be worthy of remembrance were then to be written into the book of deeds maintained by the order, and this book, called the *Livre des avenemens aus chevaliers de la Compaignie du Saint Esperit au Droit Desir*, was to be kept at all times in the order's chapel. Unlike the book maintained by the Company of the Star, therefore, that of the

---

[43] Ch. 14a,b,c.
[44] Item 17.
[45] Rule of Raymond Du Puy, ch. 10; ed. E. J. King, *The Rule, Statutes and Customs of the Hospitallers 1099–1310* (London, 1934), p. 24.
[46] Ch. 11a,b,c,d.

Knot was to be a record only of the more noteworthy deeds of the companions, and was itself part of the order's elaborate system of honours.

The book of adventures has not survived, but that it once existed we have the testimony of both Boccaccio and Villani, neither of whom was impressed with the veracity of its contents. 'He wrote in French,' wrote the former of Acciaiuoli in a letter to Francesco Nelli, 'of the deeds of the knights of the Holy Spirit, in the style in which certain others in the past wrote of the Round Table. What laughable and entirely false matters were set down, he himself knows.'[47] Villani attributed the book to Loysi himself. 'He praised and vaunted himself so much for the magnificent deeds he did in time of war and in time of peace that he plunged his listeners into astonishment and into boredom. Pleasing himself with his own praise, he had made of his tales some writings in a pompous style.'[48]

Immediately following the banquet the knights of the Knot were to gather for a business-meeting, rather grandly called a *Parlement* in the statutes.[49] At this meeting the knights present were obliged by oath to present any idea which they felt would be 'good and honourable for increasing and amending the said order', and the Prince was to have added to the statutes of the order any suggested ordinance approved by the assembled companions. The statutes were not indeed to be amended in any other way. In addition to considering proposals for new ordinances, the *Parlement* was to deal with those disputes among the companions over the proper observance of the existing rules of the order which had proved too difficult for the Prince and his Council to settle before the meeting. There is no suggestion in the chapter dealing with these questions that the *Parlement* was to consider disputes among the companions not related to the statutes, or that they were to advise the Prince on any matters not directly related to the order as such, so it would appear that (unlike the equivalent assembly of the Company of the Star), the *Parlement* of the order was not intended to function as an assembly representative of the nobility of the kingdom. This, too, was in keeping with the absolutist traditions of the kingdom, but the existence of a national parliament composed of barons would in any case have made such a function un-necessary.

It is unclear from the statutes whether the knights of the Knot were intended to fight together as a unit in the manner of the knights of the Band. The fact that they were obliged to give military aid to their Prince whenever summoned and to accompany him or any other Christian prince on a crusade to reconquer the Holy Land suggests that they might have been, and the illustrations to the statutes contain a number of panels in which several knights wearing the order's badge are depicted riding or fighting together. If they were not to fight in a body, the only irregular corporate activities in which the companions were obliged to participate

---

[47] 'Scripse in francesco de' fatti de' cavalieri del santo spedito, in quello stile che gia per addietro scripsono alcuni della Tavola ritonda, nel quale che cose da ridere et al tutto false abbia poste egli el sa.' Francesco Corazzini, ed., *Le lettere edite e inedite di Messer Giovanni Boccaccio* (Florence, 1877), p. 161. On this letter, see G. Traversari, 'Per l'autenticità dell' epistola del Boccaccio a Francesco Nelli', *Giornale storico della Letteratura italiana* 46 (1905), pp. 100–18, esp. pp. 110–12.

[48] *Cronica*, 1. X, cap. 83 (t. V, p. 131).

[49] Ch. 15.

6.4 The sword of the Knot
(reconstruction)

6.5 The device of the dove-and-rays,
as represented in the MS. of the statutes
on the shields of the companions

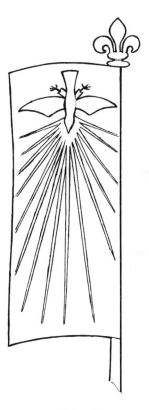

6.6 The formal habit of the Knot,
as represented in the MS. of
the statutes

6.7 The banner of the Knot, as
represented in the MS. of the statutes

were the memorial services held for their deceased brethren. In an order with 300 members such services might well have been held more often than once a month on average, so although irregular, they would have brought at least a selection of the companions together frequently enough to give them a sense of solidarity in the long period between annual Assemblies.

11 The Costume of the Companions

Like the knights of the Star, those of the Knot had several orders of dress. The most formal of these was to be worn during the annual service and (according to the illustrations) during the banquet that followed. This costume is described in the text of ordinance 7d as consisting of *seurcote, chaperon, chausses et solers tous blans*, and the accompanying illuminations represent it more clearly as consisting of white hose and white shoes; a white *jupon* with tight wrist-length sleeves; a white *cote-hardie* charged on the breast with the device of the dove-and-rays, with a dagged hem cut several inches above the knee and elbow-length sleeves continued in long dagged tippets; and a white *chaperon* with a knee-length liripipe and a wide gold band around the base of the cape, which was also dagged at the hem. This striking habit was quite different from that of the Star knights, and indeed from that adopted in any other order except the Band, being the first to substitute for the old-fashioned mantle and long surcoat of the religious orders a *jupon* and *cote hardie* of the most modish cut. Acciaiuoli similarly replaced the elaborate Saturday costume of the Star knights with a simple black *chaperon* bearing a plain white knot over sober everyday dress, and required that it be worn not as a sign of fasting but to commemorate the Passion.[50] In addition, the wording of chapter 3 implies that the costume laid down for wear by all the knights of the Company during the annual service was to be worn at all times by those who had retied their knots. Finally, a special costume of black with the inscription *J'ay esperance ou Saint Esperit de ma grande honte amender* on the breast was provided to signalize disgrace. Its colour was no doubt selected as the opposite to that of the habit of honour, and its inscription answered the honourable sentence *Il a pleeu a Dieu*.[51] All of these costumes were quite original, and evoke the knights of the Round Table in their grail-seeking mode rather than the knights of the religious orders of knighthood.

12 The Banner of the Company

Like the Company of the Star, that of the Knot was to have a banner or armorial flag which was to bear on a field of the livery-colour an image of the Company's heavenly patron, and which was to be borne in battle against the enemies of Faith and lord. Its iconography differed from that of the Star banner in that the ordinary badge of the Company, the knot, did not appear on its surface. The banner of the

[50] Ch. 2d.
[51] Ch. 11b.

Knot is officially described as *d'argent ou toute blance a un grant ray ardant ou millieu du Saint Esperit*, and is depicted in the illustrations of the statutes as an upright rectangle of white charged with the dove-and-rays device described above. Unlike Jean, Acciaiuoli said nothing about the number of companions who had to be present before the banner could be raised, but he did introduce a battle-cry to be used when it was raised, after the companion's own cry: *Au Droit Desir!* It would appear that both banner and cry were to be used by any companion who chose to do so, in a purely private capacity. Presumably it would also have been borne before any military company composed of the knights of the order as well, but the chapter makes no reference to any such unit.

13 Conclusions: The Company of the Knot

In conclusion it can be said that, although the Company of the Holy Spirit of Right Desire founded by Nicola Acciaiuoli in the name of his master Loysi 'di Taranto' was modelled closely upon the Company of the Star, and therefore resembled the latter order in many respects, the numerous modifications and wholly novel ordinances introduced by Acciaiuoli made the order he created very different in several important respects from its French original. Unlike Jean, who was principally concerned with improving the performance of the knights of his kingdom on the field of battle, Acciaiuoli seems to have been interested primarily in restoring the tarnished glory of his master's kingdom, house, and person, and he accordingly sought to create an order whose members would reflect glory upon their Prince by performing great deeds of valour and chivalry. The untying and retying of the knot, the *devise* and habit of honour, the seat at the *Table Desiree* and crown of laurel, the book of deeds and the tomb with its glorious inscription – all formed part of an elaborate system of reward for heroic action without parallel in any earlier order except that of the Star.

Jean of France had of course sought to reward acts of valour performed in his service, but while the deeds for which the knights of the Holy Spirit were to untie their knot could certainly have been performed in the service of their Prince, the retying of the knot required them to undertake a pilgrimage which was not only of no practical use to Loysi, but would actually have deprived him of their service for a period of months or years. Even more than Edward of England and Jean of France, Acciaiuoli seems to have conceived of the order he created in the image of the Round Table, whose knights brought honour to their king and country not merely by performing heroic actions in the wars of their king, but by undertaking long voyages in search of adventure, and returning to the court from time to time to tell the king and their companions what they had seen and done. Indeed, on one level the Company of the Knot was a sort of votive order whose members undertook to visit the Holy Sepulchre rather than to find the Holy Grail. Acciaiuoli's requirement that the companions of the Knot inform the king of their itinerary so that he could enquire after them at the next Assembly should probably be interpreted in the light of such a romantic conception of the order, as of course should his provision that the more notable deeds of its members be recorded in a book of 'adventures'. Both Boccaccio and Villani imply that this book, composed like the statutes in French, was written in the style of an Arthurian romance, and it was clearly intended to be a sort of collective chivalric biography.

At the same time, Acciaiuoli required the companions to undertake cliental obligations to their Prince that were far more extensive than those imposed in any earlier order. This suggests that he also hoped to use the order as a means of securing the loyalty and service of the knights who were admitted to it, and thereby to increase his master's hold upon the power which he had wrested from his wife, and had to guard against the schemes of his brothers and cousins. The order may indeed have been intended to function like a political party or faction, devoted to the interests of Loysi and his line. This would explain why Acciauoli was so indifferent to the relationships among the members themselves, and also why the order simply dissolved when Loysi died without leaving an heir of his body.

Chapter 7

The Order of the Sword
Cyprus, 1347/59–1489?

Two further knightly orders seem to have been founded by princes in the period before 1360. One of these – the *Gesellschaft in der Fürspang* or 'Society of the Buckle', said to have been founded by the Emperor Karl IV von Luxemburg in Nürnberg in 1355 – although both its size and its device were clearly inspired by those of the Garter, was certainly a confraternal order, with its own elected *Hauptmann*.[1] The only other princely order known to have been founded before 1360 is the Order of the Sword, said to have been created by Pierre de Toulouse-Antioch 'de Lusignan'[2] in 1347, when he was only the titular Count of Tripoli, and certainly maintained by him after he succeeded his father on the throne of the kingdom of Cyprus in 1359. There is some reason to think that this Order was given a monarchical constitution by its founder, but the only trace of its statutes that has survived is a summary in the diary of a fifteenth-century pilgrim of the principal obligations then undertaken by its members, and very little is known about the nature of the Order during its founder's brief reign. Because the Order survived in some form until the fall of the Cypriot monarchy in 1489, however, and because it may well have served as the inspiration for several later orders, one of

[1] On this order, (which had twenty-six knights), see F. Freiherr von Biedenfeld, *Geschichte und Verfassung aller geistlichen und weltlichen, erloschenen und blühenden Ritterorden* (Weimar, 1841), I, pp. 225–9, and Alwin Schultz, *Deutsches Leben im XIV. und XV. Jahrhundert* (Vienna, 1892), II, p. 541. The device of the society, of which several contemporary representations have been preserved, took the form of a collar differing from the English garter in having, instead of a single buckle and a single belt-end wrapped arond the circular belt and pendant below it, five identical buckles and pendant belt-ends, set equidistant from one another around the circular belt. This is in any case the form it took both on the effigy of Martin von Seinsheim (d. 1434) on his tomb in the Marienkapelle of Würzburg, and in the representation of Jan von Strolenburg in the register of the Brotherhood of St Christopher in Arlberg, compiled over a period of years in the fifteenth century. (Arthur Charles Fox-Davies, *The Art of Heraldry* [London, 1904], p. 414.) Walter Leonhard, *Das grosse Buch der Wappenkunst* (Munich, 1978), p. 332, fig. 7, gives a representation of the collar of this order alone, with a chain for attaching it to a helmet in an armorial achievement, almost certainly taken from the same register. (Figs. 7.1, 7.2.)

[2] The members of the royal house of Cyprus all used the surname 'de Lusignan' in the fourteenth and fifteenth centuries, but they were actually members of a cadet branch of the house of Toulouse (or more properly Rouergue), which had inherited the throne of Cyprus from the heiress of the Lusignans in 1267.

which was certainly monarchical, it will be useful to review briefly what is currently known of its history.[3]

The founder of the Order, the future Pierre I, had been born in 1329, and was thus a contemporary of the Black Prince rather than of his father and the other earlier founders. He was the second of the four sons of Hugues IV, King of Cyprus and titular King of Jerusalem from 1324 to 1359.[4] The island kingdom of Cyprus, filled since its conquest during the Third Crusade in the late twelfth century with French-speaking refugees from the much-reduced kingdom of Jerusalem, had been since the fall of Acre in 1291 the last major bastion of the Levantine Crusade in the eastern Mediterranean, but neither Pierre's father nor most of his barons had much enthusiasm for an aggressive war against the Infidel. Pierre, by contrast, devoted himself to the ideal of reconquering the Holy Land when he was still a youth, and 'became in pursuit of that ideal one of the most persistent knights-errant of his century.'[5] Brave, chivalrous, passionate, and tireless in the pursuit of his goal, Pierre was one of the most spectacular figures in the history of his time, and attracted not only the admiration of such writers as Froissart, Machaut, Petrarch, and Chaucer, but the personal devotion of the fanatical Carmelite Pierre Thomas and the chivalrous dreamer Philippe de Mézières.

According to Machaut (whose rhymed chronicle La prise d'Alexandrie is our principal source for Pierre's early life),[6] shortly after the death of his elder brother Guy in 1346 made him the heir aparent to his father's throne, Pierre had a vision in which Christ himself urged him to 'undertake the Holy Passage' and conquer his 'heritage'.[7] In response to this vision, Pierre, though barely seventeen years old, took the vow of a crusader, and furthermore 'made an order to attract knights of good character, who felt a devotion to the Promised Land, and also for all men-at-arms, who wished to save their souls.'[8] According to Machaut, he recruited his first knights among the noble pilgrims who came to Cyprus from the kingdoms of

---

[3] Favyn provided an account of the nature and history of this Order in his Théâtre d'honneur which was even more fanciful than usual, declaring that it had been founded by Guy de Lusignan, first King of Cyprus, in 1195, and that its collar, given to 300 barons on that occasion, was composed of loveknots interlaced with the letters S and R, standing for the motto Securitas Regni. Later authors followed him, or added other inaccurate details. The only critical account of this Order that I have found is that of Christiane Van Den Bergen-Pantens, 'Etude historique et iconographique de l'Ordre de L'Epée de Chypre', in Mélanges offerts à Szabolcs de Vajay . . ., ed. comte d'Adhémar de Panat et al., (Braga, 1971), pp. 605–10, Pl. XLVIII.

[4] On the life and reign of Pierre I, see especially Sir George Hill, A History of Cyprus (Cambridge, 1948), II, pp. 308–66. The claim of the Kings of Cyprus to the throne of Jerusalem was based on their descent from the de facto kings of the twelfth century and was superior to the purchased claims of the Angevin rulers of Naples.

[5] Sir Harry Luke, 'The Kingdom of Cyprus, 1291–1369', A History of the Crusades, ed. Kenneth Setton, Vol. III (London, 1975), p. 352.

[6] Ed. L. de Mas-Latrie (Geneva, 1877).

[7] Ibid., p. 10.

[8] 'Si fist une ordre pour attraire/ Les chevaliers de bon affaire,/ Qui avoit devotion/ En terre de promission,/ Et aussi pour toutes gens d'armes,/ Qui vouloient sauver leurs ames.' Ibid., pp. 11–12, ll. 349–54.

western Europe on their way to the Holy Places in Jerusalem.[9] Since his father disapproved of his project to lauch a new crusade, he conferred membership in this Order 'secretly, wisely, and maturely, without speaking too much and without pleading too much, by which he hoped to aid himself; for he was otherwise unable to enjoy his deed fully.'[10] Soon after this, Pierre and his younger brother Jean, titular Prince of Antioch, attempted to set out for the West to raise more men for their projected crusade, but they were arrested by agents of their father and imprisoned in Kyrenia until they were released at the request of the Pope.

If Machaut's account is not misleading (and it should be emphasised that he gives no dates for any of these events), then the Order must have been founded in secret at some time in or shortly after 1347 – about the same time the Order of the Garter was proclaimed in its definitive form. It is possible that Pierre's decision to found what seems to have been from the first an order of lay knights was inspired directly by news of the orders proclaimed in England and France three years earlier, but it is perhaps more likely that he got the idea from the Picard knight Philippe de Mézières, who arrived in Cyprus in that very year, and soon became a close friend and collaborator of the young heir to throne, barely two years his junior. Mézières had been a member of the entourage of the unfortunate first consort of Queen Giovanna of mainland Sicily when he was murdered in 1345, and in the following year had served under the Dauphin Humbert in the Battle of Smyrna, so he was probably familiar with both the Hungarian Society of St George and the Dauphinois Order of St Catherine when he arrived in the court of Cyprus. Just as importantly, after leaving the service of the Dauphin in Rhodes (headquarters of the knights of the Hospital of St John), he had gone on to Jerusalem in 1347, and there, by his own testimony, had conceived the idea of founding a new crusading order to replace all the older orders. It would be difficult to believe that he did not discuss this idea with the young Count of Tripoli after his arrival in the court of Cyprus later the same year, and Pierre's Order of the Sword may well have been the result of Mézières' ideas.[11]

Machaut implies that Pierre actually admitted some like-minded knights to his new order shortly after its foundation, but the failure of his first attempt to reach Europe and his subsequent imprisonment by his father must have placed the project to create an order of knights in abeyance for the next few years at least, and in all likelihood Pierre did not attempt to reestablish the Order of the Sword until after his father's death in 1359. Once he was securely on the throne, Pierre immediately recalled Philippe de Mézières and made him his Chancellor, and together with the Carmelite Pierre Thomas – a zealous proponent of the Levantine Crusade who in

---

[9] Ibid., p. 12, ll. 369–80.

[10] '. . . secretement/ sagement et meurement,/ sans trop parler, sans trop plaider,/ par quoy il s'en penst aidier;/ car il ne pooit autrement/ joir de son fait bonnement.' Ibid., p. 12, ll. 381–6.

[11] On the life and writings of Philippe de Mézières, see N. Jorga, *Philippe de Mézières 1327–1405. La croisade au XIVe siècle* (Paris, 1890); Abdel Hamid Hamdy, 'Philippe de Mézières and the New Order of the Passion', *Bulletin of the Faculty of Arts* (Alexandria University) 18 (1964), pp. 45–54. Mézières actually refers to the Order of the Sword – 'son gracieux ordre de l'espee', of which he was probably one of the first members – in his work *Chevalerie de la Passion* (Jorga, p. 82, n. 2).

May 1359 had been appointed Legate to the East by Pope Innocent VI – they set in motion the preparations necessary for a full-scale *Passagium Generale* to reconquer the Holy Places. Among these preparations must have been the formal restoration of the Order of the Sword, for on Pierre's seals and coins a sword replaced the sceptre borne by his predecessors, and the device of the order itself was depicted in association with the royal arms on his privy seal and on other monuments of his reign. A belt-buckle bearing the device of the Order, and presumably worn by one of its knights, has been found at Adalia on the coast of in Anatolia, which Pierre captured from the Turks during his first crusading expedition in August 1361, and held until his death.

Pierre and his two counsellors determined to launch their invasion of the Holy Land on 1 March 1364, and on 24 October 1362 set forth on a tour of the principal courts of western Europe whose primary object was to seek support for the great venture. On 29 March the three crusaders reached Avignon, and within a short time won the enthusiastic backing not only of the new Pope, Urban V – who on Good Friday (31 March) proclaimed a full-scale crusade – but of Jean 'the Good' of France, who agreed to take up the cross as the official leader of the crusade. After travelling for some months through Germany and France, Pierre arrived in London on 6 November, but was unable to pursuade Edward III to take part in the proposed *Passagium.* He returned home by way of Reims (where he attended the coronation of Charles V), Prague (where he stirred some interest in the Emperor Karl IV), Krakow (where both Kazimierz 'the Great' of Poland and his nephew Lajos 'the Great' of Hungary were won over to the idea of a Holy War), Vienna (where he enlisted the support of Duke Rudolf IV of Austria, whose brother and successor was to found a knightly order), and finally Venice, where he remained from 11 November 1364 until the end of the following June. In Venice he lodged with Federico Cornaro, who gave him 60,000 ducats for the projected crusade, and seems to have accepted membership in the Order of the Sword.[12]

Despite all this, no other prince joined the expedition finally launched by Pierre and his two counsellors in 1365. Their army was sufficient to capture Alexandria on 9 October of that year, but most of the 'crusaders' proved to be interested only in loot, and Pierre was reluctantly forced to withdraw within a few days. News of the capture of the richest city in Africa caused great excitement in the West, but in spite of this, and of further long journeys undertaken by Philippe de Mézières (to Castile and Aragon)[13] in 1366 and by Pierre himself (to Naples, Lombardy, and Greece) in 1368, no Christian prince could be pursuaded to join the King of Cyprus in another expedition.[14] Pierre himself led several successful attacks on the coast of Syria, in which the knights of the Sword may be presumed to have taken part, but there is reason to believe that even they did not live up to Pierre's high hopes for them, for it was in 1367 that Mézières started work on the first draught of the statutes of an altogether new form of military order, which he called the 'New Religion of the Knighthood of the Passion of Jesus Christ'.[15] In any case Pierre

---

[12] Van Den Bergen-Pantens, *Etude historique*, p. 606, citing K. Herquet, *Cyprische Königsgestalten des Hauses Lusignan* (Halle, 1881), p. 31.
[13] Hamdy, 'Philippe de Mézières', p. 51.
[14] Hill, *History*, pp. 355–9.
[15] See Hamdy, 'Philippe de Mézières'.

rapidly became disillusioned by the indifference of his fellow rulers to his dearest dreams, and conceived such a bitter hatred of his own barons (whose enthusiasm for the crusade seems to have been minimal) that his behaviour drove them to assassinate him on 17 January 1369. His young son Pierre was allowed to succeed him on the throne, but neither he nor any later king of Cyprus showed real interest in holy warfare, and all serious thoughts of reconquering the lost kingdom of Jerusalem were abandoned.

In these circumstances the Order of the Sword, which seems to have been conceived primarily as an instrument for the prosecution of the crusade, might very well have been suppressed, but it is clear that it was in fact maintained by all of Pierre's successors on the throne of Cyprus right down to extinction of the monarchy in 1489. Nothing is known of the order during the reign of the founder's son Pierre II (r. 1362–82), but we know the names of two knights (Simon de Sarrebrück and Antoine Thonis) who received the device of the Order from the founder's brother Jacques I (r. 1382–98); one (Nicola da Este, Marquis of Este) who received it in 1416 from Jacques's son Janus (r. 1398–1432); three (the Emperor Friedrich III in 1436, Friedrich von Hohenberg before 1449, and Hendrik t'Seraets before 1457) who certainly received it from Janus' son Jean II (r. 1432–58); and thirteen (all Netherlanders, Swiss, or Germans) who received it either from him or from one or another of the four sovereigns who succeeded him between 1458 and 1489, when the Venetian Republic persuaded the widow of Jean's son Jacques, Queen Catherine Cornaro (r. 1474–89), to resign her crown in favour of the Doge.[16]

Most of these names are known only from tomb monuments or other memorials on which the device of the Order is represented, often in association with the devices of several other knightly 'orders', but in a few cases the reception of the device was described in some form of narrative. In an account of the pilgrimage to Jerusalem undertaken by Ogier VIII d'Anglure in 1395–6, the latter recounted the circumstances in which his step-father, Simon de Sarrebrück, was admitted to the Order by Jacques I. On their arrival back in Nicosia on 4 January 1396, the members of Ogier's party were received by the king, who sent them food. A few days later, however, Simon fell ill with a fever, and by Sunday the 16th was very ill.

> And when the following Monday morning arrived, the King of Cyprus sent him his order by his knights, and he received the order and the knights very graciously and wisely, and asked the knights to recommend him to the king and to thank him for his order which he had sent him, and afterward thanked the knights for coming there . . .[17]

16 All but one of these names are given in Van Den Bergen-Pantens, *Etude historique*, but most of those she lists were first identified by C. Enlart in 'Deux souvenirs du royaume de Chypre au Musée britannique et au Musée du Cinquantenaire de Bruxelles', *Mém. de la Soc. Nat. des Antiquaires de France* 69 (1910), pp. 10–16; and Paul Ganz, 'Die Abzeichen der Ritterorden', *AHS* (1905, 1906), pp. 63–4. See also Schultz, *Deutsches Leben*, II, pp. 543–4, 548–9, figs. 556, 560, 561.
17 Ogier VIII, seigneur d'Anglure, *Le saint voyage de Jherusalem du seigneur d'Anglure*, ed. François Bonnardot, Auguste Longnon (Paris, 1878), pp. 84–7.

Nicola da Este recounted the bestowal of the collar of the Order upon himself and four fellow pilgrims by Janus in 1413 in similar terms,[18] and in 1480 the pilgrim Felix Faber described in the following terms the actions of the members of his company when they arived in Nicosia during the reign of Catherine Cornaro:

> But because the Kingdom of Cyprus still lacked a king, the nobles petitioned the lady queen to be received into the society of the Kings of Cyprus (*societatem Regum Cypri*). She summoned them to a large upper room, and when they were before her she proposed to them through an interpreter the oaths of that society, which were that they come to the defense of the Kingdom of Cyprus in its necessity, whether it was against Saracens, Turks, or Tartars. When they had given faith by hand to the queen, she gave them little swords (*gladiolos*) and permitted them to leave.[19]

From these three accounts it is clear that, by 1396 at the latest, and probably shortly after the death of the founder in 1369, the Order of the Sword was converted into a sort of pseudo-order, whose badge was conferred on noble pilgrims returning from Jerusalem, on their request, in return for a promise – no doubt recognized by both giver and receiver as wholly empty – to return to defend the kingdom should it be attacked by Muslims. It may also have been conferred by the Kings of Cyprus on other noble travellers whom they wished especially to honour.

It remains only to describe the forms taken by the device of the Order during the 142 years of its existence. As usual there are no surviving examples, and only one representation of the device dating from before 1450, but there are two descriptions dating from the founder's own reign. According to an act of 5 March 1363 by which Pierre granted certain privileges to the Genoese, the device depicted on the attached privy seal took the form of a '. . . sword unsheathed . . . to which is connected a line of letters in these words: *Pour loyoté mantenir . . .*'[20] This conforms very closely with the description given by Machaut in the chronicle cited above: 'He bore among all men a sword of fine silver, which had the pommel above . . . seated on a blue field . . . and it had around it in letters of gold . . . *C'est pour loiauté maintenir.*'[21] At Adalia, captured as we have seen by Pierre in 1361 and held by him and his son until 1373, there is a stone bearing his arms accompanied by what was certainly meant to be the badge of his order: a sword traversed by a phylactery or

---

[18] N. da Este, *Viaggio a Gerusalemme*, in *Miscellanea di opuscoli inediti o rari nei secoli XIV e XV*, Prose I (Turin, 1861), p. 138, declares that he was given 'la sua divisa della spada, con lo breve attorno che dice: Puor loauit maintenir . . . una collana d'oro lavorata, bellissima, e con un grosso zaffiro sopra alla divisa del rei'.

[19] Felix Faber, *Evagatorium in Terrae Sanctae, Arabiae, et Egypti Peregrinationem*, ed. Conrad Dietrich Hassler, *Bibliothek des literarischen Vereins in Stuttgart*, II–IV (Stuttgart, 1843–9), II, p. 42.

[20] '. . . ense evaginato . . . cui etiam est connexa una linea litterarum in hec verba: Pour l'onore (loyaoté) mantenir . . .' L. de Mas-Latrie, 'Notice sur les monnaies et les sceaux des rois de Chypre de la maison de Lusignan', *Bibl. de l'Ecole des Chartes*, 1st ser., 5 (1843–4), p. 423.

[21] Prise, p. 12, ll. 357–66.

7.1 Jan von Strollenburg, as
represented in the Arlberg *Wappenbuch*
(after Fox-Davies)

7.2 The collar of the Buckle
(after Leonhard)

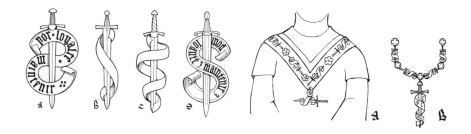

7.3 The badge of the Sword,
as represented
a. in the Grünenberg *Wappenbuch*
b. on the tapestry of Nicolas von Diesbach
c. on the stele of Nicolas von Diesbach
d. by Ganz (provenance unspecified)

7.4 The collar of the Sword,
as represented
a. in 1449   b. in 1480

scroll, whose legend is now illegible.[22] This is in fact the form normally taken by the device in representations dating from the second half of the fifteenth century, when nobles in the Germanic lands of the Empire who had completed a grand pilgrimage began to began to have it represented, along with the devices of the other 'orders' they had joined on their travels, on portraits, tomb-slabs, and stained-glass windows.[23] In all of these the motto *Pour loyauté maintenir* is represented in a narrow scroll twisted around the sword in the shape of an S or reverse S, but despite the statement by Felix Faber that this was meant to represent the word *Silence*, it is most unlikely that the form of the scroll had any significance whatever.[24] Most of the representations depict a single sword-and-scroll, and it is likely that the badge was at first always and later usually worn as a brooch, pinned to the breast of the surcoat. Nevertheless, the account of the pilgrimage of the Marquis of Este declares that he received a gold collar with a pendant saphire engraved with the Order's device,[25] and there are two representations of a collar supporting the device of the Order. The first, on the effigy of the German knight Friedrich von Hohenberg (d. 1449), depicts the collar as a band of leather or fabric about two inches wide, resting on the shoulders of the knight and terminating on his chest in a v-shaped juncture, from which the sword-and-scroll device, set horizontally rather than vertically, depends by two metal rings. The collar itself is decorated with small representations of the same device, pointing upwards, alternating with what appear to be roses.[26] In the second collar, painted around 1480 in a window in the Scharnachthal in Hilterfingen, the principal sword-and-scroll device is suspended by the pommel from a rose, which forms part of a collar proper made up of roses and lesser versions of the badge linked in alternation.[27] It may be that collars of this type were given by the kings of Cyprus to the more important pilgrims who sought entry into their 'order', but it is equally possible that there was no symbolic distinction between the two forms of the badge. Machaut assigned an elaborate allegorical significance to the sword device, but in all likelihood the sword was chosen as the badge of the Order for the obvious reason, and the motto was added to indicate that the Order was intended to promote loyalty to the crown of Cyprus as well as to promote an offensive crusade. (Figs. 7.3, 7.4.)

---

[22] F. W. Hasluck, 'Frankish Remains at Adalia', *Annual of the British School at Athens* 15 (1908–9), pp. 270–2, fig. 2.
[23] On the practice of accumulating the devices of pseudo-orders, see below, p. 483.
[24] Faber, *Evagatorium*; had this been the case, Machaut would certainly have mentioned it. The collar of the Sword has often been confused with the English collar of SS.
[25] See above, n. 18.
[26] Schultz, *Deutsches Leben*, fig. 556; Ganz, *Die Abzeichen*, p. 64, fig. 65a.
[27] Ganz, *Die Abzeichen*, p. 64, fig. 65b.

Chapter 8

The Order of the Collar
From 1518 Called
the Order of the Annunciation of Our Lady
Savoy, 1364?–Present

1 Historical Background

The grand tour of the courts of Europe undertaken by King Pierre I of Cyprus and his two counsellors between October 1362 and June 1365 undoubtedly exposed the various kings and princes through whose lands they passed to the newly revived Order of the Sword, and probably inspired the creation of several similar orders, not only by kings but by several princes of lesser rank. The first theoretically subordinate prince to create a monarchical order – Count Amé VI of Savoy – was in fact the only prince to answer Pierre's call to take part in a Crusade, and the order he founded in 1364, the *Ordre du Collier* or 'Order of the Collar', seems to have been created primarily to aid him on the crusade he finally launched in 1366. Amé had in fact founded a knightly society fourteen years earlier, but this society – called the 'Company of the Black Swan' – had been of a temporary nature, and had dissolved within a short time of its creation. Unlike that society, and most of the other orders we have just examined, the Order of the Collar was destined to survive as the sole or principal order of its founder's house throughout our period (and indeed until the present day). Like those of the Company of the Black Swan, however, the statutes of the Order of the Collar were much simpler than those of any of the earlier monarchical orders, and laid a much greater emphasis upon what we have called the fraternal relationships among its companions.

Amé[1] de Savoye, later known from his livery as the 'Green Count', had been born in 1334, and was thus a slightly younger contemporary of Pierre of Cyprus and the Black Prince, and a slightly older contemporary of Charles V of France, who as Dauphin was for some years his most dangerous rival. He was the only legitimate son of Aymon, Count of Savoy, Tarentaise, and Maurienne, and Duke of Chablais and Aosta in the largely Alpine kingdom of Burgundy, and lord of an extensive part of the neighbouring Piedmont district of the Kingdom of Italy. Since the authority

---

[1] 'Amé' was the contemporary Savoyard form of the Latin Amadeus, generally rendered into Modern French as Amédée, and into Italian as Amadeo.

of the Holy Roman Emperor as king of both of these kingdoms had long been nominal, the Counts of Savoy (as they were briefly called) had long been effectively sovereign princes in all of their dominions, and Aymon and his immediate predecessors had devoted much of their energy to welding their lands into a unified state.[2]

Amé had succeeded his father as lord of this princely state on 22 June 1342. He was then only nine years old, and the Savoyard dominions were accordingly governed by a council of regency until he was proclaimed of age on his fourteenth birthday, in January 1348. The seven years immediately following this formal accession to power were largely occupied by a bitter struggle against the French, who in the same year took possession of a neighbouring Burgundian principality, the Dauphiné of Viennois (sold to the future Charles V by the Dauphin Humbert), and whose expansionist policies posed a serious threat to the independence of Savoy. To counter the French pressure, Amé and his council decided to ally themselves with the Visconti rulers of the neighbouring Italian principality of Milan – two of whom, Galeazzo and Matteo, had been exiles in the Savoyard court until the summer of 1349. The pact concluded in that year between Savoy and Milan was strengthened in September of the following year by a marriage treaty, according to which Amé's sister Blanche was to marry Galeazzo Visconti.

The proposed marriage actually took place at Rivoli on 28 September 1350, and it seems to have been during the festivities that accompanied this event that Amé founded his first order of knighthood, the *Companie du Cigne Noir* or 'Company of the Black Swan'. Since Amé proclaimed this order only five months after the first great feast of the Order of the Garter, it is possible that he drew some inspiration from the latter event, but the order he established bore little resemblance to that of the King of England, and it is perhaps more likely that he drew his inspiration from the confraternal order of St Catherine, founded by his erstwhile neighbour the Dauphin Humbert about fifteen years earlier.

Our knowledge of the Company of the Black Swan is derived almost entirely from its statutes, of which a single copy has been preserved.[3] The statutes, setting forth the obligations of the *compangons* of the Company in eight short chapters, are followed in the manuscript by a list of the fourteen founders. The list includes the names of three *grans seignours*, whose rights and obligations are distinguished in the statutes from those of the members of lesser rank: Count Amé of Savoy himself, his cousin and former guardian Count Amé III of Genévois, and his brother-in-law Galeazzo Visconti, Lord of Milan. In addition the list includes the names of six men known to have been Savoyard officials, and three men who were members of prominent Savoyard families. Two of the men listed have not been identified, but they too were probably officers, vassals, or allies of the young Count of Savoy.[4]

The society of knights described in these statutes resembled that of the Garter only in that it was a military confraternity whose members wore a common badge,

---

[2] For the background and events of the founder's life I have relied primarily upon the recent biography by Eugene Cox, *The Green Count of Savoy* (Princeton, 1967).
[3] They were published by Luigi Cibrario in *Opuscoli* (Turin, 1841), pp. 75–77; and in Cox, op. cit., pp. 359–361.
[4] Cox, op. cit., pp. 361–362.

paid a fee to the society, evidently met once a year on a saint's day, and were bound to obey a set of corporate statutes. In all other respects the Company of the Black Swan could hardly have been more different. Where the emphasis of the Garter statutes was on ceremony and devotion, the Black Swan statutes concentrated on matters of a military nature. The 'Company' was in effect a society of brothers-in-arms or allies, bound to aid each other in military enterprises. The only requirement for entry was an ability to serve effectively as a knight without pay and whenever required. Presumably Amé was principally interested in having the companions serve him and his two allies in their struggle against the French in the Dauphiné, but in return for such service the three princes were to help the lesser companions in their private difficulties. Careful arrangements were made for the settlement of the inevitable disputes that might have disrupted the alliance and for the safe-keeping of its emergency funds. The statutes contain no reference to any permanent physical establishment, to annual festivities, to religious observances, or to services or memorials for the society's departed, and there is no indication that there was to be any presidential office, let alone one hereditary in the founder's family. Thus, despite its foundation by a prince, the Company of the Black Swan must be classed as a fraternal rather than a monarchical order.

Like most of the known fraternal orders, that of the Black Swan, created to meet an immediate military need, was probably never intended to be permanent, and in fact it seems to have disappeared from the scene within a few years of its creation. Perhaps the principal reason for its early dissolution was the movement of one of its three leaders, the Count of Genévois, into the camp of Amé's enemy the Dauphin Charles in the final months of 1350. Certainly Amé seems to have little use for his erstwhile allies after that time, and in the event it was he who came to the aid of Galeazzo Visconti, rather than the other way around.

Once he was fully in control of the affairs of his princely state, Amé quickly proved to be an extremely capable ruler, and his long reign is looked back upon as one of the most fortunate periods in the history of Savoy. Not only did he increase the extent of his principality through the annexation of territories in Burgundy and Italy, but he used both the aggressive foreign policy he conducted to win these territories, and the additional supplies of men and revenue they provided to him, to increase his authority within the state, and maintained internal peace throughout his reign by keeping possible rivals constantly occupied in his service.[5] He also assured the future independence of his princely state by securing from the Emperor a grant of immediate dependence upon the Empire itself rather than the Kingdom of Burgundy.

Like his contemporary the Black Prince, Amé seems also to have recognized from an early age the advantages to be derived from a reputation as a paragon of chivalry, and did all in his power to promote such an image. He was knighted on the field of battle in November 1352, and during the festivities that accompanied his nineteenth birthday celebration at Christmas of that year held a series of magnificent tournaments, for which he adopted a livery of solid green. Thereafter he frequently issued green clothing not only to his valets and pages but to his relatives and close companions, and from this practice came to be known as the 'Green Count'. At some point in the same period, he adopted as a badge a white

5 Cox, *Green Count*, pp. 340–9.

love-knot, identical in design to the knot that served as the principal device of the Neapolitan order of that name,[6] and the motto *fert*, which probably meant 'he bears'.[7] Thus splendidly clad in green and white, Amé in his mountain fastness practised courtly chivalry by holding sumptuous tournaments and banquets in the grand fashion set by such comtemporary monarchs as Edward of England and Jean of France, with whose courts he had frequent contact during the years between 1350 and 1363. Indeed, in 1355 he married Bonne Capet de Bourbon, the sister both of his western neighbour Duke Louis II of Bourbon and of Jeanne, wife of his southern neighbour the Dauphin Charles – who would succeed his father Jean on the throne of France in 1364. As a result of these connections Amé must have been reasonably familiar with the Company of the Star as well as with the Order of the Garter, and since his claims and ambitions in the Italian Piedmont were in direct conflict with those of Nicola Acciaiuoli, he probably knew something of the Company of the Knot as well.

Despite his chivalrous proclivities, the young Count of Savoy had not immediately responded to the papal proclamation of a general crusade against the Turks issued at the end of March 1363, and even when the King of Cyprus himself had visited his court at the beginning of June had given him only vague promises of assistance. Amé was occupied in this period with a war against his neighbour the Marquis of Saluzzo, however, and this undoubtedly prevented him from contemplating projects which would take him far from home. By the time Philippe de Mézières and Pierre Thomas arrived in Savoy around mid-December the political situation had changed, and Amé, no doubt moved by their impassioned advocacy as well as by more practical considerations, decided to take the vow of a crusader. By doing so, Amé probably hoped – for political as well as personal reasons – to share in the prestige already won in the cause of the True Faith by Pierre of Cyprus, as well as to increase his chance of salvation. In any case, he travelled to Avignon in January 1364, either to take up or to reaffirm his crusading vow in the presence of the Pope himself, and Pope Urban was sufficiently pleased with Amé's devotion to grant him the coveted prize of the Golden Rose, which was awarded each year to the individual or community judged most worthy.

2 The Foundation and Maintenance of the Order, 1364–1518

In all likelihood it was while he was in Avignon – and probably shortly after he received the Golden Rose – that Amé proclaimed his second order, that of the Collar.[8] Unfortunately, we cannot be sure of the precise date of this proclamation,

---

[6] Luigi Cibrario, *Descrizione storica degli Origini cavallereschi della Monarchia di Savoia* (Turin, 1846), pp. 5, 6.

[7] See Muratore, 'Les origines', 1910, p. 73. (Full reference in n. 8.)

[8] Since the Order of the Collar not only survived but grew steadily in prestige in the sixteenth and seventeenth centuries, it was of course known to all the early historians of knightly orders, and like the Garter and the Golden Fleece was considered worthy of extensive treatments by several writers. The early history of the Order was examined by François Capré, *Catalogue des Chevaliers de l'Ordre du Collier de Savoie dict de l'Annonciade*

for the earliest statutes of the Order (if they were ever written down) were lost by the time of the founder's grandson, Count Amé VIII, and the earliest chronicle which even mentions the Order's foundation, written more than fifty years after the event, gives no clear indication of the time. There is in fact only one unequivocal reference to the Order as such in the surviving documents written before the day of the founder's death in 1383, but there are several references to what must certainly be the badge of the Order in the financial records of the founder's household. The first of these – a statement to the effect that 362 florins had been paid in January 1364 to Italian jewellers in Avignon for '. . . fifteen collars in silver gilt made with the device of the Lord'[9] – suggests that the Order was founded at that time. The fact that all fifteen of the original companions joined or intended to join Amé on the expedition he undertook in 1366–7 in fulfilment of his crusading vow, and that no other interest bound all fifteen of them either to Amé or to one another, also supports the hypothesis that the Order was created at the same time as Amé solemnly announced his intention to take part in the *Passagium Generale* proclaimed by the Pope.

Amé had originally intended to join forces with Pierre of Cyprus in his attack on Egypt and Syria, but by the time he had arranged his affairs the Pope had been persuaded by another eastern monarch, the Greek Emperor of Constantinople Ioannes V, to direct the efforts of the western crusaders to help his embattled Empire drive back the Ottoman Turks, who had recently invaded Thrace, and now posed a threat to all of eastern Europe. Since Ioannes was the son of Amé's aunt Jeanne de Savoye, and therefore his first cousin, Amé had no objection to diverting his forces to the assistance of the schismatic Emperor, and in August 1366 retook Gallipoli on the Dardanelles.[10] During the siege of this city, two of the men later

---

(Turin, 1654); Vittorio Amadeo Cigna-Santi, *Dell'Ordine Supremo di Savoia, detto prima del Collare indi della Santissima Annunziata. Memorie istoriche.* (Turin, Biblioteca Reale, Manoscritti di Storia Patria, no. 759, [1784]); conte Luigi Cibrario, *Statuts et Ordonnances du très-noble Ordre de l'Annonciade, précédés d'une notice historique du même Ordre et suivies du catalogue des Chevaliers* (Turin, 1840); and barone Gaudenzio Claretta, *Statuti antichi inediti e statuti recenti dell'Ordine Supremo della SS. Annunziata con notizie storiche relative al medesimo* (Turin, 1881). The first really critical study of its orgins was made by Dino Muratore, 'Les origines de l'Ordre du Collier de Savoie, dit de l'Annonciade', *AHS* 23 (1909), pp. 5–12, 59–66; 24 (1910), pp. 8–16, 72–88, 372–373. The early history of the Order is briefly examined in Francesco Cognasso, *Il Conte Verde* (Turin, 1926), and in Cox, *Green Count*, pp. 180–5, 372–3. Favyn, *Théâtre*, arbitrarily dated its foundation to 1355, and this date was cited by several later authors on his authority. According to Muratore (p. 10), Capré, *Catalogue*, misinterpreting a statement in the fifteenth-century *Chronica di Saluzzo*, placed the foundation of the Order in 1362, and that date was accepted by most later authors until Muratore himself demonstrated that 1364 is the most likely date.

9 'Item [libravit] pro quindecim colariis argenti deaurati factis ad devisam Domini IIc IIIxx II florenos boni ponderis.' Turin, Archivio di Stato, 3rd section. Comptes de l'Hôtel du Comte de Savoie, rouleau 64, Account of Antoine Mayllet (19 Mar. 1361–6 Feb. 1365), f. xxxviii. Published in Muratore, 'Les origines', p. 64.

10 For an account of Amé's eastern expedition, see Deno Geanakoplos, 'Byzantium and the Crusades', *A History of the Crusades*, ed. Kenneth Setton, III (Madison, 1975), pp. 74–78.

listed among the founding members of his order – Roland de Veissy and Simon de Saint-Amour – fell in action, and the accounts of the expedition list among the expenses of the funerals provided for these knights outlays for several shields 'with the device of the collar', and for torches paid 'for the debt of the Order of the Collar'.[11]

The only other reference to the Order in a document contemporary with its founder's lifetime is to be found in his will, composed on the very day of his death, 27 February 1383.[12] Therein provision was made in the following terms for the foundation of a Carthusian monastery at the comital castle of Pierre-Châtel in Bugey:

> Amé . . . to the praise of the Lord Jesus Christ, of the Father, the Son and the Holy Spirit, and of His glorious Mother the Blessed Virgin Mary, of the saints of God, and of the whole celestial court, that they may be the propitiators of his sins, wishes, disposes, and ordains that in his castle of Pierre-Châtel there shall be made, constructed, and built a venerable *coenobium* or monastery, under the name and to the honour of the Blessed Virgin Mary, of hermit brothers of the Carthusian Order, in which there are to be and shall be ordained and must remain perpetually fifteen Carthusian brothers (in honour of the fifteen joys of the inviolate Virgin Mary), who shall be bound to celebrate in that place each day solemn masses and other divine offices for the aid of his soul and those of his predecessors, and also for the aid of the souls of the other lords and knights who have been, are, and come in the future to be of the Order of the Collar . . .

According to an item in the accounts of the comital treasury, a specially made collar was actually offered up, just as the later statutes require, during the founder's funeral at Hautecombe a few days later.[13]

The earliest description of the Order's foundation, initial membership, and constitution is that contained in the *Chronique de Savoie* of Jean 'Cabaret' d'Oronville, written at the command of Amé VIII between 1417 and 1419.[14] After describing the crimes of the Marquis of Saluzzo and the anger of the Green Count, Cabaret declared that Amé summoned numerous knights from all over his principality to his court.

[11] 'Libravit pro precio octo torchiorum cere oblate de mandato Domini ad sepulturam dictorum dominorum Sancti Amoris et Rolandi de Vaissi ultra predicta, pro debito Ordinis Colaris v florenos.' Account of Antonio Barberi for the voyage of Amé to the East, formerly in the Archives of the Court. Published in Cibrario, *Statuts et Ordonnances*, p. xv, and in Arnaud Chaffanjon, *Les grands ordres de chevalrie* (Paris, 1969), p. 213.

[12] Published in Claretta, *Statuti antichi*, pp. 14–15.

[13] 'Item, a mestre Pierre le dorier, pour l'argent, faczon et doreure des lacs et devise du collar de Monseigneur que l'on l'offrit a la sepulture Monseigneur, cuy Diex absolut, et lequel lacz estoit hostez par les gens de l'arcevesque de Tharentayse, qui en avoit pourté le dit collar, III sol. gr. tur.' Comptes Trésor Savoie, vol. 35e, f. 94v. Quoted in Muratore, 'Les origines', 1910, p. 79.

[14] Muratore ('Les origines', 1909, p. 7 n. 1) announced his intention of publishing an edition of this chronicle, preserved in several manuscripts, but according to Cox (*Green Count*, p. 353) it was still unpublished in 1967.

When they were assembled, the Count chose fourteen knights, and he himself was the fifteenth. He made an order of a collar, as of a hound, on which there were written in gold letters above *fert, fert, fert*, and at the ring of the collar there were nine knots together, one fairly close to the other. And he gave to each of the fourteen knights his own, and he himself had one. And they were fifteen in number in honour of the fifteen joys of Our Lady. And the Count had founded a monastery of Carthusians to pray to God for the salvation of the fifteen knights who bore this collar. He willed also that when one of the fifteen died, another would be put in his place. Of whom the first knight of this order was the Count Amé de Savoie ...[15]

Unfortunately, the only other chronicle to describe the foundation of the Order of the Collar at any length, that of Jean Servion,[16] was composed nearly fifty years later still, in 1464–5, and although the account it contains is considerably more detailed than that of Cabaret, the additions it makes to Cabaret's text (in general Servion's principal source for the fourteenth century) are of very dubious authority.

Almost nothing is known about the Order during the brief reign of the founder's son and successor Amé VII, known from his livery as the 'Red Count', (r. 1383–91), or during the first eighteen years of the very long reign of the latter's son Amé VIII (r. 1391–1434), who succeeded his father at the age of eight and was elevated to the status of Duke of Savoy in 1416. In the year 1409, however, Amé VIII, unable to discover a single copy of the original statutes, decided to prepare a new set of statutes for the Order, apparently based as closely as possible on those established by his grandfather. Happily for us, the original of this new constitution, sealed at Châtillon-en-Dombes on 30 May 1409, is still preserved in Turin, and contains in its prologue a brief summary of the Order's history down to that time.

We, Amé, Count of Savoy, Duke of Chablais and Aosta, Marquis in Italy, and Count of Geneva, make known to all to whom these presents shall come, that in as much as Messire Amé our grandfather of most noble memory, the high and puissant prince who died in Apulia, had to the honour of God, of the Glorious Virgin Mary, of her fifteen joys, of the saints of paradise, and of all the celestial court, established an order of the Collar in the fashion of knots (*lacz*) hanging from a collar, of which he and his successors were lords and chiefs, he being the fifteenth of the knights who wore the order; and for the constitution of the said order he had made certain constitutions and certain ordinances which they had to observe as long as they lived; of which statutes, after the death of all of these men, a complete memory does not at

---

[15] Original in French. Muratore, 'Les origines', 1909, p. 7.
[16] *Gestez et chroniques de la Mayson de Savoye par Jehan Servion*, ed. F. E. Bollati (Turin, 1879), pp. 113–116. The text of the passage in question is also given in Muratore, 'Les origines', 1909, p. 65. Several other fifteenth-century chronicles mention the foundation of the Order, but they add nothing to the information contained in Cabaret's account, which was probably their principal source.

present exist, and which have through defect of writing been allowed to fall into neglect.

And afterward our same ancestor founded a church of the Carthusian Order at Pierre-Châtel in the diocese of Belley, in which there were to be fifteen Carthusian chaplains who were to say fifteen masses every day.

The which order our said ancestor, and after him the high and puissant prince our father, maintained, observing the rules, and we also, after their deaths, up to this day.

For this reason we, the aforesaid count, with the counsel of our most dear and beloved uncle Messire Louis de Savoye, Prince of the Morea, and of our most dear and beloved cousins and vassals Messire Odde de Villars, Lord of Baux, Messire Humbert de Villars-Seissel, Lord of Saint-Hippolite and Orbe, and of our well-beloved and faithful councillors Messire Jean de la Baume, Lord of Valussin, Messire Boniface de Chalant, Marshal of Savoy, and Messire Anthoine, Lord of Grolée, wishing the contents of the rule to be fully observed and kept in times to come, have had it adapted for perpetual remembrance, establishing and ordaining all the rules which are contained in the said order, which we wish to be held and observed in times to come in the following fashion . . .[17]

This prologue implies that the Order had been maintained under its original statutes throughout the period since its foundation, and that the new statutes assigned to it below were substantially the same as those given to it by its founder. If this is true – and there is no particular reason to doubt it – it would explain why so little was recorded about the Order's activities before 1409, for the corporate activities prescribed in the new statutes were minimal, and of a sort that was not likely to attract the attention of a chronicler or to require expenditures from the comital/ducal treasury. Since these statutes seem to have remained in effect without amendment or addition until shortly before the abdication of Amé VIII from the dukeship of Savoy in 1434, it cannot be surprising that we know virtually nothing about the Order in his reign beyond the names of most of those elected to membership. On 13 February 1434, Duke Amé (who immediately following his abdication retired to a hermitage with a small group of companions whom he united with himself in a short-lived 'order' taking its name from the patron saint of Savoy)[18] added five

---

[17] Turin, Archivio di Stato, Ordini militari; Ordine della Santissima Annunziata: Mazzo I.N.4. The text of this manuscript was published by Cibrario in a Modern Italian translation in *Descrizione storica degli Ordini Cavellereschi della Monarchia di Savoia* 2 vols. (Turin, 1846), I, pp. 7–12. A transcription of the original Middle French text was published by A. Todaro della Galia, *Collezione degli Statuti Ordinanze ed Editti Editi ed Inediti del Nobilissimo Ordine Supremo della SS. Annunziata* (Palermo, 1907; 150 copies), pp. 11–15. I am currently preparing a critical edition.

[18] On the 'Order' of St Maurice, founded by Duke Amé at Ripaille in 1434 and dissolved shortly after his election to the throne of St Peter as Pope Felix V in 1439, see Marie José [de Belgique, Queen of Italy], *La Maison de Savoie. Amédée VIII, Le duc qui devint Pape* (Paris, 1962), II, pp. 101–136. The statutes of this 'order' (in reality a small confraternity of hermits) have been lost. The 'order' was revived as a monarchical order by his descendant Duke Emmanuel Philibert in 1572, and immediately annexed the remaining members and property of the old crusading Order of St Lazarus in Italy.

further *chapistres* to the original set of fifteen, but none of the new statutes altered the nature of the Order in any significant way, or required any further corporate activities. After 1434, the Order of the Collar was maintained under the same statutes and under its original name until 11 September 1518, when Duke Charles III (r. 1504–1553), great-grandson of Amé VIII and eleventh Chief of the Order in succession to its founder Amé VI, reorganized the Order completely on the model of the Burgundian Order of the Golden Fleece, and renamed it after the first of Mary's fifteen joys. Only then did the knights of the Collar begin to assemble in annual meetings in the fashion common to most earlier orders, and only then did their activities become worthy of note.

3 The Statutes of the Order

All of the later sources agree that Amé VI assigned statutes to the Order of the Collar at the time he proclaimed its foundation. If, as it appears, the Order was founded specifically to help him fulfil his recent vow to undertake a Crusade, its original ordinances must have been composed in the month or so immediately preceding the proclamation in January 1364. All we know for certain about the original statutes is that they required the Count to provide a solemn funeral for deceased companions, since the accounts of the eastern expedition declare that various items were provided at the funerals of the two knights who fell at Gallipoli 'for the debt of the Collar'. The prologue to the statutes of 1409 implies that the primitive statutes were never written down, and if this is true it can only have been because their requirements were simple enough to be committed to memory.

Though brief compared to those of most of the earlier monarchical orders, the statutes established by Amé VIII in 1409 are rather too complex to have been carried in the memory of an individual knight, but many of their more precise ordinances could well be codified versions of customs which developed in the interval between the foundation of the Order and the year in which the new statutes were promulgated, and there is no particular reason to doubt that the remainder bear a fairly close resemblance to the primitive statutes, as the prologue seems to imply. In any case they are the earliest of which we have any certain knowledge. They consist of forty-two ordinances organized into fifteen *chapistres*, most of which include precisely three ordinances. The chapters themselves are arranged by subject into four unequal groups. The first of these, consisting of chapters 1 though 4, deals with the obligations of the members of the Order towards one another during their lifetime. Chapters 5 and 6 make up a second group, dealing with the settlement of disputes among the companions, while chapters 7 through 14 constitute a third group concerned with matters arising from the death of one of the companions, including the provision of purgatorial masses, obsequies, and a permanent memorial, and the election and admission of his successor. Finally, the fifteenth chapter contains the solemn oaths of the Count and the five knights of the Order named in the prologue, for themselves and their heirs and successors, to observe the ordinances precisely and without fail.

The text of the five statutes added by Amé VIII on 13 January 1434 has been preserved in a fifteenth-century copy, now bound with a copy of the statutes of

1518 in a book preserved in Turin.[19] Each of the first three additional chapters sets forth one additional observance required of the companions following the death of one of their number. The fourth contains three ordinances establishing moral conditions for admission and continued membership in the Order, and threatening with expulsion any erring companion who failed to resign, while the fifth and last chapter requires the companions thenceforth to wear their collar at all times, and forbids them to accept membership in another princely order.

From 1434 until just before the end of the period with which we are concerned in this study, the Order of the Collar seems to have been governed by the twenty chapters just summarized, without any further additions or deletions. In 1518, however, these statutes were wholly replaced by a new and much more elaborate set, promulgated by Duke Charles III (r. 1504–53). In the prologue to these statutes, Charles declared that he had decided to alter the traditional name, device, and form of the Order out of the 'great love and singular devotion' he felt for the 'glorious Virgin Mary' and her 'joyous Annunciation', but it would appear that Charles – whose father, Duke Philippe I, had inherited through his mother Anne 'de Lusignan' a claim to the phantom thrones of Cyprus, Jerusalem, and Armenia – was also moved by a desire to make the usages of his Order conform more closely to those of the three great royal orders which then survived: the Garter of England, St Michael of France, and the Golden Fleece of the Netherlands, the Spains, and the Sicilies. In any case, the new statutes he assigned to the renamed Order of the Annunciation were not merely based upon, but for the most part copied word-for-word from those of the Golden Fleece, and differed from the latter only in the arrangement of the individual ordinances and chapters, and in the details of the ordinances concerned with such matters as the number of companions, the form of the collar and habit, the time and place of the annual assembly, and the titles given to the officers who were thenceforth to serve the Order.[20]

4 The Name, Title, and Badge of the Order

Like the Order of the Band before it, but unlike most of the other monarchical orders founded in the third quarter of the fourteenth century, the society of knights founded by Amé VI in 1364 bore the simple title 'order', and until the revolution effected by Charles III in 1518 invariably took its name from its badge rather than its patron. It appears that in the fifteenth century, when most orders had a badge in the form of a collar and the term *ordre de collier* had become a sort of generic term for the orders maintained by princes, the Savoyard order was commonly known as the *Ordre du Collier de Savoye*, but this designation was not employed in official

---

[19] Archivio di Stato, Ordine militari; Ordine della SS. Annunziata: mazzo I, n. 4. Published in Della Galia, *Collezione*, pp. 16–17.

[20] A manuscript of these statutes, possibly the original, has been preserved in Turin, Archivio di Stato, Ordini militari; Ordine della SS. Annunziata, mazzo I, n. 5. They have been published in Claretta, *Statuti antichi*, pp. 47–66, and Della Galia, *Collezione*, pp. 19ff.

documents. The official name of the Order after 1518 was *Ordre de l'Annúnciation Notre Dame*, or 'Order of the Annunciation of Our Lady', but it soon came to be referred to as the *Annonciade* or (in Italian) *Annunziata*, which literally translated means the 'annunciated one' or 'she who received the Annunciation'.

The original badge of the Order is described in the prologue to the statutes of 1409 simply as a 'device of knots hanging from a collar' (*devise a lacz au pendant d'ung collier*), and in Cabaret's chronicle as 'a collar as of a hound' (*ung colier comme d'ung levrier*) with nine knots close together (*neuf lasses ensemble*) at its ring. Not a single example of a collar of the Order antedating the reforms of 1518 now survives, but two early collars (one attributed to the founder himself) were still preserved in the Abbey of Hautecombe in 1782, and the historian Cigna-Santi has left us not only descriptions but drawings of both of them.[21] In addition, two representations of the collar dating from the fourteenth-century and eight dating from the fifteenth century have been preserved,[22] and on the basis of these and the descriptions of collars contained in inventories of the treasure of Lausanne Cathedral made in 1441 and 1535, we can arrive at quite a clear picture of the various forms assumed by the badge of the Order in our period. (Figs. 8.1, 8.2.)

As the figures indicate, the collar proper normally took the form of an oblong band of metal or fabric two or three inches wide and about twenty inches long, which was bent into a roughly circular shape so that it could be worn around the neck like the collar of a dog. It seems generally to have had some sort of clasp to close it at the back of the neck, but was often open at the front as well (or instead), where a set of links were set which served both to hold it together and to support the pendant knots. The collar thus formed was sometimes quite plain, and sometimes decorated with a row of one or more of the comital/ducal *devises*: the love-knot, the rose, and the word *fert*. The collar worn by the Bastard Humbert in his effigy of 1443, however, bears instead his personal *devise*, the Arabic word *Alahac*. By the mid-fifteenth century, at the latest, the collar sometimes took quite a different form, being made up of a series of links in the form of pods very similar to those that formed the collar of the French pseudo-order of the Broom-Pod,[23] or of leaves very similar to those of the Navarrese pseudo-order of the Chestnut Leaf, established by 1393.[24] The form of the pendant that hung from the collar onto the breast of the wearer seems to have varied considerably less, for in all of the surviving representations it consists of a metal wire about three eighths of an inch thick, which has been twisted into three love-knots set about half an inch apart, and then bent into a circle about two inches in diameter, and suspended by an

[21] For this and what follows, see Muratore, 'Les origines', 1910, pp. 72–81.

[22] Six of these are in Muratore, but additional examples are given in 'A propos du Collier de l'Annonciade' *AHS* (1911), pp. 45–6; and F. T. Dubois, 'Les chevaliers de l'Annonciade du pays de Vaud' *AHS* (1911), p. 134.

[23] See below, p. 428.

[24] See Marcel Baudot, 'Charles le Noble "roi de Cherbourg" (1387–1404) et les relations navarro-normandes de 1387 à 1430 d'après les comptes du Trésor de Navarre', *Bulletin philologique et historique*, 1969 (1972), pp. 197, 212, nos. 32, 33. A representation of what is surely the collar of this order is depicted in association with the armorial achievement of King Juan II of Navarre (r. 1425–1470), in a missal dated 1427, now preserved in New York, Morgan Library ms. 146 (f. 7).

8.1 The Collar of Savoy, a. as represented in the charter of 1382
b. as represented in the MS. of the statutes of 1409
c. reputed to be that of the founder (after Cigna-Santi)
d. surviving from the 15th century (after Cigna-Santi)

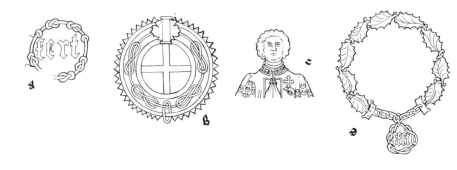

8.2 The Collar of Savoy, as represented
a. on a charter of 1399 (after Muratore)
b. in the cathedral of Chieri (after Muratore)
c. on the effigy of Humbert, Bastard of Savoy, c.1443 (after Muratore)
d. in an MS. of the chronicle of Servion, c.1465

ovoid link from the centre point of the collar in such a way that one knot falls at the bottom. By 1472, this pendant was sometimes worn suspended, like the pendants of the Golden Fleece and St Michael of France in the same period, from a simple chain.[25] In most cases both the collar and the pendant were made of silver gilt, and while the pendant was generally unadorned, the collar was often enamelled. The collar attributed to the founder is said to have been enamelled in red, and those made of leaves in green.

The collar-badge just described is of particular interest for two reasons. In the first place, it seems to have been the earliest badge of an order of knighthood to incorporate a pre-existing livery-badge (the love-knot) and verbal *devise* (the word *fert*), thus underlining the close association between membership in the Order and clientship to its founder. In addition it is the earliest known example of a form of badge that was to become very popular in the last decade of the fourteenth century, and was to become normal in princely orders of all types by the middle of the following century: the collar with pendant device. Unlike the collars of such later orders as the Golden Fleece, however, the original collar of the Savoyard order was not actually made up of lesser badges, and the plain collar was itself as much a part of the badge of the Order as the knots pendant from it. In fact the original collar was strikingly similar in its form and the manner in which it was worn both to the Castilian band and to the English garter, and was probably inspired by one or both of these badges. Like the earlier badges, it was at once visible and distinctive (especially before the wearing of collars became fashionable), and probably had no particular symbolic value. The love-knots dependent from it, on the other hand, probably represented the indissoluble bonds of fraternal love, just as the identical knot of the Sicilian order had done until two years before the proclamation of the society here in question.

The relatively simple collar just described was replaced in 1518 with a much more elaborate one modelled on that of the French Order of St Michael. The collar proper was thenceforth composed of links in which a love knot was interlaced with the letters of the word *fert*, and a small image of the Annunciation was set in the middle of the pendant. This is the form of the collar still in use.

5 The Patron of the Order

The chroniclers and Count Amé VIII agree that the Order was from the beginning dedicated, like the French Order of the Star, to the Blessed Virgin, and several aspects of its format seem to have been instituted in honour of her 'fifteen joys' – a set of mysteries associated with the Rosary, which at the time of the Order's foundation was just beginning to gain in popularity as a form of lay devotion. The fifteen knights, the fifteen priests charged with the celebration each day of fifteen masses, and even the fifteen original statutes of the Order certainly appear to reflect in their number a desire to represent the fifteen mysteries in as many ways as possible. The Order's chapel was also dedicated in the usual way to the Order's

---

[25] It is so represented in the portraits of Claude de Seyssel and Amé IX cited by Muratore, 'Les origines', p. 81.

patroness, and it is possible that a banner bearing an image of the Virgin within a nimbus of stars was regularly borne before the knights in battle. Such a banner – remarkably reminiscent of the banner of the Order of the Star – was certainly borne during the crusade of 1366.[26]

6 The Membership of the Order

Throughout the period with which we are concerned, the Order of the Collar ideally included precisely fifteen knights, including a president who from 1409 at least bore the title *Seigneur et Chef* or 'Lord and Chief'. The prologue to the statutes of 1409 declares that the founder 'and his successors' had occupied the chiefly office, but leaves implicit the attachment of the office to that of Count of Savoy or to the status of ruler of the princely state that title had come to indicate. Only in the statutes of 1518 was the chiefship formally declared to descend with the dukeship of Savoy.[27] The constitution of Amé VIII nevertheless gave considerable authority within the Order to its hereditary Chief. Not only was he to summon the other companions to the Order's irregular meetings, but he alone, with the advice (but not necessarily the consent) of the other companions, was to appoint new members, and to act as judge in cases of internal dispute. It would appear, from the action of Amé VIII in 1434, that the Chief also retained the right to clarify and amend the statutes of the Order, though nothing explicit is said on that subject.

In addition to the Chief, the Order of the Collar included fourteen ordinary members, often called *chevalliers* in the statutes, but more formally designated *freres et compaignons*. According to chapter 12 of the statutes, a candidate for appointment to a companionship had to be a *bon, vaillant, et prodome chevallier*. Chapter 20, added in 1434, further declared that no knight was to be admitted who was 'infamous for any reproach of honour'. Except for omitting any reference to noble birth (which was probably taken for granted) the qualifications were identical in essence to those required for election to the Garter. The statutes say very little about the processes to be followed for electing and inducting new companions, stating only that after the obsequies of a deceased companion had been performed, the Chief was to summon to his side those companions who were within easy reach of the chapel to advise him, and that the companion-elect was to swear to obey the statutes and to seal what was presumably the master copy with his seal.[28] No provision was made until 1434 for either the withdrawal or the expulsion of a companion from the Order once he had been admitted, but in that year Amé VIII (probably inspired by a requirement of the recently-created Order of the Golden Fleece) specified in chapter 19 that companions who committed dishonourable acts were to resign or face public expulsion. Otherwise membership in the Order was clearly intended to end only with death. Nothing was said in the statutes about membership in other orders until 1434, but in that year the fifth of

[26] Cox, *Green Count*, p. 212.
[27] Ch. 1.
[28] Ch. 12a,b,c.

the new chapters adopted declared that no companion of the Order was either to 'take or accept any other *ordre de colier.*'

Amé's decision to restrict the number of knights in his Order to fifteen – a definite and very small number – was probably inspired by the practice of the Order of the Garter, since all the other orders then existing had either a much higher limit or no limit at all. The specific number fifteen may well have been chosen for the devotional reason given, but it is interesting that it was only one greater than the number of the initial (and probably final) membership in the abortive order of the Black Swan. It was also the smallest number to which any medieval monarchical order was ever limited, and could reflect the relative smallness of the Savoyard dominions, or the comparatively low status of their ruler, a mere duke. If the proportion of knights in the population of the Savoyard dominions was comparable to that of the neighbouring kingdom of France, there were probably no more than 150 in the whole state, so the Order may well have included more than one out of every ten. The number of companions remained limited to fifteen until 1518, when Charles III added five more, in honour of the five wounds of Christ.[29] Since that time the number has never again been increased, but the Chief and his heir were eventually excluded from the count.

No official list of companions seems to have been kept during our period, and as none of the chalices or vestments meant to serve as 'perpetual memorials' to the companions long survived, the historians of the Order have been obliged to piece together a list of members on the basis of other forms of evidence, inevitably less satisfactory. The names of the fourteen original companions are known only from the later chronicles of Cabaret, Della Chiesa, and Servion, and the references to the Order in the accounts of the founder's Crusade cited above. On the basis of these sources, Muratore was able to reconstruct what may be regarded as a definitive list.[30] Four of those in his list – Amé III de Genève, Count of Genévois, Aymon de Genève-Anthon, Lord of Anthon, Antoine de Vienne-Beaujeu, Lord of Beaujeu, and Guillaume de Grandson-Saint-Croix, Lord of Saint-Croix – were close cousins of the founder, and a fifth – Hugues 'de Chalon'-Arlay, Lord of Arlay – was related to him by marriage. All five were members of important baronial families of the northern region of the Kingdom of Burgundy. Five of the others – Aymon Bonivard, Guillaume de Chalamont, Berlion de Foras, Etienne de la Baume, and Gaspard de Montmayeur – were both vassals and important officers of the Count of Savoy, and Richard Musard, an Englishman known as the 'Black Squire', was his constant companion and bodyguard. The twelfth companion, François 'Chivard' de Monthoux, a vassal of the Count of Genévois, had served with the Green Count as early as 1351. The last two companions, Roland de Veissy and Jean de Vienne, were French subjects who had served primarily in the armies of their king, but like all of the other companions except Amé of Genévois (who was probably ill and soon afterwards died) and Antoine of Beaujeu (who was engaged in the defense of his barony) they participated with the Green Count in the Crusade which he led in 1366–7. It appears, indeed, that by 1366 the Lord of Beaujeu had been replaced in the roll of the Order's membership by Simon de Saint-Amour, who died on the crusade as we have seen, but both Beaujeu and the Count of

---

[29] Statutes of 1518, Ch. 1a.
[30] 'Les origines', 1910, pp. 11–16.

Genévois sent replacements for the enterprise.[31] Certainly an intention to go on the crusade was shared by all the original companions, and although most were also Amé's cousins or retainers, the crusade was the only thing in which all fifteen were associated.

Only a partial list of the companions named to the Order of the Collar between 1364 and 1518 has been reconstructed by the historians of the Order, on the basis of official documents (such as the statutes of 1408, 1434, and 1518) witnessed by knights of the Order, an obituary roll kept at one time in the Order's chapel in Pierre-Châtel, tomb monuments, portraits, and other similar sources.[32] Of the new companions appointed during the four and a half decades between the foundation and the adoption of the first written statutes in 1409, the names of only twelve are now known, and for the seven decades between 1364 and the abdication of Amé VIII in 1434 the list includes only thirty-five names. For a similar period in the history of the Order of the Garter, the names of over one hundred companions are recorded, and as the Order of the Collar was supposed to have three fifths the membership of the English order, one would have expected a list of over sixty names. Thus, if the number of companions was normally maintained at or close to the statutory figure of fifteen, as many as half the companions named to the Order in this period may be unknown. On the other hand, it is quite possible that the number of companions was frequently allowed to fall well below the level required by the statutes (as seems to have been the case in 1568–9, when Duke Emmanuel Philibert admitted thirteen new companions in a period of eight months), so it is impossible even to estimate how many names are missing from the list.

Because of the nature of the evidence, nothing is known of the precise time or circumstances in which any of the known companions was admitted to the Order before the death of Duke Charles III in 1553, when an official list began finally to be maintained. All that can be said with certainty is that the known companions continued to be drawn exclusively from the ranks of the upper and middle nobility of Savoy and neighbouring regions, and that their number continued to include members of the comital/ducal family and important officers of the Savoyard dominions. Of the ninety-one companions known or supposed to have been admitted to the Order before the death of Duke Charles III (excluding three Counts of Savoy not known to have been appointed before becoming Chief), fourteen were members of the House of Savoy, five were the lords of neighbouring principalities (Genévois, Beaujeu, Saluzzo, and Gruyères), eighteen were Savoyard barons of the rank of count or higher (including three counts of Montrevel, and five of Challant), nine were Marshals of Savoy, and twenty-seven held some other

---

[31] Ibid., pp. 184–185, 208.

[32] Such a list has appeared in F. Capré, *Catalogue des chevaliers du Collier de Savoie dit de l'Annonciade* (Turin, 1654); *Les noms, qualités, armes et blasons des illustres chevaliers de l'Ordre de Savoie dit de l'Annonciade* (Paris, 1657); V. A. Cigna-Santi, *Serie cronologica dei Cavalieri dell'Ordine Supremo di Savoia detto prima del Collare, indi della SS. Nunziata* (Turin, 1786); Cibrario, *Statuts* (1840), pp. 139ff.; G. S. Chianale, G. B. Nicolini, *Serie dei cavalieri e ufficiali dell'Ordine Supremo della SS. Annunziata del MCCCLXVII ai nostri tempi* (Turin, 1842); and Della Galia, *Collezione* (1907), pp. 135ff. These lists all omit from the enumeration of the companions the Chiefs of the Order who succeeded before they are known to have been appointed.

high office in the central or regional government of the Savoyard state. Many fell into two or more of these categories, and only twenty-five fell into none of them. Of the latter, a few were foreign noblemen of middle rank like the founder-knight Jean de Vienne, but the great majority were Savoyard barons or members of baronial houses. Indeed, sixty-three of the companions (including thirteen of those who fit into none of the first five categories) belonged to princely or baronial families that provided two or more members to the Order in this period, and these companions belonged to only sixteen distinct houses, including that of Savoy. One of these houses (Challant) provided eight members, one (Genève) provided six, three (La Baume, Villars, and La Palù) provided four each, and three (La Chambre, Saluzzo, and Montmayeur) provided three each.

It is significant that almost every known member belonged to a family whose lands lay either within the borders of the Savoyard state or in one or another of the principalities that bordered upon it. Unlike the Orders of the Garter and the Golden Fleece, whose presidents were princes of the first rank, the Order of the Collar remained a strictly regional institution throughout our period, and indeed for some time afterward. Not until the Duke of Savoy became the *de facto* King of Sicily in 1713 did the Order begin to admit significant numbers of distinguished foreigners (mostly Spanish grandees and Princes of the Empire), and no foreign king accepted membership in the Order until more than a century after that, in 1822.

7 The Chapel and Clergy of the Order

There is no evidence that Amé provided either a chapel or clergy for the Order he had founded before the very day of his death, 27 February 1383. On that day he finally established a chapel for the Order in his castle of Pierre-Châtel in Bugey, not far from his capital of Chambéry, and created a college of fifteen Carthusian 'hermits' to serve it. As in the Order of the Garter, the priests were equal in number to the companions, and their function was to pray for them daily and perform the various funerary and purgatorial masses required by the statutes. Unlike the Garter canons, the Collar chaplains were regular rather than secular priests, but this difference was of little significance. The college or 'convent' of priests founded by Amé does not seem to have formed an integral part of the Order of the Collar – possibly because, as Carthusians, the priests were already members of another 'order'. Nevertheless, the Convent of Pierre-Châtel was very closely associated with Order, and two of the statutes of the latter were specifically concerned with maintenance of the chapel and convent through donations. Within six months of the death of any of their fellows, the companions were all obliged to give 100 florins to the Prior of the Convent for the upkeep of the Chapel.[33] This was in theory an even better source of income that the once-and-for-all entry-fee required of the knights of the Garter. Before his own death, each companion of the Collar had also to donate to the Order's clergy a chalice and a complete set of mass

[33] Ch. 7.

vestments – which together would have been worth a not inconsiderable sum.[34] The chapel and convent were also endowed and maintained by the founder of the Order and his successors as Chief from their private revenues.

The Carthusian church in the castle of Pierre-Châtel was actually constructed under Amé VII, and seems to have remained the seat of the Order from that time until 1601, when Duke Charles-Emmanuel I was obliged to cede it along with the whole province of Bugey to the King of France.

8 The Obligations of Membership

Aside from the selection of new members, the statutes of 1409 are concerned almost exclusively with the obligations that membership was to entail. Three general categories of obligations are distinguished: the mutual obligations of the companions and the Chief in life, the obligations of all members with respect to the settlement of internal disputes, and the obligations of the members arising from the death of one of their number. Of these, only the last had been the subject of extensive legislation in the earlier monarchical orders, but the first two had been prominent in the statutes of Amé's own earlier order, the Black Swan, and it was no doubt from the latter (or its sources and models) that he borrowed the ideas behind statutes 1 through 6.

The Black Swan statutes had made a distinction in obligation between the 'great lords' of the Company and the ordinary members. The Collar statutes distinguished more precisely between the obligations of the Chief and those of the companions, devoting separate chapters to the obligations of companions to Chief (1), Chief to companions (2), and companions to one another (3). The Collar companions were bound to give favour, counsel, aid, and service to their Chief, and to work to procure his honour and advantage against all but their own lords and vassals, agnates, and other relatives within the degree of first cousin.[35] The first part of their obligation was essentially similar to that of the knights of the Knot, if rather more explicitly phrased, but the second part and the reservations were quite novel in the statutes of a monarchical order. Even more novel were the obligations of the Chief to the companions, which differed from theirs to him only in omitting service and substituting the maintenance of their rights for the procurement of his advantage. The earlier monarchical orders had laid no burdens of aid or counsel whatever upon the head of the order, but Amé of Savoy made his chiefly obligations only slightly less significant than those owed to him. Finally, while the earlier founders had imposed little or nothing in the way of fraternal obligations upon the knights of their orders, Amé required each of his companions to give aid and counsel to all of his fellow companions, against all but those excepted above. He thus combined a set of reciprocal obligations similar to those undertaken by lords and retainers with another set characteristic of the very different relationship of brotherhood-in-arms.

---

[34] Ch. 9a.

[35] The reservations, pertaining to all of the obligations imposed by the first three chapters, are set out in ch. 4.

It is apparent from the nature of these obligations that the Green Count regarded his Order not primarily as an instrument for bringing his vassals and neighbours into clientship to him, but as a mutually acceptable vehicle of mutual support among all of its members, including himself. The first four statutes, in fact, reflect the reality of his situation in 1364 and of his relationship with the original companions – who were not so much his obedient subjects and clients as his faithful supporters and companions-in-arms, about to embark with him on the perilous if glorious adventure of a crusade against the Infidel. The superiority of Amé's position in the Order was justified both by his superior status as a prince and by his position as leader of the crusade, but he did not push his advantages except within the context of the Order itself.

The elaborate provisions for the settlement of disputes contained in Chapters 5 and 6 were no doubt introduced into the constitution of the Order of the Collar for the same practical reason that similar provisions had earlier been written into that of the order of the Black Swan. Amé was no doubt well aware of the propensity of most contemporary noblemen to quarrel with one another, and in order to keep his society from breaking under the pressures of internal dissension, he introduced a process of binding arbitration in which he himself (except when a party to the dispute) was to be the principal judge. If a controversy arose between two or more of the companions, those involved were bound to submit it to the judgement of the Chief, with the counsel of two or more of the companions least involved in the quarrel, and were to observe his judgement entirely.[36] If one of the companions had a dispute with the Chief himself, the latter was to do whatever he was counselled to do by at least four companions of the Order, according to reason and equity, so that neither expenses nor judicial acts would be required. If the case was obscure, the advice of two learned doctors was to be sought.[37] Of the earlier founders, only Alfonso of Castile had made similar provisions for the settlement of internal disputes.

The nine remaining chapters form a section quite distinct from the first six. They deal not with the novel questions of mutual fraternity in life, but with the more familiar subject of the obligations of the companions on the approach of their own death, and following the deaths of their fellows. Most of these duties, as presented in the redaction of 1409, seem to presuppose the existence of a chapel and a religious establishment attached to the Order, but although the founder failed to found such a chapel until the day of his death, it is likely that he had intended to do so from the beginning.

By chapter 10 of the statutes the Chief of the Order was obliged to provide for each of the companions a 'beautiful and honourable' funeral in the chapel of the Order at Pierre-Châtel, and to summon all the surviving companions who found themselves nearby at the time.[38] They for their part were obliged to attend, at their own expense and attended by two servants, to do honour to their departed comrade.[39] The Chief was to pay for four candles weighing one hundred pounds, and

---

[36] Ch. 5a,b,c.
[37] Ch. 6a,b,c.
[38] Chs. 10a,b, 14d.
[39] Ch. 14a,b,c.

for cloth of the sort used to bury a Carthusian.[40] The mourners were also to be robed for the occasion in the white *cocolla* of the Carthusians. After the service, the habits they had worn were to be donated to the real Carthusians, who thus received another regular income in kind from the companions of the Order.[41]

Following the death of a companion, each of the survivors was also obliged to have one hundred masses said for his soul within three months of learning of his death.[42] This was exactly the same number of masses as Edward of England had required of knights bachelor in his order, and was therefore within the means of all the companions of the Collar. For reasons which are not explained in the statutes, Amé also required each of his companions to bind his heir presumptive (not, as such, a member of the Order) to have a similar number of masses said for his soul.[43] It is possible that this was intended to represent among those having masses said the companion himself, who completed the mystical number fifteen. In any case the result was that every companion was to receive from the Order exactly fifteen hundred masses to speed his soul through purgatory.

Like the earlier orders we have examined, the Collar provided perpetual memorials to its members, placed as usual in the Order's chapel. On the day of his funeral, each companion was to have offered up his collar, his coat of arms, and a banner (if a banneret) or a penon (if a bachelor) of his arms, all of which were to be hung in the church and remain there as memorials to him.[44] In addition, at some time after his death the chalice and mass vestments he had donated to the chapel were to be emblazoned with his arms.[45] The offering up of the badge of the Order itself was a common feature of the practice of the earlier orders, and the armorial elements of the Collar memorial served, like the Garter stall-plate, to identify the individual whose badge was' being displayed. Not surprisingly, considering their perishable nature, none of these memorials has survived.

Although the obligations owed by the companions of the Collar to their deceased brethren were already quite extensive, three new obligations were added in 1434. Chapter 16 required the companions to wear the pendant of knots alone instead of the collar of the Order for nine days after hearing of the death of any of their number.[46] Chapter 17 required the Chief himself to offer up the late companion's collar at his funeral. Chapter 18 finally declared that thenceforth, 'to demonstrate the purity and humility of this Order', the companions were to process at funerals 'without any regard for rank', in the order of their admission into the Order. The addition of these chapters brought to eighteen the number of ordinances exclusively concerned with funerals, purgatorial masses, and memorials for the dead – nearly three eighths of the total. The Order of the Collar thus bore a far stronger resemblance to a funeral confraternity than any other monarchical order.

---

[40] Ch. 14e,f.
[41] Ch. 10c,d.
[42] Ch. 8.
[43] Ch. 13.
[44] Ch. 11.
[45] Ch. 9b.
[46] The original reads: '. . . seront tenus les freres et compaignons . . . de porter le noer et soy abstenir de porter le colier . . .'

The one remaining obligation imposed upon the companions in our period, contained in the last chapter added in 1434, was to wear the collar of the Order 'continually', 'in order to demonstrate the continuation of the Order'.

9 *Corporate Activities, Costume, and Officers*

The Green Count's most striking departure from the pattern laid down by the earlier founders of monarchical orders was his failure to require annual or otherwise regular assemblies of the companions. Indeed, it does not appear from the statutes that there was any occasion on which all of the companions were obliged to come together in one place, since even for funerals only those nearby were actually bound to come to the chapel, and it was only for funerals that they were to assemble officially at all. It appears that some sort of meeting to which everyone was at least to be summoned was to take place after each funeral, possibly to elect a successor to the dead companion, but chapter 10 is curiously obscure on this point, and nothing is said of either the form or the purpose of the gathering. In any event such meetings, if they were indeed held, must have been few and irregular. Only after 1518, when Duke Charles III revised the statutes on the model of the Order of the Golden Fleece, did the Order of the Collar meet on a regular basis in the fashion of most monarchical orders. Thenceforth, the knights met, in those years when the Chief saw fit to convene an assembly, on the eve of the Annunciation, 25 March, and comported themselves exactly as did the knights of the Golden Fleece.[47]

No doubt because the Order had neither an annual meeting nor a weekly religious observance like the Orders of the Star and Knot (or the slightly later Aragonese order of St George), the knights of the Collar in our period – alone among the knights of monarchical orders – had no official habit. In 1518 Charles III assigned to them a mantle of crimson velvet similar to that of the Golden Fleece, but until that time the only visible symbol of membership in the Order was the collar itself – which after 1434, at least, was worn all the time.

Having no corporate activities which were not religious in nature, the Order of the Collar had little need of lay officers, and in fact seems to have had none until 1518. In that year Charles III appointed a secretary, a treasurer, a master of ceremonies, and a herald called *Bonnes nouvelles* ('Good News') to serve his reorganized Order, and assigned them duties similar to those of the equivalent officers of the Burgundian order.

10 *Conclusions: The order of the Collar*

In summary, it is clear that Amé's purpose in founding a monarchical order was in some respects quite different from the purposes of the kings from whose chivalrous foundations he must certainly have borrowed both the basic idea and a number of

---

[47] Statutes of 1518, ch. 25.

particular features. Amé did not hope primarily either to promote or to reward chivalrous conduct, or to bring an unruly nobility into closer dependence on his court or person. The original members of his Order were in fact men whose loyalty he had little need to buy, and the number of companions was so small that he could hardly have hoped to influence more than a tiny fraction of his nobility through distributing memberships among them.

Of the two distinct parts into which the Order's original statutes naturally fall, it is in the first – largely derived from his own earlier foundation and essentially fraternal in nature – that the original purpose of the Order is to be found. Despite its hereditary Chief, the Order of the Collar was to begin with, in the words attributed by Servion to its founder, 'an order of brothers', bound not only by the Order's statutes, but by their no less solemn vow to take part in a crusade together. It thus partook of the characters of both fraternal and votive orders, and bore a closer resemblance to the knightly societies we have called by those names than to any of the earlier monarchical orders, with the possible exception of the Sword of Cyprus. The essentially confraternal obligations set forth in the second part of the statutes of 1409, some of which, at least, seem to have been imposed from the start, were no doubt intended both to provide a pious counterpoise to the more practical and worldly obligations of the first part – clearly appropriate in a society dedicated to the holy enterprise of a crusade – and also to extend the fraternal obligations of the 'brothers and companions' beyond the grave. The latter was in all likelihood the consideration uppermost in the founder's mind, for he did not think to impose any of the other forms of 'spiritual' exercise common to the earlier monarchical orders. No doubt the funerals, masses, and memorials prescribed in these chapters made the Order more attractive and acceptable, especially to future companions, but for the founder, at least – who did not get around to endowing a chapel for the Order until he was on his death-bed nearly twenty years later – they were obviously of secondary importance.

In spite of the very specific purpose for which the Order of the Collar was founded, it survived not only its founder, but his son and grandson, and many generations of their descendants to the present day. It is still the chief order of what is now the Royal House of Savoy, and it is the only medieval order still maintained in the family of its founder. Its longevity, like that of the Garter, is probably to be attributed in part to the prestige and longevity of its founder, in part to the fact that his dominions devolved peacefully after his death to his son and successive generations of his agnatic descendants, and in part to its small size and relatively simple nature. Although none of the Green Count's descendants had need for a fellowship of crusaders, they were not slow to realise that membership in the order they had inherited from their illustrious ancestor could be used both to encourage and to reward the loyalty of their most important vassals, officers, and allies, and they almost certainly converted the order from the votive-fraternal form given to it by its founder, and formally preserved in the statutes of 1409, into something much more like the quasi-monarchical pseudo-orders founded in France and neighbouring countries from about 1365 to 1460 or so, and typical of minor princely courts. Only in 1518 was it given the elaborate sort of neo-Arthurian constitution characteristic of the monarchical orders founded by kings.

Chapter 9

French Princely Orders Founded Before 1430:
The Order of the Golden Shield, Bourbon 1367–1410?
The Order of the Ermine, Brittany 1381–1532?

The creation of a knightly order by the Imperial prince Amé of Savoy in 1364 seems to have inspired the creation of similar societies by several other subordinate princes in both the Empire and France. These were the only states in which most princes could still act like petty kings within their lands in the fourteenth and fifteenth centuries, and thus had some real use for an expensive order of this type. Despite the fact that some dozens of princes in France and some scores of princes in Germany still presided over their own petty courts, however, only a handful of princes in either country are known to have founded a knightly order of any sort in our period, and only three founded an order which was certainly monarchical. All three of these princes were dukes and heads of cadet branches of the French royal house of Capet whose principal estates lay in France: Louis Capet de Bourbon, Duke of Bourbon; Jean Capet de Dreux-Bretagne-Montfort, Duke of Brittany; and Philippe Capet de Valois-Bourgogne, Duke of Burgundy. Only the first two founded orders before the end of the fourteenth century, and as very little is known about either of the orders in question, we shall consider them here in a single short chapter.

1 The Order of the Golden Shield: Bourbon, 1367–1410?

The founder of the first of these orders, Louis 'the Good', third Duke of Bourbon and fourth Count of Clermont-en-Beauvaisis in succession to his great-grandfather Robert, was actually a brother-in-law of the Green Count of Savoy, as well as a first cousin through his mother of King Jean 'the Good' of France and a nephew by marriage of Prince Guy of Galilee, elder brother of Pierre of

271

Cyprus.[1] Born three years after Count Amé, the future duke had been raised in the company of his cousin and exact contemporary the Dauphin Charles (who married his sister in 1350), and with Charles he had been admitted to the Company of the Star at the time of its foundation in 1352.[2] Louis' father Duke Pierre I had fallen fighting at the side of King Jean at Poitiers in 1356, and Louis had then succeeded to his lands and dignities. Most of his first eight years as duke were spent in England as a hostage for Jean's ransom, and he was only quit of this responsibility and permitted to return permanently to his own lands in October 1366.

Louis, described by Christine de Pisan as 'fair, joyful, festive, gentle in his manners, benign in his words, generous in his gifts, meritorious in his deeds,' seems to have been, like his wife's brother Amé of Savoy, a very model of knightly virtue. After many years fighting by the side of such captains as Bertran du Guesclin, he would even lead a minor crusade against the Muslims of North Africa in 1390,[3] and after his death in 1410 would be the subject of a chivalric biography comparable to those dedicated to the Black Prince and Marshal Boucicault.[4] While in England Louis must have learned a good deal about the Order of the Garter, and must have heard something about the order founded by his brother-in-law the Count of Savoy, whose lands lay very close to his own. He seems to have been deeply impressed by what he had seen and heard of the new type of knightly order, for he adopted a badge that was clearly inspired by the English garter – a belt bearing the word *Esperance* – almost immediately upon his return to the Bourbonnais,[5] and shortly after his arrival in his capital city of Moulins on New Year's Day proclaimed the foundation of his own order: the *Ordre de l'Escu d'Or* or 'Order of the Golden Shield'.

The chivalric biography, which is our only source for the nature and history of this Order, describes its foundation in the following terms:

[1] His mother Isabelle was the sister of King Philippe VI and his father's sister Marie married the luckless Prince of Galilee.

[2] See above, p. 191.

[3] See Aziz Atiya, *The Crusade in the Later Middle Ages* (London, 1938), pp. 398–454, for Louis' character and military career as well as his crusade of 1390.

[4] Jean 'Cabaret' d'Oronville, who had composed the first chronicle of Savoy for Duke Amé VIII in 1419, wrote his *Chronique du bon duc Loys de Bourbon* (ed. A.-M. Chazaud [Paris, 1876]) in 1429, apparently at the behest of the late duke's constant companion Jehan de Châtelus-Châteaumorand.

[5] According to the chronicle, on Christmas Day 1366 Duke Louis concluded an address to his barons with the following words: 'Et pour le bon espoir que j'ai en vous, après Dieu, d'ores en avant je pourterai pour devise une seinture ou il aura escript ung joyeulx mot: ESPERANCE.' (Ibid., p. 8.) This device was to remain one of the principal badges of the Dukes of Bourbon until the sixteenth century, and numerous repsentations have survived. Favyn (*Théâtre*, I, p. 781.) made of this device and another badge used by the Dukes of Bourbon, the thistle (*chardon*), an order of knighthood, which he called *Notre Dame de l'Esperance ou du Chardon*, but as Jean-Bernard de Vaivre has demonstrated ('Un document inédit sur le décor héraldique de l'ancien hôtel de Bourbon à Paris', *Archivum Heraldicum* 1 [1972], pp. 2–10) there is no evidence that either of these badges ever represented a true order of knighthood.

And on New Year's Day, the good duke got up quite early to receive his knights and gentlemen, in order to go to the church of Our Lady of Moulins. And before the duke left his chamber, he wished to admit them to a fair order that he had made, which was called the Golden Shield. And on this golden shield was a band of pearls where he had written: ALLEN. And the first to be admitted to this Order was the Lord of La Tour, Messire Henry de Montaigu, son of Messire Gille Aicelin. The second was Messire Guichard Dauphin; the third Messire Griffon de Montagu; Messire Hugues de Chastellus, Lord of Chastelmorand; the Lord de Chastel de Montaigne; the Lord de la Palice; Messire Guillaume de Vichi, Lord of Busset; Messire Philippe de Serpens; Messire Lordin de Saligny; the Lord of Chantemerle; Messire Regnault de Basserne, Lord of Champroux; the Lord of Veaulce; the Lord of Blot; Messire Guillaume de la Mothe; Messire de Fontenay, of the land of Berry; and several other knights, who received the Order of the Golden Shield. And each held himself much honoured to receive it, and not without cause. And in giving this order, the duke began to say to each one: 'My Lords, this order of the Golden Shield that I have made signifies many honourable things for all knights and others, the which I shall tell you after the divine service, and after we have dined, so that we may swear and promise them all together.'[6]

After dinner, the duke duly announced to the assembled knights what the order 'signified', and they were then obliged to swear to be as brothers to one another, living and dying together in all good works; to avoid all places where they might hear God blasphemed; to honour ladies and damsels and to hear no evil spoken of them; and to bear faith to one another, avoiding slanderous remarks. The Order's device, apparently Bourbonnais dialect for *allons*, was finally explained as signifying 'Allons tous ensemble au service de Dieu' – 'Let us all go together to the service of God'. The first of the duties imposed by Louis on the knights of his Order resembled the fraternal obligations imposed by his brother-in-law on the companions of the Collar, but if the chronicler's account is accurate, the five remaining obligations of membership in the Order of the Golden Shield entailed little more than an undertaking to behave, in the words attributed by the chronicler to Louis himself, 'comment appartient a tout honneur et chevalerie.'[7]

The chronicler (whose source was one of the founder knights he named in the paragraph quoted above) makes no reference to any annual meetings or other forms of corporate activity, and it does not appear that the Order ever had any physical or religious establishment. Like the Order of the Collar itself during the reign of its founder, the Order of the Golden Shield was thus the merest shadow of a monarchical order of chivalry, and was hardly to be distinguished after the day of its foundation from any other group of knights wearing the badge of their lord. It may perhaps be seen as representing a stage beyond that represented by the Savoyard order in the evolution from the formally constituted monarchical order to the pseudo-order, whose 'members' were not bound by any form of corporate statutes at

6 Chazaud, ed., *Chronique*, pp. 8–9.
7 Ibid., pp. 12–13.

all. Unlike the pseudo-order founded in 1394 by Duke Louis' agnatic cousin Duke Louis of Orléans (that of the Camail-and-Porcupine[8]), the Order of the Golden shield did not even impose any real cliental obligations upon its members. Indeed, so little did the Order demand of its members in the way of loyalty that several of the founder knights thought nothing of accepting membership in the Castilian Order of the Band (by that time equally undemanding) while attending upon the founder of the Order of the Golden Shield only eight years after the foundation of the latter order.[9]

I have found no direct evidence for the survival of the Order of the Golden Shield after about 1370, and it is possible that it was abandoned by Louis in favour of the belt bearing the motto *Esperance* which seems to have been converted into a pseudo-order by 1379. Cabaret's chronicle declares that in that year Duke Louis gave to the Constable Bertrand du Guesclin 'a beautiful belt of gold, very rich, of his Order of Esperance, which he put on his neck'.[10] Unlike the golden shield, the belt of *Esperance* continued to be distributed as a badge by all of Louis' successors as Duke of Bourbon in our period, and was frequently displayed in conjunction with the ducal arms.

2 The Order of the Ermine: Brittany, 1381–1532?

The next of our three orders was established by a Duke of Brittany, a principality which had once been ruled by its own ethnic kings and had always resisted the interference of the Kings of France in its internal affairs. Perhaps for this reason the order in question was somewhat more substantial than that of the Golden Shield, which seems to have been created for reasons which were largely romantic. Like the founders of several of the earlier orders we have studied, the founder of the Order of the Ermine, Duke Jean IV of Brittany, was a vigorous and capable prince who had been obliged to fight for his throne.[11] His father Jean 'de Montfort', the fourth son of Duke Arthur II of Brittany, had succeeded his mother as Count of Montfort-l'Amaury in 1322, and on the death of his older half-brother Duke Jean III in 1341 had claimed the Breton throne as the heir-male of his line. This claim had been contested by his niece Jeanne, Countess of Penthièvre – the daughter of the late duke's full brother Guy, and consort of Charles de Blois, soon to be one of the founder knights of the Star – and the duchy had been plunged into a vicious succession war in which Edward of England had taken Jean's side and recognized him as the successor to his brother in the English earldom of Richmond, and Philippe of France had taken that of Jean's opponents and confiscated his County of Montfort.

---

[8] On this order, see Hélie de Brémond d'Ars-Migré, *Les Chevaliers du Porc-Epic ou du Camail, 1394–1498* (Macon, 1938). The only clear representation of the collar of this order that I have found is in the frontispiece of Paris, B.N. fr.606, f. 1, showing Christine de Pisan offering the founder a copy of the book in which it appears.

[9] See above, p. 59.

[10] '. . . une belle seinture d'or, tres riche, de son ordre d'Esperance, laquelle il lui mit au col, . . .' *Chronique*, p. 116.

[11] On his reign, see Michael Jones, *Ducal Brittany 1364–1399* (London, 1970).

The prince in question here, born shortly before his father Jean 'de Montfort' was taken prisoner by Philippe in 1341, had succeeded to his father's claims only four years later, but it was not until twenty-four years later still, after he had defeated and killed his father's rival Charles de Blois in a battle fought outside the walls of Auray on 29 September 1364, that the new *de facto* King of France, Charles V, had recognized him as the *de jure* Duke of Brittany. Even then his relations with his French suzerain had been strained by his continued friendship with Edward of England, whose daughter he had married in 1361, and in 1374 Charles' hostility had forced him to flee once again to England. There he had remained for five years, and might have stayed for the rest of his life if Charles had not driven his highly particularist vassals into open rebellion by attempting to annex his duchy permanently to the crown of France. Duke Jean rode back to power in 1379 on a wave of Breton nationalism, and although Charles V never accorded him formal recognition, after Charles' death in September 1380 the regents for the new king, Charles VI – among whom was Duke Louis II of Bourbon – abandoned this policy, and on 4 April 1381 invited Jean to do homage to their young ward.

According to the brief account in the rhyming chronicle which is our sole contemporary source for the early history of his order,[12] Jean first distributed the *nouvelle devise* of what came to be known as the *Ordre de l'Hermine* or 'Order of the Ermine' less than three months later, on 22 June, immediately following his solemn entry into his capital city of Nantes, where he had gone to meet with the Estates of his duchy in preparation for his journey to the royal court to swear fealty to his sovereign. In the circumstances, the device, to be worn by many of his 'barons, knights, [and] squires' when they arrived in Paris, was almost certainly intended to be a symbol of Breton independence, as well as a sign of the ties between the Breton barons and their duke.[13]

Unfortunately, the next document to mention the Order, and the only one which tells us anything about its form and activities, dates from more than sixty years later. The relevant part of this document – a letter of the founder's son and successor Duke Jean V (r. 1399–1442) dated 25 November 1437, ordering his procurators general to collect the collars of the deceased members – reads as follows:

> Jean by the grace of God Duke of Brittany etc. As our most redoubted lord, the duke our father, whom God pardon, ordained and made an order of his collar, at the reception of which collar those from whom our said lord and father received the oath were held by oath to bring themselves on the day of the feast of St Michael in Monte Gargano[14] to our chapel of St Michael of the

---

[12] Guillaume de St-André, *Histoire de Jean IV*, ed. Dom H. Morice, *Mémoires pour servir de preuves à l'histoire ecclésiastique et civile de Bretagne* (Paris, 1742–6), II, cols. 356–7.
[13] This order was known to most of the antiquarian historians, but their accounts, based largely on that of Favyn in his *Théâtre*, are full of the usual glaring innaccuracies. I know of no earlier attempt to reconstruct its history on the basis of the surviving primary sources.
[14] The feast of the Apparition of St Michael on Monte Gargano in Apulia was celebrated on 8 May. Why the Order was to have met on this feast rather than that of the the Dedication on 29 September, when the battle of Auray was fought, is unclear, but it may be that it was regarded as a more suitable time of year for knightly festivities.

field near Auray, if on that day they were in our said duchy and not impeded, and for each deceased member of that collar order (*ordre de collier*) the survivors were to have said a certain number of masses for the salvation and redemption of the said deceased members, and the heirs of the said deceased members were to render the collars which those deceased members had borne, to the dean and chaplains of the said chapel, to be converted and employed in chalices, ornaments, and other good works for the said chapel; ...[15]

This very brief (and probably only partial) summary of the statutes of the Order established by its founder suggests that it was a true monarchical order, and that it was modelled in part on the Order of the Garter (since it met annually on one of the feasts of its patron) and in part on that of the Collar (since its badge took the form of a collar, and was to be returned on the death of the companion to endow the Order's chapel). Duke Jean was certainly familiar with the former order, as he had been elected to membership in it shortly after his flight to England in 1374, and had probably heard of the second.

The Chapel of St Michael in the Field near Auray, which served as the seat of the new Breton Order, was itself founded by Duke Jean IV on 16 February 1382, to commemorate the great battle by which he had first secured his throne, fought there on Michaelmas Day 1364. Since St Michael the Archangel was one of the principal patrons of knighthood in general, Jean's decision to place the Order under his patronage was doubly appropriate. Although the letters establishing the chapel make no reference to the Order of the Ermine,[16] it is likely that it was from the beginning intended to function as the headquarters of the Order founded eight months earlier. Like the chapel of the Order of the Collar at Pierre-Châtel, which was founded exactly a year after it, the chapel near Auray came eventually to be served by priests of the strict Carthusian Order, but for some time after its foundation it seems to have been staffed in the more usual fashion by a college of secular canons.

At about the same time as he founded the chapel, Duke Jean ordered the construction of a new castle, to be known as the *Chasteau de l'Hermine* or 'Castle of the Ermine', at the edge of the old royal capital of Vannes a few miles from Auray, and later made this his principal residence. The situation of the Order's seat was thus made to correspond to that of most of the earlier foundations. Sadly, nothing now remains of either the chapel or the castle, so we can learn nothing from them about either the membership or the insignia of the Order.

I have found no depiction of the collar of the Order of the Ermine contemporary with the reign of its founder, but the chronicle describes it as being composed of 'two scrolls burnished and beautiful, coupled together with two clasps, and below ... the ermine, fine in form and colour. On the two scrolls was written A *ma vie*, ... the one word white and the other black ...'[17] At some time before 1480 the

---

[15] Morice, *Mémoires*, II, cols. 1315–16.

[16] Ibid., cols. 445–6.

[17] 'Et estoit nouvelle devise/ De deux roletz brunis et beaux,/ Couplez ensemble de deux fermaux,/ Et au dessoubs estoit l'ermine/ En figure et en couleur fine,/ En deux cedules avoit escript:/ A ma vie, comme j'ai dit;/ L'un mot est blanc et l'autre noir/ ...' *Histoire*, p. 357.

9.1 The badge of the Golden Shield (reconstructed)

9.2 The ermine device in the 14th century
a. The collar (reconstructed)
b.–d. The ermine represented on ducal seals of the period

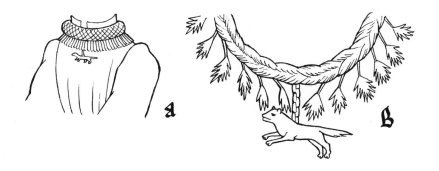

9.3 The collar of the Ermine in the 15th century, as represented
a. in the MS. of the *Histoire de Bretagne* c.1480
b. in the Grünenberg *Wappenbuch* c.1483

277

collar composed of scrolls seems to have been replaced by one in the form of an annulus apparently woven from the stems of wheat-ears, with a more-or-less continuous brush formed of the ears themselves hanging below. This is the form of the collar worn by Jean de Derval in a miniature painted about that year in which he is depicted receiving a copy of Pierre Lebaud's Histoire de Bretagne from the author,[18] and of the collar depicted in the Wappenbuch of Conrad Grünenberg,[19] completed in 1483. The significance of the ears of wheat is obscure, but Jean's choice of an ermine as the device of his order is not difficult to explain. A shield of ermine plain had been the arms of the Dukes of Brittany since 1316, and the small white beast with the the black-tipped tail from which the most prestigious of furs was taken was thus an obvious device for a Breton ducal order. Duke Jean seems to have taken a particular delight in the conceit, for he not only adopted the ermine as the badge of his Order, but displayed ermines in the spandrels of his ducal seals, and even named his new castle after the little beast. The ermines on the seals are collared and chained like dogs or monkeys, and are often accompanied by a scroll bearing his motto A ma vie – a chivalrous devise commonly associated in the period with tournaments. The ermines depicted in the two documents cited, however, have neither a chain nor a scroll.

The history of the Order of the Ermine after Duke Jean's death in 1399 is even more obscure than its history during his lifetime, and it is not certain that the Order was maintained as a true corporation even by his son. His son's letters of 1437 quoted above, though issued to enforce one of the Order's statutes, do not unequivocally indicate that the Order was still functioning at that date, but suggest rather that the Order had fallen into disuse within a few years of the founder's demise. On the other hand, the new duke and his immediate successors continued to display both the ermine and the motto A ma vie on their seals,[20] a collar with a pendant ermine was worn by at least one Breton nobleman in 1480, and the letter of Olivier de la Marche cited in the preface indicates that the ermine was still regarded as the device of an order of some sort in the time of the founder's grandson, Duke François II, the last independant ruler of Brittany (r. 1457–1488).[21] If De la Marche was correct, by the reign of the latter duke the Ermine had been reduced to the condition of a mere pseudo-order, and that may well have been its condition throughout the fifteenth century. The Order's device and motto were still employed by Duke François' daughter the Duchess Anne (r. 1488–1514), who married successively King Charles VIII and King Louis XII of France; by her daughter the Duchess Claude (r. 1514–1524), wife of Louis' successor King François I; and by their second son the Dauphin Henri, titular Duke of Brittany in succession to his mother from 1539 until his accession to the throne as King Henri II in 1547. The Duchy of Brittany had already been permanently united with the crown of France in 1532, however, and the later rulers had no use for an order of knighthood which would encourage Breton particularism.

---

[18] Paris, B.N., ms. fr.8266, f. 393v. See fig. 9.3a.
[19] Paul Ganz, 'Die Abzeichen der Ritterorden', pp. 136–7. See fig. 9.3b.
[20] See fig. 9.2b,c,d.
[21] See above, p. 12 n. 10.

Chapter 10

The Enterprise of the Knights of St George
The Lands of the Crown of Aragon,
1371/9–1410?

1 Historical Background

When Amé of Savoy founded his order of the Collar in 1364, there were still a number of royal courts in Western Christendom which had yet to acquire an order of the new monarchical type: those of Aragon, Navarre, and Portugal in the Iberian peninsula, that of Trinacria or Sicily proper in the far south, and those of Sweden, Denmark, Norway, and Scotland in the far north. The courts of Scandinavia and Scotland were both minor and peripheral to the cultural and political life of Europe, and would not see the creation of any sort of princely order until about a century later.[1] The Kings of Portugal seem to have been satisfied thoughout our period with the control they had come to exercise over the three religious orders of knighthood based in their kingdom,[2] and the Kings of Navarre (who in the fourteenth century took a more active interest in their French possessions than in their diminutive Iberian kingdom), seem to have contented themselves with a pseudo-order similar to those maintained by their agnates in France.[3] The court of Trinacria, presided over by cadets of the royal house of Aragon, does not appear to have been served by a monarchical order until after its reunion in the 1380s with that of Aragon, which had itself finally acquired its own monarchical order at some time in the 1370s when King Pere 'the Ceremonious' established the *Empresa de sant Jordi* or 'Enterprise of St George'. Like the Order of the Collar, this society appears to have been inspired by, and partially modelled upon, the Cypriot Order of the Sword, and perhaps in consequence was endowed

---

[1] See below, pp. 398–9.
[2] The Orders of St Bendict of Aviz, of São Thiago or St James of the Sword, and of Christ. I have found no evidence to support the claim made when the order was 'reestablished' by King João VI in 1808 that Afonso V had founded an 'Order of the Sword' following his conquest of Fez in 1459. I have not even found a reference to such an order in the accounts of the seventeenth-century historians of knightly orders, and Antonio Caetano de Sousa, who describes the order at some length in his *História Genealógica da Casa Real Portuguesa*, III (Lisbon, 1737), pp. 601–2, admits that there is absolutely no surviving evidence of the order's existence.
[3] The Order of the Beech-Leaf. See above, p. 258 n. 24.

with a monarchical constitution of unprecedented simplicity.

Since the accession to the throne of the first king of the Catalan dynasty of Barcelona in 1162, the kings of the small, landlocked kingdom of Aragon had been the rulers of a conglomerate of mutually independent states collectively known as the Lands of the Crown of Aragon. The dominant partner in this conglomerate was not in fact the Kingdom of Aragon but the vigorous maritime County of Barcelona or Principality of Catalonia, which until 1259 was technically a constitutant part of the Kingdom of France, and retained throughout our period a form of social and political order more like that of a large French principality than a Spanish kingdom. In addition to the Kingdom of Aragon proper the Counts of Barcelona had added to their princely state by the year 1330 the Kingdoms of Mallorca and Valencia, conquered from the Moors in 1228 and 1238; the Kingdom of Sicily proper or Trinacria, seized as we have seen from King Carlo I after the revolt of the 'Sicilian Vespers' in 1282; the Kingdom of Sardinia, granted to Jacme II by the Pope in 1297 and conquered by him by 1326; and various lesser territories in southern France and the western Mediterranean. They had, however, granted both Mallorca (in 1278) and Sicily (in 1285 and 1296), along with certain other lands, to younger sons, retaining only a loose suzerainty.

The future King Pere IV and III,[4] born in 1319, was the elder of the two sons given to King Alfons IV 'the Benign' by his first queen, Teresa Countess of Urgell.[5] Pere was only sixteen when he succeeded his father on 27 January 1336, but immediately assumed effective control of his dominions. Like his contemporary Edward of England, who had come to the throne at a similar age, he was to reign for more than fifty years, and was to devote most of his considerable energies to making war. His overriding ambition was to reunite in his own hands the various possessions of his house which had been given in apanage to cadets of his royal ancestors, and in 1343 he trumped up an excuse to confiscate the Kingdom of Mallorca from his cousin King Jacme III. He then became embroiled in a civil war in his Iberian dominions, occasioned by his attempt to change the succession law in order to allow his daughter to succeed him, and to remove the existing heir-presumptive, his brother Count Jacme of Urgell, from his office as Procurator General. This conflict culminated in the Battle of Epila on 21 July 1348, which resulted in a resounding victory for Pere's forces, but in the previous year a revolt had broken out in Sardinia which was to demand his military attention for many years, and two years later the newly-crowned Pedro 'the Cruel' of Castile launched a war against him that was to last until Pedro's own defeat and murder in 1369 at the hands of his half-brother Enrique of Trastámara – to whom Pere had long given protection and support.

It was not until after the victory of his ally Enrique of Trastámara and the final cessation of hostilities with Castile that Pere got around to founding an order of

---

[4] He was the fourth of his name in Aragon, but only the third in Barcelona, and Catalan historians commonly call him Pere III.

[5] On his life and reign, see Rafael Tasis i Marca, *Pere el Ceremonios i els seus fills* (Barcelona, 1957), and *La vida del rei En Pere III* (Barcelona, 1954). On the nobility of Aragon in the later medieval period, see Santiago Sobrequés [Vidal], *Els Barons de Catalunya* (Barcelona, 1957), pp. 142–264, and *La Alta Nobleza del Norte en la Guerra Civil Catalana de 1462–1472* (Zaragoza, 1976), esp. pp. 14–40.

knighthood for the leading members of his court. It is unclear why he had not done so earlier, for he must certainly have been familiar with the Order of the Band, founded by his neighbour and longtime enemy Alfonso of Castile seven years before his own accession, and must also have known something of the orders founded by Edward of England, Jean of France, and Loysi of mainland Sicily, who like Alfonso were his near contemporaries in age. He certainly had the requisite interest in chivalry, for he had the section of the Castilian *Siete Partidas* dealing with knighthood translated into Catalan and published under his name,[6] and his imposition upon his own court of the elaborate ceremonial regulations of the court of Mallorca after his annexation of that kingdom in 1344 led his contemporaries to bestow upon him the sobriquet 'the Ceremonious'.[7] It may be that he long felt that he enjoyed sufficient control over the religious orders of knighthood already established in his kingdom, especially the Orders of St George of Alfama and Our Lady of Montesa, both of which had been created by his royal predecessors.[8] The latter, indeed, had been founded by Pere's grandfather Jacme II in 1317 to replace the recently suppressed Order of the Temple, and was thus only ten years old when Pere ascended the throne.

2 The Foundation and History of the Enterprise

By the 1370s, however, Pere seems to have begun to feel that his court should also have an order of the new monarchical type, and at some time before 6 May 1379 he created the society he called the Enterprise of the Knights of St George. Unfortunately, the state of the documentation does not permit us to establish with any degree of certainty even the year in which this order was founded. Historians of Spain have assigned the date 16 October 1371 to the (undated) statutes, preserved in one of the registers of the royal chancellery, presumably on the basis of their position in the register,[9] but both Rafael Tasis, the most recent historian of Pere's reign, and Kenneth Setton, the most important historian of the Catalan settlements in Greece, seem to believe that it was founded at Livadia in the Greek duchy of Neopatria.[10] This would mean that the Order could not have been established until some time after 27 July 1377, when the death without male issue

---

[6] Barcelona, Archivo General de la Corona de Aragón, reg. 1529, f. 16ff. Published in *Tractats de Cavalleria*, ed. Pere Bohigas (Barcelona, 1947), pp. 97ff.

[7] See M. Durliat, *La cour de Jacques II, de Majorque (1324–1349) d'après les 'lois palatines'* (Paris, 1962).

[8] See above, pp. 17, 21.

[9] Luis Más y Gil, 'La Orden militar de San Jorge de Alfama, sus Maestres, y la Cofradía de Mossen Sent Jordi' *Hidalguía*, 6 (1958), pp. 247–56, esp. p. 253.

[10] Tasis, *La vida*, p. 350, declares that 'La Livàdia, famosa pel seu culte a Sant Jordi, esdevé residència dels cavallers de l'Ordre creada pel Rei, i com a primer nucli d'aquells ordena Lluís Frederic, Comte de Salona, Joan d'Aragó i Jofre Ça Rovira'. Setton, *Catalan Domination of Athens, 1311–1388* (Cambridge, Mass., 1948), p. 109 n. 27, had similarly declared that 'On 18 May, 1381, Don Pedro IV bestowed upon him [Lluís Frederic] the "white mantle with the red cross" of the Order of St. George, which had been previously established at Livadia'.

of the current ruler of the twin duchies of Athens and Neopatria, Pere's agnatic cousin King Federico of Sicily, led Pere to claim the whole inheritance Federico had left by will to his daughter Maria.[11]

Both Tasis and Setton appear to have arrived at their belief that the order founded by Pere was based in the castle of Livadia on the basis of the fact that that castle had long been famous for its possession of the head of St George, patron of Catalonia (which Pere had actually attempted to purchase in 1354),[12] and the fact that the three barons most responsible for the effective annexation of the two Greek duchies to the Crown of Aragon in 1379 were named to the Enterprise in a letter written by Pere to the current Vicar General of the duchies in May 1381.[13] The letter, translated from the original Catalan, reads as follows:

> En Pere, by the grace of God, King of Aragon, Valencia, Mallorca, Sardinia, and Corsica, Count of Barcelona, Duke of Athens and Neopatria, and also Count of Rousillon and Cerdagne. To our noble and beloved councillor and chamberlain, Mossen Felip Dalmau, Viscount of Rocabertí and Vicar General of the said duchies, greetings. Forasmuch as we know that our noble and dear cousin En Loys d'Aragó, Count of Malta,[14] and Mossen Jofre Ça Rovira,[15] and the noble En Johan d'Aragó,[16] dwelling in the said duchies,

---

[11] These two principalities, both products of the infamous Crusade of 1204 that had placed a 'Latin' prince on the throne of Constantinople, had been conquered at the beginning of the fourteenth century by the same company of Catalan mercenaries that had secured the throne of island Sicily for the House of Barcelona, and their leaders had decided in 1312 to turn to their former employer, the Catalan King of Sicily, to provide them with a duke. Successive Kings of Sicily had obliged by naming one of their younger sons as titular duke, but in 1355 the new Duke of Athens and Neopatria, Federico 'the Simple', succeeded to the throne of Sicily itself as King Federico III, and lacking sons he continued to hold both duchies until his death on 27 July 1377. (See Setton, *Catalan Domination*, pp. 1–17.) In his will Federico left all of his dominions to his daughter Maria, who was duly proclaimed queen and duchess, but Pere of Aragon, citing a clause in the will of the late king's grandfather excluding women from the throne, immediately claimed his whole inheritance as both suzerain and heir-male. A succession struggle certainly ensued in Sicily, and a similar struggle may also have erupted in the Greek duchies, but almost nothing is known about events in the latter between 1376 and 1379. It appears that the young queen Maria continued to exercise some authority in Athens and Neopatria from 1377 to 1379, but in the latter year King Pere, with the loyal support of his cousin Lluís Frederic 'd'Aragó', Count of Salona, Vicar-General of the two duchies, and Galcerán de Peralta, the Captain and Castellan of Athens, finally secured the annexation of the two duchies to the Crown of Aragon. (Setton, *Catalan Domination*, pp. 100–1, 110–17, and 'The Catalans in Greece, 1311–1380', in *A History of the Crusades*, ed. K. M. Setton, III, ed. Harry W. Hazard [Madison, 1975], pp. 214–15.)

[12] Setton, *Catalan Domination*, pp. 48–9, 71.

[13] Ibid., p. 114.

[14] Lluís Frederic (*alias* Luis Fadrique), also Count of Salona and Vicar General of Athens and Neopatria in 1377. He was the son of Jacme Frederic, second son of Alfons Frederic, a natural son of Federico II of Sicily who had been appointed Vicar General of Athens and Neopatria in 1317. Lluís Frederic was the third Vicar General of his line, and the most important baron in the two duchies.

[15] *Alias* Jofre Zarrovira. Captain of the County of Salona.

[16] Joan Frederic d'Aragó, co-Lord of Aigina and sometime Captain of the County of Malta,

have great affection for our honour, for which they deserve our favours and graces, by the tenor of the present [letter] we command you in our name and by our authority to place them, and each one of them, in our Enterprise of St George, and to give to each of them the white mantle with the red cross which we and the nobles and knights who are in the said Enterprise wear every Saturday, and on St George's Day. We command you to receive from each of them in our name the oath and homage relevant to the matters contained in the chapters of the said Enterprise, which you shall arrange to have given to them, sealed with our pendant seal. Given in Zaragoza, on the 18th day of May, in the year of the Nativity of Our Lord mccclxxxi. Rex Petrus.[17]

Tasis went so far as to declare that these three knights formed the 'first nucleus' of the order in Livadia. In fact, however, there is nothing in this letter or in either of the other contemporary documents that refer to the order to suggest that it was founded in Livadia, and there are a number of positive reasons for thinking that the order never had any connection either with that city or with Pere's claims to the Greek duchies. In the first place, if Pere ever effectively possessed Livadia, he held it only for a very short time, for (as Setton himself has shown) the city and castle of Livadia both fell to a company of Navarrese adventurers in the spring of 1379 – the same time the rest of the duchy recognised Pere's sovereignty – and neither was ever recovered.[18] Furthermore, not only does the letter quoted above clearly indicate that the order already had a number of members at the time of writing, but we possess another letter written on 6 May 1379 which makes it clear that the order had been founded more than two years before Pere decided to reward his supporters in Greece. This letter, sent by Pere to one of his two sons (the Infants En Joan, Duke of Gerona, and En Martí), contains an amendment to one of the chapters included in the surviving copy of the statutes:

The King. Dear son: we have ordained that even as every Friday we and all the barons, knights of our order of St George (cavallers del orde nostre de Sant Jordi), were to wear the white mantle or other upper garments of white, from this time onward we shall wear it every Saturday, so that those who out of reverence for the Passion of Jesus wish to wear black on Fridays may be able to do so. And according to what we have ordained, so shall we and those who are in our court observe it. And we have written to all our governors, that they might observe it. And so, dear son, we send to you so that you may also observe it. Given in Barcelona under our secret seal on the sixth day of May of the year mccclxxxix. Rex Petrus.[19]

---

alias Juan Fadrique. He was the son of Bonifaci Frederic, third son of Alfons Frederic, the founder of the line.

[17] Barcelona, Archivo General de la Corona de Aragón, reg. 1559, f. 8v. Published in Antonio Rubió y Lluch, Los Navarros en Grecia y el Ducado Catalán de Atenas en la Epoca de su Invasión (Barcelona, 1886), no. LI, pp. 269–70.

[18] Setton, Catalan Domination, pp. 146–7.

[19] Original and transcription published in Tasis, La vida, Pl. III (facing p. 192).

It is clear from this letter that the Enterprise of St George was well established by May 1379, and already had members spread throughout the dominions of the Crown of Aragon. It is thus most unlikely that Pere's decision to create the order was in any way connected with his claim to Athens and Neopatria, for if it had been he would harldy have waited two years before admitting to membership the three men who were at once the most important barons and officers in those duchies, and the most active proponents of his cause during the period between the summers of 1377 and 1379, when they were still in dispute between himself and his cousin Maria. In all likelihood, therefore, the Enterprise was founded at some time before the death of Federico of Sicily in 1377, and quite possibly as early as the date conventionally assigned to the statutes.

Indeed, there is at least one reason aside from the position of the statutes in the register to suspect that the order was founded around 1370. As we shall see, the principal obligations undertaken by the knights of St George were almost identical to those imposed (uniquely until then) upon the knights of the Cypriot order of the Sword, and Pere probably learned about the ordinances of that order in 1366, when the Chancellor of Cyprus, Philippe de Mézières, visited his court during his second tour of the courts of Europe.[20] It would not be at all surprising if Pere's late decision to found a monarchical order of knighthood was inspired by what he learned on that occasion about the new (and apparently very simple) Order of the Sword.

I have found no evidence to indicate that the Enterprise of St George survived its founder's death, which occurred in 1387, but as Pere was succeeded by his elder son Joan (I), and the the latter was succeeded in 1395 by his younger brother Martí 'the Humane', who ruled until his death in 1410, there is at least a strong possiblity that the Order was maintained in some form until the latter date. Martí's only son and namesake had been married in 1390 to his dispossessed cousin Maria of Sicily (daughter of Federico III) in order to solve the contest over the Sicilian succession, but the younger Martí, his wife Maria, and their son Pere all died before Martí 'the Humane' himself, and as he was the last survivor of his whole house, his death in 1410 produced a succession crisis of major proportions. This was finally resolved by the Compromise of Caspe of 28 June 1412, according to which the Infante Don Fernando 'de Antequera', Duke of Peñafiel – the younger son of the elder Martí's sister Leonor by King Juan I of Castile – was chosen to succeed as King Ferran I. The new king had already founded his own quasi-monarchical order, as we shall see, and from the time of his accession until the extinction of his line a century later, in 1516, it was that order whose insignia graced the throats of the Kings of Aragon and the more eminent members of their court. In all probablity, therefore, the Order here in question dissolved during the troubles that followed the death of the last king of the House of Barcelona in 1410.

[20] See above, p. 244.

3 The Statutes of the Enterprise

The statutes of the Enterprise of St George, uniquely preserved as we have noted in one of the registers of the royal chancellery,[21] are even simpler than those assigned to the Order of the Collar in 1409, though not as simple as those assigned to the Order of the Golden Shield. They are composed of only twenty ordinances organized into only ten chapters (distinguished by the word *Item*), introduced by the following brief prologue:

> To the service of God and of Our Lady Saint Mary, and in reverence of the blessed *Mossen* Saint George, the Lord King ordained that an enterprise (*empresa*) of nobles [i.e. barons] and knights be made in the form and manner written below, who shall be called the knights of St George (*los cavallers de sant Jordi*).

It is unclear why Pere chose to give the body of knights he referred to in his letter of 1379 as 'our order' the formal title 'Enterprise', which appears in the text of the statutes as well as the prologue; though never borne by another monarchical order, this title was applied to certain of the votive orders founded between 1390 and 1415,[22] and suggests an affinity with those romantic societies. The style 'knights of St George', on the other hand, seems to have been inspired by that of the religious orders of knighthood, which usually took at least part of their name from their patron saint. St George, the patron of knighthood in general, had long been regarded as the protector of Catalonia as well, and he was thus the obvious choice for the role of patron of the order. Neither the prologue nor any of the following chapters has anything to say either about the number of 'knights' who were to be admitted to this 'enterprise', the qualities that were to be required for membership, or the process by which they were to be selected, so it would appear that Pere meant to reserve to himself and his royal heirs the right to admit whomever they chose. Pere's use of the phrase 'nobles and knights' to describe the membership of the order, both in the prologue to the statutes and in both of the letters quoted above, nevertheless implies that the membership was to be restricted to to men of high rank who had received the accolade of knighthood.

Ten of the ordinances are concerned exclusively with the badge and costume of the Order, which were almost identical with those of the religious order of St George of Alfama. The badge was to consist of a red cross (no doubt taken from the arms attributed to St George) which was to be at least as long as the back of a man's hand and as thick as a thumbnail.[23] As was customary, this badge was to be worn

---

21 Barcelona, Archivo General de la Corona de Aragón, reg. 1232, f. 109. Published in *Colección de documentos inéditos del Archivo General de la Corona de Aragón* (Barcelona, 1847–), VI, pp. 76–78; and in Más, 'La Orden militar de San Jorge', pp. 253–4.

22 See above, p. 17.

23 Ch. 1. It is possible that this cross had a distinctive shape which allowed it to be distinguished clearly from that of the knights of the religious order of St George of Alfama, but I have found no representation of it either alone or on the mantle of the order.

10.1 The cross of the Enterprise of St George (reconstructed)

every day by the knights of the Order on their outermost garment, directly over the heart, for as long as the king lived.[24] When dressed for battle or other feats of arms, the knights were to wear at least two such crosses, one in front and one behind.[25] To encourage compliance with these rules, Pere further decreed that any knight of the Order who wore an outer vestment without a cross was to lose that garment, and the garment was to be given to the royal almoner to be sold for the benefit of the poor.[26]

The cross was also to be emblazoned over the heart on the formal habit of the order, which was to consist of a white mantle.[27] This mantle – whose colour may have represented the white field of the arms of St George, but was also that of the mantles of most of the religious orders of knighthood – was to be worn not only by those knights who took part with the king in the annual celebration of the feast of St George,[28] but all day every Friday (changed to Saturday in May 1379) by all the knights of the Order,[29] and any knight who failed to wear it on either occasion was to forfeit the outer garment he wore instead to the royal almoner, to be sold for the benefit of the poor.[30] Any *rich hom* or knight who wished to give his mantle to anyone other than another member was to remove the cross first.[31]

The obligations of the knights not related to the wearing of the badge or mantle are set forth in two ordinances in chapter 3. Both of these obligations were cliental and strictly military, and bore some resemblance to the military obligations undertaken by life-retainers in England and France in the same period, and a rather more striking resemblance to those undertaken by the knights of the Order of the Sword. At the time of their admission to the order (as the letter of 1381 indicates),

[24] Ch. 2. The implications of the last statement are unclear.
[25] Ch. 9.
[26] Ch. 7a,b.
[27] Ch. 1.
[28] Ch. 10c.
[29] Ch. 8a.
[30] Chs. 8b, 10c.
[31] Ch. 6.

all of the knights were to do homage to the king and swear that they would personally accompany the king at his expense, with such mounted men as they could muster, whenever he rode against the Moors.[32] They were also bound to come with a similar troop to the defense of the king's lands, whenever they were attacked by any foreigner.[33] They could, however, be excused from either form of service if the king saw fit to do so.[34]

The remaining ordinances are concerned with the government and corporate activities of the Order. It would appear that the Order was to be governed by the king (who bore no special title as the Order's chief officer) with the advice of twelve counsellors, four of whom were to be *nobles* or barons, and eight of whom were to be simple knights. Together they were to 'ordain all things good and profitable' for the 'Enterprise' (including, presumably, selecting new members and adopting new ordinances), but were not to alter or limit the stipulated form of service in any way.[35] Only with the consent of this body was a knight to receive the licence of the king to join any other 'enterprise, general or special'.[36] Every year, those knights who happened to be with the king on the feast of St George were to join with him in hearing vespers on the eve and both the mass and vespers on the day itself,[37] but they were not apparently to take part in any formal assembly or banquet, and the knights of the Order who were not at court were not required either to come or to celebrate the feast on their own.

Though clearly a monarchical order according to the definition we have established, the Enterprise of St George bore only a superficial resemblance to most of the earlier monarchical orders we have examined here. Unlike the knights of all of the earlier orders whose statutes are known (including the three founded by subordinate princes), the knights of Pere's Order owed no obligations whatever to one another either in life or after death, and unlike the knights of every earlier order except that of the Golden Shield, unless they happened to be in court on St George's eve, or were chosen to serve in the unprecedented office of counsellor, they were not obliged to take part in any form of corporate activity whatever. They thus had no real need for a fixed seat, and do not appear to have had one. In fact, like the Order of the Golden Shield founded only a few years earlier, the Enterprise of St George was little more than a glorified body of contractual retainers, differing from other such bodies only in having corporate statutes, officers, and a mantle, which together gave them the appearance of constituting an order of knighthood. Unlike the obligations owed by most contractual retainers, however, the specific cliental duties undertaken by the knights of St George were of such a nature that the knights might never be called upon to fulfil them. Despite their specifications, Pere's object in founding his order was almost certainly not to secure troops either for a crusade against the 'Moors' or for the defense of his dominions. Indeed, it is clear from the wording of the letter Pere wrote to the Vicar General of Athens and Neopatria that the three knights were to be admitted to the Enterprise to reward

[32] Ch. 3a.
[33] Ch. 3b.
[34] Ch. 3c.
[35] Ch. 4a,b.
[36] Ch. 5a,b.
[37] Ch. 10a,b.

them for their past services rather than to secure their services in some future conflict, and that the obligations they were to undertake were not to be taken too seriously. In all probability, therefore, Pere created the Enterprise of St George merely to provide himself with an effective but inexpensive way of encouraging and rewarding the loyalty of the principal barons and officers of his various dominions to himself and his house, and gave it the appearance of an order of knighthood dedicated to fighting the enemies of Christendom and their king only because membership in such an order would convey more honour than any other comparable form of dignity he could have invented.

Chapter 11

The Order of the Ship
Mainland Sicily (Naples), 1381–1386?

1 Historical Background

By 1380, a monarchical order had been founded in every major court of Latin
Christendom, and as most of the orders founded had so far been maintained, if only
as a pseudo-order, by the heirs of their founders, a princely order of one sort or the
other had come to be a normal feature of such courts. The Neapolitan Company of
the Knot, however, had almost certainly dissolved completely within a short time
of the death of its ostensible founder Loysi 'di Taranto' in 1362, and as neither his
widow Queen Giovanna nor either of Loysi's successors as her consort – the
dispossessed King of Mallorca Jacme IV and the German adventurer Duke Otto of
Brunswick-Grubenhagen – had shown any inclination to replace it, the royal court
of Naples had remained without a lay order of any sort for nearly two decades. This
situation was soon to be rectified by Giovanna's cousin and successor, Carlo Capet
d'Anjou-Durazzo-Gravina, who, shortly after ascending her throne as King Carlo
III in November 1381, founded a society of knights that he called the 'Order of the
Ship'. This society – which may be regarded as the first monarchical order of the
second generation – was destined to survive for an even shorter time than the
ill-fated order it replaced, but it is nevertheless of considerable interest to the
historian, for (in striking contrast to the other orders founded since 1352), it was by
far the most elaborate and ambitious of all the lay orders created by princes in our
period, and its carefully constructed statutes give a better idea of the potential of
the monarchical order as an instrument of political and military organization than
those of any other order.

The founder of the Order, Carlo 'di Durazzo', had been born in 1355, just three
years after the coronation of his cousin Loysi 'di Taranto' and the proclamation of
the Order of the Knot. He was thus himself a whole generation younger than any of
the earlier founders, and the first founder to have grown up in a world in which
monarchical orders were normal adjuncts of royal courts.[1] As we have seen, his

---

[1] There does not appear to be a critical monograph devoted primarily to Carlo's life or reign,
but Matteo Camera, *Elucubrazioni storico-diplomatiche su Giovanna Ia e Carlo III di Durazzo*
(Salerno, 1889), Alessandro Cutolo, *Re Ladislao d'Angiò-Durazzo* (Milan, 1936), and Emile
Léonard, *Les Angevins de Naples* (Paris, 1954), give brief accounts of his reign in Italy, and
Bálint Hóman, *Gli Angioini di Napoli in Ungheria* (Rome, 1938), pp. 432ff., gives an account

father, Count Loysi of Gravina, second son of Duke Giovanni of Durazzo, had been deeply involved in the internecine strife between the Durazzo and Taranto branches of the Sicilian royal house that had marked the period following the death of King Roberto in 1343. In the last years of his life Count Loysi had been in a state of almost constant rebellion against his cousins the queen regnant and her consort King Loysi, and at the time of the latter's death in 1362 had been in prison as a rebel. Shortly after this event, Count Loysi himself had died of poison, almost certainly administered to him by an agent of the two surviving Taranto brothers, who had seen in him a dangerous rival for the hand of the newly-widowed queen. His orphaned son, the future Carlo III, was at this juncture only a child of seven, and although he was now the only surviving male member of the Durazzo branch of the royal house, he posed no immediate threat to the Tarantos. He was first taken under the protection of Queen Giovanna herself, but in 1365 he was effectively adopted by his childless second-cousin King Lajos 'the Great' of Hungary (whose younger brothers had both died without issue), and later that year was brought to the Hungarian court to be raised as the heir presumptive to Lajos' throne. King Lajos was of course the head of the senior branch of the Angevin house, and like his father Károly I, the founder of the Fraternal Society of St George, he maintained a court famous throughout Europe as a school of chivalry in the traditions of northern France. Thus, though born in Italy and raised in Hungary, Carlo received an education very similar to that given French princes in the same period, and as we shall see there is some reason to believe that he was fluent in French as well as Italian and Hungarian.

Like most young princes of his day, Carlo soon found himself playing the role of pawn in the game of dynastic politics. In 1370, when he was fifteen, he was married by Hungarian contrivance to another of his second-cousins, Margherita 'di Durazzo', who – as the child of the deceased only sibling of the barren Queen Giovanna – was heir presumptive to the possessions and pretensions of the Neapolitan line of the Angevin house.[2] Thus, for a short time, Carlo had every reason to expect that following the deaths of his adoptive father and his cousin Queen Giovanna he would sit on both of the thrones currently occupied by members of his dynasty.

The birth in 1370 of the first of three daughters to the long barren wife of King Lajos, however, quickly ended his chances of succeeding easily to the Hungarian throne, and he was left dependent entirely upon his wife's expectations of following her aunt on the throne of Naples. The papal schism of 1378, precipitated in part by Queen Giovanna's refusal to recognize the election of her subject, the Archbishop of Bari, to the throne of St Peter, set off a complex chain of events which led among other things to Carlo's claiming his wife's inheritance before it was fully

---

of his reign in Hungary. Much of the historical account presented in this chapter has already appeared in the introduction to my article, 'The Middle French Statutes of the Monarchical Order of the Ship (Naples, 1381): A Critical Edition, with Introduction and Notes', *Mediaeval Studies*, 47 (1985), pp. 168–271.

[2] Margherita (d. 1412) was the fifth and youngest child of Maria of Calabria (d.c. 1367) by Duke Carlo of Durazzo (d. 1348), the uncle of the future Carlo III. Her position as heiress presumptive was due to the death or disqualification of her four older siblings.

due. The new Pope, Urban VI, quickly declared his recalcitrant vassal Queen Giovanna to be deposed for heresy and schism, and allied himself with Lajos of Hungary, who still held Giovanna responsible for the murder of his younger brother Endre, her first consort. Together Pope and king seized upon the latter's ward, the partially disinherited Carlo 'di Durazzo' (who since the death of Prince Filippo of Taranto in 1374 had been the only surviving male of the Angevin house other than Lajos himself), as the instrument of her removal. Carlo, no doubt anxious to secure what remained of his expected inheritance, agreed readily enough, and was accordingly dispatched to Naples with a large force of Hungarians and Italians. *En route* he stopped in Rome long enough to receive the crowns of mainland Sicily and Jerusalem from the Pope's own hands on 2 June 1381. Carlo's army then marched on Naples, and after defeating the forces led by Giovanna's consort Otto of Brunswick at Anagni, entered the city in triumph on 26 July. Giovanna herself (who on 29 June 1380 had formally disinherited her niece Margherita in favour of her distant cousin Duke Louis I of Anjou, the second son of Jean II of France), held out for a month in the Castel Nuovo, but was finally forced to surrender on 26 August. She was imprisoned for the next few months in the Castel dell'Ovo, the erstwhile seat of the Order of the Knot,[3] while Carlo set up his own court as King Carlo III in the nearby Castel Nuovo. There he was again crowned King of Jerusalem and Sicily on 25 November.

2 The Foundation and History of the Order, 1381–1387

It was during the festivities that followed this second coronation that, on 1 December according to the statutes, Carlo proclaimed his new order of knighthood, that of the Ship.[4] Nearly twenty years had elapsed since the extinction of the Company of the Knot. Carlo himself could have had no clear recollection of its ceremonies and feasts, but there must have been many in the court who remembered them very well, and it is likely that a copy of the order's statutes would have been available to Carlo. There can have been no thought in his mind of reviving the old order, which was inextricably associated with the rival Taranto

---

[3] She was moved to Muro in Basilicata in March 1382 and died there on 22 July, probably of strangulation.

[4] The Order of the Ship was known to most of the antiquarian historians of knightly orders on the basis the brief account of its history published in Pandolfo Collenucio's *Compendio delle istorie del Regno di Napoli* (Venice, 1539, 1541, 1552, 1613), Lib. V, p. 198: 'Feronsi poi bellissime giostre e feste, doue interuenne il Re in persona, il quale a imitazione del Re Luigi, che fe quella del Nodo, institui vna nuoua compagnia chiamandola della Nave, alludendo alla naue de gli Argonauti.' Since the publication in 1642 of Joseph Micheli Márquez's *Tesoro militar de cavallería*, it has been generally believed that the Order was formally called the 'Order of the Argonauts of St Nicholas', that it was placed under the patronage of St Nicholas of Myra (who was the patron of the kingdom and of sailors, and had as one of his attributes a ship), and that its members assembled each year on his feast day at his shrine in the Cathedral of St Nicholas in Bari in a formal habit of white, but as we shall see there is no basis in the evidence for any of these beliefs, and the Order does not appear to have had any connection whatever with the Argonauts, St Nicholas, or Bari. The Order has been virtually ignored by modern critical historians, and I know of no previous attempt to examine either its history or its statutes.

line of the royal house, the murderers of his father. Nevertheless, it can hardly be doubted that in establishing a new order so shortly after his coronation he was following the example set by Loysi on the day of his coronation in 1352, and it is evident from the content of its statutes that the Order of the Ship was partly modelled on Loysi's order. There is reason to believe that the Hungarian order of St George – to which Carlo, as the heir presumptive to the Hungarian throne, had surely been admitted by 1381 – also served as a model for Carlo's new society, though the limited state of our knowledge of that order makes it difficult to say to precisely what extent Carlo drew upon its current constitution in framing the ordinances of the order he founded.

The only contemporary documents I have found for the history of the Order of the Ship are two manuscript copies of the statutes, each of which ends with a brief description of the foundation of the Order:[5]

> The names of the companions of the order are those which follow below: First, Monsire Charles de Duras [di Durazzo], King of Jerusalem and Sicily, Prince and commencer of the Order; Monsire Loys de Anguien, Count of Conversano;[6] Monsire Charles Rous de Monhaut of Calabria;[7] Monsire Jannot Prothojudice of Salerno;[8] Monsire Gieffroy de Marsan, Count of Alife;[9] Monsire Thomas de Marsan;[10] Monsire Palamides Bochut of Naples;[11] Monsire Franchoys Guidace of Naples;[12] and Monsire Bartholome Tomacelle;[13] the which kings, counts, and knights took the order and swore even as the chapters of the order say, in the great chapel of the Castel Nuovo, on the first day of the month of December in the year of grace 1381 of the fifth indiction, in the presence of many gentlemen and great people.

I have found no evidence that the Order thus founded ever met again, or that Carlo put any part of his elaborate plan for his Order into effect, but the state of the documentation in general is such that this lack of positive evidence means very little. In fact it is more than likely that Carlo pushed forward with the plans

---

5 See below, pp. 294–5.

6 I.e., Louis d'Enghien-Brienne, Count of Conversano just to the south-east of Bari in Apulia and (from 1381) of Brienne in Champagne (d. 1394).

7 I.e., Carlo Ruffo, Count of Montalto in Calabria and Grand Justiciar of the kingdom. (Léonard, *Jeanne Ire*, I, p. 590.)

8 I.e., Giannotto Protogiudice, Count of Acerra just to the west of Naples and Grand Constable of the kingdom. (Camera, *Elucubrazioni*, p. 298.)

9 I.e., Goffredo di Marzano, Count of Alife in the Matese just to the north of Naples, probably to be identified with the baron of that name who, as Count of Squillace, was Grand Admiral of the kingdom.

10 I.e., Tommaso di Marzano, presumably a relative of the Count of Alife. His name was omitted, probably in error, from the Pennsylvania ms. of the statutes.

11 A member of the prominent noble house of Bozzuto, which had provided companions both to the Company of the Knot and to that of the Star.

12 Probably Francischello Guindazzo (or Guindaccio), a member of a family prominent among the nobility of the kingdom. (Léonard, *Jeanne Ire*, I, p. 37.)

13 Probably Bartolomeo Tomacelli, a member of another prominent noble family of the kingdom. (Ibid.)

announced in the statutes to the extent that his situation permitted, fully intending to establish the Order on a solid basis as soon as his position was secure. As it turned out, Carlo, like his cousin Jean of France three decades earlier, was obliged to spend most of his short reign fighting to keep his throne, and probably had neither the time nor the money necessary for the effective establishment of his Order. Although Giovanna herself was soon removed from the scene by strangulation or the administration of a lethal dose of some poison, her adoptive heir Duke Louis of Anjou proved more troublesome. After conquering the Counties of Provence and Piedmont – which neither Carlo nor his heirs would ever recover – Louis set out from Carpentras in the spring of 1382 with an army of more than 60,000 veterans supplied by his nephew the King of France, the Avignonese Pope, and some of the most powerful princes in Italy – including Amé 'the Green Count' of Savoy, who as we have seen was to die while serving with the expedition. Duke Louis arrived with this force before Naples itself in October of that year, and after conquering the Principality of Taranto from Otto of Brunswick, had himself proclaimed king on 30 August 1383. His triumph was short-lived, however, for while confronting an army led by Carlo and his erstwhile enemy Otto of Brunswick near Bari in September 1384 he died unexpectedly of a fever, and his army simply dissolved.

Louis' death did not immediately relieve Carlo of the obligation of defending his crown, for his former ally Pope Urban VI had in the previous year formed the mad project of conquering the kingdom of mainland Sicily either for the Holy See itself or for his nephew, and had not merely excommunicated Carlo and his descendants to the fourth generation, but had proclaimed a general crusade against him on 27 February 1385. Swift military action by Carlo forced Urban to flee to Genoa in July of that year, and his flight assured the young king at long last of the control of his kingdom.

At this point there was reason to believe that Carlo III would assume in the affairs of Italy as a whole the place once occupied by his ancestor Carlo I, for the death of Count Amé of Savoy in February 1383 and the deposition of Bernabò Visconti of Milan in May 1385 had removed the leading players from the Italian stage, and Carlo himself – well-educated, able, ambitious, and unscrupulous – seemed to contemporaries to be fully capable of playing the role. Indeed, some of the leading humanists of the day, responding to his generous patronage, were already saluting him as the master of Italy.[14]

Unfortunately, Carlo allowed himself to be seduced by his old dream of reuniting the whole Angevin patrimony in his hands. King Lajos had died on 10 September 1382, leaving Hungary to the younger of his surviving daughters, Hedwig, and Poland to the elder, Mária, but the latter had been elected to the Hungarian throne by the magnates one week later, and Hungary had been governed in her name by her mother, the Queen Dowager Erzsébet, and the latter's favourite Miklós Garay, the Count Palatine. Queen Mária had been promised by her father to Sigismund von Luxemburg-Brandenburg, younger son of the Emperor Karl IV, but her mother had her married by procuration to Louis Capet de Valois-Orléans, the younger brother of Charles VI of France, in April 1385. This marriage was opposed not merely by the adherants of Sigismund (who arrived with an army in August 1385 and forced the young queen to marry him according to her father's plan), but by a

---

[14] Léonard, *Les Angevins*, p. 475 n. 3.

faction led by Janos Horvathy, who wanted to see Mária married to Carlo's son, Ladislao. Encouraged by Horvathy, Carlo landed with an army at Zagreb on 23 October, and after forcing Mária to abdicate in his favour, had himself crowned King of Hungary as King Károly II in the capital city of Buda on 31 December.

Carlo thus achieved for a short time the dearest ambition of his immediate predecessors on the Hungarian throne. His Hungarian adventure soon proved fatal to all his hopes, however, for on 7 February 1386 he was attacked in the apartments of the queen dowager, apparently at her instigation, and died of the wounds he received a few days later. His widow Margherita had their nine-year-old son Ladislao proclaimed king as soon as news of his death reached her in Naples, but the partisans of Duke Louis II of Anjou succeeded in forcing her to flee Naples in the following year, and although Ladislao was crowned king with the blessings of the new Roman Pope, Boniface IX, in 1390, he was not finally able to regain control of his kingdom until 1399 – thirteen years after his father's death.

Ladislao proved to be a worthy successor to his murdered father, and pursued throughout his reign the same aggressive policy both in Italy and in Hungary, but there is no evidence that he even attempted to maintain his father's order. Indeed, there is evidence which suggests that Carlo's ambitious project for a monarchical order was abandoned almost immediately after his death, for his widow Margherita, in her capacity as regent, seems to have founded some sort of order of her own (that of the *Argata* or 'Spool') in 1388 – the year after her abandonment of Naples.[15] Little is known about this order, but it is hardly likely that Margherita would have established it if the Order of the Ship had survived. Ladislao died childless on 6 August 1414, leaving the throne to his sister Giovanna II (r. 1414–1435), the last of her house to reign in Naples. Before her death in 1435 she bequeathed her throne to Duke René 'the Good' of Anjou, the grandson of her father's rival, but he was soon displaced by King Alfons V of Aragon, whose ancestors had long claimed the mainland kingdom of Sicily as the heirs of the Hautevilles and the Hohenstaufen. Neither René nor Alfons had any reason to revive the Order of the Ship, and the latter's son and successor in Naples founded yet another monarchical order, as we shall see.

3 The Statutes of the Order

Most of our knowledge of the Order of the Ship is derived from its statutes, which have been preserved in at least two contemporary manuscripts. One of these, now in Turin, is a deluxe copy that appears to have been prepared within a few weeks of

---

[15] According to Cesare d'Engenio Caracciolo (*Napoli Sacra*, pp. 670–76), Queen Margherita and King Ladislao in that year '. . . instuirono la compagnia dell'Argata, & per insegna portauano nel braccio sinistro vn Argata ricamata d'oro in campo rosso, simil a quell'argate di canna e d'altro, de quali si sogliono seruire le donne ne'loro feminili esercitii: onde i Napolitani con quei vascelli andauanno perseguitando le galee della Reina.'

the foundation of the Order in December 1381;[16] the other, now in Philadelphia, is a more ordinary copy which could have been made at any time during the next four years.[17] The statutes contained in both manuscripts are expressed in the same Middle French dialect that the statutes of the Knot had been composed in thirty years earlier, and for the most part the texts differ from one another only in the phrasing and organization of the ordinances. When the obvious scribal errors in both manuscripts are corrected, both contain the same set of 383 ordinances, grouped in 153 chapters in the Turin manuscript and in 152 chapters in the Pennsylvania manuscript. Although the arrangement of the chapters in the Turin manuscript is slightly more logical, we shall here follow the organization of the Pennsylvania manuscript, which my recent edition has made available for consultation.

Although undoubtedly inspired by the earlier orders of the Knot and St George of Hungary, Carlo did not imitate his (known) models nearly as slavishly as had his predecessor King Loysi, or rather his Grand Seneschal Nicola Acciaiuoli.[18] The originality of Carlo's statutes is clear from their relative number and length alone: with 383 ordinances expressed in roughly 17,000 words, they are more than five times as long as those of the Society of St George, whose 66 original ordinances were expressed in about 1400 words, and those of the Company of the Knot, whose 72 ordinances were expressed in 3200 words. Furthermore, only 27 of the Ship ordinances (well under ten percent) correspond even approximately to the known ordinances of St George, and only seven have strikingly similar provisions. Similarly, only 41 (just over ten percent) correspond in subject matter to ordinances of the Knot, and only 35 of the 72 Knot ordinances are represented in any form among those of the Ship.[19] Carlo may have used other models for his foundation, including the orders of the Hospital of St John and of the Teutonic Knights, with which he would certainly have been familiar, but if he did use them he borrowed from their statutes only in a small way, and most of his ordinances seem to have been freely adapted from military and political practices not particularly associated in the past with orders of any kind.

The statutes of the Ship are not only more numerous than those of any earlier (or for that matter any later) lay order, but considerably better organized. Carlo arranged his chapters into nine principal groups or sections, most of them distinguished in the text by a special sectional heading. All but one of these sections are concerned with a single easily definable subject, and only one of

---

[16] Turin, Biblioteca Nazionale Universitaria, ms. L III 29. Although this manuscript was largely destroyed by the fire which swept through the Turin library in 1904, a transcription of it made just before the fire was published by Silvio Pivano as an appendix to a general article on knighthood: 'Lineamenti storici e giuridici della cavalleria medioevale', Memorie della Real Accademia delle Scienze di Torino, 2nd Ser., 50 (1905), esp. pp. 295–336.

[17] Philadelphia, University of Pennsylvania ms. French 83. For the text of this manuscript, corrected on the basis of Pivano's transcription, and for a more detailed description of both manuscripts and a discussion of their relationship to one another, see my edition 'The Middle French Statutes of the Monarchical Order of the Ship', cited above.

[18] It is of course possible that Carlo borrowed heavily from a late version of the statutes of the Hungarian Society of St George currently unknown to scholarship. See above, p. 31.

[19] See 'The Middle French Statutes', p. 204, nn. 107, 108.

the eight remaining sections contains chapters not obviously related to that subject. Like the chapters (which contain between one and sixteen ordinances), the sections vary significantly in length (from seven to forty-three chapters), and the four longest are divided into between two and eleven subsections. To facilitate reference, I have assigned Roman numerals to the sections and capital letters to the subsections, in addition to the usual numbers and letters used to distinguish chapters and ordinances.[20]

Because they are both long and well-organized, and because they constitute virtually the only evidence that survives for the nature and history of the Order as such, I shall in general follow their organization in the following commentary, deviating from it only when some more logical category imposes itself, or the arrangement of the chapters is not altogether convenient.

4 The Prologue: The Name, Badge, and Patron of the Order

By 1381 it was customary to begin the statutes of a monarchical order with a brief statement of the founder's purpose and the name, badge, and patron he had chosen for his order. The prologue which stands at the head of the statutes of the Ship differs from earlier prologues primarily in being long (1500 words) and discursive, and it must be compared to the letter founding the clerical college of the Company of the Star and the letter of election to the Company of the Knot as well as to the simple prologue which precedes the chapters of the latter order. The purpose, device, and patron are all introduced in the Ship prologue through an interlocking series of rather convoluted metaphors, involving images of flowering rods (playing on the words *verge* 'rod' and *virge* 'virgin'), three flowers 'two above and one below' (symbolic of the Trinity, the three Estates, and the royal arms of France), and a ship sailing on a troubled sea 'without sails, without masts, without banners, without anchors, without rudders, and without ropes'. The general import of the prologue can be summarized as follows. Carlo, mindful of the past glories of his Capetian house, and seeing that in his own time 'the Church was deceived, knighthood annulled, and the common people destroyed', proposed to do what he could not only to 'maintain, guard, and defend' the Catholic Faith and the three Estates, but to avenge the death of Jesus Christ and exalt his faith by passing beyond the sea to wrest the Holy Land from the hands of the Infidel.

> And since this cannot be done at all by one man without the aid of others, the said prince, moved by devotion, virtue, and faith, and by very great good, has made and ordained an order of knighthood, to the honour of the Blessed and Holy Trinity, Father, Son, and Holy Spirit, in the year of the incarnation of Our Lord Jesus Christ 1381, and in the twenty-fourth year of the age of the said lord, so that the Blessed Trinity would give him force and power to guard the Order well and loyally, as it is devised and ordained by the chapters written below, and made for this, in order to praise good knights, and to increase their name, and to exalt knighthood, and so that there would

[20] See Boulton, 'The Middle French Statutes', pp. 208–9.

be a perpetual memory of the good, and so that those who come afterwards may take example from the virtues and prowess of those deceased, and to give heart and hardiness to all to do well, and to love, honour, and hold dear the good and the valiant, and to hate and despise the bad and the cowardly, as is right, and as the Order wishes and commands, as appears clearly by the chapters.

In order that those who 'took' the Order might be known to each other and be properly united as brothers, they were to wear at all times the 'ensign and device' of the ship, denuded of all its accoutrements until such time as, by performing some notable feat of arms, they might 'garnish' it according to the rules set out later in the statutes. The prologue concludes with an elaborate justification of the ship as the 'most noble possible' badge, declaring that the device represented at once the Ark of Noah 'by which the human lineage was saved and protected'; the ships in which the Greek, Roman, and later heroes 'sought out and conquered divers lands, and acquired honour and praise and demonstrated virtue and prowess'; the Blessed Virgin Mary, the 'virginal vessel' in which the Holy Trinity and the 'three flowers' of the first metaphor 'reposed'; and the Catholic Faith itself, the vessel of the 'great fisherman' currently buffeted by tempests on the sea, which the Prince and the companions of the Order were especially to defend.

We shall return in the conclusion to this chapter to a consideration of Carlo's true purpose in founding the Order, and concentrate for the moment on what the prologue tells us about the new Order's nomenclature, badge, and patron. Curiously enough, considering its prolixity, the prologue does not explicitly name the society – which it refers to generically as an *ordre de chevalerie* – but it is clear from the prologue title and references throughout the statutes which follow that, like the Order of the Collar and most of the later monarchical orders, the society founded by Carlo was formally styled 'order' quite simply, and took its formal name, not from its patron, but from its badge alone. In the body of the statutes, however, it is frequently referred to as a *compaignie*, and the term *ordre* is used (usually in combination with the word *devise*) to designate the Order's badge.

The basic badge of the *Ordre de la Nef*, a ship stripped of its fittings, is represented in the historiated initial of the prologue in the Pennsylvania manuscript as a double-castled craft of the type generally called a cog, with a naked mast and bowsprit, set in an ovoid patch of 'sea' which does not actually obscure any part of its rounded hull (fig. 11.1). The ship itself is of gold, and the 'sea' is made up of blue and white waves. It is only the second such device of whose symbolic significance we are informed by its inventor (the first being the knot of the earlier Neapolitan order), and it is interesting to note that the symbolism explained in the prologue is decidedly complex and esoteric, and has no very obvious connexion with the Order's heavenly patron.

Despite the lengths to which Carlo went to justify his choice of a ship as the badge of his new Order, its three-layered symbolism – Jewish, pagan, and Christian – can have been only part of the reason for its selection. Equally important to Carlo's choice of a ship must have been the fact that a badge in this form, while perfectly recognizable in a totally denuded condition, could be augmented with a great variety of possible accoutrements – the sails, masts, banners, anchors, rudders, and ropes mentioned in the prologue – any or all of which could be added to it without altering its essential nature. The prologue itself makes it clear that this was Carlo's intention: that the ship was to be, like the knot of the earlier Neapolitan order, not merely a fixed sign of membership in the Order, but a device capable of visible augmentation to indicate personal achievement.[21] The knights of the Knot seem to have responded enthusiastically to the idea of an augmentable badge, and it seems to have been imitated by the founders of at least two other lay orders, one fraternal and one votive.[22] As we shall see, Carlo liked the idea well enough to devote fifteen chapters to it, and it was probably the principal reason why he chose a ship as the device of his new Order.

As was customary in confraternities, the ship-badge was evidently to be worn as a sort of brooch. For some reason Carlo did not see fit to suggest anywhere in the statutes exactly where the badge was to be worn, so it may well have been pinned to different parts of the companions' clothing, according to convenience and whim. Like the badges of most monarchical orders, however, the ship-badge was to be worn all the time, both as a constant reminder to the wearer of his membership in the Order, and as a means of advertising the Order's existence to the world at large.[23]

All but one of the earlier monarchical orders had been placed under the patronage of some celestial personage, and Carlo clearly saw no reason to depart from this custom. It is likely that his rather surprising selection of the Holy Trinity as patron was due primarily to a desire to outdo his predecessor Loysi, who had placed his order under the protection of the Holy Spirit alone, though it is also possible that Carlo, like the Black Prince, felt a special devotion to the Trinity. The Triune Godhead was to be formally honoured as the patron of the Order of the Ship in three of the established six ways: the principal annual meeting of the Order was to be held on Trinity Sunday (a feast first universally proclaimed less than half a century earlier, in 1334); the principal altar in the Order's chapel was to be dedicated especially to the Holy Trinity; and the principal mass sung in the chapel each day was to be that of the Trinity. Despite these deferential gestures, however, the Trinity seems to have been intended to serve more as a status symbol than as a genuine object of communal devotion for the knights of the Order.

5 The Membership of the Order: The Prince

Loysi di Taranto had followed the declaration of his order's purpose, patron, and title with a simple statement about the order's composition and structure. Carlo, however, made no comparable statement in his statutes, and the structure of the Order of the Ship must therefore be inferred indirectly. It is in fact quickly apparent from the statutes that the Order was to have a chief officer bearing the title *Prince* or 'Prince' and an unspecified number of members called *compaignons* or 'companions'.

---

[21] Cf. Knot chs. 3, 24, 25.
[22] The orders of the Tiercelet (chs. 6–12) and the Dragon of Foix (chs. 7–12), both founded in France. See above, pp. 15, 17.
[23] Ch. 93.

The statutes imply rather than state that Carlo himself was to be the first Prince of the Order. The title 'Prince' was probably taken from the statutes of the Knot, and the office it designated seems to have been essentially similar to the princeship of the latter society. Like every other founder of a monarchical order in our period, however, the founder of the Order of the Knot had entailed the princeship of his order to his successors as king. Carlo, by contrast, devoted a whole subsection of his statutes (III.A) to the devolution of the princely office under various possible circumstances, and made it theoretically elective rather than hereditary. To begin with, he gave to each successive Prince the right to nominate his own successor, if possible from among his own legitimate sons,[24] but in the absense of sons, from among his male agnates in general.[25] If by some chance the designated successor declined to take up the office,[26] or if the line of the founder failed entirely in all its branches, the companions were to be free to elect by a majority vote one of their own number to fill the position, 'so that the Order will not fail in default of a Prince.'[27] On learning of the Prince's death, all the companions were to assemble to make sure that a successor had been chosen, and if no choice had been made, they were to elect one then and there.[28] However the new Prince was chosen, they were to be obliged to him exactly as they had been to his predecessor.[29]

In theory, therefore, the Order of the Ship was not to have been, like the other monarchical orders, a mere appurtenance of the crown, but a distinct corporate entity which could, under certain circumstances, become entirely independent of royal control. Whether in reality Carlo was so concerned to perpetuate his foundation that he was willing to see it become a potential threat to his royal successors is another matter. On close examination, the refusal of a designated heir to serve as Prince and the failure of the whole Capetian house must seem extremely unlikely eventualities, and probably seemed so to Carlo as well. It is also unlikely, considering the nature of the Order and the extent of his intended investment in it, that either Carlo or any of his successors as king would have nominated as his successor in the princeship anyone other than his heir presumtive in the kingship. There was, therefore, no real reason to suppose that the princeship of the Order would ever have been vested in anyone but Carlo's royal heirs, and the other provisions should perhaps be regarded as a subtle ploy to create a false hope of future independence among his clients, or a feeling that they had a significant role in the governance of the Order. It may be, however, that Carlo was primarily concerned with preventing the Order from coming under the control of Duke Louis of Anjou or one of his heirs, in the all-too-likely eventuality that they succeeded in seizing the Neapolitan throne.

[24] Ch. 25.
[25] Ch. 26.
[26] Ch. 27.
[27] Ch. 28.
[28] Ch. 19.
[29] Ch. 20.

6 The Membership of the Order: The Companions

Unlike most of the earlier and later founders, Carlo did not set any specific limit on the number of ordinary members or 'companions' who could be admitted to the Order, and the statutes give the impression that, like Alfonso of Castile, he simply hoped to attract as many as possible. While most earlier founders had said very little about the selection and admission of new members, on the other hand, Carlo devoted the whole first section of his statutes – some seventeen chapters – to the qualifications required for nomination and the processes through which candidates were to be both elected and received into the Order.

The qualifications, both positive and negative, were minutely set forth. A prospective member was required to be of good character and health, a true Catholic, a knight, and a gentleman of good lineage, and was to be known as such to at least one of the companions. He was not to be a member of any religious order, a judge, a lawyer, a physician,[30] a merchant, a banker, a heretic, a schismatic, a thief, a traitor, a man of infamous reputation, a user of foul language, or a pensioner of anyone hostile to the Prince or any of the companions.[31] In short, he was to be everything the nobility then admired, and nothing it despised, and furthermore well known both as such and as a man who could be trusted by the companions not to betray them. The last qualification was doubtless the most important in Carlo's own eyes, but the others served to give the Order a public image that was at once virtuous, orthodox, and thoroughly aristocratic.

A man of such qualities who wished to enter the Order was to present himself to the Prince, who alone had the right to present him to the companions for election. Elections were to take place only during the Order's four annual feasts, at Trinity, All Saints, Christmas, and Easter, but Carlo reserved to himself the right to nominate any 'haut prince ou seigneur' at any time for election by such companions as happened to be with him.[32] Otherwise the agreement of two thirds of the assembled companions was necessary for election.[33] Carlo thus retained for himself and his successors the controlling right of nomination, while allowing the companions to refuse any nominee other than a 'high prince or lord' with whom they did not wish to associate.[34] The concession was a minor one, and no doubt worth the good-will he hoped to gain by it. Even more than the theoretical right to elect the Prince, it gave the Order the appearance of being a self-governing society rather than a body of servile clients totally dependent on their lord.

The exception from the normal rule of election of 'high princes and lords' seems to indicate that Carlo, like Edward of England and Nicola Acciaiuoli before him, saw his Order as a potential instrument of international diplomacy, and was concerned to secure the freedom of action essential in foreign policy.

---

[30] The Turin ms. omits this word from ord. 1j., and it may therefore have been added as an amendment.

[31] Ch. 2. Cf. Garter ch. 2.

[32] Ch. 1.

[33] Ch. 3.

[34] Cf. St George of Hungary chs. 20, 21; Garter, C, ch. 17.

Chapters 4 through 8 describe the ceremony of admission into the Order that was to be followed under normal circumstances. The ordinary candidate, once elected, was to present himself at one of the four annual assemblies. There the names of all the existing companions were to be read to him, and he was to pardon any of those named with whom he had a quarrel, or to submit the quarrel to the binding arbitration of the Prince.[35] The statutes were then to be read to him and he was to swear to observe them, under pain of the various penalties set forth for default.[36] He was then bound to declare before the assembled companions all his other oaths, fealties, and obligations.[37] Lastly, before being formally received into the company, he was to fast for one day, confess, and receive communion at the high mass held on one of the four great feasts.[38] Following the mass, the assembled companions and their Prince, all similarly fasted and shriven, were to kneel with him before the high altar and pray for him, while the clerks present sang the psalm *Exaudivit te dominus*, a prayer for the victory of the king in battle.[39] The statutes were then to be read to him again (an activity requiring about an hour and a half), and he was again to swear to abide by them. Finally, the Prince was to take him by the hand, kiss him, and bestow upon him the device of the Order, and the companions were to kiss him each in turn as a sign of fraternity. He was then to be regarded as a member of the Order, and his name included with the others in the book of the statutes, of which he was to obtain a copy for himself as soon as possible.[40]

Carlo seems to have designed the ceremonies of admission to the Order to accomplish two purposes in particular. He was first of all concerned to secure, by every possible means, complete obedience to the statutes. Every companion-elect was obliged to swear to obey them not once but twice, on each occasion after hearing them read aloud in the presence of all the assembled companions. No member could therefore be in a position to claim either ignorance of the rule or failure to undertake the full burden of membership, and infractions could be punished accordingly.

In addition, Carlo was unusually concerned to promote both the appearance and the feeling of solidarity among the companions, and to avoid any internal conflict. The renunciation of all quarrels and the declaration of all other obligations were clearly designed to pave the way for the more positive feelings of fraternity produced by the corporate prayer, the kiss, and the inscription of the new companion's name among the others. The solemnity of the undertaking was underscored by its religious setting – in a church, immediately following a high mass on a major feast day – and by the religious preparation undergone by both members and postulant. The badge itself, the visible symbol of his new status as a member of the brotherhood, was to be solemnly bestowed, like the accolade of the general order of knighthood, by the Prince himself. The rite of admission could hardly have been more moving if the postulant had been entering a religious order.

---

[35] Ch. 4.
[36] Ch. 5. Cf. Knot ch. 1b.
[37] Ch. 6.
[38] Ch. 7.
[39] Psalm 19/20. Cf. Knot ch. 7e.
[40] Ch. 8.

The knights of Carlo's Order may have been laymen, but their brotherhood, once entered, was to be no less sacred than that of any monastery.

Chapters 9 to 17 deal with the reception of companions-elect at times or in circumstances when either the postulant or the Prince himself was unable to be present. The Prince was to have the right to send the 'order and device' to any king, duke, prince, or other high lord, at any time he chose.[41] During the course of any of the four regular assemblies of the Order, the Prince, with the consent of two thirds of those present, could also send the 'order and device' to any knight who met the qualifications for membership.[42] More remarkably, with the consent of the same proportion of the companions present the Prince could give licence to 'any king, prince, duke, or high lord' who had been admitted or was to be admitted to companionship, to receive into the Order in the Prince's name as many knights as the latter chose to specify in the licence.[43] When sent to a companion-elect of any rank, the 'order' was to be borne by a trusted messenger known to the Prince,[44] who was also to bring to the companion-elect a complete copy of the statutes[45] and to receive his oaths.[46] The companion-elect was then to be received through the usual ceremonies, but these could be held on any convenient day, not merely during the four feasts of the Order.[47] A companion thus received *in absentia* was to send back to the Prince a copy of the oaths he had sworn, duly sealed with his seal.[48] Any companion received by an absent lord who had been given the power to admit others into the order was to receive from him a complete copy of the statutes.[49]

The contents of this subsection are more than usually novel. Of the older orders, only that of the Garter had made any provision whatever for reception *in absentia*, and no earlier order had permitted the delegation to other lords of the right either to name or to receive companions. The wording of chapters 11 and 16 is somewhat obscure, but it seems to imply that the licence sent to lords honoured with this right was to specify only the number of knights the lord could admit, leaving the choice of individuals to the lord himself. This provision seems to have been designed to make it possible to recruit members for the order in districts of Italy with which the Prince himself had little direct contact; because of the nature of the obligations associated with membership, it is extremely unlikely that any knight not resident in or near the kingdom of mainland Sicily would have accepted membership in the Order, and Carlo must surely have been aware of this.

Very little is known about the membership of the Order during its brief history. The statutes themselves, as we have seen, give the names of the first eight companions, and the Turin manuscript contains an addendum to the effect that a ninth companion, 'Messire Nichole d'Alemaigne' was admitted to the Order later

41 Ch. 9.
42 Ch. 10.
43 Ch. 11.
44 Ch. 12.
45 Ch. 13.
46 Ch. 15.
47 Ch. 16.
48 Ch. 17.
49 Ch. 14.

the same week, on Friday 6 December 1381. The presence of the arms of Malespina on the title page of the Pennsylvania manuscript of the statutes suggests that at least one member of that great family was admitted to the order as well. The antiquarian Cesare d'Engenio Caracciolo in his *Napoli Sacra*[50] listed the names of ten men who left some record of having belonged to the Order, including eight whose names are not mentioned in either manuscript of the statutes: Gurello Caracciolo, Grand Constable of the Kingdom; Arrigo Sanseverino, Count of Militio; Raimondello Orsini (d. 1406), Count of Lecce in Apulia from 1384 in succession to his brother-in-law, Pierre d'Enghien, nephew of the companion Louis d'Enghien-Brienne, and Prince of Taranto from 1393; Jean de Luxembourg-Ligny-Brienne (d. 1397), Count of Brienne and Conversano from 1394 in succession to his father-in-law, the companion Louis d'Enghien-Brienne; Angelo Pignatello; Gioanluigi Gianvilla; Tomaso Boccapianola; and Giovan Caracciolo. Both Giannotto Protogiudice, Count of Acerra, and the Grand Constable Gurello Caracciolo recorded their membership on their tombs in the Church of St Dominic in Naples. Most of the sixteen companions whose full names are known were members of important families of the *Regno*; no fewer than seven of them were counts, and the two Caracciolos belonged to a comital house. Four of them were great officers of the kingdom. Arrigo Sanseverino was an agnatic relative of Carlo's mother, the daughter of Roberto Sanseverino, Count of Tricario. All sixteen were probably close friends or political adherents of the new king. One of them (Palamides Bozzuto) belonged to a family which had provided companions to both the Star and the Knot, while three others (the Caracciolos and Boccapianola) belonged to families which had provided a known companion to the latter order, and another (Jean de Luxembourg) was the ancestor of one of the founder-knights of the Order of the Golden Fleece.

7 The Spiritual Obligations of Membership

The religious emphasis introduced in section I of the statutes was continued by Carlo in section II, headed *Les chapistres espiritueulz*. The seven chapters of the section (18–24) may be seen as an elaboration upon the rather rudimentary spiritual obligations imposed on the knights of the Star and the Knot. The statutes of both of these orders had set aside one day of the week for fasting, and prescribed a small monetary penalty for any who failed to fast.[51] The knights of the Knot had also been obliged to wear their badge in plain white on a black hood and to dress in the simplest colour possible every Friday (having fasted on Thursday), 'in remembrance of the Passion'.[52] These requirements are reflected in chapters 20, 21, and 22 of the Ship statutes. The companions of the Ship were to fast each Friday in commemoration of the Passion of the Second Person of the Trinity.[53] On the same

[50] (Naples, 1623).
[51] Knot ch. 5a.
[52] Knot ch. 2d.
[53] Ch. 20.

day they were not only to dress entirely in black,[54] but to say the Little Office of the Cross (appropriate to the day) or, if illiterate, twenty-five *Pater Nosters* and twenty-five *Ave Marias*.[55] This alone constituted a significant addition to the spiritual obligations of the earlier orders, but Carlo added three even greater religious burdens: the obligation, 'out of love and fear of God',[56] never to blaspheme,[57] and the obligation both to hear mass[58] and to say either the Office of Our Lady or the Seven Penitential Psalms (or if illiterate one hundred *Pater Nosters* and one hundred *Ave Marias*) every day of the year.[59] Failure to observe each of these requirements was provided with an appropriate penalty: confession followed by fast for blasphemy, abstention from meat for failure to hear mass, and alms for failure to pray. The effect of these additions, especially in the light of the rite of entry, was to make the Order of the Ship a far more convincing devotional confraternity than any of the previous orders had been.

It would appear from this that Carlo, unlike his predecessors, was not content to pay lip-service to the idea of religious obligations. But while some of his emphasis on daily devotion may reasonably by attributed to his own sincere piety, it seems likely that he was not unaware of the fact that the common obligations imposed upon all the knights on a daily and weekly basis would serve as a frequent reminder of their common membership in one fraternal society.

8 *Obligations Arising from the Death of a Member*

The third section of the statutes is concerned with obligations arising from the death of a member of the Order. We have already discussed the provisions of its first subsection (25–30), which deals with the question of the succession to the princeship on the demise of the Prince. The second and third subsections are devoted to the social and religious obligations of the Prince and companions following the death of the Prince (31–34) or of one of the companions (35–39).

Funerals and masses for departed members had been a feature of all but one of the earlier orders whose statutes survive, and they were undoubtedly looked upon by the companions as one of the principal benefits of membership. Carlo as usual elaborated considerably upon the arrangements of the earlier orders. He first of all provided special treatment in this respect for the departed Prince, who was to receive from each companion fifteen sung and thirty said masses if he died in bed,[60] or twice that number if he died 'in a feat of arms'.[61] The companions were to dress in black as a sign of mourning for fifteen continuous days in the former

---

54 Ch. 22.
55 Ch. 21.
56 Ch. 18.
57 Ch. 19.
58 Ch. 23.
59 Ch. 24.
60 Ch. 31.
61 Ch. 34.

circumstance, and thirty in the latter, unless one of the Order's feast days fell during that period.[62] As a perpetual memorial to each Prince, his sword and shield, borne into the chapel by the two best knights of the Order, were to be hung there immediately following those of the previous Prince.[63]

The companions themselves were to receive analogous but lesser benefits: eight sung and sixteen said masses from each of their fellows if (having confessed and communicated) they died in bed, and twice that number if they died 'in a feat of arms'. The periods for wearing black were reduced to eight and sixteen days respectively.[64] The Prince himself was obliged to double all the services owed by the other companions, and to have a solemn requiem mass sung in the chapel of the Order, just as if the body were actually present.[65]

In order that all these obligations could be carried out, the companions were further obliged to report at each assembly the death of any of the Order's members.[66] The Prince was then to acquire from the deceased companion's executor the companion's shield, which was to be hung in the chapel or chapels of the Order in a position that accorded with his 'chivalry and estate'.[67] Finally, each year on the Sunday next after Trinity, the Prince and all the companions present were to have a solemn mass sung for all the departed companions, and were to be present themselves, garbed in black, for the duration of the mass.[68]

The whole funeral programme was thus designed and set forth with the precision and refinement which characterize the statutes as a whole, and the elaborate activities prescribed would undoubtedly have served not only as a powerful inducement to join the Order, but as yet another source of corporate solidarity.

9 *The Mutual Obligations of the Members in Life*

The obligations to the dead are followed in the statutes by the obligations in life of the companions to the Prince (40–54), of the Prince to the companions (55–57), and of all the members to one another (58–61).

Though central to their nature, the obligations to the president required by the earlier orders from their ordinary members had been very simple. As usual, the statutes of the Ship were both more extensive and more specific in their requirements, and the demands they made were considerably greater. The whole section dealing with these obligations was composed like a contract of retinue, spelling out the services owed by each party in great detail. The services owed by the companions to the Prince were for the most part military, though a strong political element is also present in the specifications. First of all, each companion

---

62 Ch. 32.
63 Ch. 33.
64 Ch. 35.
65 Ch. 36.
66 Ch. 37.
67 Ch. 38.
68 Ch. 39.

was required not to oppose the Prince in any way or for any reason, except in defence of his liege lord (when this was not the Prince) or of someone who had given him a pension before he joined the Order. Under either of these circumstances the companion was obliged to inform the Prince of his position on pain of being considered perjured.[69] The companions were also bound, more positively, to aid the Prince with all their power,[70] and to serve him in all his wars according to their status, against all men but those excepted above.[71] Should any one of them be too impoverished to do so, he was obliged to inform the Prince, who could decide either to support the companion in question in a way appropriate to his status, or to quit him of his obligations.[72] Whether or not they could support themselves in a war, all the companions were obliged to report to the Prince as fully equipped as possible as soon as they heard of the outbreak of war,[73] those too sick to do so being obliged to send a suitable substitute.[74] All the companions were also bound to defend the heritage, goods, honour, and estate possessed by the Prince at the time that the statutes were promulgated,[75] and furthermore to attend upon him, if possible, at their own expense, in any attempt he chose to make to reconquer his lost heritage – specified as the whole of the Kingdoms of Jerusalem and (island) Sicily, of the Empire of Constantinople, and of the Counties of Provence and Piedmont – subject to the usual provisions for poverty and sickness.[76] They were finally called upon to avenge any 'villany, shame, or spite' against either the Prince or the Company in general.[77]

The companions were thus called upon to serve together as members of a sort of élite company comparable to that of the Order of the Band and to act individually as the agents and partisans of the Prince, to defend him in every possible way, and to increase with all their power his 'honour and estate'. Not content with the services of the companions themselves, however, Carlo sought through the next set of ordinances to impose comparable obligations on all those knighted thereafter either by the Prince or by any of the companions. Like the companions, all such knights were to be bound to accompany the Prince in person on any attempt to reconquer his lost heritage, or if unable to do so for some good reason, to send a suitable substitute. All new knights thus made were to be obliged to swear to do this, and the Prince and the companions were to swear to see that the oath was sworn.[78] If a knight thus made was unable to come because of poverty, he was to tell the Prince, who could either pay for him, or absolve him from his vow.[79] The knights made by the Prince or by any of the companions were to be obliged not to oppose the Prince in any way either openly or secretly,[80] but like the companions to

69 Ch. 40.
70 Ch. 41.
71 Ch. 42.
72 Ch. 43.
73 Ch. 44.
74 Ch. 45.
75 Ch. 46.
76 Ch. 47.
77 Ch. 48.
78 Ch. 49.
79 Ch. 50.
80 Ch. 51.

bear him honour and reverence, and to obey his commands at all times.[81] Both the companions and the knights they had made were to proclaim at all times the virtues of the Prince and the Company, and to defend both against shame and dishonour.[82] Finally, they were all called upon to report as soon as possible to the person or persons concerned any evil done to the Prince or the Company, on pain of forfeiting the Order and being reputed perjurers and traitors.[83]

These extensive obligations – for several of which a special oath was required – would have subjected the companions to the Prince to a quite unprecedented degree. Even more remarkably, they would have subjected to the Prince many other knights who were not actually companions of the Order, but were merely their clients or vassals. Carlo evidently realized that he could not hope to attract anyone into so disciplined a clientage without correspondingly great patronal obligations being imposed upon himself and his successors as Prince. The rather rudimentary obligations of most of the earlier founders towards their 'companions' – consisting for the most part of providing the order's physical establishment and paying for such ceremonies as the annual banquet – were clearly insufficient, and Carlo (like Amé of Savoy in a broadly similar situation) accordingly assumed a more active patronal role. He first of all bound himself and his successors to 'aid, maintain, and defend' all the companions against all other persons in the world, at his own expense and according to the status of the companion, in all just quarrels, except against the Church of Rome (his lord for the Kingdom of Sicily), King Lajos of Hungary (his erstwhile guardian) or any other person to whom he was bound by oaths taken before creating the Order; and in these exceptional cases he was to be obliged to obtain peace between the companion and his adversary.[84] He also bound himself as Prince to 'procure the honour and estate' of the companions, to inform them of any threats against them, and to protect them from the effects of such threats.[85] In effect, he assumed for himself obligations of support and protection which were closely analogous to those owed by the companions to him, but were more generally expressed, and lacked the strong element of subservience present in the obligations of the companions. Since Carlo can hardly have been unaware of the importance of material inducements to loyalty and service, he no doubt intended the obligation he assumed to 'procure the honour and estate' of the companions to be understood as a promise to favour them before all others when distributing offices, pensions, and fiefs.

This subdivision of the statutes ends with what amounts to a protective rider to the effect that the Prince was not bound by any chapter which did not specifically require him to swear to maintain it,[86] but this would appear to have been intended only as a general reservation, as both chapters specifying the Prince's obligations do require such an oath.

Subsection IV.C of the statutes sets forth the obligations of the companions to one another. Mutual obligations, including some sort of oath of fraternity, were an

---

[81] Ch. 52.
[82] Ch. 53.
[83] Ch. 54.
[84] Ch. 55.
[85] Ch. 56.
[86] Ch. 57.

important part of the statutes of all the lay orders I have termed 'fraternal', but of the earlier monarchical orders probably known to Carlo only the Hungarian Society of Saint George had imposed significant mutual obligations among the living. The founders of the Orders of the Star and the Knot in particular had been concerned primarily with establishing the essentially vertical patron-client relationship, and the latter had shown no interest whatever in the possibility of a horizontal relationship among the clients themselves. Like Amé of Savoy, however (if for rather different reasons), Carlo was clearly interested not merely in acquiring a number of dependents bound to him personally on an individual basis, in the fashion of feudo-vassality, but in creating an organization with strong corporate bonds, whose members were tied not only to him, but to one another. This is implicit in the Order's elaborate rites of entry, in its religious practices, and in its funeral rites, but it is made particularly clear in the list of obligations which all the members of the Order were to owe to one another.

They were bound first of all to maintain 'good company and fraternity' with each other at all times, and in all cases.[87] In addition they were to help one another actively in all 'adventures' good and bad, and especially in illness, prison, and poverty.[88] They were to hide one another's shame and dishonour, except in those cases specified otherwise by the statutes – for they were equally bound (by ch. 54 above) to reveal all cases of treason or damage to the Prince, the Company, or any of the companions.[89] The companions were finally bound in particular to aid any of their number who fell into difficulty in a battle, especially the Prince.[90]

These mutual obligations are of precisely the same type as those imposed by the fraternal orders and by the Order of the Collar, and may be seen as forming – as did the analogous obligations of those orders – one of the principal benefits to be derived from membership in the Order. Where they differ principally from those of the fraternal orders is in the very small part they occupy of the total number of obligations incurred, and in the fact that they are balanced not only by the protection of a king, but by extensive duties owed to him as protector. The strong fraternal element of the Ship statutes – probably introduced both to attract and hold the members and to create a more effective military and political force – certainly did not compromise the essentially monarchical nature of the Order.

10 The Settlement of Disputes

The five chapters of the fourth subsection of Section IV (62–66) are concerned with a practical matter commonly dealt with in the statutes of both fraternal orders and confraternities: the settlement of disputes. Like Alfonso of Castile and Amé of Savoy before him, Carlo was deeply concerned with the problem of maintaining the cohesion of his 'Company', and could not afford to ignore the possiblity of

[87] Ch. 58.
[88] Ch. 59.
[89] Ch. 60.
[90] Ch. 61.

disputes arising that would endanger that cohesion. In fact the settlement of internal quarrels weighed so heavily on Carlo's mind that he made provision for it in four separate places in the statutes: in the rite of admission, discussed above;[91] in the present subsection; and in subsections V.B and F,[92] which are concerned with the activities of the members during the Order's general assembly. The placement of the first chapters on the settlement of disputes arising after admission to the Order in a section otherwise devoted to the mutual obligations of the members would appear to indicate that Carlo looked upon the submission of disputes to his arbitration as one of the duties of membership.

Certainly Carlo as Prince was to play a large part in the process, and the first two of these statutes were phrased in such a way as to lay a large part of the obligation on him. If any 'discord, quarrel, or war' broke out among any of the companions, the Prince was to attempt to settle the question at issue, with the counsel of such of the companions as were with him.[93] Should the conflict prove difficult to resolve, one or both of the contestants could appeal the Prince's initial decision to the General Court of the Order, in the interim refraining from any active pursuit of the quarrel, on pain of forfeiture of the Order. In the Court, the question was to be settled by the Prince with the counsel of all the companions, without any possiblity of further appeal, even in the event of the non-appearance of one of the contending parties.[94]

This last provision is particularly striking. Carlo was clearly all too aware of the contemporary tendency for litigation to be carried endlessly from court to court, and sought to impose a form of discipline on the members of his Order which would prevent this disruptive process. It was an ingenious idea, not only in the context of the preservation of amity in the Order as such, but in the broader context of the peace of his kingdom, for it should have had the effect of imposing his own judicial decision in matters which all too often led to strife between over-mighty subjects.

The following statutes provided the regulation with the necessary teeth, declaring the complementary obligations of the companions. All of the companions were first obliged to assist in the settlement of quarrels among their fellows independently, but once they had failed, the contestants were themselves bound to submit their quarrel without any further action to the Prince,[95] and further to accept his judgement upon pain, not only of ejection from the Order, but of being publicly proclaimed perjured in a letter to be sent to all royal and princely courts.[96] In a case where the accuser was finally satisfied with the defense of the accused, the Prince was to have the prerogative of depriving the offender, or not, as he saw fit; otherwise the offender was apparently to be expelled from the Order.[97]

---

[91] Ch. 4.
[92] Chs. 77, 78, 92.
[93] Ch. 62.
[94] Ch. 63
[95] Ch. 64.
[96] Ch. 65.
[97] Ch. 66.

11 Other Obligations of Membership

The last two chapters of Section IV, numbers 67 and 68, form a subsection concerned with the question of loyalty to the Order. The first binds all the companions to keep the Order's secrets,[98] while the second reiterates the adjuration to report immediately all knowledge of treason 'in thought or deed' against the Prince, the Company, or any of the companions. Anyone found to be guilty of such treason was to be deprived of the 'order and device', and declared a 'perjured traitor'. A letter to this effect, declaring the specific reasons for his deprivation, was to be sent (as in the case of companions who refused to accept the Prince's judgements) to all 'princes of great estate'. Finally, (and more remarkably), the companions were bound to reveal any suspected act of treason by one of their number against anyone who was not a member of the Order, and any commpanion found guilty of such treason was to be punished by deprivation, though not by the public parading of his crimes.[99]

This latter penalty, touching upon the very sensitive spot of public honour, was one of Carlo's most ingenious innovations, and while it could not have prevented all the inevitable rash actions which would have led to its imposition, it might well have discouraged many. Deprivation alone was the most severe penalty provided by the statutes of the earlier Orders, but Carlo realized that the mere loss of the benefits of membership would not act as a sufficient deterrent, while deprivation coupled with the more positive punishment of public humiliation might prove significantly more effective.

Carlo's concern with discouraging any form of treachery within his clientage is in keeping with his general concern for cohesion, but his provision of deprivation for treason towards anyone outside the Order as well must be viewed in a different light. It suggests that he was concerned with the peace and security of his realm as a whole, and wished to extend the pacific influence of the Order as far beyond its membership as possible. In this respect the provision resembles the earlier ordinances by which Carlo had extended the influence of the Order to all those knighted by any of its members.[100]

The sixth division of the statutes – a miscellaneous collection of nine ordinances which apparently did not fit in elsewhere or had been omitted through oversight from some earlier section – contains several chapters whose provisions relate to the general matter of the obligations of the companions to the Prince, to one another, and to the society in general. The first forbids any of the companions to join any other 'company', unless forced to do so by one more powerful than himself, or by his own liege lord, on pain of deprivation.[101] Both the Star and the Knot statutes had dealt with the problem of membership in other orders, but while both had discouraged multiple allegiances,[102] neither had done so with the degree of

---

[98] Ch. 67.
[99] Ch. 68.
[100] Chs. 49–54.
[101] Ch. 114.
[102] By item 9 and chapter 16.

determination shown here. It is nevertheless significant that Carlo held no hope of preventing it altogether.

Chapter 115 adjures the companions to refrain from engaging in any 'unjust' war, defined as one in which he was not himself the victim of either dishonour or damage; if one of them did so, neither the Prince not any of the companions was to aid him. This statute is another element of Carlo's attempt to avoid conflict in his realm as a whole, though of course he may have been equally concerned to keep himself and his Order out of wars brought about through the private aggression of his clients, from which he had nothing to gain, and possibly much to lose. Its underlying principle was of course the chivalric notion of the just war.

Chapter 116 next declares that those companions who were the vassals of the Prince were not to oppose him, but to aid him in all his wars under the double obligation of their oaths of homage and as companions. This ought to have gone without saying, and its mention is indicative of the lack of faith Carlo felt in the loyalty of his vassals.

The remaining chapter (118, which rightly belongs in Section IV) reiterates the requirement that the companions aid any of their number who had fallen into prison, sickness, or poverty. It differs from the last sentence of chapter 59 only in specifying that those in trouble were to be aided only if their trouble was not of their own making, and thus appears to be a reservation similar to that dealing with 'unjust wars'.

12 The Annual General Court

In the fifth major division of the statutes, including the forty- three chapters from 69 to 111, Carlo dealt with a variety of matters, for the most part connected with the annual assembly of the Order, which he designated the General Court. In most of the earlier orders the annual assembly had been the only corporate activity in which all of the companions had been called upon to participate, but although this was not true in the Order of the Ship, Carlo nevertheless described the activities that were to take place during the assembly of his Order in unprecedented detail.

The section of the statutes dealing with the Court falls naturally into twelve subsections. Subsection V.A, comprising chapters 69 to 75, is concerned with the time and place at which the General Court was to be held, and with attendance at it. It will be recalled that the timing of the Order's four annual feasts, at Trinity, All Saints, Christmas, and Easter, was specified in chapter 1 in connexion with the reception of new companions. Carlo followed earlier precedents in adopting as the principal feast of his Order the feast of the Order's celestial patron, but although both Károly of Hungary and Alfonso of Castile had called for several annual meetings, he was alone among the later founders in requiring more than one regular meeting every year. The explanation for Carlo's addition of three minor assemblies is obvious in the light of his general concerns: he clearly felt that one yearly meeting was not enough to give his companions a sense of either their mutual fraternity or their clientship to him. The more often they assembled for communal activities, the closer would be all the bonds that bound them to him and to one another. Carlo also decided that the three days usually set aside for an assembly were inadequate for his purposes. He therefore ordained that the assembly held on the *mestre feste* was to begin on the eve of Pentecost and conclude two weeks later on the Sunday following Trinity Sunday,[103] while the minor assemblies were to begin three days before and conclude three days after after their respective feast days. In all no fewer than thirty-six days each year were to be spent in assemblies – considerably more than in any other order except the Hungarian Society of St George.

It is clear that some business was to be carried on at the three minor feasts, but the General Court proper was to be held only during the seventeen days of the 'master feast' of Trinity.[104] Unlike the meetings of most other orders, the General Court was to be held at the Order's seat only when convenient. Chapter 71 declares that the *pays* or 'country' in which the next Court was to be held was to be proclaimed in the chief city of that country during the preceding Easter feast. Carlo obviously did not wish to miss a meeting himself, and at the same time was aware that his peregrinations were likely to place him far from Naples at Trinity. Perhaps he was already contemplating some action in the prosecution of his claims to Sicily proper or Constantinople – or even to Hungary, where he eventually died. Unless illness prevented it or the licence of the Prince had been obtained, every companion was bound to attend the General Court.[105] Any companion who had not obtained a licence to absent himself, but found for some good reason that he would be unable to attend, was obliged to send his excuses in writing to the Prince, and to submit to a fine graduated according to his rank.[106] For the first such failure to appear at a General Court, a companion who was a king was to be fined 100 florins; one who was a duke or other 'prince of great estate', 80 florins; a count, 60 florins; a baron, 40 florins; and a simple knight, 20 florins.[107] For the second default, the fine was to be the same, but the companion in question was to lose his seat and his right to wear the Order's badge for one year.[108] For his third default, a companion was to be expelled from the Order, and his expulsion announced 'to all princes of great estate'.[109] Of the orders examined so far, only the Garter had comparable provisions, and its regulations were far less stringent.

The remaining subdivisions of Section V are concerned with the activities of the Prince and the companions during the tenure of the Court, which according to chapter 76 was to be held to the 'honour and profit' of the Prince and the Company. Subsection B (chs. 77–81), the first of two subsections concerned with legislative and judicial business, begins with two chapters (77 and 78) which deal once again with the settlement of internal disputes.[110] According to the first of

---

[103] Ch. 69b. The ordinance actually says that the General Court was to last for 'eight days before Trinity Sunday and eight days afterwards, but in all likelihood Trinity Sunday was itself included in this count.

[104] Ch. 69a.

[105] Ch. 70.

[106] Ch. 72.

[107] Ch. 73.

[108] Ch. 74.

[109] Ch. 75.

[110] Cf. chs. 62, 63.

these, the assembled companions were to put an end to all discords, wars, and hatreds that had arisen among them, and if they failed to do so, the Prince was to forbid the parties to the dispute to do anything against one another, and to order them to take their case before their ordinary judge and lord, on pain of expulsion. The last ordinance appears to be in conflict with what was ordained earlier, but the next chapter reiterates the earlier declaration that all questions actually placed before the Prince were to be settled without possibility of further appeal. Subsection F, consisting of chapter 92, deals with the same subject and is similarly redundant.

The next several chapters (79–81) deal with two different but related subjects: the amendment of the Order's statutes, and the punishment of those who failed to observe them. The latter subject is more fully dealt with in subsection V.D (chs. 84–87) below. Carlo approached the former subject with his usual caution, and the process of amendment and its consequences were specified with great care. If the Prince announced his intention to do so during the course of a meeting, he could at the next Court make new statutes for the Order and annul existing ones, but only with the consent of at least two thirds of the companions present.[111] The companions were to be bound by all such new statutes just as they had been by the old, and were to be absolved from obedience to those annulled.[112] Miscellaneous statute 117 adds to this that any obscurity in an existing ordinance was to be clarified by the Prince with the counsel of the companions at the General Court.

Chapters 81 and 84 to 87 set forth the method by which failure to observe the statutes was to be exposed and punished, a theme repeated in subsection V.J (chs. 95–98). The separation of these subsections appears capricious, and they may be more conveniently dealt with together. Carlo laid a much greater emphasis upon punishment in his statutes than any other founder, and this may be taken as an indication of the relative seriousness of his intentions. His regulations were demanding, and he therefore fully expected them to be broken, but he did his best to discourage as many breaches as possible by instituting penalties that were both specific and significant, and a clear-cut method for their imposition.

All those who had failed to keep any part of the statutes were to be punished in the General Court according to the nature of their fault. Those who had for some reason been deprived of the Order between meetings of the Court were to be denounced at the next session, and those who had merited but not received the punishment of deprivation were to be both deprived and denounced publicly at the same time.[113] Any of the companions present could accuse any of the others of infractions during the past year,[114] and indeed all were bound to reveal the defaults known to them, though never out of favour or rancour.[115] Any companion found to have accused one of his fellow companions falsely was to suffer deprivation and the circular denunciation regularly accompanying that disgrace.[116] Anyone justly

---

[111] Ch. 79.
[112] Ch. 80.
[113] Ch. 81.
[114] Ch. 85.
[115] Ch. 96.
[116] Ch. 97.

accused of any offence who refused to confess was to be punished in the prescribed way without mercy,[117] but anyone who freely confessed might at the discretion of the Prince in council suffer a reduced penalty, or be spared altogether.[118] The Prince was to give judgement with the advice of the companions in all important cases, but in lesser matters he could decide alone.[119] Those whom he punished by deprivation were to be publicly denounced and no longer regarded as companions by the others, who were thus absolved from any obligation to them.[120]

After the serious business of the settlement of disputes, the amendment of the statutes, and the meting out of justice, there remained one more activity to be carried out during the General Court, and that was the recounting of deeds. Every companion was obliged to recite at the Court each year not only the adventures which had befallen him since he last attended (martial and otherwise, good or bad, save only adventures in love), but the adventures which had come to anyone absent or unwilling to speak. All these adventures were then to be recorded.[121] This much Carlo lifted almost directly from the statutes of the Knot, bur probably because of the criticism Loysi had received for the absurdly exaggerated stories which inevitably found their way into his order's book of deeds, Carlo introduced a characteristic refinement. The Order of the Ship was to maintain two books of adventures. Each companion was to report to the Prince of the Order all of his recent adventures each time he met the Prince in his travels, and these adventures, along with those recounted during the General Court, were to be written down in the first book, the *Livre et Romanz des Preux* or 'Book and Romance of the Valiant (or Worthy)'. Only those adventures which later proved, after careful investigation by the Prince and companions, to be 'true and certain', were then to be transferred to the other book, the *Romans de la Nef* or 'Romance of the Ship', in which they were to be set down without embellishment. Nothing was to be written in the latter except by the express command of the Prince and the companions during the General Court.[122] The *Livre et Romanz des Preux* was to be kept with the Prince wherever he went, while the *Romans de la Nef* was to be kept (according to chapter 151) in the Order's chapel. Both books were to be produced during the General Court.[123] Anyone who was found to have lied about his adventures was to have his lie proclaimed in the Court by the heralds, and the lies were to be removed from the account.[124]

The purpose of the two 'romances', like that of the augmentable badge described below, was the encouragement of valour. It is notable that the books of adventures were among the very few elements of the Ship statutes with a truly Arthurian flavour, and they may have been introduced because Carlo thought they would appeal to the romantic tastes of his noble clients, as well as to their strong desire for public honour.

---

[117] Ch. 98.
[118] Ch. 95.
[119] Chs. 84–86.
[120] Ch. 87.
[121] Ch. 88.
[122] Ch. 89.
[123] Ch. 90.
[124] Ch. 91.

Compared to that accorded to the Court proper, the attention given in the statutes to the other two types of activity in which the companions were to participate during the course of the Order's annual meeting – the religious services and the banquet – is scant indeed. This is in complete contrast to the emphasis given to these activities in the statutes of most earlier orders, and suggests that Carlo regarded them as relatively unimportant to his goals. On Trinity Sunday each year, the Prince and companions were to hear a solemn mass and vespers, in the Order's chapel if the Court was held near enough to it, otherwise in a church of the Prince's choosing.[125] The services themselves are not described, and nothing is said about the order in which the companions were to process or sit during them. The banquet was to be held on the same day,[126] in the hall of the Order if that was convenient, otherwise wherever the Prince thought best. The Prince was to sit in the first place at the table, with the companions arranged below him 'according to their goodness and chivalry in his eyes'.[127] This arrangement has a distinctly Arthurian ring as well, but was really quite normal in a royal court of this period. Unlike the founders of the Star and the Knot, Carlo did not establish a special 'table of honour'.

Possibly by sheer coincidence, the costume Carlo assigned to his companions for wear during these festivities[128] differed primarily in the colour and the cut of the undertunic from that of the French Order of the Star, which had not been worn for nearly thirty years.[129] It consisted of a blue-green *gippon* or *cote courte*; a white *surcote* or *villain* described as knee-length and 'fairly wide', and decorated at its lower hem with a wide band of silver-gilt; red shoes with soles; and a red mantle and *chaperon* or caped hood. In the one surviving representation of a knight in this habit – in the illumination with which the Turin manuscript of the statutes begins – the founder is depicted wearing a loose ankle-length white surcoat with tight, wrist-length sleeves, and a red floor-length mantle, open at the front, with a hood (apparently attached) pulled up to conceal the back part of his head (fig. 11.2). Like the equivalent habits of the Garter and the Star, this full costume was to be worn only during the Order's annual religious services on Trinity Sunday; for the banquet that followed, the mantle and *chaperon* were to be discarded and a 'chaplet of flowers or leaves' worn on the head. It will be recalled that the right to wear a crown of leaves in the fashion of a Roman *triumphator* had been introduced by Acciaiuoli as a special honour for the companions of his Order who had untied their knots.[130] Carlo evidently liked the conceit, but extended the right to all the members of his Order equally. With the removal of the mantle and hood and the addition of the chaplet, the habit of the companions bore a striking resemblance to that worn by the knights of the Knot during the festive parts of their annual assembly, and this is unlikely to have been the result of coincidence.

Only one more group of chapters deals with matters related to the annual meeting of the Order: chapters 99 to 110. Despite his precautions, Carlo evidently

[125] Ch. 82.
[126] Ch. 83.
[127] Ch. 120.
[128] Ch. 83.
[129] See above, pp. 205–7.
[130] Ch. 14

felt that there remained a possibility that he might not be able to attend a meeting of the General Court, and so saw fit to make provisions for 'lieutenants' to preside over the Court in his place. Only Edward of England among the earlier founders had included the appointment of a lieutenant in the statutes of his foundation. The principal concern revealed in the twelve chapters in which the Ship lieutenants' powers are described is not so much the definition as the strict limitation of those powers. The Prince was to have the right to appoint in his place two or more lieutenants, but at least two.[131] They were to swear to hold the Court 'to the honour and profit of the Prince and Company', and in no way to exceed their authority as defined by the statutes,[132] on pain of arbitrary punishment by the Prince.[133] The lieutenants thus sworn in were to be empowered to 'treat with the companions of the good estate of the Company', but were specifically forbidden to receive new companions, make new statutes, or annul existing ones.[134] Should the lieutenants and the companions together agree that a new statute was desirable, they were to submit their resolution in writing to the absent Prince, who could either confirm it or reject it entirely.[135] The lieutenants could also act to settle disputes,[136] but if either party to the dispute was not content with the lieutenants' decision he could appeal it to the Prince, who could either confirm it or overturn it.[137] The lieutenants were to hold the Court in every respect as if the Prince himself were present, but they were to leave the Prince's seat vacant, and sit in the next seats below it.[138] They were to decide in what realm the next court was to be held, apparently without the consent of the Prince,[139] and to make decisions about matters that would not bear delay,[140] but were obliged to report these decisions along with all the other matters decided by the Court to the Prince.[141] When the Court over which they had presided had been dissolved, the authority of the lieutenants within the Order was to terminate completely.[142]

A subsection consisting of a single chapter (111) concludes the long section dealing with the Order's meetings, and it is concerned with the minor feasts of All Saints, Christmas, and Easter. Apart from chapter 1, this chapter contains the only reference to these meetings, and simply binds the companions to attend them unless sickness or other just cause prevented them from doing so. It prescribes no penalties for failure to appear, however, and does not describe what form the meetings were to take.

We have already dealt with several of the nine miscellaneous statutes (112–120) which follow the more orderly Section V. Two of these (112 and 113), do not in fact easily fit under any other heading. The Order was to have a common seal, to be

---

[131] Ch. 99.
[132] Ch. 100.
[133] Ch. 101.
[134] Ch. 102.
[135] Ch. 103.
[136] Ch. 104.
[137] Ch. 105.
[138] Ch. 106.
[139] Ch. 107.
[140] Ch. 108.
[141] Ch. 109.
[142] Ch. 110.

kept by the Prince and used only on the business of the Order.[143] Of the earlier founders, only Edward of England had thought to mention a corporate seal in the statutes of institution, and Carlo probably did so simply because the corporate nature of his Order required such a seal for the proper conduct of its affairs.

The next chapter returns to the subject of romantic chivalry, specifically respect for the weaker sex. Despite its importance in all of the Arthurian romances, this was a subject upon which only two of Carlo's predecessors had thought to legislate for their monarchical order. Carlo's statute demands that, except in defence of his own honour, that of his father, brother, or liege lord, of any of the companions, or of the Prince of the Order, no companion was to defame any gentlewoman, on pain of being forbidden the table at the Trinity feast.[144] A very similar penalty was provided in the Knot statutes[145] for flying from battle or doing 'any other shameful thing', and Carlo may have had that statute before him when drafting the present regulation.

13 The Banner and Company of the Order

The seventh and eighth sections of the statutes (grouped under the general heading *De fait d'armes*) are concerned with two related subjects: the Order's banner and its display, and the Order's badge, its wearing, and its augmentation. These subjects are related to one another in being both symbolic and military in nature, and are independently related to the military obligations of the companions set forth in chapters 40 and 54.

In adopting a banner for his Order, Carlo was probably following the precedent set by Jean of France and copied by Acciaiuoli. Unlike the banners of the Star and the Knot, however, the banner adopted by Carlo for the Order of the Ship bore an image not of the Order's patron, but of its badge – the ship stripped of all accoutrements and set in a patch of sea. The field of the banner was to be red, like the outer elements of the formal habit, and the ship itself gold.[146] (Fig. 11.3).

Like the statutes of the Star and the Knot, those of the Ship set forth the circumstances in which the banner of the Order could be raised. The raising of the banner was a serious matter in this period, as it indicated the status not merely of the combatant who raised it but, under the complex and formalized rules of war then prevailing, that of the encounter itself. The banner of the Ship was to be the visible symbol of the Order's corporate existence and honour in battle, and was clearly intended by Carlo to serve both as a rallying point and as a focal point for the loyalty of the companions. The banner of the Order was to be raised and borne at the command of the Prince when either he or a lieutenant appointed by him for the purpose was present with at least ten companions of the Order and at least five

---

[143] Ch. 112.

[144] Ch. 113.

[145] Knot ch. 11.

[146] Ch. 121. 'En ceste ordre et compaignie aura et sera une baniere et penon, de quoy le champ sera de guelles a une nef d'or dedens la mer, desgarnie fors que du mast.'

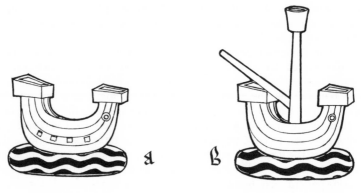

11.1 The basic badge of the Ship   a. As described in the statutes
b. As represented in the Penn. MS. of the statutes, c.1382/6

11.2 The formal habit of the Ship,
as represented in the Turin MS.
of the statutes, 1381

11.3 The banner of the Ship
(reconstructed)

318

hundred lances. It could be raised in any form of encounter with all classes of enemy, at conquests of lands, at sieges of fortified places, and (at the Prince's pleasure) at jousts and tournaments.[147] It could also be raised by a single companion, with the Prince's licence, in the crusade against the heathen in Prussia.[148] The Prince's lieutenant for the banner was to have authority equal to that of the Prince for the duration of his commission,[149] but although the companions were bound to obey him to the extent his commission indicated,[150] he could be replaced by the Prince at their behest for negligence, disloyalty, or incapacity.[151] The banner was to be given each morning to the companion present (other than a captain or marshal) who was judged by the Prince and the companions present to have performed the most notable feats of arms either since his admission to the Order or on the previous day. He was to return it each night to the Prince's keeping.[152] Whenever the banner was displayed in battle the companions present were bound to follow it and never to abandon it even for fear of death. Each companion was to act to the limit of his power in arms for the greater honour of the Order and himself.[153] Should any of the companions find himself on the opposing side when the banner of the Order was raised in battle, he was bound not to oppose it, but if his honour permitted, to change sides and fight under it.[154] A companion who deserted the banner borne either before the Prince or his lieutenant, or committed any other dishonourable deed before it, was to be deprived of the Order with the usual public denunciations. Following that initial disgrace – the heaviest penalty otherwise exacted for an offence against the statutes – he was to be brought, if possible, by the other companions present to the meeting of the next General Court of the Order, and there made to sit on the floor before the Prince and companions and made to eat out of the same bowl as a dog. He was never to be allowed to recover his membership in the Order.[155]

Carlo's treatment of the display of his Order's banner and the behaviour expected of the companions in its presence went well beyond that of any earlier founder. This was due in part to the fact that Carlo incorporated the usual penalties for 'shameful deeds' in battle under this heading, and in part to the fact that, like the founder of the Band, he intended the knights of his Order to form a sort of élite company within the royal army. This company was evidently meant to fight under its own banner and its own commander whenever the Prince had need of it, whether or not he himself could be present. Presumably the companions were to be summoned personally to serve in this company, and on the basis of the obligations they had incurred on joining the Order, would be obliged not only to come but to remain and fight for as long as the Prince required them. Since some of the companions were barons rather than mere knights, it is possible that the company

[147] Ch. 122.
[148] Ch. 126.
[149] Ch. 123.
[150] Ch. 124.
[151] Ch. 125.
[152] Ch. 129.
[153] Ch. 128.
[154] Ch. 127.
[155] Ch. 130.

of the Ship was meant to include their vassals and retainers as well – many of whom would have sworn special oaths of loyalty to the Order at the time they received the accolade of knighthood. On the other hand, since such clients could not have been compelled either to remain beyond the usual ninety days or to submit to the severe discipline required of the companions, it is perhaps more likely that Carlo had in mind a company composed primarily of the companions and their personal attendants and life retainers, who together might well have constituted a formidable force – and in theory, at least, a force upon which Carlo could rely as he could rely upon no other. Certainly such a company would have been a vast improvement upon a comparable body composed of vassals or mercenaries, which were the only alternatives available at the time.

14 The Augmentation of the Order's Badge

Like the banner, the badge of the Order of the Ship was a visible symbol of membership in the Order, and every companion was obliged by the statutes to wear it every day of the year,[156] on pain of paying to the almoner of the Order's chapel the sum of one florin per day of default, to be spent on the souls of the Order's departed companions.[157] As we have seen, however, the badge was to serve not merely as a sign of membership in the Order, but as a sign of personal honour and achievement. Just as he hoped to discourage his knights from fleeing from battle by imposing a heavy penalty, Carlo, like Acciaiuoli before him, hoped to encourage them to perform heroic deeds in his service by providing an exceedingly elaborate system of symbolic honours, clearly inspired by that of the Company of the Knot. Deeds of especial note were to be signalized through the systematic addition to the initially naked ship that was the Order's basic badge of the various accoutrements appropriate to it – that is to say, tillers, anchors, cords, masts, sails, and banners – in various colours, numbers, and sequences. Each type of item was to have a very specific significance, so that the augmented badge would contain a full account of each companion's military exploits. The whole idea was very similar to that underlying the modern military medal. As it is likely that the deeds for which the augmentations were to be granted would also have been recorded in the 'Romance of the Ship', that volume may have been intended to serve as part of the system of military honours as well.

The system of augmentations is very revealing of fourteenth-century concepts of military accomplishment, and no doubt describes the best that Carlo hoped to get from his companions in battle. Not only the symbols but the deeds for which they were to be awarded were remarkably complex. In order to add to his ship its first tiller, a companion had, in a battle in which at least 1500 of his party opposed with banner displayed at least 2000 Saracens, heretics, or schismatics, to be a good knight and among the first to attack, or the first to descend to face the enemy, unless he was an officer of arms or among his lord's bodyguard, in which cases it was sufficient for him to perform his office well, if his lord himself was a companion and

[156] Ch. 93 and prologue.
[157] Ch. 94.

fought well.[158] To add the second tiller he had only to perform as for the first,[159] but for the third or great tiller he had to act with equal valour during the conquest of Jerusalem.[160] To supply his ship with an anchor, a companion had to take part in the siege of a fortified place, of at least 500 hearths if Christian or at least 1000 hearths if Saracen, and be among the first besiegers to enter the place when it was taken. If he was among the first three to enter, he could add an anchor of gold; if among the next three, or if he thereafter performed noteworthy deeds on the captured walls, the anchor was to be of iron. The anchor was to be placed above the water of the badge if the place was Christian, and in the water if it was Saracen.[161] A single rope or cord was to be added to each companion's ship for every battle in which he acted as a good knight. The rope was to be of gold if on each side of the conflict there were at least 700 men;[162] of vermilion if 600 or more;[163] of blue if 500;[164] of white if 400;[165] of green if 300;[166] of grey if 200;[167] and of iron if there were at least 100 men on each side, one side at least having displayed a banner in every case.[168] A companion who was reputed among the best fighters of the day in such a combat with at least 800 men on each side could add to his ship a yard – of gold if the enemy was Christian, of red if Saracen.[169] A companion who, in a battle in which there were at least 1000 men on each side, and in which (unless it was against Saracens) a banner or pennon was raised, performed such notable deeds of arms that he was held to be one of the best knights of the day, could add to his ship a sail, of white if the battle was against Christians, and of red if against Saracens.[170] Those companions who had already won tillers, sail, and mast could, on the accomplishment of similar deeds, add for each further deed a banner, of white for an engagement against Christians, and of red for one against Saracens. A banner might also be added by one who, in the opinion of the Prince and companions, had borne well either the banner of the Order or his own banner as a captain or a marshal of the army.[171] Finally, a companion who overcame an opponent in single combat was to add a banner to the castle of the mast – of white if his adversary was a Christian and he had not appealed for mercy, or red if he was a Saracen.[172] (Fig. 11.4).

The deeds for which the companions of the Ship could augment their badge – almost certainly inspired by those required of the knights of the Knot in the two chapters added to the statutes of that order at its first meeting – were also very

[158] Ch. 131.
[159] Ch. 132.
[160] Ch. 133.
[161] Ch. 134.
[162] Ch. 135.
[163] Ch. 136.
[164] Ch. 137.
[165] Ch. 138.
[166] Ch. 139.
[167] Ch. 140.
[168] Ch. 141.
[169] Ch. 142.
[170] Ch. 143.
[171] Ch. 144.
[172] Ch. 145.

similar to those for which the members of the exactly contemporary fraternal order of the Male Falcon and the somewhat later votal order of the Dragon were permitted to add to their badges in similar ways. They were clearly in keeping with the romantic conceptions of chivalrous achievement then so dear to the knightly class of Western Christendom, but they were not without practical value, and Carlo had much to gain by encouraging a well-regulated sort of heroism among the members of his Order.

15 The Order's Chapel and Hall

The ninth and last section of the statutes, containing chapters 145 to 151, is concerned with a subject dealt with in the statutes of the Garter (ch. 26), but not touched upon in those of either the Star or the Knot: the Order's chapel and clergy. Though broadly similar to the religious establishments of the other fourteenth-century orders, that of the Ship was to have been provided with a quite unprecedented number of both chapels and altars. Carlo declared that he would found, in honour of the Blessed Trinity, one or several 'great and beautiful' chapels. They would be built wherever he chose to build them (possibly one in the capital of each of his principal dominions), and he would make whichever one he decided the chief among them.[173] In this principal chapel there were to be six principal altars: the first dedicated to the Trinity; the second, to its right, to Christ; the third, to the left, to the Holy Spirit; the fourth to the Blessed Virgin; and the fifth and sixth to Saint Bartholomew (on whose day Naples opened its gates to him in 1381) and Saint Louis of France (the principal saint of his dynasty).[174] The chapels were to be served by whatever clerics the Prince chose to appoint,[175] and they were to say there every day not only the canonical hours, but three masses, the first of the Trinity, the second of the Virgin, and the third of the saint of the day.[176] In the chapels the obsequies of the departed Princes and companions were to be sung according to their various estates,[177] and their shields and banners were to be hung there as a perpetual memorial to them.[178] The original copies of the statute book and of the two books of deeds were also to be kept there, presumably by the clergy.[179]

Carlo had described the other element of his Order's physical establishment, the *grande sale* or 'great hall', in the last two chapters of the section of miscellaneous ordinances. The hall Carlo envisaged for his Order was to have been similar to that planned by Jean of France for the knights of the Star. It was to be built 'in the habitation' of the Order's clergy (and presumably, therefore, next to the chapel), and was to be painted with 'the glory of the Order's chivalry'. In it the Prince was to

[173] Ch. 146.
[174] Ch. 147.
[175] Ch. 148.
[176] Ch. 149.
[177] Ch. 150.
[178] Ch. 151.
[179] Ch. 152.

have the first place, and the others were to be placed after him according to their *chevalerie* and the regard of the Prince, and especially according to their *chevalerie* since taking the Order.[180] This appears to be a description of an arrangement of seats or stalls marked with the armorial bearings of the knights, but the wording is too obscure to allow a more precise reconstruction. It is significant that the companions were to be seated according to the greatness of their accomplishments rather than either their social status or the time of their admission to the Order; Carlo was not one to miss an opportunity to reward service or achievement. The General Court and Trinity feast of the Order were to be held in the hall, if possible, once it had been built, but until then they were to be held wherever the Prince chose.[181]

In fact it is unlikely that any part of either the hall or the chapel was ever built, and the meetings of the Order were probably held at first (if any were held at all) in the Castel Nuovo. This great castle, constructed in 1283 near the harbour of Naples by King Carlo I, the founder of the Angevin dynasty, was in any case a sufficiently grand setting for the Order's festivities. Its gothic hall, designed by no less an artist that Giovanni Pisano, had been the setting for many great events, and was easily worthy of the Order.

16 Conclusions: The Order of the Ship

The statutes just examined describe what may well have been the most ambitious project of its kind in the medieval period. Carlo, in composing such elaborate rules to create a tightly-knit corps of supporters, bound both to him and to one another by the closest possible ties, had in effect written a constitution for what would now be termed a political party, of a type not dissimilar in essence from that of a modern fascist state. Its specific characteristics were of course those of its own age. Its constitution was expressed in perfectly orthodox chivalrous and Christian terms, and it had no peculiar ideology to distinguish it from any other political alliance of the time. It was to exist, in fact, solely to effect the policies and promote the interests of its leader, to whom its members were to be attached entirely out of personal loyalty or interest rather than out of any belief in the efficacy or moral superiority of his policies. Since politics in fourteenth-century Italy were largely a matter of force, most of the Order's 'political' activities were to be of a distinctly military nature, but various other forms of support were also required of its members, including what amounted to spying on their fellow barons. In all of these respects, Carlo's 'party' resembled the normal affinity of the late fourteenth century, but was atypical in the discipline of its rule – in which minutely specified obligations were reinforced by elaborate rewards and punishments – and its members were to be bound to one another as well as to their patron.

Carlo had probably taken the basic idea of creating such a 'king's party' in the form of an order of knighthood either from his step-father Lajos of Hungary or from his predecessor on the throne of mainland Sicily Loysi di Taranto. The only

[180] Ch. 119.
[181] Ch. 120.

essential difference between Loysi's conception of 1352 and Carlo's of 1381 lay in the considerable expansion in the practical obligations between Prince and companions, and the introduction of mutual obligations among the companions in life. Carlo improved upon his Sicilian model primarily by elaborating and refining its regulations, to the point where they could be truly practicable. One can have little doubt, after seeing the effort he expended upon its statutes, and the immense financial outlay it would inevitably have involved, that he seriously intended to put his projected Order into operation as an instrument of royal policy, both internal and external. Its most immediate use would have been to secure the support of the leading barons of his kingdom in his war against Louis of Anjou, but once Louis was safely out of the way he could well have employed the services of its members in the projected campaigns to reconquer the various 'lost' elements of his heritage – including the Kingdom of Jerusalem. Indeed, it is more than likely that many of its companions were called upon to take part in the expedition which did briefly succeed in winning control of the Kingdom of Hungary.

Whether or not the Order of the Ship could ultimately have served to counterbalance the aristocratic particularism and factionalism which had characterized the political life of mainland Sicily since the death of King Roberto 'the Wise' in 1343 is difficult to say, since Carlo died only four years after its foundation, and his new Order almost certainly dissolved within a short time of his death. There is nevertheless no particular reason to doubt that if Carlo had been given more time to establish and endow his foundation, it would have proved a reasonably effective instrument for the promotion of his policies and interests. Indeed, the success of the rather similar society of the Dragon, founded by his successful rival for the Hungarian throne Sigismund von Luxemburg-Brandenburg in comparable circumstances twenty-seven years later, is sufficient proof of the viability of Carlo's even more elaborate plan for a society in which chivalrous trappings disguised a form of military and political clientship that was at once more demanding and less costly than the traditional feudo-vassality which it was meant to replace.

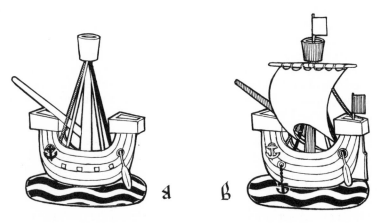

11.4 The badge of the Ship augmented (reconstructed)

Chapter 12

Monarchical and Quasi-Monarchical Orders Founded in Castile, Aragon, Austria, and Hungary, c. 1381–1433

Although the period of roughly half a century between 1330 and 1381 had seen the creation of at least nine monarchical orders of knighthood by the kings and princes of Western Christendom, three of these (the orders of the Band, the Star, and the Sword) seem to have been effectively reduced to pseudo-orders within a few years of the death of their founder, and two of the others (the Neapolitan orders of the Knot and the Ship) had dissolved completely by 1386. The dissolution of the Order of the Ship in the latter year may indeed have reduced the number of true monarchical orders still surviving in the royal courts of Western Christendom to two – the English Order of the Garter and the Aragonese Enterprise of St George – and while the former was to survive until the present day, the latter may well have dissolved on the death of its founder in the following year, and certainly dissolved before the accession of King Ferran I in 1412. In addition to these there were at least two orders founded by subordinate princes that might still have been maintained under monarchical constitutions in 1386: those of the Collar of Savoy and of the Ermine of Brittany. The first of these, apparently moribund since the death of its founder in 1382, was to be given a new lease on life in 1409, but the second was probably reduced to the condition of a pseudo-order soon after the death of its founder in 1399.

Despite the reduction or disappearance of all but two of the early orders, in the period of just under half a century between the foundation of the Order of the Ship in 1381 and that of the Golden Fleece in 1430 very few princes of any rank founded new knightly societies that appear to have conformed with our definition of a monarchical order. This is not to say that princes gave up founding orders altogether, but most of the orders founded in this period about which anything much is known were certainly not monarchical in nature. At least two of the new princely 'orders' of this period (the French royal 'order' of the Broom-Pod, probably created by Charles VI around 1388, and the 'order' of the Camail or Porcupine, founded by his brother Duke Louis of Orléans in or about 1394)[1] seem to have been pseudo-orders from the start, their founders having apparently decided that even the highly simplified sort of statutes given to the orders of the Golden Shield and St

[1] See above, p. 274 n. 8.

George of Aragon were an unnecessary encumbrance. Most of the true princely orders founded in this period whose statutes have been both preserved and discovered were either votive (like the 'enterprise' of the Prisoner's Iron created by Duke Jean of Bourbon in 1415),[2] or confraternal (like the Order of St Hubert created in 1422 with the blessings of René 'the Good', Duke of Bar).[3]

Nevertheless, a number of societies were founded in the years between 1381 and 1430 by princes in Spain and eastern Europe which either were or might have been endowed with a monarchical constitution, if only of a very simple form. Very little is known about any of these societies, so I have set forth what I have been able to discover of their histories in a single chapter, arranged geographically rather than chronologically. For the sake of convenience, I have included in the section on Austrian orders one which might have been founded slightly before 1381, and one which seems to have been founded slightly after 1430. I have concluded the chapter with a brief account of the Hungarian Society of the Dragon, whose statutes, though clearly modelled on those of the more elaborate type of monarchical order, made no reference to knighthood.

1 Castile: The Order of the Dove (1390) and the Collar of the Scale (c. 1430–1474?)

We have already had occasion to notice the foundation of the second order created in the court of Castile, that of the Holy Spirit or Dove. This order was proclaimed on 25 July 1390 by King Juan I, the son of Enrique of Trastámara and grandson of Alfonso 'the Implacable', who had been born in 1358 (three years after Carlo 'di Durazzo') and had succeeded his father in 1379. According to the chronicle of his reign, which is the only contemporary evidence I have found for the existence of this society,

> On St James' Day in the principal church of the said city of Segovia, the king declared publicly that he had ordained the wearing of a device, which he afterwards displayed there. It was in the form of a collar made like the rays of the sun; and there was on the said collar a white dove (*una paloma blanca*), which was a representation of the grace of the Holy Spirit. And he displayed a book of certain conditions which those who were to bear that collar were to fulfil. And the king took the collar and gave it to certain knights. He also made another device, which his squires wore, called the Rose (*Rosa*), and those seeking to prove their bodies *justando* wore it. When in a few days the king died, these devices were no longer worn.[4]

---

[2] See above, p. 17.

[3] See above, p. 15.

[4] *Crónica del Rey Don Juan, Primero de Castilla é de León*, ed. Don Cayetano Rosell, *Crónicas de los Reyes de Castilla desde Don Alfonso el Sabio, hasta los Católicos Don Fernando y Doña Isabel*, (Madrid, 1875), II, p. 145.

As the 'device' of the collar of the Holy Spirit was given only to knights, and those who received it had to fulfill certain conditions written out in a book, it seems likely that the collar was the badge of a true order of some sort, and it is at least possible that it was a monarchical order, founded to take the place of the still-surviving but much-reduced order of the Band. If so, it had the shortest life of any order of that class, for as the chronicle account indicates, its founder died (as a result of a riding accident) only three months after proclaiming its foundation, on 9 October 1390, and his son Enrique III, who succeeded him at the age of twelve, does not appear to have maintained it.

According to some historians, the device (if not the order) of the Holy Spirit was revived in a somewhat different form by Enrique III in 1399 (when he turned twenty-one) and bestowed by him and his successors until about 1470.[5] Certainly a collar bearing some resemblance to that created by Juan I in 1390 was displayed on their tombs and other monuments by a number of German knights who died in the second half of the fifteenth century.[6] This collar takes the form of a circlet of stylized clouds rather than rays, but has dependent from it (in addition to a series of T's set equidistant from one another all around its circumfrence) a dove in flight, represented with its head directly downwards and its back toward the viewer. The dove – almost certainly intended to represent the Holy Spirit – is attached to the circlet at its tail, and appears to be holding in its beak a disc sometimes larger than its body, charged with a cross paty. Dependent from this disk (which is probably a communion wafer) is a lion, statant or passant, represented as being about the same size as the dove. The lion could certainly represent the kingdom of Leon, but I have found no other evidence to link this collar with the lands of the Crown of Castile, and nothing other than the presence of the dove of the Holy Spirit to suggest that this collar was in any way associated with the order founded by Juan I. Indeed, as the collar of clouds and T's is almost identical to that of the Order of St Anthony,[7] it is not unlikely that the collar identified as that of the Holy Spirit is merely a variant of the collar of that society. (Fig. 12.2).

In any case the collar of the Holy Spirit was not among the three 'orders' conferred by Enrique IV on the German knight Jörg von Ehingen in 1456, which in addition to the Band included those of the 'collar of the scale' and the pomegranate.[8] Neither of the latter is actually described as the badge of an 'order' in any of the Castilian sources, including the official letter of Enrique IV by which he gave Von Ehingen the right to wear them, and what we know of the way in which they were distributed suggests that they were both pseudo-orders at most. The origin of the pomogranate device is obscure,[9] but the *devisa del collar del escama* seems to have been created by Juan II of Castile[10] at some time before Easter 1430,

[5] Paul Ganz, 'Die Abzeichen der Ritterorden', *AHS* (1905), p. 60.
[6] See Ganz, ibid., p. 61, fig. 57a,b,c; Ottfried Neubecker, *Le grand livre de l'héraldique* (Brussels, 1977), pp. 215, 218.
[7] Ganz, ibid., p. 55, fig. 47.
[8] See above, p. 63.
[9] A representation of its collar taken from the Grünenberg *Wappenbuch* is reproduced in Ganz, op. cit., p. 63, fig. 63.
[10] He succeeded his father Enrique III in 1406 at the age of one-and-a-half, and reigned until 1454.

12.1 The collar of the Holy Spirit
(reconstructed)

12.2 The collar (commonly identified
as that of the Holy Spirit of Castile)
as represented on the stele of
Nicolas von Diesbach

12.3 The collar of the Scale, as represented   a. by Ganz (provenance
unspecified)   b. by Ganz (provenance unspecified)   c. on the tombs of
Heinrich von Mallse and Jörg Perkchaimer, c.1450   d. by Leonhard

when he gave 'license' to wear the collar, and five actual collars of gold, to the Count of Cilli, brother-in-law of the Emperor Sigismund, and to four knights of his household who had accompanied him on a pilgrimage to the shrine of Santiago de Compostela.[11] Five years later, in 1435, the same king gave twenty-two collars of the scale to the German knight 'Roberto Señor de Balse' (possibly Heinpert Baron of Mallse) and certain gentlemen of his company, who had come to Spain wearing *empresas* which obliged them to perform certain feats of arms, and had jousted with a company led by the Castilian knight Juan Pimentel, Count of Mayorga. The two knights in the German company, who had requested the honour, received collars of gold, and the twenty squires received collars of silver.[12]

Two years later still, Juan is reported to have given 'his device of the collar of the scale, which he gave to very few', to his *doncel* Diego de Valera, who had just returned from a trip to the court of Albrecht, King of the Romans, King of Hungary and Bohemia, and Duke of Austria, where he had received the devices of the orders of Hungary, Bohemia, and Austria.[13] Juan's son Enrique IV 'the Impotent', who succeeded him in 1454, certainly gave the collar to Jörg von Ehingen in 1456, and may well have continued to distribute it along with the other Castilian 'orders' until his death in 1474, but it appears to have been abandoned by his sister Isabel 'the Catholic' during the civil wars which followed his death.

Clearly the device of the collar of the Scale functioned as a sort of honorific pseudo-order, and it may have been inspired by that of the pseudo-order of the Camail, which it closely resembled. Jörg von Ehingen described it in his diary as 'a broad collar overlapping like large fish-scales', and in the various representations of it that I have found (most of them on the tombs and memorials of German knights errant) it takes the form of a camail or mail shoulder-cape composed of large scales arranged in from three to eight overlapping rows.[14] When worn, it would probably have covered the lower neck and most of the upper part of the shoulders, chest, and back of the wearer, just as the very similar collar of the Camail-and-Porcupine does in several surviving representations.[15] The symbolic significance of this collar is obscure, but it would certainly have been distinctive when worn with civil attire. (Fig. 12.3).

[11] *La Crónica de serenisimo Principe Don Juan, Segondo deste nombre en Castilla y en Leon . . .*, ed. Rosell, *Crónicas*, II, p. 482.

[12] Ibid., p. 525.

[13] Ibid., pp. 533–4.

[14] See Alwin Schultz, *Deutsches Leben im XIV. und XV. Jahrhundert*, (2 vols., Vienna, 1892) figs. 551, 552, 560, and 561; Ganz, 'Die Abzeichen', fig. 62; Walter Leonhard, *Das grosse Buch der Wappenkunst* (Munich, 1978), p. 332, fig. 3.

[15] See the equestrian portrait of Charles Capet d'Artois, Count of Eu, in Paris, B.N., ms. fr.4985, f. 37v, published in D. L. Galbreath and Léon Jéquier, *Manuel du Blason* (2nd edn., Lausanne, 1977), p. 209, fig. 599.

2 Aragon: The Device of the Jar of the Salutation or Order of the Stole and Jar, 1403–1516

We noted in an earlier chapter that the Aragonese Enterprise of St George, founded by Pere 'the Ceremonious' in or about 1371, was replaced after the death of his younger son Martí 'the Humane' in 1410 by a new order that had already been founded by the Castilian prince chosen to succeed him by the Compromise of Caspe of 28 June 1412. The prince in question – the Infante Don Fernando 'of Antequera', Duke of Peñafiel, Count of Alburquerque and Mayorga, and Lord of Lara, Castro, and Haro (v. 1373–1416) – was the younger son of King Juan I of Castile, founder of the Order of the Holy Spirit, the grandson of Pere 'the Ceremonious' of Aragon, founder of the Enterprise of St George, and the great-grandson of Alfonso 'the Implacable' of Castile, founder of the Order of the Band.[16] Fernando seems to have been one of the most chivalrous as well as one of the most capable princes of his house, and during the course of the festivities surrounding the celebration of the feast of the Annunciation on 15 August 1403 in the city of Medina del Campo, he is said to have distributed to his sons and other knights the collar of his new order, which was at first called that of *la Jarra de la Salutación* or 'the Jar of the Salutation', but came to be known as that of *la Stola et Jarra*, the 'Stole and Jar'.[17]

The statutes apparently adopted on that occasion have been preserved in a manuscript in the Escorial.[18] In a lengthy prologue, Fernando, observing that 'the works of chivalry are the things most praiseworthy and precious', proclaimed the foundation in the following terms:

> to the honour and reverence of the Virgin St Mary, and in recognition of the pleasure which she received when the angel saluted her, I have taken as a device a collar of the Jar of the Salutation, from which collar descends a griffin (*Grifo*) suspended, in signification that even as the griffin is strong among all the animals, so all those of this Device must be strong and firm in the love of God and of the Virgin St Mary.

[16] On his life and reign, see I. Macdonald, *Don Fernando de Antequera* (Oxford, 1948); and Juan Torres Fontes, 'The Regency of Don Ferdinand of Antequera', *Spain in the Fifteenth Century 1369–1516*, ed. Roger Highfield (New York, 1972), pp. 114–70.

[17] This order was known to the early historians of knightly orders as the 'Order of the Lily', and in consequence has been thought to be a revival of an 'Order of (Our Lady of) the Lily', said by Favyn and Micheli Márquez to have been founded by a King of Navarre in the first half of the eleventh century, but probably imaginary. The only modern account of the order I have found is the Barón de Cobos de Belchite, 'La Antigua Orden de Nuestra Señora del Lirio (Año 1043)', *Hidalguía* 1 (1953), pp. 269–272, which is largely concerned with the imaginary Navarrese order, but does contain some useful information.

[18] Biblioteca del Monasterio del Escorial, d.m. 25, ff. 250v–258r, 'Reglas y Divisa de la Orden Militar de la Jarra, que ordenó el Infante Don Fernando, hijo del Rey Don Juan de Castilla', published in Cobos de Belchite, op. cit., p. 272.

He went on to declare that he wished his eldest son Don Alfonso or whichever of his sons succeeded him to maintain the Device under the 'rules and conditions' that followed, and to give it the '*ricos homes*, knights, squires, ladies, and damsels' he thought should belong to it. Finally, he set forth the *reglas* proper, which all the 'knights and ladies' who received the Device were to swear on the cross and gospels to follow:

First – That when they can, they are to assist at Vespers on Saturdays and feast days;
Second – That each one of them is to give food to five paupers on the day of the feast;
Third – That they are to put on the white mantle and wear the Device on solemn feasts;
Fourth – That every person who wears the Device has to swear that he will wear it for his whole life;
Fifth – That they are to put it on every Saturday.

These statutes bear a close resemblance to certain of the ordinances of the Aragonese Enterprise of St George, with which the Infante, the grandson of its founder, must surely have been familiar by 1403, and the society represented by the 'device' looks rather like a highly attenuated version of that already attenuated order. Since it had corporate statutes and a membership that was not only defined (at least partly) in terms of knightly status, but was to be distributed exclusively by its founder and his heirs, the Device of the Jar fits our definition of a monarchical order, but only barely. Like the Order of the Golden Shield (possibly still in existence in 1403), it was in fact only a shadow of a monarchical order, for its members had, as such, no formal obligations either to one another or to their chief, and took part in no truly corporate activities. Presumably Fernando meant to bestow its device on those of his vassals and household retainers whom he wished especially to honour, hoping that the gratitude they felt, and the regular wearing of the collar and mantle, would encourage those who received it to persist in the loyal behaviour for which they had been rewarded in the first place. Both he and his successors seem to have distributed it fairly freely to foreign visitors to the court of Aragon as well, for a considerable number of Germans displayed representations of the collar (or the jar alone) on their tombs and other monuments.[19] Despite the claim he made in the prologue to the statutes that he had founded the society of the Jar to promote chivalry, Fernando – no doubt influenced by the contemporary practice of the Order of the Band – opened membership in his order to ladies and damsels, but gave no hint of the circumstances in which they were to be admitted.

Since Fernando had no particular expectation of succeeding to the throne of Aragon in 1403, when he founded the order, he must initially have intended it to be a ducal counterpart to the royal orders of the Band and St George, but he did not annex it formally at that time to any of his lordships. Once he became King of

[19] Among them were Heinpert Freiherr von Mallse, Jörg Perkchaimer, Georg Leininger, Ulrich Keczel, and Niklaus von Diesbach. See Schultz, *Deutsches Leben*, figs. 551, 552, 557, 558, 560, and 561; Ganz, 'Die Abzeichen', figs. 59, 60, and 61, and Tafel VI.

Aragon and its dependencies (including island Sicily) in 1412, under the name of Ferran I, he took the order with him and made it, in practice, the sole royal order of the lands of the Crown of Aragon. Whether he ever attached the order in any formal way to the crown of Aragon is unclear, but it is more likely that the order remained throughout its history the personal property of the head of his house. Whatever its legal status, the evidence I have been able to discover suggests that from 1412 to 1516 the decidedly vestigial order of the Jar played a prominent role in the ceremonial life of the Aragonese court, and was treated in very much the way the rather more substantial orders of the Garter and the Golden Fleece were treated in the courts of England and Burgundy. According to the chronicler Alvar García de Santa Maria, who seems to have been an eyewitness, Ferran 'of Antequera' made much of the order at his coronation in Zaragoza in 1414, and had borders of jars embroidered in gold on both the dalmatic and the chasuble that he wore on that occasion.[20] He allowed the Emperor Sigismund to confer membership in it as well as his own society of the Dragon on Basilio Colalba, Marquis of Ancona, in 1413,[21] and conferred membership in it on Sigismund himself when he was in Perpignan in 1415.[22] He is also reported to have conferred the collar on the ambassadors sent to him by Ladislao of Sicily, and on Godofredo, bastard son of the King of Navarre.[23]

The founder's elder son Alfons V, 'the Magnanimous', who succeeded him in 1416 at the age of twenty-two, offered membership in the order to Duke Philippe 'the Good' of Burgundy when the latter procured his election to the Order of the Golden Fleece in 1445,[24] and had himself and the knights carrying the canopy over his chair portrayed wearing the collar of the Jar on the arch erected around the principal portal of the Castel Nuovo in Naples to commemorate his entry into that city in triumph on 26 February 1443.[25] The Jar remained the royal order of the mainland kingdom of Sicily, in succession to those of the Knot and the Ship, from that time until Alfons' death in 1458, when he was succeeded in Naples by his bastard son Ferrante (who soon founded yet another order), and in Barcelona by his younger brother Joan II. Joan (who had been King of Navarre in the right of his wife Blanche since 1425) introduced the order into that kingdom (which does not appear to have had a monarchical order before 1458), but on his death in 1479 Navarre passed to his only surviving daughter by Blanche, and the lands of the Crown of Aragon to his son by his second wife, Ferran II, later known as 'the

---

[20] Passage quoted in Cobos de Belchite, 'La Antigua Orden', p. 271.

[21] The passage of the letter by which Sigismund conferred these orders is quoted by Ashmole, *Institution*, p. 113: 'Te quem manu propria militiae cingulo & societatis nostrae Draconicae ac stolae seu amprisiae charissimi fratris nostri Regis Aragoniae insignivimus . . .' The word *amprisiae* seems to be a Latin form of the word *empresa* 'enterprise' (which in an Aragonese document of 1445 was written *emprisia*).

[22] Cobos de Belchite, op. cit., p. 271.

[23] Ibid., citing Hernán Pérez de Guzman, *La Crónica de . . . Don Juan, Secondo*.

[24] See Barcelona, Archivo de la Corona de Aragón, reg. 2654, ff. 100v–102v, reg. 2699, f. 50, cited or published in Constantin Marinesco, 'Documents espagnols inédits concernant la fondation de l'Ordre de la Toison d'or', *Comptes rendus de l'Académie des incriptions et belles-lettres* (1956), pp. 401–417.

[25] See George L. Hersey, *The Aragonese Arch at Naples, 1443–1475* (New Haven, 1973), figs. 72, 74, 75, 77, 79.

Catholic'. Ferran, whose wife Isabel 'the Catholic' had already succeeded to the throne of Castile in 1474, seems to have maintained the order of the Jar under its original statutes until his death in 1516, for the statutes were copied into a register of the Neapolitan royal chancellery covering the years 1496–1500,[26] and its insignia were proudly displayed by the German knight Florian Waldauff on a bookplate engraved by Albrecht Dürer around 1505,[27] and by the Emperor Maximilian on the triumphal arch he had engraved by Dürer's workshop in the year 1515.[28] As Isabel seems to have abandoned all of the old Castilian 'orders', the Order of the Stole and Jar may well have been treated as the principal royal order of the united kingdoms of Spain in the period between 1479 and Isabel's death in 1504, when Philippe 'the Handsome', Sovereign of the Order of the Golden Fleece, became King of Castile in the right of his wife Juana, daughter of Ferran and Isabel. The Order of the Stole and Jar seems to have been abandoned in its turn by Philippe's son Charles, who (already King of Castile as Carlos I), succeeded Ferran on the throne of Aragon in 1416.

Because the order survived for more than a hundred years, quite a number of contemporary representations of its insignia have survived, covering the period from about 1430 to 1515.[29] According to the statutes the original *Devisa* was a collar, possibly inspired directly by that of the Order of the Holy Spirit, composed of a series of jars or vases intended to represent the jar of lilies commonly set next to the Virgin Mary in depictions of the Annunciation. In the surviving representations the 'jars' take the form of bulbous pots, sometimes with and sometimes without handles, and hold three natural lilies whose heads emerge from the opening. From this rather unlikely collar was hung, by one or two fine chains, a passant griffin, sometimes gorged with a fleuron-crown, and often holding in its four paws a scroll, usually shown blank, but sometimes bearing the motto *Por so amor*, 'For love of her'. In two of the representations the griffin hangs from an image of the Virgin on a crescent moon, in one case surrounded by a glory and set into the collar itself. The collar was worn in at least two different forms: a short form (depicted on a monument of about 1430) worn upright around the standing collar of the wearer's coat; and a longer form (depicted on monuments carved after 1450), angled in such a way that it rested on the wearer's shoulders. The latter type

---

[26] A copy of this was made by Paolo Garzilo in a manuscript now in the Biblioteca Brancacciana, ms. II E, f. 12, headed: 'Capitula Ampritiae Stellae cum hydriis et moniti aureo cum Griffo pendente in laude Beatae Mariae Virginis aedita per quondam Serenissimum Dominum Ferdinandum Aragonum. Videlicet de iis quae sunt observanda ab eis de quibus dictus ordo seu ampritia tradita fuerit. Desumpta ab archivio Regiae Cancelleriae a libro intitulatu Curiae pᵒ Friderici Regis de anno 1496 usque ad anno 1500 fol. 90 a tᵒ'. Published in Giuseppe Maria Fusco, *I Capitoli dell'Ordine dell'Armellino* (Naples, 1845), p. 28. The 'stella' referred to was probably a glory surrounding the image of the Virgin.

[27] Willi Kurth, *The Complete Woodcuts of Albrecht Dürer* (New York, 1963), pp. 23, 130.

[28] *Maximilian's Triumphal Arch; Woodcuts by Albrecht Dürer and Others* (Dover: New York, 1972), p. v and Pl. 20.

[29] Some of these are reproduced in Schultz, *Deutsches Leben*, II, figs. 551, 552, 557, 558, 560, and 561; Ganz, 'Die Abzeichen', p. 62, fig. 60; and Galbreath and Jéquier, *Manuel du Blason*, p. 208, fig. 597, p. 210, fig. 601.

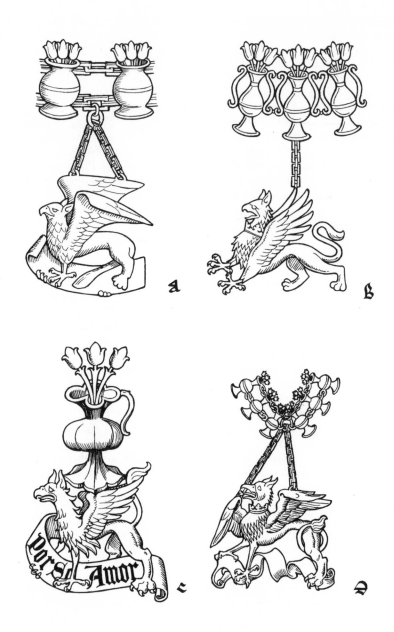

12.4 The collar of the Jar, as represented   a. on the effigy of Gómez Manrique, c.1430   b. in the portrait of Oswald von Wolkenstein, c.1480   c. in the Grünenberg *Wappenbuch*, c.1483   d. by Albrecht Dürer, c.1505?

of collar, at least, was sometimes set on what appears to be a band of fabric, and it is possible that the links of such collars were constructed of embroidery rather than metal. In paintings the collar is depicted in either gold or silver, and it is possible that (like the contemporary Castilian collar of the Scale), the collar of the Jar was given in gold to knights and in silver to squires. (Fig. 12.4).

The collar is the only form of device mentioned in the statutes of institution, but at some time before 1413 the founder seems to have assigned a secondary device to the order: a white stole first alluded to in the Emperor Sigismund's letter of that year conferring membership in the order on the Marquis of Ancona.[30] Both the collar and the stole of the order (now referred to as that of *la Stola et Jarra*) were brought by the ambassadors of Alfons 'the Magnanimous' to Philippe 'the Good' in 1446,[31] and on the arch Alfons had erected in Naples shortly after this, one of the knights in the triumphal procession wears what is certainly the stole of the order over his armour.[32] That knight and the Swiss knight Henri Blarer of St Gall (in a portrait painted in 1460) wear the stole alone,[33] but both the Castilian knight Gómez Manrique, (on his tomb effigy carved around 1430),[34] and the Tyrolian traveller Oswald von Wolkenstein, (in the portrait painted for him around 1470),[35] wear both the collar and the stole. In all of these representations the stole takes the form of a band of thick white fabric about four inches wide, and in three of the four it is worn like a sash (or the stole of a deacon) from the left shoulder to the right hip, and bears on the upper part of the left breast a small brooch, about one inch wide, in the form of the jar of lilies. The stole worn by Manrique is somewhat narrower, worn over the right shoulder, and lacks the jar. The stole device (displayed alone in a stained-glass window of the early sixteenth century)[36] bears a certain resemblance to the device of the Castilian order of the Band, which may well have inspired it (and with which it has often been confused),[37] but unlike the band it was clearly separate from the coat with which it was worn. Since it is worn alone by the only armoured knight on the triumphal arch in Naples, it is possible that it was originally intended to be worn, instead of the elaborate and valuable collar, with military attire. (Figs. 12.5-7).

According to the statutes the members of the order were also to wear a habit, described only as a *manto blanco* or 'white mantle', on solemn feasts. A mantle of the same colour was worn by the knights of all of the other Spanish orders (including the monarchical order of St George) at the time the order of the Jar was established, and Fernando no doubt prescribed such a mantle for the members of his society to associate it with those more substantial societies. It is probably

[30] See above, n. 21.
[31] Barcelona, Archivo de la Corona de Aragón, reg. 2654, f. 102v, cited in Marinesco, 'Documents espagnols', p. 405.
[32] Hersey, *The Aragonese Arch*, fig. 41.
[33] Reproduced in Neubecker, *Grand livre*, p. 220.
[34] Reproduced in Theodor Müller, *Sculpture in the Netherlands, Germany, France, and Spain, 1400-1500* (London, 1966), pl. 55. See also p. 52.
[35] Reproduced in Neubecker, *Grand livre*, p. 220.
[36] See Galbreath and Jéquier, *Manuel*, p. 210, fig. 601.
[37] For example by Ganz, 'Die Abzeichen', p. 60, fig. 55, and by Galbreath and Jéquier, loc. cit.

12.5 The collar and stole, as represented a. on the tomb of Gómez Manrique, c.1430 b. in the portrait of Oswald von Wolkenstein, c.1480

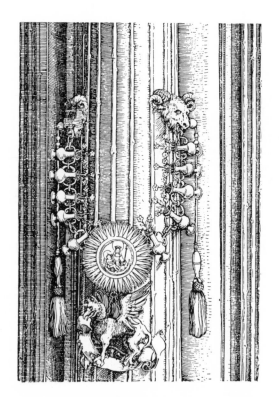

12.6 The collar of the Jar, as represented by Albrecht Dürer on the triumphal arch of the Emperor Maximilian, 1515

12.7 The stole and jar represented in a window, c.1510

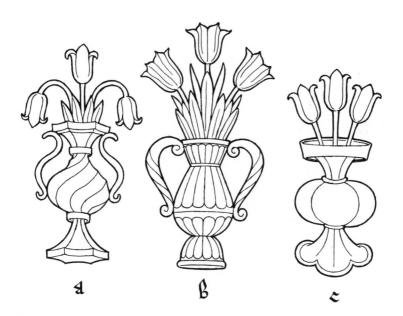

12.8 The jar, as represented a. on the stele of Nicolas von Diesbach
   b. on the tomb of Giovanni Emo (after Galbreath and Jéquier)
      c. in the window of c.1510 (after Galbreath and Jéquier)

safe to presume that the mantle of the companions of the Jar bore at least one jar embroidered on some part of its surface – either on the left breast instead of the usual cross, or arranged in the form of a border, like the jars displayed on the founder's coronation vestments – but I have found no representation of a member of the order in his mantle.

3 Austria: The Societies of the Tress (1365/86–1395?), the Salamander (c. 1390–1463?), and the Eagle (1433–1457/93)

On the opposite side of Western Christendom from Spain, three knightly societies were founded between 1365 and 1433 by successive rulers of Austria. The Dukes of Austria of the great Swabian dynasty of Habsburg, rulers of a large and growing dominical estate stretched across the whole southern part of the German kingdom, were anxious in this period to assert both their independence from the Emperors of the rival house of Luxemburg and their equality with the seven Prince Electors named by the Emperor Karl IV in 1356, so their foundation of knightly orders may have been intended in part to make them appear more like kings than the other princes of Germany. Although very little seems to be known about any of the societies they founded, what evidence I have found for their histories suggests that membership in all three was in the gift of the reigning Duke of Austria, and it is possible that all three were maintained under a monarchical form of constitution during some part of their histories at least.

The first of these societies to be founded was the *Geselschafft vom Zopff* or 'Society of the Tress'.[38] According to the preface of the travel diary composed a century later by the German knight Jörg von Ehingen, whose ancestor Burkard 'With the Tress' (v. 1348–1407) had been admitted to it, this order was founded by a Duke of Austria at some time before 1388 in honour of a beautiful lady who had cut off a tress of her hair and presented it to him as a favour.[39] The duke in question was Albrecht III, called 'With the Tress', who was born in 1348 (seven years before Carlo 'di Durazzo'), succeeded his father Duke Albrecht II as co-ruler of Austria, Carinthia, the Tyrol, and Alsace in 1358, succeeded his eldest brother the 'Archduke' Rudolf IV as head of the ducal house in 1365, and became sole ruler of the lands of his house after the death of his younger brother Leopold III in 1386.

---

[38] On this society, unknown to most of the early historians of knightly orders, see Sigmund von Birken, *Spiegel der Ehren des höchst löblichen Kayser-und Königlichen Erzhauses Österreich* (Nürnberg, 1668); S. Essenwein, 'Albertus mit dem Zopfe auf einem Glasgemälde zu St. Erhard in der Breitenau in Steiermark', *Anzeiger für Kunde der Deutschen Vorzeit*, Neue Folge 6 (1866), cols. 177–9, and 'Zur Geschichte der Zopfgesellschaft', ibid., 7 (1867), cols. 193–7; Schultz, *Deutsches Leben*, pp. 541–2; E. A. Gessler, *Anzeiger für Schweitz. Altertumskunde* 16 (1914); Ernst Girsberger, 'Die Gesellschaftsabzeichen der Sempacher-Ritter zu Königsfelden', *AHS* (1927), pp. 104–8; Ganz, 'Die Abzeichen', p. 54; Neubecker, 'Ordensritterliche Heraldik', *Der Herold*, I (1940), p. 116, n. 216; and Roman Freiherr von Procházka, *Österreichisches Ordenshandbuch* (Munich, 1974), p. 118.

[39] *The Diary of Jörg von Ehingen*, trans. and ed. Malcolm Letts (London, 1929), p. 13.

I have found nothing to indicate precisely when he founded the Society of the Tress.[40] The German historian S. Essenwein suggested that the strap depicted hanging at the back of Duke Albrecht in a stained-glass window in the church of St Erhard in the Breitenau in Styria,[41] and those depicted hanging at the backs of the knights who fell with Duke Leopold III in the Battle of Sempach fought on 9 July 1386,[42] in an heraldic manuscript once preserved in Linz[43] (and in a fresco in the Agneskapelle of the monastery of Königsfelden)[44] were meant to be the device of the Society. If this is true, the Society must have been founded before the battle. A very different form of tress is represented chained to the crested helm of the founder on one of the first folios of the book of the Brotherhood of St Christopher in the Arlberg Pass,[45] begun three years after the foundation of that society in 1390.[46] This is the latest reference of any sort that I have found to the Society of the Tress, and it seems likely that it dissolved when Duke Albrecht died in 1395.

As we have just observed, the *zopff* or 'tress' from which the Society took its name seems to have taken two quite distinct forms. One of these was a collar of gilded metal wrought in the shape of a natural tress of human hair, braided in the form of a long pigtail narrowing steadily until just before the end (which was left flowing freely) and twisted into a circle with the loose end hanging down as if it were a pendant. This is the form represented in association with the arms of the founder in the book of the Brotherhood of St Christopher, and surrounding a unidentified shield of arms bearing a gonfannon reproduced by Walter Leonhard.[47] It is also the form taken by the only actual exemplar of the device to survive, a gilded collar now preserved in the Joanneum Museum in Graz.[48] In two genealogical trees painted around 1500, now in the Hofburg in Vienna, the founder is depicted wearing the tress around his neck, with the loose end on his breast.

In the second form of the device (according to Essenwein) the *zopff* proper was completely hidden by an elaborate metal case (which in the surviving representations looks like a heavy belt about two and a half feet long) and was not twisted into a collar but simply suspended (presumably from some sort of chain, ribbon, or hook) at the back of the neck.[49] Since these straps bear no resemblance to the collars described in the previous paragraph, however, there is reason to doubt that they were meant to be the device of the Society here in question, and Ernst Girsberger has in fact argued that these appendages were merely straps to hold the

---

[40] Procházka, loc. cit., states that it was founded in 1367, but cites no evidence to suggest that date.

[41] 'Albertus mit dem Zopfe'.

[42] See Th. von Liebenau, *Die Schlacht bei Sempach* (Lucerne, 1886).

[43] 'Zur Geschichte der Zopfgesellschaft', and Ganz, loc. cit.

[44] Girsberger, 'Die Gesellschaftsabzeichen'.

[45] Reproduced in Leonhard, *Das grosse Buch der Wappenkunst*, p. 332, fig. 10.

[46] See S. Herzberg-Fränkel, 'Die Bruderschafts- und Wappenbücher von St. Christoph auf dem Arlberg', *Mitteilungen des Instituts für Oesterreiche Geschichtsforschung* 6 (1901) Ergänzungsband, pp. 355–412.

[47] Loc. cit., fig. 4.

[48] Reproduced in Procházka, op. cit., p. 122.

[49] Reproduced in Essenwein, 'Zur Geschichte', pl.; Schultz, op. cit., fig. 549; Ganz, op. cit., p. 54, fig. 46.

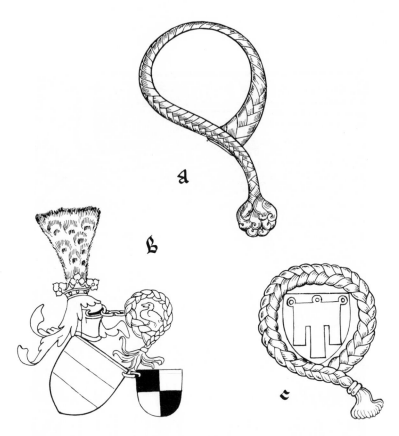

12.9 The natural form of the tress, as represented a. in the surviving
exemplar, in Graz b. in the Arlberg *Wappenbuch*
c. by Leonhard (provenance unspecified)

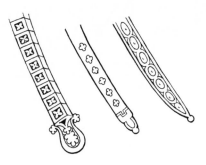

12.10 The belt-like tress, as represented in the stained-glass and fresco

12.11 Duke Albrecht 'With the Tress', represented in a window in St Erhard in der Breitenau (after Schultz)

shield or helm in place, and had nothing whatever to do with the Society of the Tress.[50] Girsberger may be correct, but the belt-like objects worn by Duke Albrecht in the window and by Count Friedrich von Zollern and several other knights in the fresco are not attached either to the helmets worn by those princes or to their shields (which they are not carrying), and appear to be both too long and too thick to have served any useful function. It is therefore much more likely that they are representations of the tress-device in an alternative form. Whether they were cases holding natural tresses is another question; their belt-like shape suggests that the form of the device they represent was inspired by the badge of the Order of the Garter (either directely or via the Luxemburg order of the Buckle), and it is possible that the collar in the form of a natural tress was a later form suggested by the name given to the belt when worn hanging down the back. If this is true, the legend about the damsel cutting off her hair cited above is probably an apocryphal story similar to that told to explain the origin of the mysterious device of the English order. (Figs. 12.9–11).

Even less appears to be known about the second of the Austrian orders founded in this period, that of the Salamander.[51] Its foundation has been tentatively attributed to Duke Leopold III, 'the Valiant', the younger brother of Albrecht III who fell at Sempach in 1386,[52] but there seems to be no evidence to support this hypothesis, and as none of the knights who fell at Sempach depicted in the Agneskapelle of the Monastery at Königsfelden is depicted wearing the device of the order,[53] it must seem unlikely. It is in fact probable that the order was created by one of Leopold's four sons, for the first three, at least, certainly belonged to it, and it was maintained in the fifteenth century in the junior, Leopoldine line of the ducal house, rather than the senior, Albertine line descended from his elder brother. The earliest surviving evidence for the order's existence appears to be the representations of the order's device in the book of the Brotherhood of St Christopher in the Arlberg Pass, in the section of the book written and painted in 1393. Therein it is associated first (on f. 6r) with the arms of the future Duke Albrecht IV 'the Marvellous' (v. 1377–1404), who was soon to succeed his father Albrecht 'With the Tress' as head of the ducal house, and then (on ff. 7v, 8r, and 9v respectively) with those of his agnatic first-cousins of the Leopoldine line Duke Wilhelm 'the Affable' (v. 1370–1406), Duke Leopold IV 'the Superb' (v. 1371–1411), and (probably) Duke Ernst I 'the Iron' (v. 1377–1424), whose arms occur next to the date 1394.[54] The device next appears surrounding the shield of

[50] 'Die Gesellschaftsabzeichen', pp. 107–8.

[51] This order was unknown to most of the early writers on knightly orders, and very little has been written about it in the last century. See K. von Sava, 'Ueber Ordens-Insignien auf deutschen Siegeln vor Kaiser Maximilian I', Anzeiger für Kunde der deutschen Vorzeit 8 (1857), cols. 290–2, 9 (1857), cols. 329–32; August am Rhyn, 'Das älteste Luzerner Stadtwappen mit dem Orden vom Salamander', Beitrag zur Kunstdenkmälergeschichte des Kantons Luzern (1938); Procházka, loc. cit.

[52] Rhyn, op. cit.; Procházka, loc. cit.

[53] Girsberger, 'Die Gesellschaftsabzeichen', makes no reference to the salamander device when discussing the devices worn by the knights in the fresco there.

[54] Von Sava, 'Ordens-Insignien', col. 292. The third and fourth are both identified with Duke Leopold IV, but as Leopold could harldly have joined twice in rapid succession, it is likely that the second name is a scribal error for Ernst. Von Sava mistakenly took the device for that of the Hungarian Society of the Dragon.

Albrecht's arms on an exemplar of his seal attached to a document written in 1396,[55] and on the seal of his cousin Duke Ernst 'the Iron' appended to documents dated 20 September 1402 and 22 November 1404.[56] Nothing is known of the order in the next several decades, but it must have survived, for Jörg von Ehingen wrote in his travel diary that Duke Ernst 'the Iron's' son Duke Albrecht VI 'the Prodigal' (who succeeded Ernst in 1424 at the age of five) admitted him into the *fürstlich geselschafft des Salamanders* or 'princely society of the Salamander' when he presented himself at the ducal court at Rottenburg am Neckar in 1454.[57] I have found no evidence to suggest that the order was maintained after Albrecht VI's death without issue in 1463, either by his elder brother Duke Friedrich V – German King as Friedrich IV from 1440 and Emperor as Friedrich III from 1452 until his death in 1493 – or by his cousin Duke Sigmund, ruler of Alsace and Tyrol from 1439 to 1489/90.

The badge of the Society of the Salamander was (as the name suggests) a representation of a salamander. In all of the surviving examples, the salamander is depicted as a long, thin quadruped with a head rather like that of a dog (or dragon) and a tail (in some examples rather short, in others fairly long) ending in a sort of bush, like that of a lion but larger. It is shown in every case as if seen from above, and twisted into a circle so that its head touches or overlaps its tail. In the Arlberg book the salamanders are left white, but their tongues are painted in red and their backs are speckled with small red (and in one case green) spots. On the seals of Albrecht IV and Ernst I the salamander encircles a shield of the arms of Austria – a method of display probably inspired by the the custom of encircling the arms of England with a garter established by Edward III of England in the 1350s. It is unclear what the salamander badge was intended to signify, but in the bestiary the beast was said to be the strongest of all poisonous creatures, and not only immune to fire, but able to put it out.[58] It is therefore more than likely that, like the griffin of the contemporary Order of the Stole and Jar, it was chosen for one or more of these impressive qualities. (Fig. 12.12).

The third of the Austrian orders – variously known to historians as the *Ordo Disciplinarum* or 'Order of (the) Disciplines', and the *Adlerorden* or 'Order of the Eagle'[59] – was founded by Duke Albrecht V 'the Magnanimous', who succeeded his

---

[55] Neubecker, 'Ordensritterliche Heraldik', p. 119, fig. 102.

[56] Ibid., fig. 103; Von Sava, 'Ordens-Insignien', col. 291.

[57] *Des Schwaebischen Ritters Georg von Ehingen Reisen nach der Ritterschaft* (Stuttgart, 1842), pp. 14–15; *Diary*, p. 26.

[58] T. H. White, ed. *The Bestiary. A Book of Beasts* (New York, 1954, 1960), pp. 182–4. As White observes, none of the characteristics imputed to the salamander in the Bestiary is found in the natural beast.

[59] This order was known to Micheli Márquez, Mendo, Ashmole, and later historians as the *Ordo Disciplinarum*, but they made no claims to know precisely what that name meant, when it was founded, or even who founded it. It has received some attention from modern historians: see Karl Heinrich Freiherr Roth von Schreckenstein, *Die Ritterwürde und der Ritterstand* (Freiburg-im-Breisgau, 1886), p. 671; Schultz, *Deutsches Leben*, p. 543; D.-K. Fromm, *Mitteilungen der kaiserliche und königliche Zentral-Kommission*, 15; and Ganz, 'Die Abzeichen', pp. 55–6. This society may be identical to that of the White Eagle, said by Favyn to have been founded by King Wladislaw (IV) of Poland in February 1325. Favyn

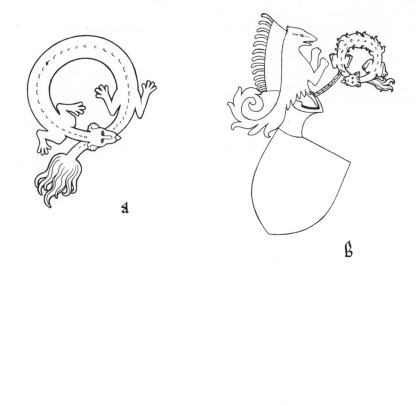

12.12 The badge of the Salamander, as represented a. in the Arlberg *Wappenbuch* b. in the same c. on the seal of Duke Albrecht IV, 1396 (after Neubecker) d. on the seal of Duke Ernst I, 1404 (after Neubecker)

father Albrecht IV 'the Marvellous' as head of the ducal house in 1404 (when he was seven), assumed the government of Austria in 1411, and spent much of his life fighting at the side of his neighbour Sigismund von Luxemburg, King of Hungary and Bohemia and King (from 1411) or Emperor (from 1433) of the Romans, against the Hussites of Bohemia and the Turks. On 28 September 1421 Albrecht married Elizabeth, the only daughter of Sigismund, and when the old Emperor died in December 1437 he suceeded him on all three of his royal thrones (although he never succeeded in gaining effective control of Bohemia).[60] Sigismund, as we shall see momentarily, had in 1408 founded the Society of the Dragon, a baronial league modelled on the older orders of knighthood, and Albrecht may well have been inspired to create the Society of the Eagle by his example.

According to the nineteenth-century historian Roth von Schreckenstein, Albrecht founded the order on 16 March 1433, two months before Sigismund's Imperial coronation.[61] The only unequivocal reference to this order that I have found in a written document of any sort is in a passage of the chronicle of the reign of the Castilian king Juan II cited above. This passage records that the Castilian knight Diego de Valera – who shortly after Albrecht's accession to the thrones of Hungary and Bohemia in December 1437 had journeyed across half of Europe to serve him in his war against the Hussites – was at some time before his departure from Albrecht's court in November 1438 given 'his three devices, which are the Dragon, which he gives as King of Hungary, the Tusinique [sic], as King of Bohemia,[62] [and] the Collar of the Disciplines with the Eagle, as Duke of Austria, in which there are three and a half marks of gold.'[63] The Augsburg patrician Sebastian Ilsung recorded in his travel diary that he had received the *gesellschaft und liberey* of King Albrecht from the hands of a knight in the city of Breslau (or Preslaw), and it is more than likely that the 'society' in question was that of the Eagle.[64] Since

---

could easily have been misled into associating this society with Poland by the fact that its device resembled the white eagle of the Polish royal arms.

[60] He was crowned King of Hungary on 1 January 1438, elected King of the Romans on 18 March of the same year, and received the crown of Bohemia in June.

[61] Loc. cit.

[62] This order was known to Mennenius and Micheli Márquez as that of the *Equites Tusini*, but neither author suggests what this name meant. The latter author asserts that it was founded by a ruler of Austria to combat the Turks and Hussites, but the passage quoted here implies that it was a Bohemian royal order. It is possible that this society was founded by Albrecht himself in 1438 to secure his claim to the throne of Bohemia – or simply as a Bohemian counterpart to his Austrian and Hungarian orders – and dissolved upon his death in the following year. This would explain why so little is now known about the order.

[63] *La Crónica de . . . Don Juan Segondo*, ed. Rosell, *Crónicas*, II, p. 534. The chapter in question is not found in all of the manuscripts, but gives every appearance of being genuine.

[64] 'Der hat um mein dienst, die ich dem h. rich gethan han, (als ich) zu sinen gnaden gen Bechem geraisset uf min kost, mich begabet mir seiner küniglichen gnaden gesellschaft und liberey; die ward mir angehenkt von eim ritter zu Pressla in der statt.' Quoted in Roth von Schreckenstein, *Ritterwürde*, p. 671.

Albrecht's energies in the 1430s were largely devoted to fighting the Hussites and the Turks, it is likely that the Society of the Eagle was formally dedicated to that end, but I have found no trace of the order's statutes, and the only other evidence for the order's nature and history seems to be the repsentations of the order's badge, found principally on the tomb monuments of various German knights errant who must have been admitted to the order, like De Valera and Ilsung, during visits to the court of the founder and his heirs. The badge is reproduced on the monuments of the knights Heinpert Baron of Mallse and Jörg Perkchaimer, who both died in 1450;[65] the knight Niclas Drugksecz, who died in 1468;[66] and the knight Caspar Hanperkhain, who died in 1520.[67] It is also associated with the arms of two unnamed Kings of Bohemia in the *Wappenbuch* of Conrad Grünenberg, completed in 1483.[68] This suggests that the order survived in some form under its founder's son Ladislaus 'the Posthumous', who was born on 22 Februrary 1440 – four months after Albrecht's own death on 27 October 1439 – and raised in the court of his cousin Friedrich V of Austria, who had been elected to succeed Albrecht as King of the Romans (as Friedrich IV) on 2 February. Ladislaus was proclaimed King of Hungary and Bohemia and actually crowned King of Hungary as László V on 15 May 1440, but was not generally recognized there until 1444, and died childless at the age of seventeen in 1457 without ever having assumed effective control of the government of any of his dominions. It would appear that the presidency of the Society of the Eagle was then assumed by his cousin Friedrich V (now Emperor as Friedrich III), who claimed his whole inheritance, but was able to attach only the Austrian portion. In both a panel and a stained-glass window set up to commemorate a pilgrimage he undertook to the Holy Sepulchre in 1462, the knight Ulrich Keczel displayed the devices of the many orders and societies to which he was admitted during his voyage, and among these is that of the Eagle.[69] If the order survived until Friedrich's death in 1493, it was immediately abandoned by his son Maximilian, who was already the Sovereign of the more illustrious order of the Golden Fleece, and seems to have felt no need for more than one such society.

The badge of the Society of the Eagle took the form of an eagle, displayed and crowned with an open crown, holding in its claws a scroll bearing the motto *Thue Recht* (sometimes completed *und scheue Niemand*), and usually pendant from a second device in the form of a clothed arm, emerging from a cloud and holding in its hand what appears to be a switch made up of sticks, in one example bent around into a circle. On the carved effigy of Caspar Hanperkhain the eagle is suspended, without the arm, from what appears to be a thick cord worn as a collar, and as De Valera refers to it as the *collar de las disciplinas con la aguila blanca* it must appear that the whole badge normally hung from some sort of collar throughout its history. The motto means 'Do right and fear no one', and the device may have been be intended to represent the arm of God chastising (disciplining?) Germany (of which the eagle

---

[65] Reproduced in Schultz, *Deutsches Leben*, figs. 551, 552.
[66] Ibid., fig. 555.
[67] Ibid., figs. 553, 554.
[68] Ganz, Die Abzeichen', p. 56, and fig. 48; and Arthur Charles Fox-Davies, *The Art of Heraldry* (London, 1914; repr. New York, 1976), Pl. LXXXIX (f. p. 281).
[69] See Schultz, *Deutsches Leben*, figs. 560, 561, pp. 548, 549.

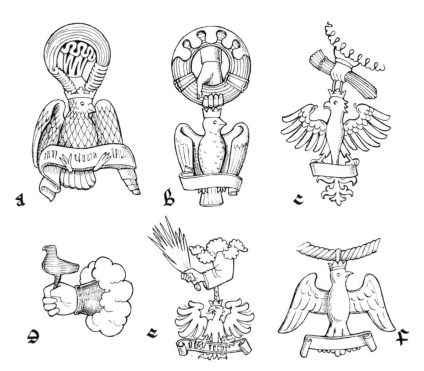

12.13 The badge of the Eagle, or the Disciplines, as represented
a. on the tomb of Heinpert von Mallse, c.1450 (after Schultz)
b. on the tomb of Jörg Perkchaimer, c.1450 (after Schultz)
c. on the tomb of Niclas Drugksecz (after Schultz)
d. in a window commemorating) Ulrich Keczel, 1462
e. in the Grünenberg *Wappenbuch*, 1483
f. on the tomb of Caspar Hanperckhain, 1520

was a recognized symbol). Alternatively, it could have been intended to represent Germans acting as God's scourge in Bohemia. According to Roth von Schreckenstein, the eagle was normally silver (rather than white, as De Valera reported), but after fighting three and four battles respectively a member of the order could change the colour first of one and then of both of its wings to gold. It was thus, like the badges of the earlier orders of the Knot and the Ship, at once a symbol of membership and accomplishment. (Fig. 12.13).

4 Hungary: The Society of the Dragon, 1408–1493?

Among the devices Diego de Valera received from King Albrecht in 1438 was that of the Hungarian society of the Dragon. This society – which as we observed above was not strictly speaking an order of knighthood – had been founded thirty years earlier by Albrecht's late father-in-law, the Emperor Sigismund von Luxemburg. Sigismund, born in 1368 (thirteen years after his rival Carlo 'di Durazzo') as the youngest son of the Emperor Karl IV (King of Bohemia and reputed founder of the Order of the Buckle), had been betrothed by his father to Mária, eldest daughter and presumptive co-heiress of his neighbour King Lajos 'the Great' of Hungary. Following Karl's death in 1378 the ten-year-old Sigismund, now Marquis of Brandenburg, joined his bride-to-be in the court of his future father-in-law, where he received an education worthy of a knight and a courtier, and acquired some degree of fluency in seven languages. As we have seen, when King Lajos died in 1382 (only months after Carlo 'di Durazzo' with his assistance seized the throne of mainland Sicily) the eleven-year-old Mária was proclaimed Queen of Hungary by the magnates, and her mother the Queen Dowager Erzsébet assumed control of the government, assisted by her favourite Miklós Garai, the Count Palatine. Setting aside her husband's will, Erzsébet had Mária married by procuration to Louis Capet de Valois-Orléans, younger brother of Charles VI of France, but Sigismund seized the young queen in August 1385, and forced her to marry him. One year after the murder of Carlo 'di Durazzo' in February 1386, Sigismund was finally elected by the Hungarian magnates to share his wife's throne as King of Hungary, and then only when he had agreed to the terms of a carefully-worded compact. On 31 March 1387 he was crowned with the Holy Crown of St István.

Sigismund's reign in Hungary as King Zsigmond was destined to be very long but far from peaceful or secure. From the beginning, a powerful party of nobles led by the baronial house of Horvathy actively supported the rival claims of Carlo's son Ladislao, and although this party was temporarily suppressed in 1395, the death of Queen Mária in that same year without issue by Zsigmond left the latter without any claim to the throne save that derived from the election of 1387. In the following year, 1396, the failure of the Crusade of Nicopolis – in which Zsigmond led the combined forces of Christendom against the Ottoman Turks – resulted in a temporary victory for his domestic enemies, and Zsigmond was forced to spend the next five years in exile. When he finally returned to Hungary in 1401, he was immediately confronted with another revolt in support of Ladislao (now King of Sicily), and he was captured by the rebels and imprisoned for a time on the rock of Siklós. While still imprisoned there, Zsigmond, recognizing that he could only regain control of his kingdom by coming to some sort of agreement with one or another of the baronial parties, concluded a pact with two great barons who opposed the Horvathys: the Palatine Miklós Garai, and Hermann II von Cilli, Count of Cilli in Styria and claimant through his mother to the royal throne of Bosnia. Shortly thereafter, Zsigmond sealed this pact by marrying Count Hermann's daughter Barbara and making her Queen of Hungary. With the aid of Garai and Cilli and their numerous relatives, vassals, and clients, Zsigmond gradually beat down his various domestic enemies, but his power was now based almost exclusively upon the support of this party, and he was obliged thenceforth to share his authority with its leaders.

It was apparently in recognition of this fact that Zsigmond – finally victorious over all his enemies – proclaimed in 1408 the foundation of the organization which should probably be called the Society of the Dragon.[70] It would appear that Zsigmond had already abandoned the Fraternal Society of St George, posssibly because most of its members, loyal to the house of its founder, had supported Carlo and Ladislao in the succession struggles of the previous twenty-six years. It is nevertheless more than likely that Zsigmond drew some inspiration from that society (to which he himself had almost certainly been admitted before the death of his father-in-law in 1382), and also from the Order of the Ship, probably introduced into Hungary by Carlo in 1385. In any case, the Society of the Dragon was clearly intended to serve, like the Order of the Ship, as the institutional embodiment of the royal faction its founder had created.

The statutes promulgated on 13 December 1408,[71] take the form of a pact or covenant between Zsigmond and his wife Barbóla on the one hand, and

[70] It is referred to in its statutes simply as a *societas* whose members were to be distinguished by the *signum draconis*, but in other contemporary documents it is designated by such names as the Gesellschaft mit dem Trakchen, the Divisa seu Societate Draconica, the Societate Draconica seu Draconistarum and the Fraternitas Draconum. This society was known to Favyn, Micheli Márquez, and most later historians as that of the Dragon Overthrown, and like the name, most of the statements contained in the works of the early historians about this order are quite inaccurate. The society has received some attention from critical historians in Hungary and Germany, but is still virtually unknown outside those countries. Brief accounts (of uneven value) are to be found in Joseph Aschbach, *Geschichte Kaiser Sigmunds I* (Hamburg, 1838), pp. 262–5; H. Luchs 'Schlesische Fürstenbilder des Mittelsalters', *Zeitschrift des Vereins für Geschichte und Altertum Schlesiens* 9 (1868), pp. 405–9; Edmund Berzeviczy, 'Adelék a Sárkány-rend ismertetéséhez' (Contribution to the Understanding of the Order of the Dragon), *Turul* 11 (1893), pp. 93–6; Franz Paul Edler von Smitmer, 'Über den Drachen-Orden', *Jahrbuch der k.k. heraldischen Gesellschaft "Adler"*, N.F. 5, 6 (Vienna, 1895), pp. 65–83; Bálint Hóman, *Gli Angioini di Napoli in Ungheria* (Rome, 1938), pp. 529–31; and Ferenc Felszeghy, Imre Rátvay, and György Ambrsóy, *A Rendjelek és Kitüntetések történelmünkben* (A History of Orders and Decorations) (Budapest, 1943), pp. 441–8. The only extensive account of its history is that of Béla Baranyai, 'Zsigmond király ú. n. Sárkány-rendje', *Századok* 40 (1926), pp. 561–91, 681–719.

[71] The statutes of the society seem to have been preserved in the original manuscript, kept since 1764 in the Hungarian National Archives (Budapest, Magyar Országos Levéltár, DL. 947[?]). They were published first by J. F. Miller among other 'Monumenta diplomatica nunc primum ex autographis edita' in *Acta Literaria Musei Nationalis Hungarici* 1 (Buda, 1818), ff. 167–90, and more recently by György Fejér, *Codex diplomaticus Hugariae* X, 4, (Buda, 1841), no. CCCXVII, pp. 682–94.

twenty-one prominent barons (generally referred to simply as *barones* throughout the document, but occasionally called *socii*), whose names are listed before their first joint declaration. In a long prologue, Zsigmond and his Queen declared that they had founded the Society (which they refer to throughout simply as *nostra societas*),

> in company with the prelates, barons, and magnates of our kingdom, whom we invite to participate with us in this party, by reason of the sign and effigy of our pure inclination and intention to crush the pernicious deeds of the same perfidious Enemy, and of the followers of the ancient Dragon, and (as one would expect) of the pagan knights, schismatics, and other nations of the Orthodox faith, and those envious of the Cross of Christ, and of our kingdoms, and of his holy and saving religion of faith, under the banner of the triumphant Cross of Christ . . . we and the faithful barons and magnates of our kingdom shall bear and have, and do choose and agree to wear and bear, in the manner of a society, the sign or effigy of the Dragon incurved into the form of a circle, its tail winding around its neck, divided through the middle of its back along its length from the top of its head right to the tip of its tail, with blood [forming] a red cross flowing out into the interior of the cleft by a white crack, untouched by blood, just as and in the same way that those who fight under the banner of the glorious martyr St George are accustomed to bear a red cross on a white field . . .

The document goes on to set forth the obligations undertaken by both parties to the pact, in alternation, but without any itemization. The barons swore eternal fidelity to the royal couple and their sons as yet unborn, and undertook to defend their persons and rights in every possible circumstance, to serve them faithfully, especially against the enemies of the kingdom, and to reveal without delay any aggression or plot against the royal family of which they had knowledge. In addition to these essentially cliental obligations, they undertook to 'observe true and pure fraternity' with all those elected to the Society, to defend one another against all aggression, and to allow the Society both to determine the amount of aid each of them was to owe to the others, and to settle all disputes that might arise among them.

In return for the cliental obligations owed specifically to them, the king and queen promised solemnly to cover the barons of the Society with honours and offices, to defend not only them but their widows and orphans from every threat, especially to their property, and to submit any disputes which arose between themselves and any member of the Society to the binding arbitration of the members. Zsigmond alone promised to decide all questions relating to the Society only after hearing the advice of at least five of its members. Finally they set forth certain general obligations which all of the barons of the Society were to undertake: to attend, if possible, the funeral of any of their number who died, or (if not) to have thirty masses said for his soul and to dress in 'lugubrious' clothing for one day; to wear black every Friday, or have five masses said for the five wounds of Christ; and to wear the device of the Society every day (unless prevented), or have five masses said.

Under these statutes, the Society of the Dragon bore a strong superficial resemblance to the more ambitious monarchical orders of knighthood founded in the previous century. Like most societies of that type, it was a corporation of eminent noblemen whose presidency was hereditarily vested in its royal founder and his heirs, and like the companions of the more elaborate monarchical orders, its *socii* wore a distinctive device and undertook, in addition to a number of mutual and general obligations of the sort characteristic of confraternities, cliental obligations similar to those of contractual retainers. Nevertheless, the Society of the Dragon differed from most previous princely orders in a number of important ways. To begin with, although the prologue to the statutes twice refers to St George, and the dragon device was ensigned with his red cross, the Society had no formal patron, and (partly no doubt in consequence of this) had no chapel or seat, and no annual or other regular meetings. More importantly, its statutes make no reference whatever to knights, knighthood, or knightliness, and if most of its members were probably knights as well as barons, it was in the latter capacity alone that they were admitted to membership in the Society. Thus, the Society of the Dragon appears to have been the first organization of its type to be conceived of in purely political terms, without even a gesture in the direction of the chivalrous ideology that had underlain all of the earlier foundations.

Aside from its failure to recognize or promote chivalry, the Society of the Dragon seems to have functioned more or less as the Order of the Ship had been intended to function, though owing to the relative weakness of its founder's position in relation to his barons, he was obliged to do more for his companions than Carlo of Sicily had meant to do. With the aid of the Draconists (as the members of the Society came to be called) Zsigmond remained securely on his throne until his death in 1437, and kept his promise to the Draconist barons by granting them not only offices and honours, but lands and castles. By the time of Zsigmond's death, some 140 of the 200 or so castellanies that had belonged to the crown at his accession had passed by donation into the hands of his Draconist allies, along with 60 of the 70 that had reverted to the crown during his reign. Only members of the Society were rewarded in this way, and there is evidence to suggest that if Zsigmond had failed to live up to his contractual obligations in this area, the Society itself would have confiscated the property in question. Society members also exchanged lands, both with the king and with one another, in order to consolidate their holdings, and concluded succession pacts like those common in princely dynasties, so that even in cases where a member died without issue, his lands would devolve upon another member of the Society. In these various ways, the Draconists steadily increased their stranglehold upon the government of Hungary, and while Zsigmond lived, the Society rather than the crown remained the true repository of public authority in the kingdom. So important did the Society become that Zsigmond (who had been elected King of the Romans in 1410 and succeeded his brother Wenzel or Václav on the throne of Bohemia in 1419) had its statutes confirmed by Pope Eugenius IV when he went to Rome to receive the Imperial crown in May 1433.[72]

As we have seen, membership in the Society was extended in this period not

---

[72] The papal letters, issued on 21 and 24 July 1433, were published by Vilmos Fraknoi in 'Genealógiai és heraldikai közleményele a Vatikáni levéltárból' *Turul* 11 (1893), pp. 7–8. The Society is therein called the *societas cum signo draconis*.

only to Hungarians, but to foreigners. The papal letters of confirmation refer in general terms to the 'princes, dukes, marquises, counts, barons, and nobles' who had been received into the Society, and we actually possess the letters by which Duke Ernst 'the Iron' of Austria accepted membership in the *Gesellschaft mit dem Trakchen* in 1409,[73] those by which membership was conferred (along with membership in the Aragonese order of the Stole and Jar) on the newly knighted Marquis of Ancona in 1413,[74] and those by which Vitautas or Vitovd, Grand Prince of Lithuania, accepted membership in August 1429.[75] We know that Vlad II, Prince of Wallachia, was received into the Society in January or February 1431, and was thereafter known as *Dracul* 'the Dragon'; his son, Vlad *Draculea* 'the Dragon's son', was the historical Dracula.[76] We also know that Christoffer (III), Duke of Bavaria and King of Denmark and Sweden (from 1440) and of Norway (from 1442) was admitted to the Society at some time before his death in 1448, since his name and arms appear among those of fifteen members of the Society commemorated in the Himmelscron monastery in Culmbach.[77] Like the pilgrims who were admitted in this period into the Cypriot order of the Sword, foreigners who accepted membership in the Society of the Dragon under its founder seem to have undertaken (at least in theory) obligations to aid the King of Hungary in his wars against the enemies of Christendom.

As we have just observed, when Zsigmond died in December 1437, he left both of his hereditary crowns to his son-in-law Duke Albrecht of Austria. Albrecht (or Albert, as he was called in Hungary) had probably been admitted to the Society at the time he married Zsigmond's daughter Erszébet in 1422,[78] and he certainly maintained the Society during his short Hungarian reign, along with the Society of the Eagle that he had founded himself only four years earlier. We have seen that Albrecht conceded membership in both orders to the Castilian knight Diego de Valera in 1438,[79] and we possess the letters he sent on 22 July 1439 to John II de Mowbray, Duke of Norfolk in England (and later a knight of the Garter), granting him the right not only to wear the device of the Society but to give it to six other noblemen.[80] We also have those by which on 10 July 1439 Albrecht named Brande Schelen to the Society, in consideration of the services performed by his uncle, Bishop Johann of Lübeck, his representative at the Council of Basel.[81]

After Albrecht's death on 27 October 1439 Hungary dissolved into a civil war between the partisans of his posthumous son Ladislaus, crowned as King László V on 15 May 1440, and King Wladyslaw III of Poland, crowned by a rival faction of barons one month later. As we have seen, Ladislaus spent the next sixteen years in

---

[73] Fejér, *Codex*, X, 4, no. CCXV, pp. 764–5.

[74] See above, n. 21.

[75] Fejér, *Codex*, X, 8 (1843), no. CCXCI, pp. 616–21.

[76] Radu Florescu and Raymond T. McNally, *Dracula: A Biography of Vlad the Impaler, 1431–1476* (New York, 1973), pp. 30–31.

[77] See Louis Bobé, *De Kongelige Danske Ridderordener og Medailler* (Copenhagen, 1950), p. 11.

[78] He had certainly been admitted by 26 March 1432, as he possessed a dragon badge by that date. See Von Sava, 'Ordens-Insignien', (1857), cols. 331–2.

[79] See above, n. 63

[80] Von Sava, 'Ordens-Insignien', (1857), col. 331.

[81] Ibid.

the court of his cousin the future Emperor Friedrich III, and it would appear that during this period Friedrich acted as the head of the Society of the Dragon, for we have letters issued by him in 1452 granting membership to Johann Franz Snardus and Johann de Schilinis (simultaneously made a doctor).[82] He may also have admitted such German knights as Baron Heinpert of Mallse (d. 1450), Jörg Perkchaimer (d. 1450), and Niclas Drugksecz (d. 1468), who displayed its device on their tombs next to that of the Society of the Eagle.[83] Like most of those conferred on foreigners by Albrecht, these memberships must have been primarily honorary. Presumably Ladislaus assumed at least nominal control of the Society when he returned to Hungary in 1453, but when he died without issue only three years later the gentry of Hungary elected as his successor Mátyás 'Corvinus', younger son of the late regent János Hunyadi, rather than the Emperor Friedrich, who claimed the throne as Albrecht's heir-male. Like his father before him, King Mátyás was consistently opposed throughout his long reign (1453–90) by the barons of the Draconic Society, but he seems nevertheless to have maintained the Society, for we possess letters by which he conferred membership in it on the Burgundian knight Jean de Rebreviettes in 1460, in recognition of his service against the Turks.[84] The German knight Ulrich Keczel seems to have been admitted to the Society during his pilgrimage to the Holy Sepulchre in 1462,[85] and the Tyrolian adventurer Oswald von Wolkenstein wears the dragon device pinned to the stole of the Aragonese order of the Stole and Jar in the portrait cited above.[86] Little else is known about the Society of the Dragon after Mátyás' election, but it seems to have survived in some form until the seventeenth century.

The device of the order seems to have taken two distinct forms: one in which the dragon appeared alone, and the other in which it was suspended from a cross, distinct from that laid along its back. In both forms the dragon itself corresponded in practice quite closely to that described in the passage of the prologue quoted above, but none of the known depictions show the cleft down the back. In the surviving examples and representations the dragon (usually depicted with four legs and folded wings) is invariably set in profile, with the body above and the tail below, and is usually facing to the sinister (the viewer's right). The dragon itself is gold and the cross on its back (if it is there at all) is red. In this form the dragon was commonly displayed by Hungarian knights encircling the shield of their arms, very much in the fashion of the English garter or the Austrian salamander (which may well have inspired it); it is so displayed on the patent issued by King Zsigmond on 19 March 1418, granting arms to András Chapy, a member of the Society.[87] According to the founder's councillor and biographer, Eberhard von Windeck, Zsigmond conferred the right to wear the dragon alone on a large number of people, but during his lifetime only twenty-four barons at a time were allowed to bear the

---

[82] Ibid.
[83] See above, p. 346 nn. 65–67.
[84] See Maurice Keen, *Chivalry* (New Haven, 1984), p. 167, where he cites Besançon, Bibliothèque Municipale, Collection Chifflet, ms. 90, f. 9.
[85] See above, p. 346 n. 69.
[86] See above, p. 335 n. 35.
[87] László Fejerpataky, 'A Chapy-czímer és a Sárkány-rend' *Turul* 1 (1883), pp. 116–119. (Fig. 12.13).

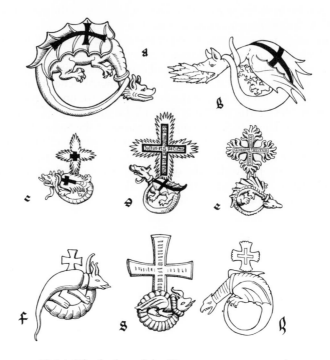

12.14 The badge of the Dragon, as represented
a. in trapunto-work in the Bayerische Nationalmuseum, Munich
b. in a window at Worb (after Ganz)
c. by Berzeviczy (provenance unspecified)
d. in the Grünenberg *Wappenbuch*, 1483 (after Berzevicy)
e. in a metal exemplar, preserved in the Kunstgewerbemuseum, Berlin
f. on the tomb of Jörg Perkchaimer, c.1450 (after Schultz)
g. on the tomb of Heinpert von Mallse, c.1450 (after Schultz)
h. on the tomb of Giovanni Emo, c.1483 (after Galbreath and Jéquier)

12.15 The dragon surrounding a shield of arms, 1419

dragon suspended from the cross.[88] Von Windeck described the greater badge of the Society as 'A dragon hanging from a cross. On the cross are [the words] O *quam misericors est deus* on the length, *Justus et pius* on the crossbar.'[89] In the letters of 1439 by which King Albert conferred membership on the Duke of Norfolk, he described the device he had sent as 'our illustrious royal society with the flaming cross extended above',[90] and the badge given to Brande Schelen in the same year was also conferred 'with the sign of the cross above'.[91] In one of the two surviving examples of the device the dragon is suspended from a simple Greek cross whose arms terminate in flames.[92] Several representations of the badge show a cross very similar to this one, with stylized flames all around its perimeter.[93] The exemplar just referred to is made of silver-gilt, and takes the form of a brooch, four centimetres high and two centimetres wide. The other exemplar, more than twice as large, is made of gold fabric, modelled in trapunto-work; it was presumably sewed to the garment on which it was worn.[94] (Fig. 12.14).

[88] See the catalogue *L'art européen vers 1400* (Vienna, 1962), no. 509, pp. 373–4.
[89] Quoted in Von Sava, 'Ordens-Insignien' (1857), col. 330.
[90] '... insignem nostram regiam societatem cum cruce flamea desuper extensa'. Ibid., col. 331.
[91] Ibid.
[92] Berlin, Ehemals Staatliche Museen Berlin, Kunstgewerbemuseum, Inv. No. 03.44. See the catalogue *L'art européen*, pp. 373–4; and Von Procházka, *Ordenshandbuch*, p. 121, and fig. 1072.
[93] Two are reproduced by Berzeviczy, 'Adalék', p. 95. On the first of these, the last word of the legend on the cross is *paciens* rather than *pius*.
[94] Munich, Bayerische Nationalmuseum. Reproduced in Von Procházka, *Ordenshandbuch*, and in Peter Hogarth, *Dragons*, (New York, 1979), p. 147.

Chapter 13

The Order of the Golden Fleece
Burgundy and the Netherlands
(and later Austria, the Spains, and
the Sicilies)
1430/31–Present

1 Historical Background

By the year 1430 – the centenary of the creation of the first truly monarchical order – the only unquestionably monarchical orders still maintained in the courts of Western Christendom were those of the Garter, the Collar, and the Stole and Jar, and no other such order had been founded since the last of these was proclaimed in 1403. Indeed, the Order of the Stole and Jar was the only certainly monarchical order known to have been been founded in the preceding half-century, and it had such simple statutes that it was barely distinguishable from the pseudo-orders that most kings had come to prefer to the older and more restrictive type of society. Its claim to be a knightly order was also weaker than that of any earlier foundation, for like most cliental pseudo-orders its membership was open not merely to knights and squires, but to ladies and damsels. Of the other quasi-monarchical societies created in the half-century before 1430, the only one founded after 1390 – that of the Dragon of Hungary – made no claim whatever either to be a society of knights, or to promote chivalrous behaviour.

All this appears to indicate that by 1390 the idea of maintaining an elaborate neo-Arthurian order, composed largely or exclusively of knights and genuinely dedicated to the promotion of chivalry, had fallen completely out of favour in most of the royal and princely courts of Europe. A number of factors no doubt combined to bring about the abandonment of this concept, so much in vogue in the preceding half-century: the marked decline between 1350 and 1390 both in the absolute number of knights in most regions and in the importance of heavy cavalry in general within princely armies; the repeated humiliation of knightly armies at the hands of burghers, yeomen, and Infidels; the virtual disappearance by 1380 of the tournament proper (with which several early orders were closely associated); the insistent attacks by moralists on the behaviour of the knightly class and even on the value of the knight as such to society as a whole; and the failure of most of the earlier monarchical orders to survive the first civil war or succession crisis that

356

followed their foundation. All of these factors must have discouraged the rulers who assumed power after about 1380 from emulating their fathers or grandfathers by founding a new order restricted to knights and closely associated with the traditions of chivalry.

Many princes must also have been discouraged by the difficulties and expenses involved in creating the elaborate housing the monarchical orders seemed to require, and the restrictions and inconveniences imposed upon the ruler himself by their statutes – which as we have seen commonly required weekly or even daily observances of all their members, and almost always required an elaborate annual meeting at a fixed time and often at a fixed place. These princes seem to have discovered that, by disposing with statutes altogether, or ignoring completely those that had been adopted by their predecessors, they could create an 'order' that would give them many of the real advantages their predecessors had received from their monarchical orders, without any of the liabilities. The prince who distributed the device of such a pseudo-order as that of the Broom-Pod could still reward and secure the loyalty and services of his barons and officers, surround himself on festive occasions with noblemen in his livery, and honour foreign visitors to his court, and could do so with no restrictions and only limited expenditure. In all likelihood even the highly successful Order of the Garter – by 1400 the only order that still held regular meetings – continued to operate under its foundation statutes largely because they had placed very few burdens either upon its Sovereign or upon its members, and because its founder (almost alone among the founders of the fourteenth century), had actually succeeded in providing it with both the buildings and the income it needed to function without constant subventions from general funds. Nevertheless, attendance at its meetings was very poor after 1413.

By the end of the fourteenth century many ordinary knights must have been reduced to despair for the future of their estate and calling, under attack from every side, but chivalry was too deeply embedded in aristocratic culture to die as suddenly as this, and in the first decade of the fifteenth century certain princes set in motion a major chivalric revival by trying once again to recreate in their courts the pristine chivalry which had existed (according to the romances that still made up a large part of their libraries) in various past ages. Most prominent among the promoters of this revival – recently described as a sort of 'medieval Renaissance' – were the Valois Dukes of Burgundy, who exalted chivalry in their court at least partly to dispel the crisis of confidence felt by their noble vassals.[1] It should come as no surprise to us, therefore, that the year 1430 saw the proclamation in the court of Burgundy of a new monarchical order on the old, neo-Arthurian model, explicitly restricted to knights and calculated to promote chivalrous values and behaviour: the *Ordre de la Thoison d'Or* or 'Order of the Golden Fleece'. It is perhaps more surprising that the statutes with which this order was endowed by its founder – though clearly modelled on those of the two relatively simple fourteenth-century societies still maintained as monarchical orders at the time of its foundation – were more elaborate than those of any previous order save the abortive Sicilian order of the Ship, and that the new order was quickly provided with support staff and facilities comparable to those of the Garter. At least partly as a result of these early

[1] See C. A. J. Armstrong, 'The Golden Age of Burgundy: Dukes that Outdid Kings', in *The Courts of Europe*, ed. A. G. Dickens (London, 1977), pp. 55–75, esp. pp. 69–71.

endowments, the Order of the Golden Fleece, though founded by a mere duke, was to become by the end of our period the sole order of more than half the kingdoms of Europe, and was to survive as the principal order of at least one such kingdom up to the present day. Its early history, obviously of particular interest to historians of the countries in which it was and is maintained, is better documented than that of any other medieval order, and has been set forth at some length several times in the last century or so.[2] In consequence, I shall present here only a rapid summary, referring the reader to other works for a more detailed narrative.

The founder of the Order of the Golden Fleece was the third of the Valois Dukes of Burgundy, Philippe III Capet de Valois-Bourgogne, known to history as 'the Good'. Philippe's grandfather, Duke Philippe 'the Bold'[3] (youngest son of Jean 'the Good' of France, the founder of the Company of the Star, and himself one of the founding knights of that order), had been given the recently-lapsed Duchy of Burgundy by his father in 1363. He had acquired a claim to the inheritances of both Louis III 'de Mâle', Count of Flanders, Artois, Nevers, and Rethel in France, and of the Imperial County Palatine of Burgundy, and of Jean III 'the Triumphant', Duke of Brabant and Limburg in Germany, when he married Louis' only daughter by Marguerite of Brabant in 1369. Philippe 'the Bold' actually assumed control of the former inheritance immediately following the death of Count Louis in 1384, and of half of the latter by an arrangement made in 1396. By the time of his death in 1402, the annexation of these and other lesser territories had made Philippe 'the Bold' the lord of a dominical estate comparable in extent to those of the Counts of Savoy and the Dukes of Austria, and most of this estate was passed on to his eldest son Jean 'the Fearless'.[4] Jean had acquired claims to still more territories through his marriage to the daughter of Duke Albrecht I of Bavaria (son of the Emperor Ludwig by Margaretha of Hainault and Holland), and after his murder in 1419 his only son Philippe 'the Good' used these claims to annex the Imperial Counties of Hainault, Holland, Zeeland, and Namur in the 1420s.[5] By one means or another, Philippe

---

[2] More has been written about the Order of the Golden Fleece than about all the other lay orders put together. Probably the best list of relevant works is that by the Vicomte de Ghellink Vaernewyck, 'Bibliographie de l'Ordre de la Toison d'Or', *Bulletin de l'Académie royale d'Archéologie de Belgique* (1907), pp. 212–76, but it is now out of date, and was not complete even when it was written. The best history of the Order in the fifteenth and sixteenth centures is still that of the Baron de Reiffenberg, *Histoire de l'Ordre de la Toison d'Or* (Brussels, 1830), which is based in large part on the Order's own records. Rather less valuable are Baron H. Kervyn de Lettenhove, *La Toison d'Or; Notes sur l'institution et l'histoire de l'Ordre (depuis l'année 1429 jusqu' à l'année 1559)* (Brussels, 1907), and Luc Hommel, *L'Histoire du Noble Ordre de la Toison d'or* (Brussels, 1947), which are the principal modern works with any pretension to scholarship that deal with the Order in a general way. Articles dealing with particular aspects of the Order's history in the period under review are cited in the notes below. See also the brief but insightful discussion of the Order in M. G. A. Vale, *War and Chivalry* (Athens, Georgia, 1981), pp. 38–51.

[3] On his life see Richard Vaughan, *Philip the Bold: The Formation of the Burgundian State* (London, New York, 1962, 1979).

[4] On his life see Richard Vaughan, *John the Fearless: The Growth of Burgundian Power* (London, New York, 1966).

[5] On his life see Richard Vaughan, *Philip the Good: The Apogee of Burgundy* (London, New York, 1970).

also acquired possession of the French counties of Boulogne, Auxerre, Mâcon, Bar-sur-Seine, and Ponthieu in the same decade, along with most of the province of Picardy, and in 1430 added to these lands the important Duchy of Brabant. In theory Philippe held all of his lands as a vassal either of the King of France or of the Emperor, but in practice he was virtually independent throughout his reign, and since much of his princely estate was located in the most populous and industrialized region of northern Europe, he was one of the richest princes of any rank in Western Christendom by the end of 1429 – far richer, indeed, than many who wore royal crowns.

Philippe's father and grandfather had not been content with the power and wealth which had flowed to them from the lordship of their own principalities, but had sought to increase both by controlling the central government of France during the long minority and subsequent spells of insanity of their nephew or cousin King Charles VI. This policy had led first to a head-on conflict with that king's brother, Duke Louis of Orléans (founder of the pseudo-order of the Camail or Porcupine), and after Louis' murder by agents of Jean 'the Fearless' in 1407, to a bitter civil war between the parties of Burgundy and Orléans, the invasion and partial conquest of France by Henry V of England in 1415–19, and the assassination of Duke Jean himself by an agent of the Dauphin Charles (the future Charles VII) in 1419. Partly no doubt to avoid a similar fate, and partly to concentrate on his policy of territorial aggrandizement, Philippe 'the Good' withdrew from active interference in the internal affairs of France, and until 1435, when he finally committed himself to his agnatic cousin King Charles VII, strove to maintain a precarious balance in his relationships with the two contending parties in the last and most destructive phase of the Hundred Years War. His ultimate goal was to achieve complete sovereignty in his feudal dominions (which his father and grandfather had already provided with a central government modelled on that of France), and he carried on long negotiations to this end with the Emperor Sigismund, who alone had the power to make him a king. Although Philippe failed to achieve this goal, his cautious policies and a certain amount of sheer good luck brought a measure of peace and prosperity to his subjects in what was in many countries a very troubled period, and enabled him to devote an increasing proportion of his energies to the development of a court that, if never royal, was nevertheless to become the most brilliant in Christendom. It was at this, the creation of magnificent feasts and beautifully orchestrated ceremonies, that Philippe particularly excelled, and the almost Byzantine ritual of his court was to be the principal legacy of Burgundy to early modern Europe.[6]

As we have already noted, chivalrous conceptions played a central role in the life of the Burgundian court from early in the reign of Philippe's father, Jean 'the Fearless', and under Philippe himself chivalrous behaviour was encouraged not only by the precise rules of court etiquette and the staging of ever more elaborate jousts and 'passages of arms', but by the distribution of prose versions of numerous epics and romances, newly translated from Old into Middle French, which were intended to provide ideal models as well as general inspiration. Philippe's enthusiasm for the romantic conception of chivalry promoted by these works seems

[6] On his court, see O. Cartellieri, *The Court of Burgundy* (London, 1929); Vaughan, *Philip the Good*, pp. 127–63; and Armstrong, 'The Golden Age'.

to have been perfectly genuine, for he often took part in jousts himself, and in 1425 actually went into training for a judicial duel *à l'outrance*. He also longed to prove himself an *athleta Christi* in the tradition of Pierre of Cyprus, the Green Count of Savoy, and Louis of Bourbon, and as late as 1454 staged an elaborate banquet known as the 'Feast of the Pheasant' in order to proclaim his intention of leading a crusade.

It was thus almost inevitable that Philippe – the 'Grand Duke of the West' as he came to be called – should decide to emulate Arthur, Charlemagne, and the crusaders of the previous century by creating his own knightly order. His frequent dealings with Henry VI of England and Amé VIII of Savoy (both of whom were his immediate neighbours and closely related to him by marriage) had no doubt made him perfectly familiar with the orders of the Garter and Collar, and as we have seen, he was actually elected to membership in the former order, and given a copy of its statutes, in 1422.[7] In addition, his father's archenemy Duke Charles of Orléans maintained throughout his long life the pseudo-order of the Camail or Porcupine founded by his father in 1394, and its mere existence must have encouraged Philippe to establish an order that would completely outshine it.[8]

2 The Foundation and Maintenance of the Order, 1430–1519

It is unclear precisely when Philippe 'the Good' decided to found an order of knighthood, but the occasion which provided the necessary setting for the proclamation of the Order was his wedding to his third wife, Isabella of Portugal, which took place at Sluys on 7 January 1430. The splendid festivities which followed in nearby Bruges, capital of Philippe's County of Flanders, culminated in a series of tournaments held in the market-place, and these concluded with the proclamation itself. According to the chronicler Jean le Fèvre, Philippe's King of Arms for Flanders announced the foundation of the Order on that occasion in the following terms:

> Then hear, princes and princesses, lords, ladies, and damsels, knights and squires, the Very High, Very Excellent, and Very Puissant Prince, My Lord the Duke of Burgundy, Count of Flanders and Artois, Count Palatine of

[7] The contemporary writer Georges Chastellain declared that Philippe had founded his order to enable him to evade accepting membership in that of the Garter, which would have tied him too closely to the English side in the current civil war. (*Oeuvres*, ed. Baron Kervyn de Lettenhove [Brussels, 1865], p. 216.) This may well have been a factor in Philippe's decision, but it is unlikely to have been the only or even the most important one.

[8] Philippe's grandfather Philippe 'the Bold' had distributed collars supporting a golden tree to several members of his family and household a few months before his death in April 1404, and this may have been intended to function as a pseudo-order similar to those of the Broom-Pod and Camail. His son Jean 'the Fearless' seems to have abandoned it immediately after his accession, however, and there is no sign that the device of the plane (*rabot*) spewing shavings that he distributed as a livery badge was ever called an 'order'.

Burgundy, Count of Namur, etc., makes known to all that for the reverence of God and the maintenance of our Christian Faith, and to honour and exalt the noble order of knighthood, and also for the following three reasons: first to do honour to old knights, who for their high and noble deeds are worthy of being recommended; second, so that those who are at present still capable and strong of body and do each day the deeds pertaining to chivalry shall have cause to continue from good to better; and third, so that those knights and gentlemen who shall see worn the order which shall be mentioned below should honour those who wear it, and be encouraged to employ themselves in noble deeds, and to nourish themselves on such customs, that by their valiance they may acquire good renown, and deserve in their time to be chosen to bear the said order; my said lord the Duke has today undertaken and founded an order which is called 'the Golden Fleece', in which, with and besides the person of my lord the Duke himself, are twenty-four knights, gentlemen of name and arms without reproach, born and procreated in legal marriage, of whom a declaration of the names and surnames follows . . .[9]

Le Fèvre lists the names of only twenty-three knights who received the collar of the new 'order' at the time of its proclamation, but we know from other sources that twenty-four were in fact admitted, one of whom was shortly thereafter expelled for cowardice.[10] After listing these names, the King of Arms concluded the proclamation with the following statement: 'To the which knights above-named my said Lord gives to each of them a collar made of firesteels, from which depends the Golden Fleece; and it is the intention of my said Lord the Duke to make shortly the ordinances pertaining to the said Order.' It is clear, therefore, that at the time the new order was proclaimed, Philippe had not yet provided for it any sort of constitution, and for some time thereafter it remained no more than a pseudo-order.

The first formal meeting of the Order of the Golden Fleece did not take place until late in the following year. On 30 November 1431 – the feast day of St Andrew, the patron of Burgundy – Philippe met with eighteen of the knights he had appointed nearly two years earlier, in the city of Lille in southern Flanders. There he finally presented them with the statutes (which he had had drawn up in the interim by his councillor Jean Germain, and had himself sealed as letters patent three days earlier), and the twenty-two knights still remaining in the Order took the oath of obedience contained in them either in person or by the procuration of one of those present. At the same meeting the first four officers of the Order were also sworn in, and a chapter was held during which two knights were expelled from the Order and two more were elected to fill the vacancies created by death and expulsion. The Order's corporate existence thus dates effectively not from 10

---

[9] Jean le Fèvre, sire de St-Rémy, *Chronique*, ed. R. Morand (Société de l'histoire de France, 2 vols., Paris, 1876, 1881), II, pp. 172–173. Le Fèvre was the Order's first king of arms, and was therefore peculiarly well-placed to know the details of its statutes and history.

[10] Le Fèvre omits the name of the Lord of Montagu, who is listed by the chronicler Monstrelet as the fourth companion after the duke. See *La chronique d'Enguerran de Monstrelet*, ed. L. Douët d'Arcq (Société de l'histoire de France, 6 vols, Paris, 1857–1862), IV, pp. 373–374.

January 1430 but from 30 November 1431 – the day on which the statutes were first promulgated, accepted, and put into operation.

The subsequent history of the Order can be summarized only very briefly here. The Order was maintained by its founder in very much its original form until his death on 15 June 1467, nearly four decades after its proclamation. So well established was the Order by that time that Philippe's son Charles 'the Rash' assumed without hesitation the sovereignty of the Order (to which he had been elected shortly after his baptism in 1433), and maintained it essentially unchanged (at least on paper) throughout his brief and turbulent reign.[11] Charles' untimely death in the Battle of Nancy on 5 January 1477 might have spelt the end of the Order, for he had left only an unmarried daughter to succeed him, and his archenemy, King Louis XI of France, promptly claimed both the reversion of the Duchy of Burgundy as a lapsed apanage, and the control of the whole Burgundian inheritance in his capacity as the natural guardian of Charles' daughter Marie (v. 1457–1482). Louis succeeded in occupying the two Burgundies, but Marie saved herself and her heritage by marrying Maximilian von Habsburg, the only son of the Emperor Friedrich III. The marriage was solemnized on 18 August 1477, and Maximilian immediately undertook the defence of his wife's dominions. Neither Maximilian (who between 1489 and 1493 succeeded to the Counties of Alsace and Tyrol, the Duchies of Styria, Carinthia, and Carniola, the Archduchy of Austria, and the kingship of the Romans) nor any of his descendants ever succeeded in regaining the Duchy of Burgundy, but he did maintain himself in the possession of the rest of the Burgundian dominions, and never surrendered his claim to the whole inheritance of the Valois dukes. In token of this claim Maximilian not only assumed the title 'Duke of Burgundy', but had himself installed as the third Sovereign of the Order of the Golden Fleece, by then the preeminent symbol of the Burgundian dynasty, on 30 April 1478.

The Order thus survived the first crisis in its long history, only to be faced with a second crisis less than five years later. In March 1482 the Duchess Marie herself died prematurely, leaving all her possessions – including the right to the sovereignty of the Golden Fleece – to her son Philippe, who was just over three years old. Despite the claims made on Philippe's behalf by some of the companions of the Order, who chafed under Maximilian's sovereignty, Maximilian not only continued to govern his late wife's dominions during the minority of his son, but also retained for two years the sovereignty of the Order of the Golden Fleece. In 1484, however, he resigned this office in favour of the six-year-old Philippe (IV as titular Duke of Burgundy), who retained it until his own untimely death in 1506, and actually assumed the government of the Order in May 1491. In 1496 the eighteen-year-old Philippe, by then called 'the Handsome', was married through his father's contrivance to Juana (later called 'the Mad'), daughter of King Ferran 'the Catholic' of Aragon and Sicily and Queen Isabel 'the Catholic' of Castile and Leon. The death of Juana's only brother in 1497 made her the heir to the several thrones of both her parents, and on her mother's death in 1504 Juana succeeded her as Queen of Castile and Leon. Philippe himself, already lord of the Burgundian dominions and heir to those of his father's house of Habsburg, was immediately

---

[11] On his life and reign, see Richard Vaughan, *Charles the Bold: The Last Valois Duke of Burgundy* (London, New York, 1973).

proclaimed king consort as Felipe I, and from that time onwards every Sovereign of the Order of the Golden Fleece was to be King of Castile as well as titular Duke of Burgundy.

Philippe himself died prematurely only two years later, on 26 September 1506, leaving his Burgundian inheritance to his elder son, the six-year-old Charles (II of Burgundy). Despite his youth, Charles was immediately recognized as the Sovereign of the Order of the Golden Fleece, though it was not until ten years after his accession, in October 1516, that he was old enough to preside over a meeting of the Order. Two years later still, following the death on 23 February 1516 of his maternal grandfather Ferran 'the Catholic', Charles was proclaimed King of Castile, Leon, Aragon, Navarre, and the two Sicilies (as Carlos I, Carlo IV, etc.) in association with his mother Juana (who since 1504 had been completely mad), and on 12 January 1519 he succeeded his paternal grandfather Maximilian as lord of the Austrian dominions. Later that year he was elected Emperor of the Romans in succession to Maximilian, as Karl V. Charles II of Burgundy thus became at nineteen the most powerful prince in Christendom. Since he chose not only to maintain the Order of the Golden Fleece as a society through which to unite the nobilities of his many lands, but to abandon all the other lay orders to whose presidency he had a claim (including the Band, the Stole and Jar, and the Eagle), the originally Burgundian order emerged as the most important such society in Christendom. It was destined to retain that preeminence for the next four centuries.

Charles continued to maintain the Order of the Golden Fleece in essentially the form established by its founder until 1555, when he resigned the sovereignty along with the lordship of his Spanish and Burgundian dominions to his son Philippe (v. 1527–1598). Under Philippe (V as titular Duke of Burgundy, Felipe II as King of the Spains) the Order met only once, in 1559, and under his successors it never met at all. After 1559, indeed, the Order was effectively reduced to a state that was not very different from that of a pseudo-order, although the continued existence of its statutes and corporate officers gave it a semblance of its original monarchical nature. In this reduced condition the Order has been maintained continuously to the present day. Since the death of its ninth Sovereign, Charles III (Carlos II of Spain), in 1700, it has been divided into two distinct branches, one Spanish (maintained by the heirs of Charles III's successor as King of Spain, Felipe V Capet de Bourbon-La Marche-Anjou), and one Austrian (maintained by the heirs of Charles' successor in the old Burgundian dominions, the Emperor Karl VI von Habsburg). Although only its Spanish Sovereign (King Juan Carlos I of Spain) is now a sovereign prince, it is only in its Austrian branch (presided over by the Archduke Otto von Habsburg-Lothringen) that its traditional constitution is still retained, even in theory.[12]

---

[12] On the modern history of the Order, see José Romero de Juseu y Lerroux, Marqués de Cardenas, El Toisón de Oro: Orden dinástica de los Duques de Borgoña (Madrid, 1960).

3 The Statutes of the Order

The statutes of the Order required that each companion be given his own copy of
the statute book when he was informed of his election, and as this regulation seems
to have been carried out with reasonable regularity, numerous fifteenth-century
manuscripts of the statutes of the Order of the Golden Fleece have been preserved.
Most of these contain, not the version adopted by the original companions in
November 1431, but a slightly later version that resulted from the only major
revision of the Order's constitution, recommended by a committee of five knights
appointed during the seventh chapter of the Order in December 1445. The
principal effect of this revision was the separation from the body of the statutes of
all the articles particularly concerned with the duties of the Order's four officers,
and the relegation of these articles to a second, separately numbered division.
Possibly the only surviving copy of the original form of the statutes is text A of the
Hague ms. 76 E 14, which (as it does not contain the amendments made at the
chapter of 1440) may safely be dated to the first decade of the Order's existence.[13]
Since the revised version of 1445 (with the exception of three very minor
amendments made in 1436 or 1440) was identical in substance to the version in the
Hague manuscript, and since it remained in effect (with further minor alterations)
through the remainder of the period with which this study is concerned, my
references to the statutes will follow the revised order – which has the added
advantage of being more logical.[14]

The revised version of the statutes consists of a prologue and 243 distinct
ordinances, organized into 95 articles or chapters. The statutes are thus almost
twice as long as those of the Garter, which in their oldest redaction had only 138
ordinances. The orginal version of the statutes seems to have been written in the
Burgundian dialect of French, and this is the language in which they are expressed
in most of the surviving manuscripts. By the end of the fifteenth century, however,
the statutes had been translated into Latin, Dutch, and German for the benefit of
the many companions whose native tongue was not French.[15] The statutes are
commonly preceded in manuscripts by a table of contents in which each chapter or
article is identified by a number and title, and with the exception of the first and
fourteenth, each chapter in the text begins with the word 'Item'.

In the prologue, Duke Philippe expressed his purposes for founding the Order in
terms rather different from those of the proclamation of 1430:

---

[13] I am grateful for this information to Mr C. A. J. Armstrong.

[14] On the surviving statute-books see G. Dogaer, 'Des anciens livres des statuts manuscrits
de l'Ordre de la Toison d'Or', in Publications du centre européen d'études burgondo-médianes, 5
(1963), pp. 65–70. The analysis of the statutes given below is based on three almost
identical versions: that contained in the chronicle of Jean le Fèvre (op. cit., II,
pp. 210–254); that printed in G. W. von Leibnitz, Mantissa codicis juris gentium (Hanover,
1700), vol. II, pp. 17–31; and that in London, British Library, Harley ms. 6199. I have
indicated where these versions differ in substance. I also consulted the copy that once
belonged to Claude de Toulongeon (elected to the Order in 1481), which contains the later
amendments. This is now Paris, B.N., ms. fr.1281.

[15] Dogaer, op. cit., p. 66.

We Philippe, by the grace of God Duke of Burgundy . . . make known to all present and to come, that for the very great and perfect love that we have for the noble estate and order of knighthood, of which from very ardent and singular affection, we desire the honour and increase, by which the true Catholic Faith, the faith of our mother, the Holy Church, and the tranquility and prosperity of the public may be, as far as possible, defended, guarded, and maintained; we, to the glory and praise of the Almighty, our Creator and Redeemer, in reverence of his glorious mother the Virgin Mary, and to the honour of my lord Saint Andrew, Apostle and Martyr; to the exaltation of virtues and good habits; on the tenth day of January in the year of Our Lord 1429 [O.S.], which was the day of the solemnization of the marriage between us and our most dear and beloved companion, Elizabeth, in our city of Bruges, we did undertake, create, and ordain, and by these presents do undertake, create, and ordain an order and fraternity of knighthood, or amiable company of a certain number of knights, which we wish to be called the Order of the Golden Fleece, under the form, condition, statutes, manner, and articles which follow.[16]

This prologue is followed immediately by the statutes proper, which as we have noted were divided into two separately numbered divisions. The first, made up of sixty-seven chapters containing 170 ordinances, is concerned primarily with the companions of the Order, and the second, made up of twenty-eight chapters containing seventy-three ordinances, is concerned with the Order's four principal officers. The chapters of the former division are arranged in seven sequences or sections, but these are never distinguished in any way in the manuscripts.
    The first section, made up of the twelve ordinances comprised in chapters 1 to 3, deals with the general structure of the order, the qualifications required for membership, and the form and wearing of the Order's badge. The second section, including the twenty-eight ordinances of chapters 4 to 12, sets forth the reciprocal obligations of the Sovereign and the companions. The third section, composed of the fifteen ordinances of chapters 13 through 21, deals with questions related to the Order's membership and structure. Chapters 22 to 28, making up the fourth section, contain twenty-two ordinances concerned with the Order's general Assembly, and more particularly with its religious elements. The fifth section, composed of the twenty-four ordinances of chapters 29 to 40, is concerned with the various forms of activity that were to take place at the business meeting or 'chapter' held during each Assembly. The sixth section of the statutes, comprising the fifty-four ordinances of chapters 41 to 62, is both the longest and the last which deals with a single general subject – in this case the election and admission of new companions. The last five chapters of the division dealing with the companions, chapters 63 to 67, are made up of fifteen ordinances concerned with a number of questions which did not fit into any of the earlier categories: purgatorial masses, the support of the Order's king of arms, the procedures to be followed if the Sovereign died leaving only a minor son or daughter to succeed him, the jurisdiction of the Order over cases involving the companions, and the interpretation and alteration of the statutes.

[16] Le Fèvre, op. cit., pp. 210–211.

These miscellaneous chapters are followed by the separately numbered division of the statutes concerned with the Order's officers. The first five of these chapters (which I shall number O.1 to O.5) contain eight ordinances concerned with the *Chancelier* or Chancellor of the Order; the next five, O.6 to O.10, contain seventeen ordinances concerned with the office of *Tresorier* or Treasurer; chapters O.12 through O.14 contain thirteen ordinances concerned with the office of *Greffier* or Registrar of the Order; and chapters O.15 through O.17 contain nine ordinances concerned with the office of the Order's King of Arms, who was to be called *Thoison d'or*. This division concludes with twenty-six ordinances concerned with the election and induction of each of these officers, organized into the eleven chapters numbered O.18 through O.28.

As we shall see, the statutes of the Order of the Golden Fleece bear an obvious resemblance to those of the Garter, but contain a number of elements which, though wholly lacking in the Garter statutes, are prominent in those of the Collar. Since Philippe was certainly familiar with both of these orders, the numerous points of similarity may reasonably be supposed to be the result of conscious imitation on Philippe's part, rather than mere coincidence. It is also possible that Philippe drew some inspiration from what he knew of the statutes of the Company of the Star (described in some detail in the chronicles of Le Bel and Froissart), and from the contemporary practices of the Aragonese Order of the Jar, with whose insignia, at least, he must have been familiar by 1430. It is unlikely that he knew anything about the statutes of any of the other earlier foundations.

4 The Name, Title, and Badge of the Order

Like both the Order of the Garter and the Order of the Collar by 1430, the new Burgundian order was officially styled 'order' quite consistently, and equally consistently took its name from its badge rather than its patron. Philippe was nevertheless able to refer to it in the preface to the statutes as 'un ordre et fraternité de chevalerie, ou aimable compaignie', which indicates clearly enough that the term 'order' was still regarded as being equivalent to 'fraternity' and 'company', as it had been nearly a century earlier.

The badge of the Order of the Golden Fleece, like those of the Collar and the Jar, consisted of a collar with a device pendant at the front. Also like the badge of the Collar (and like that of no other earlier order) the badge of the Golden Fleece incorporated an independent device, used by the founder both before and after the foundation of the Order as a regular livery-badge. In the case of the Golden Fleece, however, the collar itself was made up of a series of identical examples of this livery-badge, following the fashion which had developed for the display of such badges in the last two decades of the fourteenth century. The badge in question here consisted of a more or less elaborate golden *fusil* or fire-steel (whose inwardly-curling finger rings gave it the general form of a Lombardic capital B, the initial of Burgundy) and an adjacent piece of flint of ovoid configuration, from which issued, either on all sides or merely from above and below, a number of formalized flames commonly represented in their natural colours.[17] Sometimes smaller flames or sparks were represented as emanating from the fiery flint, and a verbal *devise* was also occasionally associated with the badge: *Ante ferit quam flamma micet* – 'It strikes before the flame spurts forth'. This badge was probably adopted by Philippe shortly after he succeeded his father (whose principal badge had been a plane spewing shavings),[18] and was certainly in use by April 1425, since it was displayed on a horse trapper and a tent purchased by Philippe for use in a duel with the Duke of Gloucester to be held on St George's Day of that year.[19]

The description of the collar in the statutes is not entirely clear, but in practice the collar of the Order was invariably constructed of paired gold fire-steels (each about one inch square) with interlocking finger rings, alternating with smaller flints emitting metallic flames, generally gold in examples from the fifteenth century. Pendant from this collar, sometimes from a fiery-flint of special configuration, was a representation in plain gold of the flayed skin of a wooly ram: the golden fleece itself. The whole collar bore a strong general resemblance to that of the Jar, and it is not unlikely that the latter served as a model. The statutes specify that it was to be made of gold, and was never to be enriched with jewels – a rule presumably introduced to maintain a semblance of equality among the companions when they assembled each year.[20] (Fig. 13.1).

There is no reason to believe that the flint-and-steel device had any special significance in the context of the iconography of the Order. It was simply the founder's personal badge, with its own peculiar (and cryptic) symbolism, and was introduced in accordance with contemporary custom as an indication of his preeminence and proprietorial interest in the Order. As a livery-badge it could have been worn in exactly the same fashion had the Order never been thought of, and could have supported a variety of other badges. It was the pendant alone that was peculiar to the Order, and its symbolic significance was completely distinct from that of the collar proper. (Fig. 13.2).

It was almost certainly to the golden fleece of Kolkhis, carried off in classical legend by Jason and the Argonauts, that the pendant device adopted by Philippe 'the Good' in 1430 was initially intended to allude. Such an allusion was unquestionably apt, for the fleece of this legend was a marvellous prize won only through heroic endeavour of precisely the sort the Order was founded to promote,

---

[17] The collar is described in ch. 3 of the statutes as: '. . . ung colier d'or a nostre devise: c'est assavoir, par pieces a façon de fusilz touchans a pierres dont partent estincelles ardantes, et au boult d'icellui colier pendant semblance d'une thoison d'or.'

[18] F. Deuchler, 'Zur Burgundischen Heraldik und Emblematik', *Die Burgunderbeute and Werke Burgundischer Hofkunst* (Berne, 1969), p. 36, shows that Philippe had adopted it by 1422. According to E. E. Rosenthal. 'The invention of the columnar device of the Emperor Charles V at the court of Burgundy in Flanders in 1516', *Journal of the Warburg and Courtauld Institutes* 36 (1973), p. 204, the device had first been adopted in 1396 in connection with a vow to avenge the capture of Jean 'the Fearless' by the Turks in the Battle of Nicopolis.

[19] See Vaughan, *Philip the Good*, p. 39, citing a contemporary account book. For an example of its independent use after the foundation of the Order, see the illumination in Paris, B.N., ms. fr.12476, where it is set at the foot of the page between the words of the ducal motto *Autre Naray*.

[20] Ch. 3a,f.

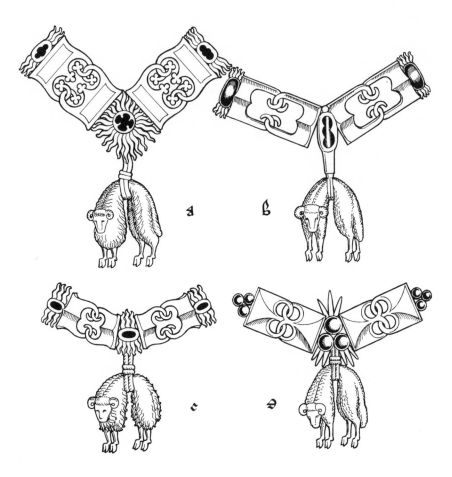

13.1 The collar of the Golden Fleece, as represented
a. in a contemporary portrait of the founder
b. in the portrait of the founder by Rogier van der Weyden,
Royal Palace, Madrid
c. in the portrait of Anthoine, bastard of Burgundy,
in the Musée des Beaux-Arts, Brussels
d. in the portrait of the future Emperor Karl V
in the Church of St Sauveur, Bruges

and won moreover by the joint efforts of a company of noble heroes. Most of the contemporary writers in fact assert that it was the fleece of Jason that the badge of the Order represented, but several of them report that within a short time after the Order's proclamation – possibly at the first meeting, in November 1431 – the Order's first Chancellor, Jean Germain, Bishop of Nevers, protested at the use of a pagan device as the badge of a Christian order, and suggested that the fleece was really that of the biblical hero Gideon.[21] Gideon's fleece, however, was neither golden nor a reward for valour, but a device he employed for testing the intentions of God, and the arrogation to the Order of the Gideon legend was therefore artificial at best. Later in the century a whole series of historical and mythical fleeces were invoked on behalf of the Order, but such symbolism-after-the-fact is of little interest to us here. The search for a Christian interpretation of what was undoubtedly a purely pagan device is interesting only in that it reveals how seriously the whole matter was regarded in the light of the Order's pretensions to be a fraternity dedicated to upholding the Christian faith.[22]

Like the badges of most of the earlier orders, the collar of the Golden Fleece was to be worn by the companions of the Order every day, on penalty of paying a fine for each failure.[23] Philippe also (with characteristic concern for detail) formulated elaborate regulations to deal with the various situations that might arise in which the collar might not or could not be worn, and what was to be done if the collar were lost. The fleece alone could be worn in battle, pendant from a simple chain, and the whole collar could be laid aside if damaged, or if a long voyage or illness made it necessary, but it was never to to be given away, pawned, or alienated for any reason.[24] If a companion lost his collar in an honourable action, or through capture, the Sovereign was to give him a new one at his own expense, but if he lost it in any other way he was bound to have a new one made at his own expense within four months, or as soon as possible.[25]

The novel regulations permitting the non-wearing of the collar and those stating the companions' obligations with respect to its loss or alienation were no doubt necessitated by the peculiar weight and monetary value of the heavy gold collar, though the ordinance allowing the companions to wear the fleece suspended from a simple chain may have been inspired by Henry V's similar ordinance permitting the Garter knights to wear a blue ribbon instead of their garter while dressed for battle. After Philippe's death the practice of wearing the fleece on a simple chain with civilian clothes as well as with armour seems to have become quite

---

[21] See Judges vi. 36–40 for the story of Gideon's fleece.

[22] On the symbolism of the golden fleece see G. Doutrepont, 'Jason et Gédéon, patrons de la Toison d'Or,' *Mélanges Godefroy Kurth* II (Liège, Paris, 1908: Bibl. de la faculté de philosophie et lettres de . . . Liège, fasc. 2). See also V. Tourneur, 'Les orgines de l'Ordre de la Toison d'or et la symbolique des insignes de celui-ci,' *Bulletin de l'Académie royale de Belgique, Lettres*, 5e sér., 42 (1956), pp. 300–323. Guillaume Fillastre, Bishop of Tournai and Chancellor of the Order from 1461 until his death in 1473, wrote a collection of histories related to the Order entitled *Six manieres de la Thoison d'or*, of which a copy is now preserved in Paris, B.N., ms. fr.139.

[23] Ch. 3b. The fine was 8s per day.

[24] Ch. 1c–e.

[25] Ch. 40 (a,b).

common,[26] but it was never considered correct in our period, and at the chapters held in 1473 and 1484 the companions found guilty of the practice were reprimanded. The rule forbidding the enriching of the collar with precious stones was also increasingly ignored by those companions who could afford it, and some later collars are positively encrusted with jewels.[27]

Like the garter of the English order, the collar of the Order of the Golden Fleece came within a short time of the Order's foundation to be depicted encircling the shield of arms in representations of the armorial achievements of its companions. The earliest known representation of the collar used in this way as part of the founder's own armorial achievement is on a votive plaque set by Philippe's consort Isabella in the Charterhouse of Basel in 1438,[28] but thereafter the arms of the Dukes of Burgundy and their heirs rarely appeared without the collar of the Order, and it became one of the most important elements of Burgundian heraldry. The custom of the Golden Fleece was later imitated by members of most other orders of chivalry, and in the sixteenth century even the knights of the Garter sometimes surrounded their pictorial shields with their order's new collar, rather than, or in addition to, the original badge of the order.

The collar was to be given to each knight at the time he was received into the Order, but because of its great value, it was to be returned to the Sovereign if the companion was expelled from the Order before his death,[29] or after his death by his heirs or representatives,[30] and given to his successor. Anyone deprived in absentia was to be informed of his obligation by letters, and if he refused to surrender his collar, the Sovereign was to proceed against him in whatever way seemed appropriate.[31]

5 The Patron of the Order

In conformity with what had become the invariable custom of monarchical orders, the Order of the Golden Fleece was placed under the patronage of a particular celestial personage, under whose banner its princely founder made war, upon whose feast day the Order itself held its meetings, to whom its corporate chapel was dedicated, and whose mass was its principal annual service. The patron chosen by Philippe, St Andrew the Apostle, had long been the particular protector of the Dukes of Burgundy, whose palace chapel at Dijon, built by Duke Hugues III in 1172 and magnificently enriched by his successors, contained important relics of the saint. The saltire-cross of St Andrew – frequently made up of ragged staves and generally depicted in red on a white field – was as important a badge of the founder

[26] See for example the portrait of Antoine, 'Grand' Bastard of Burgundy, published in Vaughan, *Philip the Good*, Pl. 6, facing p. 190.
[27] See Kervyn de Lettenhove, op. cit., p. 22.
[28] See Paul Post, 'Ein Verschollenes Jagdbild Jan van Eycks,' *Jahrbuch der preussischen Kunstsammlungen*, 52 (1931), p. 123.
[29] Ch. 37a.
[30] Ch. 39.
[31] Chs. 37b, 38.

13.2 The device of the flint-and-steel

13.3 The cross of St Andrew with flints and steels

as the fiery-flint-and-steel, and the two devices were frequently represented in association by Philippe and all his *de facto* and *de jure* successors as duke. Nevertheless, the cross had no official connexion with the Order as such, and as we shall see, St Andrew himself was given little other recognition by the Order after the first ten years of its existence. (Fig. 13.3).

6 *The Membership of the Order: The Chief and Sovereign*

The structure of the Order of the Golden Fleece, as described in the statutes, was clearly based upon that of the Garter. Like the latter, it was to have been made up of limited college of lay knights called *compagnons* or 'companions' supporting a parallel college of canons and (in theory at least) a college of poor knights, all under the presidency of an hereditary *Souverain* or 'Sovereign'.

Philippe chose to augment the presidential title of Sovereign assumed by Edward III with the additional title of *Chef* or 'Chief', previously peculiar to the head of the Order of the Collar, but it is generally under the title of Sovereign alone that the statutes refer to the head of the Burgundian Order. The duties, prerogatives, and privileges of the Chief and Sovereign of the Order as such were also similar in nature to those of the head of the English order, but were more limited in extent. With the advice of such companions as were with him, he determined the time and place of the Order's general assemblies, presided over the meetings of the chapter, sat in judgement of internal disputes and cases of infraction of the statutes, and proceeded against those who refused to surrender their collars. When it was necessary to choose a new companion, he announced the election, received the oaths of the electors before they voted, and received the oath of the companion-elect before formally admitting him to the Order. His voice in the election counted for twice that of any other companion, and he could in the case of a drawn election either cast a deciding vote or hold another ballot. He also presided over the elections of new officers, and received their oaths of office. He alone could interpret or amend the Order's statutes. He took the place of honour in formal processions, in the choir of the church in which the Order's services were celebrated, and in the room in which the chapter was held. Finally, he was formally required to provide the Order's physical facilities and the bulk of its finanacial endowment, and paid for the various festivities associated with its assemblies. In all these respects his office was both monarchical and proprietary, and resembled its English analogue. Unlike the Sovereign of the Garter, however, his voice in the election of companions and officers was strictly limited, he did not have a voice in the appointment of any but the first canons attached to the Order's chapel, and his costume was not distinguished in any way from that of the other companions. Why Philippe chose to limit his power and status in these ways is not clear, but it is possible that, because he was a mere duke rather than a king, he felt it would be wise to create a more fraternal and egalitarian image for his Order, so as to make it more acceptable to important barons and to princes who were equal or superior to him in rank.

Like the Sovereignty of the Order of the Garter, that of the Golden Fleece was explicitly annexed by its founder to the lordship of his principal dominion: the

Duchy of Burgundy.[32] Unlike any of the earlier founders except Carlo of Sicily, Philippe sought to secure the continuity of his order in certain circumstances in which the normal hereditary succession to the presidential office might be interrupted – specifically, the death of a Sovereign leaving only a minor son or an unmarried daughter to succeed him. Philippe was more determined than Carlo to secure the sovereignty of the Order to his own heirs and successors, however, as he required the companions to elect from among their own number not a Sovereign but a temporary regent, whose office was to cease when the Sovereign's minor son came of age and was knighted, or his daughter was married to a knight capable of assuming the office.[33] As we have seen, this provision saw the Order through its first succession crisis, which occurred only forty-seven years after the Order was proclaimed, but as it did not specify what was to be done if the heiress herself died while her husband was Sovereign, it could not prevent the dispute that broke out on the death of the founder's granddaughter Marie as to whether the sovereignty ought to remain with her widower Maximilian for life, or devolve immediately upon their infant son Philippe, during whose minority a new regent would have to be elected by the companions from among their own number. In the event, Maximilian resigned the sovereignty but retained effective control of the Order as regent until his son came of age, but these events nevertheless demonstrate forcibly how important a carefully-constructed and clearly-worded succession-law was to the continuity of such a society, and to the avoidance of successional disputes and even schisms. Philippe's rule was sufficiently careful to maintain the continuous existence of the Order, but not farsighted enough to avoid controversy and ultimately schism. He did not foresee the possibility that the dominion in terms of whose possession alone he defined the succession, the Duchy of Burgundy, would alone be lost to all of the heirs of his body, and it was thus impossible to determine in the dispute that ultimately arose between the heir male and the heir general of his great-great-grandson Charles II which of them ought to be Sovereign of the Order. On the basis of the statutes, the person with the best claim to be Sovereign of the Order during most of the period after the death of Charles 'the Rash' in 1477 was in fact the King of France, the *de facto* Duke of Burgundy.

7 The Membership of the Order: The Knights, Brothers, or Companions

The principal college of the Order of the Golden Fleece, that of the companions, was defined in terms which were clearly derived from the Garter constitution. Like the Garter companions, the *chevaliers* or *compaignons* of the Order (or *freres*, as they were also called after the *freres* of the Collar) were all to be gentlemen of name and arms without 'reproach', who had received the accolade of knighthood.

---

[32] After the loss of Burgundy it would be claimed that the sovereignty of the Order was meant to be extraterritorial, but this is contradicted by Philippe's unequivocal declaration in ch. 1c: '. . . nous, en nostre temps, seront le chief et souverain; et, après nous, nos successeurs, ducz de Bourgoingne'.
[33] Ch. 65a–c.

Philippe added that they were also to be of legitimate birth, thus restricting the college to men whose nobility was by contemporary standards both complete and unblemished in any way.[34] Philippe was obviously looking for more positive personal qualities as well, for before listing the founding knights in chapter 18 of the statutes, he declared that he had chosen those listed 'for [their] sense, prowess, virtues, and good customs . . . and the confidence [he had] in their loyalty and perserverance in good deeds and honourable works'. This statement implies that the companions of the Golden Fleece, like those of the Garter, were expected to be paragons of knightly virtue.

It would appear that it was originally Philippe's intention to have twenty-four companions in his Order in addition to the Sovereign – exactly one fewer than in the Order of the Garter. He apointed twenty-four members in January 1430, named one more shortly thereafter to replace one who had died, and held elections at the chapters of 1431 and 1432 to restore the number of companions to twenty-four. He also increased the number of canons in his palace chapel by letters of January 1432 from twenty to twenty-four, obviously intending their number to match that of the companions. At the Order's third chapter, however, held in Dijon in November-December 1433, Philippe held elections to fill not only the two seats which had fallen vacant, but six new places, bringing the total number of companions to thirty in addition to himself, and this is the number specified in all the surviving statute books. It is not clear why Philippe decided to increase the number by so small an amount, but in all likelihood he, like Edward of England in 1349, simply wanted to include certain specific individuals without waiting for others to die, and altered the constitution accordingly.[35] The number was maintained at thirty until the reign of the fifth Sovereign of the Order, the Emperor Karl V, who raised it to fifty during the first chapter of his sovereignty, in 1516, in order to accomodate the vastly increased number of his subjects.[36]

The mode of electing and admitting new companions is set forth in the statutes of the Golden Fleece with an unprecedented degree of precision; indeed, the section dealing with these two subjects contains fully one third of the chapters and nearly a third of the ordinances in its division.[37] The election procedure described in chapters 41 to 50 differed from that of the Garter in a number of significant ways. In the first place, the elections of companions were to take place only during the Order's regular assemblies rather than within a stated period of time after the death of a companion.[38] Like Carlo of Sicily before him, Philippe probably introduced this regulation to avoid the difficulties involved in calling irregular assemblies, which even in the English order were seldom summoned in practice, but once the assemblies started to fall more than one year apart (as they did after

---

[34] Ch. 1b.

[35] Chs. 1a, 18. After listing the first twenty-three companions, the latter chapter declares: 'Et le surplus, pour accomplir ledit nombre de xxx chevaliers [de l'ordre] sans le souverain, reservons a estre mis en icelle ordre, au prochain cappitre, ou aultre subsequent, a le election de nous et des compaignons dudit ordre'. It is possible that the wording of this chapter was altered at the chapter held in 1432.

[36] See Leibnitz, *Mantissa*, p. 34, no. 7.

[37] Chs. 41–62.

[38] Chs. 42b, 44a.

1440) the rule operated against the maintenance of the full complement of companions, and it is surprising that it was not altered. In order that the companions might have an opportunity to deliberate on the choice of new companions, and that those who could not come to the meeting could give their ballots to procurators, the companions were to be informed by letter before each meeting if an election was to take place, and how many new companions were to be elected.[39] The introduction of proxy voting obviated the need for defining a quorum and allowed all the companions to participate in every election, so that this rule was a distinct improvement on the Garter regulations. In making nominations the companions were required to submit one name only for each vacancy, without any special regard for rank.[40] Philippe made the nominating procedure separate from the election, so that the names of all the nominees could be known to all those present, and anyone unacceptable could be rejected before the voting.[41] He also introduced a special oath to be sworn by each companion in the hands of the Sovereign before each election, to encourage the electors to cast their votes with as little prejudice as possible for the person who seemed most likely to serve the Order best.[42] As in the Order of the Garter, the election was apparently carried by the candidate who had received the largest number of votes rather than a majority.[43] The Sovereign of the Order normally had two votes, but if there was a tie he could either cast a third vote to break it, or hold a second ballot, in which the votes of those absent would simply be re-counted.[44] If there was not a tie, however, he was obliged to proclaim whoever was thus chosen by the whole body of companions, and did not have the discretionary powers of the Garter Sovereign.[45] In theory, therefore, the Sovereign of the Golden Fleece had a great deal less to say about the membership of his order than any previous chief. In practice, however, he often exercised a decisive role in the electoral process through informal means. Charles 'the Rash', for example, railroaded the election of the Duke of Savoy in 1468, and successfully opposed that of the Count of Neuchâtel in 1473.[46]

After the elections which increased the number of companions to thirty in 1433, no further elections were necessary until 1440, when four new companions were duly chosen to replace four who had died during the previous year. Thereafter elections were held at every meeting, largely because after 1440 the chapter of the Order met at such long intervals that it was almost inevitable that several of the companions would die between meetings. Because of the infrequency of elections, the number of companions repeatedly fell well below the full complement required by the statutes, and at the meetings held during the reigns of the founder and his son after 1440, the number of vacancies that had to be filled were respectively six, six, four, six, nine, and seven.[47]

[39] Ch. 42a–c.
[40] Ch. 42b.
[41] Ch. 45 (a,b).
[42] Ch. 46 (a–c).
[43] Ch. 41b.
[44] Ch. 49e,f.
[45] Ch. 49d.
[46] See Vaughan, *Charles the Bold*, p. 104.
[47] The times and places of the Order's meetings, the numbers present, the numbers elected, and the main items of business dealt with at each one are all given in Reiffenberg, *Histoire*. It

Every companion-elect was to be informed of his election and given a copy of the statutes so that he could decide whether to accept the election,[48] in the fashion reserved in the English order for foreign princes, but only foreign princes were to be given the Order's collar before their admission,[49] and even they had both to send a letter of acceptance and to promise to come in person to the next convenient chapter of the Order (or at least to the Sovereign himself) to be formally inducted; induction by proxy was not permitted.[50] Both the rite and the oath of entry into the Order were set forth with an explicitness approached only in the statutes of the Ship. Indeed, the rite was very similar to that adopted by Carlo of Sicily fifty years earlier, being designed to impress the companion-elect with both the nature and the solemnity of his undertaking, and to ensure that he could under no circumstances claim either ignorance of the statutes or failure to undertake the full burdens of membership. The companion-elect was first to declare his willingness to join the Order before the Sovereign and as many companions as could be assembled, and was then to swear, on his faith, oath, and honour, with his hands between those of the Sovereign, to defend the high lordships and rights of the Sovereign;[51] to work to uphold the honour of the Order with all his power;[52] to surrender his collar (if for any reason he was expelled) within three months, never to wear it again, and to bear no ill-will towards any of the companions as a result;[53] to accomplish willingly and without rancour the punishments adjudged to him;[54] to come to the chapters or appoint a proxy for them; to obey the Sovereign in all matters reasonably touching the Order;[55] and to obey all of the statutes, which he had already read, and which were then read to him.[56] After touching the cross and Gospels,[57] the companion-elect was then to place himself before the Sovereign, who was to place the collar around his neck and receive him verbally into the Order, describing its high purpose, and concluding with an invocation of the Trinity. To this the newly admitted companion was to respond 'Amen. May God give me grace', after which each of the other companions present was to kiss him as a sign of perpetual love.[58] Finally, as in both the English and the Savoyard order, he was to pay a specified sum of money to buy vestments and other ornaments for the chapel, or to donate vestments and ornaments of the same value.[59] The sum

---

is interesting to note that for about three decades there were actually thirty-two companions: the Emperor Maximilian and his son Philippe 'the Handsome' counting as one while the latter lived.

[48] Ch. 50b,c,d.
[49] Ch. 51a,b.
[50] Ch. 51c,d.
[51] Ch. 52.
[52] Ch. 53.
[53] Ch. 54.
[54] Ch. 55.
[55] Ch. 56.
[56] Ch. 57.
[57] Ch. 58b.
[58] Ch. 59.
[59] Ch. 62.

payable at this time (40 *escus d'or* or 72 marks) was not graduated according to rank as it was in the English order, and the Fleece statutes say nothing about the status of a companion-elect who had not been formally admitted or had not paid his entry-fee.

Once he had been admitted to the Order, a new companion was to retain his membership for life,[60] unless for some reason he himself wished to resign[61] (an eventuality not contemplated by any earlier founder), or he committed a crime of such gravity that the other companions voted to expel him. The contemporary Garter statutes contained no provision for suspension or expulsion (though as we have seen knights were actually expelled from that order on occasion for treason), but the founders of the Band, the Star, the Knot, and the Ship had all prescribed expulsion as the penalty for cowardice in battle. To this crime (which he defined in terms of the contemporary laws of arms as flight from a battle in which banners had been raised)[62] Philippe added heresy,[63] treason,[64] and such other 'enormous' offences as the Sovereign and companions might decide were deserving of the supreme penalty.[65] The honour of the Order as a whole was thus to be preserved from any possible 'reproach'.

Philippe and his successors seem to have taken the ordinances just summarized quite seriously, for a number of companions were accused of offences punishable by expulsion during the course of the fifteenth century, and nine were in fact expelled. We have already observed that one of the knights named to the Order at the time of its proclamation – Jean de Neuchâtel-Montagu – was declared to have forfeited his membership at the very first chapter of the Order held in November 1431. In fact both he and another companion – Louis de Chalon-Arlay, Prince of Orange – had been deprived of the Order before the chapter by the founder himself, who accused them of having violated one of the statutes of the Order by fleeing from the field after the disastrous Battle of Anthon in the Dauphiné, fought on 11 June 1430. Despite appeals made by both companions at the chapter of 1431 on the grounds that they had been ignorant of the statute in question (which at the time may not even have been written down), the duke's sentence was upheld, and the Prince of Orange never even received his collar.[66] At the first chapter of the reign of Duke Charles 'the Rash', held in May 1468, the companion Jean Capet de Valois-Bourgogne-Nevers, Count of Nevers and Etampes, a cousin of the duke who had allied himself with the duke's archenemy the King of France, was expelled for treason, and his arms were duly removed from the Order's chapel. At the second chapter held under the sovereignty of Duke Maximilian in 1481, no fewer than five companions were expelled for bearing arms against the Sovereign, and one further

---

[60] Ch. 13.

[61] Ch. 16c, which suggests as a possible reason for resigning a failure of the Sovereign to answer an injury the companion had suffered at his hands.

[62] Ch. 16a.

[63] Ch. 14.

[64] Ch. 15, omitted by error from the version included in the chronicle of Le Fèvre.

[65] Ch. 16b.

[66] On the principle of expulsion for cowardice see Armstrong, 'La Toison d'or et la loi des armes', *Publications du centre européen des études burgondo-médianes*, 5 (1963), pp. 1–7.

companion was excluded for the same reason at the chapter held in 1491. The relative rarity of such expulsions may probably be explained by a desire on the part of the successive dukes not to lose valuable clients and allies for anything less than compelling reasons.

The question of precedence within a monarchical order had been raised in the fourteenth century only in the Garter statutes, which had decreed (in keeping with the prevailing notion of the equality that ought to exist among all knights) that each new companion was to assume the position occupied by the companion he had replaced, without regard for rank. Precedence had become a more burning issue by 1430, however, and Philippe's careful regulations concerning the matter reflect its increased importance. Four separate factors – civil rank, time of admission to knighthood, time of admission to the Order, and time of birth – were taken into consideration, and the relative position of each knight was determined in accordance with these factors considered in that order.[67] With respect to civil rank, however, only the distinction between great princes bearing the titles emperor, king, or duke, on the one hand, and noblemen of lesser station, on the other, was to be taken into consideration. Philippe no doubt felt that his own equals and superiors had to be treated with especial consideration, as it would otherwise have been unlikely that they would accept election to the Order. As a result of this regulation, the position of each companion in processions and in the chapel and chapter-house must have changed more or less significantly from one meeting to the next, and no companion could have been regarded as the successor to any other.

According to the original version of the statutes, membership in the Order, once accepted, was to be exclusive, the companions being forbidden to join any other order of any sort without the consent of their fellows.[68] This rule, of course, was almost identical in its implications to regulations contained in the statutes of most of the earlier orders – the Garter and Collar being notable exceptions. At the chapter of 1440, however, qualifications were appended to this statute to the effect that a prince who was himself the head of an order could retain that order on election to the Golden Fleece, while the Sovereign of the latter Order could likewise accept membership in other orders. This double-edged amendment was introduced in order to allow Philippe to exchange orders with his former archenemy Duke Charles of Orléans, elected to the Golden Fleece during the course of the same chapter, but it was almost inevitable that some such provision would be added to allow Philippe to conduct foreign policy in a world where membership in such orders was used as a token of friendship and alliance between princes.

One of the duties of the registrar of the Order was to record every election on the day it took place, and as most of the records of the Order have survived, we are better informed about the membership of the Order of the Golden Fleece than about that of any other medieval order.[69] The first twenty-four companions of the

[67] Ch. 17.
[68] Ch. 2.
[69] Lists of the companions are to be found in Reiffenberg, pp. 513ff., and Payer von Thurn, *Liste nominale des chevaliers de l'Ordre illustre de la Toison d'Or depuis son institution jusqu' à nos jours* (Vienna?, 1904).

Order, appointed by Philippe in January 1430 and listed in the statutes, were all officers, councillors, or prominent vassals of the founder in one or another of his various principalities, fairly evenly distributed geographically. Indeed, despite the Order's formal identification with Burgundy, only eight of the first companions were from either of the two Burgundies, and before the loss of those dominions in 1477 only six more Burgundians were elected to the Order.[70] Until the sovereignty of the Emperor Karl V the largest proportion of the companions were subjects of the duke's numerous dominions in the Low Countries, the richest and most populous region of the Burgundian commonwealth, and it is clear that the Order was intended to be broadly representative of the different provincial nobilities of that commonwealth, rather than of Burgundy proper.

From the time of its proclamation, the Order of the Golden Fleece included in addition to knights who were regarded as subjects of the Sovereign a number of men whose most important fiefs, at least, were held of lords other than the Duke of Burgundy, and were therefore effectively 'foreigners'. At first the 'foreign' companions were all barons of middle rank in either France or the Empire who spent much of their time in the court and service of the Duke of Burgundy: the Counts of Dammartin, Saint-Pol, and Ligny and the Prince of Orange, appointed in 1430, the Count of Mörs, elected in 1431, and the Count of Virneburg, elected in 1433. No other such barons, and no lords of higher rank, were admitted to the Order before 1440, but in that year Philippe engineered the election of four French princes – the Dukes of Orléans, Brittany, and Alençon, and the Count of Comminges – all of whom must be regarded as friends or allies rather than mere clients of the Burgundian duke. At the next chapter of the Order, held in December 1445, the first king was elected to the Order in the person of Alfons V 'the Magnanimous' of Aragon and the two Sicilies, and after lengthy negociations he was persuaded to accept his election.[71] Thereafter a very high percentage of those elected were foreign princes and even kings, though important vassals of the Sovereign continued to be admitted to the Order throughout its history.

Altogether some sixty-four companions were appointed or elected under the founder's sovereignty,[72] of whom two (Alfons V of Aragon and the two Sicilies and his brother and successor Joan II of Aragon, Navarre, and island Sicily) were kings, six were dukes or titular princes,[73] and seventeen were or later became counts. During the ten-year reign of his son Charles, fifteen new companions were elected, including three kings (Edward IV of England, Ferrante I of mainland Sicily, and Ferran II of Aragon, Castile, and island Sicily), one duke (Philippe of Savoy) and four counts or barons of equivalent rank, three of whom were foreign. Sixteen

---

[70] See J. Richard, 'La Toison d'or dans les deux Bourgognes,' *Publications du centre européen des études burgondo-médianes*, 5 (1963), pp. 47–52.

[71] See Constantin Marinesco, 'Documents espagnols inédits concernant la fondation de l'Ordre de la Toison d'or', *Comptes rendus de l'Académie des Inscriptions et Belles Lettres* (1956), pp. 401–17.

[72] Two of these, the Prince of Orange, named in 1430, and the Count of Terreno, elected in 1456, are not included in the official list.

[73] The others were Johann, Duke of Cleves, and Jean, titular Prince of Antioch and regent of Cyprus.

companions were elected during the brief sovereignty of Maximilian of Austria, none of whom was a foreign prince and only four of whom (including Maximilian's infant son Philippe) were counts, but under Philippe 'the Handsome' the thirty-one companions elected included four kings or future kings (his grandfather the Emperor Friedrich III, his son Charles, and both Henry VII and Henry VIII of England), two dukes or future dukes, and nine counts. The first two chapters of the reign of Charles II (or Karl V), which fell at the very end of our period, saw the election of thirty-nine companions, whose number included no fewer than five kings (François I of France, Manuel I of Portugal, Lajos II of Hungary and Bohemia, Christian II of Denmark, Norway, and Sweden, and Zygmunt I of Poland), one future king, eleven dukes or princes of equivalent rank (including eight Spanish grandees), and eleven counts. Thereafter very few men below the rank of count were elected to membership. By 1520 the Order had thus succeeded in becoming élite in the highest possible sense – a society, not of mere knights, but of lords and princes, drawn from all over Western Christendom. In this development, too, it had followed the lead given by the Order of the Garter.

It should finally be noted that nearly half of the companions appointed or elected before 1520 – 84 out of of 166 – belonged to one or another of the nineteen families that provided more than one member to the Order in the same period. Three of these families (those of Capet, Croy, and Luxemburg) provided ten members each to the Order before 1520, one family (Lannoy) provided seven, three (Habsburg, Lalaing and Neufchâtel) provided five each, six (Berghes, Borsele, Brimeu, Châlons, Egmont, and Toulonjon) provided three each, and seven families (Baume, Crèvecoeur, Hornes, Melun, Nassau, Savoye, and Vergy) provided two each. As one would expect, all of these were important princely and baronial families closely associated with the Burgundian court throughout the fifteenth century.

8 The Obligations and Privileges of Membership

Companionship in the Order of the Golden Fleece entailed a number of obligations, most but not all of which were set forth in the second section of the statutes. As usual they may be divided into three categories: obligations to the Sovereign as such; obligations to one another; and obligations of a general nature. To the Sovereign the companions were bound to bear good and true love,[74] and to give active aid whenever he acted in defence of himself, his own territories, his vassals or subjects, or the Church, in person if possible, but otherwise by a reasonable substitute, unless there was an obvious impediment.[75] They were also to obtain his licence before setting forth on any long voyage or engaging in a war,[76] and to inform him if they intended to engage in military service with a foreign

[74] Ch. 4a.
[75] Ch. 5.
[76] Ch. 7a.

prince.[77] The first of these provisions seems to represent a watered-down version of the first chapter of the Collar statutes, the second an augmented version of the twenty-seventh chapter of the Garter statutes. Both were mitigated for those companions who were not exclusively vassals of the Sovereign, who were allowed to serve their liege lords against him in their native lands, and even (in certain carefully specified circumstances) in an attack on the Sovereign's lands,[78] and were required only to inform the Sovereign of their intentions to travel or make war.[79] Even with these qualifications, the obligations of the companions of the Golden Fleece to their Sovereign were much more significant than the corresponding obligations of the Garter companions, but somewhat less extensive (at least in theory) than those of the knights of the Collar.

The companions' obligations to one another, including the Sovereign, were much more extensive. Each companion was bound in life to bear 'good and true love' to all his fellows;[80] to inform them of any evil that was said about them;[81] to aid them against those who had done them any harm, especially when the matter was submitted to their judgement and the accused refused to cooperate;[82] to save their lives when they were captured in battle;[83] and (if allowed) to release any companion he captured himself, unless the captive was the commander of the enemy force.[84] Should the captor's lord refuse to allow the release of the captured companion, the captor was to refuse to fight further and quit his lord's service.[85] These obligations, typical of brotherhood-in-arms, were probably inspired by the similarly fraternal third chapter of the Collar statutes; certainly they stand in marked contrast to the single, purely negative mutual obligation of the Garter knights, not to make war on one another for pay. Their introduction was consistent with Philippe's apparent desire to make his Order more egalitarian and less obviously centred on its princely founder, and also with his declared intention to promote the highest standards of chivalry.

Perhaps because he had imposed much heavier obligations on his companions in life than were required in the Garter statutes, Philippe felt that he ought to impose smaller obligations upon them to the Order's dead. The fifteen masses he required each survivor to pay for as soon as he had heard of the death of any of his fellows[86] were in any case considerably fewer than the one hundred masses demanded by the Collar statutes and the one hundred to one thousand demanded by those of the Garter. The number fifteen was much closer to the numbers of masses required by

---

[77] Ch. 12a.

[78] Ch. 11. They were permitted to attack the Sovereign only if they were constrained to do so, their lord was personally present, and they informed the Sovereign by sealed instrument of their intention to do so.

[79] Ch. 7b.

[80] Ch. 4b.

[81] Ch. 4d. He was also bound to warn the defamer of his obligation to do this.

[82] Chs. 9, 10. The latter specifies that the companions were to give every possible assistance to their fellows who were subjects of the Sovereign, and such assistance as they could to those who were not.

[83] Ch. 12b.

[84] Ch. 12c,d.

[85] Ch. 12e.

[86] Ch. 63a.

the defunct orders of the Star (one), the Knot (seven), and the Ship (twenty-four to ninety), but this was almost certainly coincidence. In keeping with his egalitarian policy, Philippe did not require a special number of masses either for or from the Sovereign, who was to be treated as an ordinary companion in this respect as in so many others. Philippe did add one new obligation to the dead: at the offertory of the mass for the dead held on the day after the Order's solemn feast, each companion was to present, either in person or by proxy, a wax candle decorated with the arms of a deceased companion.[87]

The companions finally had certain duties simply as members of the Order: (1) to submit disputes among themselves, either in person or by procuration, to the arbitration of the Chapter;[88] (2) to maintain the honour of the Order with all their power;[89] (3) to attend the assemblies of the Order or appoint a proxy;[90] (4) to submit willingly to the criticisms and punishments imposed by the Order;[91] (5) to obey both the statutes and the Sovereign in all matters pertaining to the Order;[92] (6) to pay a sum of 15 solz for the Order's chaplains at the same time as they paid for masses for each recently-deceased companion;[93] (7) to pay a sum of one noble (a Flemish coin worth one pound of Tours) at each Chapter for the support of the Order's king of arms;[94] and (8) to keep secret all the proceedings of the Chapter.[95] The first, second, and sixth of these obligations seem to have been borrowed from the statutes of the Collar,[96] the fourth, fifth, and seventh from those of the Garter.[97] The obligation to submit disputes to binding arbitration, found in the Ship as well as the Collar statutes, was the most significant non-mutual duty of the companions, and Philippe no doubt introduced it for the same reason as the earlier founders: to maintain internal harmony.

The Sovereign of the Order also owed a number of obligations to the companions which were peculiar to his office. He was to 'advance' their 'power, honour, and profit',[98] to inform a majority of them before undertaking any but a secret or pressing military enterprise, and to ask for their advice on the matter.[99] The first obligation, probably taken from the Collar statutes,[100] simply formed a counterpoise to the companions' duty to defend their Sovereign's lordships and rights. The other two in effect altered the duty of giving counsel (imposed by the constitutions not only of the Collar, but of the Star, the Knot, and the Ship) into an obligation of the Sovereign to receive counsel from the companions under similar circumstances. The result of this alteration was to increase considerably the

[87] Ch. 27d.
[88] Ch. 8.
[89] Ch. 53.
[90] Chs. 23, 56a.
[91] Chs. 54, 55.
[92] Chs. 56b, 57.
[93] Ch. 63b,c.
[94] Ch. 64b.
[95] Ch. 30.
[96] Collar chs. 5, 1, 7.
[97] Garter ch. 24, and letters creating the office.
[98] Ch. 4c.
[99] Ch. 6
[100] Collar ch. 2.

rights of the members of the Order with respect to the Order, and it can only be explained in terms of Philippe's desire to create a society in which all the members bore equal burdens. The obligation to inform and receive counsel before going to war was thus probably intended to balance the obligation imposed upon the companions to inform the Sovereign and to receive his permission before making war or going on a long voyage. It was nevertheless a truly remarkable concession for Philippe to make voluntarily, and shows how high a place the Order held in his estimation.

Even more remarkable, however, was Philippe's concession to the Order of the right to judge its own members, not merely in cases of infraction of the statutes, but in all cases whatsoever, without the possibility of appeal.[101] This privilege – similar to that granted the knights of St George in Hungary a century earlier – removed the companions completely from the regular judicial system, and made them answerable, like the Peers of France and England, only to their fellows. Such a privilege alone would have made membership in the Order extremely attractive to the gentlemen of Philippe's dominions, but its wider implications were denied by Philippe's successor Charles 'the Rash' on the very first occasion on which one of the companions was charged with a crime against the state. At the eleventh Chapter of the Order, held in Bruges in 1468, the authoritarian Charles, having arrested three of the companions on charges of lèse-majesté, declared that thenceforth the Order was to have neither the cognizance nor the right of punishment except in cases of honour, and that he alone had criminal jurisdiction over his subjects.[102] This high-handed declaration, typical of Charles' approach to government generally, was accepted at the time by the cowed companions, and later attempts of companions to claim the protection of the Order (of which the most famous was that of the Counts of Egmont and Horn in 1568) were invariably ignored. Clearly the privilege conceded was too great to be tolerated by a prince as jealous of his prerogatives and determined to have his way as Charles, and once challenged by Charles as Sovereign, could not be maintained. Ultimately, all of the privileges of the companions depended entirely upon the will of the Sovereign, who could interpret the statutes in whatever way suited him.

Perhaps to offset some of the effects of his declaration of 1468, Charles decreed at the next Chapter of the Order, held in May 1473, that the knights of the Order were thenceforth to enjoy a right of precedence in the Burgundian court immediately after the relatives of the duke, and a number of other privileges of a similar nature.[103] Such a substitution of honorific for practical privileges was typical of the policies maintained by most contemporary princes with respect to their most powerful subjects.

[101] Ch. 66.
[102] Reiffenberg, op. cit., pp. 46ff.
[103] Ibid., pp. 81–83.

9 *The Assembly, Chapel, and Clergy of the Order*

Like those of most of the earlier orders, the knights of the Golden Fleece were initially intended to meet in a formal Assembly, to be held annually (in keeping with the practice of the Order of the Garter) on the feast of their patron saint.[104] The format of the St Andrew's Day Assembly described in the statutes of the Order (which constituted their only truly corporate activity) was clearly based fairly closely upon that of the Garter, though Philippe as usual did not copy his model slavishly. It will be recalled that the Garter Assembly consisted of a meeting of the Chapter followed by attendance at vespers on the eve of the feast day; attendance at the high mass of the patron, a banquet, and vespers on the feast day itself; and attendance at a solemn requiem for the Order's dead on the day following the feast. Philippe altered these arrangements[105] only in replacing the second vespers with a vigil for the dead,[106] transferring the Chapter-meeting from the eve to the day following the feast,[107] and adding a third mass, that of the Virgin, on the day following that[108] – thus extending the proceedings from three days to four. He also introduced certain new actions into the mass for the dead,[109] and specified that the psalm *De profundis* and the prayer for the dead were to be said at the end of it. None of these changes was of great significance.

Philippe did prescribe the procedure that was to be followed at the Chapter meeting much more specifically than Edward of England had done. He assigned to the Chapter of the Order of the Golden Fleece three principal orders of business: the examination of the general conduct of each of the companions, including the Sovereign; the judgement of cases of infraction of the statutes or the commission of any other crime alleged against one of the companions, and the selection of appropriate punishments up to and including expulsion; and the election of new companions to replace those who had died or been expelled. In addition the Chapter on occasion adopted amendments to the statutes, but the founder had reserved to himself and his heirs the right to interpret any obscurity in the existing statutes, and declared that certain chapters were never to be altered.[110]

Like the procedures for electing new companions (which we have already examined) the public examination or 'correction' of conduct is described in great detail in the statutes. The Chancellor was to ask each companion in turn to leave

---

[104] Ch. 22.
[105] Chs. 24b, 25a,c–e, 26.
[106] Ch. 27b.
[107] Ch. 29a.
[108] Ch. 28.
[109] Ch. 27d–f. At the offertory of this mass, each companion was to present in person or by proxy a wax candle decorated with the arms of the companion for whom it was offered, and the Registrar was to read out a list of the Order's dead.
[110] Ch. 67b–d. The chapters in question were 1 (on the Order's structure), 2 (on membership in other orders), 4, 5, 8–17 (stating the companions' more important obligations and the rules governing expulsion and precedence), 41 (requiring elections), and 52–58 (the companions' oath). In fact, chapters 1, 2, 8–17, and 41 were all either amended or ignored before the end of the sixteenth century.

the room in which the Chapter was meeting.[111] When he had left, the Sovereign was to ask each of those remaining, beginning at the bottom and working upwards, to declare on oath what he knew or had heard of what the companion had said or done since the last Chapter that was contrary either to the honour of knighthood or to the statutes of the Order.[112] The companion was then to be recalled, and if he had been found by a majority of those present to be guilty of any offence, he was to be punished by the Sovereign.[113] When all of the companions present had been examined in this way, the proxies were to be examined in the place of those absent, and finally the Sovereign himself was to submit to examination, in order to set a good example to the others.[114] If anyone present was indicted for offences for which deprivation was prescribed, he was to be tried then and there, and either deprived or pardoned.[115]

This process was similar in both principle and method to the public recounting of deeds which took place at the Chapters of the Star, the Knot, and the Ship, and was clearly designed to promote chivalrous behaviour. In the Order of the Golden Fleece, however, the procedure was shorn of its romantic trappings and treated in a strictly businesslike manner. The emphasis was also shifted from the rewarding of honourable deeds to the punishment of dishonourable ones. Indeed, far from receiving some sort of augmentation to his badge, the knight who had done well was merely commended by the Chancellor and encouraged to keep up the good work.[116] The real function of the Chapter during the 'correction' was to act first as a sort of grand jury and then as a panel of judges, first indicting, then trying, and finally sentencing those companions who had done less than what was expected of noble knights *sans reproche*. No founder since Alfonso of Castile a century earlier had shown such a concern for promoting what Philippe in the Prologue called 'virtues and good habits' among the companions. Perhaps the most remarkable aspect of the whole business, however, was that the Sovereign himself was to be subjected to the same examination *in absentia* as the other companions: another example of Philippe's determination to minimize the Sovereign's special status.

In the event, Philippe's carefully worked out plan for the Order's Assembly proved overly ambitious, and had to be modified in a number of ways. As we have noted, the Assembly was initially supposed to meet every year on St Andrew's day, which was the last day of November. It was in fact held on that day only seven times: annually from 1431 to 1436, and again in 1440. In the years from 1437 to 1439 and from 1441 to 1444, various circumstances made it impossible for Philippe to hold any general meeting of the Order, and in 1445 the companions, complaining in a Chapter held two weeks late of the shortness of the days at that time of year, the coldness of the weather, and the length of the journeys some of them had to make, declared that thenceforth the Assembly would be convened on the second of May rather than the last day of November, and every three years

---

[111] Ch. 31b.
[112] Ch. 32.
[113] Ch. 33.
[114] Ch. 34.
[115] Ch. 36a.
[116] Ch. 35.

rather than annually, unless the Sovereign felt an extra meeting was needed.[117] Even this reduced frequency proved impossible to maintain, however, and the only remaining Assemblies of Philippe's reign were held on 2 May in 1451, 1456, and 1461, at intervals of six, five, and five years respectively. Under Philippe's successors as Sovereign, Assemblies of the Order were held even less frequently – in 1468, 1473, 1478, 1481, 1491, 1501, 1505, 1516, and 1518 in our period, or on average about once every seven years. Altogether only twenty-three Assemblies were convened in the 128 years that elapsed between the first in 1431 and the last in 1559. Furthermore, after the founder's death in 1467, the meetings were not even held on 2 May, for his son Charles declared at the Chapter of 1468 that thenceforth chapters were to be convened by the Sovereigns 'at such season of the year and at such interval of years as their affairs would permit'.[118] Until 1491, the Assemblies were always held within a few weeks of 2 May, but after that they were summoned at whatever time of year suited the increasingly peripatetic Sovereign. In 1531, indeed, the knights actually met for the eighth and last time on St. Andrew's Day.

Philippe also attempted to give his Order a fixed seat on the Garter model in the chapel of his palace at Dijon in northern Burgundy, and initially required that the Assembly meet there.[119] Philippe had proclaimed his intention of founding services for the Order in his chapel in Dijon in the letters patent of November 1431 promulgating the statutes,[120] and two months later, in January 1432, by letters dated at Rethel, he 'chose, decerned, and determined, and established irrevocably and forever, the place, chapter, and college' of the Order of the Golden Fleece in the palace chapel, 'a notable church founded by very great devotion and miraculous cause'. In that chapel, from 25 March 1432 onward, a different mass was to be celebrated for the Order every day of the week: on Monday, the mass for the souls of the departed; on Tuesday, the Mass of the Angels; on Wednesday, that of St Andrew; on Thursday, that of the Holy Spirit; on Friday, that of the Cross; on Saturday, that of Our Lady; and on Sunday, that of the Holy Trinity. Four general solemn *obits* were to be said each year for the Order's dead, and the various services connected with the Assembly on St Andrew's Day were to be conducted there, wherever the Assembly itself convened. The funerals of the companions were also to be held there, as was customary, and for a payment of ten *livres tournois* per annum a companion could also be interred in the chapel. Since the foundation for the support of poor knights was mentioned in the same chapter of the statutes as the chapel,[121] it may be assumed that, like its Garter counterpart, it was to have been attached to the chapel as well, but there is no evidence that any provisions for

---

[117] Ch. 22, as amended in 1445.

[118] See Leibnitz, op. cit., p. 33, no. 2.

[119] For this and what follows see P. Quarré, 'La chapelle du duc de Bourgogne à Dijon: "Lieu, Chapître, et Collège" de l'Ordre de la Toison d'or,' *Publications de centre européen d'études burgondo-médianes*, 5 (1963), pp. 56–64; and Reiffenberg, op. cit., p. 16.

[120] Ch. 20a.

[121] Ch. 20b. The ordinance reads: '. . . et aultre fondacion du vivre et substentacion des povres chevaliers, et edifficacions a ce pertinentes et necessaires, ainsi que declairiés est en noz lettres sur ce ce faictes'. This must be a reference to the letters attaching the canons to the Order.

poor knights were ever made by Philippe or any of his successors, either in Dijon or anywhere else.

The foundation statutes decreed that – in accordance with the current practice (though not the rule) of the Order of the Garter – the armorial achievements of the companions were to be set over their stalls in the chapel.[122] Armorial plates were first attached to the stalls of the companions in the collegiate church of St Donatian at Bruges in preparation for the second Chapter of the Order in 1432, and for the third Chapter, which actually took place in Dijon in the following year, similar wooden panels painted with the armorial bearings of the knights were in fact set over the stalls of the canons in the choir of their official chapel. One of the duties of the Order's Treasurer was to replace the panels of those companions who had died with those who had been elected to their places. The removal of the panels, of course, did not reflect current Garter usage, but the panels taken down were in practice preserved and hung elsewhere in the chapel (in keeping with the custom of the Order of the Collar with respect to collars, arms, and banners) as 'perpetual' memorials to the companions represented by them.

By his letters of January 1432 Philippe also increased the number of canons attached to the chapel from twenty (at which it had been fixed by Duke Eudes III in 1214) to twenty-four, in order to equal (in the fashion of both the Garter and the Collar) the number of companions. The canonical college was from that time onward to be dedicated primarily to the service of the Order, to which it was in theory attached almost as securely as the College of St George's Chapel, Windsor was to the Order of the Garter, and the canons of Dijon were given a yearly income of 780 *livres tournois* for performing the services required for the well-being of the companions.

Despite these provisions, the Order of the Golden Fleece assembled only once during its long history at the ducal chapel in Dijon, and although the specified services were continuously performed (despite the sequestration of the Duchy of Burgundy in 1477 and the consequent alienation of the chapel from the Order) until 1791 (when the French Revolution brought about the dissolution of the college of canons), the companions themselves had very little to do with their official seat. After the ninth Chapter in 1456, no new panel was ever set up in the choir there, though after the eleventh meeting in 1468 the panel most recently removed was returned to its stall to replace that of the Count of Nevers, who had been expelled from the Order. The panels remained in this state until 1802, when the chapel and all but one of the panels were finally destroyed by fire.[123]

Thus Philippe's attempt to establish a regular time and place for the Order's Assemblies and a permanent centre for the Order's religious activities came within a few years to naught. The companions actually met irregularly and in a location which was only consistent in that it was never the same for two consecutive meetings.[124] This is not to say that Philippe's plans for the Order's Assemblies were wholly frustrated, however. On the contrary, not only did the Order meet at

---

[122] Ch. 21.

[123] Quarré, op. cit., p. 63.

[124] The seventeen meetings of our period were held in Lille, Bruges, Dijon, St Omer, Ghent, Mons, The Hague, St Omer, Bruges, Valenciennes, Bruges, Bois-le-Duc, Malines, Brussels, Middelburg, Brussels, and Barcelona respectively.

relatively short intervals for more than a century, but its meetings were invariably attended with great pomp, and generally followed the programme set forth by Philippe in the statutes. The relatively copious evidence that survives clearly indicates that, while the full programme was not always included and the prescribed order of procedure was not consistently followed, every one of the various activities Philippe had planned for the Assembly was in fact carried out at most of the Assemblies convened in the fifteenth and sixteenth centuries.

Perhaps the most complete and detailed description of the Assembly as a whole that we now possess is that contained in a long letter written by Olivier de la Marche, Captain of the Guard and *Mantre d'Hôtel* under Duke Charles 'the Rash', to Charles' grandson Duke Philippe 'the Handsome', explaining to the young duke on the basis of his own experience how to organize and hold an Assembly of the Order.[125] De la Marche first describes how the church should be set up before the feast. The Treasurer and King of Arms were to have *tableaux* or panels of the arms of all the companions, living and dead, painted and set up over the stalls in the choir, arranged according to the rules of rank and precedence set forth in the statutes, fifteen to a side. The Panels of the kings were to be larger and more ornate than the others, and those of the deceased companions were to include only the shield of arms, not the crested helm. The seat and panel of the Sovereign of the Order were to be set higher than all the others, next to the door in the rood-screen at the west end of the choir, and presumably facing the altar. Before them was to be set a bench on which the four officers could sit during the services. The *hostel* in which the Order was to meet was to be similarly prepared. Five different rooms were required for the secular activities of the companions during the Assembly: a retiring room for the companions; a retiring room and audience chamber for the Sovereign; a room in which the Treasurer could display the treasure of the Order and dispense and collect the companions' robes; a room in which the Chapter or 'Conclave' could meet; and a dining hall for the feast and other meals. In the Chapter room were to be set up a canopied throne for the Sovereign and similar thrones for any kings who happened to be present, two upholstered benches for the companions (who were to sit in the same arrangement as in the chapel), and a shorter bench for the officers (who were to sit facing the Sovereign). In the hall there was to be a great table at which the companions were to sit for the feast on the first day, in the fashion of the knights of the Round Table and of several of the earlier monarchical orders.

De la Marche goes on to enumerate the duties of the cooks and waiters in great detail, setting forth what courses should be served at the banquet and how each was to be presented. Finally he describes how the activities of the companions themselves were to be arranged, including the processions to and from the church, the sermon and offering at the mass of St Andrew, the banquet and the other meals, and the Chapter itself. His description of these activities is too lengthy even to summarize here, but it may be said that it corresponds very closely in its general outline to the programme of activities prescribed in the statutes. De la Marche's description of how an Assembly should be held is confirmed by a variety of other sources, including a number of pictorial representations of the first Chapter set as a

---

[125] *Mémoires d'Olivier de la Marche*, ed. H. Beaune, J. D'Abaumont (Paris, 1888), iv, pp. 158–189.

frontispiece in many of the surviving statute-books, in keeping with the requirement of chapter xx.[126]

We are relatively well informed on what was actually discussed at the Chapter of the Order from the capitular minutes themselves, maintained (albeit rather carelessly) by successive Registrars of the Order, and (unlike the equivalent records of all previous orders) preserved intact to the present day.[127] From them we learn not only that the electoral procedures set forth in the statutes were observed with care, but how many votes each companion received, and what persons were nominated but not elected. We also learn that the statutes requiring the Sovereign and companions to submit to the 'correction' of their faults and transgressions against the statutes and the code of chivalry were regularly obeyed. The process was taken particularly seriously by Charles 'the Rash', who used the two Chapter-meetings of his reign to lash out against those companions whose loyalty and devotion to him were not all he desired. At the Chapter held in Bruges in 1468, less than a year after his accession, Charles not only had Count Jean of Nevers expelled for treason, but accused Antoine and Jean de Croy and their nephew Jean de Lannoy of saying insulting things about him, procuring a false horoscope to convince his father of his bad character, promising King Louis of France not to allow Charles and his father to be reconciled, attempting after Duke Philippe's death to take Boulogne, Namur, and Luxemburg from Charles himself, and allying themselves with the traitorous Count of Nevers. He similarly had Henrik van Borselen, Lord of Veere, accused of accepting an office and pension from King Louis, his archenemy, and ordered to return those favours. Other companions received a more personal form of criticism from their fellows at this Chapter, with or without ducal urging. Charles' own half-brother, Antoine Bastard of Burgundy, though praised for his 'valour, prowess and prudence, and several other good habits and virtues', was severely reproved for his open fornication and adultery, which were unworthy of a Christian knight. Charles himself did not escape the Chapter unscathed. The companions, after extolling in a most obsequious fashion 'the most noble virtues, good sense, generosity, prudence, valour, and prowess of his person', ventured rather hesitantly to criticize him for speaking too sharply to his servants, becoming too emotional when talking about other princes, working too hard and thus endangering his health, oppressing his subjects with military exactions, breaking his pledged word, and failing to end his wars as quickly as possible. Charles replied to all these charges with his usual belligerence, but submitted to criticism again at the next Chapter, and heard the same complaints expressed in more elaborate terms. The minutes record that the Emperor Karl V still submitted to the criticism of the knights of the Golden Fleece in the middle of the next century.

The minutes of the Chapters also record attempts by the Order to end disputes among its members, just as the statutes required. After hearing charges made against the Dukes of Guelders and Cleves of warring on one another in 1468, the assembled companions resolved to send the registrar of the Order with one of their

---

[126] See, for example, the illumination at the head of the 'second book' of the Order, now designated Brussels, Bibliothèque royale de Belgique, ms. no 9027–9028.

[127] The original is preserved in the Archiv des Ordens vom Goldenem Vliesse, Vienna. Its contents are summarized in Reiffenberg, op. cit., passim.

number to order the two dukes to conclude a truce immediately and either appear in person before the Sovereign as soon as possible or be summoned to appear before the next Chapter to answer for their failure to do so. Similar attempts at reconciliation were made at other Chapters, not always with notable success.

The companions also discussed more general political matters at the Chapter meetings, and on rare occasions issued joint declarations or resolutions. In 1456, for example, they sent a joint letter to King Charles VII of France on the subject of a crusade which Duke Philippe hoped to lead.[128] Such declarations seem to have been both rare and ineffectual, however, and there is no evidence that the Order as such played an important role in either the internal or the external affairs of the Burgundian commonwealth.

10 The Habits of the Companions

During certain of the activities of the Assembly, including the Chapter, the knights of the Golden Fleece were required to wear a formal costume or habit. Not surprisingly, since the Order of the Collar had no peculiar habit until 1518, the habit of the Order of the Golden Fleece seems to have been based primarily on that of the Garter, but certain details may have been borrowed from the habits both of the Order of the Jar and of the defunct Company of the Star. Like the habit of the Garter, that of the Golden Fleece consisted until 1473 of a mantle and *chaperon* only, the garments worn underneath the mantle being undefined in the statutes.[129] The statutes specify only that both mantle and *chaperon* were to be made of red cloth-of-scarlet, and that the mantle was to be floor-length, lined in *menu-vair*, and decorated with a rich border composed of *fusils*, flints, sparks, and fleeces. Not only the colour, fabric, and lining of this mantle, but its cut and the manner of its wearing were identical to those of the Company of the Star; unlike the mantle of the Garter, which was by 1430 certainly worn with the opening at the front and tied at the neck with long cords, that of the Golden Fleece was worn with the opening at the right side, and the two sides were sewn together from the neck-opening to the point of the right shoulder. This was in keeping with contemporary French fashion, but in combination with the decorative and symbolic border which took the place of the single badge embroidered on the breast of the Garter mantle (a feature possibly borrowed from the mantle of the knights of the Jar) it gave the whole habit an appearance very different from that of the Garter habit, and this may well have influenced its design. If one may judge by the representations of the Chapter statutorily prefixed to the statutes in most manuscripts, the *chaperon* was always worn in the form of a hat, with a fashionable roundlet inserted to give it the appearance of a sort of turban. Because of this its borders were not normally edged in gold embroidery, and it merely relected the red colour of the mantle. From 1431 to 1473 the mantles and *chaperons* were always made of the materials initially specified, but at the Chapter held in the latter year, Charles 'the Rash' decreed that thenceforth they should be made of crimson velvet

---

[128] See Vaughan, *Philip the Good*, p. 172.
[129] Ch. 25b.

lined with white satin – the fabrics of which the Garter mantles had by this time come to be made. The gold-embroidered border of the mantle, which statutorily contained the various elements of the Order's collar, also on occasion contained the personal motto of the Sovereign. Under Philippe 'the Good' this was *Aultre n'aray* ('I shall have no other'), adopted on the occasion of his wedding and the proclamation of the Order, and equally applicable to both wife and Order.[130] Charles 'the Rash' adopted the more cryptic motto *Je l'ay emprins* ('I have undertaken it'), sometimes expanded with the phrase *Bien en advienne* ('May it come out well').[131] The Order itself, however, had no verbal *devise*.

Like the knights of the Knot, but unlike those of either the Garter or the Collar, the knights of the Golden Fleece always had a second habit, consisting of a black mantle and *chaperon*, for wear during the Order's more somber functions: specifically the vigil and requiem for the dead held during the course of each Assembly.[132] The regular red habits were worn, like the equivalent habits of the Garter, while taking part in any other formal activity associated with the Order,[133] with the single exception of the extra mass of the Virgin, at which they could dress as they pleased.[134] In both orders of dress, the collar of the Order seems to have been worn over the mantle, in keeping with the requirement that it be worn at all times in public. This practice was later imitated by the Orders of St Michael, the Garter, and the Collar.

Unlike the statutes of all the earlier orders we have studied except those that survived in 1430, the statutes of the Golden Fleece did not at first specify what garments were to be worn by the knights under the formal mantle. It appears from the surviving representations of the first Chapter that the knights normally wore a full-length *houppelande* or gown with simple tubular sleeves under their mantle. Sometimes this garment was of the same colour as the mantle, but frequently it was of whatever colour the individual companion chose. In 1473, Charles 'the Rash' not only decreed that the gown worn under the regular mantle was thenceforth to be of crimson velvet, but established a third order of dress for the companions, consisting of a gown of white damask and a *chaperon* of crimson velvet, for wear during the mass of the Virgin.[135] He also decreed that thenceforth the regular habit of the companions (which they had been required to pay for themselves until that time)[136] was to be provided by the Sovereign at his own expense.

---

[130] See Vaughan, *Philip the Good*, p. 172.
[131] See, for example, the illumination cited above in n. 126. See Deuchler, loc. cit.
[132] Ch. 27a,c.
[133] Chs. 25a,b, 26a, 29d.
[134] Ch. 28a.
[135] Ch. 28a, amended.
[136] Ch. 25b.

11 The Officers of the Order

When the Chapter was not in session, the business of the Order was conducted in the usual fashion by the Sovereign assisted by the Order's four officers, who were all required to swear to do their office properly and secretly.[137] Of the earlier foundations, only the Garter had been provided with regular corporate officers – consisting by 1430 of a Prelate, a Registrar, a Keeper of the Seal, and a King of Arms. The four officers Philippe attached to the Order of the Golden Fleece (and whose qualifications and functions he defined with characteristic and unprecedented thoroughness in the second division of the revised statutes of 1445) corresponded only approximately to those of his model.

The *Chancellier* or Chancellor of the Golden Fleece seems to have combined in his office the status of the Prelate with the function of the Keeper of the Seal of the English order, for, being 'of great responsibility', the office was reserved to prelates and doctors of theology or law. The Chancellor was to keep the common seal of the Order in a locked coffer, and was not to apply it to any document touching the honour of any companion except by the express command of the Sovereign in the presence of six other companions. He was also to preside over the examination and election of the companions, to audit the accounts of the Treasurer during each Assembly, and to act as the spokesman of the Sovereign or his Deputy during the Chapter.[138]

The *Tresorier* or Treasurer performed some of the functions of the Dean of the Garter canons, but his office was probably modelled on the equivalent officer of collegiate churches and confraternities. He was to have the keeping of all the Order's 'charters, privileges, orders, writings, muniments, and acts' and of its 'jewels, relics, ecclesiastical adornments and vestments, tapestries, and library' (all of which he was to display during every Assembly). He was further to keep the mantles of the Sovereign and companions, and to set up and remove the armorial panels of the companions in the Order's chapel. He was to have control over both the income and expenditures of the Order, to keep proper records of both, and to render an account of all his actions at each meeting of the Chapter. He was also to send a notarized copy of every document pertaining to the Order both to the Order's chapel and to the *Trésor de Chartres* of Burgundy. Finally, he was to read out a list of all the order's benefactors at each Chapter, so that the companions might pray for them.[139]

Unlike the Registrar of the Garter, who was always a canon of St George's, the *Greffier* or Registrar of the Golden Fleece was to be either a prebendary of the Order's chapel or some other 'notable and able clerk', either clerical or lay. In addition to keeping two copies of the Order's statutes (one for the chapel and one for the chapter house) and to recording the proceedings of the Chapters in the fashion of the equivalent Garter officer, he was also charged with maintaining a record of all the 'laudable and honourable deeds' of the companions, as reported to

[137] Ch. 19.
[138] Chs. O.2–O.6.
[139] Chs. O.7–O.11.

him by the Order's fourth officer, the King of Arms.[140] Thus the founder of the Golden Fleece revived the romantic custom of keeping a book of deeds, common to the defunct orders of the Star, the Knot, and the Ship, from the first of which he may possibly have borrowed the idea.

The King of Arms, who was responsible for collecting the information for this book, was also charged with bearing the Order's messages. In most respects his office (like his title *Thoison d'Or*) was based directly on that of Garter King of Arms, and like Garter he was made the chief heraldic officer of all his lord's dominions as well as of the Order to which he was particularly attached. The Sovereign was to give him an enamelled badge (*esmail*) bearing the ducal arms, which he was to wear throughout his life.[141]

Whenever any of the four offices fell vacant through death or resignation, it was to be filled by an election involving the Sovereign and at least six companions held in the presence of the other officers, and the person chosen to fill the office was to be informed of his election and received into it if he accepted it in very much the way the companions themselves were informed and received.[142] It is not clear to what extent these procedures were followed in practice, but all four offices have been filled almost continuously from the first meeting of the Chapter to the present day.[143] Like the Prelates and later the Chancellors of the Order of the Garter, the first five Chancellors of the Order of the Golden Fleece were all bishops, but the statutes did not require episcopal status, and the sixth Chancellor, elected in 1504, resigned his office to take the bishopric of Autun. Fittingly enough, the six Treasurers of the Order in our period were all prominent financial officers of the Burgundian dukes, while most of the six Registrars were ducal secretaries. The three Kings of Arms in our period were all well-educated minor vassals of the Dukes of Burgundy who had served as heralds before being promoted to the highest office in their profession in the Burgundian dominions.

According to the statutes, the officers of the Order were obliged to provide themselves with habits suitable for wear at the various functions in which they had to take part. The habit of the officers was not formally defined in the earliest versions of the statutes, but it appears from the representations of the first Chapter of the Order that until 1473 the Treasurer and Registrar attended that function, at least, dressed in a habit very similar to that of the companions, consisting of a plain red mantle worn open at the right over an *houppelande*, and a sugarloaf hat instead of a *chaperon*. The Chancellor seems to have worn his episcopal vestments on these occasions, including a cope and mitre, while the King of Arms seems to have worn only a simple *houppelande* or even a short *cote-hardie*. At the Chapter held in 1473, however, Charles 'the Rash' declared that thenceforth all four officers were to wear habits which (except for the absence of a border around the mantle) were to be exactly like those worn by the companions, and that all three forms of habit were to be provided to each officer at the time of his induction.

---

[140] Chs. O.12–O.14.

[141] Chs. O.15–O.17.

[142] Chs. O.18–O.28.

[143] A complete list of the Order's officers, with short biographies, is given in F. Koller, *Au service de la Toison d'or (les officiers)*, (Dison, Belgium, 1971).

12 Conclusions: The Order of the Golden Fleece

We must now attempt to answer the final questions: What was the Order of the Golden Fleece? What functions did its founder intend it to perform? and How well did it perform them? There can be no doubt that (despite borrowings from other sources) the Order of the Golden Fleece was essentially a Burgundian version of the Order of the Garter, for its structure and activities bore a close resemblance to those of the latter order. Like its English model, it was a co-optive corporate society of a specific and relatively small number of well-born lay knights, organized on the constitutional model of a confraternity, with an hereditary 'Sovereign', four corporate officers, a corporate seal, a corporate chapel in which each knight had his own stall marked with his arms, and a college of canons initially equal in number to the knights, whose principal function was to offer up prayers and masses on the knights' behalf. It was also intended to have a college of 'poor knights' like that of the Garter, though this was never established. Like the 'companions' of the Garter, the 'companions' of the Golden Fleece owed certain obligations both to their 'Sovereign' and to each other both in life and after death, and initially met every year on the feast day of their patron saint in an 'Assembly' which constituted their only corporate activity, and which consisted of a 'Chapter', a banquet, and several religious services.

Despite these points of resemblance – too numerous to be the result of coincidence – the Order of the Golden Fleece was not a mere replica of the Order of the Garter. On the contrary, it differed from its principal model in a number of significant ways. In the first place, its Sovereign, while retaining a greater influence than any other member in the affairs of the Order, had far less formal control over the election of both members and officers than the Garter Sovereign, and was in general treated more like the other companions. Secondly, the companions of the Golden Fleece, while owing a much smaller number of purgatorial masses, owed much more significant military and political obligations both to their Sovereign and to one another than the companions of the Garter, and had to submit to a much more rigorous examination of their conduct during each Chapter. Finally, while the companions of the Garter always met annually at the chapel of their patron saint, those of the Golden Fleece met irregularly, at times and places convenient to the Sovereign, and paid relatively little attention to the chapel or cult of their heavenly patron. The general effect of these changes was to de-emphasize the religious elements which the Order of the Garter had taken on with its confraternal format in favour of the more pragmatic political elements of retaining and fraternity-in-arms.

The alteration of emphasis was due to Philippe's rather different purpose in creating a monarchical order, and is indeed the principal indication of what that purpose was. Where Edward of England had wanted merely to reward knightly prowess, to increase his own prestige, and to cement the generally good relations that he enjoyed with his principal commanders, Philippe – who certainly shared those goals – clearly had more practical objects in mind as well. He wanted not only prestige but loyalty and service from his 'companions', and was willing to provide adequate compensation in exchange. It appears that he also wanted to use the Order as an organ to unite the separate and formerly antagonistic nobilities of his numerous principalities in bonds of mutual fraternity, and to create what amounted to a peerage of the Burgundian state as a whole. Of the earlier founders, Edward of England had been virtually alone in having no need to promote either loyalty or unity, and Philippe was forced both to borrow from other sources and to invent freely in order to seek these ends. Like his ancestor Jean 'the Good' of France, Philippe also wanted to promote chivalrous behaviour and to exalt the status of knight, and provided elaborate mechanisms to accomplish these ends wholly lacking in the primitive statutes of the Garter.

As usual, it is very difficult to judge the true effectiveness of the Order in accomplishing the goals for which it was founded. Although most of its members did indeed serve Duke Philippe and his heirs quite faithfully, it is not clear that they did so in obedience to their oaths as companions, and as we have seen, a number of companions – especially those who were not subjects of the Burgundian dukes – paid little attention to the obligations they had undertaken on joining the Order when those obligations conflicted with their own political interests. Furthermore, while many of the companions exercised considerable influence in the internal affairs of the Burgundian dominions, this was primarily because the dukes tended to secure the election to the Order of those closest to them, rather than because they found that those who happened to be elected to the Order were exceptionally trustworthy. Recent historians of Burgundy have been inclined to minimize the political significance of the Order as such, largely on the grounds that its very restricted membership prevented its Sovereigns from influencing more than a handful of persons at any time.[144] It could not even accomodate all those of importance in the central government of the Burgundian commonwealth: of the twenty-nine members of the ducal council enumerated in a household *ordonnance* of 1438, only ten (albeit ten of the most influential) were also members of the Order.[145] The Order was too small and had too many barons and princes among its members for it to be of much use as an élite bodyguard for the duke or as a unit of the field army, and although the very preponderance of barons and princes might have made it useful for recruiting troops, I have found no evidence that it was ever employed in this way.

The very limitation on membership, however, combined with the policy of promoting the election of counts, princes, and even kings which the dukes maintained throughout our period, gave the Order an immense and international prestige, which naturally reflected back both on the Sovereign and on the companions individually. In a period in which formal honours were increasingly valued by the members of most Western Christian nobilities as a sign of status within their social estate, membership in the Order of the Golden Fleece came to be coveted and sought after by many princes of middle rank, and far from despised even by kings and emperors. Henry VII of England even had his portrait painted wearing the collar of the Order, rather than that of his own order of the Garter.[146] The succession of the Order's fifth Sovereign, Duke Charles II, to the thrones of

---

[144] See for example Vaughan, *Philip the Good*, pp. 162, 172.

[145] Ibid., p. 172.

[146] The portrait, attributed to Master Michiel Sitium, is now in the National Portrait Gallery. A photograph of it was published by the Royal Academy of Arts in *Kings and Queens AD 635–1953* (London? 1953?), p. 14.

the Spains and the Sicilies in 1516 removed the difficulties that had inevitably arisen from the fact that the head of the Order was a mere duke, for thenceforth its Sovereigns were not only kings but kings of many rich kingdoms. That Charles even as Emperor continued to regard membership in the Order as one of the highest dignities within his disposal is surely an indication of the esteem in which the the Order had come to be held by the time of his accession, as well as a sign of the continuing usefulness of the Order as a political instrument.

The usefulness of the Order in the sixteenth century, however, seems to have had little to do with its elaborate statutes or even with its magnificent ceremonies (by then seldom held). It lay, rather, in its value as a symbol of royal favour. It was at least partly in recognition of this fact that its sixth Sovereign, Felipe II of Spain, ceased to hold the statutory Assemblies and elections after 1559, and converted the Order from a true fraternity to a mere dignity, entirely at the disposal of its 'Sovereign'. It was in this form, wholly different from the form given to it by its founder, that the 'Order' survived thereafter. As a true monarchical order the Order of the Golden Fleece survived only to 1559.

Chapter 14

The Order of the Ermine
Mainland Sicily (Naples), 1465–1494/1501

1 Princely Orders Founded between 1430 and 1465

The romantic revival of chivalry promoted by the Dukes of Burgundy spread throughout much of Western Christendom during the first decades of the fifteenth century, and its effects persisted well into the following century. One aspect of this revival was a renewed interest among the greater princes in true orders of knighthood, and it can hardly be doubted that the various orders founded by princes in the decades between 1430 and 1470 were inspired (like the chapters added to the statutes of the existing order of the Collar in January 1434)[1] by the foundation in the former year of the Order of the Golden Fleece.

Only one new princely order is known to have been founded in the 1430s – the Society of the Eagle, established as we have seen by Albrecht von Habsburg, Duke of Austria, in 1433 – but no fewer than four were certainly founded between 1440 and 1450: the *Selschapp unser Liuen Frowen* or 'Society of Our Lady' (commonly known as the Order of the Swan), established in 1440 by Friedrich II von Hohenzollern, Elector-Marquis of Brandenburg;[2] the *St. Hubertus-Orden* or 'Order of St Hubert', created in 1444 by Gerhard V von Hengebach, Duke of Jülich and Berg and Count of Ravensberg;[3] the *Ordre du Croissant* or 'Order of the Crescent', founded in 1448 by René I Capet de Valois-Anjou, 'the Good', sometime (and still

---

[1] See above, p. 258.

[2] Statutes in Rudolf Graf von Stillfried, *Der Schwanenorden: Seine Ursprung und Zweck, seine Geschichte, und seine Alterthümer* (n.t.p., 18??), pp. 29–41. Studies of its early history are to be found in that work and in Theodor Däschlein, *Die Schwanenorden und die sogenannte Schwanenordens-Ritter-Kappelle in Ansbach* (Ansbach, 1927). The members of this order wore an elaborate collar composed of instruments of torture holding hearts, from which depended first an effigy of the Virgin seated on a crescent moon and then, below that, a swan set in an annulet of cloth.

[3] Statutes published by T. J. Lacomblet in *Archiv für die Geschichte des Niederrheins* (7 vols., Dusseldorf, 1832–), I, pp. 400–403. According to M. Gritzner, *Handbuch der Ritter- und Verdienstorden* (Leipzig, 1893), p. 15, the statutes were first given by Gerhard's son Wilhelm IV in 1476. The members of this order wore a collar composed of hunting-horns (an attribute of St Hubert) bound by love-knots. A list of its members with illustrations of their arms has been preserved in Munich, Staatsbibliothek, cod. icon. 318. See Lorenz Rheude, 'Das Bruderschaftsbuch des St. Hubertus-Ordens', *Das Herold* (1915), p. 31.

titular) King of mainland Sicily, Duke of Anjou, Lorraine, and Bar, and Count of Provence and Maine;[4] and the Society of St Jerome, established in 1450 by Friedrich II von Wettin, 'the Mild', Elector-Duke of Saxony, Marquis of Meissen, and Landgrave of Thuringia (the brother-in-law of the Emperor Friedrich III).[5] Although all of these orders resembled that of the Golden Fleece in having elaborate statutes designed to promote knightly conduct, the first three were certainly and the fourth probably confraternal rather than monarchical in nature. Why their founders should have shied away from giving them hereditary presidencies is unclear, especially as all four orders seem to have been closely associated with their founder's court, and the Order of the Crescent was endowed with a constitution which resembled that of the Golden Fleece in most other respects. Like Philippe 'the Good' of Burgundy, all four of the founders were subordinate but effectively independent princes of the Empire of the highest rank: three were dukes, and three prince-electors of the Empire. Indeed, by 1450 all four of the electoral dynasties of Germany (the houses of Wittelsbach, Hohenzollern, Wettin, and Habsburg) had created an order of some sort (though the Wittelsbach Order of St Anthony, founded in 1384, was not conspicuously knightly).[6]

The wave of romantic enthusism for chivalry that gave rise to these orders was followed by a period of fifteen years in which only one new order of any sort seems to have been created by a Christian prince – the Confraternity of the Virgin Mary or Order of the Elephant, probably proclaimed in 1457 by Christian I von Oldenburg, King of Denmark, Norway, and Sweden – but the five years from 1465 to 1470 witnessed the creation of at least four new orders, all of which were also

[4] Statutes published by the Comte de Quatrebarbes in *Les Oeuvres complètes du bon roi René* (Paris, 1845), pp. 51–79; studies in Emile Perrier, *Les chevaliers du Croissant: Essai historique et héraldique* (Vannes, 1906); Jacques Levron, *Le bon roi René* (Paris, 1972), pp. 161–70; and M. G. A. Vale, *War and Chivalry* (Athens, Georgia, 1981), pp. 51–62. The knights of this order, which was dedicated to St Maurice, wore a curious badge in the form of a gold crescent about a foot long bearing the motto *Loz en croissant*, with a crescent of mail, silver above and gold below, dependent from it. This was worn suspended under the right upper arm, as if it were a piece of armour for the armpit. The device is clearly represented in the manuscript of the life and passion of St Maurice sent by the Venetian general Jacopo Marcello to Jehan Cossa, Seneschal of Provence, in 1453. See J. J. G. Alexander, *Italian Renaissance Illuminations* (New York, 1977), pp. 54–9.

[5] On this order see Paul Ganz, 'Die Abzeichen der Ritterorden', AHS, (1906), p. 57. According to Ganz, the members of this society, based in a church in Meissen, were obliged to defend the Church. They wore a collar bearing the words *O wie gross ist der Glaube, den der h. Jeronimus gelert hat und gepredigt*, from which depended a representation of a cardinal's hat whose cords were partially obscured by a lion passant – the attributes of St Jerome. A representation of this device appears in Conrad Grünenberg's *Wappenbuch* next to the arms of the Elector-Duke of Saxony.

[6] On this order, founded by Albrecht I, Duke of Bavaria at Straubing and Count of Holland and Zeeland, (fifth son of the Emperor Ludwig V), see Camille Enlart, *Manuel d'archéologie française* (Paris, 1916), III, pp. 405–6; and Ganz, 'Die Abzeichen', pp. 54–5. It is often confused with the religious order of St Anthony based in the Dauphiné of Viennois. What is presumed to be the collar of the Wittelsbach order, a pilgrim's belt with a pendant T-cross and bell, was depicted on the statue of Jean, Duke of Brabant, in Amsterdam, and in the portrait painted by Jan van Eyck of Johann III von Wittelsbach, Bishop of Liege, third son of the founder, who died in 1425.

founded by kings: the *Ordine del Arminio* or 'Order of the Ermine', founded by Ferrante d'Ivrea-Bourgogne-Trastámara-Aragón-Sicilia, King of mainland Sicily, in 1465; the *Ritterorden St. Jörgens* or 'Knightly Order of St George', founded by the Emperor Friedrich III von Habsburg in 1468 and confirmed by the Pope on 1 January 1469;[7] the *Ordre Monsieur Saint Michel Archange* or 'Order of My Lord St Michael the Archangel', founded by Louis XI Capet de Valois, King of France, in 1469; and the Order of St Andrew, or of the Thistle, probably founded by James III Stewart, King of Scots, in or shortly after 1470.[8] Of these five societies, the third was a religious order, whose members had to take an oath of chastity and obedience, and the last was almost certainly a cliental pseudo-order. The first may well have been a monarchical order, however, and the other two certainly were, at least in intention. I shall therefore examine each of these orders in turn.

2 The Confraternity of the Virgin Mary or Order of the Elephant: Denmark, Norway, and Sweden, 1457?–1523?

Very little seems to be known about the early history of the Danish (or Scandinavian) confraternity of the Virgin Mary, more commonly known to historians as the Order of the Elephant.[9] The founder, Christian I – whose ancestors had been nothing more than Counts of Oldenburg in northern Germany

[7] On the history of this order, see especially Joseph von Bergmann, 'Der St. Georgs-Ritterorden vom Jahre 1469–1579', *Mitteilungen der k.k. Central-Commission zur Erforschung und Erhaltung der Bandenkmale* 13 (Vienna, 1868), pp. 169–74. The device of this order, based in Millstatt, is commonly said to have been an effigy of St George slaying the dragon, pendant from a shield of the arms of the saint, often set into a quatrefoil. (See Ganz, 'Die Abzeichen', p. 53.)

[8] On the history of this order, long believed to have been founded by Achaius King of the Picts, and since its revivals in 1687 and 1703 (with true monarchical constitutions) the principal order of Scotland, see Sir Thomas Innes of Learney, Lord Lyon King of Arms, 'The Foundation of the Most Ancient and Most Noble Order of the Thistle', *Ordenskunde, Beiträge zur Geschichte der Auszeichnungen* 11 (Berlin, 1959), pp. 84–90; and Charles Burnett, 'Reflections on the Order of the Thistle', *The Double Tressure, Journal of the Heraldry Society of Scotland* 5 (1983), pp. 39–42. Burnett postulates that the Order may have had its origin in the 'Ordre de la Licorne' given by James III to the Flemish knight Sir Anselme Adornes, but in all likelihood the unicorn was an independent livery-badge which James conferred in the usual way both before and after his foundation of the order, and was called an 'ordre' just because that term was commonly used to describe princely badges in the fifteenth century.

[9] Although this Order is still the principal order of the crown of Denmark, very little seems to have been written about its early history. See Louis Bobé and the Arthur Jensens Forlag, *De Kongelige Danske Ridderordener og Medailler* (Copenhagen, 1950), I, pp. 11–16; P. J. Jørgensen, *Danish Orders and Medals* (Copenhagen, 1964), p. 15; Paul Hieronymussen, *Orders and Decorations in Europe* (London, New York, 1967), p. 145; and Arnaud Chaffanjon, *Les grands ordres de chevalerie* (Paris, 1969), pp. 261–76. The last is the most detailed account, and is the only one supported by citation of the primary sources. Unfortunately, Chaffanjon does not indicate the location of any of the sources he cites, and I have been unable to consult copies of any of them.

– had been elected to the throne of Denmark on the death of the childless king Christoffer III von Wittelsbach in 1448, and had consolidated his position by marrying the latter's widow, Dorothee von Hohenzollern. Shortly after that, he had secured election to the throne of Norway as well, and in 1457 he finally acquired the last of Christoffer's three crowns, that of Sweden. There is evidence to suggest that it was during the festivities that surrounded his coronation in Stockholm in the latter year that Christian first distributed the collar of what was to become the Order of the Elephant, though the form of the collar in this period is unknown.[10] What is presumed to be the same collar is mentioned as pertaining to a 'confraternity of the Virgin Mary' in a bull sent by Pope Sixtus IV to King Christian on 20 April 1474 and in a letter of indulgence issued in his favour on 14 January 1478.[11] The confraternity itself is first mentioned in the charter issued by Christian himself on 9 October 1464 by which he provided a clerical establishment for a chapel that he had just had built in the Cathedral Church of Roskilde just west of Copenhagen, apparently to serve as the seat of the confraternity, and that charter seems to be the principal surviving evidence for the nature of the order in the fifteenth century. According to this document, the chapel, dedicated to St Anne, the Holy Trinity, the Virgin Mary, and the Three Kings, was to be served by one canon and two vicars, who were say four masses every day at three altars, for the king, the queen, their children, and all those 'who wear the decoration of the confraternity and have worn it'. The charter also specifies that the members of the confraternity, whose number was limited to fifty, were to follow the mass with care, to give to charity, and to have their collar returned to the chapel after their death, along with the sum of five florins for the divine service.[12]

All of this suggests that the Confraternity of the Virgin Mary was indeed a monarchical order, though in the absence of the statutes of the society itself it is impossible to be sure that it had either an hereditary president or any formal association with knighthood. It does not seem to have been modelled very closely on the Order of the Golden Fleece (which had more priests and fewer lay members, and did not admit women), and as its founder's wife was the niece of the founder of the confraternity commonly called the Order of the Swan, which was also dedicated to the Virgin, it is possible that that society served as a model. In any case, it seems to have functioned like a monarchical order, for according to a letter written in 1538 by Ove Bilde, Bishop of Aahus, to Hans Friis, the chancellor of the founder's grandson Christian III, both the founder and his son Hans (who succeeded him in 1481 and reigned until 1513) wore the collar of the society themselves throughout their lives, and distributed it not merely to 'lords, princes, knights, gentlemen, ladies, and damsels of noble birth', but to such foreign kings as Henry VIII of England and James V of Scotland, and to the envoys of these and other princes who came to their court.[13] There is apparently some evidence that Hans' son Christian II continued to distribute the collar of the Elephant during the

---

[10] According to Chaffanjon, Les Grands Ordres, p. 272, it is mentioned in a diploma issued to Eduardo Giustiani in 1457 and a letter of King Christian sent to the 'prince' of Mantua (presumably Lodovico III Gonzaga, second Marquis) in 1462.

[11] Ibid., p. 266.

[12] Ibid., pp. 266–7.

[13] Ibid., pp. 271–3.

14.1 The effigy of King Hans, wearing the collar of the Elephant, 1513

first years of his troubled reign, at least,[14] but after his overthrow by his cousin Frederik (I) in 1523 the confraternity seems to have fallen victim to the Lutheran reform, and the collar does not seem to have been conferred again until 1580, when it was revived (in a much simplified form) by Frederik II.

According to Bilde, the device of the confraternity was an elephant set within a crown of thorns pierced with three nails, but there is no direct evidence for the elephant device before 1508, when the future Christian II granted to the office of Provost of the Cathedral of Roskilde a shield of arms whose principal charge was an elephant with a tower on its back.[15] The earliest representation of the collar itself – and indeed the only one certainly contempory with the existence of the confraternity – seems to be that on the tomb effigy of King Hans, set up after his death in 1513 in the Church of St Knud in Odense.[16] The king is there portrayed wearing a collar made up of pairs of elephants-with-towers set head-to-head, alternating with what appear to be spurs. From this depends a round medallion bearing an image of the Virgin and Child. In all likelihood this was the form taken by the collar from the time of its first distribution in 1457, for no other comparable

---

[14] Hieronymussen, *Orders*, p. 145.
[15] Chaffanjon, *Grands Ordres*, pp. 265, 267–9.
[16] Reproduced in Bobé, *Ridderordener*, p. 12.

collar is known to have changed much in our period once its form was established. The significance of the elephant has long puzzled historians, since the beast has no obvious association with any part of Scandinavia, but it was probably adopted (like the griffin of the Aragonese order) as a symbol of strength, or because elephants were said in the bestiary to be enemies of dragons, and the dragon was a symbol of Satan.

3 The Order of the Ermine: Historical Background

The Order of the Ermine (not to be confused with the Breton order of exactly the same name and dedication founded in 1380) was the last of a long series of knightly orders founded in our period by the occupants and claimants to the throne of the mainland Kingdom of Sicily. As we have seen, following the apparent dissolution of the Order of the Ship in 1386, Carlo's widow Margherita and their son Ladislao seem to have founded the *Compangnia dell'Argata* or 'Company of the Spool' in 1388, immediately after their flight from the kingdom. Both the nature and the history of this 'company' are obscure, but it is at least possible that it was introduced into Naples when Ladislao finally regained his father's throne in 1399, and that it was maintained by him until his premature death in 1414. I have found no evidence of the existence of any order in the court of Naples during the reign of his sister Giovanna II, however, so this 'company' may well have been as short-lived as its immediate predecessor. Giovanna had been married to Duke Wilhelm 'the Affable' of Austria (who as we have seen was a knight of the Salamander), but he had died without issue in 1406, and shortly after succeeding to the throne she had married a cadet of the ducal house of Bourbon, Count Jacques of La Marche. He was only given the style Vicar General and Duke of Calabria, however, and the kingdom was effectively governed throughout Giovanna's reign by a succession of her favourites and lovers. Since Giovanna, the last of her house, was forty-five and childless when she came to the throne, both Alfons 'the Magnanimous' of Aragon and island Sicily and Duke Louis III of Anjou had high hopes of being named her heir, but Louis, whom she personally favoured, died fighting a war she had provoked in November 1434, and when Giovanna herself finally died two months later, on 2 February 1435, she bequeathed her lands to Louis' brother and successor as Duke of Anjou and Count of Provence, René 'the Good', already Duke of Lorraine and Bar.

René was duly proclaimed king, but when he was found to have been imprisoned not long before by his cousin Duke Philippe 'the Good' of Burgundy (who claimed the Duchy of Lorraine), his rival Alfons quickly sent an army to seize the kingdom by force. Although René finally arrived in Naples in 1438, he was forced to fight Alfons' forces continuously until 2 June 1442, when he finally withdrew in despair to Provence. In a Parliament held at Benevento Alfons 'the Magnanimous' was duly proclaimed king with succession to his illegitimate son Ferran or Ferrando (generally known in Italian as Ferrante), and entered Naples in a neo-classical triumph in February 1443. He ruled there (as Alfonso I) until his death on 7 June 1458, and although René of Anjou attempted a new invasion in 1453 (five years after founding the Order of the Crescent), Alfons retained effective control of the kingdom throughout this period. Like Roberto 'the Wise' a century earlier, Alfons had a genuine passion for both learning and splendour, and attempted to draw the turbulent barons of his kingdom to the seat of royal power by maintaining a brilliant court. As we noted above, Alfons introduced into Naples and its kingdom the Order of the Stole and Jar, founded by his father, which thus became the fourth order maintained by a *de facto* King of mainland Sicily.

Alfons died without legitimate issue, leaving most of his possessions to his younger brother Joan, already King of Navarre, but in keeping with the proclamation of 1442, the crown of Naples was allowed to pass to his legitimated bastard Ferrante (born in 1423), who had been married to the niece of his father's principal supporter, Giannantonio Orsini, Prince of Taranto, and had already begun to assume the reigns of government.[17] Unfortunately, Ferrante's succession was not recognized by Pope Calixtus III, overlord of the kingdom, and he was immediately forced to beat back an attempt by his agnatic cousin Carlos, Prince of Viana (elder son of his uncle King Joan), to seize the throne. In this contest Ferrante managed to secure the support of most of the barons, and after Calixtus' death in August 1458 was recognized by his successor Pius II (who was well disposed towards him). Then his wife's uncle the Prince of Taranto and his brother-in-law the Duke of Sessa (who had married his sister), evidently resentful of the centralizing policies of his house, entered into negotiations with Jean, titular Duke of Calabria – the son of Ferrante's other rival, René of Anjou – and in October 1459 Jean's army landed with their aid on the northwestern coast of the kingdom. Almost immediately most of the baronage rose up against Ferrante, and for the next five years the country was torn by a vicious civil war, in which Ferrante was consistently supported only by the Pope, by Alessandro Sforza of Pesaro, younger brother of the Duke of Milan, (whose son and daughter had been married to Ferrante's daughter and son), by Cosimo de' Medici of Florence, and by Federigo da Montefeltro of Urbino (who married Sforza's daughter). After a decisive victory at Troia in the autumn of 1462, however, Ferrante convinced both Taranto and Sessa to return to obedience, and by 1464 the Angevins had once again been forced to withdraw.

For the next twenty-one years Ferrante ruled from Naples with an iron hand, treating anyone who opposed him with merciless severity. Indeed, despite promises of amnesty, he had many of the leaders of the rebel forces in the recent civil war (including Sessa) arrested and summarily executed, and in general kept his word to his barons only when it was expedient to do so. His behaviour was no worse than his situation called for, however, and he seems to have been a courageous captain as well as a capable ruler. He was also an important patron of humanistic arts and letters, and like his father maintained a brilliant court.

---

[17] On his reign, see Emilio Nunziante, 'I primi anni di Ferdinando d'Aragona e l'invasione di Giovanni d'Angio', *Archivo storico per le Provincie Napolitane* 18–23 (1892–98); and Ernesto Pontieri, *Per la storia del regno di Ferrante I d' Aragona re di Napoli* (Naples? 1947?).

4 The Foundation and History of the Order

It was in 1465, the year following his triumph over his enemies, that Ferrante proclaimed the foundation of the fifth monarchical order to be maintained in the court of Naples, the *Ordine dell'Arminio*. Although this order is mentioned in a number of contemporary documents, most of what is known about it is contained in its statutes, symbolically promulgated on 29 September, the feast of its celestial patron, the Archangel Michael.[18] Both the timing of the proclamation and the nature of the obligations imposed by the statutes suggest that Ferrante founded the order to secure the newly-won loyalty of his principal barons, and to reduce dissensions among them, but it can hardly be doubted that his decision to found a relatively elaborate knightly order was influenced by his own election to the Order of the Garter at some time between 1461 and 1463. Certainly the order he founded resembled the Garter much more than it did his father's very simple order of the Stole and Jar, to which he must have been admitted many years earlier. Curiously enough, Ferrante's order bore an even closer resemblance to the Order of the Golden Fleece, to which Ferrante was not elected until 1473.

Aside from the statutes, I have found only two contemporary documents that refer even obliquely to the Order of the Ermine. The first of these is a letter of Galeotto Carrafa, representative of the Marquis of Mantua at the court of Naples, written to his lord on 3 October 1474. In this letter, which describes the journey to the court of Burgundy of Ferrante's younger son 'lo Illustrissimo signor don Federico', Carafa declared that

> The said Illustrious Lord will bear the *enpresa de lo Armellino*, of which the Majesty of the Lord King was the founder, and which he will bear to the Duke of Burgundy, because the duke sent his own, that is, of the Fleece, to his aforesaid Majesty by one of his bastard brothers, . . .[19]

In an anonymous diary of the year 1487, the diarist recorded that 'In the same year, Signor Virginio Ursino received the *impresa* of the Lord King, the ermine, and that of the House of Aragon.'[20]

The only other evidence for the history of the Order that I have found is pictorial. The device of the ermine appears (along with several of the other devices

---

[18] Although this order was known to such early historians of knightly orders as Le Mire (who called it the Order of St Michael), Micheli Márquez, and Paca, very little of consequence has been written about it. The only works I have found that deal with it at any length are the Abbot di Blasi, 'Lettera intorno all'ordine dell'arminio', *Nuova Raccolta degli Auttori Siciliani* I (Palermo, 1788); and Giuseppe Maria Fusco, *Intorno all'Ordine dell' Armellino da Re Ferdinando I. d'Aragona all' Archangelo S. Michele Dedicato* (Naples, 1844), and *I Capitoli dell' Ordine dell'Armellino, messi a stampa con note* (Naples, 1845); the brief notice by D. L. Galbreath in his 'Deux ordres de chevalerie du moyen-âge', *AHS* (1927), pp. 24–5, is based largely on the early accounts, and passes on their mistakes.

[19] Mantua, Archivio di Stato, *Esteri*, XXIV, 3, published in Pontieri, *Per la storia*, pp. 69–70.

[20] Quoted in Fusco, *Intorno all'ordine*, p. 26, n. 3: 'Eodem anno [1487], il Signor Virginio Ursino pigliò la impresa del signor Re l'Armellino, e quello de casa de Aragona.'

14.2 The collar of the Ermine, as
represented in the Divine Comedy of
the Duke of Urbino
a. the whole collar   b. the links

14.3 The bust of King Ferrante in
the Church of Monteoliveto, Naples

14.4 The ermine device, as represented
a. in the Divine Comedy of the Duke of Urbino
b. on the doors of the Castle Nuovo, Naples
c. on the bust of King Ferrante

14.5 The flaming chair and sprouting stock, as represented
a. on the doors of the Castel Nuovo, Naples
b. on the bust of King Ferrante

405

used by Ferrante) on the title page of a manuscript prepared for Ferrante in 1471,[21] on that of another manuscript prepared for him in 1476,[22] on the bronze doors he had made in 1474–77 for the arch his father had inserted between the towers of the Castle Nuovo,[23] and on a number of coins bearing the founder's name and those of his son Alfonso II and his grandson Ferrante II.[24] Both the ermine device and the whole collar are represented in a manuscript of the *Divina Commedia* prepared for Federigo da Montefeltro, Duke of Urbino, in 1477 or 1478,[25] and (in a modified form) in the manuscript of the statutes of the Order issued in the Castel Nuovo (according to a statement on the last folio) on 15 April 1486,[26] and the founder was protrayed wearing yet another version of the collar in a bronze bust made for him by Guido Mazzoni between 1489 and 1492.[27]

The fact that a copy of the statutes was issued in April 1486 indicates that the Order of the Ermine was still maintained as a true monarchical order nearly twenty-one years after its foundation, and as Ferrante had no known reason to abandon it in the last eight years of his reign, and still wore its collar in this period, it is more than likely that it survived in that condition until his death in January 1494. Whether it survived much beyond that is another question, however, for although Ferrante was followed on his throne by his son Alfonso II, the latter, faced with an invasion by Charles VIII of France (to whose father Louis XI the last of the Angevin line had left his claim to Naples in 1481), abdicated in favour of his son Ferrante II, who was displaced in the same year by the victorious Charles. Ferrante succeeded in driving out the invaders in the summer of the following year, 1496, but died at the height of his triumph on 7 September, leaving the throne to his father's younger brother Federigo. Both Alfonso II and Ferrante II continued to display the ermine as a badge on their coins, which suggests that they maintained the Order in some form until the latter's deposition in 1495, but Federigo is not known to have displayed the ermine device, so the Order may well have dissolved during the brief reign of Charles VIII as Carlo IV of Sicily.[28] In any case, barely four years after his accession Federigo's agnatic cousin Ferran 'the Catholic' of Aragon concluded a treaty with the new King of France, Louis XII, by which the two rival claimants agreed to conquer the kingdom from Federigo, and divide it between them. On learning of Ferran's treachery following their joint invasion in 1501, the unfortuante Federigo surrendered to Louis, who had conquered the northern half of the kingdom, and went off into exile in France, leaving Louis and Ferran to fight

---

[21] Paris, B.N., ms. latin 12947, Andrea Contrario, *Reprehensio sive objuratio in calumniatorem divini Platonis*, f. 3; reproduced in *Dix siècles d'enluminature italienne (VIe–XVIe siècles)* (Paris, B.N., 1984), no. 154, pp. 174–6.

[22] Paris, B.N., ms. latin 12946, Bessarion, *Adversus Georgium Trapezuntium calumniatorem Platonis defensionum opus*; reproduced in ibid., no. 153, pp. 173–4.

[23] Reproduced in George L. Hersey, *The Aragonese Arch at Naples, 1443–1475* (New Haven and London, 1973), Pls. 57, 61, 62; commentary pp. 42–4.

[24] See Fusco, *Intorno all'Ordine*, p. 29 and passim.

[25] Rome, Biblioteca Apostolica Vaticana, ms. Urb. Lat. 365, ff. 1r, 97r; reproduced in J. J. G. Alexander, *Italian Renaissance Illuminations* (New York, 1977), Pls. 23, 25.

[26] London, B.L., ms. Add. 28,628.

[27] Naples, Museo Nazionale, reproduced in a drawing in Fusco, *Intorno all'Ordine*, p. 3, and in a photograph in Pontieri, *Per la storia*, Pl. facing p. 464.

[28] Fusco, *Intorno all'Ordine*, pp. 34–6.

for control of the whole kingdom. After three years of fierce fighting the last French garrison surrendered to Ferran's forces 1 January 1504, and the kingdom was once again annexed to the Crown of Aragon.

If the Order of the Ermine had survived the reign of Ferrante II, it certainly dissolved on the abdication of Federigo in 1501, for there is clear evidence that the French royal order of St Michael was maintained in Naples during the brief reigns of Charles VIII and Louis XII as the kingdom's sixth monarchical order, and that the leading barons of the kingdom were admitted to it.[29] This order too was swept away in 1503, and after a brief period in which the Aragonese order of the Jar was restored to Naples, the Burgundian order of the Golden Fleece was finally introduced, as the seventh monarchical order maintained in the court of Naples, in 1516. Unlike all of its predecessors, which dissolved almost immediately following the death or expulsion of their founders, the Golden Fleece was destined to remain there, with one brief interruption, until the kingdom was again detached from Spain in 1738, when it was replaced by the so-called 'Constantinian' Order of St George still maintained by the head of the Sicilian royal house today.[30]

5 The Statutes of the Order

The statutes of the Order of the Ermine have been preserved in at least two manuscripts: one, of uncertain date and with a text in Italian, was evidently kept in the archive of the Abbey of the Holy Trinity in Cava, and its text was published in 1845 by Giuseppe Maria Fusco;[31] the other, with the text translated into Latin, is the manuscript of 1486 just referred to, now in the British Library.[32] Aside from being expressed in different languages, the texts contained in the two manuscripts

[29] A letter signed by Bernardino di Sanserverino, Prince of Bisignano, Troiano Caracciolo, Prince of Melfi, and Andrea Matteo d'Acquaviva, Duke of Atri, was sent to Louis XII on 12 November 1511 along with the collars of the French order given to those men, explaining why they felt obliged to resign their membership. See Fusco, Intorno all'ordine, pp. 16–17, and below, pp. 446.

[30] On the early history of this curious order, supposed to have been founded by Constantine 'the Great', and later transformed into a religious order of knighthood under the Rule of St Basil with a mastership attached hereditarily to the chief of the sometime imperial house of Angelos, see the Marqués de Villareal de Alava, La Maison royale des Deux Siciles, l'Ordre Constantinien de Saint Georges, et l'Ordre de Saint Janvier (Madrid, 1964). According to that work (p. 356), there is absolutely no unequivocal reference to this order in any document prior to the bull Quod alias of Pope Julius III, issued on 17 July 1551 in favour of two Greek noblemen, Andreas and Hieronumos Angelos, who claimed to be the heirs of its earlier masters. Since neither knighthood nor religious orders were known in Eastern or Orthodox Christendom, it is extremely unlikely that any such order was founded by a Greek prince before the fall of Constantinople in 1453.

[31] I Capitoli, pp. 11–26. Extracts had been published earlier by Di Blasi, 'Lettera intorno all'ordine dell'arminio', and on the basis of the latter by Fusco himself. Unfortunately, neither author gives the precise location or number of the manuscript, so I have been unable to consult it.

[32] Ms. Add. 28,628.

are virtually identical, and the Latin text was probably translated directly from the Italian. In each manuscript, the statutes proper are preceded in the usual way by a prologue, in which the founder proclaimed the foundation of the Order, and set forth his official reasons for doing so.

> In the name of the Holy and Undivided Trinity, Father, Son, and Holy Spirit. Be it known that we Ferrando of Aragon, by the grace of God King of Sicily, Jerusalem, and Hungary, thinking many times in our mind that nothing was so suitable for princes as to give worthy examples of themselves, and especially to those who have the rank of knighthood,[33] in order to train them to virtue, to the end that they will more willingly take up, at need, the defense of the orthodox faith, and of the Most Holy Roman Church; and furthermore to the praise and glory of Almighty God, and the exaltation of our faith, and in honour of Saint Michael the Archangel; by the tenor of the present [document], we ordain the following order of knighthood (*ordine de milicia, militie ordinem*), to be called the Order of the Ermine, in which there shall be twenty-seven brothers and companions and not more; of which Order we and our successive heirs and successors in that kingdom of Sicily shall be Chief. And in order that the name may be consonant with the fact, we establish the said order of knighthood under the following most honest chapters and most holy constitutions, which are full of religion and knightly observance (*observancia militare, militarem observantiam atque virtutem*), for which those who observe•them will receive praise not only from men but from Immortal God, and the prize of future life.

The statutes proper consist of some 137 ordinances organized into only 33 *capitoli* or chapters, distinguished in both manuscripts by simple titles of the form *Capitulo primo/ Capitulum primum*, and so forth, set in the breaks between paragraphs. The numbers of both the ordinances and the chapters are just under those of the statutes of the Garter in 1465 (respectively 147 and 36), and as Ferrante must have had his own copy of the latter when he formulated those of his own order, it is unlikely that this relationship is wholly coincidental. Nevertheless, only 32 of the 137 ordinances of the Ermine correspond in subject-matter to ordinances of the Garter, so the Garter statutes seem to have served only as a very general model. Exactly twice as many of the Ermine ordinances – some 64 – correspond at least approximately to ordinances of the Golden Fleece, so Ferrante must have had a copy of the statutes of that order available to him as well. This was probably the exemplar that had been given to his father when he was elected to the Burgundian order in 1445, or a copy made from it, but it could also have been the copy given to one of the three other Italian knights elected to that order before 1465, the Counts of Ariano and Golisano (elected in 1451) and the Count of Terreno (elected in 1456).[34] Nevertheless, more than half of the ordinances of the Order of the Ermine (70) bear no resemblance to any ordinance either of the Garter or of the Golden

---

[33] '. . . chi hanno gradu di milicia . . .'

[34] I assume the last two counts were Italians, as their counties are not listed among those erected in either Castile or Aragon before 1500. Unfortunately, there is nothing resembling a complete list of Italian titles of dignity in this period.

Fleece, and only two of these resemble any of the five known ordinances of the Aragonese order of the Jar. Thus, unless they were based on a late version of the statutes of the latter order unknown to us (which is certainly possible), the statutes of the Ermine were largely original, at least in detail.

Except within chapters and sequences of chapters based on those of either the Garter or the Golden Fleece, the organization of the statutes is quite original. For the most part the order of the chapters follows a continuous logical progression throughout, so that there are no sharp breaks of the sort that exist between what we have called sections in the statutes of most earlier orders. Nevertheless, ten sequences can be distinguished. The first, comprising the eleven ordinances of chapters 1 and 2, is concerned principally with the celebration of the two annual feasts of the Order's patron saint. Sequence two, including the thirteen ordinances of chapters 3 through 6, sets forth the spiritual and fraternal obligations of the members. The forty-one ordinances of chapter 7 (the longest single chapter in the statutes of any order), form the third sequence, which describes in great detail the ritual to be followed when a new member was inducted. The fourth sequence is made up of four chapters (8 through 11), but has only twenty ordinances, concerned with the form of the Order's habit and collar, and the circumstances in which they were to be worn. The fifth sequence, containing the forty-five ordinances of chapters 12 through 15, deals with the loss of the collar, its return after the wearer's death, the circumstances in which a member might be deprived of his collar, and the procedures to be followed at his trial (the sole subject of the thirty ordinances of chapter 14). Sequence six, comprising the thirteen ordinances of chapters 16 and 17, deals with the election of new members, and informing them of their election, and sequence seven, made up of the thirteen ordinances of chapters 18 through 21, is concerned with matters related to the Order's chapel and clergy, including masses to be said for deceased members. Chapter 22, dealing with the military obligations of the members, itself forms a short eighth section of only five ordinances, while chapters 23 through 25 form a sequence of nine ordinances concerned with the members' obligations to inform and inform upon one another and themselves, and chapters 26 through 33 form a miscellaneous group of nineteen ordinances concerned with such questions as the qualifications required for admission, the settlement of disputes, support for impoverished members, and membership in other orders. Unlike those of earlier orders, many of the chapters begin with a brief prologue justifying the ordinances that follow. Chapter 4, for example, begins with the declaration: 'And because we know the Holy Roman Church to be the foundation of all Christian religion, and similarly because, both by our own zeal and from the example of the past kings our predecessors in this kingdom, we have a singular care for the Christian Republic of which the Roman Church is the head, we wish and ordain . . .' Otherwise they differ from those of the Garter and the Golden Fleece primarily in detail and in the precision with which they describe certain particular activities.

6 The Name, Title, and Patron of the Order

Like the English and Burgundian societies upon which it was based, the society of knights founded by Ferrante of Sicily was officially entitled 'order' and took its name from its badge rather than its heavenly patron. Nevertheless, as the last passage of the prologue just quoted suggests, Ferrante was more concerned than any previous founder to give his order a pious as well as a chivalrous image, and made more of the patron he had chosen than either Edward of England or Philippe of Burgundy. After declaring solemnly that 'after Almighty God, Jesus Christ our redeemer, and his blessed mother the Virgin Mary, we consecrate and dedicate this Order to the aforesaid Saint Michael the Archangel, whom we take as protector of the Order and all its companions', Ferrante went on to declare that the Order was to observe not only the principal feast of the Archangel, that of the Dedication, on 29 September,[35] but also, so that 'nothing would be lacking in honour of the said St Michael', the feast of his Apparition (on Monte Gargano in Apulia), on 8 May.[36] In addition, according to a passing reference in chapter 18, the church or chapel of the Order was to be dedicated to the Archangel, and the nine canons attached to it (whose number was chosen to represent the nine orders of angels)[37] were to say at least one mass in honour of St Michael every day of the year.[38] Despite this, the insignia of the Order seem to have included no reference whatever to the patron of the Order.

The fact that the Archangel had appeared within the confines of the kingdom, and was in consequence the object of considerable popular veneration, made his choice as patron of the new knightly order doubly appropriate, for St Michael was of course regarded as the very archetype of knighthood. It is also possible that Ferrante felt a particular devotion to the Archangel, for he used his image on many of his coins, and had himself portrayed wearing a medal bearing his image on his hat in the bust by Mazzoni referred to above. It is curious that Ferrante should have chosen to dedicate his Order of the Ermine to the patron of the still-existing Breton order of the same name, which was the only earlier order placed under the protection of the captain of the heavenly hosts, but as he had no obvious reason to imitate the Breton order, it is likely that his choices of both device and patron were made in ignorance of the fact that they had already been taken by another order; as we shall see, his reason for choosing the ermine as a device was completely different from that of the Duke of Brittany.

[35] Ch. 1a,b.
[36] Ch. 2a.
[37] Ch. 19a.
[38] Ch. 19f.

7 *The Structure and Membership of the Order*

The general structure of the Order of the Ermine was very similar to those of the English and Burgundian orders upon which it was almost certainly modelled. It was to be composed of a college of exactly twenty-seven knights (one more than the Garter and four fewer than the Golden Fleece), supported by a college of canons attached to the Order's chapel, and served by three corporate officers. The number of knights was presumably fixed at the odd figure of twenty-seven because Ferrante wanted the lay college to be roughly the same size as those of the two orders he was using as models, and found that twenty-seven was the only number in that range which could be related in any meaningful way to nine, the number of the orders of angels, which he used for most other symbolic purposes related to the Order. Included among the twenty-seven knights was the president of the Order, who was to bear the titles *Capo* and *Superiore* – the Italian equivalents of the titles *Chef* and *Souverain* borne by the Duke of Burgundy as head of his order.

The office of Chief and Sovereign (as we may call it in English)[39] is as usual ill-defined in the statutes, but the prologue declares quite clearly that it was to be attached to the crown of mainland Sicily, and its holder was to play a role in the affairs of the Order broadly similar to those played by the equivalent officers in the English and Burgundian orders. The Sovereign was to determine which candidate for membership should be elected in cases where no candidate received two thirds of the votes;[40] to preside over the cermony by which companions-elect were to be inducted into the Order;[41] to appoint all of the canons;[42] to preside over the various elements of the annual Assembly,[43] over special meetings called to determine if a companion should be expelled from the Order,[44] and over the ceremony of expulsion itself;[45] to determine how best a companion captured by the Infidel should be aided;[46] to modify the requirements of the statutes in any way he chose in order to accommodate foreign companions;[47] and to be the object of certain special obligations on the part of the other companions, including one of loyalty.[48] Since nothing is said about such matters in the statutes, it would appear that he was also to provide the physical facilities necessary for the Order's various activities, to pay for its annual festivities, and to provide the collars and habits of the companions, but like the Sovereigns of the Garter and the Golden Fleece, he was not to bear the full burden of supporting the chapel and its clergy.[49]

The twenty-six ordinary members of the lay college of the Order are called

[39] Like the title *souverain* in the Garter statutes, the title *superiore* is rendered in the Latin version of the Ermine statutes as *superior*.
[40] Ch. 16e–g.
[41] Ch. 7
[42] Ch. 19b.
[43] Chs. 11d–g, 23c, 24b,c, 27a.
[44] Ch. 14a.
[45] Ch. 14p–r.
[46] Ch. 6c.
[47] Ch. 32.
[48] Ch. 13a–c.
[49] Ch. 7hh–jj.

confratri et compagni in the prologue, and are referred to in the chapters as *confratri* or (more rarely) *cavaleri*. All three terms are merely Italian versions of the titles applied to the knights of the golden Fleece, and although *confratri* is the term most commonly employed, as that word has no precise equivalent in English I shall call them 'companions'.

The personal qualities required in a candidate for admission to the Order are set forth in chapter 26.

> [a] And considering that the nobility of blood is of great value to perfect virtue and glory and the opinion of men, although he who is virtuous may be noble in himself (*da per se*), we ordain that this Order must be given to famous and noble men, not to the ignoble and vile; [b] either to such men as are noble from their antecedents (*da li suoi antiqui*), [c] or to such men as have earned nobility by their toil and industry, [d] provided that this earned nobility is of such a nature that it can be assimilated to noble lineages. [e] And it is necessary that those who shall take the Order be made knights beforehand.

The Order was thus restricted in the usual way to noblemen who had received the accolade of knighthood, but was left open to men whose nobility had been earned (and presumably conferred by royal letters) rather than inherited from knightly ancestors. No other order in our period made such a concession to the newly ennobled, and it must be assumed that Ferrante had certain particular individuals in mind when he modified the usual requirements in this manner. Perhaps because he wanted to include in the Order a number of men who had recently been in rebellion against him, Ferrante also failed to specify that candidates for membership in his Order were to be 'without reproach', but instead required those who had been admitted to confess and purge themselves if they committed any action worthy of reproach.[50]

The first companions were presumably appointed to the Order by its founder, but thereafter, whenever a companion died or was expelled from the Order, his successor was to be elected by the surviving companions in a process that appears to have been a compromise between those of the two orders Ferrante used as models.[51] As in the English order, the companions were to meet in a special conclave summoned by the Sovereign at some convenient place, apparently soon after the death or expulsion rather than during the annual Assembly of the Order. After attending a divine office in honour of their patron, the assembled companions were to submit their votes to the Chancellor of the Order in a sealed letter. As chapter 28 required every companion to appoint a procurator or proxy with full powers to represent him whenever he could not attend any function of the Order, it would appear that those who could not get to the conclave were to send their sealed letters to or with their proxies, but this is not specifically stated. Whoever received the votes of two thirds of the companions (presumably including those absent and apparently including the Sovereign), was to be declared elected. If (as was much more likely) fewer than eighteen votes were cast for a single candidate, the

---

[50] Ch. 23a,b.
[51] Cf. Garter ch. 18, and Golden Fleece chs. 41, 48, and 49.

Chancellor was to inform the Sovereign, who was either to supply the votes necessary to elect the candidate who had the largest number of votes, or in cases where several had the same number, to choose whichever of them he pleased.[52] As usual, this procedure seems to have been designed to give the appearance of internal democracy, while effectively guaranteeing the Sovereign the final word in most elections.

The companion-elect who was not present at the time was to be informed of his election in very much the way set forth in the statutes of both the Garter and the Golden Fleece, though reserved in the former order for foreign companions and those on campaign abroad. The Secretary of the Order was to compose a letter to inform the absent companion-elect of what had happened, and this was to be taken to him by the Order's King of Arms, along with a copy of the statutes. The King of Arms or his deputy was to ask the companion-elect if he accepted his election, and to require him to come to the Sovereign's court to receive the insignia in the formal ceremony of induction. Unlike the founders of the Garter and the Golden Fleece (but, coincidently, like his own predecessor Carlo 'di Durazzo'), Ferrante decided to permit induction *in absentia* (presumably to accommodate foreign princes), and declared that the Sovereign could send the insignia of the Order 'honourably' to anyone he chose. As we have seen, he sent an embassy led by his younger son to deliver the insignia to the Duke of Burgundy in 1474, the year after he himself was given the insignia of the Golden Fleece by the bastard brother of the same duke.

The rite by which the companion-elect who was not a sovereign prince was to be inducted into the Order is described in the statutes with unprecedented precision in chapter 7. On the day the ceremony was to be held, the companion-elect was to go to the royal palace with the most solemn company possible, and from there was to process with the Sovereign and such companions as the latter could gather, all wearing the habit of the Order, to the church in which the ceremony was to take place. The insignia of the Order that were to be given to the new companion were to be placed by the royal chamberlain and keeper of the wardrobe in the sacristy of the church, under the guard of the herald of the Order, and the latter officer was to bear them into the church on his arm as soon as the service began, and take them to the right corner of the altar. There the Chancellor of the Order was to take the mantle and collar and place them on the altar, leaving the King of Arms with the white gown. Between the Epistle and the Gospel, two or three of the most distinguished persons who accompanied him were to lead the companion-elect to the sacristy, where the King of Arms was to vest him with the gown. They were then to lead him back to the altar, where after kneeling to adore God, he was to turn and bow first to the king, and then (if he was not a king, emperor, or illustrious duke), to the other companions. He was then to be taken by the Chancellor to a low stool just below the seat of the junior companion, and after he had sat there momentarily, he was to be brought back to the Sovereign or (in his absence) his Vicar. Then the Chancellor or the royal chamberlain was to take the mantle from the altar and give it to the King of Arms, who was to bring it to the Sovereign. The latter was then to place it on the new companion. At the Offertory, the Sovereign or his Vicar was to go to the place of the Offertory, and

---

[52] Ch. 16.

the candidate was there to swear with his hands between those of the Sovereign that he would observe diligently the chapters and instructions of the Order, of which a copy was to be held nearby either by the Chancellor or Secretary of the Order (if the Sovereign was present) or by a notary public (if he was represented by a Vicar). When this was done, the Sovereign was to take the collar (brought to him by the Chancellor or Secretary) and place it around the neck of the new companion, making the following declaration:

> For your great virtues, the Order takes you as its brother, and in sign of this I give you these insignia, certain that, through these your virtues, this our amiable company will be ennobled, to the service and praise of Almighty God, and to the exaltation of the Holy Roman Church, and the augmentation of the Order and of your fame. And may it be fortunate and auspicious.[53] In the name of the Father, the Son, and the Holy Spirit.

The newly-received companion was then to kiss the king or his Vicar as a sign of faith, and if he broke his promise thereafter, he was to be reputed perjured. All of the other companions present were then to kiss him, as a sign of their fraternal love.

The service then continued with the Offertory. After the Sovereign had made his offering to the priest, the new companion was to offer a sum of nine *ferrandini*, in honour of the nine orders of angels, which were to be used to support the Order's chapel. Once the Sovereign had again taken his seat, the other companions present were to process to the altar in order of rank to make their oblations (which seem to have been meant to serve as annual contributions to the Order),[54] and were then to return to their seats. On this occasion, the new companion was to be seated in the first place, next to the Sovereign, but thereafter he was to sit in the choir with the others.

This solemn and elaborate ritual was clearly calculated to impress upon the new companion (and indeed the other companions present) the importance of his undertaking, and the greatness of the honour he was receiving. Since we have no contemporary descriptions of the ceremonies by which new companions of the Garter and Golden Fleece were inducted, it is impossible to know to what extent it was original, but in all likelihood it was based at least partly on what Ferrante was able to learn of the practices of both orders.

Whether these procedures for electing and inducting companions were ever in fact followed is unknown, as is the number of knights actually admitted to the Order, for none of the Order's corporate records appears to have survived, and we have nothing resembling an official list of members. The only list I have been able to discover is that compiled by Aniello Pacca, and augmented slightly by Giuseppe Fusco,[55] on the basis of various items of evidence, both documentary and archaeological. According to Fusco, the Order included at some time during its thirty-year history, in addition to the founder himself, his son Alfonso, Duke of Calabria (the future Alfonso II); the latter's son Ferrante, Prince of Capua (the

---

[53] 'Quod felix faustumque sit.'
[54] Cf. Golden Fleece ch. 63b,c.
[55] *Intorno all'ordine*, pp. 26–7.

future Ferrante II); the founder's son-in-law, Ercole I da Este, Duke of Ferrara (r. 1471–1505);[56] Galeazzo-Maria Sforza, Duke of Milan (r. 1465–76); his uncle Alessandro Sforza, Prince of Pesaro (d. 1473); Roberto di Sanseverino, Prince of Salerno; Francesco del Balzo, Duke of Andria, the founder's cousin; Giulio Antonio d'Acquaviva, Duke of Atri; Troiano Caracciolo, Duke of Melfi; Antonio Piccolomini, Duke of Amalfi, nephew of Pope Pius II and cousin of the founder; Orso Orsini, Duke of Asoli and Count of Nola; Antonio della Rovere, Duke of Sora, nephew of Pope Sixtus IV; Pietro Guevara, Marquis of Il Vasto, Grand Seneschal of the kingdom, and cousin of the founder; Innico (or Iñigo) d'Avalos, Count of Monte Odorisio, Chamberlain of the kingdom (a knight of the Garter from 1467); his son Alfonso d'Avalos, Marquis of Pescara; Onorato Gaetano, Count of Fondi; Ferdinando Guevarra, Count of Belcastro; Alfonso Guevara, Count of Archi; Marino Caracciolo, Count of Sant'Angelo; Giacomo Caracciolo, Count of Burgenza; Virginio Orsino (admitted in 1487, the same year he was made a companion of the Stole and Jar);[57] his son, Giovanni Giordano Orsino; Roberto Orsino, Count of Tagliacozzo and Alba; Diomede Carrafa, Count of Maddaloni; Scipione Pandone, Count of Venafro; Andrea di Capua, son of the Count of Altavilla; Matteo di Capua, Count of Palene; Antonio Carrafa, Lord of Mondragone; Galeazzo Caracciolo, Lord of Vico; Domizio Caracciolo, Lord of Rodi and Governor of Calabria; Galeotto Carrafa, Lord of Tirioli, and cousin of the founder; Guevara de Guevara, Lord of Arpaia and Governor of the valleys of Benevento; Luigi d'Aquino, Lord of Castellini; Alberico Carrafa; and Giacomo Carrafa della Spina, Lord of Castelvetere. To this list may be added the names of Charles 'the Rash', Duke of Burgundy (elected, as we have seen, in 1474), and Federigo da Montefeltro, who in the same year that he was made Duke of Urbino and *Gonfaloniere* of the Church (1474), was elected to both the Order of the Garter and the Order of the Ermine.[58]

Not surprisingly, this list (which is probably correct as far as it goes) contains the names of many of the most important princes in Italy in the period of the Order's existence, including Ferrante's principal allies in the war against the Angevins. Considering the sources on which it was reconstructed, it cannot be surprising that it contains only the names of men who belonged to one or another of the leading princely and baronial families of the day. Indeed, twenty-two of the known companions who were subjects of the founder belonged to only six baronial families (those of Avalos, Capua, Caracciolo, Carrafa, Guevara, and Orsini), and three of these families furnished four or more companions each. No fewer than twenty-nine of the thirty-seven companions listed were princes, dukes, or counts, and while some of the mere *signori* may have been simple knights, most were probably barons. It is thus unclear whether the Order ever included any knight below the rank of baron. It is equally unclear whether the Order ever included anyone above the rank of duke, but as Ferrante arranged for the election of the Duke of Burgundy to the

---

[56] According to Pigna, *Storia della famiglia da Este*, lib. VIII, 'Quin Rex ipse [Ferrante], de sua, deq. Pontificis approbatione cum Hercule egit, et rem confecit, misso Ferrariam Joanne Antonio Carrafa per quem etiam Alpini muris pellem equestris ipsius ordinis insigne transmissit.'

[57] Fusco, *Intorno all'ordine*, p. 26, n. 3.

[58] Alexander, *Italian Renaissance Illuminations*, p. 84.

Order within a year of receiving the collar of the Golden Fleece, it is more than likely that he did the same for Edward IV of England, who had procured Ferrante's election to the Garter several years before he even founded his Order, and he may well have exchanged orders with his agnatic cousin and neighbour Ferran 'the Catholic' (younger half-brother of his erstwhile rival the Prince of Viana), who succeeded to the thrones of Aragon and island Sicily in 1479.

It would appear that membership in the Order, once assumed, was normally to cease only with death, but Ferrante, emulating Philippe of Burgundy rather than Edward of England, made provision in the statutes for the expulsion from the Order of companions who committed certain shameful acts. The shameful acts listed by Ferrante, however, were all forms of disloyalty to the Sovereign of the Order – the only offense for which knights of the Garter had ever been expelled. After stating in the prologue to chapter 13 that 'nothing is more detestable to a knight than the vice of infidelity, which merits the privation of all orders and dignities', Ferrante declared that any companion who broke faith with his natural lord, committed the crime of treason or *laesa maiestas*, or abandoned his lord in war, especially after the sign of battle had been given and the banners had been unfurled, was to defend his actions either in person or by proxy at the next meeting of the Chapter. If he failed to do so, or if the reasons he gave for his actions were deemed inadequate, he was to be deprived of the 'knighthood of the Order' (*milicia del ordine*) and of its insignia, which he was to send back immediately to the Sovereign or his Vicar. For some reason, Ferrante chose to qualify this rule by adding that it applied only to the companions who fought 'in the armies' and not to the 'captains of the armies'. The implications of this qualification are obscure, as it is difficult to believe that Ferrante would have been more inclined to overlook the flight of a captain than that of an ordinary combatant.

None of the earlier founders had seen fit to describe the procedures by which offences against the statutes were to be tried, but Ferrante – perhaps hoping to avoid confusion and disputes – devoted the first seventeen ordinances of chapter 14 to precisely that subject, and spelled out the process in considerable detail. Whenever any knight of the Order was indicted for an act for which deprivation was prescribed, the Sovereign and such companions as happened to be with him were to choose two companions of the Order to act as judges, and to summon them to preside over the trial. One of the Order's three officers, or a procurator appointed by the Sovereign, was to act as prosecutor, the Chancellor or Secretary was to act as notary, and the King of Arms was to act as summoner and notifier. The last-named officer was to cite the accused personally, if he could find him, but if not he was to cite him publicly in the court of his lord (presumably in most cases the Sovereign himself). He was to inform the accused of the crime for which he was to be tried, and to tell him that if he failed to appear within a specified time before the judges appointed, he was to be expelled. A suitable procurator was then to be named by the judges to defend the accused companion. On the appointed day, the various officers were to assemble and deal with the case 'as the Order and reason required'. In determining the case, the statutes of the Order were to take precedence over reason and all other enactments, and a copy of them was to be kept available, but the judges could also make use of 'imperial' laws and ordinances, (presumably the *Corpus juris civilis*) and of the laws of arms as they were generally understood. When the trial was over, the judges were to report their verdict to the

Sovereign and the other companions currently in court, and they would then decide whether to expel the accused companion or not.

No previous founder had said anything about the rite by which a companion condemned to expulsion was to be expelled from the Order either, but Ferrante, obviously hoping to discourage acts of treason and cowardice by every means at his disposal, described the ritual to be followed in his Order in some detail in the last thirteen ordinances of chapter 14. If the Sovereign and companions voted for expulsion, they were to dress in full-length vestments of black cloth, and were to pronounce the sentence solemnly. If the convicted companion was actually present, he was to be deprived personally of the insignia of the Order, but if he was not, the procurator who had represented him at his trial was to take in his hands his collar and vestments, and act in his place. First the vestments were to be taken from him, and the King of Arms was to cry out: 'With such punishments must knights who are traitors and violators of the Order be punished'. Then the collar itself was to be taken, and the companion was to be driven from the court, and the King of Arms was to cry out: 'This man is no longer worthy of anything through which he might be numbered among the knights of this Order'. If the condemned man was not actually present, the King of Arms was then to seek him out, duly instructed by the Tribunal, and was to inform him that he had been expelled, and explain why. He was then to require him to return his collar and vestments, and if he refused, the Sovereign was to proceed against him according to the advice of the majority of the Chapter.

The ritual of expulsion was similar in broad outline to that employed to degrade a knight from the general order of knighthood, and may well have been similar to those actually employed in the Orders of the Garter and Golden Fleece. It was clearly calculated to humiliate the convicted companion as thoroughly as possible, and formed a natural counterpoise to the ritual of initiation, which was intended to do the companion-elect the greatest possible honour. Even the form of the expulsion ceremony echoed that of its honourable counterpart. Whether any companion of the Order was ever subjected to this ritual degradation is unknown, but when the general behaviour of the barons of the kingdom in that period is considered, it must appear more than likely that several were thus ceremoniously cast out.

Unlike Philippe of Burgundy, Ferrante made no provision for resignation from the Order, and treated precedence among the companions only in the context of the chapter describing the induction ritual. In the last two ordinances of that chapter, however, he implied that a distinction was to be made in his Order similar to that made in the Order of the Golden Fleece, between ordinary companions, who were apparently to be seated in accordance with the time of their admission to the Order, and companions with the rank of 'king, emperor, or illustrious duke', whose place was to be determined by the Sovereign and Chapter. The exemption from the normal rule of 'illustrious dukes' as well as kings and emperors could only have been inspired by the custom of the Golden Fleece, and was no doubt meant to pertain exclusively to those dukes who were effectively sovereign princes, rather than the numerous dukes subject to the crown of Naples.

Ferrante also emulated Philippe of Burgundy when he forbade the companions of his Order who were not emperors, kings, or illustrious dukes to join any other order.[59]

---

[59] Ch. 30.

He went beyond any earlier founder, however, when he declared that, in order that the 'dignity, integrity, and authority of the Order might be greater, and so that the companions be reputed to have this Order to their greater praise', no one who asked for the Order could be accepted into it.[60] This rule was obviously designed to prevent unseemly competition for places, and to underscore the exclusive character of the Order. Ferrante evidently felt no fear that he would have difficulty finding knights willing to assume the burdens of membership.

8 The Obligations and Privileges of Membership

The companions of the Ermine undertook a variety of obligations, some of which were similar to those undertaken in the same period by the companions of the Garter and the Golden Fleece, and some of which were quite different. In fact, most of the obligations differed significantly in detail from those imposed in any earlier order, and were presumably invented by Ferrante (or his principal advisors for the project) to accomplish some particular goal.

The cliental obligations of the companions to the Sovereign imposed by the statutes were very modest, and bore a closer resemblance to those imposed in the Order of the Garter than to those imposed in any other order. The fact that any companion who broke faith with his lord, committed treason against him, or deserted him on the field of battle, was to be expelled from the Order, implies that the companions who were vassals or subjects of the Sovereign, at least, were obliged to be loyal to him, but they took no positive oath of loyalty, so their membership did not formally require anything of them in this area beyond what they already owed as subjects and vassals. The companions did swear to obey the chapters and instructions of the Order,[61] but there is nothing to suggest that they undertook to obey the Sovereign in matters not directly relevant to the specific requirements of the statutes. Moreover, the only circumstance in which the companions as such were obliged to serve the Sovereign of the Order in any active way was one unlikely to occur with any frequency, if at all. If the Sovereign went to war against the enemies of the Christian faith, every companion subject to him was obliged to go into the field with him, unless prevented by some reasonable cause. Those who were not his subjects were to be informed of his intention to wage war, but were not obliged to come. To mitigate the effects of this obligation still further, Ferrante undertook on behalf of himself and his successors as Sovereign to pay all those companions who served in such a war according to their rank.[62] Since Ferrante is not known to have had any serious ambitions to undertake a crusade, he probably included this requirement merely so that both he and the companions could boast of having undertaken a crusading vow, still evidently regarded as an undertaking essential for chivalric perfection. The knights of the earlier Neapolitan order of the Knot had undertaken a very similar obligation.[63] Ferrante for his part

---

[60] Ch. 33.
[61] Ch. 7y.
[62] Ch. 22.
[63] Knot ch. 9a,b.

assumed no further patronal obligations to the other companions of his Order in his capacity as Sovereign.

The fraternal obligations imposed by the statutes were rather more extensive than those imposed by the statutes of the Garter, but less significant than those undertaken by the knights of the Golden Fleece. Like the companions of the Burgundian order, the *confratri* of the Ermine were bound to reveal to their fellows anything they knew of that might prove harmful to them.[64] They were also obliged to do everything in their power to secure the release of any of their number who, either in war or while travelling, fell into the hands of the Infidel, and were to use all of their strengths, faculties, and goods to this end. The Sovereign was to decide whether to employ force or money, and if he chose the latter, every companion was to give as much as the Sovereign and a majority of the other companions decided was just.[65] Finally, the companions were all to contribute from their own resources to the support of any of their number who, through no fault of his own, was reduced to poverty. The Sovereign and Chapter were to determine what such a companion was to receive, on the basis of his dignity, case, condition, and virtue.[66] A similar obligation had been undertaken by the Prince of the earlier Neapolitan order of the Knot,[67] but Ferrante's ordinance was probably inspired by the colleges of poor knights called for in the statutes of both the Garter and the Golden Fleece.[68]

The companions also undertook one obligation to those of their number who died, but it too was modest compared to those undertaken by the knights of most earlier orders. On learning of the death of any of his fellows, each companion was to have a mass for the dead (including the collect for the Christian departed) said in his name by each of nine priests – possibly but not necessarily the canons of the Order's chapel.[69] Only the Companies of the Star and the Knot had required fewer masses from their members, and they had been meant to have more than ten times as many members. The small number owed by each knight individually was offset to some extent but the fact that the canons of the order (whose salary was paid by the companions) were also to say masses for every companion who died, and each deceased companion was to have received as a result exactly 477 purgatorial masses – a respectable if not extraordinary number.

Ferrante may have imposed relatively light cliental and fraternal obligations on the knights of his Order because he wanted to impose relatively heavy obligations of other types. Some of these were essentially obligations to the Order as a whole, and were similar to those undertaken by the knights of most earlier orders, but others involved acts of piety and chivalry not demanded in most of the orders we have studied.

To begin with, the knights of the Ermine were required not merely to celebrate both of the feasts of their celestial patron, but to refrain, from the vespers of the vigil of the principal feast (i.e., Michaelmas) to the vespers of the feast day itself,

---

[64] Ch. 25a.
[65] Ch. 6.
[66] Ch. 29.
[67] Knot ch. 13.
[68] Garter ch. 6, Golden Fleece ch. 20.
[69] Ch. 20.

from 'all mundane works and exercises', and from 'all secular business not related to the feast, games, plays, jousts, or other exercises of arms, save in case of necessity'.[70] They were further required to make a lenten fast on the eve of the principal feast, to confess their sins either on that day or before the high mass of the feast day proper, and to receive communion at that mass.[71] All of the companions who were subjects of the Sovereign were obliged to take part in the corporate celebration of the principal feast unless they had some reasonable excuse, and any who could not take part (presumably including foreign companions) were obliged (like the knights of the Garter in the same situation) to attend a comparable service wherever they happened to be.[72] Any companion who failed to celebrate the principal feast properly was to have thirty masses celebrated for the souls of the deceased companions, and to ask the pardon of the companions assembled at the next Chapter, either personally or by procuration; anyone who failed to celebrate the feast of the Apparition was to feed nine paupers.[73] All of the companions were in any case to feed nine paupers at some time during the period between Chapters.[74]

In addition to these essentially pious duties, the companions were to undertake several obligations characteristic of chivalry. They were first of all to swear not only to obey the Roman Church, 'the foundation of the whole Christian religion', but to defend Christianity, refusing no difficulty or danger, and omitting no action which would serve to preserve its dignity. These things they were to do specifically so as to be 'judged defenders and warriors (*propugnaturi*)' of the Faith.[75] Furthermore, 'because the principal obligation of the knight is to defend wards (*pupilli*), widows, and other powerless persons', they were to undertake to defend all such persons, in keeping with the circumstances, and the power and dignity of the persons involved, and were especially to defend the wards and widows of the other companions of the Order.[76] No earlier order had imposed comparable duties, but Ferrante was obviously determined to make his Order a formal embodiment of what he saw as the essential traditions of chivalry, and did not hesitate to spell out what those traditions were.

Ferrante also imposed various obligations upon the companions that were calculated to maintain the highest standards of behaviour among them. These, too, were quite original in detail. Any companion who committed an act other than treason or flight from the field for which he became publicly infamous, or which caused some blemish of reproach to be attached to the College of the Order, was bound either to bring or to send an excuse for his action to the Sovereign as soon as possible, and at the next meeting of the Chapter was to tell his colleagues what he intended to do to purge himself of the infamy. If he failed to do this, he was to suffer a penalty allotted to him by the Sovereign and Chapter, appropriate to his crime.[77] If

[70] Ch. 1c.
[71] Ch. 3a–c.
[72] Ch. 11j,i.
[73] Ch. 2b–e.
[74] Ch. 3d.
[75] Ch. 6.
[76] Ch. 5.
[77] Ch. 23.

any companion dissimulated his infamy, or failed to send his excuses to the Sovereign, the first of his colleagues who became aware of his failure was to tell him that he was defamed, and was obliged to confess and purge himself. If he refused, the admonitor was to inform the Sovereign and the companions with him (whether or not assembled in Chapter), and any companion who failed to do this was to be punished by the Sovereign and Chapter.[78] Similar obligations had been imposed on the knights of the Golden Fleece, but they had not been required to excuse themselves, and had been required to denounce their fellows only during the correction session of the Chapter itself, not all year.[79]

Ferrante was also concerned with maintaining harmony among the companions of his Order (whose number included many of the most powerful and quarrelsome barons in the kingdom), and he accordingly required all of the companions to bring any dispute they had to the Sovereign and Chapter, or (if the Chapter was not in session) to the Sovereign himself, before going to war. Both parties were to place their cases before the Sovereign, and were obliged to accept the judgement he rendered. Any who did not were to be punished by the Sovereign and Chapter, according to the decision of the majority of those assembled. If the Sovereign was far away when the dispute erupted, the companions nearby were obliged to do everything in their power to prevent the disputants from coming to blows until the Sovereign had returned.[80] These obligations were very similar to those imposed by Philippe of Burgundy in the eighth chapter of his statutes.

The one remaining obligation imposed on the companions not related to the insignia of the Order was an obligation to keep all the secrets of the Order. This seems to have been inspired by the essentially similar duty imposed in the thirtieth chapter of the statutes of the Golden Fleece.

9 The Chapel, Clergy, and Officers of the Order

Like the two orders upon which it was modelled, the Order of the Ermine was to have had its own chapel, dedicated to its heavenly patron. Like the chapels of the two earlier orders, the *Ecclesia de S. Michaele* was to have been fitted with *sedi* or stalls whose number corresponded to that of the companions of the Order, and each companion was to affix a shield of his arms to one of these stalls, and hang a banner of his arms above it,[81] in keeping with the current practice of the Order of the Garter.[82] It is not clear from the statutes whether Ferrante intended to construct a church specifically for this purpose, or to attach the Order to an existing church dedicated or rededicated to St Michael, but no such church is known to have been founded by him, and Fusco – pointing out that no church dedicated to St Michael is known to have existed in Naples in the period – postulated that the Order actually met in the chapel of the Passion of the Church of

[78] Ch. 24.
[79] Golden Fleece chs. 31, 32.
[80] Ch. 27.
[81] Ch. 18.
[82] See above, p. 147.

the Mount of Olives (Monteoliveto) not far from the Castel Nuovo in Naples – the chapel in which the bust of Ferrante wearing the collar of the Order was originally placed.[83] Wherever the Order actually met (if indeed it met anywhere on a regular basis), nothing now remains of the stalls or stall-plates of the companions.

The chapel of the Order was to have been served in the usual way by a college of canons. Unlike the founders of the three existing orders with comparable colleges, Ferrante made their number equal that of the nine orders of angels rather than that of the companions, perhaps because nine priests could be supported more easily than twenty-seven. The nine canons (who were all to be named by the Sovereign alone) were charged with saying at least one mass in honour of St Michael every day of the week, and on the weekday on which the feast of St Michael last fell were in addition to say the *missa maiore*.[84] Finally, whenever one of the companions died, each of the canons was to say twenty-seven masses for his soul (in addition to the nine each of the twenty-six surviving companions was to have said).[85] For their regular services to the Order, the canons were to be paid a salary by the companions, at a rate to be decided by the Sovereign and Chapter.[86] Whether any such canons were ever actually appointed is unknown.

Like the founders of the Orders of the Garter and the Golden Fleece, Ferrante attached to his order a number of corporate officers, but chose to define their roles only within the context of chapters dealing with activities in which they had some share. The officers mentioned in the statutes bore the titles *Cancellero*, *Secretario*, and *Araldo* or *Re d'arme*, and their duties probably corresponded fairly closely to those of the Chancellor, Registrar, and King of Arms of the Order of the Golden Fleece. Ferrante seems to have felt no need for an officer equivalent to the Usher of the English order, and assigned the duties of the Treasurer of the Burgundian order to the royal chamberlain and keeper of the wardrobe.[87] In all likelihood all three offices were actually filled throughout the history of the Order, but nothing whatever is known of their occupants.

10 The Corporate Activities of the Order

The companions, canons, and officers of the Order of the Ermine were required by the statutes to take part in a number of corporate activities, both regular and irregular. The only regular activity involving the companions and officers was the general meeting of the Order, which was to be held annually on St Michael's day,[88] in keeping with the custom of the Garter rather than that of the Golden Fleece. Like those of the Golden Fleece, the statutes usually refer to these meetings as *Capitoli* or 'Chapters', but in fact the Chapter proper was only one of the activities in which the members and servants of the Order took part during the Michaelmas

---

83 *Intorno all'ordine*, p. 20.
84 Ch. 19a–d, f.
85 Ch. 21.
86 Ch. 19e.
87 Ch. 7c refers to the 'regio Camerlingo et guardaroba del Re.'
88 Ch. 11.

celebrations, and for the sake of clarity I shall refer to the meeting as a whole as the Assembly of the Order. The organization of the Ermine Assembly was probably very similar to that of the Garter, but as nothing is said in the statutes of when the Chapter proper was to be held, and no banquet is even mentioned, it is impossible to be sure. Chapter 11 says merely that the companions were to process in their collars and habits to the services held on the eve at vespers, and in the morning and evening of the feast, and were to dress in the same way during the Chapter. The statutes say nothing about any activities on the day following the feast, so it would appear that the Assembly was to last for only twenty-four hours.

The statutes imply that the Chapter was to be held in the usual way during the course of the annual Assembly, but unlike those of the Golden Fleece they say nothing about when or where it was to be convened or how the meeting was to be organized, and the subjects with which the Chapter was to deal are discussed in various chapters scattered throughout the statutes. The subjects mentioned are ransoms for captive members,[89] support for impoverished members,[90] the shameful acts of companions who had refused to confess,[91] the excuses of companions who had committed such acts,[92] the acts of penance or penalties required to purge such acts,[93] and the settlement of disputes among the companions.[94] It does not appear that there was to be anything equivalent either to the correction session of the Golden Fleece or to the recording of heroic deeds maintained by that and several earlier orders. Nothing is said about the amendment of the statutes, and there is no evidence that any amendment was in fact made during the Order's thirty-year history.

The annual Assembly was the only activity in which all of the companions were expected to take part, but those companions who were either in court or within a short distance of it were also expected to convene within a short time of the death of a companion to elect and induct his successor, and to convene whenever necessary to choose judges for, pass sentence upon, and formally expel those companions who had been accused and convicted of one of the offences for which expulsion was prescribed. Those companions who could not participate in any of these activities were to be represented by the procurators they had appointed, in keeping with the practice of the Order of the Golden Fleece.

11 The Collar and Habit of the Order

The collar of the Order – whose form seems to have been inspired by those of the Orders of the Jar and the Golden Fleece – is described and explained in unusual detail in chapter nine of the statutes.

[89] Ch. 6d.
[90] Ch. 29a.
[91] Ch. 24b.
[92] Ch. 13d.
[93] Chs. 23c, 24c.
[94] Ch. 27a.

The collar we wish to be made in this way, that is that it be wholly composed of stocks (*stipiti*), that is trunks of trees, into the top of which are inserted two shoots (*ramicelli*), which are beginning to throw out leaves, and similarly of chairs (*sedie*), from which flames are bursting forth, in such a way that they are joined together, that is, one stock and then one seat, and in this way the whole collar shall be composed. From which collar shall depend in front of the chest an image of a white ermine (*Arminio*), of enamelled gold, at the feet of which shall be a scroll with this word: DECORUM.[95] And let each understand what our intention is: with the image of the sprouting stock, [we signify] that which is converted into a better and more worthy seed (or race); and by the purest beast (*animal mundissimo*), we signify to our companions that only what is decent, just, and honest must be done, and let what is according to nature and the condition of each be perpetual.

The collar was thus a symbol of purification and renewal appropriate to the situation in which the Order was founded, and to the high standards of conduct set by its statutes. The device Ferrante did not explain in the statutes, the burning chair or throne, was an existing livery-badge that Ferrante had inherited from his father,[96] and was presumably included to indicate Ferrante's proprietary interest in the Order. Its significance is unknown.

No exemplar of the collar of the Order is known to have survived, but I have found two contemporary representations of it, and there may well be others. The first representation is in a copy of the *Divina Commedia* prepared for Federigo da Montefeltro, Duke of Urbino, in 1477 or 1478.[97] This collar, placed around Federigo's shield in the way the collar of the Golden Fleece was by this time commonly displayed, is depicted entirely in gold, and is composed of stocks or stumps giving off very small leafy shoots, alternating with burning thrones that look rather more like buildings than chairs. The ermine, suspended from two adjacent stocks by a fine chain, is represented standing on a compartment or slice of turf, with a blank scroll held in its right forepaw and passing behind its neck and over its back. The other representation of the collar, on the bronze bust of Ferrante referred to above, is quite different.[98] Here the ermine, devoid of both compartment and scroll, hangs by two converging chains from a collar composed of two interlaced vines, which frame a series of ovoid spaces filled, not merely with sprouting stocks and flaming chairs, but with representations of two of Ferrante's other devices, an open book (another badge inherited from his father) and a diamond mount, arranged in almost random order.[99] Since this collar does not correspond with the official desription in a manuscript of the statutes copied only a few years earlier, its

---

[95] 'Seemliness' or 'propriety'.

[96] It is depicted in a marginal medallion of a copy of Justin's *Epitome historiarum philippicarum Pompei Trogi*, prepared for Alfons not long before his death in 1458, along with the device of the jar of lilies and that of the open book, which Ferrante also employed. See *Dix siècles*, no. 150, p. 170.

[97] Alexander, *Italian Renaissance Illuminations*, Pl. 25.

[98] See above, p. 407.

[99] From his right shoulder to his left the order is: mount, book, stock, chair, mount, book, mount, stock, chair, mount, book.

peculiarities are probably the result of artistic licence.

Ferrante often displayed the various elements of the collar alone, and many more representations of these than of the collar as a whole have come down to us. On the great doors he added to his father's triumphal arch on the Castel Nuovo, the ermine, holding in its mouth a long and curly scroll bearing the word PROBANDA ('Worthy of esteem') is set in the central inner medallion directly below the medallion bearing the royal helm and crest, and the chair and stock are set in the outer medallions of the same door opposite the crest and the ermine respectively. The corresponding medallions of the other door bear Ferrante's shield of arms, the book, the mount, and a knot-device he also employed as a badge. A white ermine standing on a white scroll bearing the legend PROBANDA is depicted along with all the other devices on the first page of a manuscript prepared for him in 1471,[100] and a white ermine almost surrounded by a coloured scroll bearing the word PROBANDA was similarly depicted in company with the flaming chair on the first page of a book prepared for Ferrante in 1476.[101] The ermine is also represented alone in Federigo da Montefeltro's Dante, standing on a compartment with a blank scroll over its back, and surrounded by the garter of the English order, of which Federigo was also a companion.[102] The ermine is finally represented bearing a scroll with the word DECORUM on the first folio of the manuscript of the Latin version of the statutes, issued in 1486, and on a number of coins bearing the names of Ferrante and of his son Alfonso II.[103]

Chapter 10 of the statutes declares that the collar was to be worn from the first to the second vespers of the Order's two annual feasts, and on one day of every week of the year. Each year the weekday on which the collar was to be worn was to be that on which the previous feast of Michaelmas had fallen. This rule was quite different from that of most earlier orders, and must have been based on the custom of the Aragonese order of the Jar, which required its members to wear their collar only on Saturdays and major feasts. The knights of the Ermine were also required to wear their collar in battle, but if the whole collar was found inconvenient, they were permitted to wear the ermine alone – presumably dependent from a simple chain. This was of course a modification of the rule of the Golden Fleece, whose companions were permitted to wear the fleece alone in battle, in place of the collar which they were otherwise required to wear all the time. Any knight of the Ermine who failed to wear the collar on one of the specified occasions was to feed one pauper.

Since the collar was valuable, Ferrante also emulated Philippe of Burgundy by formulating a rule dealing with its loss, and by requiring its return after the death of the companion to whom it had been given. Ferrante declared in chapter 12 that, if the collar was lost in battle, it was not to be replaced without the licence of the Sovereign, and in chapter 15 specified that within four months after a companion's death, his heirs were return his collar and habit to the Church of St Michael or some other appropriate place, and present them either to the Sovereign himself or his Vicar. If they failed to do this they were not to be quit of the obligation

100 Dix siècles, no. 154, p. 174.
101 Ibid., no. 153, p. 173.
102 Alexander, Italian Renaissance Illuminations, Pl. 23.
103 Fusco, Intorno all'ordine, p. 29, n. 1.

undertaken by them at the time the companion was inducted, and were to suffer whatever penalty the Sovereign and Chapter decided was fitting.

When engaged in the Order's business, the companions of the Order were also to wear a habit, which is described in chapter 8 in the following terms:

> The mantle (*mantello*) of the Order which the companions shall wear shall be split and open on the right side, of carmine shaved satin, falling to the heels, and shall be lined with skins of ermine and joined (*inserrato*) at the neck. The gown (*veste*) below the mantle shall be of white silk, falling to the heels.

This habit seems to have been inspired by that of the Golden Fleece rather than that of the Garter, but was peculiar in lacking any hood or insignia, and in including a garment of a specific material, colour, and length to be worn under the mantle. It was apparently to have been supplied by the Sovereign, and returned to him along with the collar after the death of the companion who received it. I have found no contemporary representation of a knight of the Order wearing any element of this habit.

12 Conclusions: The Order of the Ermine

The Order of the Ermine was clearly based on the contemporary Orders of the Garter and the Golden Fleece, and differed from them only in ways which reflected the special circumstances and concerns of its founder at the time of its foundation. Ferrante seems to have created the Order partly to strengthen and improve the good relations he had established with the leading barons of his kingdom in the period since the end of the recent civil war, and partly to improve the behaviour of the barons themselves. It would otherwise be difficult to explain the unprecedented emphasis placed by Ferrante in the statutes of the Order on both Christian and knightly virtue, and upon punishment for conduct unbecoming a Christian knight, for Ferrante himself – whose ideas of government were not essentially different from those of his contemporary Machiavelli – was hardly a paragon of virtue of either sort. Ferrante seems to have hoped that, if on one hand he paid his barons the highest honours and set before them the highest standards of conduct he understood, and on the other hand threatened them with comparable disgrace if they failed to live up to those standards, and especially if they betrayed him in any way, he could at least curb their natural tendencies to viciousness, quarrelsomeness, and treachery. Both his goal and his method were not very different from those of St Bernard of Clairvaux when, more than three centuries earlier, he composed a rule for the knights of the new order of the Temple. It may be doubted that Ferrante had much success in reducing vice and promoting chivalry among his barons, but as the rest of his long reign was characterized by internal peace, the Order may well have served its primary purpose of encouraging loyalty.

Chapter 15

The Order of St Michael the Archangel France, 1469–1790

1 Historical Background

By 1469, the only royal courts in Western Christendom without an order of knighthood at least theoretically endowed with a written rule were those of France, Scotland, Bohemia, and Poland. The last three kingdoms existed on the cultural and political periphery of Christendom, and none of them is known to have produced a true order of knighthood of any sort until long after the Reformation. The failure of the royal court of France to produce a true knightly order in the period of just over a century since the effective dissolution of the very ambitious order of the Star in 1364 is considerably more surprising, since France was not only the richest and most populous kingdom in Christendom, but the source of the chivalrous literature and much of the chivalrous culture that had inspired the creation of monarchical orders in other kingdoms, and was moreover the home throughout the fifteenth century of several princely orders maintained by cadet branches of the royal house – the Orders of the Ermine of Brittany, the Camail or Porcupine of Orléans, and the Golden Fleece of Burgundy.

The explanation for this failure to create a second order of knighthood is no doubt to be found in the fact that, after the dissolution of Jean II's Company of the Star, his son Charles V (who was relatively indifferent to chivalry) and his grandson Charles VI developed an alternative system of cementing the patrono-cliental relationship between themselves and their most eminent subjects based on the unlimited distribution of badges and livery-uniforms – a system that persisted until the death of Charles VII, the son of Charles VI, in 1461. Colette Beaune[1] has recently demonstrated that, although distinctive livery-badges and colours had first been introduced into France from England in the reign of Jean II himself, it was only after the accession of Charles V in 1364 that they were used extensively in the royal court. She has further shown that, after what seems to have been a period of experimentation (in which the badge of the defunct Company of the Star was treated as a sort of pseudo-order), a truly revolutionary system was finally introduced by Charles VI in 1382, under which all members of the *compaignie du roy* from the king and the princes of the blood royal down to the humblest servants

---

[1] 'Costume et pouvoir en France à la fin du Moyen Age: Les devises royales vers 1400', *Revue des Sciences Humaines* 183 (1981), pp. 125–146.

were constantly dressed in costumes of particular colours and bearing particular devices. Through most of the long reign of Charles VI, (which lasted until 1422) the king and his councillors decided at some point in every year what colours and devices would be worn by the court, and had hundreds of vestments in those colours and bearing those devices – their material, decoration, and cut varying according to the rank of the recipient – distributed to the courtiers. An appearance of equality and fraternity was thus imposed upon the members of the king's retinue, similar to that which had been imposed by Arthur on the knights of the Round Table, and by the founders of monarchical orders upon their 'companions', but based solely upon their common clientship to the king rather than upon their common status of knight. Indeed, one of the advantages of the new system was that it was not restricted to knights, or even to members of the male sex.

Most of the devices adopted by Charles VI to serve as livery-badges were employed only for a short period of time, and reflected the current preoccupations of the king or the dominance of one or another of the political factions of the greater nobility, but certain devices (for reasons that are usually far from clear) were distributed and displayed over a long period of time, and came to be recognized as standard symbols of royal authority and favour. Most important among these were the *geneste* or broom-plant, adopted by Charles V as a badge towards the end of his reign[2] and inherited by his son, and the winged white stag, a modified version of the very similar device of Duke Louis of Bourbon, chosen by Charles VI himself at some time before 1388.[3] The former device, little used during Charles' minority, was apparently brought to the fore by the return of the so-called 'Marmousettes' in 1388, and was displayed thereafter in a variety of forms, including flowers and branches as well as the more familiar pods (*cosses*).[4] At about the same time, Charles seems to have decided to distribute a collar composed of paired broom-pods, with a similar pair as a pendant,[5] to certain selected members of his entourage, as a sign of his special favour, and although no corporate statutes are known to have been associated with it at any time, this collar was referred to as that of the 'Order' of the Broom Pod.[6] It was perhaps the first honorific pseudo-order

---

[2] Paris, B.N., ms. fr.3886, f. 94. (But see below, n. 7).

[3] Beaune, 'Devises', p. 143.

[4] Ibid., p. 144.

[5] Several representations of this collar have survived. The earliest is perhaps that worn by Richard II of England (and woven into his *houppelande*) in the famous Wilton diptych, painted around 1396 (published in Jacques Dupont and Cesare Gnudi, *Gothic Painting* [Geneva, New York, 1979], pp. 166–7); it is also represented (alternating with the Bourbon pseudo-order of the Belt) on a chasuble now preserved in the Musée de tissus de Lyon; in a miniature on the first page of a copy of Christine de Pisan's *Le livre du chemin de longue etude*, where it is worn by Charles VI and of two of his courtiers, (now Brussels, Bibliothèque royale de Belgique, ms. 10,983, published in Camille Gaspar and Frédéric Lyna, *Les principaux manuscrits à peintures de la Bibliothèque royale de Belgique* [Paris, 1937], I, Pl. CI); and in a similar miniature on the first page of a manuscript of her *Poesies*, where it is worn by two courtiers but not by the king (Paris, B.N., ms. fr.836, published by Camille Couderc, *Album de Portraits d'après les collections du département des manuscrits* [Paris, 1909], LIII, no. 2).

[6] Very little of value has been written about this 'order'. Favyn contended that it had been founded by King Louis IX at his coronation in 1226, but I have not found the slightest evidence of the use of the broom by a French king as a simple badge, let alone the device of

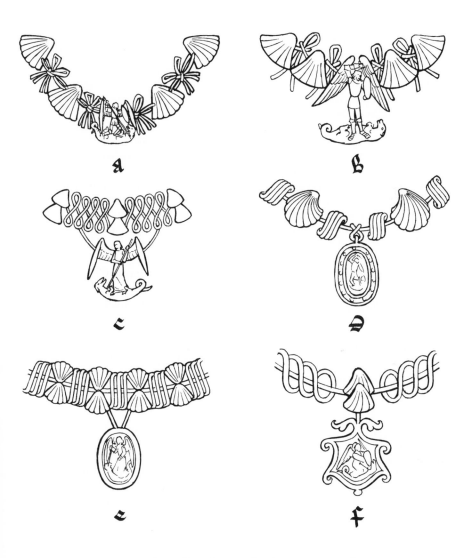

15.1 The collar of St Michael, as represented
a. in the earliest MS. of the statutes, B.N., fr. 19819
b. in B.N., ms. Clairambault 1242
c. in B.N., ms. fr. 19818
d. in the portrait of Charles VIII in the Musée Condé, Chantilly
e. in B.N., ms. fr. 19815
f. in B.N., ms. fr. 19246

deliberately founded as such. An average of twenty persons a year received this collar in the four years for which records have been preserved (1388, 1390, 1399, and 1400), and when this is compared to the 491 *houppelandes* embroidered with interlaced sprigs of broom and may that were distributed to the court as a whole in the last of these years, its honourable character is clear. In fact, unlike the bestowal of ordinary badges, the bestowal of this collar was normally accompanied by a royal letter granting the recipient the right to wear it thenceforth as a sign of royal favour.[7]

The collar of broom-pods – which was worn by the king himself and distributed on occasion to other kings and princes as well as to simple squires of his household[8] – seems to have served the purely honorific functions of the monarchical orders until Charles' death in 1422, when the country was temporarily divided between Henry VI of England, the son of his adoptive heir, and his only surviving son Charles, recognised in the southern half of the kingdom as Charles VII. In his much-reduced court at Bourges, Charles VII continued to wear livery-colours and badges much as his father had done, but he rarely distributed livery-uniforms except to members of his household proper and of his armed forces. Although he retained the winged stag as a device throughout his reign, I have found no unequivocal evidence for his use of the broom-pod either as a simple device or as the badge of a pseudo-order, and he may well have abandoned it altogether, either immediately

---

an order, before the last years of the reign of Charles V. See the Comte de Marsy, 'La collection de décorations militaires françaises du Musée d'Artillerie', *Revue nobiliaire, héraldique, et biographique* ser. 3, 2 (1877), pp. 115–17.

[7] Three such letters have been preserved in eighteenth-century copies in Paris, B.N., ms. fr. 3886, f. 94, entitled 'Patentes par lesquelles le collier de l'ordre de la Cosse de Geneste est accordé à G. de Belleville, V. de Lichtereielde, et R. de Mauny, 1378–1406'. The first of these letters, published by Favyn, *Théâtre*, should probably be dated 1388, but if the date is correct, the 'order' must have been founded by Charles V rather than his son. The third letter, issued on 7 March 1406, (also preserved in Paris, B.N., ms. Dupuy 662, f. 286), reads as follows: 'Charles etc. Sçavoir faisons que nous, a plein informez de la bonne et noble generation dont nostre amé sergent d'armes Robert de Mauny, escuier, est issu et procreé, a icelui avons donné et octroié, donnons et octroions de grace especial par ces presentes, congé et licence de [sic] doresnavant il puist et luy loyse porter le collier de nostre Ordre de la Coste de Genestre, en tous lieux et par toutes places, festes et compaignies qu'il lui plaira et bon lui semblera. En tesmoin etc.' This letter was published in Douët d'Arcq, *Choix de pièces inédites relatives au règne de Charles VI*, (Paris, 1863), I, p. 287.

[8] Charles seems to have given it to Richard II of England and his uncles the Dukes of Lancaster, Gloucester, and York, at some time during the year 1396, when Richard took his daughter as his second wife, for the account of the royal *Argentier*, Charles Poupart, records the gift. At the wedding itself, Charles is said to have worn the collar himself, and to have given *colers de son liveree de broincoddes* to the Duchesses of Lancaster and Gloucester, the Countess of Huntingdon, and to the Duke of Lancaster's daughter, Joan. For these documents, see Maude Violet Clarke, 'The Wilton Diptych', *Fourteenth-Century Studies*, ed. L. S. Sutherland and M. McKisack (Oxford, 1937), pp. 278–84. Charles also bestowed the collar on Ferran I of Aragon, receiving in return the collar of the Jar. See J. Vieillard and L. Mirot, *Inventaire des lettres des rois d'Aragon à Charles VI* (Paris, 1942), nos. 9, 20, pp. 107–10.

after his accession, or at some later date.[9] His elder son Louis XI, who succeeded him in 1461, reacted strongly against most of his father's policies, and gradually abandoned the whole practice of wearing and distributing livery-badges and uniforms.[10] By the time he founded the Order of St Michael in 1469, the system which had prevailed in the French court since the dissolution of the first French order was in disarray, and the pseudo-order which had partially replaced the Company of the Star had almost certainly been abandoned. The time was thus ripe for the creation of a new order.

2 The Foundation and Maintenance of the Order, 1469–1515

Louis XI (born in 1423, and thus an exact contemporary of Ferrante of Sicily), was in most respects an unlikely person to found an order of chivalry of any kind. A machiavellian politician who preferred the company of lowborn favourites to that of his noble vassals, his opinion of the traditions of chivalry in general was probably lower than that of any of his predecessors on the throne, and unlike any of his predecessors he normally eschewed all forms of courtly pomp. That Louis should have gone to the trouble of founding an elaborate monarchical order, eight years after his accession to the throne, at a time when he had no particular triumph or other great event to signalize, can only indicate that he felt some practical political purpose would be served by doing so.[11]

In fact there can be little doubt that Louis founded the Order of St Michael primarily to serve as a political counterfoil to the Order of the Golden Fleece, which in the previous year had passed under the sovereignty of the prince who was to be for nearly a decade Louis' most dangerous opponent: Duke Charles 'the Rash' of Burgundy. In the spring and summer of 1469, indeed, Louis was working very hard to woo his own brother Duke Charles of Berry (to whom he had just given the recently reconquered Duchy of Guyenne) away from the political camp of the Duke of Burgundy, who had long posed as Charles' friend and ally. Apparently on the advice of his uncle Duke René of Anjou (the founder of the Order of the Crescent, with whom he spent several weeks of that same summer), Louis invited his brother to visit him at his castle of Amboise in July, and there sought to win him over by entertaining him in a princely fashion with tournaments and other knightly amusements. On 1 August these chivalrous festivities culminated in the

[9] The only representation of the collar I have found in the period after the death of Charles VI is on the tomb-slab of Giovanni Emo of Venice, who died in 1483. (Reproduced in D. L. Galbreath and Léon Jéquier, *Manuel du Blason* [Lausanne, 1977], fig. 597, p. 208.) He could easily have received the collar from Charles VI when he was young. A collar later identified as that of the Broom Pod was also represented in the *Wappenbuch* of Conrad Grünenberg, completed about the same year, but it is sufficiently different from all others known that it may be the device of some altogether different body. (Reproduced in Paul Ganz, 'Die Abzeichen der Ritterorden', *AHS* [1905], p. 135.)

[10] Beaune, 'Devises', p. 145.

[11] On his life and reign see P. Champion, *Louis XI* (Paris, 1927), 2 vols.; Paul Murray Kendall, *Louis XI, The Universal Spider* (New York, 1971); and P.-R. Gaussin, *Louis XI, un roi entre deux mondes* (Paris, 1976).

proclamation of Louis' new Order, to which Charles of of Guyene was the first to be appointed as a companion, along with Jean, Duke of Bourbon and Auvergne.[12] Probably because he had little time to come up with anything very original, the statutes Louis assigned to the new society by letters patent issued on that very day were largely identical to those of the Golden Fleece. Aside from the two princes of the blood, the statutes list thirteen other knights as founding members of the Order (twelve of whom were captains of the royal *Compaignies d'Ordonnance* created by Louis' father to serve as the core of the royal army),[13] but at least one of these, Antoine de Chabannes, Count of Dammartin and *Souverain Maître* of Louis' household, did not receive formal notification of his election until the following 26 October, and it is entirely possible that most of the others learned of their appointment at about the same time.[14]

Although the circumstances surrounding its foundation have long been well known, the history of the Order of St Michael in the decades following its foundation has been obscure until very recently, when my own research and that of Philippe Contamine began to throw some light on the subject.[15] According to the statutes, the Order was to have met every year in a solemn Assembly held on the feast day of its patron saint, 29 September, in the chapel of the monastery of Mont Saint-Michel off the coast of Normandy – the principal shrine of its patron in France – but although preparations were begun in December 1470 for an Assembly to be held (according to Sforza de Bettini, the Milanese ambassador) in March 1471, and both habits and armorial panels were provided for this meeting,[16] it would appear that no proper Assembly was held at any time or in any place during its founder's reign. Presumably Louis was prevented by the pressure of events from attempting to convene a second meeting that year, and when Charles of Guyenne (whom he had just reminded of his obligation not to join another order)[17] died suddenly on 12 May of the following year, more than five months before the next Michaelmas feast, Louis may well have decided that so expensive an undertaking was no longer necessary to accomplish the purposes the Order was still capable of serving.

---

[12] Statutes, prologue and ch. 2.

[13] On these companies and their captains, see Philippe Contamine, *Guerre, état, et société à la fin du Moyen Age. Etudes sur les armées des rois de France, 1337–1494* (Paris, 1972).

[14] *Lettres de Louis XI*, ed. E. Charavay, J. Vaesen, and B. de Mandrot, IV (Paris, 1890), no. CCCCLXIII, pp. 41–3.

[15] Although well known to the early historians of knightly orders, the first work to deal with any aspect of the Order's first century in a critical way was comte L.-E. de Colleville and F. Saint-Christo, *Les ordres du roi* (Paris, 1925), which contains in addition to a cursory narrative of the Order's history a very useful list of the members and officers of the Order based on contemporary evidence. Of the biographers of Louis XI referred to in note 11 above, only Champion had anything much to say about the Order. The paper by Philippe Contamine, 'L'Ordre de Saint-Michel au temps de Louis XI et de Charles VIII', *Bulletin de la Société nationale des antiquaires de France 1976* (Paris, 1978), was the first narrative of the Order's history in this period based on a thorough examination of the surviving primary sources, and was the basis for my own more recent research.

[16] See Contamine, 'L'Ordre de Saint-Michel', pp. 217–20.

[17] Ibid., p. 225.

Not everyone concerned was happy with this state of affairs, however, and Louis apparently received a number of complaints from companions that he had failed to act in conformity with the statutes. In a letter dated 16 September 1476, Louis himself admitted to the companion Antoine de Chabannes (who seems to have enquired about the subject) that 'great affairs' had prevented him from holding the feast of the Order since the time of its foundation, and declared that he wanted strongly to convene a meeting, 'as much to give advice on putting into it the number of knights which it lacks, as to provide for many other things which are necessary to it.'[18] Despite the regret expressed in this letter, Louis made it clear that he had no intention of holding an Assembly at any time in the near future, and went on to ask Chabannes for his approval of the 'election' to membership of Pierre de Rohan-Gié, Count of Porcien and Marle. Chabannes seems to have got the message, and in a second letter not only approved Louis' choice, but thanked the king very humbly for asking his advice on the matter.

Chabannes was apparently not the only knight to complain of Louis' failure to put most of the statutes into effect, for only three months after he sent the letter just cited, on 22 December 1476, Louis issued letters patent promulgating no fewer than sixty new ordinances for the Order, clearly intended to satisfy as many as possible of the complaints he had received without actually holding an Assembly, and to mollify the companions by increasing their privileges. After proclaiming the 'very perfect and singular love' that he felt for the Order, Louis declared in the prologue to these letters that he had vowed to found and endow a College of priests to pray for the Order.

> And so that the said Order might by continual observance be better, more easily, duly, and honourably sustained, (which by default of good policy, duly kept and observed, might fall into decadence, inconsequence, and mis-prision, which would be slander and a charge against the conscience, honour, and *ravallement* of our reign, and of the noble estate of knighthood, and a damage to the whole commonwealth), we wish with all our power to provide for what has been said, and avoid all variations and indignities; and [also] that the high deeds of us and our said knights, bothers of the said Order, may be able, shall come, and shall be in truth composed in true writing, worthy of being chronicled and placed in the Treasury of the Order, even as is said by the said institution of the latter; and that the faults, which by human frailty may suddenly occur, contrary to the observance of the said statutes of the Order, as it is said, may be promptly, softly, and honestly represented to us, as Chief and Sovereign, by the said knights, brothers and members of the said Order, in order that the whole might be corrected and amended easily and amiably, to the honour of the said Order; and to keep and observe the laudable ceremonies, required and ordered for the decoration and exaltation of the said Order: we have been remonstrated by the said knights and our brothers of the said Order, that it is suitable, very necessary, and expedient to create, ordain, and institute an office for the said Order, beyond the four offices instituted at the said institution of the said Order, and to place in the

[18] *Lettres de Louis XI*, VI (Paris, 1898), no. DCCCCXXXII, pp. 87–8.

exercise of this office a prudent, wise, virtuous, and experienced knight, garnished with prowess and virtue in truth, who shall have the express and special charge of the things hereafter specified and declared ...

The new officer thus created, called the *Prevost Maistre de Ceremonies*, was to act as a sort of executive officer for the Order, and to see to it that the requirements of the statutes, including the establishment of a college of priests, were actually carried out. Louis immediately appointed to this office Jean d'Albert, Baron of Montelus, who was indeed an experienced knight, but despite Louis' vow the latter was unable to extract from him the funds necessary to endow a canonical college.

Nevertheless, as his letter to Chabannes indicates, after the autumn of 1476 Louis XI did attempt to carry out (or enforce) the specifications of the statutes he had adopted as far as was possible without convening a formal meeting. Not only does he appear to have consulted each of the companions individually, either in person or by letter, when he wished to make a new appointment,[19] but he refrained from appointing to the Order more men than the statutes called for, or men whose standing was less than that they required. It would appear that he also appointed suitable men to fill at least three of the four offices called for in the original statutes: the office of Chancellor was given successively to the Bishop of Langres and the Archbishop of Reims, both dukes and Peers of France, while the office of Treasurer was given to a knight whose son and successor was the Treasurer of France, and the office of Registrar was given to one of his personal secretaries.[20] In sum, he seems to have maintained the Order on very much the same basis as the Savoyard Order of the Collar had been maintained before the establishment of its chapel, (and as the Order of the Golden Fleece was maintained in the long periods between meetings), albeit in violation of certain of its more important ordinances.

By the time of Louis' death on 30 August 1483, the Order of St Michael had acquired sufficient prestige that his daughter Anne, Lady of Beaujeu, upon whom the regency devolved during the long minority of her brother Charles VIII, planned to hold a formal Assembly on the first Michaelmas following Charles' coronation on 30 May 1384. This Assembly, however, was first postponed and then cancelled due to political rivalries that came to a head in September 1484, and no further attempt to convene a formal meeting of the knights was again made during Charles' reign.[21] Nevertheless, the Order continued to exist in much the same condition as

---

[19] In addition to the correspondance just cited, we have a letter to Louis from the founding companion Jean d'Estouteville, written on 8 October (probably in 1481) in response to a letter from Louis asking him to approve the 'election' of Jean du Pont. (Paris, B.N., ms. fr.15540, f. 66. See Contamine, 'L'Ordre de Saint-Michel', pp. 222–4.)

[20] Ibid., p. 221; Colleville, Saint-Christo, *Les ordres*. Only a partial list of the Order's officers in this period had been constructed, and the precise dates on which most were appointed are unknown.

[21] According to Olivier de la Marche (who was in a good position to know the truth), the companions of the Order never assembled for a chapter during the first thirty years of the Order's existence. In the letter written to Philippe 'the Handsome' cited in the last chapter he wrote: 'King Louis of France and King Charles, his son, and the present King Louis raised up an order or device which is called the Order of Saint Michael; but up to the present there is no fixed number, although several notable knights bear this order; but for myself and my understanding, I could not call it an order, because there is no number of knights, and the

it had under Louis XI, and in 1496 Charles actually tried to put into effect the statute adopted by his father twenty years earlier that called for the establishment of a college of priests to serve the Order. The college founded by his charter comprised twelve canons, twelve chaplains or vicars, six choristers, three clerks, four ushers, and five musicians, and the chapel of Saint-Michel du Palais in Paris (more conveniently situated than the remote monastery of Mont Saint-Michel) was made over entirely to it. A bull of approbation for this foundation was sought and obtained from Pope Alexander VI in November of the same year,[22] and the prebends were designated, but in the end the endowment needed to support them could not be found before Charles' death on 8 April 1498, and the project foundered once again for lack of funding.[23]

The Order seems to have been maintained in much the same way under Charles' immediate successors, his cousins Louis XII, formerly Duke of Orléans (r. 1498–1515) and François I, formerly Count of Angoulême (r. 1515–1547). Under François' son and successor Henri II (r. 1547–1559), what seems to have been the first Assembly of the Order's history was held at Lyon at Michaelmas 1548,[24] and the seat of the Order was formally transferred by letters of 15 August 1555 to the royal castle of Vincennes, on the outskirts of Paris, for the greater convenience of the court. Nevertheless, during Henri's reign the Order began to grow rapidly in size. Although the statutes still limited the number of companions to the figure of thirty-six fixed by the founder in 1469, Henri II during his twelve-year reign (increasingly disturbed by feuding between Catholic and Protestant noblemen) appointed at least 101 new companions. This inflated rate of appointments increased exponentially during the reigns of Henri's two elder sons. François II (r. 1559–1560) appointed at least twenty-four companions during his reign of only seventeen months. His brother, Charles IX (r. 1560–1574) is known to have appointed seventeen companions in both 1561 and 1563, and fifty-six in 1564. In order to accommodate some, at least, of these new knights, Charles formally raised the official number of companions from thirty-six to fifty (the current number of the knights of the Golden Fleece) by letters of 3 April 1565.[25] After four years of relative restraint, however, he proceeded in 1569 to create no fewer than 151 new companions of the Order, and continued to appoint similar numbers in the five remaining years of his reign.[26]

---

feast has never been held, nor have the knights assembled; wherefore I say that it is nothing but an obligation by which the king of France obliges several knights in his service.' *Epistre pour tenir et celebrer la noble feste de la Thoison d'Or*, ed. H. Beaune and J. D'Arbaumont in *Mémoires d'Olivier de la Marche*, IV (Paris, 1888), pp. 161–162.

[22] Paris, B.N., ms. n. acq. fr.9760, f. 184.

[23] Most of the relevant documents are to be found in Paris, B.N., ms. fr.25188. See Contamine, 'L'Ordre de Saint-Michel', pp. 234–5.

[24] Paris, B.N., ms. Clairambault 1242, pp. 1705–13.

[25] Published in Comte Garden de Saint-Ange, *Code des Ordres de Chevalerie* (Paris, 1819; reissued with a preface by Hervé baron Pinoteau, 1979), pp. 151–4.

[26] See Colleville, Saint-Christo, *Les ordres du roi*, for a list of the knights appointed. Letters dealing with appointments to the Order in this period are to be found in Paris, B.N., ms. fr.3241, ff. 81–2, 3244, f. 132, and 3943, f. 17.

By the first centenary of its foundation, therefore, the Order of St Michael had definitively lost what remained of its character as a strictly limited, co-optive confraternity, and had become a mere pseudo-order, whose badge was distributed by its royal 'Sovereign' as a symbol of royal favour to as many men as he chose. So widely was this badge distributed, indeed, that it soon lost its value even as a sign of favour, and Charles IX's brother Henri III (r. 1574–1589), after attempting to restore its value by greatly reducing the number of creations (to two in 1574, six in 1575, and so forth), finally gave up, and in December 1578 proclaimed a new order, dedicated to and named after the Holy Spirit. The older Order was not suppressed, however, and membership in the new Order of the Holy Spirit (which was to have one hundred members) was actually restricted in large part to those who were already companions of the Order of St Michael. The latter order was maintained in this subordinate state until the Revolution of 1789, when both of the *ordres du roi* were officially abolished along with all other such distinctions. Although both orders were 'revived' under new statutes after the Restoration of 1815, the new orders were also discarded after the July Revolution of 1830, and since the latter date have been effectively defunct except as pictorial adjuncts to the arms of successive pretenders to the throne.

3 The Statutes of the Order

Like those of several earlier orders, the statutes of St Michael required that each new companion be given his own copy of the statute-book at the time he was informed of his election, and a number of fifteenth- and early sixteenth-century statute-books prepared for particular companions have come down to us. Those prepared for the founder's brother Charles, Duke of Guyenne,[27] and for Jean, Duke of Bourbon and Auvergne[28] – both of which can be recognized by the arms they bear on the first page – naturally contain only the text of the statutes adopted in 1469, but most of the surviving copies contain in addition to these the chapters added by Louis XI in 1476.[29]

Though differing in such particulars as the dedication, badge, and costume prescribed, and in the arrangement and division of the individual items, the statutes of the Order of St Michael adopted by Louis XI in 1469 were for the most part textually identical with those of the Golden Fleece, as revised in 1445. Their contents may therefore be indicated most economically in a table of concordance.

[27] Paris, B.N., ms. fr.19819. See Paul Durrieu, *Une peinture historique de Jean Fouquet; le roi Louis XI tenant un chapitre de l'Ordre de Saint-Michel* (Paris, 1891).
[28] Paris, B.N., ms. fr.5745.
[29] Among these are ibid., mss. fr.19246, 19815, 19818, and Clairambault 1242, pp. 1421–69. See Paul Durrieu, *Les manuscrits à peinture des statuts de l'ordre de Saint-Michel* (Paris, 1911). The primitive statutes have been published several times: in André Favyn, *Le Théâtre d'Honneur et de Chevalerie* (Paris, 1620), pp. 616–637; André Briçonnet, *Statuts de l'Ordre de Saint-Michel* (Paris, 1725); in the *Ordonnances des rois de France de la troisième race*, xvii, pp. 236–55; and in Comte Garden de Saint-Ange, *Code des Ordres de Chevalerie*, pp. 92–135.

Table 14.1

A Concordance of the Statutes of the Order of St Michael (M) with those of the Order of the Golden Fleece (F). (P = Prologue)

M	F	M	F	M	F	M	F
P	= P	17	= 62	34	= 27+	51	= 54,55
1	= 1,2	18	= 63	35	= 28,29,30	52	= 56,57,58
2	= 18	19	= 20a	36	= 31,32	53	= 59
3	= 3a–c	20	= 21	37	= 33	54	= 60
4	= –	21	= O.1	38	= 34	55	= 61
5	= 3d	22	= O.2,O.6	39	= 35	56	= O.18,O.19
6	= 4	23	= O.3	40	= 36	57	= O.20
7	= 5	24	= O.12,O.13	41	= 37,38	58	= O.21
8	= –	25	= O.14	42	= 39	59	= O.22
9	= 6+	26	= O.7	43	= 40	60	= O.26
10	= 7	27	= O.8	44	= 46,47,49cd	61	= O.23–25
11	= 8,9	28	= O.9–11	45	= 42	62	= O.27–28
12	= 10	29	= O.15–17, 64	46	= 44	63	= 65
13	= 11	30	= –	47	= 49ab,50a	64	= 66
14	= 12	31	= 22, 23	48	= 50bc	65	= 67a
15	= 13–16	32	= 24,25	49	= 51	66	= 67b
16	= 17	33	= 26	50	= 52,53		

Omitted from M: F.19, 20b, 43, 45, 48, O.4

As table 14.1 indicates, a few minor amendments were made by Louis in the substance as well as in the organization of the statutes he so largely plagiarized. Five of the Fleece statutes were omitted altogether from the constitution of the Order of St Michael: Chapter 19, introducing the four officers, chapter 20b, calling for a body of poor knights to be supported by the canonical college, and chapters 43, 45, 48, and O.4, prescribing certain details of the election procedure. None of these was of any particular importance however, and their omission merely made the statutes somewhat less precise when dealing with these matters.

Louis also added three chapters of his own invention, and significantly augmented another. In chapter 4 he added to the situations in which the great collar of the Order could be replaced by a simple chain, allowing the companions to wear the chain while going on a journey, staying in their own homes, hunting, or doing anything private and informal. In chapter 8 Louis increased the obligations of the Sovereign of the Order to the companions by requiring him to promise to maintain each of the companions in his dignities, lordships, and all his other rights and prerogatives, against anyone who might attempt to take them. By chapter 30 he confirmed the four officers of the Order in their offices and official possessions for life (in keeping with his general policy on the tenure of royal offices), and assured them of royal protection and justice even against the Sovereign and companions of the Order. Finally, in statute 34, Louis altered the colour of the mantle to be worn by the Sovereign during the two services for the dead from black to violet, thus distinguishing his costume, on those occasions only, from that of the other companions. Except for these rather unimportant alterations, the primitive statutes of the Order of St Michael differed from those of the Golden Fleece only when dealing with the strictly specific aspects of the new Order's patronage and iconography, which we shall examine in the remaining sections of this chapter.

The additional statutes promulgated by Louis by letters patent issued on 22 December 1476 comprise some sixty ordinances, organized into thirty-one chapters numbered 67 to 97 in most manuscripts, of which the last merely requires that they be annexed to the original set of statutes in all copies produced thenceforth.[30] Unlike the statutes of institution, most of these ordinances are relatively novel, and they contain most of the features of the Order which can be considered original to its founder. The great majority are concerned at least partly with the new office of *Prevost Maistre des Ceremonies* – an office without parallel in any other monarchical order, created as we have seen to act as a sort of executive officer or chief of staff for the Order.

The first fourteen ordinances, included in chapters 67 through 79, set forth the principal duties of the office. The *Prevost* or 'Provost', who was to enjoy a status comparable in every respect to that of the original four officers,[31] was above all to expedite in every way the establishment of the college of canons, the collection of its revenues, the construction of its buildings, and the performance of the divine office by its clergy.[32] He was also to keep careful watch over the behaviour of the companions of the Order, and if any of them committed a minor infraction of the statutes, he was to inform the companion, as well as to report it to the Registrar so that he could record it for presentation at the Chapter as he was required to do.[33] In addition he was to be informed of the death of each companion, so that he could order the statutory services for him.[34]

Chapters 80 to 87 describe in twenty-four ordinances the ceremony by which newly elected companions were to be received into the Order – a ceremony in which the Provost was to play a leading role. The ceremony called for in these chapters is similar to that described the statutes of the Neapolitan order of the Ermine, and it is possible that Louis drew his inspiration from a copy of those statutes which had by some route or another come into his hands. When a companion-elect was to be received, the Provost was to inform the companions presently in court that they were to present themselves for the ceremony at a particular time and place, unless they could give him a legitimate excuse.[35] The companions present were to be seated in the statutory order in the church appointed, and during the high mass (celebrated if possible by the Chancellor of the Order), the collar and habit to be conferred were to be laid before the king's seat on a sheet of red satin or taffeta, and censed when the priest censed the altar.[36]

---

[30] Published in Saint-Ange, *Code des Ordres*, pp. 136–150.
[31] Chs. 68, 70, 71. Ch. 69 merely reiterates the qualifications required announced in the prologue.
[32] Chs. 72–76.
[33] Chs. 77, 78.
[34] Ch. 79.
[35] Ch. 80.
[36] Chs. 81, 82.

After the king had made his offering, the Provost was to lead the senior companion present to bring in the companion-elect, who was to make his offering of one gold piece, followed by the other companions in order.[37] When the mass was over, the companion-elect was to be brought before the king, and after he had taken the oath prescribed and the king had given him the collar, the Provost was to bring him the habit, and either give it to the knight himself, or give it to the king to give to the knight. Whoever vested the knight was to say while doing so the following words: 'The Order vests and covers you with the habit of the amiable Company and fraternal Union, to the exaltation of our Catholic faith, in the name of the Father and the Son and the Holy Spirit'. To this the knight was to reply: 'In the name and praise of God, and to the honour of the said Order, may it be done'. The new companion was then to be led before the altar by the senior companion present, and after he had prayed there for a while, the Provost was to divest him of his habit, and give it back to the treasurer of the Order.[38] When the ceremony was over, all of the clothing the new companion had worn under the habit was to be given to the Provost, in payment for his services at the ceremony.[39] The ceremony thus described, though simpler than that used in the Order of the Ermine, was clearly designed to accomplish the same purpose, and it can hardly be doubted that Louis included it to satisfy those companions who felt that Louis had shown the Order too little honour in the first eight years of its existence.

The next two chapters, 88 and 89, add to the regular duties of the Provost, requiring him to keep a record in a 'little book' of everything he heard to the honour of the Order and its members, and to collect such information from the Order's King of Arms. At the end of each year he was to give this book to the king, so that he could provide whatever was necessary for the Order. Since the Registrar had been required (by chapter 24) to keep a similar book, this rule was merely a modification of a custom borrowed from the Golden Fleece. There is no evidence that either book was ever kept, but it is certainly possible that both were maintained, at least for a few years, and have simply been lost.

The ten ordinances of chapters 90 through 93 are more original in dealing with the status and income which the Provost (and incidently the other officers) were to enjoy thenceforth. In order that one of the officers of the Order could be with him at all times, Louis declared that the Provost was to be included among the ordinary councillors and officers of the royal household, and was to receive the usual rights and emoluments of a domestic officer. When the college of canons was properly endowed, he was also to draw from its income a salary of 600 *livres parisis* (a considerble sum), but until then was to receive an annual pension of 1000 *livres tournois*.[40] The other officers were to receive similar salaries from the income of the college: the Chancellor 800 l.p., the Treasurer 600, the Registrar 400, and the King of Arms 200.[41] Louis probably chose to include these ordinances in the statutes in order to assure the complaining companions that the Order was to be placed on a more solid footing than it had had until that time. No doubt he felt

---

[37] Ch. 83.
[38] Chs. 84, 85.
[39] Ch. 86.
[40] Chs. 90–92.
[41] Ch. 93.

that it would be easier to find the money to support five officers from year to year than to endow a college of canons in perpetuity.

Chapters 94 and 95 turn to a completely new topic, not obviously related to the office of Provost in any way: the patrono-cliental relationship between the Sovereign and the companions. To placate still further the companions who had felt slighted by his cavalier treatment of the Order, Louis promised that thenceforth he and his successors as Sovereign were to be be bound to maintain all of the companions 'in very loyal love', according to their qualities, to give them 'competent and reasonable pensions', 'to prefer them before all others in honours, offices, and charges', and furthermore 'to increase, augment, and remunerate them duly and liberally according to their merits and services'. In return for these remarkable concessions (no more than implicit in the statutes of most earlier orders), Louis required the companions to comply with the 'requests, pleasures, and reasonable wishes' of the Sovereign of the Order, and 'in all sweetness and cordial love, to employ themselves to accomplish [his] good and honest pleasures, without prejudice to their honours and conscience'. The effect of these two statutes was to convert the companions into something very like life-retainers of the King of France, bound to serve the latter not merely when he acted to defend the faith, the Church, or the kingdom (as required in chapter 6), but whenever called upon, so long as the service was honourable.

In chapter 96, Louis finally sought to deal with future complaints by requiring the companions to submit to the Provost of the Order, in person, by letter, or by messenger, any complaints they might have either about things ordered by the Sovereign, or about reports of their conduct. The Provost was then to report such complaints to the Sovereign, who was to act upon them as he saw fit. Louis thus placed his new lieutenant for the Order between the companions and himself.

4 The Patron, Name, Badge, and Costume of the Order

The nomenclature and iconography of Louis' new Order differed from that of the Golden Fleece in a general way in centring on the Order's heavenly patron rather than on its badge. In the prologue to the statutes, Louis expanded upon Duke Philippe's bare reference to his patron, St Andrew, in the following terms, declaring that he had founded the Order to the glory of God, in reverence of the Blessed Virgin,

> ... and to the honour and reverence of Saint Michael the first knight, who in God's quarrel battled against the ancient Enemy of the human race, and cast him out of heaven, and who has always guarded his place, and preserved and defended his oratory, called Mont Saint-Michel, without ever suffering it to be taken, subjected, or placed in the hands of the ancient enemies of our realm ...

As we have seen, the Archangel Michael had long been thought of in this fashion as a sort of celestial knight. Moreover, although St Denis was the principal patron of France, the Archangel's cult at Mont Saint-Michel had long been an important one in the kingdom, and as the passage above suggests, the fortified abbey, never taken by the English in the long war which had only recently ended in victory, had become the preeminent symbol of resistance to foreign invaders. Charles VII had in fact chosen to display an image of St Michael battling the Devil on his standards, and St Michael has thus become a recognised patron of the French monarchy.[42] Finally, the Archangel himself had appeared (among other heavenly personages) to Jeanne d'Arc, under whose inspired leadership the signal victory of Orléans had been won on one of his two annual feasts. St Michael was thus a highly appropriate patron for a French royal order – especially one founded to oppose the influence of the virtually foreign Duke of Burgundy.

The Archangel was honoured in the new Order not only in the same ways that St Andrew had been in the Burgundian order – that is, by the timing of its corporate assembly and the dedication of its corporate chapel and principal mass – but in the location of its seat at his principal shrine, and in its corporate name and device.[43] The monarchical orders founded in England, France, Sicily, and Aragon in the previous century had all taken the name of their heavenly patron as part, at least, of their formal designation, but it is not clear that any of them but the last had been commonly known by this name, and none had taken as its principal device an image of the patron himself. Louis broke with this tradition by adopting as the badge of his Order 'an image of *Monsieur* Saint Michael on a rock'. The rock was almost certainly meant to represent Mont Saint-Michel, since it was not part of the standard iconography of the Archangel. Representations of the badge made during Louis' reign (most of which are to be found on the frontispieces of the surviving statute-books) show a cut-out low-relief figure of a winged knight in armour, but without a helmet, standing on a small dragon (a symbol of Satan)[44] only rarely supported by a rock.[45]

According to the statutes of institution, this image was to be set into the middle of a collar of gold, made of cockles (*coquilles*) tied one to the other with a double knot, seated on *chainettes* or *mailles* of gold. The cockle-shells were generally represented more or less as in nature, and were invariably arranged (when closed) with the broad ends outwards. The knots were depicted with four loops and four loose ends, and were arranged so that the two outer loops were inserted into or behind the shells, while the two middle loops curled upwards to balance the four ends hanging below the central knot. The shells and knots were always about the same size, but the image of St Michael and the dragon was generally several times larger than the other elements, and hung below them when the collar was worn. Under the first two Sovereigns of the Order the image of St Michael was usually

---

[42] Beaune, 'Les devises', p. 145. A tapestry showing the winged stag supporting a standard bearing the image of St Michael was reproduced by W. R. Stæhelin, 'Symbolischer Wandteppich zum Gedächtnis an die Stiftung des St. Michael-Ordens 1469', *AHS* (1925), pp. 80–82.

[43] Louis also named his King of Arms 'Mont Saint-Michel'.

[44] See the representation of the collar of the Order on the first page of B.N., ms. fr.19819, published in Chaffanjon, *Les grands ordres*, p. 22.

[45] The only representation I have found that includes the statutory rock is that in B.N., ms. fr.19817.

freestanding and set into rather than suspended from the collar, but after the accession of Louis XII in 1498 it was normally set into an oval medallion, also of gold, which was hung from the collar by a link passing either through a shell or the loop of a knot.[46] After the accession of François I in 1515, a slightly different form of collar (possibly introduced as a variant under Charles VIII)[47] also came into general use. The shells were now represented more like scallops than cockles, and were commonly shown either wide open or doubled, one being placed over the other in such a way that only the upper and outer edges of the latter were revealed. Finally, the 'double knots' of the original collar were replaced by rather longer elements of similar gold cord arranged in a series of three to five shallow reversed S-curves over a single or double transverse cord which connected the adjacent shells.[48]

Like the collar of the Golden Fleece, the collar proper of the Order of St Michael seems to have had no particular significance as a symbol of the Order. The shell, the badge of the pilgrim, was apparently a device favoured by the founder, who collected saints' medals. The knots seem for once to have had no significance at all, and were probably introduced simply to bind the shells together in an aesthetically pleasing way. As we have seen, identical knots were soon to be employed to unite the garters in the new collar assigned by Henry VII to the Order of the Garter, which was clearly inspired by that of St Michael.

In most of the early statute-books, the collar of the Order is depicted partially or wholly encircling the shield of arms of the companion for whom the book was prepared, in keeping with the custom of the Golden Fleece, and by the end of the century the collar was regularly displayed in this fashion around the shield of the royal arms, however it was displayed.[49] Louis XII had his portrait painted wearing the collar of the Order in 1514,[50] and thereafter the Kings of France were rarely portrayed without it. Within a short time of the foundation of the Order its collar thus came to function as one of the most important symbols of the French monarchy. Not surprisingly, it came to be displayed in similar ways by the companions of the Order, who adopted the title *chevalier de l'ordre du roy*.

The formal costume assigned by Louis to the companions of the Order for wear on formal occasions conformed rather more closely than the collar to its Burgundian model. It was identical except in colour, material, and the details of its embroidery. The costume consisted of two elements only: a floor-length mantle of white damask, embroidered with a border of gold shells and knots as in the collar, and lined in ermine; and a *chaperon* of crimson velvet, exactly like that worn by the knights of the Golden Fleece. Red and white were the colours of Louis' livery, and they were no doubt chosen for that reason. The statutes specify that the *chaperon*

---

[46] See the portraits published in Chaffanjon, op. cit., pp. 23, 24, 25, 26.

[47] He is portrayed wearing such a collar in a portrait now in the Musée Condé, Chantilly, reproduced in Chaffanjon, op. cit., p. 25, but the portrait could have been painted after his death.

[48] See the collar on f. 11 of Paris, B.N., ms. fr. 19815.

[49] See for example the frontispiece of Robert Gaguin, *Compendium super Francorum gestis* (Paris, 1501), published in Beaune, 'Costume et pouvoir', Pl. 4.

[50] Reproduced in Desmond Seward, *Prince of the Renaissance. The Life of François I* (London, 1973), p. 37.

was to be worn either on the head or on the neck, but the representations of the companions in the habit of the Order which were painted on the opening page of most of the statutes-books (in emulation of the usage of the Golden Fleece) show all the companions wearing it in the late fifteenth-century fashion, slung over their right shoulder with the *cornette* or liripipe hanging down the front.

Twelve habits conforming precisely to the statutory description were in fact made for Louis in preparation for the meeting of the companions he planned to hold in March 1471, but finally cancelled. They were then put into storage until 1484, when they were brought out again to be worn at the Michaelmas Assembly planned for that year. Sixteen new sets of vestments were made at that time, since the Order then had thirty companions, and two of them – the Kings of Denmark and Scotland – were not expected to come. One of the new mantles (presumably that made for the young king himself) was described as being of 'German work'. None of these new habits, however, was ever worn.[51]

5 The Membership of the Order

Like the Order of the Golden Fleece, the Order of St Michael consisted in theory of a fixed number of lay knights called 'companions' presided over by an hereditary president with the double title 'Chief and Sovereign', and initially administered by four corporate officers. Louis deviated from his model in this area only in raising the theoretical number of companions from thirty-one to thirty-six, including the Sovereign. Like most of his initial modifications, this was probably introduced primarily to distinguish his Order from that of his enemy of Burgundy, though the fact that the number was higher rather than lower suggests that it was also meant to symbolize his superior rank. The number of companions remained theoretically fixed at thirty-six until 1565, when it was raised to fifty by Charles IX.

Whether the number of companions ever actually reached the official limit of thirty-six in our period is unclear. Unlike most of the earlier founders, Louis chose to appoint only fifteen of the thirty-five ordinary companions called for at the time of the Order's proclamation, and gave them the right to elect the twenty needed to complete the complement. The elections of these and all subsequent companions were supposed to be held during the meetings of the Order's chapter in accordance with a procedure which differed only in a few minor details from that of the Golden Fleece. In fact, as we have seen, this procedure was never followed in our period, and Louis and his successors continued to appoint new companions, after consulting the surviving members on an individual basis. Unfortunately, no official record seems to have been kept of who was appointed to the Order in this fashion, and it is not clear precisely when most of those who are known from other sources to have been companions of the Order under its founder and his immediate successors were actually elected or admitted. Moreover, the lists of members that have been reconstructed are almost certainly incomplete, so it is impossible to

---

[51] Contamine, 'L'Ordre de Saint-Michel', pp. 219–20, 227–8.

comment except in a very general way on either the size or the nature of the Order's membership in our period.[52]

In addition to two royal dukes, the fifteen original companions included four counts and several barons, but the thirteen non-royal knights were almost certainly chosen primarily on the basis of their official rather than their social status, for twelve of them were captains of royal *compaignies d'ordonnance*, and they included the Constable, the Admiral, and both Marshals of France, the Grand Master of the Household, and the royal governors of four of the most important provinces in the kingdom. Louis seems to have persuaded his uncle Duke René of Anjou to join in June or July 1471,[53] and offered membership to Duke Charles of Burgundy in the following November (in exchange for membership in the Order of the Golden Fleece), but was refused.[54] Offers of membership in the Order were also refused by Duke François of Brittany and Duke Adolph of Guelders, but King Christian I of Denmark, Norway, and Sweden, his son and successor King Hans, and King James III of Scotland all accepted membership in the Order at some time in this period. Of the remaining knights certainly admitted to the Order under the founder after the initial proclamation, not one was a duke, but several were titled barons, and the rest seem to have been either lesser barons or substantial knights. Like the original companions, those appointed after 1469 were drawn from all over the kingdom, but in certain periods political considerations led Louis to favour certain regions over others. Thus in 1472 Louis seems to have decided to use the Order to secure the loyalty of some of the leading barons of separatist Brittany,[55] some of whom probably wore the collar of the Breton ducal 'order', and when the sudden death of Charles 'the Rash' in 1477 gave him an excuse to seize the Duchy of Burgundy, he appointed a whole group of Burgundians to the Order, including several who were already knights of the Golden Fleece.[56]

Under Charles VIII, the Order was opened up to the princes of the blood, who with a few exceptions had been excluded by his father. Duke Louis of Orléans (the future Louis XII) was certainly admitted on 14 October 1483, shortly after Charles' accession, and Contamine has argued that most of the other princes who are known to have been members later in the reign – including Pierre of Beaujeu, Gilbert of Montpensier, François of Vendôme, Charles of Angoulême, and Jean of Nevers – were appointed to the order at about the same time, so that they could take part in the Assembly planned for the following Michaelmas.[57] Thereafter princes, both French and foreign, made up a large proportion of the Order's

---

[52] It would appear that the dates given in Colleville and Saint-Christo, *Les ordres du roi*, are unreliable, as they conflict in a number of cases with those documented by Contamine. For example, they place René of Anjou among the original companions, and assign the election of Louis of Orléans (and seven other princes of the blood) to the period before 1480.

[53] *Lettres de Louis XI*, IV (Paris, 1890), no. DLXXXIV, pp. 247–8. René was specifically allowed to continue wearing the device of the Order of the Crescent, which he had founded himself.

[54] K. Bittmann, *Ludwig XI. und Karl der Kühne. Die Memoiren des Philippe de Commynes als historische Quelle*, I (Göttingen, 1964), p. 566.

[55] Contamine, 'L'Ordre de Saint-Michel', pp. 223–5.

[56] *Lettres de Louis XI*, VI (Paris, 1898), no. MLXI, pp. 279–80.

[57] 'L'Ordre de Saint-Michel', pp. 226–7.

membership, and after the conquest of mainland Sicily by Louis XII in 1501, several of the most prominent princes of that kingdom accepted membership, only to resign it when Ferran of Aragon expelled the French forces once again. Nevertheless, men of lesser rank – mostly holders of important offices – continued to be appointed as well. A list of living knights of the Order compiled in 1556 (the only such list I have found) includes the names of the Emperor, four kings (including the Sovereign), six dukes (one foreign), six titled barons of lesser rank (two of them foreign), and five knights without a title of dignity.[58] The whole list includes only twenty-four names, and it is not unlikely that the number of companions commonly fell well below the statutory figure of thirty-six before that time.

Since we have no reliable list of members, it is of course impossible to know whether all of those admitted to the Order had received the accolade of knighthood, but it is significant that the founder's own son and successor, who became the Sovereign of the Order at the age of thirteen in August 1483, was not yet a knight, and was only admitted to that status (by Duke Louis of Orléans) on the day of his coronation, 30 May 1484.[59] In the meantime he had certainly received Duke Louis himself into the Order, and probably several other princes, which indicates that knighthood was considered no more essential for exercising the jurisdictional functions of the office of Sovereign than episcopal consecration was for exercising the jurisdictional functions of the office of bishop. It also indicates that companionship in the Order was still conceived of as quite distinct from knighthood in the more general sense, and that membership in the Order did not make one a knight.

There is no evidence to suggest that any companion was ever inducted into the Order in our period with the elaborate rite prescribed for such occasions in the statutes, but the knights who accepted appointment to the Order were required to swear the oath of membership and receive the collar either from the king himself or from an envoy sent to them by the king.[60]

As we have seen, several princes to whom membership was offered by Louis XI turned it down, presumably because they did not wish to accept the obligations to the Order's Sovereign imposed by the statutes. Indeed, Duke François of Brittany, when offered the collar in 1470, made it quite clear in his reply that he could not accept membership in the Order, not only because of the personal animosity he felt toward several of its companions, but because membership would place him in too close a dependance upon the King of France.[61] These refusals imply that the requirements of the statutes were taken quite seriously in our period, and this impression is confirmed by the text of the letter written on 12 November 1511 by the only companions known to have resigned from the Order before 1515: the Neapolitan barons Bernardino di Sanseverino, Prince of Bisignano, Troiano Caracciolo, Prince of Melfi, Andrea Matteo d'Acquaviva, Duke of Atri, and

[58] Paris, B.N., ms. Clairambault 1242, p. 1841.
[59] Contamine, 'L'Ordre de Saint-Michel', p. 226.
[60] Ibid., pp. 221–2.
[61] His reply is published in Briçonnet, Statuts, pp. 75–9. See also J. de Roye, Chronique scandaleuse, ed. B. de Mandrot (Paris, 1894), I, p. 234.

Giovanni Tommaso Carrafa, Count of Maddaloni, who had all been appointed to membership by Louis XII during his brief reign in Naples.

> Sacred [and] Most Christian Majesty, ... During the time when we were your subjects, you deigned to include us in your most honoured Order of the glorious St Michael, the statutes of which we have observed without violation, and with the whole integrity pertaining to knights. At the present, [as] the conditions of the time have so changed things that we find ourselves vassals and lieges of the Catholic King, our lord, we fear the situation has become such that our sincerity must be denigrated by the calumnious opinion of the people, and because it is necessary for good knights to be as clear of bad opinion as devoid of sin, moved by lawful and reasonable causes, we send by the Magnificent Messer Palatio, the bearer of this letter, to restore to your Majesty the abovesaid Order and collar, with every obligation appertaining to the said Order, as by you was graciously given. Given etc.[62]

This statement is the only indication I have found that the companions of the Order attempted to carry out those obligations of companionship which did not involve attendance at meetings, but there is a strong probability that, like these great barons, most of the knights of the Order tried to fulfil all of the obligations they had assumed with membership which did not conflict with what they perceived as their vital interests.

6 Conclusions: The Order of Saint Michael the Archangel

When he founded the Order of St Michael in 1469 to keep his brother from falling into the clutches of his rival Charles 'the Rash' of Burgundy, Louis XI – though personally contemptuous of chivalry and hostile to most of the knightly class of his kingdom – probably intended it to be a French equivalent of the Order of the Golden Fleece, and meant to convene the Assemblies called for in the statutes at reasonably short intervals, if not every year. Various events made it impossible to convene such an Assembly before the death of his brother in 1473, however, and when Charles 'the Rash' himself died in 1477, Louis – who disliked ceremonies and probably had no desire to give the noble companions any real influence over the affairs of the Order – apparently decided that there was no longer any reason to hold such an expensive gathering. To placate the companions, whose statutory right to elect their fellows and otherwise participate in the governance of the Order he thus abrogated, he conceded additional privileges to them, but at the same time increased the service they owed to him, and, in theory at least, converted them into life-retainers of the King of France. Louis may well have been sincere when at the same time he proclaimed his intention to provide the companions with a chapel in which the funerary masses owed to them could be said, and a college of clerks to serve it, for this would have added to their sense of dignity without in any

---

[62] Published in Giuseppe Maria Fusco, *Intorno all'Ordine dell'Armellino*, (Naples, 1841), pp. 16–17, n. 4.

way reducing his power, but he obviously did not place the funding of such a college high on his list of priorities, and neither he nor any of his immediate sucessors (who inevitably had less interest in the Order than its founder) succeeded in finding the necessary capital.

The Order of St Michael thus existed without a clerical college, a corporate seat, or corporate activities of any kind for nearly eight decades. It was not thereby reduced to the condition of a pseudo-order, however, for Louis and his successors in our period seem to have observed the ordinances restricting membership to a limited number of noble knights, and on occasion at least attempted to enforce other ordinances. The companions, for their part, seem to have taken the oaths they swore to obey the statutes quite seriously, and presumably considered themselves bound to aid their fellows as well as their Sovereign in the ways the statutes specified. Furthermore, although Louis himself was at best indifferent to the traditions of chivalry, the men he was obliged to appoint to the Order seem to have had a much more positive view of the ethos of their estate, and may well have enjoyed being seen as members of an élite body of noble knights created in the image of the Round Table. Thus, though it was hardly part of its founder's intention either to create a true fraternity of knights, or to promote among his clients the ideals of chivalry, he may well have succeeded in doing both of these things, as well as in creating an élite body of retainers bound to his service by both honour and interest.

Chapter 16

Epilogue
Developments from 1469 to 1525

The Order of St Michael the Archangel seems to have been the last monarchical order of knighthood to be founded by a Christian prince of any rank before the beginning of the Reformation in the years around 1520. In fact, no true lay order of knighthood of any sort is known to have been founded by a lay prince[1] in the period of nearly eleven decades between 1469 and 1578, when the quite unchivalrous order of the Holy Spirit was created to take the place of the ruined Order of St Michael.[2] The explanation for the lack of new foundations during the five decades between 1469 and 1520, at least, is not to be sought in a decline in the enthusiasm felt by the princes and barons of Europe for chivalry, for most of the evidence suggests that the chivalric Renaissance begun by the Dukes of Burgundy in the first decades of the fifteenth century continued well into the sixteenth century, and was little affected by the Lutheran and Calvinist reforms. Nor is it to be found in a decline in the value placed by princes in the monarchical order as a form of institution, for as we have seen, both Charles III of Savoy and Henry VIII of England gave the orders founded by their fourteenth-century ancestors new and more elaborate constitutions in 1518 and 1519 respectively, and Henri II of France held the first formal meeting of the Order of St Michael in 1548.

In fact, the explanation for the total lack of foundations between 1469 and 1578 is almost certainly to be found in the fact that by 1470, virtually every major court in Europe had a knightly order adequate to its needs, and the fact that during the following half century or so the number of royal courts in Europe declined markedly as a result of various personal unions, so that many of the existing orders were no longer necessary. After the marriage of Queen Isabel of Castile to her cousin Ferran, heir to the throne of Aragon, the old Castilian orders of the Band and the Collar of the Scale were discarded, and from that time until Isabel's death in 1503, the Aragonese Order of the Jar seems to have been the sole lay order of their united

---

[1] The only knightly order known to have been founded by a lay prince in this period was that of St Stephen, established by Cosimo de'Medici, second Duke of Florence, in 1561. It was a religious order, modelled on that of St John, but its mastership, like those of the religious orders of knighthood in Spain after 1523, was attached to the crown of its founder.

[2] The new Order was not formally conceived of as a society of knights, for the statutes of the Order contain no reference to knights or knighthood. See Comte Garden de Saint-Ange, *Code des Ordres de Chevalerie* (Paris, 1819), pp. 24–77.

court. Ferran's annexation of mainland Sicily in 1504 and of cis-Pyrenean Navarre in 1512 reduced still futher the number of royal courts, and substituted the Order of the Jar for the Sicilian order of the Ermine. It would appear that the Austrian order of the Eagle was similarly discarded when Maximilian von Habsburg, who had married the heiress of the Dukes of Burgundy in 1478, succeeded to the thrones and pretensions of his father the Emperor Friedrich III in 1494, and introduced into the Austrian lands the Order of the Golden Fleece. Maximilian's son, Philippe 'the Handsome', ruler of what remained of the Burgundian dominions and Sovereign of the Order of the Golden Fleece, introduced the latter order into the court of Castile when his wife Juana succeeded her mother Isabel as Queen in 1504, and when his son Charles succeeded Juana's father Ferran 'the Catholic' in 1516, the Golden Fleece replaced the Jar in the united courts of Aragon, Navarre, and the two Sicilies as well. The death of the last Jagellonian king of Hungary and Bohemia in battle against the invading Turks in 1526 made Charles' younger brother Ferdinand a contender for the thrones of what remained of those two kingdoms, and eventually (by 1538) introduced the dynastic order of the Golden Fleece into their united court – which on Charles' abdication in 1556 was merged with that of Austria. Thus, by 1538, the originally Burgundian Order of the Golden Fleece had come to serve as the sole lay order of no fewer than nine formerly separate states, now held by the brothers Charles and Ferdinand of Habsburg. The three kingdoms of Scandinavia were similarly served by a single order, that of the Elephant, until the Lutheran reform (which was hostile to its Catholic rather than its chivalrous character) brought about its dissolution in the 1520s. England, Savoy, and Scotland all remained independent and thus retained their own orders throughout the sixteenth century, though the Scottish pseudo-order of the Thistle may have fallen into disuse except as a decoration for the royal arms after the triumph of Calvinism in the 1560s. That left only Poland and Portugal, neither of which is known to have produced a royal order of its own before the end of the seventeenth century,[3] and the Order of the Golden Fleece was imposed on the court of Portugal in 1580, when the kingdom was annexed to Castile.

By 1525, therefore, there were only four monarchical orders left in Europe – those of the Garter, the Collar or Annunciation, the Golden Fleece, and St Michael – but these orders either served or would soon serve the courts of almost all of the kingdoms in which the royal house continued to adhere to some form of the Catholic faith. It is worth noting that by 1520 all four of the surviving orders, though founded at widely separated dates (1349, 1364/1409, 1430, and 1469), had been endowed with remarkably similar statutes, under which a college of between twenty and fifty lay 'companions' headed by a prince with the title 'Sovereign' or 'Chief and Sovereign' were served (at least in theory) by four or five corporate officers (including a chancellor, a registrar, and a king of arms) and a college of priests attached to a chapel dedicated to the order's heavenly patron, and supported (except in the case of the Order of St Michael) a body of 'poor knights'. To this

---

[3] The Polish royal order of the White Eagle was founded in 1713, and the Portuguese royal order of the Tower and the Sword was founded in 1808. At the time, their founders claimed to be reviving orders founded in the fourteenth and fifteenth centuries, but I have found no evidence for the existence of these orders in our period.

extent, at least, the three junior orders were all modelled (either directly or indirectly) on the Order of the Garter, which was by far the most successful of the fourteenth-century foundations, and the only one to survive under its original statutes into the fifteenth century. The statutes of the three junior orders also retained elements – mainly patrono-cliental and fraternal obligations peculiarly lacking in the statutes of the Garter – that had their origin in the statutes assigned to the Order of the Collar in 1409, but by 1520 both the Order of the Collar itself and the Order of St Michael derived these elements of their statutes directly from the statutes of the Order of the Golden Fleece, upon which their own had been either modelled or remodelled. The revised statutes of the Garter also contained ordinances that had first appeared in the statutes of both the Golden Fleece and St Michael. The similarities among the four orders at the end of our period were thus the result of a complex process of mutual imitation, in which first the Order of the Garter and then the Order of the Golden Fleece served as the principal model.

The form that these orders had assumed (at least on paper) by 1520 seems to have proved adequate to the needs of all successive generations of Sovereigns until the end of the eighteenth century, for no further changes of any consequence were introduced into the statutes of three of the orders before 1790,[4] and almost identical statutes were given to the Order of the Thistle in 1687, the Order of the Elephant in 1693, and the Order of the Bath in 1725. In practice, however, the statutes of the continental orders requiring regular assemblies and the election of new companions came to be ignored during the second half of the sixteenth century by their royal sovereigns, and all three were effectively reduced to a condition not very different from that of the cliental pseudo-orders in the period we have studied here. By 1570, the power and dignity of all Christian kings had been so much raised above that of their baronial subjects that it was no longer either necessary or useful for them to associate with barons on terms of equality and fraternity, and the chivalrous ideology which infused the statutes of the monarchical orders had finally been displaced by a courtly ideal more suited to the absolute subordination of noble courtiers to their prince. Thereafter, the orders were useful merely as sources of distinguished decorations that could be bestowed upon men of sufficient rank to reward their loyalty or service to the prince; other, more efficient means had been invented for attracting, compelling, and organizing that service in the context of the sovereign and bureaucratic state.

---

[4] The exception was the Order of the Collar, or of the Annunciation, which received new statutes from Duke Emmanuel Philibert in 1570.

Chapter 17

Conclusion:
The Monarchical Orders of Knighthood
1325–1520

I have now traced the development of the monarchical orders of knighthood from their origin in the second quarter of the fourteenth century to the eve of the Reformation, and have examined in some detail the history and nature of each of the thirteen orders of this class whose statutes I have been able to discover. In this final chapter I intend to examine the same orders in a more general way, to place them within the context of the culture and society that gave rise to them, and to assess their value to those who founded, maintained, and belonged to them in the years before 1520.

1 Foundations and Founders

The idea of creating an order of lay knights attached to a royal court seems to have occurred independently to kings at opposite ends of Western Christendom in 1325 and 1330: Károly I of Hungary and Alfonso XI of Castile. Both of these kings created lay orders that bore a strong superficial resemblance to orders of the traditional religious type, and there is some reason to believe that they not only used such orders as general models, but drew part of their inspiration to create a knightly order from the recent foundation of successors to the Order of the Temple in Portugal (1317) and Aragon (1319). Both kings also gave their order a confraternal form of constitution, and borrowed certain features of the fictional order of the Round Table, so the monarchical order was from the first a hybrid of all three forms of society. It is not clear that any later foundation was inspired solely by the Fraternal Society of St George of Hungary (though the Neapolitan order of the Ship and the later Hungarian society of the Dragon almost certainly borrowed from its statutes), but the decision of Edward III of England to reestablish the Round Table in 1344 was almost certainly based upon what he had just learned of the Castilian order of the Band, and the latter must therefore be regarded not only as the first truly monarchical order, but as the ancestor of most subsequent orders of that type. Edward of England's Round Table project and the Order of the Garter it eventually gave rise to stand in a similar relationship to most of the later orders, for they undoubtedly inspired the creation of the French company of the Star in 1351, and probably served as the direct inspiration for the foundation of the German confraternal society of the Buckle in 1355, the Savoyard order of the Collar in

1364, the Bourbonnais quasi-order of the Golden Shield in 1367, and the Breton order of the Ermine in 1381. The Company of the Star for its part served as the direct model for the first Neapolitan order of the Knot in 1352 and the indirect model for the second Neapolitan order of the Ship in 1381. The creation of the Order of the Garter in 1348 may also have inspired Pierre of Cyprus to create his order of the Sword in the same year (though this is much less clear), and the latter order probably served as the principal model for the Aragonese enterprise of St George in 1371/5. The Order of the Golden Fleece was directly modelled on the Orders of the Garter and the Collar (the only full-fledged monarchical orders still surviving at the time it was founded in 1430), while the Order of the Ermine of Sicily was modelled in 1465 upon those of the Garter and the Golden Fleece, and the Orders of St Michael (in 1469) and the Annunciation (in 1518) lifted most of their ordinances directly from those of the Golden Fleece.

As this rapid survey of their affiliation suggests, the period of roughly half a century between 1325 and 1381 saw the foundation of a lay order of monarchical or quasi-monarchical type in almost every royal court in Western Christendom where a romance language was a common medium of communication (the only exceptions being the courts of Navarre and Portugal), and in the courts of two French-speaking dukes who, though vassals of the Emperor and the King of France respectively, were nevertheless effectively sovereign within their extensive dominions. The year 1381 itself saw the creation of the first order founded to replace an order which had dissolved, but in the period of just under half a century between that year and the foundation of the Order of the Golden Fleece in 1430, the only order founded anywhere in Europe that certainly had a monarchical constitution was the vestigial order of the Stole and Jar, founded by a cadet of the royal house of Castile in 1403, and soon transferred to the royal court of Aragon. Successive Dukes of Austria – like the Counts of Savoy and Dukes of Brittany effectively sovereign princes anxious to assert their independence from their royal lords – founded three orders that might have been monarchical in the 1380s and '90s, and in 1433, but for some reason the other princes of Germany preferred confraternal orders to those of the neo-Arthurian type favoured by their romance-speaking cousins. Even among the highly Gallicized princes of the Imperial house of Luxemburg only Sigismund, then (1408) Marquis of Brandenburg and King of Hungary, founded a quasi-monarchical order, and although it replaced the defunct society of the knights of St George, its statutes made no reference to knighthood or chivalry. In fact, the territory within which monarchical orders were maintained increased very little after 1381, for three of the four courts in which unquestionably monarchical orders were founded or introduced after that date – those of Aragon, mainland Sicily, and France – had already had at least one such order attached to them. The exception was the (French-speaking) court of Burgundy, which only emerged as an important and virtually independent state in the decade or so immediately preceding the foundation of the Order of the Golden Fleece in 1430. An order that may have been monarchical was finally established in or about 1457 in the court of the united kingdoms of Denmark, Norway, and Sweden, which had just been reunited under a new German dynasty, but this order is just as likely to have been confraternal, like the orders founded by other German princes in the same period.

The fully developed, neo-Arthurian monarchical order may thus be seen as an institution both characteristic of and possibly peculiar to the courts of kings and effectively sovereign dukes whose mother (or ancestral) tongue was a romance language.[1] The creation of such orders in the courts of almost all of the princes in this category in the half-century between 1330 and 1381, and particularly in the two decades between 1344 and 1364, may plausibly be linked both to the keen interest most such princes took in all the uses of chivalry in that period, and to the simultaneous adoption in many of the same courts of ever more detailed household ordinances, increasingly elaborate rules of etiquette and ceremony, and constantly varying modes of dress, ultimately including livery uniforms in particular cuts and colours. Since the orders founded in the four decades between 1430 and 1469 were all modelled either directly or indirectly on two of the early orders, and their statutes contained very little that had not been included among the ordinances of at least one of the orders founded by 1381, the monarchical order can also be described with some justice as a form of institution both invented and largely perfected in the middle decades of the fourteenth century, which to a greater or lesser extent epitomized the chivalrous culture of the romance-speaking courts of that period.

Although a desire to be in fashion or to possess an institution which had come to be characteristic of the courts of sovereign princes undoubtedly played a part in the decision of many princes to found a monarchical order of knighthood, there is reason to believe that such desires were rarely uppermost in the minds of founders at the time they made their decision to establish an order of their own. As we have seen, most of the founders created their order in reponse to a very particular political situation, often quite pressing, and tailored the statutes of the order to suit their perceived needs in that situation. Five of the founders – Károly of Hungary, Alfonso of Castile, and Loysi, Carlo, and Ferrante of mainland Sicily – had just succeeded in securing or consolidating their power against considerable opposition from rivals or overmighty subjects, and founded their orders primarily to strengthen their hold on their leading subjects in anticipation of further difficulties. Edward of England, by contrast, had just won a brilliant victory at Crécy which appeared to vindicate his claim to the throne of France, and created his Order of the Garter to commemorate that victory, to reward and celebrate the prowess of the most eminent members of the different knightly strata of his armies, and to enhance his own image as the heir of the legendary king Arthur. Edward's enemy Jean of France, for whom the Battle of Crécy had been a humiliating defeat, founded his Company of the Star as soon as possible after his accession to promote both loyalty and higher standards of knightly conduct among the knights of his realm. Pierre of Cyprus and Amé of Savoy both founded orders to form the core of the force they hoped to lead on a crusade to reconquer the Holy Land. Philippe of Burgundy created the Order of the Golden Fleece on the occasion of his second wedding primarily to bind together in his service the leading members of the nobilities of the various mutually independent dominions he and his immediate predecessors had acquired, and Louis of France created his Order of St Michael primarily to act as a foil to the Order of the Golden Fleece at the height of his rivalry with Charles 'the

---

[1] Károly of Hungary and Edward of England were both members of French dynasties, and were brought up speaking Italian and French respectively, but their descendants spoke those tongues only as second languages.

Rash' of Burgundy. Only Pere of Aragon and Fernando of Peñafiel, who ultimately succeeded him, seem to have decided to found a monarchical order without any particular occasion or need, and the orders they founded, intended merely to honour their more important vassals and officers, were by far the simplest and least demanding.

Because they were founded for such very different reasons, the monarchical orders, while sharing a number of characteristics which gave them a strong family resemblance, differed from one another in many very important ways. This was especially true of the orders founded in the fourteenth century, which at first glance, at least, appear to have had little in common besides a broadly confraternal form of constitution (which they shared with thousands of other societies of extremely varied types) and an hereditary presidency. The differences among the orders defy easy classification, though rough divisions can be made between the orders that were intended to be very large and those that were meant to be relatively small, between those with very elaborate statutes and those whose statutes were relatively simple, and between those which made heavy demands upon their members and those in which the demands were relatively light. Since these classes overlap one another in various ways, it will be more useful to consider the similarities and differences among the various orders we have studied under the various headings I have used throughout this study.

2 The Names and Titles

The form of corporate designation which was ultimately to prevail among the monarchical orders was actually adopted by the founder of the first true order of this class, Alfonso of Castile, who gave his foundation the title 'order', previously peculiar (in the relevant sense) to religious orders, and a name taken from its distinctive device. The founder of the second order, Edward of England, seems to have been unsure of the propriety of this very novel form of nomenclature, and protected himself by giving it the alternative titles 'company' and 'society' (which were used by corporate bodies of all kinds, including many confraternities) and by giving it an alternate name taken from that of its patron saint (a type of name common among both confraternities and religious orders of knighthood). The next two founders (Jean of France and Loysi of Sicily) rejected the first form of designation altogether, and gave their foundations the more modest title 'company' and a name derived from that of their patron followed by an attribute peculiar to the order – in the first case the newly-adopted name of the order's seat, which was itself inspired by the Arthurian legend. Thereafter most founders, taking their lead from the Garter, gave their foundations the title 'order' and a name taken from its badge, but the first Aragonese order was given the peculiar title 'enterprise' (which seems to have taken on the same meaning as 'order'), and both it and the second French order took their name from their patron (whose effigy the latter used as its badge). The titles 'company' and 'society' survived throughout our period as alternative designations for most of the monarchical 'orders', and were commonly used by knightly orders of the confraternal type. *Gesellschaft*, the German word for 'society', seems in fact to have been used of the various German orders in preference to the more Latinate term *Orden*. It is clear that, by 1360 at the latest, all three titles were generally regarded as synonymous when used to describe a body of knights.

3 The Patrons and Their Cult

Religious orders and confraternities of all kinds were invariably placed under the protection of some heavenly personage, usually chosen because of his supposed interest in the locality or profession of the founders, and it was only to be expected that most of the princes who founded monarchical orders of knighthood would establish a similar form of relationship with an appropriate member of the celestial hierarchy. In fact, it is surprising that several of the orders we have examined – the Band, the Sword, and the various Austrian orders – are not known to have been given a patron by their founders. Six of the remaining orders were dedicated to one or the other of the two principal patrons of knighthood: three of them to St George (who was also the patron of two religious orders and several confraternal orders of knights), and three to St Michael the Archangel. Two of the orders dedicated to the soldier-martyr of Lydda (the Garter and St George of Aragon) were founded in kingdoms which had long had a particular devotion to that saint, and two of those dedicated to the captain of the heavenly hosts (the Ermine of Sicily and St Michael of France) were founded in the kingdoms which contained his principal shrines. Another three orders (the Star, the Collar, and the Stole and Jar) gave their corporate devotions to the Blessed Virgin Mary, who as the Queen of Heaven was also an appropriate object for the devotion of chivalrous knights. The remaining orders were given patrons with no particular chivalric associations. One order (the Knot) was dedicated to the Holy Spirit, whose cult had been promoted in the founder's court by the Spiritual Franciscans; one (the Ship) was dedicated to the Holy Trinity, for whom a feast day had only recently been created; and one (the Golden Fleece) was dedicated to St Andrew, the traditional patron of the founder's principal dominion.

The heavenly patron was generally honoured (in those orders which acknowleged one) in all of the ways conventionally employed in confraternities. Even if the order did not take its name from that of its patron it dedicated its chapel to him and celebrated his principal feast or feasts with suitable corporate devotions. All but four of the orders whose statutes we have examined (the Band, the Ship, the Golden Fleece, and the Ermine of Sicily) eventually included a symbol or an effigy of their patron among their insignia, and several orders (including the Golden Fleece) displayed such a symbol or effigy on their corporate banner or on a banner closely associated with the order. Two orders (those of the Collar and the Ermine of Sicily) even fixed the number of their companions and priests on the basis of numbers associated with their patron.

Despite all this, the relationship of the knights of all monarchical orders to their patron seems to have been largely formal, and there is little to suggest that they really expected the patron to do very much for them. In fact, the principal function of the patron in most orders was probably to give the order the appearance of piety.

4 The Prince Presidents

The characteristic feature of the monarchical orders of knighthood – the feature which alone distinguished them from confraternities and true orders of knighthood of all other types – was of course a presidency that was both life-long and hereditary. Not all of the orders founded by princes in our period were endowed with a presidential office of this type, which was not at all common in corporate bodies other than dominions, but almost all of the kings who founded true lay orders of knighthood before 1520 seem to have felt that the only way they could be sure of retaining sufficient control over their order for themselves and their successors on the throne was to give the order a presidency annexed in perpetuity to their crown or their house. In fact, all but two of the princes who founded monarchical orders (Carlo of Sicily and Ferran of Aragon) explicitly or implicitly attached the presidency of the order to the crown of their principal dominion, so that whoever succeeded them on the throne could assume control of the order without any opposition, even if he was not the natural heir either of his predecessor or of the founder. Carlo of Sicily, no doubt fearful that his order might come under the control of his rival Louis of Anjou or one of his heirs if he annexed its presidency in the usual way to his crown, gave the president the right to name his successor from among his own legitimate sons, or if he had no sons, from among his male agnates in general, but there is little reason to believe that either he or any of his successors as king would have chosen to bequeath the presidential office to anyone other than his natural heir. Ferran 'of Antequera' had founded the Order of the Stole and Jar before he had any expectation of succeeding to the throne of Aragon, so it can hardly be surprising that he implicitly entailed the right to appoint the members of his vestigial order (which had no real corporate organization) to the heirs of his body, without reference to any particular status. In practice, however, both he and his successors as king treated the order as an adjunct of the crown of Aragon.

Confraternities were normally governed by officers with strictly limited powers elected for a short period of time, but the religious orders of knighthood were all ruled by 'masters' with extensive authority who, once elected, usually retained their office for life. Thus, though the historical precedent for the attachment of the presidency of a knightly order to a royal crown was undoubtedly found in the Arthurian legends, the most useful model for the sort of presidency the founders of monarchical orders clearly wanted to create was the office of master in one or more of the religious orders. There is reason to believe that the earliest founders did in fact use this office as a model, to the extent that the very different nature of their orders permitted, and in most of the orders we have examined the president performed almost all of the major functions normally performed by the master in a religious order – including receiving new members, convening and presiding over the order's chapters, appointing its officers, overseeing its affairs, and leading its members in battle. Unlike the master of a religious order, however, the president of a monarchical order was obliged to provide out of his own pocket both the order's physical facilities, and most or all of the money necessary to pay the order's clergy and lay officers, and furthermore to defray the full costs of the order's regular and irregular assemblies. As a sovereign prince, he was also obliged to devote most of his time to matters in no way concerned with the order as such. To this extent, at least, his position was closer to that of the fictional kings Arthur and Perceforest in the societies of the Round Table and the Frank Palace. In some orders the president was also required to provide the badges and habits of the companions, which constituted a sort of livery, and in most orders the whole relationship between him and the companions of the order was broadly similar to that between an English lord and his life retainers.

In many respects, therefore, the presidency of a monarchical order was an office *sui generis*, and most founders signalized their recognition of its peculiar nature by giving it a title not used for any other office. Pere and Ferran of Aragon do not seem to have adopted any special title in respect of the orders they founded, and it is not clear what title, if any, was used by the presidents of the orders whose statutes I was unable to discover. Among the founders of the orders whose statutes we have examined, only Alfonso of Castile adopted for himself and his successors the traditional title 'master' (which was currently borne by many kinds of functionary, high and low); all later founders preferred some elegant synonym, suggestive at once of superiority and of lordly or monarchical powers. Edward of England took the title *souverain*, which he clearly regarded as equivalent to the Latin *superior*, but his rival Jean of France preferred the title *prince*, and that title was adopted by the founders of the orders of the Knot and the Ship, which were modelled upon that of the Star. Amé of Savoy adopted the double title *seigneur et chef*, and Philippe of Burgundy, whose order of the Golden Fleece was modelled on those of the Garter and the Collar, combined the titles of both their presidents in the double title *chef et souverain*. This title in its turn was adopted by the founders of the Orders of the Ermine of Sicily (in the form *capo et superiore*) and St Michael, and by the reformer of the Order of the Collar, so that by the end of our period every president bore the title 'sovereign' and most bore the title 'chief'.

In the orders we have studied, the position of the president was marked primarily by the special place he occupied in processions and in the chapel, hall, and chapter house. In most orders (all, in fact, except the Garter and St Michael), the insignia and costume worn by the president were identical with those worn by the ordinary members, and where distinctions were made they were of a very minor nature.

5 The Knights, Brothers, or Companions

Like the knights of the fictional societies of the Round Table and the Frank Palace, the ordinary members of the monarchical orders of knighthood invariably formed, with the president of their order, a true college, in which only the president himself enjoyed any rights which raised him above the others. Unlike the religious orders of knighthood, most monarchical orders had no offices which could be held by their members, and no order divided its members into classes distinguished by special titles or insignia. Some orders did give special treatment to members who were sovereign princes, and others fixed the size of entry fees or fines, or the number of masses owed to deceased companions, on the basis of precise civil rank, but most orders paid relatively little attention to such external distinctions, and arranged

457

their ordinary members on the basis of their precedence within the order itself, or their chivalrous achievements.

The term most commonly employed to designate the ordinary members of the orders we have examined was 'knight'. In fact, this term was used to refer to the ordinary male members in the statutes of every one of the orders, including those that did not require formal knighthood for admission. Perhaps because the title 'knight' did not in itself suggest membership in a collegiate body, however, certain terms indicative of collegiality were also commonly employed. The title 'brother' (*frater*, *confrater*, or *frere*), probably borrowed from the religious orders of knighthood, was used to designate the members of the Hungarian society of St George, and the members of the Orders of the Collar, the Golden Fleece, the Ermine of Sicily, and St Michael, but the title most commonly employed was 'companion' (*socius*, *compaignon*, *compagno*), applied to the members of the Garter, the Knot, the Collar, the Ship, the Golden Fleece, the Ermine, and St Michael. In several orders all three titles were used, either in random alternation or in various combinations.

In keeping with the general custom of confraternities, admission to the status of companion in most of the orders we have examined was restricted to persons who possessed certain particular qualities, but these qualities were generally set forth rather tersely in the statutes. Not surprisingly, the only quality explicitly required of a prospective companion by more than half of the orders was formal knighthood, which all but two of the orders we have studied required for admission (though not for election). The statutes of both the Castilian order of the Band and the initially Castilian order of the Stole and Jar imply that squires as well as knights could be admitted to full membership, and the first order certainly admitted a number of men who did not receive the accolade until some years after their reception. It is perhaps worth noting here that admission to an order did not itself entail admission to knighthood, and that while some founders are known to have knighted companions-elect immediately before receiving them into their order, no order made any formal provision for conferring knighthood upon its members.

Since only men could be knights, those orders that were formally restricted to knights were *ipso facto* restricted to men as well, but in practice the Order of the Garter regularly admitted high-born ladies to some sort of associate status from 1376 to 1495, and the statutes of the Aragonese order of the Stole and Jar explicitly opened the order to 'ladies and damsels' as well as to squires. Perhaps because knighthood was generally bestowed in that period only on men of noble birth, only three of the fourteenth-century orders – the Band, the Garter, and the Ship – listed nobility of blood among the qualities required for membership, and in the first order this quality was actually substituted for knighthood. All three of the major fifteenth-century foundations we have examined – the Orders of the Golden Fleece, the Ermine, and St Michael – required candidates to be noble, but the second explicitly permitted the admission of men who had been ennobled for their 'toil and industry', probably to allow the induction of certain notable *condottieri* whom the founder wished to reward. It is significant that, unlike orders founded in later centuries, no order specified either the number or the identity of the ancestors from whom the hereditary nobility they required was to be derived; presumably anyone reputed noble in the land of his birth was considered acceptable in most orders. Alfonso of Castile required candidates for admission to the Order of the

Band to be vassals of either the king or one of his sons, and his fellow Iberian Pere of Aragon required all knights admitted to his Enterprise of St George to do homage to him, but no other founders saw fit to enact a similar restriction. It is likely that most of the later founders had less confidence in the efficacy of the seigniorio-vassalic bond than Alfonso, and felt that the oaths of loyal service imposed by the statutes of their order were sufficient for their purposes. Furthermore, most founders clearly hoped to attract distinguished foreigners into their order, and did not want to put any unnecessary obstacles in the way.

In addition to these formal qualities, a few orders also required certain more personal qualities in candidates for election, but these were defined only in the most general terms in the statutes of every order except that of the Ship, and seem to have been mentioned primarily to give the order the appearance of excluding all but the most worthy members of the knightly class. The prologue to the Band statutes declared that only the 'best' knights and squires were to be admitted to the order, but failed to specify the nature of the superiority expected. Several later orders – the Garter, the Collar (from 1434), the Ship, the Golden Fleece, and St Michael – explicitly excluded from membership any knight who had committed an act worthy of *reproche*, and the Order of the Star may have done the same, but only the statutes of the Ship specified the acts deserving such 'reproach' before 1519, when Henry VIII declared the acts for which expulsion had been prescribed by the founder of the Golden Fleece – flight from battle, heresy, and treason – to be those enormous enough to merit exclusion. Philippe of Burgundy also formally excluded from his order knights of illegitimate birth, and legitimacy was therefore required for election to the Orders of St Michael and the Annunciation. No other quality was formally demanded of candidates in the statutes of any order save that of the Ship, probably because most founders did not wish to place inconvenient restrictions upon their freedom to secure the admission of their relatives, friends, and allies.

Neither the religious orders of knighthood nor most forms of confraternity had set limits on the number of their ordinary members, but the founders of all but five of the true monarchical orders (the Band, the Sword, St George of Aragon, the Ship, and the Stole and Jar), no doubt emulating the practice of the knightly societies described in the Arthurian romances, (but possibly influenced by the normal practice of colleges and collegiate churches), declared that their order was always to include a specific number of knights. The first founder to do so was Károly of Hungary, whose limit of fifty may have been inspired by the number of knights assigned by Robert de Boron to the Society of the Round Table. Edward III initially intended to create an order of 300 knights – the number of members in the fictional society of the Frank Palace – and both his rival Jean of France and the latter's cousin Loysi of mainland Sicily assigned similar limits to their orders. The former at first planned to establish an order of 200 knights, but later decided to raise the limit to 500, while the latter set himself a goal of 300. All of these limits were very high in relation to the number of knights currently living in the kingdoms ruled by these princes, and if achieved would have created companies of knights as large as those maintained by the greatest of the religious orders of knighthood at the height of their power. It must be presumed that the three kings in question set such high limits in order to exert as wide an influence as was practically possible through the order, while at the same time preserving some semblance of selectivity. In all likelihood the five founders who set no limit at all on the number of knights that could be admitted to their order had a similar idea in mind. Whether in reality any of these orders ever included much over a hundred knights is to be doubted, however, and Edward of England, who had set the fashion for high limits in his project of 1344, ultimately decided to found a much smaller society, initially restricted to twenty-four and finally to twenty-six companions, including himself. This very low limit may well have been chosen primarily in order to avoid the expense of building a special building to house the order, as he had actually begun to do, but since Edward had no real need for a large body of knights attached to his court, he lost nothing and may well have gained a good deal by making his order more exclusive. Most of his contemporaries seem to have felt that inclusiveness would be more useful than exclusiveness, however, and between 1349 and 1430 only one other founder – Count Amé of Savoy – imposed a similar limit on the number of companions.[2] By 1429, however, the only full-fledged monarchical orders still surviving were the two with low limits, and the three certainly monarchical orders founded after that year were all given limits based on that of the Garter: thirty-one, twenty-seven, and thirty-six, respectively. Of all the figures chosen as limits, only those of the Collar and the Ermine were certainly chosen for symbolic reasons; the others seem to have been adopted either arbitrarily, or for reasons that were purely practical. It is worthy of note that while Edward of England – who presided over the principal ceremonies of his order from a stall in the order's chapel opposite that of his son and heir – limited his order to an even number of knights, most of the later founders adopted odd numbers, presumably so that they could sit or process alone before the pairs of ordinary companions.

Confraternities of most types required that new members be chosen through some sort of election, and in keeping with this general practice, most of the founders of monarchical orders gave the current companions a role in the selection of successors to companions who had died or had otherwise left the order. Only the founders of the Orders of the Band, the Knot, the Sword, and the Stole and Jar retained to themselves and their heirs an unrestricted power of appointment, and the last society was little more than a pseudo-order throughout its history. In some orders – the Garter, the Collar, the Ship (in certain cases), and the Ermine of Sicily – the election was supposed to take place at a special chapter held within a short time of the loss of the member to be replaced, but in most the election was to be held during the course of the next regular assembly of the order, even if that was not to be convened until several years later.

Like those of most other sorts of confraternity, the rules governing the process of the election varied significantly from one order to another. The Order of the Garter required each companion present to submit a list of nine candidates, including three titled barons, three simple barons or bannerets, and three knights bachelor, but the knights of the Golden Fleece, the Ermine of Sicily, and St

---

[2] It is perhaps worth noting here that two orders founded by princes in this period that did not conform to our definition of a monarchical order had similar limits: the Order of the Buckle, founded by the Emperor Karl IV in 1355 had twenty-six members, and the Society of the Dragon, founded by King Zsigmond of Hungary in 1408, had twenty-four principal members.

Michael were each required to submit only one name, and in the Society of St George of Hungary and the Order of the Ship the king alone could present candidates for election. The founders of the last two orders and that of the Band expected postulants to present themselves to the king in keeping with the custom both of the religious orders of knighthood and of ordinary confraternities, but most of the other orders made no provision whatever for active postulancy, and the statutes of the Sicilian order of the Ermine specifically forbade the admission of any knight who had actively sought membership in the order.

The formal role of the prince-president in the electoral process also varied greatly from one order to another: the Sovereign of the Garter could ignore the votes of the ordinary companions completely, while the Sovereigns of the Golden Fleece, the Ermine, St Michael, and the Annunciation were all obliged to declare elected any candidate who had received the required plurality of the votes cast, and could decide the outcome only in the case of a tie. It would appear that the founders of the last four orders placed this formal restriction upon their right to name members to the order primarily in order to give the companions the feeling that they were not just clients of their prince-president, but equal members of a self-governing *collegium* over which he merely presided. In practice the prince-presidents whose rights were thus restricted almost certainly let it be known before the conclave whom they wished to see elected to the order, and it is most unlikely that many candidates favoured by the president of any order were excluded, or that many he opposed were actually admitted to the order.

In most of the orders we have studied, at least, a candidate who had been declared elected was formally received into the society through some sort of ceremony. In the statutes of the orders founded before 1381 this ceremony is not described in any detail, but it is clear that in these as in the later orders it was ordinarily to take place in the presence of the prince-president, and was to involve swearing an oath of obedience to the statutes (and in some orders supplementary oaths of loyalty and fraternity), and the reception of the insignia and/or habit of the order from the president's hands. To this extent, at least, the induction ceremonies of the monarchical orders were essentially similar to those employed to admit new knights to the religious orders of knighthood. The Order of the Ship and all of the orders founded after 1429 required companions-elect to pass through extremely elaborate induction rites, clearly designed to impress upon them the importance of the order and the seriousness of their undertaking.

Several orders had special rules governing the induction of foreign princes, who would obviously find it difficult to come to the court of the order's president to take the oaths of membership. The Order of the Garter permitted installment by proxy, while those of the Ship and the Ermine of Sicily permitted foreign princes to be inducted *in absentia* by a special envoy of the Prince, and the Order of the Golden Fleece and the later orders patterned on it allowed foreign princes to defer their induction until the next convenient chapter. Two of the orders we have examined – those of the Ship and the Stole and Jar – also permitted foreign princes who had been admitted to the order to induct other foreign companions *in absentia*, and in the former order, at least, the foreign prince could apparently be given the right to choose the companions he was to induct, up to a certain specified number. By 1475 the Orders of the Garter and the Golden Fleece, finding that most foreign princes elected to membership never got around to having themselves admitted as the statutes required, had also adopted the practice of investing such princes in their own courts, and this was to be the norm thereafter.

It is difficult to generalize with any confidence about the actual membership of the orders we have studied, because extensive lists of members have been reconstructed only for five of them – the Band, the Garter, the Collar, the Golden Fleece, and St Michael – and only those compiled for the Garter and the Golden Fleece are even approximately complete. A mere handful of the members of most of the remaining orders have been identified with any degree of certainty, and we know nothing whatever about the others. We also know almost nothing about the precise time or circumstances of the admission of most of those companions whose names *are* known in the period before 1420, and even after that date our knowledge of these matters is restricted entirely to the Orders of the Garter and the Golden Fleece. Our ability to deduce why particular companions were chosen in preference to other possible candidates, especially in the first nine decades of our period, is thus severely limited. Nevertheless, it is possible to make a few general observations about the sort of men who were actually admitted to the monarchical orders in our period.

Although only Edward of England required the companions of his order to nominate knights from all three strata of the nobility, there are a number of reasons to believe that most of the fourteenth-century founders hoped to attract knights of all ranks into their orders, including knights bachelor of relatively humble origins. The very high membership goal set in some of the early orders could not have been reached without including a significant number of simple knights, and the failure of some founders to set any limit on membership suggests that they too hoped to secure the membership of a large number of minor knights. Presumably these early founders wanted either to give their order the appearance of being representative of the knightage of their realm as a whole, to extend the influence of the order as widely as possible, or to recruit as many knights as possible for a body they hoped would serve them in various active ways, and felt obliged for one or more of these reasons to include a certain number of ordinary knights, in addition to barons and princes.

From the beginning, however, the two higher strata of the nobility seem to have been disproportionately represented in all of the orders whose membership is known, and the proportion of the places occupied by members of the princely and baronial classes grew more or less steadily throughout our period. Fully two thirds of the sixty-three men known to have been admitted to the Order of the Band before 1350 were neither *ricos omes* nor cadets of *ricos omes*, but only two fifths of the twenty-five knights named to the Order of the Garter in 1349 were knights bachelor, and fewer than a quarter of the thirty-seven knights elected during the remainder of the founder's long reign still held that rank when they died. The forty-four companions elected under Henry VI between 1422 and 1461 included four kings, six princes, sixteen higher peers, and eleven barons or lords of Parliament, but only five men who ended their days as simple knights – just over one in nine. Similarly, while more than two thirds of the ninety-one men known to have been elected to the Order of the Collar before 1553 were drawn from one or another of the sixteen princely or baronial families that provided that order with more than one companion in our period, all but five of the companions admitted between 1440 and 1553 belonged to one of these families, and all five of these men were also either princes or barons. The Order of the Golden Fleece, founded when the encroachment of the upper nobility was already well advanced in the older orders, admitted very few mere knights bachelor even in the earliest years of its history, and by the end of our period was made up almost entirely of kings, princes, and titled barons.

A number of different factors no doubt contributed to the gradual exclusion of the lesser knights from the monarchical orders, including the marked decline between 1330 and 1430 in the number of men of less than baronial rank who received the accolade, the gradual conversion of knighthood from a functional status into a dignity associated primarily with the upper nobility, and the relatively low limit placed on membership in most of the certainly monarchical orders that survived into or were founded in the fifteenth century. The prince-presidents naturally wanted to include in their orders the men whose service, loyalty, or friendship they felt the greatest need either to reward or secure, or whose presence would add the greatest possible lustre to the order itself, and although close friendship or truly exceptional service might occasionally lead them to arrange the admission of a knight of no great wealth or station, in the vast majority of cases it made more sense to admit a man of exalted rank.

Since the barons and princes of the later medieval period belonged with very few exceptions to patrilineages that had been of at least knightly standing for several centuries, it can be said with reasonable confidence that the great majority of the men admitted to the monarchical orders before 1520 were not merely of noble birth, as the statutes of several orders required, but in fact nobles of what would later be termed 'ancient extraction'. Men of less than knightly ancestry *could* acquire simple nobility and even receive the accolade of knighthood in our period, but no recently ennobled knight is known to have been admitted to a monarchical order before 1520, and the great majority of the simple knights so far identified as companions of these orders were certainly members of old knightly or baronial families. The monarchical orders may thus be seen as bastions of a nobility that was as venerable for its antiquity as it was for its exalted rank.

Although a high and growing proportion of the membership of most orders was drawn from the upper strata of the nobility, it would appear that in all of the orders except perhaps those of the Star and the Knot, only a small proportion of the baronial class of the founder's realm or realms was ever included at any particular time, and only the most exalted members of the local hierarchy ever acquired a strong claim to be admitted by customary right. Indeed, the only class of persons whose members were admitted almost without fail into most orders was that composed of the sons of the prince-president. Partly no doubt to associate the order as closely as possible with the royal house, and partly in order to make membership more attractive (or acceptable) to their most exalted vassals and neighbours, the presidents of most orders secured the admission of each of their sons as soon as they felt them to be old enough. Alfonso of Castile (who did not require the members of his orders to be knights) seems to have inducted his sons while they were still in the cradle, but most later founders were more patient, and waited until their sons were at least capable of walking in processions. The youngest son of Jean of France included among the founding knights of the Company of the Star was nine at the time, but no prince under the normal age of knighthood was elected to the Garter until 1377, when the future kings Richard 'of Bordeaux' and Henry 'of Bolingbroke' were elected at the ages of nine and ten respectively, and no prince under nine was admitted to the order until 1475, when Edward IV secured the election of his sons Edward and Richard, then only four and two years old. His decision to break with precedent in this way may have been due to the example of Philippe of Burgundy, who had had his only son and eventual successor Charles 'the Rash' elected to the Order of the Golden Fleece in November 1433, only a few weeks after his birth.[3] Despite the practice of Burgundy and England, however, Louis XI of France does not seem to have had his only son Charles elected to the Order of St Michael before his own death in 1483, when Charles was thirteen, and none of his successors had a son to admit to the order before 1517.

Aside from the sons of the prince-president, no one was assured of election or appointment to any monarchical order, but a close relationship by blood or marriage to the prince seems to have increased one's chances considerably in those orders for which we have extensive lists of members. High social rank also increased the likelihood of being elected, and in England, Savoy, and the Burgundian state successive holders of certain titles were admitted with great regularity. The holders of certain important offices – especially the military offices of constable, marshal, and captain – were also elected with considerable regularity to those orders for which we have extensive lists of members. This was in keeping with the overtly military character of most monarchical orders.

Except in the rather peculiar order of the Sword, most of the knights known to have been elected or appointed to each of the orders we have studied were subjects of the prince-president in one or another of his dominions, and several early founders – Károly of Hungary, Alfonso of Castile, Jean of France, and Alfons of Aragon – expressed no interest in admitting any foreign knights. These founders seem to have thought of their orders exclusively as instruments for influencing the behaviour of their own vassals or rere-vassals, but most of the other founders evidently felt that their orders could also be used as instruments of propaganda and tools of diplomacy throughout Western Christendom, and not only made provision for the admission of eminent foreigners, but actually secured the election of several foreign knights. The Order of the Garter seems to have been the first established order to admit foreign knights, but the Company of the Knot and the Order of the Collar soon followed suit, and the Order of the Sword may well have been made up primarily of foreigners throughout its history. Most of the later orders seem also to have admitted a certain number of knights who were not subjects of the prince-president, and a high proportion of the knights admitted in the fifteenth century to both the Order of the Garter and the Order of the Golden Fleece (nearly a third of those elected after 1430 to the former order) were technically foreigners.

At first, most of the foreign knights admitted to monarchical orders seem to have been drawn from the two lower strata of the knightly class, and although the statutes of both the Garter and the Ship made special arrangements for the reception of foreign princes, no effectively sovereign prince is known to have

---

[3] According to the chronicler Enguerrand de Monstrelet (*Chronique*, ed. L. Douët d'Arcq, V [Paris, 1861], p. 81), Charles was given the collar of the order 'sur le fons', just after his baptism, but he could not have been formally admitted to the order until after the chapter held on St Andrew's Day a week or two later.

accepted membership in an order maintained by another prince before 1375, and only four are known to have done so before 1403. All four of these princes were dukes (one French and three German), and all four were admitted to the Order of the Garter. Six more foreign princes were elected to the Garter between 1402 and 1440, including five kings, and early in the same period the Kings of Aragon and Hungary exchanged memberships in the monarchical or quasi-monarchical orders they had founded in 1403 and 1408 respectively. Philippe 'the Good' of Burgundy similarly exchanged orders with Alfons 'the Magnanimous' of Aragon in 1445 (if only after considerable negotiation), but there is no evidence that either he or his son Charles 'the Rash' accepted membership in any other order before 1471, when Charles was elected to the Garter, and no King of England is known to have accepted membership in any foreign order before 1468, when Edward IV was elected to the Golden Fleece. Since no foreign prince is known to have accepted membership in the Savoyard order of the Collar in our period, and only Charles 'the Rash' of Burgundy is known to have exchanged orders with Ferrante of Naples, the practice of exchanging memberships in monarchical orders, which was later to be a standard element of international diplomacy, must be regarded as exceptional before the last decades of our period.

In every order we have studied, companions-elect who had passed through the rite of induction were expected to retain their membership and fulfil all of its obligations until death removed them from the world, but most of the orders founded after 1380 made some provision for the expulsion or 'deprivation' of members who had committed some dishonourable or treasonable act, and the Order of the Golden Fleece also permitted its companions to resign. In fact, a number of companions are known to have been expelled from both the Order of the Garter and that of the Golden Fleece, and several foreign companions are known to have resigned from the former order in order to avoid conflicts of allegiance.

As we noted in the introduction, it was customary in most of the countries in which monarchical orders were established for men who had received the accolade of knighthood to write the title 'knight' or its equivalent immediately after their surname. This practice persisted throughout our period, but so far as I have been able to discover it was not until the last decades of the period that knights who had been admitted to monarchical orders began to indicate that fact by adding after the title 'knight' either the name of their order or some equivalent phrase such as 'de l'ordre du roi'. Clearly the status of knight continued to be thought of as quite independent of the status of companion at least until the end of the fifteenth century, but it is nevertheless surprising that, in a period as sensitive to titular distinctions as the later Middle Ages, it took so long for the members of these exalted bodies to find a suitable form of title to indicate their membership.

6 *The Obligations and Privileges of Membership*

Like the religious orders and confraternities on which they were modelled, the monarchical orders all imposed obligations of various sorts on their members. Both the nature and the extent of these obligations varied considerably from one order to another, however, according to the founder's conception of the order and the goals he had in mind when formulating its statutes. Taken as a whole, the obligations of the companions fall into five principal categories: (1) cliental; (2) fraternal or mutual; (3) corporate; (4) moral and spiritual; and (5) chivalric.

It has long been recognized that one of the principal purposes of most monarchical orders was to promote loyalty to the founder and his heirs. In fact, all but two of the orders we have examined – the Garter and the Stole and Jar – sought to secure some form of service from the ordinary companions to the prince-president, and all but the second of these imposed specific cliental obligations, designed either to supplement or replace the traditional obligations of feudo-vassality. The nature and extent of the cliental duties explicitly imposed differed to a remarkable extent from one order to another, and in some orders (notably the Hungarian society of St George) such obligations were only implied in the statutes. In two of the earliest orders – St George of Hungary and the Star – the sole or principal service demanded of the companions to the prince was loyal counsel, and four later orders – the Knot, the Collar, the Golden Fleece, and St Michael – specifically mentioned counsel among the services expected of the companions. Every order except the Garter, the Star, and the Stole and Jar, however, demanded more active forms of aid and service from the companions, in addition to, or in place of, counsel. In the statutes of the Knot and the Collar the form this service was to take was not clearly specified, and it would appear that the founders of these orders expected the companions to assist them in all of their affairs by every means available to them. The statutes of the Ship also required the companions to aid their president 'with all their power', and to defend his 'honour and estate', but like those of all of the remaining orders they were primarily concerned with military service. Nine of the thirteen orders whose statutes we have studied imposed some form of military service on the companions, and in four of these orders – the Band, the Knot, the Collar, and the Ship – the companions seem to have undertaken to serve their president in arms whenever and for as long as he required. In the remaining five orders the companions were required to fight for their president only when he acted in defense of his own lands or vassals (St George of Aragon, Fleece, St Michael), or the Church (Fleece, St Michael), or either led or took part in a crusade against the Infidel (Sword, St George of Aragon, Ermine of Sicily). Five orders – the Garter, the Star, the Knot, the Golden Fleece, and St Michael – also imposed obligations designed to give the prince-president some control over the movements and activities of the companions. All five required their members to seek the permission of the president before going on any long voyage, and the last two required their members to obtain the president's licence before engaging in a private war.

While confraternities of other types rarely if ever imposed what could be classified as cliental obligations, they almost invariably imposed a number of obligations of the sort that we have called 'fraternal'. Since the monarchical orders were all organized on the confraternal model, it was perhaps inevitable that most of them would require their companions to assume at least one obligation to their fellow companions in general, in addition to those owed specifically to the prince-president. In fact it is surprising that the founders of two of the twelve orders we have examined in detail – Pere and Ferran of Aragon – imposed no fraternal obligations whatever upon their companions. These founders clearly had no interest in the corporate character of their respective orders, or in the relationships among their members, but the other founders (hoping no doubt to disguise to some extent the companions' subordination to themselves) all tried to present their orders as 'amiable companies' of equal brothers, on the model of the Round Table and the Frank Palace. Several of them also had strong pragmatic reasons for wanting to promote close friendship and cooperation among all of their companions. These founders accordingly did everything they could think of to promte both the appearance and the reality of fraternity among their companions, and introduced into the statutes of their orders a variety of mutual obligations of the sort characteristic of both confraternities in general and of the peculiarly military relationship called 'brotherhood-in-arms'. These obligations fall naturally into two broad categories: those owed to companions who were still living, and those owed to companions who were dead.

The Company of the Knot imposed no obligation upon its companions towards their fellow companions in life, and the only such obligation imposed by the Order of the Garter was to refrain from serving against their fellows for pay, but most of the remaining orders imposed rather more extensive obligations towards the living. Like the Order of the Garter, the two earlier orders (St George and the Band) imposed a negative obligation (possibly derived from the vassalic oath of fealty) not to harm fellow companions. Both of these orders and three others – those of the Ship, the Golden Fleece, and St Michael – required their companions to take a special oath of love and loyalty to their fellow companions, very similar to that undertaken by brothers-in-arms. Six orders, including four of these (St George of Hungary, the Ship, the Golden Fleece, and St Michael) and two others (the Collar and the Ermine), required their companions to give some form of aid and support to their fellows in times of peace, and all of these orders save that of the Ermine also adjured them to give aid to their fellows in war as well. The Company of the Star may also have imposed such an obligation, but this is not entirely clear.

In addition to these broad obligations (usually defined in very general terms), several orders required their companions to undertake certain specific obligations to one another before their deaths. The orders of St George of Hungary, the Ship, and all three of the orders founded after 1429 imposed a duty to secure the release of fellow companions who had for one reason or another been captured and imprisoned, and the orders of St George of Hungary and the Band both required their members to settle any quarrels that developed between other members. The Order of the Band also adjured its members to attend the weddings and knightings of their fellows. Finally, the Order of the Ermine of Sicily required all of its members (rather than the prince-president alone) to support any of their fellows who, through no fault of his own, had been reduced to poverty.

The provision of masses for recently deceased members was required in most forms of confraternity, and in keeping with this custom all but three of the twelve monarchical orders whose statutes we have examined (the three Spanish orders) imposed such an obligation upon their companions. The number of masses demanded from each companion varied significantly, from one, in the Company of the Star, to 800, owed by foreign kings who were companions of the Garter. In the orders of the Garter and the Collar the number of masses owed by each companion of the lowest rank was 100, but in all of the remaining orders it was under twenty-five, and the average number was only eleven – a rather low figure for the period, especially when the rank of the companions is considered. No other form of obligation to dead companions was imposed in most of the orders, but the orders of the Band and the Collar also required their members to attend the funerals of their deceased brethren, and the former required them to dress in a dark coat for ten days as a sign of mourning.

Like confraternities in general, most monarchical orders required companions-elect to undertake on oath a certain number of obligations to the order as a whole: to obey its statutes, to promote its interests, to take part in its meetings, elections, and other corporate activities, to keep its secrets, to submit to its criticism and carry out the penalties it imposed for infractions of the statutes or failures to live up to the standards expected of them, and to obey its judgements. Obligations of this sort can be considered more usefully under the heading of corporate activities. In this context the most interesting corporate obligations imposed by the monarchical orders were those of refraining from joining other comparable societies, of resigning when possible from those previously joined, and when resignation from other such societies was not possible, of putting the order in question first. Such obligations – explicitly imposed only by the founders of the Star, the Knot, the Ship, the Golden Fleece, and St Michael (but added to the statutes of the Collar in 1434) – were clearly intended to strengthen the hold of the order (and therefore the prince-president) upon the ordinary companions.

Devotional confraternities commonly imposed a variety of moral and 'spiritual' obligations on their members in addition to that of participating in the corporate celebration of the patron's annual feast, and the founders of most monarchical orders included one or more obligations of this sort among the ordinances they assigned to their foundation. It is difficult to tell in most cases whether these obligations were included primarily because they were felt to be appropriate in a society organized on the confraternal model and dedicated to a saint, or because a knight, to be considered truly chivalrous, had to behave in keeping with at least the minimum standards of piety currently expected of laymen. Both the types and the number of spiritual obligations imposed in the monarchical orders varied greatly. The most common type involved regular spiritual exercises of some sort. Four orders (St George of Hungary, the Band, the Ship, and the Stole and Jar) required their members to attend a religious service (usually a mass) either once every day or on a certain day every week; two (the Ship and the Stole and Jar) required them to recite certain prayers with similar regularity; two (the Star and the Knot) imposed a weekly fast; and three (the Star, the Knot, and the Ship) required their companions to wear a special habit on a certain day each week. In addition to saying twenty prayers and attending mass every Friday, the Society of St George (which imposed the most extensive list of spiritual obligations) required its members to adopt a sad expression and give a penny to the church on that day, and to adopt a happy expression every Sunday. Four other orders (the Garter, the Collar, the Golden Fleece, and St Michael) similarly required their companions to make regular donations to the order's chapel for the support of the clergy. Only one order (the Stole and Jar) required a regular donation of money to the poor, but five orders (the Star, the Knot, St George of Aragon, the Ship, and the Ermine) set forth such a donation as an alternative to one of the other exercises required of the companions, or as a fine. The sums demanded were in every case relatively small, and no order can be regarded as having a very important charitable function. Only two orders (the Band and the Ship) required their members to behave in keeping with specific moral precepts, but several others (the Golden Fleece, the Collar after 1434, the Ermine, and St Michael) effectively required their members to avoid behaviour of the sort that would be considered dishonourable or grossly immoral, by threatening them with punishment for such behaviour.

A majority of the orders we have studied (all but the Garter before 1519, the Collar before 1434, and the Stole and Jar) also imposed at least one obligation that could be regarded as chivalrous rather than broadly Christian – though only two orders (the Band and the Ermine) imposed more than two such obligations. Most of the chivalrous obligations were essentially military in nature, though the more important (at least in theory) had a strong religious element. The orders of St George of Hungary, the Ship, and the Ermine all required their members to defend the Church (though none of them specified under precisely what circumstances), while those of the Knot, the Sword, St George of Aragon, the Ship, and the Ermine required them to take part (in certain carefully specified circumstances) in a crusade against the Infidel. The last order was alone in requiring its members to defend the weak in general, and only that of the Band required them to defend ladies in particular. The Orders of the Band and the Ship also enjoined repectful behaviour towards ladies, but only the former imposed other forms of courtly behaviour. Finally, several orders effectively required their companions to display courage, if only by threatening to punish cowardice. The Company of the Star may have required its members to swear never to retreat more than a certain distance when engaged in a battle, and five later orders (the Knot, the Golden Fleece, the Ermine, and St Michael, and after 1518 the Collar) threatened their companions with severe penalties if they fled from a field of battle.

Flight from battle was by no means the only action for which some form of penalty was prescribed in the statutes of the monarchical orders. Roughly half of the orders we have studied in detail (St George of Hungary, the Band, the Garter, the Knot, the Ship, and the Ermine) set forth specific penalties for failure to wear the order's badge or habit at one of the required times, for failure to perform the required spiritual exercises on a particular occasion, or for failure to attend the order's principal annual assembly or to take part in other corporate activities. The penalty set forth for such infractions as these usually took the form of a fine of some sort, but in some cases a sign of disgrace or act of contrition was either added or substituted. For more serious offences – including refusal to accept the arbitration or judgement of the order, treason or *laesa maiestas*, and flight from battle – the usual penalty was formal expulsion from the order, and the Order of the Ship added to this a circular denunciation. Most orders also reserved the right (either explicitly or implicitly) to punish other offenses, both against the statutes and against the unwritten conventions of chivalrous conduct, as the president and companions saw fit.

The real burdens of membership differed from one order to another even more than the foregoing analysis suggests, for the obligations imposed in some orders were not only few in number but relatively light, while those imposed in others were at once numerous and heavy. Setting aside those which arose from the requirement to take part in the order's corporate activities (which we shall consider in another section), the positive obligations of the knights of the Garter were largely financial, while those of the knights and squires of the Stole and Jar were entirely spiritual. Those of the knights of St George of Aragon were almost entirely military, but while in theory they might have been quite onerous, they were of such a nature that the members of the order would rarely if ever be called upon to fulfil them. The knights of all the other orders whose statutes we have examined, however, undertook a set of obligations which would have required a considerable amount of time and effort to fulfil with even a moderate degree of consistency, and in many cases involved the risk of life and limb. The greatest burdens of all were undertaken by the knights of the orders of St George of Hungary, the Band, the Knot, and the Ship, who might well have been called upon to spend most of their time carrying out the cliental and fraternal duties they had undertaken on joining their order.

The burdens of membership in most of the orders we have studied were counterbalanced by formal benefits of several different types; only the two Aragonese orders promised no such benefits whatever to their members. Among the benefits explicitly set forth in the statutes of the ten remaining orders, the most common were those which were operative only after the companion's death: a funeral, prayers and masses designed to hasten the passage of his soul through purgatory, and a permanent memorial of some kind. Only the orders of the Star, the Knot, the Collar, and the Ship promised their members a funeral mass, but nine of the ten orders promised purgatorial masses (the exception being the Order of the Band), and most of them promised regular prayers either from the companions themselves or from the clergy of the order's chapel. All but the first two orders (St George of Hungary and the Band) also promised some form of memorial in the order's chapel, and the Company of the Knot promised its members a tomb as well. Benefits of most of these types were common in confraternities of all kinds, and with the exception of the memorials, those promised by most orders were not particularly impressive by contemporary standards. We have no way of knowing whether the funerals, prayers, and masses promised were actually provided in most orders with any degree of consistency, but it may be significant that no order appears to have provided the memorial promised before about 1420, and that even after that date memorials were set up only by the Order of the Garter – whose members supplied their own.

The formal benefits the companions of most orders could expect to enjoy before death were derived for the most part from the patronal and fraternal obligations of the president and the other companions. Only one patronal obligation was clearly articulated in the statutes of any of the the first five orders: the Sovereign of the Garter undertook to give preference to his companions in all honourable enterprises. The presidents of four out of the five later orders, however, promised their companions more active forms of support, very similar to those promised to a vassal or life-retainer. The Chief of the Collar promised favour, counsel, and aid to his companions, and the maintenance of their rights; the Prince of the Ship promised to aid, maintain, and defend his companions, to procure their honour and estate, and to inform them of threats against them; and the Sovereigns of the Golden Fleece and St Michael promised to advance the power, honour, and profit of their companions, and to consult them before going to war. In seven of the ten orders, as we have just observed, the companions promised to give similar forms of aid and support to one another – the exceptions being the Band and the Garter (whose companions had merely to refrain from harming one another), and the Knot. The potential value of the forms of support promised by the orders of St George of Hungary, the Star, the Collar, the Ship, the Golden Fleece, and St Michael was very great, and even if only a fraction of what was promised was actually delivered, the companions would probably have considered themselves well compensated for their services.

Some orders offered other forms of benefit to their companions, in addition to or in place of aid and support in their affairs, and a number of these could have been of considerable practical value. The orders of the Star, the Knot, and the Ermine – in keeping with a custom common to many confraternities – all promised to provide suitable maintenance to any companion who became too old or too poor to support himself. The founder of the Order of the Band initially exempted its members from the payment of any extraordinary tax levied on the lands they held from the king and his sons, but as noble land in general was exempted from taxation in Castile this privilege was not very useful, and was soon rescinded. The founders of the orders of St George of Hungary, the Golden Fleece, and St Michael formally removed the knights of their orders from the jurisdiction of all courts except that of the order itself, and in 1518 the Chief of the Order of the Collar did likewise. This privilege put the companions of these four orders on a judicial level with the peers of the realm in England, and would have been very useful if it had been enforced.

The remaining privileges were purely honorific, but even they were not of negligible value. Six of the ten orders – those of the Star, the Knot, the Ship, the Golden Fleece, and St Michael, and from 1518 that of the Collar – were to have maintained one or more books in which the deeds of the companions, like those of the knights of the Round Table and the Frank Palace, were to be recorded for posterity, and this would certainly have appealed very strongly to the desire of most knights to be seen and remembered as heroes. In 1473 the knights of the Golden Fleece were also granted a special precedence in the ducal court, next after the members of the ducal house itself, and a similar privilege was later extended to the members of the other surviving orders. Given the growing obsession of most nobilites with rank and precedence, this privilege, too, must have been valued very highly by a majority of the men admitted to these orders.

7 The Clergy and Poor Knights

Like the religious orders and confraternities on which they were modelled, most of the monarchical orders we have studied were to have been served by a body of clergy, closely associated with if not formally attached to the order, and dedicated primarily or exclusively to the spiritual welfare of the companions, both living and dead. Only the statutes of St George of Hungary and the three Spanish orders make no mention at all of such a body. Almost nothing is known about the clerical colleges that were to have been attached to the orders of the Star, the Knot, and the Ship, though it is possible that the first was to have been made up of the twenty-four canons specified in the papal letter of June 1344. The number of priests in the bodies attached to the Orders of the Garter and the Collar reflected the number of the companions in those orders (twenty-four, soon raised to twenty-six in the former, fifteen in the latter), and the number of the canons of the Golden Fleece seems to have reflected the original number of the companions (twenty-four), but the number in the college attached to the Order of the Ermine (nine) was based on that of the angelic orders, and the number proposed for the priests of St Michael (twenty-four) was probably based on that of the Golden Fleece. Very few confraternities would have had as many as nine priests in their sole employ, so the much higher figure adopted by most founders must have been chosen at least in part to emphasize the superiority of the order to ordinary confraternities.

While it is at least possible that most founders succeeded in attaching a body of clergy to their order, we know that Louis XI and his immediate successors failed to establish the college that was to have served the Order of St Michael, and it is more than likely that several other founders – including Jean of France and both Loysi and Carlo of mainland Sicily – did not get around to funding such a body before death brought an end to all their plans. In fact, the only clerical colleges that were certainly established were those associated with the orders of the Garter, the Collar, the Ermine of Brittany, and the Golden Fleece, and the second of these was not effectively established until after the death of the founder. The colleges founded by Edward of England, Jean of Brittany, and Philippe of Burgundy were composed of secular canons, while that founded by Amé of Savoy on his deathbed was made up of Carthusian hermits, and that attached to the Breton order was later converted into a convent of Carthusians as well.

The principal duties of all of the priests forming these colleges, whatever their clerical status, were to say daily masses and offices in the order's chapel, to officiate at the services held during the order's regular assemblies, and to say the prayers and masses called for in the statutes both of the order and of their own college, principally for the benefit of the companions. In return for performing these functions, they were given an income (to be drawn largely or entirely from the endowment of the college) and provided with lodgings at the seat of the order, where they were generally required to reside.

Two orders – those of the Garter and the Golden Fleece – were to have had attached to their clerical college a body of poor knights, who in the former order at least were to have been equal in number to the priests and the companions, but neither order succeeded in finding the funds necessary to support such a body before the end of our period, and only the former order is known to have maintained any poor knights at any time.

8 The Officers

Although most orders employed the services of a body of priests, relatively few adopted the practice common among confraternities of employing non-members of the society as officers. In fact, in the period before 1430 only three monarchical orders are known to have named corporate officers of any sort: the Hungarian society of St George, which was effectively governed by two *iudices*, one clerical and one lay; the Aragonese enterprise of St George, which was to have been governed by twelve 'counsellors' chosen from among the knights; and the Order of the Garter, which initially appointed a 'keeper of the order's seal' from among its companions and a 'registrar' from among its canons, and retained the services of the Bishop of Winchester *pro tempore* in the largely honorific office of 'prelate'. By 1351, however, Edward of England had created a second office to be held by an employee rather than a member of his order – that of usher – and in 1415 his successor Henry V added a third, that of king of arms. Since Philippe of Burgundy modelled his order of the Golden Fleece directly on that of the Garter, he naturally provided it with a similar complement of officers, but formally detached all four of the offices he had created – chancellor, treasurer, registrar, and king of arms – from the colleges of companions and priests. Later in the century both Ferrante of mainland Sicily and Louis of France attached comparable sets of officers to the orders they created on the model of the Golden Fleece (three in the former and four, later raised to five, in the latter), and in 1518 Charles of Savoy added four similar officers to the old order of the Collar, which he had reformed on the model of the Golden Fleece. Thus by 1520 a complement of four or five external (or mainly external) officers, exceptional until 1465, had become the rule among the surviving monarchical orders.

Unlike the colleges of clergy, the officers formally attached to at least four of the five orders just listed were certainly appointed with some regualrity, and it is more than likely that those attached to the remaining order (that of the Ermine) were actually appointed as well. Like the canons and lesser clerics, they normally played a prominent part in the annual assembly of the order they served, at which they commonly processed and sat as a group apart from the companions. Those whose offices were not honorific also served the order in an active way between meetings, and through their activities provided continuity to the order's corporate existence. Most were simultaneously employed by the king in other capacities, unrelated to the order, and the kings of arms were expressly charged with the oversight of all of the other heralds in the president's realm or dominions.

9 The Buildings

All three of the forms of society that served as models for the monarchical orders – religious orders, confraternities, and fictional societies of knights – normally had some form of corporate headquarters, more or less permanently located in a particular building or set of buildings, and all but five of the princes who founded monarchical orders – Károly of Hungary, Alfonso of Castile, Pierre of Cyprus, and

Pere and Ferran of Aragon – certainly intended to provide their order with at least one seat of this general type. The headquarters establishment of religious orders and confraternities normally included among its buildings both a chapel and a hall, and it would appear that all of the remaining founders intended their order to have at least one chapel, and that most intended it to have a hall as well.

Five of the nine founders who certainly meant to give their orders seats announced their intention to establish the seat in a particular place at the time they founded the order, but four of the eight – Amé of Savoy, Jean of Brittany, and Carlo and Ferrante of Sicily – deferred the decision to a future date, and the places ultimately chosen by the last two (if any) are not known. Five of the seven founders whose choices are known (all but Jean of Brittany and Louis of France) established the seat of their order in an important castle or manor-house situated in or near their capital city. Jean of Brittany established the seat of his order in a chapel built for the purpose on the field where he had first secured his throne, but soon built a new castle-palace only a few miles away, at the edge of the old capital city of his duchy. Louis of France attempted to give his order a seat in the fortified monastery of Mont-Saint-Michel, the principal shrine of the order's patron in the kingdom, but quickly discovered that this was too far from the capital, and may have held the order's only meeting in our period in a chapel dedicated to the patron in the royal palace in Paris. Thus in every case for which we have adequate information, the seat of the order was effectively situated in close proximity to the principal seat of the royal or princely government, and in or near a palace where the court could be housed and entertained in a particularly elaborate fashion.

Since chapels, halls, and buildings suitable for housing large bodies of clerics were not only expensive but could hardly be constructed in less than a decade, every founder except Jean of Brittany initially made over to his order for its exclusive use certain existing structures within the palace complex, including the principal chapel. Some founders, at least, probably thought of this as a stop-gap measure, and fully intended to provide their foundation with a whole new set of buildings constructed specifically to serve its needs and contribute to its glory, but only Edward of England and his successors appear to have succeeded in doing this. The buildings actually conceded to the monarchical orders were nevertheless very grand compared to those of ordinary confraternities, and when refurbished especially for their use must have seemed fully worthy of the exalted societies they served.

The knights of the fictional orders of the Round Table and the Frank Palace had seats permanently assigned to them around the the great round tables which occupied much of their respective halls, marked with their names or armorial bearings, and most of the founders of monarchical orders intended to provide their companions with seats similarly marked. The founders of the orders of the Star and the Ship meant to establish the seats in their order's hall, in keeping with the literary tradition, but Edward of England, despairing of his original project to construct a huge round hall to house the restored Round Table, introduced the practice (no doubt inspired by one common in collegiate churches) of placing these seats in the choir of the chapel rather than in the hall, and most of the remaining founders decided to follow his lead rather than that of his legendary predecessors. The method of marking the seat or stall currently occupied by a companion varied somewhat from one order to another. In the Order of the Garter, the sword, crested helm, and armorial banner of each knight were hung over his stall; in those of the Star, the Knot, the Ship, the Golden Fleece, and St Michael (and after 1518 the Collar) his armorial achievement was to be painted over his seat (on moveable panels in the last two cases); and in the Order of the Ermine of Sicily, a shield and banner of his arms were to be hung over his stall.

In several orders the chapel was also meant to house the memorials promised to the companions in the statutes. In the Order of the Garter this took the form of a small metal plate enamelled with the companion's armorial achievement that was to be affixed to the back of his stall after his death, and the deceased companions of the Golden Fleece were commemorated with similar panels bearing a shield of their arms alone, hung from the stall for the duration of each assembly. In the order of the Knot, however, the memorial was to have consisted of the companion's sword bearing the order's badge on its pommel, in the Order of the Collar of his collar and a coat and banner of his arms, and in the Order of the Ship of a shield of his arms, in each case hung like a votive offering somewhere in the chapel. Of all of these 'perpetual' memorials, only those of the knights of the Garter have survived, and it is not certain that any of the others were ever in fact set up.

10 The Corporate Activities

All but one of the monarchical orders whose statutes we have examined required their members to take part in at least one form of activity that could reasonably be described as 'corporate' – an activity, that is, in which the members took part as a body, rather than on an individual basis. Only the vestigial Aragonese order of the Stole and Jar failed to require participation in any such activity. By their very nature, corporate activities could only take place when some or all of the members were gathered in some form of assembly, either regular or irregular. In a majority of the remaining orders most or all of the activities prescribed were to have been carried out during general assemblies of the order (variously termed *assemblé*, *court general*, and *chapitre* or *capitulo*) convened at more or less regular intervals, ranging from several months to several years. Only one of the remaining orders – that of the Collar – was not intended to assemble on a regular basis in our period, and only one order – the quasi-monarchical order of St George of Hungary – held minor assemblies as often as once a month.

Most confraternities held a general assembly exactly once each year, on the feast-day of their patron saint, and this practice was adopted by a majority of monarchical orders. The knights of the orders of St George of Hungary, the Band, the Garter, the Star, the Knot, St George of Aragon, and the Golden Fleece were all initially intended to meet once annually for a period which included the principal feast-day of their heavenly patron (if the order had one). The founders of the first two orders, however, seem to have decided not long after the creation of their order that one yearly meeting was not sufficient for their purposes, and decreed that their orders would thenceforth meet at least three times each year, at intervals of roughly four months, and Alfonso of Castile declared that his order was to meet every two months if possible. Carlo of Sicily intended from the outset that his order of the Ship meet four times every year, at somewhat uneven intervals, but required only those companions who were near the court to attend the three minor meetings; his successor Ferrante required all of the knights of his order of the Ermine to assemble twice a year, on each of its patron's annual feasts. Before 1445, every order that held general assemblies was intended to convene one at least once a year, but in that year the knights of the Golden Fleece decided that the dispersal of the companions made it too difficult for them to assemble every year, and declared that thenceforth they would meet only once every three years. This rule was adopted in 1469 for the Order of St Michael, and in 1518 for the reformed order of the Collar, so by the end of our period the Order of the Garter was the only order whose statutes still required an annual assembly.

We know nothing about the frequency with which assemblies were actually held by most orders, but the fact that even the reduced rate decreed by the Order of the Golden Fleece in 1445 could not be sustained, and that the Order of St Michael never succeeded in holding a single general assembly in our period, suggests that other orders may well have met less frequently than they were supposed to. Only the Order of the Garter is known to have met virtually every year.

Not only the frequency but the duration of the assemblies the monarchical orders were supposed to hold varied significantly. Those of St George of Hungary, the Band, the Knot, St George of Aragon, and the Ermine of Sicily were probably to have lasted for twenty-four hours or less, beginning in the last two cases (at least) at vespers on the eve of the feast-day, and concluding in every case on the feast-day itself. The assembly of the Garter began in a similar fashion on the eve of the feast-day, but did not dissolve until after a special service held on the day after the feast, and those of the Golden Fleece and St Michael did not dissolve until after a second special service held on the second day following the feast, roughly sixty hours after they were first brought to order. The knights of the Ship were to have spent still more time in assemblies: two full weeks at the principal annual assembly, and six days at each of the three minor assemblies, for a total of thirty-six days a year.

The general assemblies held by most confraternities included three principal forms of activity: religious services, a business meeting, and a banquet. The assemblies of the monarchical orders we have studied, which were clearly based on those of the more ordinary forms of confraternity, invariably included activities of the first type, and generally included all three; only that of the Aragonese order of St George seems to have consisted solely of spiritual exercises. The religious services always included a solemn mass in honour of the patron of the order or the kingdom, held on the morning of the feast day, and commonly included the office of vespers either on the eve or the day of the feast, or both. The assemblies of the orders of the Garter, the Golden Fleece, and St Michael (and after 1518 of the reformed order of the Collar) all included in addition a solemn requiem mass for the order's departed members, and those of the last three included a third mass, in honour of the Blessed Virgin. All of these services were to have been sung, if possible, in the order's chapel and by its clergy, who were presumably to occupy the stalls below those of the companions. In two early orders – those of the Garter and the Star – companions who could not get to the annual assembly were required to attend similar services on the appropriate days.

Services of this sort offered an opportunity not merely for corporate devotion and prayer, but an occasion for particularly spectacular pomp and ceremony. The companions were invariably required to wear their most formal costume throughout the principal services, at least, and were generally required to process solemnly in pairs not merely to and from the chapel, but at some point during the principal service as well. During the service, they sat in the stalls marked by their armorial achievements, looking like a cross between the knights of the Round Table in conclave and the Knights Templar in choir; those of the Knot even held their swords in their hands. Since there can be little doubt that the clergy of the order were also meant to be dressed in their richest vestments during the course of these services, they and the processions with which they began and ended must have been among the most splendid ceremonies of the year in the courts of the prince-presidents.

The banquet held during the course of the assembly must also have been an occasion for ceremonial pomp and lavish display, characterized by a rather less serious tone. In all probablity every assembly included at least one formal banquet – the only regular corporate activity attributed to the fictional societies of the Round Table and Free Palace – but our sources tell us little or nothing about those held by most orders. The orders of the Star and the Knot, emulating the practice of the fictional societies, placed the most outstanding knights of the year at a special table of honour during the annual banquet, and the latter order had in addition a special table of disgrace, but no other order made any special concession to the Arthurian tradition. Some orders required their companions to wear a version of the order's habit during the banquet, but others allowed them to wear whatever they liked.

The serious business of the annual assembly was conducted during the course of the meeting referred to as the 'chapter' or 'parliament', which unlike the other forms of activity was usually held behind closed doors, either in the hall or in some convenient chamber. Several distinct orders of business were commonly dealt with during the course of an annual chapter. Taken as a whole, they included the consideration of the finances and general situation of the order; the elucidation of the existing statutes and the adoption of amendments to them; the settlement of disputes among the members; the reporting, recording, and reading of the companions 'adventures'; the examination of the members' conduct and the assignment of penalties for infractions of either the statutes or the code of chivalry; and the election and admission of new companions. With the exception of the business concerned with the 'adventures' of the companions (included in the chapters only of the orders of the Star, the Knot, and the Ship), all of these activities were normally included in the annual chapters of ordinary confraternities, and in all likelihood most of them were included in the chapters of all of the monarchical orders, even though the statutes do not always make this clear. Many of them were simply necessary for the proper functioning of a corporate organization of almost any sort, and the founders of the monarchical orders must have realised that the techniques traditionally employed by professional confraternities to maintain harmony and professional standards among their members could be used to promote peace, discipline, loyalty, and valour among the knights of their orders.

In addition to (and in one case in place of) regular general assemblies, a few monarchical orders held, or were meant to hold, irregular special assemblies to deal with matters which the founders thought too urgent to postpone for more than a month or so. Two orders – those of the Garter and the Ermine of Sicily – were to have held special assemblies within a specified time of the death of a companion to elect his replacement, presumably so that the number of companions would not long remain below the number fixed in the statutes. The Order of the Ship similarly permitted the Prince to hold special meetings of those companions who were currently with him to approve the election of 'high princes and lords', presumably so that he could conduct a more efficient foreign policy. The Order of the Collar, which held no regular assemblies before the reform of 1518, provided solemn funerals for its members, and required those members who were nearby not only to attend, but to take part in some sort of assembly immediately afterwards – possibly to elect a successor to the deceased companion. Finally, the Order of the Ermine of Sicily was to have held special assemblies to try companions accused of certain serious crimes, and to expel those who were convicted.

The only other forms of corporate activity in which the companions of monarchical orders were asked to take part were those characteristic of their knightly profession: tournaments, jousts, and military campaigns. In fact, very few orders required their members to participate *as a body* in any of these activities. It is likely that the companions of most orders were invited to join in knightly sports of various kinds during the course of the festivities that commonly accompanied their annual assembly, but only the knights of the very early orders of St George of Hungary and the Band were actually required to take part as a team in jousts or tournaments even on those occasions, let alone whenever summoned to do so. Similarly, while a majority of the orders – all but the Garter, the Stole and Jar, and possibly the Star – required their members to take part in serious military campaigns of some sort, only the orders of the Band and the Ship required them to serve as part of a unit composed largely or exclusively of companions; in the other orders, fighting could not be regarded as a truly corporate activity.

11 The Badges and Insignia

Like the religious orders and confraternities on which they were modelled, but unlike the fictional orders of knighthood, the true monarchical orders all required their members to wear at least one distinctive 'device', 'ensign', or 'badge'. Indeed, as we have seen, most orders took their usual name from that of their device, and the devices became so closely associated with the societies they represented that by 1380 they were commonly referred to by the same terms used to designate the societies themselves: 'order', 'enterprise', and 'society'.

In the first century of our period, the devices adopted took a great variety of forms. The first two orders, those of St George of Hungary and the Band, initially adopted devices that were inseparable from the the mantle or coat that constituted the order's habit, and bore no resemblance either to any earlier device or to one another: a Latin inscription on the left breast in the former, and a wide band of contrasting colour applied or painted sash-wise across the chest, shoulder, and back of the coat in the latter. The Castilian 'band' seems to have inspired a whole series of devices in the form of a detached strap, wrapped around some part or other of the body, all adopted between 1346 and 1412. The first of these was of course the garter of the English order, which was probably the direct model for most of the others. The garter took the form of a small belt – probably meant to represent the belt of knighthood – with a cryptic inscription of the sort that had recently become popular for display in tournaments, and was worn in both a three-dimensional form buckled about the leg below the knee, and in a two-dimensional form set either alone or in a semé fashion on the various elements of the companions' habit. Two later orders – the princely confraternal order of the Buckle, founded in 1355, and the honorific pseudo-order of the Belt of *Esperance*, founded in 1365 – adopted a badge in the form of a belt, complete with buckle and grommets, but in each case had it worn around the neck rather than around the leg. The simple strap-like collar of the Order of the Collar, founded in 1364, was almost certainly inspired by the garter device, as was the belt-like pigtail that hung down the back of the knights of the Tress around 1390, and it is possible that the knot device adopted in 1352 by the founder of the Company of the Knot was at least partly inspired by the garter as well – although it was not actually wrapped around any part of the body. The arm-band worn by the members of the obscure Neapolitan order of the Capstan or Spool in the 1380s also formed part of this series of zoniform devices, which seem to have been peculiar to knightly orders. Finally, the broad white baldric assigned to the initially Castilian order of the Stole and Jar shortly after its foundation in 1403 (possibly as a vehicle for the display of the jar device with armour, in place of the metallic collar) was surely based directly upon the original band device itself.

A number of orders founded between 1351 and 1408 were assigned a badge in the form of a metallic brooch – the traditional form of pilgrims' badges, and of those worn by the members of ordinary confraternities. The enamelled gold star adopted by Jean of France in 1351 was the first badge of this type certainly associated with a monarchical order, but the sword device given to the Order of the Sword around 1347, the ship device assigned to the Order of the Ship in 1381, the salamander device associated with the second Austrian order around 1395, the dragon device worn by the members of the quasi-monarchical order of the Dragon from 1408, and the jar of lilies worn pinned to the stole of the Order of the Stole and Jar after 1412, all took the form of metallic brooches, and were all worn either pinned or sewn to the breast of the outermost garment. In all likelihood the knot of the Company of the Knot – which was certainly worn in this fashion – usually took this form as well. Unlike the devices of the first type, those worn like a brooch resembled the livery badges adopted for use in England and France after about 1360 in taking the form of some easily recognizable object or beast, and in having some kind of symbolic significance external to the order itself. The significance itself was often less than clear, but was in some cases explained at length in the order's statutes.

By 1300 the knights of the religious orders of knighthood had all come to be distinguished by a cross – the badge of the crusader – of some peculiar form and colour, applied or embroidered on the left breast of their coat and mantle. Probably because they did not wish to have their 'orders' of lay knights confused with the older orders of monk-knights, very few founders of monarchical orders included a cross of any kind in the badge they assigned to their foundation, and only one founder – Pere of Aragon – adopted a cross alone as the badge for regular wear. Pere's order, of course, was dedicated to and named after St George, whose attributed arms were a red cross on a white shield, so a red cross was the most obvious badge for the order, but as there was already a religious order in Aragon whose knights displayed the red cross of St George on their white habits, it is surprising that Pere chose to have his cross embroidered or applied in the traditional way on the coats and mantles of his knights. The only other monarchical orders to make use of a cross in our period were also dedicated to St George, but both of these – the Hungarian society of St George, and the English order of the Garter – displayed it on a shield, and the knights of the latter order only wore it on their formal mantle, surrounded by a garter. The senior members of the quasi-monarchical society of the Dragon suspended their dragon device from a fiery cross, bearing a Latin inscription, but this bore little resemblance to the crosses of the religious orders.

The fourth general form of ensign adopted by monarchical orders in our period – the collar composed of metallic links with a breast-pendant – evolved gradually between 1364 and 1430, and its popularity in the fifteenth century owed a good deal to the general vogue for collars of this type that prevailed after about 1390. The collar of the Savoyard order of that name had included from the start a pendant made up of comital badges, but the first collar to have as its pendant the device from which the order took its name was that of the Breton order of the Ermine, founded in 1381, and the first to be composed of separate links (as distinct from a pair of metallic straps) was that of the French pseudo-order of the Broom-Pod, created around 1386. The links of which the latter collar was composed were identical in form to the pendant itself, but the links of the ephemeral Castilian order of the Dove (proclaimed in 1390) took the quite distinctive form of sun-rays, while those of the pseudo-order of the Camail and Porcupine (created in 1394) took the form of a dozen or so interlocking rows of mail, and those of the pseudo-order of the Collar of the Scale (created shortly before 1430) took the form of overlapping rows of metal scales. The first collar to be composed of links in the form of a device different from that dependent from it was the collar of the Stole and Jar, created in 1403, and it was almost certainly the model for the next such collar, assigned in 1430 to the Order of the Golden Fleece. Such was the prestige of the latter order that most of the princely orders founded after 1430 (the most notable exception being that of the Crescent of Anjou) were given collars of precisely this form. By 1495 the Order of the Garter was the only surviving monarchical order whose insignia did not include a collar, and it was not long after that that Henry VII decided to conform to the new norm by assigning to his order a collar clearly modelled upon that of the French order of St Michael. In 1518 the Duke of Savoy similarly brought his order into line by substituting elaborate symbolic links for the simple band which had long formed the encircling part of the collar from which the order had taken its name.

The word 'collar' (Middle French *colier*) is derived from the French word for 'neck' (*col*), and the earliest collars seem to have been worn around the neck like a dog-collar (as one contemporary remarked) or a modern clerical collar, with the pendant resting on the upper part of the breast. By about 1450, however, collars had come to be worn in a somewhat longer form, arranged in such a way that the links rested on the shoulders at the base of the neck, and the pendant hung (often from a V-shaped juncture) at the centre of the breast. This form (still relatively convenient for daily wear) persisted until about the end of the fifteenth century, when some collars (notably the English collar of SS)[4] began to be represented in a much longer form, which rested on the outer part of the shoulders and hung across the lower breast at the front. The latter, rather impractical type of collar seems to have become normal by the end of our period, and still persists today.

The links forming the collars of the fifteenth-century orders usually took the form of a pre-existing livery-badge which continued to be used even after the foundation of the order as a general symbol of adherence to the founder and his house. The collar of the Savoyard order had incorporated such a badge in its pendant as early as 1364, but no other order made use of a pre-existing badge until 1430, when Philippe of Burgundy formed his collar of fiery flints and *fusils*. In some orders (the Ermine of Brittany, the Golden Fleece, the Ermine of Sicily, and St Michael) the device from which the order took its name formed the pendant, but in others (the Collar, the Stole and Jar, and the Garter) it was used to form the collar itself.

It is not clear that any knightly order suspended an effigy of its patron from its collar before 1444, when an image of St Hubert kneeling before the stag was hung from a collar of horns by Duke Gerhard of Jülich, but in the second half of the fifteenth century the practice spread rapidly. A representation of the Virgin standing on a crescent moon was often incorporated into the collar of the order of the Stole and Jar after 1450, Christian I of Denmark probably hung a similar image of the Virgin from his collar of elephants in 1457, Louis XI of France made an image of St Michael slaying a devil in the form of a dragon the pendant of his order's collar in 1469, Henry VII of England suspended an image of St George slaying the dragon from the new collar of his order around 1500, and Charles III of Savoy placed an image of the Annunciation within the circlet of love-knots that had long formed the pendant of his order's collar in 1518. Thus by 1520 such an effigy formed part of the insignia of all but one of the surviving monarchical orders – that of the Golden Fleece.

Insignia of all four types were in some cases accompanied by a verbal *devise* or motto, of the sort commonly associated with tournament devices and livery-badges. The badges of the orders of the Garter, the Knot, the Sword, the Collar, the Ermine of Brittany, the Stole and Jar, and the Ermine of Sicily all had some sort of motto inscribed on them or set next to them, either directly or on a scroll.

Like most modern 'orders', which have breast 'stars', ribands, and neck badges in addition to their medieval collars, many orders in our period had more than one form of badge, but the different forms rarely had any peculiar symbolic significance, and when they had, it was of a different sort from that assigned to the different forms of badge in most modern orders. Some badges had variable forms. The band of the Castilian order could be halved to indicate disgrace, the knot of the Sicilian order could be untied and retied to indicate (with appropriate changes in the accompanying legend) progress towards the order's ostensible goal, and the ship of the Sicilian order and the eagle of the Austrian order could be augmented to indicate martial achievement. Two of the badges worn pinned to the breast on formal occasions – the star and the knot – were also worn in miniature versions,

4 See Arthur Gardner, *English Medieval Sculpture*, (Cambridge, 1951; reissued New York, 1973), pp. 339–40, for examples.

either alone or in combination with the breast badge, the former on a ring and the latter on the pommel of a sword. In the fifteenth century several orders decreed that the normal form of their badge or collar (in most cases rather elaborate and expensive) could be replaced with a simpler version when the companions were dressed for fighting or hunting: thus a simple ribbon could be substituted for the embroidered belt of the English order after 1422, the jar of lilies of the order of the Stole and Jar could be worn on a stole (very like a modern riband) rather than as part of a metallic collar, and the collar-pendants of the orders of the Golden Fleece, the Ermine of Sicily, St Michael, the Garter, and the Annunciation could be worn suspended from a simple chain. The knights of two early orders – the Garter and the Knot – wore on their most formal habit, either in combination with or (in the case of the latter) instead of their normal badge, an entirely unrelated device symbolic of the order's patron. Around 1500 the Order of the Garter became the first order to have not merely a zoniform badge and a breast badge but also a collar (composed of representations of the breast badge alternating with livery-badges with a pendant effigy of the patron), all of which could be worn at the same time with the order's formal habit. No other order would acquire a set of insignia of comparable complexity before the seventeenth century.

Unlike the badges of modern orders, which must conform very closely to an officially established pattern or model, the badges of the monarchical orders of the fourteenth and fifteenth centuries were merely required to conform (like the charges on an armorial shield) to a verbal description. Since these descriptions were often rather vague, and since individual companions were generally permitted (and sometimes required) to have their own insignia made up at their own cost by any jeweller they chose, the form taken by the badges of most orders varied considerably from one example to another, and in all likelihood the size, material, and enrichment varied just as much. Unfortunately, most of what we know about the actual form taken by the badges of monarchical orders before 1520 is derived in almost every case only from representations, primarily in manuscripts, on tombs, and after about 1450 in painted portraits. Not one single exemplar of the device of any certainly monarchical order is known to have survived from the period before 1490, and the devices fabricated during the remaining thirty years are now represented by a single garter.[5] Most of the others must have been dismantled and melted down to make new jewels.

Even representations of the insignia of our orders contemporary with the existence of the order are surprisingly rare, especially for the period before about 1430. Before that date, for reasons which are not entirely clear, very few companions chose to have themselves represented on their tombs (or anywhere else for that matter) wearing the badge of their order, and the custom of displaying the badge in some form of association with the arms and crested helm developed very slowly. Although we know from documentary sources the garter was displayed encircling the arms of Edward III shortly after the foundation of the order, I have found no surviving representations of the royal arms encircled by the garter antedating that on the monument of Robert Hallam, Bishop of Salisbury, who died

---

[5] It is possible that some of the earliest surviving collars of the Order of the Golden Fleece also date from the fifteenth century, however, and there are several surviving exemplars of the badge of the Society of the Dragon.

17.1 The garter encircling the arms of Henry V on the tomb of Robert Hallam, Bishop of Salisbury, c.1416 (after St. John Hope)

17.2 The tombstone of Baron Heinpert von Mallse, 1450, his arms accompanied by the badges of the Eagle, the Dragon, the Scale, St George of Austria, the Jar, and the collar of SS (after Schultz)

17.3 The tombstone of an unknown knight in Neuberg, his arms accompanied by the badges of the orders of St George of Austria, the Sword of Cyprus, the Dove (?), and the Jar (after Schultz)

17.4 The tomb of the knight Jörg Perckhaimer, his arms accompanied by the badges of the orders of the Dragon, the Eagle, the Jar, the Scale, and the collar of SS (after Schultz)

17.5 The collar of the Golden Fleece encircling the arms of Maximilian of
Austria as King of the Romans, by Dürer, 1504

17.6 The arms of Florian Waldauff, accompanied by the collars of the orders of the Stole and Jar of Aragon (dexter) and of the Swan of Brandenburg (around the shield), and by the English royal livery-collar of SS, by Dürer, c.1520

17.7 Unidentified arms accompanied by the device of the Order of the Stole and
Jar of Aragon, by Dürer, c.1520

in 1416,[6] and while examples of this usage dating from the reigns of the successors of Henry V are not difficult to find, even the royal arms continued to be displayed without, more often than with, an encircling garter until the reign of Henry VIII – the first monarch to display the garter on any of his seals. The earliest example of a garter used in conjunction with the arms of an ordinary companion of the order I have found is that on the the the monumental brass of Thomas, Lord Camoys, who died in 1419, but although Lewis Robsart, Lord Bourchier, displayed five shields of his arms encircled by garters on his tomb, erected in Westminster Abbey at some time after his death in 1431,[7] I have found very few further examples of this usage dating from the fifteenth century. Even on the armorial stall-plates set up by the companions in the order's chapel at Windsor garters were never depicted before 1470, and rarely depicted between that date and the accession of Henry VIII in 1509. Similarly, the earliest known (and only medieval) representation of a knight of the Collar wearing the collar of that order dates from about 1443, and there is not one single example of the collar encircling a shield of arms antedating the year 1518, when the order was reformed. In fact, the only orders other than the Garter whose devices were certainly displayed in formal association with arms before 1415 were the (possibly confraternal) Austrian orders of the Tress and the Salamander, whose badges were painted in the 1390s chained to the arms of various members of the ducal house in the register of the confraternity of St Christopher of the Arlberg Pass. The device of the latter order was also depicted encircling the shields of Dukes Albrecht IV and Ernst I on seals attached to documents written in 1396 and 1404 respectively. The dragon of the Hungarian order founded in 1408 was displayed encircling the arms of its members by 1419, and the collar of the Golden Fleece was displayed in this way by the founder of the order by 1438, but in general the depiction of the insignia of knightly orders in conjunction with arms seems to have been exceptional before about 1450, when German knights errant began to display the devices of all the orders they had been admitted to during their travels (mostly honorific pseudo-orders) on their armorial tomb-stones. Even after that date the use of the insignia of monarchical orders in this way remained remarkably rare, and only the knights of the Golden Fleece seem to have displayed the badge of their order with any regularity before 1500.

Considering the very prominent place the devices of the surviving orders were to occupy in the heraldry and pageantry of the courts of their respective presidents in the next few centuries, when the royal arms and those of the companions were almost never displayed without the garter or collar, it is difficult to understand why such devices were not used more frequently in the period before 1520, when the orders themselves were generally more important. As we have seen, however, the companions of most orders were equally slow in adopting the habit of describing themselves as knights of the order in question, and this practice was clearly related to that of displaying the order's device.

In the great majority of the orders we have examined, the companions were required by the statutes to wear at least one form of the order's badge whenever they appeared in public, as a sign of their membership. Only the Castilian order of the

---

[6] See W. H. St John Hope, *Heraldry for Craftsmen and Designers* (London, 1913), fig. 155, p. 265.

[7] St John Hope, *Heraldry*, fig. 134, p. 223.

Band, the Aragonese order of the Stole and Jar, and the Sicilian order of the Ermine required their members to wear their badge on only one day each week. There is some evidence that the knights of the Garter, at least, did not wear their badge as often as they were supposed to, especially before 1422, and in all likelihood the knights of other orders were at least equally remiss in this respect.

12 The Formal Habits

Most monarchical orders also resembled both religious orders and confraternities in requiring their members to wear a formal habit of some sort on certain occasions specified in the statutes. Only the knights of the Collar seem to have had no peculiar costume before the very end of our period, and even they were required to wear the habit of a Carthusian hermit during the funerals for which alone they assembled as a body. In the order of the Band the habit seems to have consisted simply of a civil or military surcoat, ultimately red in colour, to which the band device was attached, but in all the remaining orders except that of the Knot the habit included or consisted exclusively of a floor-length mantle of the sort traditionally worn by the knights of the religious orders. In fact, it is clear that most founders wished to associate the knights of their new model orders, both in their own minds and in those of the public at large, with the monk-knights of the older orders, still regarded as models of religious chivalry. Mantles of the same cut were increasingly worn on formal occasions by princes, peers, and judicial officers, as the principal element of their robes of estate, so the mantle worn by the companions of the monarchical orders would also have served to associate them visually with the holders of other important dignities.

The mantle of the Knights of St George of Hungary was black, like that of the knights of the Hospital of St John, and those of the two Aragonese orders and the French order of St Michael were white, like the mantles of all the other religious orders, but those worn by the knights of the Star, the Ship, the Golden Fleece, the Ermine of Sicily, and (from 1518) the Annunciation were red, like most robes of estate, and that of the Garter was blue. Only in the Order of St Michael did the colour correspond to that of the founder's normal livery. The mantles of the knights of the religious orders bore on their left breast the peculiar cross of their order, but among the knights of the lay orders only those of the Garter and those of the Aragonese order of St George wore a mantle charged in this way in our period; in the other orders the regular badge was simply pinned to or hung over the mantle when it was worn. In place of a breast badge, the mantles of the orders of the Golden Fleece, St Michael, the Annunciation, and possibly the Stole and Jar, were enriched with a wide embroidered border representing the elements of the order's collar, running all the way around the outer hem, but those of the other orders seem to have been quite plain. Mantles seem in general to have been cut from some high quality cloth — at first usually woolen cloth-of-scarlet, but by 1475 usually silk satin or velvet — and were usually lined in fur or fabric of some contrasting colours: ermine, vair, or satin. The mantles of the knights of the Garter and the Ship were worn with the opening at the front, like those of the religious orders, but those of the knights of the Star, the Golden Fleece, the Ermine of Sicily, St Michael, and the Annunciation were all worn, like a classical chlamys (and like the robes of estate worn in France), open on the right side.

Before the year 1465, only the orders of the Star and the Ship specified the nature, form, or colour of the garments that were to be worn below the mantle, and in each of these orders the principal undergarment was a white *surcote* of old-fashioned length and cut, probably meant to suggest the coat worn by the knights of the religious orders. The knights of the Garter may well have worn a similar surcoat in the fourteenth century, but its form and colour were not fixed by the statutes, and seem to have varied from one year to the next. Aside from the mantle and surcoat, the items composing the formal habit of all three orders were those of the ordinary civil costume of the period: *chaperon* or caped hood, worn in the normal way before about 1390 over the surcoat and possibly over the mantle; *cote* or undertunic, worn under the surcoat and covered except for the sleeves below the elbow; and hose, visible only below the knee. Only the knights of the Knot (who had no mantle) wore a short surcoat of the new tailored style. The knights of the orders founded after 1429 wore a floor-length gown rather than a surcoat under their mantle, but its form, colour, and fabric were not fixed until the period 1465–73. The knights of the Golden Fleece and St Michael were also to have worn a caped hood like that of the Garter knights, but by 1430 it had long been the fashion to wear this garment as a sort of turban, and by 1465 hoods were normally worn slung over one shoulder by the liripipe, with the headpiece hanging down the back. The vestigial hood of the knights of the Garter (the only one of our orders whose habit is still worn) is even yet carried in this way.

Unlike the badge of the order, the habit was meant to be worn only on certain formal occasions connected with the order. In general it was to be worn during the religious services held during the course of each of the order's regular assemblies, and was in some orders to be worn during the chapter as well. Some orders specified that their companions were also to wear the habit during the course of assemblies called for special purposes, and the Order of the Stole and Jar (which held no formal assemblies) required them to wear it on all solemn feasts. The earlier Aragonese order had required its members to wear their habit on a certain day each week, and that of the Band was to have been worn on at least one day every week. The Company of the Star similarly required its members to wear a special version of their habit on a certain day each week. Finally, the knights of the Garter were expected to don their mantle whenever they came to the order's seat.

Unfortunately, we know very little about the actual appearance of the habits of any of the orders in the first century of our period, and even less about when they were actually worn. Even in the second century of our period only the habits of the knights of the Golden Fleece and St Michael – depicted in the frontispiece to most of the manuscripts of their statutes – are really well documented, and it appears that the latter, though made up, were never actually worn by the companions in our period.

13 A Final Assessment

In order to assess the potential value of the monarchical orders to their presidents, one must consider them in relationship to the purposes for which they were founded, to the other methods and institutions currently available to fulfil the same or similar purposes, and to the general level of administrative sophistication prevailing in the period when they were founded. One must also bear in mind the beliefs and values both of their founders and of the men they were meant to include among their ordinary members.

The only purpose common to all of the orders we have studied was to encourage loyalty to the founder and his heirs on the throne, both among those actually admitted to the order and among those who might aspire to membership. In order to achieve this goal, the founders all offered certain significant benefits to companions and would-be companions whose loyalty remained unimpeachable, and threatened those whose loyalty fell short of their expectations with the loss of those benefits, and often with more serious penalties as well.

The principal benefit conferred by admission to a monarchical order was of course prestige or 'honour'. Since the members of the contemporary knightly class generally placed a very high value upon public honour, it was probably at least as powerful an inducement to loyalty as most forms of practical advantage, and there can be no doubt that most founders were fully aware of this when they created their orders. Honour was of course conferred on every companion merely by admitting him to membership in an exclusive society presided over in person by a sovereign prince, but most founders were not content with this, and did everything they could think of to increase the prestige conveyed by membership. By stating the high personal qualities theoretically required in all candidates for admission, by restricting the society to knights or men of noble birth or both, by limiting the number of members, and by associating the order in some way with the legendary societies of heroes depicted in the Arthurian romances, the founders attempted to convey the impression that everyone admitted to the company was a veritable paragon of chivalry, in the tradition of Lancelot, Galahad, and the Nine Worthies. No doubt a few minor knights with exceptional reputations for prowess were admitted into many orders primarily to shore up the image of the order as a worthy successor to the Round Table, and lend the lustre of their deeds to the other, less heroic members. Most founders also associated the companions of their orders with the heroic knights of the religious orders by giving them a formal habit that included a mantle, and by requiring them to take what amounted to a crusader's vow. Furthermore, like Arthur and Perceforest, the founders of monarchical orders conferred honour upon those admitted to their orders, by treating them as colleagues and brothers, rather than mere subjects or clients, by wearing the same badge and habit, and (toward the end of our period) by displaying the badge of the order in conjunction with their arms. In addition, in most orders the companions could count among their colleagues not only the king or duke himself, but the latter's sons and brothers, and in some orders a number of foreign princes and even kings. Few barons would have felt less than eager to associate on terms of near equality with men of such exalted rank, for honour and status were closely associated in contemporary minds. Of course the status of companion was itself a sort of dignity, comparable in important respects to the dominical dignities of duke, count, and so forth which were first conferred as part of a real system of honours in exactly the same period, and for very much the same reason. Like those statuses, that of companion was conferred by the ruler himself in most orders in an impressive public ceremony, and commonly conveyed to its recipient not only distinctive robes (of very similar cut, colour, and material to those worn by princes), but a definite precedence in court. Unlike those dignities, the dignity of companion also entailed the right to wear a distinctive badge at all times and to display it in association with one's armorial bearings, to display one's armorial bearings themselves in the chapel of the royal palace, and to be commemorated there after one's death by a permanent memorial of some sort. With all of these features in its favour, the monarchical order was really without equal as an instrument for conferring honour on its members.

Although designed primarily to confer honour, monarchical orders could also be used to confer disgrace upon those of their members who failed to live up to their obligation, whether explicit or implicit, to be loyal to their prince president. Most orders prescribed expulsion as the penalty for the more flagrant forms of treason, and several orders – most notably the Ship and the Ermine of Sicily – heaped shame upon the traitor's head in various formal ways. If public honour was highly desirable, public dishonour must have been equally undesirable to most contemporary knights, so the threat of such penalties ought to have served to discourage disloyal acts in all but the most difficult situations.

In addition to honour, all monarchical orders provided their members with at least one practical benefit which, though not spelled out in any statute, was nevertheless quite real: the right to associate on intimate terms with the king or duke and the members of the inner circle of his friends and advisors, who were invariably admitted to the order. In a society in which advancement was determined far more by personal relationships than personal accomplishments, this was a very important right, for it inevitably put the companion in a strong position to lobby for appointments both for himself and for his relatives and friends. Such an advantage, combined with the honours entailed in membership, and the various spiritual benefits offered by all but the three Spanish orders, must surely have been regarded by those fortunate enough to be elected to a monarchical order as more than adequate compensation for past loyalty and service, and must have served as a powerful incentive to further behaviour of the same sort.

Most founders, however, wanted to use their order not merely to encourage loyal service in a general way, but to engage the services of the companions, at least in certain types of situation, either on an individual or a corporate basis. In order to do this, they introduced into the statutes not only specific cliental and patronal obligations, which together constituted something very like a life-contract of retinue, but in most cases supplemented these with fraternal obligations, and in some cases added still further practical privileges such as exemption from taxation and from the regular system of courts. Most founders also made use of the confraternal custom of examining the conduct of members and rewarding and punishing them on the basis of their behaviour to enforce compliance with their statutory obligations. Depending on how one looks at it, they may be said to have introduced the characteristic features of retaining by contract into the existing, egalitarian form of knightly confraternity, or to have taken advantage of the characteristic features of confraternities in general, and knightly confraternities in particular, to impose order, discipline, and cooperation upon the members of what would otherwise have been an unorganized group of life retainers, and to provide them with various advantages they could not otherwise have enjoyed. This fusion of two previously unrelated institutions was surely as ingenious as St Bernard's idea of fusing the equally unrelated institutions of knighthood and monasticism two centuries earlier, even if it has not generally been appreciated as such by scholars. The practice of retaining by life contract, widely used throughout the same period in both England and France, seems to have been regarded as a very effective means of securing the services of those retained, and there is no obvious reason why the monarchical order would not have been at least as effective. It is true that few founders mentioned any monetary payment for the services required, but it is not unlikely that some form of payment was actually given to those companions who answered the summons to service, and even if it was not, the various benefits to be derived from membership in the order – which commonly included promises of aid and support from the ruler and the most influential members of his court – might well have been regarded as more valuable in the long run than a mere salary.

The nature of the services required or expected by the founders of the different orders varied considerably, in accordance with the needs they felt at the time they formulated the statutes. The first true monarchical order, that of the Band, was clearly intended to function primarily as an élite military unit, comparable to those provided by the religious orders of knighthood, to be used against both domestic rebels and the Moors of Granada. Given the state of military organization in Castile in the middle decades of the fourteenth century, the idea of creating a lay order for this purpose was perfectly sound, and as Alfonso insisted in the statutes that the knights of the order maintain a high level of military discipline and participate in frequent tournaments in order to develop both their martial skills and their ability to fight as a unit, there is every reason to believe that the order quickly became at least as effective a force as the older orders. It is very likely that the knights of the Cypriot order of the Sword were intended to fight in the same way as part of their founder's crusading army, and at least possible that the knights of the Star and the Knot were meant to fight on occasion as units of the royal army, but the only other order whose statutes clearly imply that its members were to form some sort of company in battle was that of the Ship. It is unclear why most later founders rejected the rather obvious idea of using their order as a sort of élite military company, especially as many specialized companies of soldiers – crossbowmen, archers, halberdiers, bombardiers, and so on – were created in the same general period. It may be that most founders felt that they had a compelling need for an order that would include their most important vassals and officers, and that such men could be put to much better use commanding their own companies than fighting as part of a company composed largely of princes and barons. Certainly the goal of encouraging the service of the mighty was in direct conflict with that of creating a useful military unit, and most founders seem to have decided that the former was more important.

The goal of rewarding important barons was not incompatible with a requirement that they serve in arms at the head of their own company of vassals and retainers, however, and most orders did require this, if only implicitly. The circumstances in which this service was to be exacted varied greatly. Some orders – St George of Hungary, the Ship, and the quasi-order of the Dragon – were founded by princes who faced a serious challenge to their authority from within their kingdom, and such orders were clearly intended to function primarily as political parties or factions. The members of these orders were probably expected to support the prince president against his domestic rivals and enemies without any specific request to do so, and to join their forces with those of the president whenever summoned. In these orders military service would have been frequent, undirected, and probably unpaid except when expressly requested, and would have included such activities as recruiting, garrisoning castles, and spying, as well as taking part in campaigns and sieges. Aside from the general function of encouraging loyalty to the prince, the most important functions of these orders as such were to bring the various commanders together for relatively frequent consultations with the prince and one another, to encourage cooperation among them, to discourage defection or treasonous dealings with the enemy, and to provide a system of rewards and punishments for their actions, comparable to those maintained by modern armies. Given the importance of the ideology of chivalry and the lack of any alternative forms of organization at the time, the idea of creating a king's party in the form of a knightly order or aristocratic confraternity must appear quite promising, for such an institution was at least as likely to secure the loyal service of barons as any other at the prince's disposal, and the peculiar benefits it provided could be supplemented (in keeping with the patronal obligation to promote the interests of the companions) with whatever offices, fiefs, and pensions were currently at the prince's disposal. Moreover, unlike the grant of a fief, the concession of membership in such an order alienated no jurisdictional rights or income, and could easily be rescinded if the services promised were not performed, and unlike the grant of a money-fief or non-feudal pension, it did not absolutely require the payment of any money. Of course no combination of promises, concessions, and threats, however sincerely made, could have prevented the defection of princes and barons who felt that the enemies of the president were going to achieve his removal from the throne, but as long as the balance of forces was not impossibly against the president, the various forms of oversight imposed by these orders ought to have served to discourage not only treason but neutrality among their members.

Six founders seem to have felt sufficiently secure against domestic enemies not to require their companions to serve them constantly as members of an armed faction, but still wanted them to serve whenever they or their successors had need of them, especially in campaigns to defend their lands or vassals against foreign enemies, or to reconquer lost territories. The founders of the orders of the Knot, the Collar, St George of Aragon, the Ship, the Golden Fleece, and St Michael all imposed such an obligation, at least upon those companions who were their subjects. The practical importance of this service to the president inevitably varied according to the size of the order and the frequency of such campaigns. In the orders of the Knot and the Ship, which were probably intended to include well over a hundred important barons, and were founded by princes with serious pretensions to foreign territories, it may well have been taken very seriously. For the presidents of the relatively small orders of the Collar, the Golden Fleece, and St Michael, the obligation of the members to serve them in battle was of rather less importance, but as almost all of the members of these orders who were not officers were important barons its value was not necessarily negligible. For most of the men in question, it would have been no more than a supplement to the obligations undertaken as vassals, officers, and retainers, but in a society where loyalties were precarious every tie helped, and the solemn oaths taken by the companions in the presence of their fellows could not be set aside lightly. It may be that the members of the more limited orders – and indeed those of the unlimited order of St George of Aragon – were rarely called upon to perform military service on the basis of their oath of membership alone, but the mere existence of the obligation would have made it difficult to refuse other forms of summons.

Six founders – those of the orders of the Sword, the Knot, St George of Aragon, the Ship, the Dragon, and the Ermine – explicitly required the members of their order to take part in some sort of war against the Infidel, but their motives for doing so were far from uniform. Pierre of Cyprus seems to have founded his order primarily to act as the core of the army he hoped to lead in a general crusade to reconquer the Kingdom of Jerusalem – whose throne he claimed as the lineal heir of the former kings – and it is entirely possible that the knights of the Sword never undertook any obligation except to fight the Infidel, either in an attack on their lands or in defence of the Kingdom of Cyprus. The three kings of mainland Sicily who imposed similar obligations also claimed the throne of Jerusalem, and it is just possible that both Loysi (or at least Nicola Accaiuoli) and Carlo actually had some hope of leading a crusade to reconquer it, but such an expedition was not high on the list of priorities of either prince, and it is most unlikely that Ferrante had any serious plan to make good his decidedly dubious claim. Similarly, Pere of Aragon required the knights of his order to take part in any expedition he led against the Moors, but there is no reason to believe that he was planning to lead such an expedition. Thus, in all likelihood, these four founders included the obligation to take part in a crusade primarily to associate their orders with the religious orders of knighthood, and allow their members to call themselves crusaders. Sigismund or Zsigmond of Hungary, on the other hand, founded his society of the Dragon at least partly to shore up the defenses of his kingdom against the growing menace posed by the Ottoman Turks, and undoubtedly expected his barons to take part in campaigns against them. It is not without significance that the princes who actually did lead crusades in the fourteenth century – Alfonso of Castile, Humbert of Viennois, Pierre of Cyprus, Amé of Savoy, Louis of Bourbon, and Zsigmond of Hungary – all founded lay orders of knighthood, but only two of these princes seem to have required their companions to take part. It may be that the more serious crusaders recognised the weaknesses of a lay order as an instrument for carrying on an offensive foreign war of any sort; even the Order of the Sword, whose knights did not have far to travel to fight the Infidel, does not seem to have been particularly successful as an instrument of the crusade, although we can only infer this from the decision of its promoter Philippe de Mézières to found an order of a very different type.

The one remaining form of service demanded by the founders of monarchical orders was loyal counsel. This service was specifically required in the statutes of the orders of St George of Hungary, the Star, the Knot, the Collar, the Golden Fleece, and St Michael, and there is reason to believe that the founders of all of these orders (with the possible exception of Loysi of Sicily and Louis of France) hoped that their order would function at least in part as a sort of council representative of the nobility of their kingdom or dominions. Indeed, this may well have been the principal function envisioned by both Károly of Hungary and Jean of France for their respective foundations. None of these princes had access to any other assembly that included the leading members of the nobility from throughout their dominions, so the regular chapters of the order (which met more frequently than any other comparable body except the privy council itself) might well have proved a useful forum for the discussion of important affairs of particular concern to the nobility. Even when the prince was not really interested in the opinions of his barons, and intended to follow a certain course of action whatever they initially suggested, it was useful to give the appearance of consultation, and the chapter provided an opportunity for the prince to present his views and to attempt, at least, to win over those who showed signs of opposition. Such a body could also be used as a forum for airing grievances felt by the companions both towards the prince and towards one another, and for forstalling and settling quarrels which might have led to civil disorders, and it is very likely that these founders – who provided more or less elaborate mechanisms for settling disputes among the members – had these purposes in mind as well. Finally, the meetings of the chapter could be used to create fellow feeling among barons drawn from many different regions who had previously had no real contact with one another, and could thus help to unite the lands of a prince like Philippe of Burgundy. The order could not, of course, include more than a fraction of the nobility of its president's lands, but it could contain, like the English House of Lords, the most important members of the nobility, and in addition a few representatives of its lower strata. The companions of the order could thus constitute a sort of peerage within the nobility of the president's dominions (conveniently unrestricted by the boundaries between kingdoms and principalities). There is reason to believe that some founders, at least, conceived of the companions of their order in very much that way, for they endowed them with the judicial privilege characteristic of peerages: the exclusive right to judge their own members in all cases in which they were involved.

The two remaining functions the monarchical orders were intended by their founders to perform were closely related: the 'exaltation' of chivalry, and the promotion of chivalrous behaviour among the companions. Most founders probably sought to use their order to 'exalt' chivalry in order to identify themselves and their houses as closely as possible with the nobility as a social class and with its characteristic ethos and values. By placing themselves at the head of a body clearly modelled on the ancient company of the Round Table, formally restricted to knights *sans reproche* and obviously intended to embody the same knightly ideals, these princes no doubt hoped to appear at once as patrons and paragons of chivalric virtue in the image of Arthur, and thus more than worthy of the respect and loyalty of their noble subjects and princely allies. They may have hoped, indeed, to use their order as they used the tournament, to coopt the ethos of the nobility to their own advantage, and to place themselves firmly at the head of, rather than outside, the noble class of their kingdom or dominions as a whole.

The goal of promoting chivalrous behaviour was probably seen by most founders as but one way among many of exalting chivalry and thus enhancing their own standing, but some founders almost certainly saw this as an independent goal of equal or greater importance. Three of the four earliest orders – those of St George of Hungary, the Band, and the Star – had among their primary functions the promotion of conduct in keeping with the norms of chivalry, not only among their members, but among the nobles of their respective kingdoms in general. Their founders clearly felt that some, at least, of the standards of conduct demanded by the knightly code, if strictly enforced, could actually prove to be of great political and military utility to the crown. Courage and prowess were still essential qualities in captains as well as knights of the rank and file, and loyalty was a virtue (all the more prized in this period for its rarity) that was equally important in soldiers and civil officers. Even courtesy was of some political value, for it reduced the ever-present risk of quarrels among the king's own adherents. Both Károly of Hungary and Alfonso of Castile were probably interested in encouraging all of these virtues among their noble subjects, whose behaviour in the period immediately before the foundation of the order certainly left much to be desired; Jean of France was concerned primarily with improving knightly conduct on the field of battle. In all likelihood all three of these princes, and quite possibly others among the founders, hoped that the high standards of conduct enforced within their order would percolate down to the other members of the nobility, who could reasonably have been expected to emulate the behaviour of the most honoured members of their class.

In practice, the founders of monarchical orders 'exalted' chivalry on the one hand by exalting the order itself, and on the other by associating the order as closely as possible with chivalric values and symbols, by demanding chivalrous conduct from its members, by honouring those knights who behaved in keeping with the highest ideals of chivalry, and by punishing those who did not. Most orders were dedicated to the recognized patrons of knighthood, and provided various opportunites for the display of shields, banners, and helms bearing the personal arms and crests of the companions – insignia closely associated with chivalry both on the battlefield and in the lists. The later orders also maintained kings of arms – who had emerged by 1400 as the high priests of the cult of chivalry – to make sure that these sacred ensigns were correctly displayed, and to keep a record of the companions' ancestry and noble deeds. Most orders actually required their members to perform one or two specific types of action traditionally associated with knighthood, including honouring and defending ladies and orphans, defending the church, and taking part in crusades, and one order even encouraged its members to wander about in search of adventures and to go on a pilgrimage to Jerusalem. Otherwise the practices used to promote chivalrous conduct were inseparable from those used to honour it. Worthy acts by a non-member could of course be recognized simply by election to the order, but within the order such acts were commonly rewarded with praise during the course of the annual chapter, and in some orders by recording them for posterity in the order's book of 'adventures' (a collective chivalric biography of decidedly Arthurian form), by an augmentation to the order's badge (which thus functioned like a modern military medal), and (or) by a seat at a special table of honour, or near the prince president, during the order's annual banquet. Unworthy acts could similarly be punished during the course of the chapter by criticism or denunciation, and by the imposition of a penalty, including such forms of dishonour as the reversal of a shield of arms, being forbidden to wear the order's badge or habit, having to wear a special habit symbolic of disgrace, and having to eat apart from the other companions. Especially unworthy acts could be punished by expulsion from the order, effected through a more or less solemn ceremony designed to heap as much dishonour as possible on the companion's head, and in one order accompanied by a general denunciation. Although relatively few forms of behaviour were either explicitly enjoined or explicitly forbidden in the statutes of most orders, there is reason to believe that many orders expected their members to maintain high standards of conduct both in court and on the battlefield, and did not hesitate to criticise or punish behaviour which they deemed unworthy of a chosen knight. Whether any order succeeded in converting all or even most of its members into the exemplars of chivalric virtue they were supposed to be may be doubted, but their efforts to do so must have won them the respect of many contemporaries, and they were almost certainly regarded as the principal institutional embodiments of the secular ideals of chivalry. There is also some evidence that they served to promote heroic conduct in the service of the prince president – one of the principal objects of the founders of the orders of the Star and the Ship – though in the case of the former order this heroism seems to have proved fatal to the rest of the founder's plans.

The monarchical order of knighthood was thus a complex and highly flexible institution in which elements derived from a number of contemporary organizations were ingeniously interwoven with others taken from the Arthurian romances and the practices of the contemporary knightly class, and which could be used to accomplish a variety of quite distinct goals. Although every one of these societies was intended to encourage and reward loyal service to the founder and his heirs, and to confer a politically useful aura of chivalry upon the president and his court, some were also meant to serve as élite military companies, some as political parties or factions, and some as instruments for securing the advice, cooperation, good behaviour, and unification of the nobility. None of these goals could be regarded as frivolous, and as I hope I have shown, the orders were generally provided with mechanisms which could in theory have achieved them.

The question we must deal with finally is whether they did in fact achieve any of these goals, to the extent that any human institution can reasonably be expected to do so. Unfortunately, we know too little about the histories of most of these orders to make such a judgement with any confidence. It could be argued that as most of the fourteenth-century orders either dissolved or were reduced to the condition of pseudo-orders before the end of the century, those orders, at least, were ultimately failures. Against this, however, we must set the fact that, with the exception of the orders of the Star and the Ship, whose founders were removed from power before they had had time to establish them properly, every order seems to have been preserved in some form at least until the extinction of the heirs male of the founder's body, and may well have functioned as it was intended to at least until its founder's death. The orders of St George of Hungary, the Band, St George of Aragon, the Ship, and the Ermine seem to have dissolved as a result of major political upheavals which removed their founder's heirs, at least temporarily, from the throne, so their collapse cannot be used to argue that they had never functioned properly before those cataclysmic events. Indeed, the very fact that men in such difficult situations as Carlo and Ferrante of Sicily and Zsigmond of Hungary decided to found elaborate new orders to succeed others which had dissolved suggests that the earlier orders had been at least reasonably successful, and we know that the Society of the Dragon established by the last of these princes remained a major power in the state until the death of his son-in-law three decades later. There is also some evidence to suggest that companions took their membership oaths at least as seriously as they took any other such oath even in the fifteenth century, for several companions felt obliged to resign from the Garter, the Golden Fleece, and St Michael in order to avoid being compromised, and knights of various ranks are known to have refused election to the Garter and St Michael in order to avoid being bound too closely to their royal presidents.

There are thus grounds for concluding that most of these orders were successful in achieving at least some of the goals their founders had set for them. By the end of our period, however, the only practical functions these orders were still capable of performing more effectively than any other type of institution at the disposal of their prince presidents were those of rewarding and encouraging loyal service among the members of the uppermost strata of the nobility, and the four orders which survived in 1525 – those of the Garter, the Collar or Annunciation, the Golden Fleece, and St Michael – were all preserved thereafter almost exclusively to perform those functions. Along with the other knightly orders that survived the social and political upheavals of the sixteenth century, however, the monarchical orders continued to serve at least one further function, whose importance to society as a whole was almost certainly greater: that of preserving into the post-medieval period a fossilized remnant, at least, of the chivalric ethos they had been created to epitomize. By some time in the seventeenth century (the precise date has yet to be established), the formal status of knight itself was effectively preserved in most continental countries exclusively in the context of 'knightly' orders, whose statutes continued to demand that their members receive the accolade before their formal induction; only in the British realms was the status of 'knight bachelor' still conferred upon men who were not to be admitted to any special 'order' of knights. Since all but a handful of the orders then extant – including all of the religious orders of the Iberian kingdoms – had been converted into monarchical orders through the attachment of their presidency to a royal or princely crown,[8] it could be said that by that time the monarchical order was, in most of Europe, the principal or sole remaining repository of the traditions of knighthood.

For reasons I have already suggested, very few new 'knightly' orders of any sort were founded between 1470 and 1687.[9] During that period of more than two centuries, therefore, the chivalric tradition was carried primarily by orders that had been founded in the period when knighthood was still a functional military status, and chivalry a living social code, but the knightly order was in some danger of becoming nothing more than a relic of a vanished culture. In 1687, however, James VII of Scotland (who in his capacity as James II of England was Sovereign of the Order of the Garter) decided to 'revive' for the benefit of his Scottish subjects the defunct Scottish order of the Thistle, and to endow it with statutes based directly on those of the Garter. Like the foundation of the Order of the Garter itself

---

[8] The principal exceptions were the knights of St John, since 1530 based in Malta, and the Teutonic Knights.

[9] Aside from the Orders of St Stephen of Tuscany (1561) and the Holy Spirit of France (1578), the only certainly knightly orders founded by lay princes in this period were those of Our Lady of Mount Carmel (France, 1607, united with the schismatic French branch of the Order of the Hospital of St Lazarus in 1608), of the Precious Blood (Mantua, 1608), and of Amaranta (Sweden, 1645).

nearly three and a half centuries earlier, James' action seems to have set off a whole new wave of similar foundations. In the twenty-two years between 1693, when Louis XIV of France created a third order for his kingdom, and 1715, when the Marquis of Baden founded an order for his principality, no fewer than eleven neo-monarchical orders were either established or endowed with statutes for the first time by European princes – especially those who for one reason or another had not inherited such an order from their predecessors on the throne.[10] After 1715 the rate of creations dropped off considerably until about 1802, when Napoléon created his Legion of Honour, but this set of another wave of new foundations. Thereafter new 'orders' composed of 'knights' or 'companions' were to be created with considerable regularity, not only by monarchical régimes, but by republics of the most diverse political ideologies, right up to the present day. Before the end of the nineteenth century the custom of creating and maintaining such orders had spread from Europe to its former colonies (from 1811)[11] and to the lands of Asia and Africa (from 1851),[12] and by the First World War practically every sovereign state in the world maintained at least one, and often three or more such 'orders'. As all of these hundreds of orders were modelled at least partly on the monarchical orders we have studied, it could be said without exaggeration that those orders have proved to be the most successful instrument ever devised for rewarding and encouraging service to the state.

[10] The orders founded or endowed with statutes in this period included the following: St Louis, France, 1693; the Elephant, Denmark (1457), statutes 1693; the Dannebrog, Denmark (1671), statutes 1693; St Michael, Bavaria, 1693; St Andrew, Russia, 1698; the Black Eagle, Prussia, 1701; the Hunt, Wurtemberg, 1702; the Thistle, Scotland (revived again) 1703; Sincerity (or the Red Eagle), Prussia, 1705, 1712; St Hubert, Bavaria, (revived) 1708; the White Eagle, Poland, 1713; Fidelity, Baden, 1715.
[11] Orders were founded in Haiti in 1811, Brazil in 1820, and Bolivia in 1836.
[12] Orders were founded in Turkey in 1851 and 1879; in Siam in 1861, 1869, and 1887; in Cambodia in 1864; in Japan in 1875, 1877, 1888, and 1890; and in China in 1882.

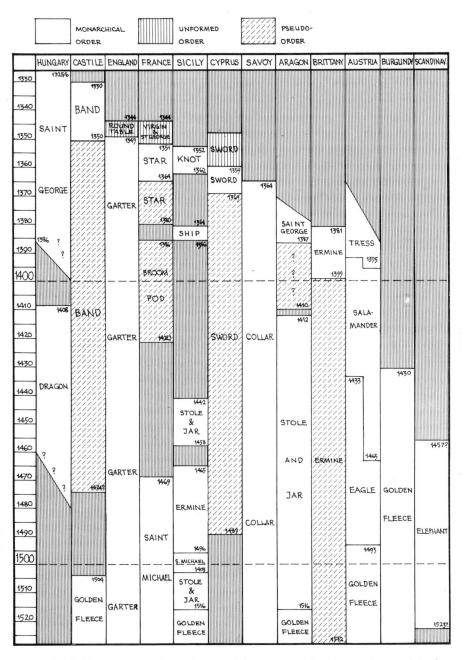

Table 17.1 Comparative chronology of the monarchical orders maintained in the twelve states in which such orders were founded, 1325–1525

Abbreviations

AHS	Archives Héraldiques Suisses
AKDV	Anzeiger für Kunde der deutschen Vorzeit
Annales	Annales: Economies, Sociétés, Civilisations
BEC	Bibliothèque de l'Ecole des Chartes
BIHR	Bulletin of the Institute of Historical Research
BSNAF	Bulletin de la Société nationale des antiquaires de France
CMH	The Cambridge Medieval History
EB	The Encyclopaedia Britannica
EHR	The English Historical Review
FMLS	Forum for Modern Language Studies
PCEEBM	Publications du centre européen des études burgondo-médianes
RNHB	Revue nobiliaire, héraldique et biographique
TRHS	Transactions of the Royal Historical Society
ZRP	Zeitschrift für Romanische Philologie

Bibliography

Manuscript Sources

London, British Library, Additional ms. 28,549
———— Additional ms. 34,801
———— Cotton ms. Julius C.IX
———— Cotton ms. Nero D.II
———— Cotton ms. Vespasian A.XX
———— Egerton ms. 3713 (Willement's Roll)
———— Harley ms. 564
———— Harley ms. 5415
———— Harley ms. 6199
———— Royal ms. 15 E 6
———— Stowe ms. 594 (Bruges' Garter Book)
———— Stowe ms. 668
London, Public Record Office, E101/390/9
———— E101/391/1
———— E101/391/14
———— E101/394/16
———— E372/207/50
New York, Morgan Library, ms. 146
Oxford, Bodleian Library, Ashmole ms. 764
———— Ashmole ms. 813
———— Laud ms. misc. 716
Paris, Archives Nationales, J 169
———— JJ 81
———— K 1731
———— KK 8
Paris, Bibliothèque Nationale, ms. Clairambault 1242
———— Dupuy 662
———— esp. 33 (anc. 464)
———— esp. 150 (anc. 466)
———— esp. 335 (anc. 465)
———— fr. 139
———— fr. 813
———— fr. 1281
———— fr. 2815
———— fr. 2904
———— fr. 3241
———— fr. 3244
———— fr. 3294
———— fr. 3886

—— fr. 3943
—— fr. 5225
—— fr. 5228
—— fr. 5241
—— fr. 5605
—— fr. 5745
—— fr. 13533
—— fr. 15540
—— fr. 19815
—— fr. 19818
—— fr. 19819
—— fr. 19246
—— fr. 21447
—— fr. 22288
—— fr. 22289
—— fr. 24108
—— fr. 25188
—— fr. 31794
—— fr. 33006
—— n. acq. fr. 3294
—— n. acq. fr. 9760
—— n. acq. fr. 12663
—— n. acq. fr. 16251
Philadelphia, University of Pennsylvania, ms. French 83
Turin, Archivio di Stato, Mazzo I. N. 4.
Turin, Biblioteca Nazionale Universitaria, ms. L. III. 29
Turin, Biblioteca Reale, Manoscritti di Storia Patria, no. 759 (Cigna-Santi, Vittorio Amadeo. *Dell'Ordine Supremo di Savoia, detto prima del Collare indi della Santissima Annunziata. Memorie istoriche* [Turin, 1784])

Printed Sources (Primary)

Adam of Murimuth. *Adae Murimuth' Continuatio Chronicarum*, ed. E. Maunde Thompson (London, 1889)
Anciens statuts de l'ordre hospitalier et militaire du Saint Sépulchre de Jérusalem, suivis des Bulles, Lettres-Patentes et Réglemens authentiques du dit Ordre (Paris, 1776)
d'Anglure, Ogier VIII, seigneur. *Le saint voyage de Jherusalem du seigneur d'Anglure*, ed. François Bonnardot and Auguste Longnon (Paris, 1878)
Anstis, John. *The Register of the Most Noble Order of the Garter . . . called the Black Book* (2 vols., London, 1724)
Archivo General de la Corona de Aragón. *Colección de documentos inéditos del Archivo General de la Corona de Aragón* (Barcelona, 1847–), VI
Bernard of Clairvaux. *Liber ad Milites Templi de Laude Novae Militiae*, ed. J. Leclercq, H. M. Rochais in *S. Bernardi Opera*, III (Rome, 1963)
Boccaccio, Giovanni. *Le Lettere edite ed inedite de Messer Giovanni Boccaccio*, ed. Fr. Corazzini (Florence, 1877)
Bohigas, Pere, ed. *Tractats de Cavalleria* (Barcelona, 1947)

Boulton, D'A. J. D., ed. 'The Middle French Statutes of the Monarchical Order of the Ship (Naples, 1381). A Critical Edition with Introduction and Notes', *Medieval Studies* 47 (1985), pp. 168–271

Bouvet, Honoré. *L'Arbre de Batailles*, ed. and tr. G. W. Coopland as *The Tree of Battles of Honoré Bonet* (Liverpool, 1949)

Busby, Keith, ed. *Raoul de Hodenc: Le Roman des Eles. The Anonymous Ordene de Chevalerie. Critical editions with introductions, notes, glossary, and translations* (Amsterdam, Philadelphia, 1983)

Cartulaire général de l'ordre des Hospitaliers de St-Jean de Jérusalem (1100–1310), ed. J. Delaville Le Roulx (4 vols., Paris, 1894–1906)

Cartulaire général de l'ordre du Temple 1119–1150. Recueil des chartes et des bulles relatives à l'ordre du Temple, ed. le marquis d'Albon (Paris, 1913)

de Caumont, Nompar II, seigneur. *Voyaige d'oultremer en Jherusalem l'an 1418 par le seigneur de Caumont*, ed. le marquis de la Grange (Paris, 1859)

Chandos Herald. *The Life of the Black Prince by the Herald of Sir John Chandos*, ed. M. K. Pope, E. C. Lodge (Oxford, 1910)

de Charny, Geoffroy. *Livre de Chevalerie*, ed. Joseph-Marie Bruno Constantin, baron Kervyn de Lettenhove, in *Oeuvres de Froissart*. I, iii, pp. 463–533 (Brussels, 1873)

—— *A Critical Edition of Geoffroy de Charny's Livre Charny and the Demandes pour la joute, les tournois et la guerre*, ed. Michael Anthony Taylor (Ph.D. dissertation, Univ. of N. Carolina, Chapel Hill, 1977)

Chastellain, G. *Oeuvres*, ed. Joseph-Marie Bruno Constantin, baron Kervyn de Lettenhove (Brussels, 1865)

Chevalier, Cyr Ulysse Joseph, ed. *Choix de documents historiques inédits sur le Dauphiné. Collection de cartulaires dauphinois*, 7 (Montbéliard, Lyon, 1874)

Chronicon Angliae . . . autore monacho quodam Sancti Albani, ed. E. Maunde Thompson (London, 1874)

Chronicon Siculum incerto authoris ab anno 1340 ad annum 1396 in forma diarii ex inedito codice Ottoboniano Vaticano, ed. Josephus de Blasiis (Naples, 1887)

Chronique des règnes de Jean II et de Charles V, ed. R. Delachenal. Société de l'histoire de France (4 vols., Paris, 1910–20)

Chronique des quatre premiers Valois, ed. S. Luce (Paris, 1862)

Cibrario, conte Luigi, ed. *Statuts et Ordonnances du Très-Noble Ordre de l'Annunciade* (Turin, 1840)

—— . *Notizia storica del Nobilissimo Ordine Supremo della Santissima Annunziata, Sunto degli Statuti, Catalogo dei Cavalieri* (Florence, 1869)

Claretta, barone Gaudenzio, ed. *Statuti antichi inediti et statuti recenti dell'Ordine Supremo della SS. Annuziata con notizie storiche relative al medismo* (Turin, 1887)

Clement VI, Pope. *Lettres de Clément VI*, ed. E. Déprez. *Bibliothèque des Ecoles françaises d'Athènes et de Rome*, sér. 3, vol. 3 (Paris, 1901)

Crónica del Rey Don Alfonso el Onceno, ed. Francisco Cerdá y Rico (Madrid, 1787)

Diez de Games, Gutierre. *El Victorial. Crónica de Don Pero Niño, Conde de Buelna, por su Alférez Gutierre Diez de Games*, ed. Juan de Mata Carriazo (Madrid, 1940)

Diez de Games, Gutierre. *The Unconquered Knight: a Chronicle of the Deeds of Don Pero Niño*, trans. Joan Evans (London, 1928)

Douët-d'Arcq, L., ed. *Choix de pièces inédites relatives au règne de Charles VI.* Société de l'histoire de France, I (Paris, 1863)

Duellius, R. *Miscellanea* (Vienna, 1723–24)

von Ehingen, Jörg. *Reisen nach der Ritterschaft des Schwaebischen Ritters Georg von Ehingen,* ed. F. Pfeiffer, Bibliothek des literarischen Vereins in Stuttgart, 1 (1842)

———. *The Diary of Jörg von Ehingen,* trans. Malcolm Letts (London, 1929)

Faber, Felix. *Evagatorium in Terrae Sanctae, Arabiae, et Egypti Peregrinationem,* ed. C. D. Hassler (Stuttgart, 1843–49)

Fejér, György, ed. *Codex Diplomaticus Hungariae, Ecclesiasticus ac Civilis* (11 vols., Buda, 1829–1844)

Foedera, conventiones, litterae et acta publica inter reges Angliae et alios, ed. T. Rymer et al. and Record Commission (4 vols. in 7 parts, London, 1816–69)

Froissart, Jean. *Chroniques,* ed. Joseph-Marie Bruno Constantin, baron Kervyn de Lettenhove. (25 vols. in 26, Brussels, 1867–77)

Fougières, Estienne de. *Estienne von Fougières livre des manières,* ed. Joseph Kremer, *Ausgaben und Abhandlungen aus dem Gebiete der romanischen Philologie* XXIX (Marburg, 1887)

Fusco, Giuseppe Maria, ed. *I capitoli dell'Ordine dell'Armellino, messi a stampa con note* (Naples, 1845)

Garden de Saint-Ange, le comte, ed. *Code des Ordres de Chevalerie du Royaume* (Paris, 1819; reissued with an introduction by baron Hervé Pinoteau, 1979)

Geoffrey le Baker. *Chronicon Galfridi le Baker de Swynebroke,* ed. E. Maunde Thompson (Oxford, 1889)

Geoffrey of Monmouth. *The History of the Kings of Britain,* trans. Lewis Thorpe (London, 1966)

Gollut, Louis. *Les Mémoires de la République Séquanoise et des Princes de la Franche Comté,* ed. Ch. Duvernoy (Arbois, 1864)

Grünenberg, Conrad. *Des Conrad Grünenberg, Ritters und Burgers zu Constenz Wappenbuch,* ed. Rudolf, Graf Stillfried-Alcántara, and Ad. M. Hildebrandt (3 vols., Görlitz, 1875)

Jacotin, A., ed. *Preuves de la maison de Polignac* (2 vols., Paris, 1898–1905)

John of Salisbury. *Johannis Sareberiensis episcopi Carnotensis Policratici sive de nugis curialium et vestigiis philosphorum,* ed. Clemens C. I. Webb (Oxford, 1909)

Kurth, Willi, ed. *The Complete Woodcuts of Albrecht Dürer* (New York, 1963)

Lacomblet, T. J., ed. *Archiv für die Geschichte des Niederrheins* (7 vols., Düsseldorf, 1832–70)

de la Marche, Olivier. *Mémoires d'Olivier de la Marche,* ed. H. Beaune, J. D'Arbaumont (4 vols., Paris, 1883–88)

Le Bel, Jean. *Chronique,* ed. J. Viard, E. Déprez (Paris, 1904)

Le Febvre, Abbé, ed. *Mémoire pour servir à l'histoire de France du quatorzième siècle contenant les statuts de l'ordre du S. Esprit au Droit Désir ou du Noeud* (Paris, 1764)

le Fèvre, Jean, sire de St-Rémy. *Chronique,* ed. R. Morand. (2 vols., Paris, 1876–81)

von Leibnitz, Gottfried Wilhelm. *Mantissa codicis juris gentium* (Hanover, 1700)

El Libro de la Confradía de Santiago de Burgos, ed. Faustino Menéndez Pidal de Navascues (Bilbao, 1977)

Livre des faicts du bon messire Jean le Maingre dit Bouc⋯aut, ed. J. Michaud, B. Poujoulat. Nouvelle collection des mémoires, II (Paris, 1857)

López de Ayala, Pedro. *Crónicas de los reyes de Castilla Don Pedro, Don Enrique II, Don Juan I, Don Enrique III, por D. Pedro López de Ayala, Chanciller Mayor de Castilla*, ed. Eugenio de Llaguno Amirola (Madrid, 1779)

Louis XI of France. *Lettres de Louis XI*, ed. E. Charavay, J. Vaesen, and B. de Mandrot (Paris, 1890)

de Machaut, Guillaume. *La Prise d'Alexandrie ou chronique du roi Pierre I de Lusignan*, ed. L. de Mas Latrie (Paris, 1877)

de Mézières, Philippe. *La Sustance de la Chevalerie de la Passion de Jhesu Crist*, ed. Abdel Hamed Hamdy, 'Philippe de Mézières and the New Order of the Passion', *Bulletin of the Faculty of Arts (Alexandria, Egypt)* 17 (1963), pp. 45–54; 18 (1964), pp. 1–41, 43–104

——. *Letter to King Richard II: A plea made in 1395 for peace between England and France*, ed. G. W. Coopland (New York, 1976)

——. *Le Songe du Vieil Pelerin*, ed. G. W. Coopland (Cambridge, 1969)

de Laurière, Eusèbe Jacob, et al., eds. *Les Ordonnances des rois de France de la troisième race* (21 vols., Paris, 1723–1849)

Llull, Ramon. *Libre que és de l'Orde de Cavalleria*, ed. Pere Bohigas in *Ramon Llull, Obres Essencials*, I (Barcelona, 1957), pp. 515–545

——. *Livre de l'ordre de chevalerie*, ed. Vicenzo Minerrini (Bari, 1972)

——. *The Book of the Order of Chyvalry*, trans. William Caxton, ed. A. T. P. Byles (London, 1926)

Luchino del Campo. *Viaggio a Gerusalemme di Niccoló da Este [1413]*, ed. G. Ghinassi in *Collezione di opere inedite o rare dei primi tre secoli della lingua* 1 (Turin, 1861), pp. 99–160

Maximilian's Triumphal Arch: Woodcuts by Albrecht Dürer and Others (Dover, New York, 1972)

Miller, Jac. Ferd., ed. 'Monumenta diplomatica nunc primum ex autographis edita', *Acta literaria Musei Nationalis Hungarici* 1 (Buda, 1818), pp. 149–204

de Monstrelet, Enguerran. *La chronique d'Enguerran de Monstrelet*, ed. L. Douët d'Arcq (6 vols., Paris, 1857–62)

d'Oronville, Jean. *La Chronique du bon duc Loys de Bourbon par Jean d'Oronville*, ed. Alphonse M. Chazaud (Paris, 1876)

de Poitiers, Aliénor. *Les Honneurs de la Cour*, ed. Charles Nodier, in La Curne de Sainte Palaye, *Mémoires sur l'ancienne chevalerie* (Paris, 1826)

René d'Anjou. *Oeuvres complètes du roi René*, ed. le comte de Quatrebarbes (Paris, 1845)

La Règle du Temple, ed. Henri de Curzon (Paris, 1886)

Rosell, Cayetano, ed. *Crónicas de los reyes de Castilla desde Don Alfonso el Sabio, hasta los Católicos Don Fernando y Doña Isabel* (Madrid, 1875)

The Rule of the Spanish Military Order of St. James 1170–1493. Latin and Spanish Texts, ed. Enrique Gallego Blanco (Leiden, 1971)

The Rule, Statutes, and Customs of the Hospitallers 1099–1310, trans. E. J. King (London, 1934)

de Saint-André, Guillaume. *Histoire de Jehan IV*, ed. Dom Hyacinthe Morice [de Beaubois], *Mémoires pour servir de preuves à l'histoire ecclésiastique et civile de Bretagne*, II (Paris, 1744)

Scala Chronica, ed. J. Stevenson (Edinburgh, 1836)

Servion, Jean. *Gestez et Chroniques de la Mayson de Savoye par Jehan Servion*, ed. F. E. Bollati (Turin, 1879)

Las Siete Partidas, trans. Samuel Parsons Scott, intro. Charles Sumner Lobinger (New York, 1931)

Spicilegium . . . olim editum opera, ed. Dom Luc d'Achery (3 vols., Paris, 1723)

Statuten des Deutschen Ordens, ed. M. Perlbach (Halle, 1890)

Todaro della Galia, A., ed. *Collezione degli statuti, ordinanzi ed editti del nobilissimo Ordine della SS. Annunziata* (Palermo, 1907)

Vegetius Renatus, Flavius. *L'art de chevalerie. Traduction du 'De re militari' de Végèce par Jean de Meun*, ed. Ulysse Robert (Paris, 1897)

———. *Knyghthode and Bataile. A XVth Century Verse Paraphrase of Flavius Vegetius Renatus "De Re Militari"*, ed. R. Dyboski and Z. M. Arend (London, 1935)

de Viel Castel, comte Horace [de Salviac]. *Statuts de l'Ordre du Saint-Esprit au Droit Désir ou du Noeud* (Paris, 1853)

Villani, Matteo. *Cronica*, ed. Ignazio Moutier (Florence, 1877)

Wace. *Le Roman de Brut*, ed. I. Arnold (Paris, 1938–40)

Wappenbücher vom Arlberg, ed. Otto Hupp (Berlin, 1937)

White, Theodore H. *The Bestiary. A Book of Beasts* (New York, 1954, 1960)

Printed Sources (Secondary)

Ackermann, Gustav Adolph. *Ordensbuch sämtlicher in Europa blühender und erloschener Orden und Ehrenzeichen* (Annaberg, 1855)

Alexander, J. J. G. *Italian Renaissance Illuminations* (New York, 1977)

Altamira, Rafael. 'Spain, 1252–1410', CMH VII, pp. 567–598

Alvarez de Araujo y Cuéllar, Angel. *Recopilación Histórica de las Cuatro Ordenes Militares* (Madrid, 1866)

d'Alauzier, L. 'Une association des seigneurs du Quercy en 1380', *Annales du Midi* 64 (1952), pp. 149–151

Allmand, C. T. *Society at War: The Experience of England and France During the Hundred Years War* (Edinburgh, 1973)

Am Rhyn, August. 'Das älteste Luzerner Stadtwappen mit dem Orden vom Salamander', *Beitrag zur Kunstdenkmälergeschichte des Kanton Luzern* (1938)

Anglo, Sydney. 'The Courtier: The Renaissance and changing ideals', *The Courts of Europe: Politics, Patronage, and Royalty, 1400–1800*, ed. A. G. Dickens (London, 1977)

Anstis, John. *Observations Introductory to an Historical Essay upon the Knighthood of the Bath* (London, 1725)

Anon. 'A propos du Collier de l'Annonciade', *AHS* (1911), pp. 45–46

Archer, Thomas Andrew and Walter Alison Phillips. 'Templars', *EB* (11th ed., 1911), XXVI, pp. 591–600

Armstrong, C. A. J. 'La Toison d'Or et la loi des armes', *PCEEBM* 5 (1963) pp. 1–7

──── . 'The Golden Age of Burgundy: Dukes that outdid kings', *The Courts of Europe: Politics, Patronage, and Royalty, 1400–1800*, ed. A. G. Dickens (London, 1977)

L'Art européen vers 1400 (Vienna, 1962)

von Aschbach, Joseph, Ritter. *Geschichte Kaiser Sigismunds* (4 vols., Hamburg, 1838–45)

Ashmole, Elias. *The Institution, Laws, and Ceremonies of the Most Noble Order of the Garter* (London, 1672; repr. in facs. 1971)

D'Assemani, Michael H. A. *The Cross on the Sword: A History of the Equestrian Order of the Holy Sepulchre of Jerusalem* (Chicago, 1944)

Atiya, Aziz Suryal. *The Crusade in the Later Middle Ages* (London, 1938)

──── . *The Crusade of Nicopolis* (London, 1934)

Auerbach, E. 'The Black Book of the Garter', *Report of the Society of the Friends of St George's* v, no. 4 (1972–3), pp. 149–153

Baranyai, Béla. 'Zsigmond király úgynevezett Sárkányrendje', *Századok* 40 (1926), pp. 561–591, 681–719

Barber, Richard. *Edward, Prince of Wales and Aquitaine: A Biography of the Black Prince* (London, 1978)

──── . *The Knight and Chivalry* (London, 1970; second ed. Cardinal 1974)

Barbet de Jouy, Henri. *Notice des objets composant le musée des souverains* (Paris, 1866)

Barker, Ernest. 'The Teutonic Order', *EB* (11th ed., 1911), XXVI, pp. 676–679

Barron, Oswald. 'Heraldry', *EB* (11th ed., 1911), XIII, pp. 311–330.

Bascapè, Giacomo C. *Gli Ordini Cavallereschi in Italia; Storia et Diritto* (Milan, 1972)

Baudot, M. 'Charles le Noble, "roi de Cherbourg" (1387–1404) et les relations navarro-normandes de 1387–1430 d'après les comptes du trésor de Navarre', *Bulletin philologique et historique* (1969), pp. 193–212

Beaune, Colette. 'Costume et pouvoir en France à la fin du Moyen Age: Les Devises royales vers 1400', *Revue des Sciences Humaines* 183 (1981), pp. 125–146

de Belloy, P. *De l'origine et l'institution des divers Ordres de Chevalerie, tant ecclésiastiques que prophanes* (Paris, 1653)

Beltz, George Frederick. *Memorials of the Order of the Garter* (London, 1841)

Bennet, Jean. *La mutualité française. Des origines à la révolution de 1789* (Paris, 1981)

Benninghoven, Friedrich. *Der Orden des Schwertbrüder. Fratres milicie Christi de Livonia* (Cologne, 1965)

Benson, Larry Dean. *Malory's Morte Darthur* (Cambridge, Mass., 1976)

──── . and John Leyerle, eds. *Chivalric Literature. Essays on Relations between Literature and Life in the Later Middle Ages* (Kalamazoo, 1980)

von Bergman, Joseph. 'Der St. Georgs-Ritterorden vom Jahre 1469–1579', *Mitteilungen der k.k. Central-Commission zur Erforschung und Erhaltung der Baudenkmale* 13 (Vienna, 1868), pp. 169–174

Bertrand de la Grassière, P. *L'Ordre Militaire et Hospitalier de Saint-Lazare de Jérusalem* (Paris, 1960)

Berzeviczy, Edmund. 'Adalék a Sárkány-rend ismertetéséhez', *Turul* 11 (1893), pp. 93–95 von Birken, Sigmund. *Spiegel der Ehren des höhst löblichen Kayser- und Königlichen Erzhauses Österreich* (Nürnberg, 1668)

Bittman, K. *Ludwig XI. und Karl der Kühne. Die Memoiren des Philippe de Commynes als historische Quelle* (Göttingen, 1964)

di Blasi, Abbot. *Lettera intorno all'ordine dell'arminio.* Nuova Raccolta degli autori Siciliani, I (Palermo, 1788)

Boalt, Gunnar; Robert Erikson; Harry Glück; and Herman Lantz. *The European Orders of Chivalry* (Stockholm and Carbondale, Ill., 1971)

Boase, T. S. R. *Death in the Middle Ages: Mortality, Judgement, and Remembrance* (London, 1972)

Bobé, Louis. *De Kongelige Danske Ridderordener og Medailler* (Copenhagen, 1950)

Böhme, Johann Gottlob. *De ordine draconis instituto a Sigismundo Imperatore* (Leipzig, 1764)

Bornstein, Diane. *Mirrors of Courtesy* (Hamden, Conn., 1975)

Bossuat, A. 'Un ordre de chevalerie auvergnat. L'ordre de la Pomme d'or', *Bulletin historique et scientifique de l'Auvergne* (1944), pp. 93–98

Boswell, A. B. 'The Teutonic Order', CMH VII (1932), pp. 248–269

Boucher, F. 'Les conditions de l'apparition du costume court en France vers le milieu du xive siècle', in *Recueil de travaux offerts à M. Clovis Brunel* (Paris, 1925), pp. 183–192

Boulton, D'Arcy Jonathan Dacre. *The Origin and Development of the Curial Orders of Chivalry, 1330–1470* (D.Phil. thesis, Oxford, 1975)

——. *Dominical Titles of Dignity in France, 1223–1515; A Study of the Formalization and Hierarchization of Status in the Upper Nobility in the Later Middle Ages* (Ph.D. thesis, University of Pennsylvania, 1978)

de Brémond d'Ars-Migré, Hélie. *Les Chevaliers du Porc-Epic ou du Camail, 1394–1498* (Mâcon, 1938)

Bümke, Joachim. *The Concept of Knighthood in the Middle Ages*, trans. W. T. H. and E. Jackson (New York, 1982)

Burnett, Charles. 'Reflections on the Order of the Thistle', *The Double Tressure, Journal of the Heraldry Society of Scotland* 5 (1983), pp. 39–42

Camera, Matteo. *Elucubrazioni Storico-Diplomatiche su Giovanna Ia Regina di Napoli e Carlo III di Durazzo* (Salerno, 1889)

Capré, François. *Catalogue des Chevaliers de l'Ordre du Collier de Savoie dict de l'Annonciade . . .* (Turin, 1654)

Capré, François. *Les noms, qualités, armes et blasons des illustres chevaliers de l'Ordre de Savoie dit de l'Annonciade* (Paris, 1657)

Carrafa, Giovanni Batista. *Historia del Regno di Napoli* (Naples, 1572)

Carsten, F. J. *The Origins of Prussia* (Oxford, 1954)

Cartellieri, Otto. *The Court of Burgundy* (London, 1929)

Castan, Auguste. *Les origines de la chevalerie franc-comtoise de Saint-Georges* (Besançon, 1884)

Catalán y Menéndez-Pidal, Diego. *Un cronista del siglo XIV: La Gran crónica de Alfonso XI: Hallazgo, estilo, reconstrucción* (Canaria, 1955)

Cazelles, Raymond. *Société politique et la crise de la royauté sous Philippe de Valois* (Paris, 1958)

——. *Société politique, noblesse et couronne sous Jean le Bon et Charles V* (Geneva, 1982)

Chaffanjon, Arnaud. *Les Grands ordres de chevalerie* (Paris, 1969)

Champion, Honoré. 'L'ordre du Croissant', *RNHB* n.s. 2 (1886), pp. 503–509

Cheetham, Nicolas. *Medieval Greece* (New Haven, 1981)

Chianale, G. S., and G. B. Nicolini. *Serie dei cavalieri e ufficiali dell' Ordine Supremo della SS. Annunziata del MCCCLXVII ai nostre tempi* (Turin, 1842)

Cibrario, conte Luigi. 'Delle società popolari e degli aspize de' nobili nelle città libere piemontesi e specialmente della società di S. Giorgio di Chieri', *Studi Storici* (Turin, 1851)

—— . *Descrizione storica degli Ordini cavallereschi della Monarchia di Savoia* (Turin, 1846)

—— . *Opusculi* (Turin, 1841)

—— . *Sigilli dei Principi di Savoia* (Turin, 1834)

Cigna-Santi, Vittorio Amadeo. *Serie cronologica dei cavalieri dell'Ordine Supremo di Savoia detto prima del Collare, indi della SS. Annunziata* (Turin, 1786)

Clarke, Maude Violet. 'The Wilton Diptych', *Fourteenth Century Studies*, ed. L. S. Sutherland and M. McKisack (Oxford, 1937), pp. 271–292

Clay, R. M. *Mediaeval Hospitals of England* (London, 1909)

Clayton, Muriel. *Catalogue of Rubbings of Brasses and Incised Slabs* (London, 1968)

Clément, Joseph-H.-M. C. *L''Escu d'or' et l'ordre de 'Nostre Dame', institués par Louis II, duc de Bourbonnais* (Moulin, 1900)

Clephan, Robert Coltman. *The Tournament: Its Periods and Phases* (London, 1919)

Cline, R. H. 'The Influence of Romances on Tournaments of the Middle Ages', *Speculum* 20 (1945), pp. 204–211

de Cobos de Belchite, el barón. 'La Antigua Orden de Nuestra Señora del Lirio (Año 1043)', *Hidalguía* 1 (1953), pp. 269–272

Cognasso, Francesco. *Il Conte Verde* (Turin, 1926)

—— . 'Ordine della SS Annunziata', *Enciclopedia Italiana di Scienze, Lettere ed Arti* (1929), III, pp. 409–411

Cohen, Gustave. *Histoire de la chevalerie en France au Moyen Age* (Paris, 1949)

Collenuccio, Pandolfo. *Compendio delle historie del regno di Napoli* (Venice, 1539, 1613)

Colleville, Ludovic-Etienne, comte de, and François Saint-Christo. *Les Ordres du roi . . .* (Paris, 1925)

Colón, German. 'Premiers échos de l'Ordre de la Jarretière', *ZRP* 81 (1965), pp. 441–453

Colvin, Howard Montague, ed. *The History of the King's Works*, II (London, 1963)

Contamine, Philippe. *Guerre, état et société à la fin du moyen âge; Etudes sur les armées des rois de France 1337–1494* (Paris, 1972)

—— . *La Guerre au Moyen Age* (Paris, 1980)

—— . ed. *La Noblesse au Moyen Age XIe–XVe siècles. Essais à la mémoire de Robert Boutruche* (Paris, 1976)

—— . 'L'ordre de Saint-Michel au temps de Louis XI et Charles VIII', *BSNAF* 1976 (Paris, 1978), pp. 212–238

—— . 'Points de vue sur la chevalerie en France à la fin du moyen âge', *Francia* 4 (1976), pp. 255–285

511

Coornaert, E. 'Les Ghildes médiévales', *Revue historique* 99 (1948), pp. 22–55, 206–46

di Costanzo, Angelo. *Storia del Regno di Napoli* (Naples, 1581)

Couderc, Camille. *Album de portraits d'après les collections du département des manuscrits* (Paris, 1909)

Coville, A. *Les premiers Valois et la Guerre de Cent Ans (1328–1422)* (Paris, 1911)

Cox, Eugene L. *The Green Count of Savoy* (Princeton, 1967)

Cross, F. L., and E. A. Livingstone, eds. *The Oxford Dictionary of the Christian Church* (2nd edn., London, 1974)

Cunnington, C. Willet and Phyllis. *Handbook of English Mediaeval Costume* (2nd edn., London, 1969)

Cutolo, A. *Re Ladislao d'Angiò-Durazzo* (Milan, 1936)

Dacier, M. 'Recherches sur l'établissement et l'extinction de l'ordre de l'Etoile', *Mémoires de Littérature tirés des registres de l'Académie royale des Inscriptions et Belles-Lettres* 39 (1777), pp. 662ff

Däschlein, Theodor. *Der Schwanenorden und die sogenante Schwanenordens-Ritter-Kapelle in Ansbach* (Ansbach, 1927)

Daumet, Georges. 'L'Ordre castillan de l'Echarpe', *Bulletin hispanique* 25 (1925), pp. 5–32

Fox-Davies, Arthur Charles. *The Art of Heraldry. An Encyclopaedia of Armory* (London, 1904)

——— . *Heraldic Badges* (London, 1907)

Delaville Le Roulx, J. 'Les statuts de l'ordre de St-Jean de Jérusalem', *BEC* 48 (1887), pp. 341–356

del Carmen Carlé, María. 'Infanzones e hidalgos', *Cuadernos de Historia de España* 33–34 (1961), pp. 56–100

Demay, Germain. 'Note sur l'ordre du Camail ou du Porc-Epic', *BSNAF* (1875), p. 71

Deuchler, F. 'Zur Burgundischen Heraldik und Emblematik', *Die Burgunderbeute und Werke Burgundischer Hofkunst* (Berne, 1969)

Diaz Martín, Diego Vicente. *Los Oficiales de Pedro I de Castilla* (Valladolid, 1975)

Dickens, A. G., ed. *The Courts of Europe: Politics, Patronage, and Royalty, 1400–1800* (London, 1977)

Dogaer, G. 'Des anciens livres des statuts manuscrits de l'ordre de la Toison d'or', *PCEEBM* 5 (1963), pp. 65–70

Doutrepont, G. 'Jason et Gédéon, patrons de la Toison d'Or', *Mélanges Godefroy Kurth* (Liège, Paris, 1908), II, pp. 191–208

Dubois, Frédéric-Th. 'Les chevaliers de l'Annonciade du Pay de Vaud', *AHS* 25 (1911), pp. 78–83, 129–140

Duby, Georges. 'Les origines de la chevalerie', *Ordinamenti militari in Occidente nell'alto medioevo* (Settimane di studio del Centro italiano di Studi sull'alto medioevo 15.1–2, Spoleto, 1968)

——— . *The Chivalrous Society*, trans. C. Postan (London, 1979)

——— . *Les trois ordres ou l'imaginaire du féodalisme* (Paris, 1978)

Dufourcq, Charles-Emmanuel, Jean Gautier Delaché. *Histoire économique et sociale de l'Espagne chrétienne au Moyen Age* (Paris, 1976)

——— . 'Les royaumes chrétiens d'Espagne au temps de la "reconquista" d'après les recherches récentes (1948–1969)', *Revue historique* 504 (1972) pp.

Dumont, P. 'L'ordre de l'Ecu d'or', *Bulletin de la Société d'émulation du Bourbonnais* 26 (1923), pp. 46–49

Dunham, W. H. (Jr.). *Lord Hastings' Indentured Retainers, 1467–1483. The Lawfulness of Livery and Retaining under the Yorkists and Tudors, Transactions of the Connecticut Academy of Sciences* 39 (New Haven, 1955)

Dupont, Jacques, and Cesare Gnudi. *Gothic Painting* (Geneva, New York, 1979)

Dupuy de Clinchamps, Philippe. *La chevalerie* (Paris, 1961)

Durliat, M. *La cour de Jacques II de Majorque (1324–1349) d'après les 'lois palatines'* (Paris, 1962)

Durrieu, Paul, comte. 'Les manuscrits à peinture des statuts de l'Ordre de Saint-Michel', *Bulletin de la Société française de reproduction de mss. à peintures* (1911), pp. 19–47

———. 'Une peinture historique de Jean Fouquet. Le roi Louis XI tenant un chapître de l'ordre de Saint-Michel', *Gazette archéologique* 14 (1889), pp. 61–80

d'Engenio Caracciolo, Cesare. *Napoli Sacra* (Naples, 1623)

Enlart, Camille. 'Deux souvenirs du royaume de Chypre', *Mémoires de la Société nationale des antiquaires de France* 69 (1910), pp. 10–12

———. *Manuel d'archéologie française* (Paris, 1916)

Essenwein, A. 'Albertus mit dem Zopfe auf einem Glasgemälde zu St. Erhard in der Breitenau in Steiermark', *AKDV* (1866), pp. 177–179

———. Zur Geschichte der Zopfgesellschaft', *AKDV* (1867), pp. 193ff

Evans, Joan. *Dress in Medieval France* (Oxford, 1952)

———. *Pattern: A Study of Ornament in Western Europe, 1180–1900* (Oxford, 1931)

Adam Even, Paul. 'Les fonctions militaires des hérauts d'armes: Leur influence sur le développement d'héraldique', *AHS* (1957), pp. 2–33

Fabritius, Albert. *Ordnernes og Ordenskapitlets Historie. De Kgl. Danske Ridderordner og Medailler* (Copenhagen, 1965)

Favyn, André. *Le Théâtre d'Honneur et de Chevalerie: ou l'histoire des ordres militaires des Roys et Princes de la Chréstienté* (Paris, 1620)

Federici, Domenico M. *Istoria de' cavalieri gaudenti* (Vinegia, 1787)

Fejérpataky, László. A Chapy-czímer és a Sárkany-rend' *Turul* 1 (1883), pp. 116–119

Fellowes, E. H. *The Knights of the Garter, 1348–1939* (Windsor, 1939)

———. *The Military Knights of Windsor, 1352–1944* (Windsor, 1944)

Felszeghy, Ferenc, Imre Rátvay, and György Ambrózy. *A Rendjelek és kitüntetések történelmünkeben* (Budapest, 1943)

Fleckenstein, Josef, ed. *Das ritterliche Turniere im Mittelalter. Beiträge zu einer vergleichenden Formen- und Verhaltensgeschichte des Rittertums* (Göttingen, 1986)

Florescu, Radu, and Raymond T. McNally. *Dracula: A Biography of Vlad the Impaler 1431–1476* (New York, 1973)

Flori, Jean. 'Chevalerie et Liturgie: remise des armes et vocabulaire "chevaleresque" dans les sources liturgiques du XIe au XVe siècle', *Le Moyen Age* 84 (1978), pp. 247–278, 409–492

———. *L'essor de la chevalerie XIe–XIIe siecles* (Geneva, 1986)

———. *L'idéologie du glaive. Préhistoire de la chevalerie* (Geneva, 1983)

——— . 'La notion de chevalerie dans les Chansons de Geste du XIIe siècle: étude historique de vocabulaire', *Le Moyen Age* 81 (1975), pp. 211–244, 407–445

——— . 'Les origines de l'adoubement chevaleresque: étude des remises d'armes et du vocabulaire qui les exprime dans les sources historiques latines jusqu'au début du XIIIe siècle', *Traditio* 35 (1979), pp. 209–272

——— . 'Pour une histoire de chevalerie: l'adoubement dans les Romans de Chrétien de Troyes', *Romania* 100 (1979), pp. 21–53

——— . 'Sémantique et société médiévale: le verbe adouber et son évolution au XIIe siècle', *Annales* 31 (1976), pp. 915–940

de Foras, comte Amédée. *Chevaliers de l'ordre du Collier de Savoie, dit de l'Annonciade, appartenant au duché de 1362 à 1860* (Grenoble, 1878)

Forey, A. J. 'The Order of Mountjoy', *Speculum* 46 (1971), pp. 250–266

——— . 'The Military Order of St Thomas of Acre', *EHR* 92 (1977), pp. 481–503

Foulet, Lucien. 'Sire, Messire', *Romania* 71 (1950), pp. 1–48, 180–221; 72 (1951), pp. 31–77, 324–376, 479–528

Fowler, Kenneth. *The Age of Plantagenet and Valois* (London, 1967)

——— . *The King's Lieutenant. Henry of Grosmont, First Duke of Lancaster 1310–1361* (New York, 1969)

Fox, John. *A Literary History of France: The Middle Ages* (London, New York, 1974)

Fraknói, Vilmos. 'Genealógiai és heraldikai közlemények a vatikáni levéltarból', *Turul* 11 (1893), pp. 1–8

Frappier, Jean. 'Le Graal et la chevalerie', *Romania* 75 (1954), pp.

Fronner, Karl. 'Die Ordensinsignien auf mittelalterlichen Grabsteinen', *Mitteilungen der k. k. Central-Commission zur Erforschung und Erhaltung der Baudenkmale* 15 (1870), pp. cxiv–cxix

Fusco, Giuseppe Maria. *Intorno all'Ordine dell'Armellino, da Rè Ferdinando I d'Aragona all'Arcangelo S. Michele dedicato, ragionamento* (Naples, 1844)

Gabriel, A. L. 'A Statute Book of the Order of St. Michael in the Pierpont Morgan Library, New York City', *Miscellanea codicologica F. Masai dicata . . .* (Ghent, 1979), pp. 481–489

Galbreath, Donald Lindsay. 'Deux ordres de chevalerie du moyen âge', *AHS* (1927), pp. 24–28

——— . 'Sigilla Agaunensia', *AHS* (1925), pp. 57–61

——— . and Léon Jéquier. *Manuel de Blason* (Lausanne, 1977)

Gallego Blanco, Enrique. *The Rule of the Spanish Military Order of St. James 1170–1493. Latin and Spanish Texts, Edited with Apparatus Criticus, English Translation, and a Preliminary Study* (Leiden, 1971)

Galway, Margaret. 'Joan of Kent and the Order of the Garter', *University of Birmingham Historical Journal* 1 (1947), pp. 13–50

Ganshof, François-Louis. 'Qu'est-ce que la chevalerie?' *Revue générale belge* (1947), pp. 77–86

Ganz, Paul. 'Die Abzeichen der Ritterorden im Mittelalter', *AHS* (1905), pp. 28–37, 52–67, 134–140; (1906), pp. 16–25

Gardner, Arthur. *English Medieval Sculpture* (2nd edn., Cambridge, 1951)

Gaspar, Camille, and Frédéric Lyna. *Les principaux manuscrits à peintures de la Bibliothèque royale de Belgique* (Paris, 1937)

Gaussin, P.-R. *Louis XI, un roi entre deux mondes* (Paris, 1976)

Gayre of Gayre and Nigg, Robert. *Heraldic Standards and Other Ensigns: Their Development and History* (London, 1959)

de Ghellink Vaernewyck, le vicomte. 'Bibliographie de l'ordre de la Toison d'Or', *Bulletin de l'Académie royale d'Archéologie de Belgique* (1907), pp. 212–276

Gibbs, Vicary, and H. R. Doubleday, eds. *The Complete Peerage of England, Scotland, Ireland, Great Britain, and the United Kingdom, Extant, Extinct, or Dormant* (2nd edn., London, 1910–1959)

Girouard, Mark. *Life in the English Country House: A Social and Architechtural History* (London, 1980)

Girsberger, Ernst. 'Die Gesellschaftsabzeichen der Sempacher-Ritter zu Königsfelden', *AHS* (1927), pp. 104–108

Gransden, Antonia. 'The Alleged Rape by Edward III of the Countess of Salisbury', *EHR* 87 (1972), pp. 333–344

Grassotti, Hilda. *Las Instituciones Feudo-Vasalláticas en León y Castilla* (2 vols., Spoleto, 1969)

Gritzner, Maximilian. *Handbuch der Ritter- und Verdienstorden* (Leipzig, 1893; repr. Graz, 1962)

Guenée, Bernard. *L'Occident aux XIVe et XVe siècles: Les Etats* (Paris, 1971)

Gutton, Francis. *La chevalerie militaire en Espagne. L'Ordre de Calatrava* (Paris, 1955)

Haenle, S. *Urkunden und Nachweise zur Geschichte des Schwanen-Ordens* (Anspach, 1876)

Hasluck, F. W. 'Frankish Remains at Adalia', *Annual of the British School at Athens* 15 (1908–9), pp. 272ff

Heers, Jacques. *L'Occident aux XIVe et XVe siècles: Aspects économiques et sociaux* (Paris, 1970)

Hélyot, P. *Histoire des ordres monastiques, religieux, et militaires et des congrégations séculaires, VIII Congrégations séculières, ordres militaires et de chevalerie, qui ne sont soumise à aucune des règles de religion* (Paris, 1719)

Herder, J. G. *Der Orden Schwertbrüder* (Cologne, 1965)

Hersey, George L. *The Aragonese Arch at Naples, 1443–1475* (New Haven, 1973)

Herzberg-Fränkel, S. 'Die Bruderschafts- und Wappenbücher von St Christoph auf dem Arlberg', *Mitteilungen des Instituts für Oesterreichische Geschichtsforschung* 6 (1901), pp. 355–412

Hewitt, H. J. *The Organization of War under Edward III 1338–62* (Manchester, 1966)

Hieronymussen, P. *Orders and Decorations of Europe* (London, 1967)

Hill, Sir George. *A History of Cyprus* (4 vols., London, 1940–52)

Höfler, Otto. 'Ulrich von Lichtensteins Venusfahrt und Artusfahrt', *Studien zur deutschen Philologie des Mittelalters Friedrich Panzer zum 80. Geburstag . . . dargebracht*, ed. R. W. Kienast (Heidelberg, 1950)

Hoffmann, Henri. *Les monnaies royales de France, depuis Hugues Capet jusqu'à Louis XVI* (Paris, 1878)

Hogarth, Peter. *Dragons* (New York, 1979)

Hóman, Bálint. *Gli Angioini di Napoli in Ungheria* (Rome, 1938)

——. 'Hungary, 1301–1490', *CMH VIII* (Cambridge, 1936), pp. 587–619

Hommel, Luc. *L'Histoire du noble ordre de la Toison d'Or* (Brussels, 1947)

Hope, W. H. St. John. *Heraldry for Craftsmen and Designers* (London, 1913)

515

————. *The Stall Plates of the Knights of the Garter, 1348–1485* (London, 1901)

Houseley, N. J. 'Politics and Heretics in Italy: Anti-Heretical Crusades, Orders, and Confraternities, 1200–1500', *Journal of Ecclesiastical History* 33 (1982), pp. 193–208

d'Hozier, Jean-François-Louis. *Chevaliers bretons de Saint-Michel depuis la fondation de l'ordre en 1469 jusqu'à l'ordonnance de 1665* (Nantes, 1884)

————. *Les Chevaliers de Saint-Michel de la province de Poitou* (Vannes, 1896)

Hüber, Alfons. *Geschichte Österreich* (7 vols., Gotha, 1885–1921)

Huizinga, Johan. 'The Political and Military Significance of Chivalric Ideas in the Middle Ages', *Revue d'histoire diplomatique* 35 (1921), pp.

————. *The Waning of the Middle Ages* (1st English edn., London, 1924)

Hunt, Tony. 'The Emergence of the Knight in France and England, 1000–1200', *FMLS* 17 (1981), pp. 93–114

Innes of Learney, Sir Thomas. 'The Foundation of the Most Ancient and Most Noble Order of the Thistle', *Ordenskunde, Beiträge zur Geschichte der Auszeichnungen* 11 (Berlin, 1959), pp. 84–90

Jackson, W. H. 'The Concept of Knighthood in Herbort von Fritzlar's Liet von Troye', *FMLS* 17 (1981), pp. 131–145

Javierre Mur, Aurea L. *Privilegios reales de la Orden de Montesa en la Edad Media* (Madrid, 1945)

Jones, Michael. *Ducal Brittany 1364–1399* (London, 1970)

Jørgensen, P. J. *Danish Orders and Medals* (Copenhagen, 1964)

Jorga, N. *Philippe de Mézières, 1327–1405, et la Croisade au XIVe siècle* (Paris, 1896)

Keen, Maurice. 'Brotherhood in Arms', *History* 47 (1962) pp. 1–17

————. *Chivalry* (New Haven, 1984)

————. 'Huizinga, Kilgour, and the Decline of Chivalry', *Mediaevalia et Humanistica* 8 (1977), pp. 1–20

————. *The Laws of War in the Middle Ages* (London, 1965)

Kalff, Friedrich Johannes. *Funktion und Bedeutung des Ordens vom goldenen Vlies in Spanien vom XVI. bis zum XX. Jahrhundert; ein Beitrag zur allgemeinen Ordensgeschichte* (Bonn, 1963)

Kendall, Paul Murray. *Louis XI. The Universal Spider* (London, 1971)

Kervyn de Lettenhove, Henri Marie Bruno Joseph, baron. *La Toison d'Or: Notes sur l'institution et l'histoire de l'Ordre, 1429–1559* (Brussels, 1907)

Kilgour, Raymond Lincoln. *The Decline of Chivalry, As Shown in the French Literature of the Late Middle Ages* (Cambridge, Mass., 1937)

Koller, F. *Au service de la Toison d'Or (Les Officers)* (Dison [sic], 1971)

de la Chênaye des Bois, François-Alexandre Aubert. *Dictionnaire de la Noblesse* (2nd edn., 15 vols., Paris, 1770–1786)

de La Roque de la Lontière, Gilles-André. *Du ban et de l'arrière ban* (Paris, 1676)

Le Bras, G. 'Les confréries chrétiennes: Problèmes et propositions', *Revue historique de droit français et étranger*, 4e sér., 19, 20 (1940–41), pp. 310–363

Lee, Lawrence, George Seddon, and Francis Stephens. *Stained Glass* (New York, 1976)

Lehoux, Françoise. *Jean de France, duc de Berri. Sa vie, son action politique (1340–1416)* (4 vols., Paris, 1966–1968)

Le Mire, Aubert (*alias* Albertus Miraeus). *Origine des chevaliers et ordres militaires* (Antwerp, 1609)

Léonard, Emile G. *Les Angevins de Naples* (Paris, 1954)

————. *Boccace et Naples* (Paris, 1944)

————. *Histoire de Jeanne Ie, reine de Naples, comtesse de Provence* (2 vols., Paris, 1932–37)

Leonhard, Walter. *Das grosse Buch der Wappenkunst: Entwicklung, Elemente, Bildmotive, Gestaltung* (Munich, 1978)

Lessurios. *Histoire de l'ordre du Saint Sépulchre, son origine, son but et sa destination* . . . (Maestricht, 1872)

Levron, J. *Le Bon Roi René* (Paris, 1972)

Lewis, N. B. 'An Early Indenture of Military Service, 27 July 1287', *BIHR* 13 (1935–36), pp. 85–89

————. 'Indentures of Retinue with John of Gaunt, Duke of Lancaster, Enrolled in Chancery, 1367–1399', *Camden Miscellany* 22 (1964), pp. 77–112

————. 'The Organization of Indentured Retinues in Fourteenth Century England', *TRHS* ser. 4, 27 (1945), pp. 29–39

————. 'The Recruitment and Organization of a Contract Army. May to November, 1337', *BIHR* 37 (1964), pp. 1–19

Lewis, P. S. 'Decayed and Non-Feudalism in Later Medieval France', *BIHR* 37 (1964), pp. 156–184

————. 'Une devise de chevalerie inconnue, créée par un comte de Foix: le Dragon', *Annales du Midi* 76 (1964), pp. 77–84

————. *Later Medieval France: The Polity* (London, 1968)

Lichnowsky, Eduard Maria, Fürst. *Geschichte des Hauses Habsburg* (8 vols., Vienna, 1836–44)

von Liebenau, Th. *Die Schlacht bei Sempach* (Lucerne, 1886)

Lobineau, Dom Gui. *Histoire de Bretagne* (Paris, 1707)

Lods, Jeanne. *Le Roman de Perceforest* (Geneva, Lille, 1951)

Lomax, Derek W. *La Orden de Santiago: 1170–1275* (Madrid, 1965)

Loomis, Roger Sherman. 'Arthurian Influence on Sport and Spectacle', *Arthurian Literature in the Middle Ages*, ed. R. S. Loomis (Oxford, 1959), pp. 553–559

Loomis, Roger Sherman. 'Chivalric and Dramatic Imitations of Arthurian Romance', *Medieval Studies in Memory of A. K. Porter* (Cambridge, Mass., 1931), I, pp. 79–97

Louda, Jiří, and Michael Maclagan. *Lines of Succession. Heraldry of the Royal Families of Europe* (London, 1981)

Luchs, H. 'Schlesische Fürstenbilder des Mittelalters', *Zeitschrift des Vereins für Geschichte und Altertum Schlesiens* 9 (1868), pp. 405–409

Luke, Sir Harry. 'The Kingdom of Cyprus, 1291–1369', *A History of the Crusades*, ed. Kenneth M. Setton, III, ed. Harry W. Hazard (Madison, 1975), pp. 340–360

Lutrell, A. 'The Aragonese Crown and the Knights Hospitallers of Rhodes, 1291–1358', *EHR* 76 (1961), pp. 1–19

Lyon, Bryce D. *From Fief to Indenture. The Transition from Feudal to Non-Feudal Contract in Western Europe* (Cambridge, Mass., 1957)

————. 'The Money Fief under the English Kings, 1066–1485', *EHR* 66 (1951), pp. 161–193

McFarlane, K. B. 'Bastard Feudalism', *BIHR* 20 (1943–45), pp. 161–180

McKendrick, Melveena. *Ferdinand and Isabella* (New York, 1968)

McKisack, May. *The Fourteenth Century* (Oxford, 1959)

McMillan, Ann. 'Men's Weapons, Women's War: The Nine Female Worthies, 1400–1640', *Mediaevalia* (1979), pp. 113–139

Marie José [de Belgique, Queen of Italy]. *La Maison de Savoie II, Amédée VIII; Le duc qui devint Pape* (Paris, 1962)

Marinesco, C. 'Documents espagnols inédits concernant la fondation de l'Ordre de la Toison d'Or', *Comptes rendues de l'Académie des inscriptions et Belles-lettres* (1956), pp. 401–417

——— . 'Les origines de la Toison d'Or et du Voeu du Faisan, 1454', *Le Flambeau* 39 (1956), pp. 382–384

Marks, Richard, and Ann Payne. *British Heraldry from its Origins to c. 1800* (London, 1978)

de Marsy, le comte. 'La collection de décorations militaires françaises du musée d'artillerie', *RNHB*, 3e sér., 2 (1877), pp. 109–128, 361–375

de Mas Latrie, L. *Histoire de l'Isle de Chypre sous le règne des Princes de la maison de Lusignan* (3 vols., Paris, 1841–55)

——— . 'Notice sur les monnaies et les sceaux des rois de Chypre de la maison de Lusignan', *BEC* 5 (1843–34), pp.

Mas y Gil, Luis. 'La Orden Militar de San Jorge de Alfama, sus Maestres, y la Confradía de Mossen Sent Jordi', *Hildaguía* 6 (1958), pp. 247–256

Mathew, Gervase. *The Court of Richard II* (London, 1968)

——— . 'The Ideals of Knighthood in Late Fourteenth-Century England', in *Studies in Medieval History Presented to Frederick Maurice Powicke*, ed. R. W. Hunt, W. A. Pantin, R. W. Southern (Oxford, 1948), pp. 354–362

Maurice, Jean-Baptiste. *Blason des Armoiries de tous les chevaliers de l'ordre de la Toison d'Or* (The Hague, 1667)

Mendo, Andrés. *De ordinibus militaribus disquisitiones canonicae, theologicae, morales, et historicae* (Lyon, 1648, 1668)

Menestrier, François. 'De la chevalerie ancienne et moderne', *Collection des meilleurs dissertations relatifs [sic] à l'histoire de France*, XII (Paris, 1826)

Mennenius, Franciscus. *Deliciae Equestrium, sive militarium ordinum et eorundem origines, statuta, symbola, et insignia* (Cologne, 1613)

Micha, Alexandre. La Table ronde chez Robert de Boron et dans la Quête du Saint Graal', *Les Romans du Graal aux XIIe et XIIIe siècles. Colloques internationaux du centre national de la recherche scientifique* III (Paris, 1956), pp. 119–136

Micheli Márquez, Joseph. *Tesoro militar de cavalleria* (Madrid, 1642)

Meiss, Millard. *French Painting in the Time of Jean de Berry: The Late Fourteenth Century and the Patronage of the Duke* (2 vols., London, 1969)

Melville, Marion. *La vie des Templiers* (Paris, 1951)

Monti, G. *Le Confraternite Medievali* (Venice, 1927)

Morel, J. 'Une association des seigneurs gascons au quatorzième siècle', *Mélanges . . . dédiées à Louis Halphen* (Paris, 1951), 523–534

de Moxó, Salvador. 'De la nobleza vieja a la nobleza nueva. La transformación nobiliaria castellana en la baja edad media', *Cuadernos de Historia* 3 (1969), pp. 1–210

————. 'La nobleza castellano-leonesa en la Edad Media. Problemática que suscita su estudio en el marco de una historia social', *Hispania* 30 (1970), pp. 5–68

Müller, Theodore. *Sculpture in the Netherlands, Germany, France, and Spain, 1400–1500* (London, 1966)

von Müller, Otto. 'Stemmi di Cavalieri del Santo Sepolcro del XV Secolo', *Rivista Araldica* (1909)

Muños de San Pedro, Miguel, conde de San Miguel. 'Los caballeros de Nuestra Señora de Salor', *Hidalguía* 2 (1954), pp. 449–460

Muratore, Dino. *La fondazione dell'ordine del Collare della SS. Annunziata* (Turin, 1909)

————. 'Les origines de l'ordre du Collier, dit de l'Annonciade', *AHS* 23 (1909), pp. 5–12, 59–66; 24 (1910), pp. 8–16, 72–88, 372–373

Neubecker, Ottfried. *Le grand livre de l'héraldique* (Paris, Brussels, 1977)

————. 'Ordensritterliche Heraldik', *Der Herold* 1 (1940), pp. 17–48, 83–176, 220–245

Newton, Stella Mary. *Fashion in the Age of the Black Prince. A Study of the Years 1340–1365* (Woodbridge, Suffolk, 1980)

Myers, A. R. *The Household of Edward IV. The Black Book and the Ordinance of 1478* (Manchester, 1959)

Nicolas, Sir (Nicholas) Harris. *History of the Orders of Knighthood of the British Empire* (4 vols., London, 1842)

————. 'Observations on the Institution of the Most Noble Order of the Garter', *Archaeologia* 31 (1846), pp. 1–163

Anon. *Notice historique sur l'ordre de Saint-Hubert de Lorraine et du Barrois* (Paris, 1852)

Nunziante, Emilio. 'I primi anni di Ferdinando d'Aragona e l'invasione di Giovanni d'Angiò', *Archivio storico per le provincie napolitane* 18–23 (1892–98)

O'Callaghan, Joseph F. *A History of Medieval Spain* (Ithaca, London, 1975)

————. *The Spanish Military Order of Calatrava and its Affiliates. Collected Studies* (London, 1975)

de Oliviera, M. 'A Milicia de Evora e a Ordem de Calatrava', *Lusitania Sacra* 1 (1956)

Ollard, S. L. *The Dean and Canons of St. George's Chapel* (Windsor, 1950)

d'Orlac, C. 'Les chevaliers du Porc-Epic ou du Camail, 1394–1498', *RNHB* n.s. 3 (1867), pp. 337–350

Orlandini, Ugo. Le croci cavallereschi negli stemmi dei secoli XV e XVI', *Rivista Araldica* (1913), pp. 303–305

Painter, Sidney. *French Chivalry. Chivalric Ideas and Practices in Medieval France* (Baltimore, 1940)

Pannier, Léopold. *La Noble Maison de Saint-Ouen, la villa Clipiacum et l'Ordre de l'Etoile* (Paris, 1878)

Pastoureau, Michel. *Traité d'héraldique* (Paris, 1979)

Patterson, Linda. 'Knights and the Concept of Knighthood in the Twelfth Century Occitan Epic', *FMLS* 17 (1981), pp. 194–198

Payer von Thurn, R. *Der Orden vom Goldenen Vlies* (Zurich, Leipzig, Vienna, n.d.)

————. *Liste nominale des chevaliers de l'Ordre illustre de la Toison d'Or depuis son institution jusqu'à nos jours* (Vienna?, 1904)

Perrier, Emile. *Les chevaliers du Croissant. Essai historique et héraldique* (Vannes, 1906)

Perroy, Edouard. *La Guerre de Cent Ans* (Paris, 1945)

Pescador, Carmela. 'La caballería popular en León y Castilla', *Cuadernos de Historia de España* 33–34 (1961), pp. 101–238

Pétiet, René. *Contribution à l'histoire de l'Ordre de St-Lazare de Jérusalem en France* (Paris, 1914)

Piaget, A. 'Le Livre Messire Geoffroi de Charny', *Romania* 26 (1897), pp. 394–411

Pidoux de la Maduère, baron A. 'Le Noble ordre de St Georges au comté de Bourgogne', *Rivista de Collegio araldico* (1905), pp. 464–472

de Pierredon, comte Michel. *L'ordre équestre du Saint-Sépulchre de Jérusalem* (Paris, 1928)

Pinoteau, baron Hervé. *L'héraldique capétienne* (Paris, 1954–)

Pipponier, Françoise. *Costume et vie sociale: la cour d'Anjou XIVe–XVe siècle* (Paris, 1970)

Pivano, Silvio. 'Lineamenti storici e giuridici della Cavalleria Medioevale. Studio di storia del diritto pubblico che accompagna la publicazione del Codice dell'Ordine "Della Nave" guasto dall'incendio della Biblioteca Nazionale di Torino', *Memorie della Real Accademia delle Scienze di Torino* ser. 2, 15 (1905), pp. 255–336

Pontieri, Ernesto. *Per la storia del regno di Ferrante I d'Aragona, re di Napoli* (Naples?, 1947?)

Poquet, B. *Histoire de Bretagne* (Rennes, 1913)

Post, Paul. 'Ein verschollenes Jagdbild Jan van Eyks', *Jahrbuch der preussischen Kunstsammlungen* 52 (1931), pp. 123ff

Pouy, Ferdinand. *Peinture et gravure représentant le roi Charles VI et les chevaliers de l'ordre de l'Espérance, Ph. d'Artois, Enguerrand de Coucy, &c, dans l'église des Carmes à Toulouse, 1389* (Amiens, 1888)

Powell, J. Enoch, and Keith Wallis. *The House of Lords in the Middle Ages. A History of the English House of Lords to 1540* (London, 1968)

Prestage, Edgar. *Chivalry: A Series of Studies to Illustrate its Historical Significance and Civilizing Influence, by Members of King's College, London* (London, 1928)

Prince, A. E. 'The Indenture System under Edward III', *Historical Essays in Honour of James Tait* (Manchester, 1933), pp. 238–297

——— . 'The Payment of Army Wages in Edward III's reign', *Speculum* 19 (1944), pp. 137–160

von Procházka, Roman, Freiherr. *Österreichisches Ordenshandbuch* (Munich, 1974)

Prutz, Hans. *Die geistliche Ritterorden. Ihre Stellung zur kirchlichen politischen, gesellschaftlichen, und wirtschaftlichen Entwicklung des Mittelalters* (Berlin, 1908)

Quarré, P. 'La chapelle du Duc de Bourgogne à Dijon: "Lieu, Chapître, et Collège" de l'Ordre de la Toison d'Or', *PCEEBM* 5 (1963), pp. 56–64

Rabino, M. H. L. 'Le Monastère de Sainte-Catherine (Mont-Sinaï), souvenirs épigraphiques des anciens pèlerins', *Bulletin de la Société royale de géographie d'Egypte* 19 (1935), pp. 121–126

Rassow, P. 'La Confradía de Belchite', *Anuario de historia del derecho español* 3 (1926), pp. 200–226

de Reiffenberg, le baron. *Histoire de l'Ordre de la Toison d'Or* (Brussels, 1830)

Renouard, Yves. 'L'Ordre de la Jarretière et l'ordre de l'Etoile: Etude sur la genèse des ordres laïcs de chevalerie et sur le développement de leur caractère national', *Le Moyen Age* 55 (1949), pp. 281–300

Richard, Jean. 'La Toison d'Or dans les deux Bourgognes', *PCEEBM* 5 (1963), pp. 47–52

de Riquer, Martín. *Cavalleria fra Realtà et Letteratura nel Quatrocento* (Bari, 1970)

———. *L'Arnès del cavaller; Armes i armadures catalanes medievals* (Barcelona, 1969)

Roberts, A. K. B. *St George's Chapel, Windsor Castle, 1348–1446* (Windsor, 1947)

Romero de Juseu y Lerroux, José. *El Toisón de Oro; Orden dinastica de los duques de Borgoña. Historia, soberanos, constituciones y caballeros* (Madrid, 1960)

Rosenthal, E. E. 'The invention of the columnar device of the Emperor Charles V at the court of Burgundy in Flanders in 1516', *Journal of the Warburg and Courtauld Institutes* 36 (1973), pp. 158–230

Rossi, Ettore. 'The Hospitallers at Rhodes, 1306–1421', and 'The Hospitallers at Rhodes, 1421–1523', *A History of the Crusades*, ed. Kenneth M. Setton, III, ed. Harry W. Hazard (Madison, 1975), pp. 278–339

Roth von Schreckenstein, Karl Heinrich Leopold Eusebius, Freiherr. *Die Ritterwürde und der Ritterstand. Historisch-politische Studien über deutsch-mitteralterliche Standesverhältnisse auf dem Lande und in der Stadt* (Freiburg-im-Breisgau, 1886)

Rubió y Luch, Antonio. *Los Navarros en Grecia y el Ducado Catalán de Atenas en la Epoca de su invasión* (Barcelona, 1886)

Ryder, Alan. *The Kingdom of Naples under Alfonso the Magnanimous* (Oxford, 1976)

Saffroy, Gaston. *Bibliographie généalogique, héraldique et nobiliaire de la France, des origines à nos jours, imprimés et manuscrits* (3 vols., Paris, 1968–75)

del Saltillo, el marqués. *Catalogo de la exposición de la heraldica en el arte* (Madrid, 1947)

Sanders, Ivor J. *English Baronies. A Study of their Origin and Descent 1086–1327* (Oxford, 1960)

Sansovino, Franceso. *Della origine dei Cavalieri, Libri IV, con gli 'Statuti et leggi della Giarettiera, del Tosone, di S. Michele e della Nunziata* (Venice, 1570)

von Sava, K. 'Über Ordens-Insignien auf deutscher Siegeln vor Kaiser Maximilian I', *AKDV* N.F., 4 (1857), pp. 289–292

Schultz, Alwin. *Deutsches Leben im XIV. und XV. Jahrhundert* (2 vols., Vienna, 1892)

Scudieri Ruggieri, Jole. *Cavalleria et Cortesia* (Modena, 1980)

Sczaniencki, M. *Essai sur les fiefs-rentes* (Paris, 1946)

Selden, John. *Titles of Honor* (London, 1614)

Servais, Victor. *Notice historique sur l'ordre de Saint Hubert du Duché de Bar* (Paris, 1868)

Setton, Kenneth M. *Catalan Domination of Athens, 1311–1388* (Cambridge, Mass., 1948)

———. 'The Catalans in Greece', *A History of the Crusades*, ed. K. M. Setton, III, ed. Harry W. Hazard (Madison, 1975), pp. 167–224

Seward, Desmond. *The Monks of War: The Military Religious Orders* (London, 1972, 1974)

────── . *Prince of the Renaissance. The Life of François I* (London, 1973)

Shaw, William Arthur. *The Knights of England. A Complete Record from the Earliest Times to the Present Day of the Knights of all the Orders of Chivalry in England, Scotland, and Ireland, and of the Knights Bachelors* . . . (2 vols., London, 1906)

Simon, E. *The Piebald Standard* (Cassell, 1959)

Riley-Smith, Jonathan. *The Knights of St John in Jerusalem and Cyprus, 1050–1310* (London, 1967)

von Smitmer, Franz Paul, Edler. 'Über den Drachenorden', *Jahrbuch der k.k. heraldischen Gesellschaft "Adler"*, N.F. 5, 6 (Vienna, 1895), pp. 65–83

Sobrequés Vidal, Santiago. *Els Barons de Catalunya* (Barcelona, 1957, 1961)

────── . *La Alta Nobleza del Norte en la Guerra Civil Catalana de 1462–1472* (Zaragoza, 1976)

de Sousa, Antonio Caetano. *História Genealógica da Casa Real Portuguesa* (Lisbon, 1737)

Squibb, G. C. *The High Court of Chivalry* (Oxford, 1959)

Staehelin, W. R. 'Symbolischer Wandteppich zum Gedächtnis an die Stiftung des St. Michael-Ordens 1469', *AHS* (1925), pp. 80–82

von Stillfried, Rudolf Maria Bernhard, Graf. *Der Schwanenorden. Seine Ursprung und Zweck, seine Geschichte und seine Alterthümer* (Halle, 1845)

Stubbs, William. *The Medieval Kingdoms of Cyprus and Armenia. Two lectures delivered Oct. 6 and 29, 1878* (Oxford, 1878)

Suárez-Fernández, Luis. *Nobleza y Monarquía. Puntos de vista sobre la historia castellana del siglo XV* (Valladolid, 1959)

────── . *Juan Ier, rey de Castilla (1379–1390)* (Madrid, 1955)

────── . *El canciller Pedro López de Ayala y su Tiempo (1322–1407)* (Vitoria, 1962)

Summonte, Giovanni Antonio. *Historia della Città e Regno di Napoli* (4 vols., Naples, 1601–1643, 1640–1675)

Tasis i Marca, Rafael. *Pere el Ceremoniós i els seus Fills; el sigle XIV* (Barcelona, 1957)

────── . *La vida del rei En Pere III* (Barcelona, 1954)

Torres-Fontes, Juan. 'The Regency of Don Ferdinand of Antequera', *Spain in the Fifteenth Century, 1369–1516; Essays and Extracts by Historians of Spain*, ed. Roger Highfield (New York, 1972), pp. 114–170

Tourneur, V. 'Les origines de l'Ordre de la Toison d'Or et la symbolique des insignes de celui-ci', *Bulletin de l'Académie royale de Belgique, Lettres* 5e sér. 42 (1956), pp. 300–323

Toy, Sidney. *The Castles of Great Britain* (4th edn., London, 1966)

Traversari, G. 'Per l'autenticità dell'epistola del Boccaccio a Francesco Nelli', *Giornale storico della Letteratura italiana* 46 (1905), pp. 100–118

Tumler, P. Marian. *Der Deutsche Orden* (Vienna, 1965)

de Vaivre, Jean-Bernard. 'Un document inédit sur le décor héraldique de l'ancien hôtel de Bourbon à Paris', *Archivum heraldicum* (1972), pp. 2–10

de Vajay, Szabolcs. 'L'héraldique hongroise', *AHS* (1960), pp. 6ff

Vale, Malcolm G. A. *Charles VII* (London, 1974)

────── . 'A Fourteenth Century Order of Chivalry: the "Tiercelet"', *EHR* 82 (1967), pp. 332–344

────── . *War and Chivalry. Warfare and Aristocratic Culture in England, France, and Burgundy at the End of the Middle Ages* (Athens, Georgia, 1981)

Vale, Juliet. *Edward III and Chivalry. Chivalric Society and its Context 1270–1350* (Woodbridge, Suffolk, 1982)

Van Den Bergen-Pantens, Christiane. 'Etude historique et iconographique de l'Ordre de l'Epée de Chypre', *Mélanges offerts à Szabolcs de Vajay* . . . (Braga, 1971), pp. 605–610

Van der Veldt, James Herman. *The Ecclesiastical Orders of Knighthood* (Washington, 1956)

Van Luyn, P. 'Les milites dans la France du XIe siècle', *Le Moyen Age* 77 (1971), pp. 5–56, 192–238

de Vargas-Zúñiga, Antonio, marqués de Siete Iglesias. 'Titulos y Grandezas del Reino', *Hidalguía* 1 (1953), pp. 8–24, 217–232, 453–468; 2 (1954), pp. 9–24, 213–228, 421–436, 629–644, etc.

Vattier, Am. 'Fondation de l'ordre de l'Etoile', *Comité archéologique de Senlis* 2e sér. 10 (1885), pp. 37–47

Vaughan, Richard. *Charles the Bold. The Last Valois Duke of Burgundy* (London, 1973)

——— . *John the Fearless. The Growth of Burgundian Power* (London, 1966)

——— . *Philip the Bold. The Formation of the Burgundian State* (London, 1962)

——— . *Philip the Good. The Apogee of Burgundy* (New York, 1970)

Vergil, Polydore. *Polydori Vergilii Urbinatis Anglicae Historiae libri XXC* (Basel, 1534)

Vicens i Vives, Jaume. *Els Trastámares (Segle XV)* (Barcelona, 1956)

Vicente Cascante, Ignacio. *Heraldica general y fuentes de las armas de España* (Barcelona, Madrid, 1956)

Vielliard, Jeanne, and Léon Mirot. *Inventaire des lettres des rois d'Aragon à Charles VI* (Paris, 1942)

Villanueva, L. T. 'Memoria sobre la Orden de Caballería de la Banda de Castilla', *Boletín de la Real Academia de Historia* 73 (1918), pp. 436–465

de Villareal de Alava, el marqués. *La Maison royale des Deux Siciles, l'Ordre Constantinien de Saint Georges, et l'Ordre de Saint Janvier* (Madrid, 1964)

Wagner, Anthony Richard. *Heralds and Heraldry in the Middle Ages. An Inquiry into the Growth and Armorial Function of Heralds* (Oxford, 1939; 2nd edn. 1956)

——— . *Heralds of England* (London, 1967)

——— . 'The Order of the Garter 1348–1948', *Annual Report of the Friends of St George's Chapel* (Windsor, 1948), pp. 11–15

Weber, Annemarie. *Der Österreichische Orden vom Goldenen Vlies. Geschichte und Probleme* (Bonn, 1971)

Williams, Neville. *Henry VIII and His Court* (London, 1973)

Woodward, John. *A Treatise on Heraldry, British and Foreign* (London, 1892)

Wright, L. P. 'The Military Orders in Sixteenth and Seventeenth Century Spanish Society. The Embodiment of a Historical Tradition', *Past and Present* 43 (1969), pp. 54–70

Yarwood, Doreen. *English Costume* (2nd edn., London, 1961)

Denholm-Young, Noël. *The Country Gentry in the Fourteenth Century with Special Reference to the Heraldic Rolls of Arms* (Oxford, 1969)

——— . 'Feudal Society in the Thirteenth Century: The Knights', *Collected Papers on Medieval Subjects* (Oxford, 1946)

———. 'The Tournament in the Thirteenth Century', *Studies in Medieval History Presented to Frederick Maurice Powicke* (Oxford, 1948), pp. 240–268
de Zeininger, H. C. 'L'Ordre de l'Eperon d'Or', *AHS* (1939), pp. 91–95
Ziegler, Philip. *The Black Death* (London, 1970)

Index

Sovereign princes are listed under their first name in the language of their principal dominion; subordinate princes and titled barons are listed under the name of their principal dominion; others are generally listed under their surname (ignoring the particles de, von, van, etc.). Princes are given full genealogical names in accordance with the principles set forth on page xii.